# *The Crimean War*

*A Clash of Empires*

# THE CRIMEAN WAR

## A CLASH OF EMPIRES

By

Ian Fletcher

and

Natalia Ishchenko

SPELLMOUNT
Staplehurst

*British Library Cataloguing in Publication Data:*
A catalogue record for this book is available
from the British Library



ISBN 1-86227-238-7

First published in the UK in 2004 by
Spellmount Limited
The Village Centre
Staplehurst
Kent TN12 0BJ

Tel: 01580 893730
Fax: 01580 893731
E-mail: enquiries@spellmount.com
Website: www.spellmount.com

1 3 5 7 9 8 6 4 2



Typeset in Palatino by MATS, Southend-on-Sea, Essex
Printed in Great Britain by
T.J International Ltd
Padstow, Cornwall

# Contents

# *List of Maps*

# *A Note on Spellings (or what's in a name?)*

The majority of authors of books about the Crimean War, written in the English language, begin with a short explanation about their policy on spellings. Should it be Balaclava or Balaklava? Sebastopol or Sevastopol? Tchernaya or Chernaya? We are no different and have adopted a policy of consistency above all else, using the correct spellings of the relevant words (we have the French to thank for introducing the letter 'b' into Sevastopol). Thus, Sevastopol and Balaklava appear as such, a policy we have extended even to the original writings of men such as Russell and to the official despatches written by the Allied commanders who used the incorrect spellings of these places. Rather than appear to be inconsistent, and not wishing to employ '[sic]' throughout we have simply altered the spellings of the original writings.

# Introduction

The Crimean War. Has there ever been a war that has caused historians so much grief as to its correct name? It is virtually impossible to open a book about the war without first reading the author's own views on what the Crimean War should really have been called. And this is no different. 'The Crimean War', 'The War against Russia', 'The Eastern War', the list goes on. The question is understandable for the Crimean War extended from the freezing waters of the Baltic, to the sickly plains of the Danube and Bulgaria, to the Crimea itself, and to the far flung reaches of the Pacific and China. Was it a world war? Not really. Certainly, the Seven Years' War and the Napoleonic Wars spanned greater areas and involved more nations, in addition to which the fighting, both on land and on sea, was far more intense and prolonged.

It is important that we consider national perspective when debating the name. 'The War with Russia', for example, is all very well if you happen to be French or British, but what if you're Russian? In Western and Russian historical literature the war of 1853–6 is called either 'The Crimean War' or 'The Eastern War', although the name 'The Eastern War' originated in the west and it was some years before it took root in Russia. After all, if you are Russian neither the Baltic Sea nor the Danube are in the east; they are west, whilst the Crimean peninsula is not east, it is south. Neither is The White Sea in the east, it is north. Thus, from the point of Russian geography the name 'The Eastern War' is not correct. However, the name 'The Crimean War' is not strictly a correct term either, for the military events took place not only in the Crimea. Nevertheless, it is a convenient term for the name of the war owes itself to the area of the main military effort, for as Professor Winfried Baumgart so rightly says, 'It [the Crimea] was certainly the most important theatre of war where the military decision was to be forced.' It is a view shared by the great Russian historian, Eugenie Tarle, who also considered 'The Crimean War' to be the appropriate name, again owing to the concentrated military effort between 1853 and 1856. Another noted historian to apply the name 'The Crimean War' to the conflict between 1853 and 1856 was Karl Marx's great friend, Frederick Engels, who compared the war to the Russo–Turkish

War of 1877, which was fought on the Danube. To distinguish the two from each other he applied the term 'The Crimean War' to the events of 1853–6.

The debate does not stop with the name, of course, for many cannot even decide upon the actual date of the war. Did it begin in 1853, 1854 or 1855? Again, much depends upon your nationality. One of the more recent British books, published in 2004, commemorates the 150th anniversary of the declaration of hostilities. This, of course, is fine if you're British or French, but what about the Russians and Turks? After all, they began their own 150th anniversary commemorative events in 2003, the year when they declared war. And what about the Sardinians? 2005 will mark the anniversary of their first setting foot in the Crimea. The situation is no different from other conflicts. For example, if you happen to be Russian, the Second World War (or The Great Patriotic War) began in 1941.

The question of national perspective is an important one, for many works on the Crimean War have been dogged by the problem. There cannot be many people in Britain today, for example, who do not have at least some idea of what the Charge of the Light Brigade was, or who Florence Nightingale was. But mention the Charge to the average Russian and you'll be met with blank stares. Even the more learned Russians, and the people of the Crimea itself, give little thought to the event. It means very little. But how many Britons have ever heard of Nakhimov or Totleben, both of whom are great heroes to the people of the Crimea today. It is all a question of national perspective. Which brings us very nicely to this book. There has not, in the century and a half since the Crimean War raged, been a book on the war written by authors on opposite sides of the conflict. There have been books on the war in general, on the French, the British and the Russians. There have been books written about the Russians by British authors. But never has there been an Anglo–Russian effort until now.

The origins of this book owe themselves to a meeting late on a very dark night at Simferopol Airport in October 2002 when a group of British tourists arrived to begin a battlefield tour of the Crimea. One of them was the British author of this book, whilst the Russian author was amongst those waiting to welcome them. During the following ten days it became clear that the Crimean War was viewed from very different perspectives both in the Crimea itself and in Britain. Nowhere was this more evident than when the group visited Balaklava. Guiding the group was Patrick Mercer, one of the great authorities on the war, and himself the author of two fine works on the Battle of Inkerman. Standing on the Sapoune Ridge, not far from where Lord Raglan watched the destruction of his light cavalry, Patrick turned to the group and announced simply, 'Ladies and gentlemen, you are now looking at the most famous site in British military history.' Well, no matter what our views were as to the merits and the relative importance of the Charge of the Light Brigade it was one of those moments when the hair really did stand up on the back of your neck. The moment was not shared by our Russian hosts, however, who shrugged their shoulders and wondered why a crazy, hair-brained gallop should constitute one of England's finest hours.

There were more revealing insights into both British and Russian perceptions of the Crimean War as the tour progressed. When we visited the tombs of the four great Russian admirals in St Vladimir's cathedral, Sevastopol, we were surprised (pleasantly) to hear the custodian constantly refer to Russia's enemy as France, although it was somewhat sobering to discover that the British Army barely warranted a mention. Considering the sizes of the respective Allied armies at the outset of the war, however, this is not surprising. Nevertheless, it was yet another reminder that there is always more than one side to the story and that there was more to the Crimean War than 'The Charge' and Florence Nightingale. Indeed, as we will discover in this book, Russia had their own heroes and heroines inside Sevastopol, like surgeon Pirogov, Dasha Sevastopolskaya, and the famous Sisters of Mercy. And so, it seemed obvious that the best thing to do was to write the first Anglo–Russian account of the war.

The perception today of the Crimean War in Russia and the Ukraine is a very complicated question, more for the Ukraine than for Russia. In the middle of the nineteenth century it was, of course, one state, Russia, and the greater part of modern Ukraine was part of the Russian Empire, called Malorossiya (Small Russia). The war in general, and the defence of Sevastopol in particular, was regarded in Russian society as a just and heroic one, being the defence of their native land and homes. For this reason the war generated a great number of real national heroes across the whole spectrum of Russian society, from the high command (Kornilov, Istomin, Nakhimov, Khrulev, Totleben), to the ordinary soldiers (Ignatiy Shevchenko, Pyotr Koshka), to the doctors (Pirogov, Hubbenet) and to the nurses (Dasha Sevastopolskaya, Ekaterina Bakunina, the Sisters of Mercy of the Community of the Cross).

These heroes – and there were many more besides – fought for their people and for their land, and their struggle was born of a sense of genuine patriotism, for few of the participants gave any thought to the motives that drove the czar to war. After all, he was their emperor, and they trusted him. There were, of course, intelligent and educated officers and doctors who thought it necessary to criticise the actions of their government and the poor organisation of governmental departments during the war, but the overwhelming majority saw the Crimean War as their sacred duty to defend their land. And so today, when the diplomatic details of the Crimean War are practically forgotten by many in Russia, the defence of Sevastopol is not viewed as a defeat. Moreover, few Russians believe that Sevastopol ever was a British, French or Turkish city but that it always remained a Russian city, though only a few believe that it was exchanged for the Turkish fortress, Kars, which had been taken by the Russians in November 1855.

In spite of a widespread knowledge today amongst the people of Russia, the Ukraine and the Crimea of many details of the Crimean War the basic events themselves remain on the periphery of their social conscience. Indeed, it is a remarkable fact that many people – particularly those in the Crimea itself – view the defence of Sevastopol and the Crimean War of 1853–6 as separate events. It is a situation summed up nicely by the Polish renegade Mikhail Tchaikovsky, who wrote that, 'the siege of Sevastopol could be compared with the siege of Troy,' this being direct comparison to the great siege of antiquity which is usually divorced from the greater wars between the Greeks and Trojans. It is indeed strange that many in the Crimea do not consider the events which are depicted today in the famous Panorama in Sevastopol (the unsuccessful Allied assault of 18 June 1855) in the same light as the Crimean War itself, but they are viewed as very separate events. Moreover, the people of the Crimea today – and especially the people of Sevastopol – view the 349 days of the defence of their town as a victory of the Russian will. Thus, it was given the epithet, 'heroic', and is called today 'The heroic defence of Sevastopol.'

The overwhelming majority of this book deals fairly and squarely with the war in the Crimea and, in particular, the fight for Sevastopol. It was, of course, the main theatre of operations between 1853 and 1856. But our story does not only concern the Crimea itself, for we examine events on the Danube in 1853 and 1854. These would certainly have a bearing on the performance of the Russian Army in the Crimea. The areas we do not cover in any great depth are the peripheral theatres, such as the Baltic, Kars and the Pacific. It is true that a great deal of thought was given to strategy in the Baltic between 1854 and 1856, at least by Britain and France, for it is extremely doubtful whether the Sultan of Turkey or, in fact, any of the Turkish people, gave any thought whatsoever to affairs here. Again, it all depends upon the national perspective. The region was, however, extremely important to Russia also, but apart from Allied attacks on a couple of the Baltic forts the strategic thinking far outweighed actual fighting, and there was certainly none of the drama that ensued at Sevastopol.

As with any book on military history it is important to have an understanding of the ground where the events took place. Thus, this book benefits from having one of the authors living in the Crimea whilst the other made six extensive trips to the battlefields in an eighteen month period. These visits, in all weather, to the old battlefields were one of the most enjoyable aspects of our research. On Balaklava Day in 2002 we stood in the pouring rain at the old British memorial whilst thunder and lightning boomed and forked overhead. Twice we have walked the line of the British attack at the Alma river, including crossing the river itself, once in temperatures exceeding ninety degrees. We have also stood knee-deep in snow in the Great Redoubt in twenty degrees below freezing. At Inkerman we have climbed the St Clements ravine, have clawed our way through the trees to the remains of the Sandbag Battery, and have stood on Shell Hill in two feet of snow. We have also explored the Malakhov, stood on the commanding Mamelon, and looked out from the now peaceful Redan, whilst standing within the old Allied lines on Victoria Ridge and Green Hill in winter certainly left a deep impression as to how terrible it must have been in the winter of 1854–5. In addition to fieldwork the book has benefited from the use of rare Russian sources found in archives in the Crimea, amongst which are Czar Nicholas II's own collection of Fenton photographs and other volumes relating to the Crimean War.

Writing a book such as this, with the authors separated by thousands of miles, isn't easy, although the internet has certainly made life much easier than it would have been a few years ago. It has also been made easier by many friends and colleagues who have gone out of their way to help us. These include Vladimir Kazarin, vice-premier of the Crimean Republic and professor of the Taurida National Vernadsky University; Nina Kolesnikova, director of the Tavrika Scientific Library in Simferopol, who allowed us full access to the collections within her charge; Lyudmila Golikova, the leading scientific staff-member of the Museum of Heroic Defence and Liberation of Sevastopol; Vladimir Shavshyn, Head of Department of the preservation of monuments of Sevastopol city administration; we also thank the staffs of the Tavrika Scientific Library, and the famous Panorama and the Museum of Heroic Defence and Liberation of Sevastopol; David Grant, our editor for the extensive use of his red pen; Larissa Kazachenko, of Southern Tour, who first brought us together; Patrick Mercer, the only man who can really make any sense of the Battle of Inkerman; Jane Robinson, for much useful information on Mary Seacole; James Falkner, for valuable and enjoyable discussions as to British military tactics and thought; Gary Ashley, Simon Jervis, Matt Deadman and Mick Crumplin, for the loan of rare materials; David and Janet Bromley, for the loan of contemporary plates; and last but not least, Maggie Magnusson, of the Library of the Corps of Royal Engineers, Brompton.

Natalia Ishchenko and Ian Fletcher,<br>Simferopol and Rochester, 2004.

# CHAPTER ONE
## *Russia and the Eastern Question*

All things considered, England was a happy place when the nineteenth century reached its halfway mark. There were, of course, the usual trade disputes and movements for improved working conditions, but all in all England was in fine shape. The monarchy in France might well have been swept aside two years earlier, and an undercurrent of revolution been flowing throughout Europe, but such matters were for foreigners. England enjoyed peace, it flexed its industrial might with ease and pride, and when the Great Exhibition, housed within the magnificent Crystal Palace, was opened by Prince Albert at Hyde Park in 1851 it demonstrated to the world that England was a genuine technological and industrial powerhouse.

Fox-Talbot made great strides in the development of the world of photography, the pre-Raphaelites dazzled the art world with their exotic imagery, and the novels of Dickens, Thackeray and the Bronte sisters were devoured by a readership with an insatiable appetite. Steam trains boiled their way across the country along hundreds of miles of railway lines, whilst telegraphs sent messages singing along the wires faster than any omnibus or train could previously carry them. First class cricket was on the increase, and the St Leger, Derby and Oaks drew ever-increasing crowds of race goers. At Ascot, the czar of Russia presented the Gold Cup to the winning jockey, a task he had performed since 1845 when the prize had been known as the Emperor's Cup. It was a duty that he would perform for the last time in 1853. The presentation had been rather ironic, as the czar's country had been unable to offer the Great Exhibition a single item for display, not that this came as too much of a surprise to many people. After all, did anybody really know what went on inside the mysterious and massive Russian empire? What they did know was that both Britain and Russia had withstood the tide of revolution that had swept through Europe in 1848, a tide that had brought the spectre of a Bonapartist France to loom large just twenty miles across the English Channel. The invasion threat of 1803–5 might well have been a distant memory, but there were enough Britons alive to know that the French couldn't be trusted.

Following the fall of France and Napoleon Bonaparte in 1815, the country was occupied by the victorious Allied armies, an occupation which ended in 1818. Louis XVIII, having been in exile during Napoleon's Hundred Days Campaign in 1815, was back on the throne but was succeeded in 1824 by Charles X. The revolutionary period in the late eighteenth century had obviously left its mark, for when Charles attempted to restore absolutism the population rose up, leading to the July Revolution of 1830. Louis Philippe was then enthroned, remaining as head of state until 1848. However, during his reign Louis Philippe had twice, in 1836 and 1840, thwarted insurrections led by Prince Louis Napoleon, the nephew of Napoleon Bonaparte. In fact, the failure of the second revolt led to Louis Napoleon being imprisoned but he escaped in 1846 and made his way to England.

Louis spent two years in London, biding his time and keeping a watchful eye on events in France. The king was growing increasingly unpopular and in 1848 revolution broke out yet again. Louis chose his moment and returned to Paris on 27 February 1848, three days after the unpopular Louis Philippe had abdicated. Another brief flirtation with democracy followed and on 10 December 1848 Louis Napoleon contested the presidential election. Three days later the results showed that Louis had won with a handsome majority. In fact, he had completely overwhelmed his main opponent, the unpopular General Cavignac, receiving some 5,434,226 votes, almost four million more than Cavignac. One week later, on 20 December Prince Louis Napoleon was sworn in as president.

Although Cavignac's unpopularity was a major factor in Louis Napoleon's victory, there was little doubt that the magic of his name was what really saw him home. A Bonaparte at the head of France! It was just what the French people believed they needed to drag them from the past thirty years of restlessness and discontent, and give them a confidence lacking since the great days of his uncle's First Empire. But if Louis thought he could lead France back along the old Napoleonic road to glory he was sadly mistaken, for the trail came shuddering to a quick and sobering halt. As president of the Second Republic, he was limited by law to just one term, hardly long enough for him to make good the promises of glory and the new order which would restore France to its rightful place as a European power. Frustrated in his attempts to pass a constitutional amendment that would allow him to remain as president for more than one term, Louis planned a *coup d'état*.

There was little doubt that Louis would have the support of the people, but could he rely on the army? Given that the head of the French Army openly mocked him, this was unlikely. Louis needed his own man to convince the army of the wisdom of backing a Bonaparte, and that man was Brigadier-General Leroy de St-Arnaud, future commander of the French forces in the Crimea. The *coup* duly took place on 2 December 1851 and was a complete success.

The legislative assembly was subsequently dissolved and in January 1852 a new constitution ensured that Louis would remain in power for an extended term. It also gave him the sort of power that had allowed his uncle to rule at the beginning of the century, the new assembly consisting largely of a collection of sycophants, whilst any opposition, particularly in the press, was suppressed. Throughout the rest of the year Louis consolidated his position to the extent that, in November 1852, a plebiscite approved the establishment of the Second Empire. Louis Napoleon now became Emperor Napoleon III.

The spectre of another Bonaparte ruling as emperor in France set the alarm bells ringing across the English Channel. Politicians and press were united in their anxiety, with many sections of society voicing strong concerns about the new order in France. Indeed, when the foreign secretary, Lord Palmerston, offered his congratulations to the French ambassador, Count Walewski, he suddenly found himself out of a job: the prime minister, John Russell, duly sacked him. How ironic it was that less than sixteen months later the two lifelong enemies and ultra-wary, uneasy neighbours, would be going to war, side by side, to battle for 'poor little Turkey'.

But what of the Allies' future enemy? Few people in Britain knew much about the huge Russian empire. Not that too many cared. Suffice to say there were marked differences between the two nations in the first half of the nineteenth century. Britain was a land where the rights of the individual were largely respected and where the people enjoyed freedom of speech. It was a powerhouse of thought and design, where the genius of great men pushed back the boundaries of technology, and where industry forged ahead to consolidate Britain's reputation as the workshop of the world.

Russia, on the other hand, suffered from the ills of an ailing, corrupt and backward-looking form of government. It was a land where the rights of the individual, and freedom of thought and speech were certainly not respected and where ambivalence and contradiction characterised everyday life. It was a backward agrarian country, in which industrial development was impeded by serfdom. Laws were old, unenforceable and largely ignored and there was a lack of education. The census of 1836 showed a total population of fifty-two million people, including twenty-five million serf peasants, eighteen million state peasants, and nine million of all other classes. This latter number included 272,000 clergy and 128,000 merchants. In effect, Russia was a country in which a largely powerless and rural population of forty-three million people was ruled by a relatively small group of the nobility, the clergy, the merchants and the petty bourgeoisie. It was a country of erratic government, intent on national aggrandisement and quick reward, and a country of serfdom, which certainly projected a less-than-flattering image to the rest of the world.

Despite this, Russia was a justifiably proud nation, which still gloried in its great victory over Napoleon. In 1812 Russia's vast lands had swallowed up the Grande Armée and had played a great part in Napoleon's final downfall. During the French invasion Russia's powerless, uneducated people had demonstrated tremendous heroism in defending their country, for although they laboured and suffered under the burden of serfdom, they nevertheless loved their country and, along with the Russian Army, helped to defeat Napoleon.

Russia also enjoyed a rich cultural life, and with writers such as Krylov, Pushkin, Lermontov and Gogol it was a golden age for Russian literature, and literary salons were all the rage. The works of these latter three writers were particularly important, for they promoted progressive ideas with respect to both the reorganisation of the country and the abolition of serfdom. Any serious attempts at reform, however, needed to be inspired from the top echelons of Russian government, and in Czar Alexander I Russia had just such a ruler to cure the country of its ills and to reform the laws that governed the vast empire.

Born in 1777, Alexander began his reign on 12 March 1801. Throughout the early years he was greatly influenced by the liberalism of his Swiss tutor, Frédéric César de La Harpe. Indeed, in his first manifesto the young emperor promised to rule over the Russian people 'according to the laws and heart of his wise grandmother', the grandmother in question being Catherine the Great. He was acutely aware of what he considered to be the great barrier to Russian social organisation, what he called the 'despotism of our governing'. Consequently, the main objective of his government became the establishment of a strict legality instead of individual despotism. It was fortunate, therefore, that Alexander's advisors and the people who helped him in these reforms were imbued with the progressive ideas of the eighteenth century and were also well acquainted with the political system in the west.

Alexander understood that serfdom had to be abolished and took the first step towards its abolition in February 1803, when the government issued its 'free ploughman' edict. Accordingly, landowners could sign agreements with their peasants to liberate whole settlements or families with land. Alexander also suppressed the secret police and abolished the tortures to which prisoners were subjected during interrogation. He also abolished the equally brutal corporal punishments. Alexander allowed the nobles to travel abroad without restrictions, he opened new universities in St Petersburg, Kazan and Kharkov, and founded a Commission, under the chairmanship of M M Speransky, for the establishment of the first Russian constitution. Alexander founded new ministries to replace the old ones and established a Council of State, which discussed drafts of all new projects prior to sending them for the emperor's approval. But despite his good intentions, Alexander encountered opposition to his reforms and many of them were not implemented, largely to placate a nervous nobility. The events of 1812 to 1815 tired Alexander and by the end of the Napoleonic Wars he was, though still only 38 years old, tired and grey-haired. His government was much changed also, as were its policies, whilst the legislative reforms were nearly stopped. Indeed, Speransky's Commission was disbanded and Speransky himself exiled. It was all a great struggle for Alexander.

In 1818 there were student disorders in Germany and, in the 1820s, revolution in Spain and unrest in Italy. These events gave Alexander genuine concern for Russian domestic stability, so much so that he issued a Censorial edict, directed against the 'spirit of free-thinking and pseudo wisdom' in Russian universities and in the Russian press. He appointed Count Arakcheev to domestic Russian affairs, the count persecuting liberal ideas with fanatical cruelty. Indeed, such was the dismay at these repressions that clandestine political organisations were formed, the so-called 'Decembrists', largely from officers who had served in the Napoleonic Wars and who had been exposed to the influence of western liberal ideas.

The death of Alexander on 19 November 1825 was the cue for the Decembrists to begin their revolt, in effect the well-educated nobility against the czarist regime. Alexander had no children and it was unclear who would be a successor to the throne. Next in line was Alexander's brother, Constantine, but he had secretly renounced the throne back in 1822 on account of the fact that he had a Polish wife. Consequently, Alexander's other brother, 31 year-old Nicholas, succeeded him. The Decembrists fixed their day of revolt for 14 December, the day when the army was to pledge an oath of allegiance to the new emperor. The revolt was cruelly suppressed, however, and the leaders, once arrested, were sent to the gallows.

Once he had succeeded his brother one of Nicholas's priorities was to revise many of the laws which had been passed years before and which were badly in need of revision. The bureaucrats who ruled in Russia left many laws open to abuse. Consequently, the Code of Laws, which ran to some fifteen volumes, was compiled. He also tried to ensure that domestic affairs were debated openly, much of the business having been previously discussed in secret. Some useful acts were passed, particularly in 1842, 1847 and 1848, which concerned the rights of serfs. But despite these moves Nicholas remained very much an autocratic ruler. His period of rule, which was to last until 1855, was marked by repression and fear and by a very liberal use of his much-hated secret police, whilst his government violently punished those who tried to defend human rights and liberties. These included the poet Polezhaev, who was sent into the army after writing a satirical drama, 'Sashka'. Then there was the future outstanding critic, Belinsky, who was expelled from his university in 1832 for his anti-serfdom drama 'Dmitry Kalinin', and the writer Gertsen, who was exiled to the north of Russia in 1835. There was also a clampdown on the press. In 1834 Polevoy's magazine, *The Moscow Telegraph*, was shut down, as was Nadezhdin's magazine, *Telescope*, two years later.

As the middle of the century approached, Russia found itself in the grip of a struggle for change. There were the Slavophiles, those who sought a return to the pre-Peter the Great regime, a rejection of the European way of development and who wished to unite all the classes on the basis of a peasant community. Then there were the westernisers, who blamed Russia's troubles on the fact that the country was not 'European' enough. Amongst the latter were men such as Botkin, Granovsky and Ketcher, who called on the government to follow the European way of development, and to master the western forms of social and political life.

And yet, despite this uphill struggle for reform Russia remained firmly rooted in the past. There were no great or significant changes in the everyday lives of the people during the first half of the nineteenth century, and whilst other nations took great strides along the road to development, Russia's infrastructure remained positively static. In 1851 there was still only one major railway, from Moscow to St Petersburg, and that was only opened that year. Roads were as bad as they had been in England a century before, and despite its size and large population, the development of Russian industry can be said to have been almost non-existent. Little wonder then, that Prince Albert and Queen Victoria failed to find any Russian exhibits in the Great Exhibition that same year. Nicholas had simply been unable to present anything.

But whilst Nicholas and Russia continued to sail along on a sea of internal domestic strife, foreign affairs took a decidedly more sinister and threatening turn. During the Napoleonic Wars, Russia's forces, despite defeats at the hands of Napoleon, demonstrated their great powers of recovery, as we have already seen, destroying the Grande Armée in 1812. In 1826, and after he had been czar for barely a year, Nicholas went to war with Persia and as a result of the war which lasted two years Russia gained control of part of Armenia and the Caspian Sea. No sooner had the war with Persia ended than Russia was at war again, this time with Turkey. The war ended the following year with Russia gaining the eastern coast of the Black Sea and the mouth of the Danube. Closer to home, Nicholas brutally suppressed the Polish uprising in 1830–1 and afterwards revoked the Polish constitution and Polish autonomy. There were no more major conflicts involving Russian arms for almost twenty years, although the czar's troops did help Austria crush the revolution in Hungary in 1849.

But it was the so-called 'Eastern Question' and matters concerning the apparent break-up of the waning Ottoman Empire that began to take up an increasing amount of Nicholas' time. Until now, Russian foreign policy had been concerned mainly with what might almost be termed regional disputes. The wars with Turkey and Persia were largely localised affairs, neither of which drew in any more troops than were required to settle matters along Russia's borders. The imminent break-up of the Ottoman Empire was another matter, however, and Russian expansionism, in all its sinister form, was about to ignite a real clash of empires.

The Crimean War was a long time in starting. Even though many could see it coming it took almost four years for the deep-rooted arguments to fester and develop into a full-blown war. From the moment France chose to revive and re-assert its old religious rights in the Holy Land until the declaration of war by France and Britain in March 1854, diplomats tried in vain to solve what was possibly, in retrospect, an insurmountable problem. Indeed, up to the declaration of war, the intrinsic differences between the disputants taxed and ultimately defeated even the most experienced diplomats involved in negotiations. And it was not only diplomats who struggled with the various causes of the war. It vexed historians, such as the great chronicler of the Crimean War, Alexander Kinglake, who used the entire 519-page first volume of his great history to set out in detail the causes of the war.

Like all of his predecessors on the Russian throne since Peter the Great, Czar Nicholas II sought Russian supremacy in the Black Sea and access to the Mediterranean. But in order to achieve this it was necessary for Russia to control both the Bosphorus and the Dardanelles, the straits which led the way into the Black Sea. His 'peaceful' attempts to take a firm hold of these key straits proved unsuccessful, but in 1828 he was afforded the opportunity of controlling them when he went to war with Turkey. The war ended the following year with the Peace of Adrianopole, which deprived Turkey of the eastern coast of the Black Sea and a part of Turkish Georgia. But it still did not give Russia control of the two strategically important straits.

A second chance was not long in coming, however, for in 1831 the Egyptian pasha, Mehemet Ali, rebelled against Turkey. Nicholas, rather than take advantage of the weakening state of the Ottoman Empire, supported the Turkish sultan Makhmud instead and in 1833 he sent Admiral Lazarev's squadron to help the Turks, a move which naturally drew the previously suspicious empires closer together. The Turkish sultan now looked to Russia for future protection and a mutually beneficial treaty, the Unkyar-Iskelesiy Treaty, was signed, which permitted Russian warships to traverse the Bosphorus and the Dardanelles. These straits were now effectively closed to the warships of other countries. This, of course, was a situation that did not suit either Britain or France whose governments soon began to try to break down Russian's influence with Turkey.

In 1839 the Egyptian pasha rebelled again, a rebellion that was put down with the help of Britain, Austria, Prussia and Russia, all of whom sought to gain influence with the Turks. Under the terms of the London Convention of 1841 Russia was deprived of many of its gains from the previous agreement. Turkey, on the other hand, after having settled the crisis with Egypt, soon began to feel its dependence on Russia as a burden. It wanted to rid itself of Nicholas' influence, something which was achieved by the middle of the nineteenth century, largely as a result of the help given by both Britain and France.

The situation now in Turkey was unacceptable to Nicholas who resented foreign influence from two major European powers in a waning empire so close to the southern tip of his own empire. Russian influence in Turkey had to be reasserted, by either diplomacy or war. One way or another, the question of Russian influence, of the straits and of supremacy over the Black Sea had to be resolved. In reality, there was only one way – war. But in order to take control of the Bosphorus and assert Russian influence on the Black Sea region it was necessary for Nicholas to have both a strong army and a fleet. In reality he had neither. The Russian empire in the early 1850s may well have been a vast one but its industry was massively under-developed and was far inferior to the advanced Western European countries. As a result it was impossible to equip its army with the necessary modern arms, equipment and ammunition. Indeed, although this was not the only reason for Russia's future defeat in the Crimea, it was certainly a major contributory factor.

Of course, the Crimean War would not be decided purely on land. Naval power would also be a factor in both the course and outcome of the conflict. At the outset of the Crimean War Nicholas' son, the Grand Prince Konstantin Nikolayevitch, had examined the state of both the Baltic and Black Sea fleets. It appeared that the latter fleet was the superior of the two, largely through the efforts of Admiral Lazarev, who had been appointed to command in 1833. During the eighteen years since he had become commander of the Black Sea fleet and ports he had worked tirelessly to improve the situation in the Black Sea. Sixteen liners and more than 150 ships of other types were built, including steamer-frigates and steamers with iron hulls. A unique five-stage dock and workshops were built in Sevastopol, coast batteries were erected, the Admiralty was founded, Sevastopol marine library was established and an advanced naval school founded.

At the outbreak of the Crimean War the Black Sea fleet consisted, as did the Baltic fleet, only of sailing vessels and a few battle paddle-boats, but those ships which were created by Admiral Lazarev were of perfect construction, had good armament and experienced crews. Lazarev planned to do much more but many of his plans were destroyed by conservatism and by the short-sightedness of Nicholas' government, not to mention the lack of money. For example, a Russian artilleryman,

Lekhner, came up with a design for a 68-pounder gun, based on the British 68-pounder. The naval authorities refused to allow money to be used for the design and development of the gun, however, and so Lazarev himself was forced into subsidising its testing, after which he ordered it to be added to the Russian armaments. In addition to the lack of funds for artillery, under-funding for the Russian shipbuilding programme meant that Lazarev was unable to provide any large, modern paddle-steamers at a time when Britain, France and even Turkey had equipped their fleets with such ships.

Nevertheless, despite these constraints Admiral Lazarev managed to create a reasonably strong Black Sea fleet, which was much stronger than the Turkish fleet. At that time the high-powered 120-gun sailing ship *Twelve Apostles* was built, but otherwise everything was very difficult owing to the lack of money and a shortage of timber for building. Unfortunately, the emotional and physical strain on Lazarev inevitably told on his health. He also developed cancer of the stomach and in 1851 he died whilst in Vienna. He would be sadly missed by the Russians during the Crimean War. Of course, war was still some way off at the time of Lazarev's death. Nicholas was anxious to assert his influence over the weakening Turkish empire, but as yet there was still no legitimate reason for him to mobilise his army and take up arms against the Sultan's armies. That was, however, until a minor squabble arose in the Holy Land between two sets of monks.

The dispute in the Holy Land was over certain religious rights relating to the possession of the keys to the Church and Grotto of the Nativity in Bethlehem, and to the maintenance of the Church of the Holy Sepulchre in Jerusalem. Under the conditions of a treaty, known as 'the capitulations', drawn up in 1740, France had become recognised as the protector of the Latin Church in eastern lands which, amongst which duties, gave them custody of the Holy Sepulchre. The privileges enjoyed by France had long since ceased to be of any real concern to the French, but the struggle between Mehemet Ali and the sultan in the 1830s enabled Christians to visit the Holy Places for the first time in centuries. As the Czar was nominally the protector of Christians in Turkish dominions, Nicholas naturally began to develop a keen interest in Turkish affairs once more. But in 1850 France, taking note of the situation in Turkey and keen to deny Russia a foothold in Turkish domestic affairs, decided to revive its claim, a move that did not go down too well with its Russian rivals. Remarkably, this trivial and seemingly insignificant little quarrel would escalate into something far more serious than a dispute between two sets of monks supported by France and Russia.

But it was only a *casus belli*, for the religious quarrel very soon became the excuse for a struggle between French and Russian diplomats for influence on the Turkish Empire. The initial dispute was not over the rights to worship in either Orthodox or Catholic churches, since neither was prohibited. The whole sorry business came down to the ungrounded, petty and litigious old dispute between Greek and Catholic monks over who must repair the broken dome in Jerusalem and who must possess the keys to the Bethlehem cathedral, which was not even locked with the keys anyway. There was also a dispute about what star to put in the Bethlehem cave, Catholic or Orthodox. These discussions were absurd even to the most ardent theologian. But for Nicholas I the 'struggle for the Holy Places' was a very advantageous and popular cause and he was quick to seize upon it. With the help of this slogan he began a radical revision of Russian–Turkish relations, although to the rest of Europe it was clear that it was a becoming a battle of wills between the French emperor, Napoleon III, and the Russian czar.

Napoleon III was afraid of the possibility of the resurrection of the quadruple union (Russia, Britain, Austria and Prussia) that defeated his uncle, Napoleon Bonaparte, in 1814–15, and was provoking and knowingly stirring up the religious quarrel. In response, Nicholas tried to persuade Europe that the Russian people were deeply worried about the religious issue and that he was under great pressure from his peoples' deep religious feelings. In fact, Napoleon was seeking the most trivial of reasons for declaring war with Russia and used any excuse to further his argument, even the tiniest and most artificially created. Indeed, he even cited the disrespectful way in which Nicholas referred to him in his letters, calling him 'Mon ami', instead of the usual 'Mon frère'. This may seem trivial today, but in the obsessively protocol-bound society of the mid-nineteenth century, it was a real slight.

One of Nicholas' main mistakes was that he considered Britain to be Russia's friend and believed that it would never become an ally to France, its implacable enemy. A chapter in the anonymous treatise of one well-informed diplomat was called 'The Causes of Nicholas' Blindness' and Nicholas' conviction that an alliance between Britain and France was absolutely impossible was identified in the treatise as his fatal mistake. Nevertheless, Nicholas was absolutely sure of his own diplomatic infallibility. Throughout his thirty-year reign he had selected a servile court circle and systematically dismissed honest, straight-thinking and law-abiding people. Lies and flattery, and feigned optimism permeated Nicholas' court, which was unpleasant and dangerous, shamelessly making a fool of the czar who would become angry when told sad truths but yet could never react to a lie if it was what he wanted to hear. This was typical of 1852, the last 'safe' year of Nicholas' reign.

Endless parades, military festivities for no apparent reason, manoeuvres in Krasnoye Selo (The Red Village) and various other demonstrations of Russian military power in 1852 not only attracted the attention of the British Ambassador Sir George Hamilton Seymour but, as he admitted, worried him also. Seymour understood their political purport, but Nicholas' 'sabre rattling' in St Petersburg was aimed, first of all, at Turkey, not Britain. Moreover, the czar and his military commanders were confident that a Russian attack on Constantinople would be successful, but only with the benefit of complete surprise. This they didn't have, largely on account of the British ships in the region which would detect Russian preparations as soon as they had begun.

Therefore, Nicholas had to solve the main diplomatic problem: how to neutralise the only antagonist who could defend Turkey. He considered Prussia and Austria to be his obedient allies. France, on the other hand, might react with hostility, but would Napoleon III really risk his shaky throne to take on Russia? This left only Britain. War with Britain would be a very dangerous business indeed, but Nicholas came up with a daring – some would say preposterous – plan that he hoped would entice Britain into agreeing to carve up the decomposing Turkish Empire.

Britain, ever empire conscious, might be lured into his web of intrigue by the attraction of protecting the overland route to her possessions in India. Nicholas' proposal might shock the British, but he hoped they would give it serious consideration. There was, after all, little to lose. Between January and February 1853, Nicholas had several meetings in St Petersburg with Seymour during which he broached the subject of the state of the Turkish empire. He didn't set out any specific proposals but pointed out – if it ever needed pointing out – that Turkey was 'a sick man', and that they must consider the probable future collapse of the Ottoman Empire. Britain and Russia, he said, should make arrangements beforehand in order to avoid any disputes over territories that would inevitably follow. It was a proposal akin to disposing of a sick man's belongings before he was actually dead.

Nicholas suggested to Seymour and the British government that the Danubian Principalities of Moldavia and Wallachia, already having formed a separate state under Russia's protectorate, should continue to live as such, and that Serbia and Bulgaria should do likewise. He stated how conscious he was of the importance of Egypt to Britain, and said he would not oppose any move by Britain to take control of the country, adding that he could see no reason why Crete should not become a British possession also. It was pure and simple 'horse-trading'. Seymour listened to the czar's proposals in silence. He was shocked by Nicholas' openness and by the significance of his proposals. The meeting between Nicholas and Seymour marked the beginning of a continuous and fast changing chain of events that led Europe and Russia down the road to a bloody catastrophe.

Nicholas' proposals for the amicable division of Turkey were, predictably, met with hostility in London. The British government was quick to see the dangers of such policy. Russian control of the Dardanelles and the Bosphorus would put Russia in an extremely strong position and turn the Black Sea into a virtual Russian lake. It would also appear to be the prelude to the capture by Russia of Turkey. Indeed, the close geographical proximity would allow the huge Russian land army to operate with ease. Turkey would simply be swallowed up. Russia would then have domination over Persia, and control of the overland route to India. This, naturally, gave great cause for concern in London. It simply wouldn't do.

The British government was well aware of Nicholas' mistaken opinion regarding the impossibility of Britain joining its old enemy France in an alliance against Russia and did its best to persuade him of it, provoking him and almost goading him. This was not done through official documents but in personal letters, and in the outpourings of British ministers, ambassadors and other authorities. It was as if they were daring him to mobilise his army.

Napoleon's hand was strengthened when he finally won the quarrel for the Holy Places, after which he performed the ceremony of passing the keys to the Jerusalem and Bethlehem churches to the Catholic bishop with 'provocative ostentation'. Given his increased feelings of isolation and frustration one can well imagine Nicholas' reaction to this setback, but it did not deter him in his efforts to assert Russian influence over Turkey. Indeed, in February 1853 Nicholas despatched the 66 year-old Prince Alexander Menshikov to Constantinople in order to re-establish the privileges of the Orthodox Church in the Holy Places. More sinister, however, were the demands which he carried with him for a protective treaty similar to the Unkyar-Iskelesiy Treaty. This Menshikov was to negotiate in secret.

Menshikov's mission to Constantinople marked the beginning of the end as far as hopes of a long-standing agreement between all parties and a subsequent peace were concerned. The antagonistic Menshikov succeeded in little but the ruffling of his hosts' feathers. Even his arrival in Constantinople was antagonistic, arriving as he did in a Russian warship. Throughout his mission, which lasted until 21 May, Menshikov displayed little tact or respect, but a lack of protocol and a fierce determination to do his master's bidding. Menshikov had seen a great deal of action during his time in the service of Czar Nicholas, but his brusque manner was more suited to the battlefield than the bargaining table. The many skilful diplomats in Constantinople parried his every move and showed that, at the court of the Turkish sultan at least, the pen – or rather the spoken word – was indeed mightier than the sword.

Lined up on the opposite side of the negotiating table to Menshikov was the British ambassador to the Porte (the Turkish government), Lord Stratford de Redcliffe. Known to the Turks as 'the Great Elchi', Redcliffe was an experienced diplomat and a man with enormous influence within the Porte. Indeed, there was no man living outside Turkey who knew more about the affairs of the Ottoman Empire and of its society. The French ambassador, de la Cour, was only recently appointed and his experience at dealing with the Turks paled when compared with Redcliffe. To begin with, there was slight tension between the British and the French. Indeed, the French history of the Crimean War is critical of the British stance, accusing it of being gullible and expressing sympathy for Russia's claims, unlike the French who remained cautious and suspicious. Bazancourt wrote:

> Thus England, who had become mediatress in this grave debate, saw, without fear, the arrival of the Russian ambassador in Turkey. She blindly believed in the protestations of Russia, and in her desire to arrest this conflict, which brought in question the most solemn interests; and she could not but believe them. What a striking contrast the menacing, hostile, and disdainful attitude of this envoy [the French] presents to the confident tranquillity of England![1]

Despite this unease, both British and French ambassadors were soon deep in negotiations with Menshikov. The Russian envoy's demand that Nicholas be recognised as protector of all Christians in the Turkish dominions was met with polite but firm rebuttal. The Turkish foreign minister's reply was:

> It is unquestionable that a government, which, upon a subject so grave as this, should sign an engagement with another government, would do an act entirely opposed to international rights, and would totally obliterate the very principle of its independence.[2]

Turkey could not allow a foreign power to wield such influence within the sultan's realm, although it would nevertheless strive to remove any disadvantages the Christians might have endured and would address any grievances they might have. This response was endorsed on 20 May at a conference of the British, French, German and Austrian ambassadors. Menshikov's proposal that Turkey conclude a protective treaty with Russia along the lines of the Unkyar-Iskelesiy Treaty was also flatly rejected. The embittered Menshikov, suspicious in particular of British motives and believing that Turkey was merely a puppet controlled by the British hand, then broke off both negotiations and relations, and sailed away from Constantinople on 21 May.

Nicholas now raised the stakes by informing the Porte that unless Turkey accepted Menshikov's proposal he would send his troops across the Pruth river and into the Danubian Provinces. In fact, Nicholas had already issued orders to Prince Gorchakov to make preparations for the

Russian 4th and 5th Corps to cross the frontier and invade Moldavia and Wallachia. Fortunately, both Britain and France pre-empted Nicholas' threat and ordered their fleets to move to Besika Bay, at the entrance to the Dardanelles, where they assembled on 14 June. Eighteen days later, Gorchakov crossed the Pruth. How the Russians fared against the Turks will be soon discovered.

The spectre of war now loomed larger than ever before, but still negotiations dragged on and proposals were submitted in London, Paris, Constantinople and St Petersburg. The fact that Russian troops had crossed the Pruth appeared to be a catalyst for war, but in fact they were entitled to do so under the terms of a treaty that allowed them to enter the provinces if they thought it necessary to preserve order. With events dragging Europe inexorably to war, it was decided to hold a conference of all the main powers in Vienna. Austria, being the closest European power to the scene of potential conflict and having the more immediate concern for the future, threw in its lot with Britain and France, supporting Turkey against Russia, and condemning the crossing of the Pruth by Russian troops. Notes flew back and forth between the various countries, but as each formula for peace was proposed and then rejected, either by Turkey or Russia, war appeared more inevitable than ever.

The most significant of all the communiqués was the famous 'Vienna Note' of 31 July 1853, thrashed out between Britain, France, Austria and Prussia, and put before the czar for his approval. This note, which in effect bound Turkey to the conditions of the 1774 treaty of Kutchuk-Kainardji, and to the Adrianople Treaty of 1829, was certainly advantageous to Russia. Indeed, when the conditions were known to Czar Nicholas the Vienna Note was accepted by him, giving all concerned renewed hope that a conflict could be avoided. However, they had not considered the influential and crucial views of the British ambassador, Lord Stratford. Furthermore – and more remarkably – none of the four powers had bothered to consider Turkey's views on the Vienna Note. It was a fatal error.

Despite the requests from London to Lord Stratford that he recommend the acceptance of the note to the sultan, the 'Great Elchi' could not hide his true feelings, and when he presented the note to the sultan he did so with a heavy heart, knowing that it would not be in Turkey's interests to accept it. Nevertheless, he did what was required of him as a representative of the British government. He did his duty and urged its acceptance. Lord Stratford pointed out to the sultan that all four of the major powers supporting Turkey recommended acceptance of the Vienna Note, and that even Czar Nicholas had agreed to its terms. He also urged the sultan to come to a speedy decision as a delay might prove dangerous to Turkey. But what Lord Stratford did not do was venture his own private opinion, and it was this that the sultan and the Porte really wanted to hear. His opinion was not forthcoming, but the Great Elchi's look and silence said more than words could ever express.

> There was that in his very presence which disclosed his violation; for if the thin disciplined lips moved in obedience to constituted authorities, men who knew how to read the meaning of his brow, and the light which kindled beneath, would gather that the Ambassador's thought concerning the Home Governments of the five great Powers of Europe was little else than an angry 'quos ego![3]

The Porte studied the Vienna Note carefully before, somewhat predictably, adding some amendments. On 19 August the Porte made it known that unless its amendments were added they would be unable to accept it. Inevitably, these alterations proved unacceptable to Russia. The lengthy negotiations between Britain, France, Austria and Prussia had been in vain. Given the fact that they had not sought the views of the Porte this is not surprising. The sticking point once again centred upon Turkey's refusal to grant Russia protective rights over the Orthodox Church in the Turkish Dominions. The negotiations had gone full circle. The disputants were back to square one and with little hope of a settlement war was now virtually inevitable.

It should also be asked what the Turkish people thought of all the negotiations, the Notes and of the comings and goings of the various delegations to Constantinople. Turkey may well have been dubbed 'the sick man of Europe', with its empire truly in decay, but its people were not content to simply lie back and allow the Russians to walk all over them and over the people ostensibly under their protection in the Danubian Provinces. They inevitably reached the point where they had to take matters into their own hands and stand up for themselves. Cynics would, of course, point to the fact that Turkey's stance against the might of the Russian Empire was emboldened by the fact that it had the support of both Britain and France, even though the governments of both these countries were still working to avert war. But Turkish popular opinion, stoked up by their religious leaders, would not be assuaged. On 4 October 1853, and despite an increase in frantic diplomatic activity, Turkey went ahead and declared that, unless the czar withdrew his troops from the Danubian Provinces within two weeks, a state of war would exist between the two countries. The 'sick man' was standing up for himself.

The German historian, Winfried Baumgart, hit the nail on the head, when he wrote that Turkish public opinion led to the outbreak of war. 'It was not,' he added, 'as many contemporaries, foremost among them the Tsar, and many historians to the present day maintain, the secret doings and alleged warmongering of the British ambassador, Stratford de Retcliffe.'[4] It would indeed appear that the conference in Vienna and all the diplomatic activity that followed had been superfluous. The seeds of war had been well and truly sown when the czar moved his troops across the Pruth. 'That once done, the War God was loosed from confinement.'[5]

NOTES

1 Bazancourt, the Baron de, (trans. by Robert Howe Gould). *The Crimean Expedition, to the Capture of Sebastopol. Chronicles of the War in the East* (London 1856), I, xx.
2 Ibid, I, xxiv–xxv.
3 Kinglake, Alexander William. *The Invasion of the Crimea: Its Origin, and An Account of its Progress down to the Death of Lord Raglan* (London 1863), I, 352.
4 Baumgart, Winfried. *The Crimean War 1853–1856* (London 1999), 14.
5 MacMunn, Sir George. *The Crimea in Perspective* (London 1935), 14.

# CHAPTER TWO
## *The Day of Reckoning*

The refusal of Nicholas to pull his troops back across the Pruth and Turkey's subsequent declaration of war left the British and French governments in no doubt that they were drifting inexorably towards war with Russia. But there was still time, perhaps, to avert a conflict. Despite the worsening situation between Turkey and Russia Britain in particular was still hopeful of avoiding being drawn into the unfortunate although seemingly inevitable conflict developing in the east. However, France now began to put pressure on Britain to move her fleet from Besika through the Dardanelles. The French emperor had lived in England long enough to know how British public opinion could be used to sway a government's actions. With the Turks having declared war against Russia, and with both the British people and the influential British press voicing their support for the sultan, Napoleon decided to use this to his advantage. He urged Britain to move her fleet forward, a move which would naturally meet with the approval of the British people. On the other hand, the prime minister, Lord Aberdeen, regarded this as somewhat premature. He also knew that such a move would leave Britain and France in breach of the Straits Convention of 1841, under the terms of which the Dardanelles and Bosphorus were closed to foreign ships by Russia. Nevertheless, Lord Aberdeen, unwilling to risk alienating popular opinion and coming under increasing pressure from Napoleon's ambassador, Count Waleski, agreed to instruct the British fleet to move through the Dardanelles. On 22 September the fleets duly glided slowly through the straits and thus another step was taken along the road to war.

The Russian ambassador in London, Baron Brunnov, naturally protested against this move, citing the treaty of 1841 and accusing both Britain and France of pushing Europe to the brink of war. The usual protests went in and, as usual, were fended off by the British foreign secretary, Lord Clarendon. Czar Nicholas knew that the time for talking was at an end. Even Russia's experienced and hitherto optimistic foreign secretary, Count Nesselrode, reacted with dismay. He had done his best but now even he began to suspect the British government of a 'settled purpose to humiliate Russia'. Russia responded to this aggressive act by ordering the Black Sea Fleet to put to sea and by the middle of November it was actively patrolling the area, capturing any Turkish vessels it happened to chance upon. This in itself was bad enough, but on 30 November came the crucial act that finally nailed all hope of averting war.

The Turkish port of Sinope lies on the southern shore of the Black Sea, about 340 miles east of Constantinople. Barely 200 miles north across the Black Sea lies the great Russian naval base of Sevastopol. Four weeks had passed since Turkey had officially declared war on Russia, and although there had been fights between the two sides on the Danube, there had yet to be any real clash to stir passions in France and Britain. That all changed, however, when the 51 year-old Admiral Paul Nakhimov sailed from Sevastopol in his flagship, the *Imperatrista Mariia,* along with two ships of the line in order to discover the whereabouts of a Turkish fleet that had been reported heading east from Constantinople to the Caucasus, carrying weapons and supplies to their troops. If Russia was going to stand any chance of success in the war, command of the Black Sea was vital. This naturally involved the neutralisation of all hostile Turkish shipping there. On 24 November Nakhimov duly discovered the Turkish ships in the port of Sinope where they were taking shelter from bad weather. One can imagine the consternation the sight of Russian ships caused amongst the Turks, and it came as a great relief to them when, after a short time, the ships turned and sailed away.

The arrival of Russian ships certainly set alarm bells ringing in Sinope, and requests for reinforcements were quickly despatched to Constantinople by the Turkish commander, Osman Pasha. The problem was that Sevastopol was closer to Sinope than Constantinople. If the Russian ships did decide to return it would be a race against time to determine who arrived first: the Russians or the Turkish reinforcements. The answer was not long in coming. Just six days after the first alarm Russian ships were sighted once more, but this time Nakhimov brought with him not only his own flagship and the two ships that had accompanied him on 24 November, but a further four ships of the line and two frigates, mounting between them some 720 guns. Sitting invitingly at anchor in the small harbour of Sinope was the Turkish flotilla consisting of seven frigates, a sloop, a steamer and some transports. Outgunned and covered only by some relatively weak shore batteries, the Turkish ships were at the mercy of Nakhimov's guns, seventy-six of which were capable of firing modern explosive shells, and for the next hour or so they provided wonderful target practice for the Russian flotilla.

Although the Turks opened fire first, the 'engagement' quickly became a very one-sided affair and the destruction and slaughter in the harbour was terrible. Try as they might, the Turkish ships had no answer to the firepower of the Russians, who sent shell after shell flying in to explode amongst Osman Pasha's helpless ships.

> The combat was terrible, ferocious, for on the side of the Turks the contest was hopeless; they did not fight to conquer, but to die with honour. An hour after sunset this sanguinary combat still continued; and the burning town, of which various quarters had been fired by the bombs of the enemy's vessels, illuminated with baneful light the terrible spectacle.[1]

The Turks' desperate situation became even more hopeless when the Russian Admiral Kornilov arrived with three steam-powered warships to compound their misery. Even when the Turkish guns tried to hit back they found it impossible to see their targets owing to the clouds of black smoke that billowed from the burning wrecks of their own ships clogging the harbour. Consequently, Russian casualties were slight. The same could not be said of the Turks, however, for it is claimed that as many as 4,000 Turkish sailors were killed, either by the fire of the Russian guns or by drowning. Many more were consumed by the fires that engulfed part of the town, whilst several hundred others were taken prisoner, including Osman Pasha himself. Not a single Turkish ship struck its colours, and rather than see their ships taken by the enemy, Kadri-Bey, the captain of the 60-gun *Mizamie*, along with Ali-Bey, captain of the 50-gun *Navik*, are said to have blown up their own ships. The Russian ships remained off Sinope until the following day when they sailed north to Sevastopol to report what was a crushing victory for the czar's navy. The Turks, on the other hand, were left to count their dead and try as best they could to restore order in the town. The single remaining Turkish ship, the *Taif*, commanded by an Englishman, was then despatched to Constantinople to deliver the shocking news to a stunned sultan.

News of the disaster at Sinope reached both London and Paris on 11 December and was greeted with horror. It was not so much the fact that thousands of Turkish lives had been lost but rather that British honour had been stained. Britain had pledged to protect Turkey. Instead, the Russians had simply sailed across the Black Sea and had dealt a crushing blow against the Turkish navy. Where, wondered the British people, was the 'Nelson touch' when it was needed? The same reaction was felt in Paris. Like Britain, France had pledged its protection to Turkey and thus Sinope was seen as an affront to French martial prowess. Predictably, there was outrage amongst the French and British people who quickly clamoured for revenge.

The legality of any French or British armed response to the Russian attack at Sinope was brought sharply into focus by a circular, issued by Count Nesselrode four weeks earlier, on 31 October 1853, and issued to various Russian ambassadors. This stated that, although the Turks had declared war, Russia would refrain from any hostile response. On the face of it, therefore, the attack by Nakhimov at Sinope represented a breach of this promise, at least it did in the eyes of both the British and French publics. However, Nesselrode had also said that Russia would not take the offensive unless Turkey attacked, and as Omar Pasha had been active along the Lower Danube the Russians were well within their rights to attack Turkish shipping. After all, it had been the Turks who had declared war, not Russia.

The clamour for action continued in both France and Britain, where the people demanded their fleets be sent into the Black Sea to teach the Muscovites a lesson. The French, in particular, seemed hell-bent on hostilities, but while French domination in the Black Sea was almost as bad as Russian domination, the British government continued to waver over taking decisive steps to curb the Russians. But Napoleon's pressure and his demands for action were relentless. He proposed that Britain and France should send their fleets into the Black Sea and oblige all Russian ships, save for merchantmen, to return to Sevastopol. 'The proposal of the French Emperor,' wrote Kinglake, 'closed in like a net round the variegated group which composed Lord Aberdeen's Ministry, and gathered them all together in its supple folds.'[2] Indeed, at one point France threatened to go it alone if Britain would not join them in a coalition against Russia. This, Britain simply could not allow. And so, despite efforts in London and Paris, and in Vienna, where envoys from Britain, France, Austria and Prussia met to try and find a solution to the 'Eastern Question,' war drew ever nearer. Lord Aberdeen, coming under increasing pressure from both his own cabinet and the French, finally bowed to the inevitable and gave orders for the British fleet to sail out into the Black Sea.

At St Petersburg on 12 January 1854, Czar Nicholas was informed that British and French ships of the line had sailed out from Constantinople with the intention of requiring all of his ships, save for merchantmen, to return to Sevastopol. Any flickering hopes that a peaceful settlement might yet, at this very, very late hour, be pulled from the fire, were now well and truly doused. Even a spirited but eventually fruitless mission to St Petersburg by a group of Quakers, led by Joseph Sturge, could not convince the czar to pull back from the brink of war. On 6 February the Russian ambassadors to Britain and France, Brunnow and Kesilev, were on their way back to St Petersburg, Nicholas having recalled them both after receiving the news of the Allied fleet's movement into the Black Sea. The move was reciprocated by France and Britain, whose ambassadors departed St Petersburg soon afterwards. By the middle of the same month, British troops were being earmarked for Malta, from where they would continue on to Constantinople. The sudden, although not unexpected displays of martial pageant, as the regiments paraded before the admiring public, brought about a wave of patriotic fervour, whilst the clamour for war reached fever pitch.

On 27 February 1854, and with all possible diplomatic solutions having been submitted and rejected, Britain and France finally issued an ultimatum to the czar of Russia. The ultimatum called upon Nicholas to agree – within six days of its delivery – for the withdrawal of all Russian troops from the Danubian Principalities by 30 April. If no reply was forthcoming or if it he refused to do so, Britain and France would declare war on Russia. Sadly, but perhaps predictably, Czar Nicholas did not deem the summons worthy of reply. In fact, it was not until 19 March that Nesselrode finally let it be known that Nicholas had refused the ultimatum. And with that, the great peace that had lasted in Europe since the Waterloo Campaign of 1815 was shattered. On 27 March Emperor Napoleon announced to the Senate and to the Legislative Assembly that France was at war with Russia. In London the same day, Queen Victoria spoke to Parliament informing it that negotiations with Russia had been broken off. The following day, Britain also declared war on Russia.

The first British troops despatched to the east had left England's shores in February 1854, sailing initially to Malta. Amongst the first to leave London were the Coldstream Guards, whose last action had been at Waterloo in 1815 when they defended the crucial fortified farm of Hougoumont. Fighting alongside them on that momentous day were the 3rd Foot Guards. Their descendants, the Scots Fusilier Guards, departed for the east soon after the Coldstreamers, as did the 3rd Battalion of the Grenadier Guards. The three Guards regiments would form a Guards Brigade under Brigadier General Bentinck. The sight of these bearskinned regiments marching off to war through the streets of London brought back fond memories for many older residents of the country's capital. For the majority, however, it was a new experience.

By the end of May the majority of the British troops destined to fight in the Crimea had arrived in Turkey. There were two main bases for the army. The first was at Scutari, situated on the eastern side of the Bosphorus. Here a barracks provided shelter for the troops, none of whom had been issued with tents. Scutari would become the site of the infamous hospital into which the sick and wounded were brought from the Crimea. Thousands would die there. The other base was at the peculiarly named peninsula in the Dardanelles. It meant little to the men of 1854 but to their descendants of 1915 it was a place that few would care to remember. It was Gallipoli.

But before we begin following the fortunes of the British Army, said to have been 'the finest army ever to leave England's shores', we must go back eighteen months to a day that would long remain in the memories of those who witnessed it. It was a day that saw the burial of one of Britain's greatest soldiers. This in itself may not appear to have too much direct bearing on the story of the Crimean War, but given the plaudits heaped upon the departing British troops bound for the east it will be worth recalling if only to identify one of the root causes of the mismanagement that would so affect the performance of Queen Victoria's army in the Crimea.

The day in question was 18 November 1852. Foreign news and the developments in the east concerning Russia's intimidating stance against Turkey were forgotten for the day. The streets of London were lined with thousands upon thousands of people, who waited silently in the gloomy, wet weather, to pay their respects to one of the greatest men in British history. The Duke of Wellington had passed away two months earlier at the grand old age of 83 after over half a century of service to his country. He had not only lived through one of the country's most dramatic periods, but he had commanded Britain's army to countless victories in the Iberian Peninsula, and capped his brilliant military career by defeating Napoleon Bonaparte himself on the field of Waterloo in June 1815.

It was said that 'half of England' rode in the procession. Indeed, the immense funeral cortege included no fewer than three thousand infantry, eight squadrons of cavalry and three batteries of guns. Other than the muffled sound of drums and the clanking of the gun carriages, the pavements were silent, with only the echoed cries of 'hats off' breaking the forbidding silence as the huge funeral car, draped in black and gold, rolled slowly by. Eventually, the cortege arrived at St Paul's Cathedral where, amidst careful ceremony, the great man, arguably the greatest soldier in British history, was laid to rest alongside another of the country's heroes, Horatio Nelson, who had been interred there almost half a century before.

Wellington had enjoyed a magnificent and almost unparalleled military career, during which he had barely lost a gun, let alone a battle. The harrowing retreat from the city of Burgos to the Portuguese border in the late autumn of 1812 had been the one and only blemish on an otherwise untarnished record. There was, naturally, a price to be paid for the great and glorious days enjoyed by Wellington and his army, but it was not the normal price one usually expected to pay. Whilst there was, of course, the usual 'butcher's bill' payable in blood, there was a far more significant price to be paid, by the British Army in particular, for Wellington's great success. With Napoleon secure and imprisoned on the remote island of St Helena and with Europe seemingly at peace at last after over twenty years of almost constant war, the British Army, called by Wellington in 1813, 'the most complete machine . . . now existing in Europe', was allowed to slip into a period of lethargy and slow decay. In short, the once proud army that had defeated Napoleon just forty years earlier had become a fossil.

The British Army at the outset of the Napoleonic Wars had been much like a blunt instrument which, mainly through years of campaigning in the Peninsula, had been honed to a very sharp weapon. Now, after almost forty years of inactivity, save for small and relatively insignificant campaigns in China, India and southern Africa, the cutting blade had been allowed to rust. True, the army had achieved some very notable victories during this period, but these had only served to obscure the decline of its prowess. Furthermore, they had not been gained against a professional European army.

But if the decaying system was to blame for the unacceptable state of the British Army, one of the root causes lay with the man who was now carried amidst great pomp, ceremony and grief to his tomb in London's great cathedral. For despite his many great attributes, the Duke of Wellington had one great failing which, forty years after the end of the Peninsular War, was to have a profound effect on the conduct of the unhappy war into which Britain had now drifted less than two years after his death.

When we refer to the British Army of the Napoleonic period as being 'Wellington's army', we do so purely and simply because it was indeed that; it was *his* army, and such was the tight rein upon which he kept it, that nobody, not even his senior officers, ventured to act without his say so. Even on the battlefield, orders that would normally be expected to be delivered by the hand of a staff officer were frequently delivered by Wellington himself. Take Salamanca as a glowing example, where the commander-in-chief rode three miles across that glorious, dusty plain, to deliver an order that one would have expected to have been delivered by a dragoon. This was all very well, but it did little for the confidence and abilities of those around him. As the historian of the Crimean War, Kinglake, put it:

> for in proportion as the great Duke's comprehensive grasp and prodigious power of work made him independent and self-sufficing, his subordinates were of course relieved from the necessity, and even shut out from the opportunity, of thinking for themselves'.[3]

This style of command had a profound effect on his lieutenants when he was not present. At the Battle of Roncesvalles, in July 1813, for example, two of Wellington's best generals, Cole and Picton, finding themselves fighting without their great chief, let their nerves get the better of them and began a headlong and unnecessary retreat which ended almost at the walls of Pamplona, a French objective. It drew a stinging rebuke from Wellington who, whilst admitting that they fought like heroes when he was present, accused them of behaving like children when he was not. But it was a problem of his own making. There was neither scope nor opportunity for Wellington's lieutenants to act on their own initiative and demonstrate any ability they might have themselves, not, at least, without bringing down a stiff rebuke from him. Indeed, it was not unusual to find officers placed under arrest for acting without orders, such was Wellington's firm grip on his army. [4]

There was little escaping the Duke's domineering presence even in peacetime. Twice, in 1837 and 1849, the Duke opposed with success reforms in the administration of the army. Even after Wellington had ceased to be commander-in-chief – he had been re-appointed in 1842 at the age of 73 following Lord Hill's death – his massively influential shadow was still cast over Horse Guards. Little wonder, then, that when Wellington died in 1852 the British Army is said to have breathed a sigh of relief.

The Duke might have gone, but his legacy remained and with it a dearth of talented, energetic officers at senior level. The army found itself devoid of the sort of young officers with which Wellington had defeated Napoleon. Indeed, Wellington was just 39 years old when he began his Peninsular campaign, whilst his staff and divisional heads were either of a similar age or were a few years younger. It was, in fact, a very young army in terms of age. But where were their successors? The intervening years had not been kind to the British Army, largely due to the Duke's method of command, his opposition to reform, and to years of inaction. Consequently, the army went off to the Crimea to fight its first European war for forty years, led by a group of elderly gentlemen many of whom had last seen action fighting alongside the Duke forty years before.

On 10 April 1854 66 year-old Fitzroy James Henry Somerset, who, after Wellington's death, had been raised to the peerage with the title Lord Raglan, was appointed to lead the British Army during the coming campaign. His appointment was no surprise. He was Master-General of the Ordnance and one of the most respected and experienced men in the army, having served under Wellington in the Peninsula and at Waterloo, where a French cannonball took off his right arm. With the loss of this arm he was forced to teach himself the art of writing with his left hand, something which he did quickly and successfully. After the post-Waterloo peace his next two positions were as Secretary with the British Embassy in Paris and, afterwards, Secretary to the Master-General of the Ordnance. In 1825 he travelled to St Petersburg as secretary to the British ambassador, the Duke of Wellington, and two years later was appointed Military Secretary at Horse Guards, a post he was to hold down for the next twenty-five years. With the death of Wellington in 1852, he was appointed Master-General of the Ordnance, followed by his elevation to the peerage.

Lord Raglan's appointment to command the expedition to the east perhaps demonstrates the problems inherent in the British Army. At 66, Raglan was not a young man. Indeed, British armies had, in the past, been commanded by men who were younger than Raglan, and yet been criticised as being too old for command in the field.[5] Sir Hew Dalrymple, for example, was 53 when he superseded a young Sir Arthur Wellesley in the Peninsula in 1808, his age frequently being the source of much comment. 'He had not seen a stricken field for upwards of fourteen years,' wrote one historian, 'and never as a General.'[6] Raglan's record was worse still. Wellington himself was 39 years old when he commanded for the first time in the Peninsula, whilst Britain's other great commander, the Duke of Marlborough won the first of his four great battles – Blenheim – at the age of 54, and was 61 when he fought his last action at Bouchain. Old men may very well make good use of themselves at Horse Guards but, with a few exceptions, they do not fight great battles.

Raglan's age conspired against him, as did his physical condition. For no matter how well he might have overcome the loss of his right arm, it is unlikely that he was really up to facing the rigours of the coming campaign, a campaign that would be fought in the harshest of conditions. One might also consider his psychological condition. At the age of 66, Raglan was well past the average life expectancy for the time. Having experienced the greatest and bloodiest of 'recent' battles – Waterloo – not to mention several severe actions in Spain, he could not have looked upon the coming campaign with the same relish as men half his age.[7] Indeed, even his own family expressed doubts – in private – about his appointment. 'Under any circumstances,' wrote the Countess of Westmorland, 'I should deeply regret seeing Fitzroy, at his age and with his indifferent health, undertake a life so different from that he has been accustomed to for thirty-eight years.'[8]

Despite his service under Wellington, Raglan had never before commanded men in the field. There were few alternatives, however. The commander-in-chief of the army, Lord Hardinge, could hardly go. Such was the state of the British Army at the outbreak of the Crimean War that Raglan was, quite simply, the only man for the job. Ironically, it was from the war against Russia that there would emerge many of the better officers who would lead the army through the traumas of the Indian Mutiny in 1857. Sadly, the British Army of the Crimean War was not afforded the luxury of a similar campaign that might have rooted out shortcomings and have provided an invaluable period of 'training'.

Lord Raglan's quartermaster-general was Sir Richard Airey, although it was a position accepted only after the army arrived in Bulgaria. Once again, Airey was a man with no real military experience, although by all accounts he was a very talented man. Indeed, Wellington himself had an extremely high opinion of him, and there was no better judge than Wellington when it came to the position. In the Peninsula, the post of quartermaster-general – in effect, the chief of staff – was held for the most part by Sir George Murray, who not only demonstrated just how important it was, but showed how effective an army could be with the right man in the job. Murray was Wellington's right-hand man and remains a massively underrated soldier. It is unfortunate that the Crimean War failed to yield a man of similarly brilliant talents.

Commanding the engineers was a man who had been born so long ago that the American colonies were still under British rule at the time. Sir John Burgoyne was 72 and had first seen service as early as 1800, at a time when Napoleon Bonaparte had yet to declare himself emperor of the French. Burgoyne's massive experience made him the perfect choice as chief engineer, although it has to be asked what had happened to the younger generation of Royal Engineers?

James Filder, another veteran of the Peninsular War, held the position of Commissary-General. Filder had seen Wellington develop an extremely efficient system of supply and transport, but only after disastrous initial failings. Similar problems would emerge in the Crimea, where all of the usual shortcomings within the department were cruelly exposed. Feeding garrisons up and down the country at home was one thing. But feeding an army overseas whilst on campaign proved to be quite a different matter, and Filder's undermanned and overworked department was, sadly, to receive a large slice of the blame for the fiasco that befell the army in the Crimea.

Despite the shortcomings of the departments and the senior officers, the men of the regiments themselves were in relatively good order. It was fortunate that, the year before the outbreak of the Crimean War, a large camp had been established at Chobham in Surrey. Here, during a period of three months, thousands of infantry and cavalry, along with artillery and engineers, underwent a period of training, supervised by yet another great veteran of the Peninsular and Waterloo campaigns, Lord Seaton.[9] It was here that great deficiencies were exposed, particularly within the artillery, deficiencies which were largely corrected. 'Unfortunately', as the great historian of the British Army was moved to write, 'there were other shortcomings which were not corrected.'[10] Happily, the same historian was moved to comment that the troops sent out from England with Raglan in 1854 were, 'probably as fine a lot of men, for their numbers, as ever were put into the field'.[11]

The numbers to which Fortescue refers were not exactly great. The initial strength of the British Army in the Crimea was just over 21,000, about one third of the number the French managed to put into the field. British numbers would fall drastically during the campaign – the lowest figure being around 13,000 – largely owing to sickness, with the number rising in the early summer of 1855 to around 32,000, although again the French vastly outnumbered these, fielding some 120,000 men.

The infantry regiments were organised into five divisions. The 1st Division was commanded by the Duke of Cambridge, and consisted of two brigades, the first being the 3/Grenadier Guards, the 1/Coldstream and the 1/Scots Guards, and the second, the so-called Highland Brigade, being the 42nd, 79th and 93rd Highlanders. The 2nd Division, commanded by Major General Sir De Lacy Evans, consisted of the 1st Brigade, being the 41st, 47th and 49th, and the 2nd Brigade, being the 30th, 55th and

95th. The 3rd Division was commanded by Major General Sir Richard England, its first brigade consisting of the 1st, 38th and 50th, and the 2nd Brigade being the 4th, 28th and 44th. Major General Sir George Cathcart commanded the two brigades of the 4th Division. The 1st Brigade consisted of the 20th, 21st and 57th, and the 2nd Brigade, the 63rd, 68th, two companies of the 46th and the 1/Rifle Brigade. Finally, the Light Division, commanded by Major General Sir George Brown, consisted of the 1st Brigade, being the 7th, 23rd and 33rd, and the 2nd Brigade, the 19th, 77th, 88th and 2/Rifle Brigade. Each division was accompanied by two field batteries of artillery, except for the Light Division, which had a troop of Royal Horse Artillery and one field battery.

Unfortunately, Raglan was not alone amongst the army's senior officers in being devoid of recent – or indeed any – military service. Of the five divisional infantry commanders despatched to the Crimea, four – Brown, Evans, England and Cathcart – had fought in the Peninsular, Waterloo or American campaigns, almost forty years earlier. Two of these – Cathcart and England – had seen further service in the Kaffir or Afghan Wars, and one – Evans – in the Carlist Wars. Brown had seen no further action since Waterloo. The fifth divisional commander, the Duke of Cambridge, had no real military experience whatsoever.

It was a similar situation with the cavalry, which was to be commanded by Lord Lucan, whose only 'active service' had come whilst attached to the staff of the Russian Army in Bulgaria in 1828. The cavalry contingent, numbering around 2,500, was divided into two brigades; the Heavy Brigade was commanded by General James Scarlett and consisted of the 1st (Royal) Dragoons, the Scots Greys, the 6th Dragoons, 4th Dragoon Guards and the 5th Dragoon Guards. The Light Brigade, commanded by the notorious Lord Cardigan, consisted of the 4th and 13th Light Dragoons, 8th and 11th Hussars, and the 17th Lancers. The cavalry division was accompanied by one troop of horse artillery. Neither commander of the two cavalry brigades had ever been in action before. Indeed, Cardigan had seen more action skirmishing with various unfortunate officers under his command, incidents which were covered regularly and with irritating frequency in the pages of the British press, much to the dismay of an exasperated Horse Guards.

On the whole, the fighting regiments of the British Army were in good shape. That the men were strong and healthy there is no doubt. Nor was their courage ever to be questioned. But, like the senior officers, there was a marked lack of experience amongst the regimental officers. This was not surprising, since only six of the twenty-five regiments earmarked to travel to the east had seen action during the previous thirty years. Once again the lack of any kind of active service overseas was to have a detrimental effect on the majority of officers who, whilst happy enough to play at soldiers at home, nevertheless lacked any experience of the smoke and fire of battle.

Indeed, the difference between the British Army and their French allies was summed up nicely by one historian who wrote, 'The English were led by gentlemen, the French by officers'.[12]

Given their experience, or rather lack of it, one cannot fail to recall Wellington's famous comment on the officers sent by Horse Guards to lead his own divisions in the Peninsula, forty-odd years earlier. 'When I look at the list of officers with whom I am expected to fight the French', he noted dryly, 'I tremble'. He could think himself fortunate that he was not being handed such a pack as that which now looked to the campaign in the east. Reflecting ominously on this, on the condition of the British Army, and on the manner in which the government and Horse Guards had allowed the rot to set in, the historian of the British Army wrote, 'the day of reckoning for all the follies . . . was now close at hand'.[13]

NOTES

1 Bazancourt, the Baron de, (trans. by Robert Howe Gould). *The Crimean Expedition, to the Capture of Sebastopol. Chronicles of the War in the East* (London 1856), I, xxxiii.

2 Kinglake, Alexander William. *The Invasion of the Crimea: Its Origin, and An Account of its Progress down to the Death of Lord Raglan* (London 1863), I, 381.

3 Ibid. II, 16.

4 At the Battle of Waterloo on 18 June 1815, for example, Sir Hussey Vivian refused to move his brigade of light cavalry to assist the stricken Union Brigade which was being badly mauled before his very eyes, fearing that Wellington would have him placed under arrest for acting without orders.

5 Dalrymple was 53, for example, at the time of the notorious Convention of Cintra in 1808. Historians, critical of his undoubted mismanagement of the business, frequently refer to his age. 'An elderly gentleman,' is one of the more common epithets applied to Dalrymple.

6 Oman, Carola. *Sir John Moore* (London 1953), 489.

7 The authors are indebted here to Patrick Mercer, author of the superb study of Inkerman, *Give Them a Volley and Charge!* We enjoyed an interesting conversation during a visit to the battlefield of the Alma in October 2002, during which Patrick, himself an ex-Regular soldier, expressed doubts as to whether Raglan really 'fancied' it, or whether he was 'up for it,' to use modern jargon. Raglan may well have had moral courage but was he still psychologically suffering from the years of past combat and from the loss of his arm? At 66 years of age it is quite possible that Raglan lacked both the psychological and physical strength to command on the battlefield.

8 Sweetman, John. *Raglan: From the Peninsula to the Crimea* (London 1993), 170.

9 Lord Seaton served with distinction in the Peninsula and at Waterloo as Sir John Colborne. His brigade was virtually annihilated at Albuera on 16 May 1811. He went on to command the 52nd Light Infantry, who played a decisive part at Waterloo in defeating the Imperial Guards towards the end of the day.

10 Fortescue, The Hon J W. *A History of the British Army* (London 1899), XIII, 30.

11 Ibid. XIII, 42.

12 Vulliamy, C E.*Crimea: The Campaign of 1854–56* (London 1939), 68.

13 Fortescue, *History of the Army* XIII, 30–31.

# CHAPTER THREE
## *The Sick Man Bites Back*

The phrase 'the sick man of Europe' is one that is used unsparingly in virtually all histories of the Crimean War. It is one which sums up the waning star of the once mighty Turkish Empire, but is a phrase which ought to be used with caution, for even though the sun was sinking slowly on the Turkish Empire its armies continued to show that they were far from unhealthy. Indeed, they held their own quite comfortably during heavy fighting in the latter half of 1853 and the first half of 1854. Even as British and French troops began to assemble in Turkey, the Turks themselves were engaged along the Danube, fighting a relatively successful campaign against the invading Russians.

The Russians had crossed the Pruth on 3 July 1853 with 58 year-old Prince Mikhail Dmitrievitch Gorchakov commanding almost 80,000 troops from the 4th Corps and part of the 5th Corps. Gorchakov reached Bucharest twelve days later and set up his headquarters there. This advance by almost two Russian army corps was, however, intended to be nothing more than a demonstration in support of the czar's ongoing diplomatic moves, and was designed to put pressure on the sultan. The Turks naturally responded with their own ultimatum that, if the Russians did not evacuate the Principalities, they would declare war, which they did on 23 October.

Within a week of their declaration of war the Turks deployed their troops in defensive positions in a series of towns along the Danube, between Kalafat in the west and Silistria in the east. The key fortress in the west was Vidin, and in order to protect the approaches to it from the north some 10,000 Turkish troops themselves crossed the Danube and deployed near Kalafat. On 2 November the Turkish commander, Omar Pasha, ordered a further 10,000 troops to cross the Danube in the centre on what might be termed an armed reconnaissance. The troops were to push forward and if they met with little opposition were to try and advance upon Bucharest itself. The move led to a fierce clash at the village of Oltenitsa where, on 4 November, General Petr A Dannenberg attempted to drive Omar Pasha back from their retrenchments. In Omar Pasha's account:

> The Russians advanced with coolness and resolution almost to the brink of the trench; and on this account their loss was considerable, amounting to 1,000 men killed, and double the number wounded. The engagement lasted four hours – from noon till 4pm.[1]

The Russian attack achieved little, other than heavy casualties sustained during a day of hard fighting, although it is doubtful whether the number of casualties was as high as Omar Pasha claimed. Indeed, only 236 were killed and 734 wounded according to the Russians.

Further skirmishes followed during the coming days, although wet weather hampered operations, and despite continued Russian pressure Omar Pasha's men held their own relatively comfortably. With the onset of bad weather, and with the Russians seemingly held in check, Omar Pasha recrossed the Danube on 15 November leaving only Kalafat and the island of Mokan in Turkish hands. Farther east, the Russians consolidated their positions around Bucharest, but there was little more action along the Danube and the year petered out with both sides settled into their positions as the bad weather continued. Thus satisfied with the state of affairs Omar Pasha returned to his headquarters at Shumla, fifty miles west of Varna.

The fighting on the Danube had been conducted against a backdrop of threatened Austrian and Prussian intervention on the side of the Turks. The region did, after all, sit on the fringes of the Austrian Empire, and whilst Vienna took a detached view of the fighting elsewhere in the Black Sea, such as the Caucasus, it certainly took far more interest in events unfolding along the Danube. Nevertheless, despite warnings from Vienna Nicholas ordered his generals to continue the campaign and as 1853 drew to a close Colonel Alexander Baumgarten and a Russian force marched easily along newly-made roads to Csitate, nine miles from Kalafat, apparently with orders to 'annihilate the pagans'.

Baumgarten ordered his men to dig entrenchments and fortify their position at Csitate and await reinforcements before moving on Kalafat. Unfortunately for them, the Turks moved first. On the evening of 5 January 1854 Ismail Pasha and Selim Pasha marched out of Kalafat at the head of thirteen battalions of infantry and three regiments of cavalry, numbering just over 11,000 men, along with twenty-eight guns. They were followed soon after by a reserve under Ahmed Pasha. The force halted for the night a few miles from Csitate at a village called Maglavit. The Turks were supposed to rest there and get some sleep, ready for the attack the next morning, but it was so bitterly cold that the men preferred to stand around and try to stay warm, stamping their feet, blowing on their hands and slapping their arms against their sides. Indeed, it came as something of a relief when orders were given to march next morning.

When Ismail Pasha's men approached Csitate shortly before 7 am there was not a soul to be seen nor a sound to be heard. But the Russians were

THE CRIMEAN WAR. AREAS OF OPERATION 1853 - 56
Frontiers 1853
Deployment & operations of Russian forces
Deployment and operations of Allied forces
Major Russian troop movements
Fortresses
Large Fortresses
Deployment of Austrian, Prussian and Swedish armies
Area ceded by Russia through Paris peace treaty 1856
NORWAY
SWEDEN
KOLA
White Sea
ARCHANGEL
Dvina
Solovetskie Islands
ULEABORG
BRAHESTAD
GAMLAKARLEBY
ABO
HELSINGFORS
VIBORG
BOMARSUND
STOCKHOLM
SVEABORG
ST. PETERSBURG
REVAL
KRONSTADT
RIGA
Baltic Sea
DUNABURG
DANZIG
PRUSSIA
MOSCOW
NOVOGEORGIEVSK
WARSAW
IVANGOROD
CHERNIGOV
KIEV
LEMBERG
ZHITOMIR
KHARKOV
Don
Dnepr
AUSTRIA
CHOTIN
Dnestr
Volga
EKARINODAR
IASI
KINBURN
ODESSA
GENICHESK
YEISK
Danube
WALLACHIA
BUCHAREST
EUPATORIA
KERCH
STAVROPOL
Caspian Sea
VIDIN
ISMAIL
SIMFEROPOL
NOVOROSSIJSK
SEVASTOPOL
SHUMLA
VARNA
Black Sea
SUKHUM
VLADIKAVKAZ
TIFLIS
CONSTANTINOPLE
SINOPE
KARS
ALEKSANDROPOL
TREBIZOND
ERIVAN
TURKEY
ERZURUM

not completely taken unawares. Indeed, their guns were primed and ready, and no sooner had the first Turkish troops entered the town than the guns opened up, the flashes from the muzzles lighting up the gloomy morning. Ismail quickly brought up his own guns in support and the fight turned into an artillery duel, with the Turks apparently having the best of it. Ismail himself was one of the first to enter the village, with bullets flying all round him. He had two horses killed beneath him during the day but came through with just a slight wound in the arm. His men rushed on into Csitate and engaged in some fierce hand-to-hand fighting with the Russians, with the bayonet being the principal weapon. The correspondent of *The Daily News* witnessed the fight and admired the bravery of the Russian officers who,

> . . . seeing no escape, and scorning to yield, pulled down their caps tightly on their foreheads, and rushed with mad despair to meet their death. Streams of blood ran down from the houses into the streets; the spaces around them were covered with bodies, heaped one upon another; and, to add to the horror of that dreadful scene, a number of pigs, which had got loose in the confusion, were seen making a revolting meal upon the dead, as yet scarcely cold.[2]

By midday the Russians had been completely and bloodily driven from the village and took up a position in some retrenchments they had dug on a hill overlooking the place. The fight then became one between the two sides' artillery, with the Turks having the best of it, so much so that the Russian commander took the decision to retreat. However, he was prevented from doing this by Turkish cavalry which began to encircle them and threaten their escape route. Fortunately for the Russians a large force of reinforcements, estimated at some 10,000 with sixteen guns, appeared in the distance, forcing the Turkish commander, Ahmed Pasha, to turn about and face this new threat. The Russians were thus released from their ordeal on the hillside and instead watched as their comrades attacked the Turks as they advanced along the Kalafat road. Ahmed's men were caught between the two Russian forces but their artillery did great execution amongst the attacking columns, gradually driving the Russians back. The Turks had been actively engaged all day, after having marched throughout the night. Exhausted by eight hours of fighting and with their ammunition running low Ahmed Pasha decided to withdraw his force and return to Kalafat. The Russians also withdrew. Losses are said to have been around 338 killed and 700 wounded on the Turkish side, with the Russians admitting 831 dead and 1,190 wounded. Tactically, the battle had been drawn, although from a strategic point of view it prevented the Russians from approaching Kalafat, which in turn ensured the safety of the vital fortress of Vidin.

The onset of spring in 1854 brought about renewed vigour in the czar's war plans. Despite increasing Austrian disquiet and a build up of Austrian troops on the Serbian frontier Nicholas ordered Gorchakov to cross the Danube along its entire length between Vidin and Silistria, with the capture of these two fortresses being a priority. By the end of March Gorchakov's 45,000 troops, commanded by General Alexander Luders, had crossed the Danube and had overwhelmed the Turks in the Dobrudscha – today a region of northern Bulgaria and southern Rumania – sustaining remarkably light casualties. Amongst their successes was the capture of the fortress of Tultscha, or Tulcea as it called today. The town commanded the Danube and three of its branches that flowed into the Black Sea. Two days later the Russians took another of the Danubian towns, Matschin, giving them a somewhat tenuous hold of the Upper Danube.

But despite these successes, Gorchakov did not press home his advantage, for in the midst of the operations he received orders from Field Marshal Ivan Paskevich in Warsaw not to advance beyond Matschin. This was on account of news he had received of a massive build up of Austrian troops – over 250,000 men – on the frontiers of Moldavia and Wallachia. If Gorchakov pressed on too deeply into the Danubian Principalities he risked the wrath of Austria and a consequent attack upon his rear and flank. Nevertheless, Gorchakov continued to move, if at a somewhat leisurely pace, against Silistria. So serious did Paskevich consider the situation, however, that he decided to travel from Warsaw to join Gorchakov in front of Silistria where he would assume overall command of the operation.

When we reflect upon the age of the British commanders in the Crimean War it should be noted that the problem was not just confined to the British Army. Indeed, Paskevich had seen action against the French way back in 1805, fighting at the Battle of Austerlitz. He had also served at Ulm, Borodino and Leipzig. Unlike the majority of the British commanders, however, the end of the Napoleonic Wars did not bring about an end to his career. He subsequently saw action in the Turkish and Persian wars, he helped put down the insurrection of 1831, and fought in Hungary in 1849–50

Paskevich had apparently set himself a deadline of 1 May to take Silistria, but it was not until the last week of April that he even reached the place at the head of around 40,000 troops. If Paskevich's age and the tardiness of his approach to Silistria gave the garrison the impression that the siege would be a trifling affair, they were sadly mistaken. By all accounts, Paskevich pressed on with the siege with a vigour which belied his years. Indeed, the great historian of the Crimean War, Kinglake, said that he, 'pressed the siege with a vehemence which seemed to disdain all economy of the lives of his soldiery'. But if Paskevich hoped to take the weakly-garrisoned town quickly he was to be disappointed.

Silistria was a strong fortress town with a population that varied wildly between 10,000 and 25,000 and which had taken the Russians six months to capture during the Russo–Turkish war of 1828–9. The town was enclosed within strong walls with ten bastions giving protection to the curtain walls and enfilading fire along the ditches. The ditch itself was twenty-five to thirty feet wide and twelve feet deep, with both the scarp and counterscarp being revetted with masonry. These fortifications were certainly strong enough to withstand a siege, but the fortress was made even more powerful by a series of outworks or forts situated to the west, east and south of the town, the largest of which was the Medjidie. But the most famous of the forts, basically a crude earthwork, was the Arab Tabia, so called because it was mainly protected by three battalions of Arabs, sent by the viceroy of Egypt. As siege operations often present problems of time for both besieged and besieger it was vital that the defenders made every effort to retard the attackers' operations. The longer Silistria remained in Turkish hands the more danger there was to the Russians from any troops which might be marching to relieve the place. Thus, the fight for control of topographical features that would make the besiegers' operations easier always took on a more vital aspect. The hill protected by the Arab Tabia was one such feature. Indeed, it would become what might be termed 'a battlefield magnet' as fierce fighting raged for possession of it.

The governor of Silistria was Mustafa Pasha who, although his bravery was never in doubt, lacked the kind of inspirational leadership demanded of situations such as sieges. The Turkish government was not unaware of his shortcomings in the motivation department, however, and it sent a Prussian officer in the service of the sultan, Colonel Grach, to help in the defence of the place. Sadly, Grach brought little of the experience one would expect from an officer in the Prussian service. He was an excellent artillery officer but had no idea how to supervise the defence of the place. Fortunately for Mustafa Pasha, Grach was not the only foreigner, for two young English officers, a Captain Butler of the Ceylon Rifles, and Lieutenant Naysmith of the East India Company, had somehow contrived to be inside Silistria when the Russians attacked. Naysmith and Butler – who were to emerge as two of the great heroes of the siege – managed to exert considerable influence over the garrison who began to draw great confidence from the two men's presence. The garrison itself numbered around 12,000 men, with fifty guns.

The Russian siege operations at Silistria were superintended by General Karl Schilder, ably assisted by 35 year-old Lieutenant Colonel Francis Totleben, the future hero of the siege of Sevastopol. On 28 April Paskevich made his first assault on the outworks of the town, after which he summoned the governor to surrender. This was no more than a formality, however, for although it has been known for fortresses to surrender after an outwork has been taken, Silistria was more than capable of holding on. Moreover, the Russians would need to take virtually all of the outworks before they could think about summoning the town to surrender. The attack on 28 April was driven off, and after Paskevich's summons had been refused there was a lull in the proceedings. This lasted until 11 May when the first Russian shells came screaming into the town, causing a great deal of panic amongst the people, many of whom were living in shelters and caves dug beneath the ground. According to Naysmith, the garrison's reply to this fire was extremely effective, particularly the mortar fire, which burst to good effect above the Russian batteries.

Paskevich opened his first parallel – way behind schedule – on 18 May and soon afterwards the main Russian bombardment commenced. Three days later the first Russian assault was made, but was beaten back with heavy loss, largely as the result of a mine which killed and wounded hundreds of the attackers. Four days later the Russians took advantage of a tremendous hailstorm to attack the Arab Tabia for the first time but this too was driven off. Another attack was made on the Arab Tabia before dawn on 29 May and on this occasion the attacking Russian troops succeeded in getting inside the work before being repulsed. A second attack the same day similarly failed before the Russians tried again, this time with a massive force, only to be driven off yet again. On this occasion they were pursued as far as their own works where the Turkish – or rather Albanian – troops set about filling as many of the Russians trenches as possible before returning to their fort. This kind of 'sortie' was extremely important. It was vital that Mustafa Pasha kept up an aggressive defence, for if he just sat back and prayed for relief – without doing anything to help himself – the likelihood was that, eventually, Silistria would fall. By following up the beaten Russian troops and destroying the enemy works he not only demonstrated a moral superiority but retarded the Russians' operations. The garrison's losses on 29 May were sixty-five killed and 112 wounded, a far lower figure than that admitted by the Russians, some 270 killed and 422 wounded. Amongst the Russian casualties was Paskevich himself who, along with two other generals, was wounded. Two were killed in the assault.

The Russian bombardment continued during the next few days, as they completed their second parallel. But whilst the anxiety of the garrison in Silistria increased as the Russian works crept ever closer, another, more dangerous problem began to worry Mustafa Pasha – being a shortage of ammunition. Indeed, he offered bounties to any person bringing in spent Russian cannon balls, a move which prompted the children of Silistria to chase the shot 'as coolly as if they had been cricket balls'. Sadly, Mustafa Pasha was not to be bothered by the shortage of ammunition for much longer, for on 2 June he was mortally wounded by a piece of shrapnel from a bursting shell. His place was then taken by Hussein Pasha. That same afternoon, 8,000 reinforcements arrived and camped in the open close to Fort Medjidie. It was a most welcome addition to the garrison.

Five days later Rifaat Pasha arrived to assume command of the town, bringing with him another British officer, Colonel Simmons, of the Royal Engineers, along with Captains Ballard and Fearon. The fighting continued, however, with several hard fights taking place outside the walls of the town. During one such fight, Paskevich was again apparently wounded, this time more seriously, by a cannon ball which struck him in the hip. Some accounts say it was his shoulder, whereas others suggest he was not wounded at all. If it was his hip he was lucky to escape with his life. Whatever the truth the close shave had been too close for comfort for him. He ordered a carriage and took off across the Danube, leaving Prince Gorkachov to assume command. Two days after Paskevich's departure, more Turkish reinforcements arrived in the shape of Behram Pasha's division, consisting of four battalions of infantry, one battalion of chasseurs, 400 Arab cavalry and six guns. Lieutenant Meynell of the 75th Regiment was also with them. These reinforcements weakened the Russians' grip on the town even further.

On 13 June the two British officers, Naysmith and Butler, were to have led two columns in a sortie against the Russian lines, but the attack was halted when Butler was wounded. In what was to prove the last entry in his diary – a remarkable one – Butler wrote:

> whilst the necessary arrangements were being made, we all went up to Ylanli. I crept into a new embrasure, for the purpose of examining the enemy's parallel on which the sortie was to be made. Whilst doing so, I was struck by a rifle-bullet in the forehead; but, thanks to a thick skull, and the ball having just passed through part of the parapet not yet cut through, it did not penetrate the bone, although it left a tolerable hole, and made me feel rather funny. This put a stop to the sortie, at least for some days.[3]

Sadly, the wound proved worse than at first thought. Butler's condition quickly worsened and on 21 June he died.

The Russian bombardment continued with great intensity between 20 and 22 June, causing severe damage to the town, but little else. Further Turkish reinforcements had been received and the Russian stranglehold on Silistria – if it could ever be called that – was effectively broken. When the garrison looked out on the morning of 23 June they saw with relief and delight that the Russians had made off in the night. The parallels and the camp were deserted. Despite intense pressure and a virtually incessant enemy bombardment, the garrison of Silistria and its outworks had held firm. It is estimated that the Russians threw over 50,000 shells into the town and its works during the siege which had lasted forty days. Three miles of

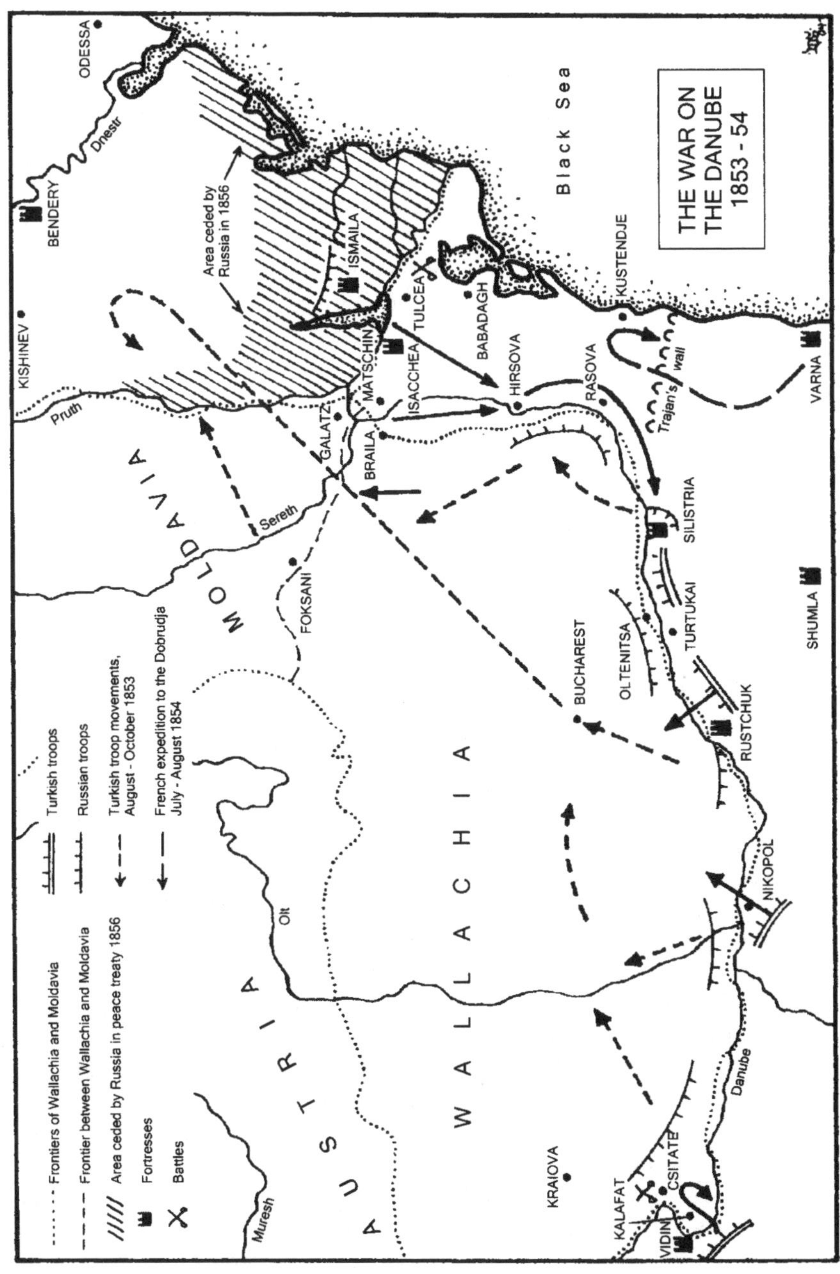
THE WAR ON
THE DANUBE
1853 - 54
Frontiers of Wallachia and Moldavia
Frontier between Wallachia and Moldavia
Area ceded by Russia in peace treaty 1856
Fortresses
Battles
Turkish troops
Russian troops
Turkish troop movements, August - October 1853
French expedition to the Dobrudja July - August 1854
Black Sea
ODESSA
Dnestr
BENDERY
KISHINEV
Pruth
Area ceded by Russia in 1856
ISMAILA
TULCEA
BABADAGH
MATSCHIN
ISACCHEA
GALATZ
BRAILA
HIRSOVA
RASOVA
KUSTENDJE
Trajan's wall
VARNA
SILISTRIA
SHUMLA
TURTUKAI
OLTENITSA
RUSTCHUK
BUCHAREST
NIKOPOL
M O L D A V I A
Sereth
FOKSANI
W A L L A C H I A
A U S T R I A
Olt
Muresh
KRAIOVA
KALAFAT
CSITATE
VIDIN
Danube

works were constructed also. It was all to no avail. In fact, it cost the Russian army some 10,000 men. Turkish losses were put at around 1,400.

June had not been a happy month for the Russians. Their setback at Silistria had come at a time when Prussia, and particularly Austria, were seriously threatening to intervene in the fighting on the Danube if the czar did not withdraw his troops. For although Nicholas pulled his troops back from Wallachia he not only remained in Moldavia but sent in reinforcements. When he advanced his troops to several towns close to the Austrian border, the Austrians responded by sending troops to the frontiers of both Transylvania and Galicia as a precaution. This potentially dangerous situation for the Russian czar became all the more worrying for him when the king of Prussia said, quite bluntly, that unless Russian troops were withdrawn from the Danubian Principalities he would declare war on Russia. It did not help matters either when, following a meeting between Omar Pasha, St Arnaud and Lord Raglan at Varna – the French and British commanders had sailed there in mid-May – it was agreed that some 55,000 troops would be moved from the Bosphorus to reinforce the Turks on the Danube. Although the effect of this accumulation of bad news for Nicholas forced him to give orders for a withdrawal, the real catalyst for the move was their failure at Silistria for without possession of both Silistria and Vidin Nicholas could not possibly hope to sustain his position on the Danube.

The rearward movement of the Russians spurred the Turks into action, and in following up the czar's retreating troops caught them at Giurgevo on 5 July. The Turkish troops were commanded by Hassan Haki Pasha and coming up to Rustchuk on the Danube, they discovered a Russian force consisting of twelve battalions of infantry, supported by cavalry and artillery, and commanded by General Soimonov, across the river at Giurgevo. The Danube was very wide at this point but the Turks intended to 'leapfrog' the river using three small islands which effectively divided the width of the river. The crossing on 5 July was made to the island of Mokan which was protected by just a few men. Initially, the Turks were flung back by a combination of musketry and artillery from the main bank of the river, but by the end of the day they had established themselves on the island and had dug batteries for four guns.

Two days later Hassan Pasha sent further troops across, this time to attack the island of Radovan. This force included a brigade of irregular light infantry commanded by a British general named Cannon, a former Sepoy officer who had also seen service with the British Legion in Spain. There were other British officers too, including Captains Bent and Burke, of the Royal Engineers, Lieutenant Meynell of the 75th, Colonel Balfour Ogilvie and Lieutenant Colonel Hinde of the 65th Bengal Infantry, Captain Arnold of the 3rd Madras Light Infantry, and Lieutenant Ballard of the Bombay Engineers. Following the attack on the 5th, it was reported that the Russians had struck their tents and were in fact moving off. On the face of it there appeared little point in undertaking a hazardous river crossing against enemy troops well positioned and armed with guns. Nevertheless, the Turks were bent on throwing back the invaders and determined to make their crossing. Despite their misgivings, the British officers joined in the attack, on 7 July, which got underway shortly after dawn with General Cannon, known to the Turks as Beyram Pasha, leading the way.

Despite intense firing from the defenders, the Turks and their British allies succeeded in taking and occupying several earthworks and their guns, but the Russians were in superior numbers and retook the positions after some very bloody fighting, during which both Meynell and Arnold were killed. Lieutenant Burke was killed shortly after, leading another detachment across the river. He had apparently leapt from his boat only to find himself coming under heavy fire from the Russians, forcing him to dig a makeshift shelter in the sandy river bank. It was of little use, however, for he was found the next morning with four bullet wounds, one of which had entered the back of his skull and exited via his chin.

The fight for the river bank was evidently fiercely contested, with a great deal of hand-to-hand fighting taking place. At length, a detachment managed to secure a position, prompting a strong counter-attack by the Russians. At least four bayonet charges were made by the Russians to try and drive the ever-increasing number of Turks back from their side of the river. But the Turks, 'with pious and warlike cries . . . sallied over their new-made parapets, brought their bayonets down to the charge, forced mass after mass to give way, and finally pressed the retreat'.[4]

It was approaching 7pm before the Russians decided enough was enough. Soimonov realised he could not hold back the thousands of Turks now establishing themselves on his side of the river and so gave the order to withdraw, which the Russians did in good order. And when the sun came up on 8 July the Turks looked to the north and saw nothing but the debris of a retreating army. Casualties for the battle at Giurgevo were very heavy indeed. Some estimates put the number of Turkish dead and wounded at 1,500, with the Russian losses amounting to 342 killed and 470 wounded. The larger number of Turkish casualties perhaps reflects the intensity of the Russian fire on the Turks as they attempted to cross the Danube.

When news of the Russian setback at Giurgevo reached Czar Nicholas he was mortified. A defeat against Turkish troops was bad enough, but against Turkish troops led by a motley band of British soldiers was unbearable. 'I can understand Oltenitsa', wrote the czar,

> I can even understand that Omar Pasha should have been able to hold against me his lines at Kalafat – I can partly account for the result of

> those fights at Csitate – I can understand Silistria – the strongest may fail in a siege – and it chanced that both Paskevich and Schilders were struck down and disabled by shot – but, but, but, that Turks – mere Turks – led on by a General of Sepoys and six or seven English boys – that they should dare to cross the Danube in the face of my troops – that, daring to attempt this, they should do it, and hold fast their ground – that my troops should give way before them; and that this – that this should be the last act of the campaign which is ending in the retreat of my whole army, and the abandonment of the principalities. Heaven lays upon me more than I can bear'.[5]

With the threat of Austrian and Prussian intervention looming ever larger, and with the probability of an advance into the Principalities at some stage by British and French troops, Nicholas took the decision to withdraw from the Danube, and on 24 July Gorchakov duly received the czar's order. On 1 August the Russians left Bucharest and by 7 September the entire Russian army, save for garrisons left behind in the fortresses of Tultscha, Isacchea and Matschin, was back across the Pruth river. And even these garrisons were gone by the end of the following month. Fifteen months of campaigning had got the Russians nowhere and had achieved nothing, save for the antagonism of various European powers. But there was one positive result; many of the czar's troops had gained vital combat experience during their campaign on the Danube, experience that the British troops in particular lacked. It would stand them in good stead during the fighting in the coming months.

Given the circumstances, the czar's decision to withdraw from the Danube was a sensible one. There was no use staying in the Principalities and waiting to be attacked in front, flank and rear. The Turks had risen from their sickbed and had demonstrated great staying power by thwarting the Russians, and even taking the offensive against them, although one wonders what the result might have been had not the Austrians, Prussians, French and British been hovering in the background. Nevertheless, Nicholas felt confident of dealing the Turks such a blow as would bring the sultan 'to his senses'. A victory against Turkey would have changed the situation in the east quite dramatically. But it was the Austrian presence that gave Nicholas most cause for concern. Indeed, the prospect of having to fight a war on two fronts, against the Turks and Austrians, would have caused Russia tremendous problems. Thus, the order to withdraw was his only real option.

The problem was that it now left Nicholas exposed to attack by the Allies who very soon would be knocking on the door of his vital Black Sea port, Sevastopol. The awful truth must now have dawned upon Nicholas. His over-confidence bordered upon arrogance, whilst his belief in Russia's infallibility, in her might and in her ability to overcome her adversaries was equally unshakeable. But he had underestimated his enemies. The Turks had thrown him back, the Austrians were poised to move given the slightest provocation, whilst the British and French navies steamed easily and unopposed along the coast of the Crimea. Nicholas suddenly realised that Russia was no longer on the offensive but was well and truly on the defensive.

NOTES

1 Tyrell, Henry. *History of the War with Russia* (London n.d.), I, 53.
2 Ibid, I, 109.
3 Ibid, I, 173.
4 Kinglake, Alexander William. *The Invasion of the Crimea: Its Origin, and An Account of its Progress down to the Death of Lord Raglan* (London 1863), II, 59.
5 Ibid, II, 62–3.

# CHAPTER FOUR
# *The Great Expedition*

Whilst the fighting had been raging on along the Danube, the British and French armies had been waiting patiently in the Bosphorus while their commanding officers decided their next step. We have already met Lord Raglan, commander in the chief of the British Army. But what of the French leader? Born in 1801, Marshal Leroy de Saint-Arnaud had joined the French Army in 1816, a year after Waterloo. His career was not particularly outstanding and he had, in fact left the army and travelled to England where he had an unhappy time living amongst the down and outs in London's Drury Lane area. He rejoined the army after the 1830 revolution and five years later was despatched to serve in Africa under General Bugeaud and it was here that he began to learn his trade during fierce fighting in the French colonies. He fought in every major action in Algeria against the Kabyles tribes between 1837 and 1851, was severely wounded, and won the Legion of Honour. His reputation made, he returned to France in 1851 and the following year was made a Marshal of France. By this time he was French minister of war, a post he was to hold until his appointment as commander-in-chief of the French Army in the East. For a man whose career had spanned fourteen years of hard campaigning in Algiers, Saint-Arnaud failed to impress many of his allies, despite his good grasp of the English language which naturally stood him in good stead. Indeed, his appointment owed as much to his political opportunism as it did to his military skill, he being the leading figure behind Napoleon's *coup d'état* in December 1851. He was also suffering badly from stomach cancer and, as we shall see, would survive barely a fortnight in the Crimea. The historian of the British Army, Fortescue, perhaps best – and ominously – summed up Saint-Arnaud. 'Brave, dashing and unscrupulous . . . quite unfit for the command of a large force against a disciplined enemy.'[1]

Given the turbulent history that existed between France and Britain it is not surprising that there was an element of mistrust between the two armies and their commanders. Britons had been fighting the French for centuries. Indeed, barely forty years had past since Wellington had crushed Napoleon Bonaparte at Waterloo. Amongst the British people there had always been the nagging fear that the revolutions that dogged

France during the first half of the nineteenth century might prove the catalyst for yet another projected invasion of old Albion. There were (and still are) those who simply could not come to terms with siding with the old enemy. Indeed, it is a measure of these deep-rooted traditions that Raglan, conditioned to seeing dark blue masses opposite him during the Peninsular and Waterloo campaigns, would on more than one occasion mistakenly refer to the Russians as the French.

The trio of Allied commanders was completed by the Turkish commander, Omar Pasha, a very amenable and capable man who quickly gained the respect of his allies. Born in Croatia, Michael Lattas, to give him his real name, served in the Austrian army before leaving for Constantinople, where he joined the Turkish army. His rise to prominence within the sultan's army was mainly due to patronage secured during his time at a military school in Constantinople. His marriage to one of the richest heiresses in the city also helped him. Given the extent of the sultan's empire and the upheavals, both military and political, that wracked the empire, it is not surprising that Omar Pasha was so active. Blessed with such important patronage and with military skills to match, it was not long before he was serving on the Danube and within a few short years was appointed commander-in-chief of the Turkish army. As the situation in the east became increasingly volatile, Omar Pasha found himself at the heart of operations in the Danubian Principalities, Moldavia and Wallachia, monitoring a situation that grew increasingly worse until, in 1853, hostilities finally broke out between Turkey and Russia.

Omar Pasha set up his headquarters at Schumla, from where he directed the Turkish army during its struggle on the Danube in 1853 and 1854. Fifty miles east of Schumla and situated on the Black Sea coast was the port of Varna, and it was here on 18 May that the ships *Berthollet* and *Caradoc* arrived with the respective commanders of the French and British armies on board. It was the first time that the three commanders had met. Raglan and Saint-Arnaud had endured an indifferent meeting in Paris the previous month, with the two men and their entourages sizing each other up, but this was the first time that Omar Pasha had been involved in the discussions. The meeting lasted five hours and must have been very strange indeed. Saint-Arnaud asked Omar Pasha to explain himself in Italian, a language which the latter spoke more fluently than French. Saint-Arnaud then translated it for the benefit of Raglan, whilst an interpreter likewise translated everything for Omar Pasha. Given the strong Russian presence in the Danubian Principalities it was only natural that the Turkish commander asked the British and French to come to Bulgaria to help throw back the czar's armies. Indeed, he grew quite animated at one point, getting to his feet and stressing in broken but intelligible phrases the need for Raglan and Saint-Arnaud to send troops to help him relieve Silistria.

> I have almost the certainty of beating the Russians, if they should attack me, but is it possible that the French and English, who are upon Turkish territory at Gallipoli, within twenty days march of Varna (or twenty-four hours by sea), will leave me blockaded here, deprive themselves of the assistance of a fine army which can fight well, and allow us to be crushed by the Russians, when, united, we might drive them to the other side of the Danube, and save Turkey?[2]

Omar Pasha's impassioned plea for help 'produced a profound effect' on all those present at the meeting. The problem was that both British and French armies were woefully short of cavalry and artillery, whilst the old problem of obtaining transport surfaced again to dog Raglan as it had dogged his old master in Spain and Portugal forty-odd years earlier. Nevertheless, despite the shortcomings in the mounted arms of their armies, both Raglan and Saint-Arnaud agreed to send troops to Varna from where they would march north towards Silistria.

Encouraged by Saint-Arnaud's enthusiasm Raglan returned to Constantinople and gave orders for the embarkation of two divisions for Varna. However, he was none too pleased when, on 4 June, Saint-Arnaud informed Raglan that he had decided to change his plans. Instead of taking the offensive and marching to the relief of Silistria, the French commander decided he would take up a defensive position behind the line of the Balkan hills with his right at Varna and Bourgas, the centre at Karnabad and Aidos, and the left at Tamboli watching the defiles of the mountains, and holding themselves ready to repulse the Russians the moment they should have passed them. Such a plan would leave the garrison at Silistria well and truly isolated. It is remarkable that Saint-Arnaud really did think that the Russians would come pouring down from the defiles of the Danube, intent on causing mayhem in Bulgaria.

An exasperated Raglan naturally refused to alter his plans. His troops were, after all, already on their way north to Bulgaria. Never one to display outward signs of great emotion Raglan was, nevertheless, firm and unbending and as usual his polite firmness won the day. With his hand thus forced, Saint-Arnaud relented, and he agreed to revert to the Allies' original plan to march north and help the beleaguered defenders of Silistria. The irony of all this was, of course, that whilst all of the wranglings and arguments were going on at Varna and in Constantinople, the fate of Silistria and, indeed, the war in the Danube Principalities, was being decided by a combination of Turkish aggression and Austrian threats. Thus, by the time the Allies were ready to march north to the Danube the war in this theatre was as good as over.

During the first weeks of June British and French steamers puffed their way across the fringes of the Black Sea, ferrying the Allied troops from their bases in the Bosphorus and the Dardanelles to Varna. Here, amidst glorious weather, the two old enemies began to fraternise whilst their leaders decided what to do next. The course of action was decided upon by the arrival of a messenger on 24 June, who turned up at Lord Raglan's headquarters with the news that the Russians had given up the siege of Silistria and had begun to withdraw across the Danube. This prompted the British commander to despatch Lord Cardigan on a reconnaissance to verify the information and to make an appraisal of the situation on the Danube. The 'soreback patrol', as it became known was a complete farce. Cardigan took with him just over 200 British cavalry and a few Turks for good measure and duly took off to see what was happening at Silistria. Sure enough, the place was free of Russian troops. But instead of returning immediately, Cardigan took himself and his men off on a 'sightseeing tour' and did not return until 11 July, by which time his men were in a terrible state. Nevertheless, Cardigan confirmed that the Russians were nowhere to be seen, and when news arrived later on of a complete withdrawal by the Russians from the Danubian Principalities it seemed as if the object of the Allies in the region, namely to thwart any Russian designs on the Danube and against Constantinople, had been accomplished.

It wasn't only the British who conducted fruitless expeditions to the north. On 22 July the French General, Yusuf, left Varna at the head of his 3,000 Spahis, bound for the Dobrudscha. An earlier reconnaissance by General Desaint had discovered that there might be as many as 10,000 Russian troops and thirty-five guns still in the region. General Yusuf was to lead his men on what amounted to a raid, but he was not to become embroiled in any long drawn-out campaign, as it looked increasingly likely that the Allies would be leaving soon for the Crimea. Saint-Arnaud told both Yusuf and Espinasse, who followed with the 1st Division:

> Do not lose sight of the fact, that you cannot remain long in the Dobrudscha. You must only appear there, observe the enemy, endeavour to take a few posts, and, your presence once detected, retire and retrace your steps to the neighbourhood of Mangalia, where you will receive orders.[3]

Yusuf was to be followed north by Espinasse's 1st Division, Bosquet's 2nd Division and the 3rd Division under Prince Napoleon. They were to go no farther than Kustendje, reconnoitre the area and then return to Varna.

The French force set off into a bare wilderness, with nothing but grassy plains covered with wild flowers and weeds as far as the eye could see. On 27 July the French advanced guard had the better of a clash with some Russian cavalry. 'It was the first time that I saw them [his men] under fire,' wrote Yusuf, 'and I was so pleased with them, that I resolved to advance the next day, and to attack the enemy vigorously.'[4] He didn't have to wait long, for on the following day just north of Kustendje, a far more serious fight took place between two regiments of Bashi-Bazouks and some Russian Cossacks. The French irregulars once again had the better of the encounter but only after some hard fighting. Yusuf planned to follow up his success by undertaking a night march, but when the order to assemble was given few answered, for his force had been suddenly struck down by cholera which spread quickly and silently through the ranks of his men, with no fewer than 150 dead and 350 dying within the hour. 'There was no longer a question of fighting, or of seeking an enemy who constantly disappeared at their approach, – but solely of escaping from the pestilence.'[5]

General Espinasse's column had likewise been decimated by cholera. Hundreds lay dead or dying in the camp, whilst many of those who dug the graves for their comrades were often struck down themselves before they had even completed their melancholy task. On 31 July 45 year-old General Canrobert, of whom more later, arrived at Kustendje on board the *Cacique*. As soon as he laid eyes on the terrible spectacle before him he gave orders for the immediate withdrawal from the area. Nearly 2,000 sick were put aboard ships which sailed from Mangalia taking them back to Varna, whilst the remainder continued their deathly march by land. The tragic expedition, called by William Russell of *The Times* 'one of the most fruitless and lamentable that has ever occurred in the history of warfare', is reckoned to have cost the French around 7,000 men. Indeed, it had achieved absolutely nothing other than the thousands of deaths. Russell also recorded that the Bashi-Bazouks, tired of rigorous and continuous French drill and discipline, began to desert in their droves, as a result of which General Yusuf was 'obliged to admit his complete failure'.[6]

The security of the Danubian Principalities did not spell an end to proceedings in the east. Far from it. It only served to remove one more obstacle preventing an invasion of the Crimea, which was the British government's real desire. The Russians might well have been thwarted on the Danube but it still left unresolved the matter of Russian power in the Black Sea. Despite the Russian withdrawals there was not the slightest possibility of the Allies returning home, not with a substantial build up of troops at Varna and certainly not with the public at home clamouring for a strike against the great Russian naval base at Sevastopol. The destruction of the base was now the number one priority amongst the people and, indeed, the press, with *The Times* and its fiery editor, John Thaddeus Delane, in particular thundering out its war cries, reminding everyone of the outrage felt after Sinope and of the more recent insult to British naval pride at Odessa, where Russian batteries fired at a British ship, HMS *Furious*, which had arrived to bring off British consulate staff, even though the ship was flying a white flag of truce. It was all fuel for the fire, and it was a fire that neither Raglan nor Saint-Arnaud could ignore.

There was little point in the Allies returning home if the Russian Black Sea Fleet was left free to roam the waters with impunity and threaten British and French interests in the region. No, something would have to be done to destroy the base, and so it was that the expedition to the Crimea and the attack on Sevastopol were decided upon. This course of action was nothing new. Indeed, on 10 April the Secretary of State for War, the Duke of Newcastle, had written to Raglan that the object of the war would probably be a strike against Sevastopol. On 29 June Newcastle followed this up with another letter, written after news of the failed Russian incursions into the Danubian Principalities had been received, in which he instructed Raglan to prepare for the siege of Sevastopol. In his dispatch, which reached Raglan on 16 July, Newcastle reminded the British Commander-in-Chief that although his first duty had been, 'to prevent, by every means in your power, the advance of the Russian army on Constantinople', the real object was 'to undertake operations of an offensive character, and that the heaviest blow which could be struck at the southern extremities of the Russian empire would be the taking or destruction of Sevastopol'. Newcastle then pointed out that the retreat of the Russian army across the Danube, 'had given a new character to the war'. As the safety of Constantinople was, 'for a time at least, secured,' he said, Raglan was to, 'concert measures for the siege of Sevastopol'.[7]

Raglan and his officers were only too aware of the dangers of rushing into a campaign before reliable intelligence could be gathered and whilst they were still relatively unprepared. But the letter was couched in veiled intimations from the government, which made it quite clear that whilst Raglan was at liberty to postpone any invasion of the Crimea the government would not be too pleased if he chose to do so. The Duke of Newcastle instructed Raglan to besiege Sevastopol, but added, 'unless, with the information in your possession but at present not known in this country, you should be decidedly of the opinion that it could not be undertaken with a reasonable prospect of success'.[8] Newcastle went on to inform the British commander that the queen herself had complete confidence in him and in his 'gallant' army. Having made it clear that the queen, her government and the British public expected great things from Raglan and his army – and in good time also – Newcastle then went on to point out that, 'Her Majesty's Government will learn with regret that an attack, from which such important consequences are anticipated, must be any longer delayed,' and added,

> . . . the difficulties of the siege of Sevastopol appear to Her Majesty's Government to be more likely to increase than diminish by delay; and as there is no prospect of a safe and honourable peace until the fortress is reduced and the fleet taken or destroyed, it is, on all accounts, most important that nothing but insuperable impediments

> – such as the want of ample preparations by either army, or the possession of a force in the Crimea greatly outnumbering that which can be brought against it – should be allowed to prevent the early decision to undertake these operations'.[9]

In other words, the government was offering Raglan the freedom to decide upon two options – to attack immediately or to delay if he thought fit. The reality was, however, that the government did not mind what Raglan chose to do, provided it was not the latter.

We may well imagine Raglan's exasperation upon receipt of Newcastle's dispatch. It was an unenviable position in which to be placed. His better judgement advised against attacking before adequate preparations could be made. It would be best to wait until the spring of 1855. On the other hand, if he delayed he risked being recalled and having somebody else, 'a more pliant instrument', placed in command. Raglan turned to one of his most trusted friends, 66 year-old Sir George Brown, who commanded the Light Division. The two men sat quietly at the table whilst Brown carefully read the dispatch. Raglan then asked him what he thought of it. Brown responded by asking Raglan what information he had on the Russian forces in the Crimea and what the strength was of the defences around Sevastopol, to which the latter replied that neither he nor Saint-Arnaud had any.

Like Raglan, Brown was a veteran of the Peninsular War and as such had lived and served in the shadow of the Duke of Wellington. Even now, forty years since the war in the Peninsula had ended, and almost two years after the duke's death, the two men still found it hard to tear themselves from the influence of their former great leader. As he sat back in his chair, Brown said:

> You and I are accustomed, when in any great difficulty, or when any important question is proposed to us, to ask ourselves how the Great Duke would have acted and decided under similar circumstances. Now, I tell your Lordship that, without more certain information than you appear to have obtained in regard to this matter, that great man would not have accepted the responsibility of undertaking such an enterprise as that which is now proposed to you![10]

But whilst Brown expressed doubts as to the wisdom of an early attack on Sevastopol, he was also realistic enough to understand the unenviable position which Raglan found himself in. Despite the reservations both he and Raglan harboured he was under no illusion as to what Raglan had to do.

> I am of the opinion that you had better accede to the proposal, and come into the views of the Government, for this reason, that it is clear

> to me, from the tenor of the Duke of Newcastle's letter, that they have made up their minds to it at home; and that, if you decline to accept the responsibility, they will send some one else out to command the army who will be less scrupulous and more ready to come into their plans.[11]

The historian, Kinglake, who was with Raglan, argued that the threat of being replaced and recalled to England carried no weight when Raglan made up his mind to attack Sevastopol. But it was a factor that he undoubtedly could not ignore. Nor did he refrain from considering what Wellington would have done. The truth is that war and politics virtually always go hand in glove, and war has been correctly termed 'an act of policy'. It was certainly the case in the Peninsula where Wellington carried out the wishes of his government to the letter, particularly in 1813 when his plans were very much dictated by events elsewhere in Europe. The difference was that Wellington was a far more political animal than Raglan ever was. After all, Wellington, when plain Sir Arthur Wellesley, was still Secretary of State for Ireland when he landed in Portugal in the hot summer of 1808 to begin his campaign. Therefore, he had far more influence with Lord Liverpool's government than Raglan did with Aberdeen's. Indeed, for much of the Peninsular War it was Wellington himself who drove and guided the government on the best course of action. After giving the matter some considerable thought Raglan decided to do what he thought his old master would have done. He would carry out his government's wishes and attack Sevastopol. How much influence public opinion had on his decision we will never know, but it should not be discounted. But the real pressure had arrived in the form of Newcastle's dispatch. One suspects that Raglan, acutely aware of the problems an invasion would bring, of the lack of intelligence, and of the unsatisfactory state of his army, ultimately took the decision to attack Sevastopol partly because he considered it possible but mainly on political grounds, as Newcastle himself would later acknowledge. From a military standpoint, however, it was a questionable decision.

On 18 July a conference was held at Saint-Arnaud's headquarters at which Raglan announced his decision to attack Sevastopol. Present at the meeting were Raglan and Saint-Arnaud, and Admirals Hamelin, Bruat, Lyons and Dundas. There was no representative from the Turks, however. The French commander had already expressed his reluctance for the plan, but declared his support for the venture. But then, the French had expressed reservations about virtually everything Raglan had suggested. They had been against the plan to help Silistria and were very critical of the way in which they considered the British to be too greatly influenced by public opinion rather than the realities of the political and military situation on the ground. Indeed, Bazancourt openly claimed the decision had been taken as a result of 'the pressure with which they [the English] were harassed by the London newspapers'. Nevertheless, once the decision had been made Saint-Arnaud wrote to his minister of war expressing his full support. 'The decisions which the Council assembled at my quarters have adopted,' he wrote, 'must be considered as definitive; and I devote all my activity and all my care to prepare for their execution.'[12]

It says much for Raglan's quiet, polite and yet very firm powers of persuasion that he was able to convince all those present at the meeting of the wisdom of a seemingly hazardous expedition to the Crimea. The truth was that he didn't. Raglan was well aware that some were against attacking before the spring of 1855, so rather than have the meeting degenerate into a debating chamber as to the wisdom of attacking Sevastopol, Raglan instead limited it to a discussion on how the Allies would invade the Crimea. Raglan's main concern was the lack of reliable intelligence about the Russians, and what sort of opposition he could expect to find in the Crimea. It was decided, therefore, to undertake a reconnaissance of the Crimean coast in order to determine a suitable place for disembarkation. Remarkably, the reconnaissance would be conducted not by staff officers but by some very senior Allied officers. The French sent General Canrobert and Colonel Trochu, along with one engineer, Leboeuf, and one artillery officer, Sabatier, whilst Raglan sent Sir George Brown, Lieutenant Colonel Lake of the Royal Horse Artillery, Captain Lovell of the Royal Engineers, and Captain Wetherall of the Quartermaster-General's department. The ship itself was steered by 'no common hand', as Kinglake put it, but by Admiral Sir Edmund Lyons himself. On 19 July, and with the reconnaissance party once aboard, the steamer *Fury* puffed its way out into the Black Sea bound for the Crimean coast.

With the *Fury* underway Allied leaders had time to reflect upon the decision to attack Sevastopol. Although there had been no discussion of the plan on 18 July there were still some dissenting voices. Indeed, even Saint-Arnaud, who had thrown his weight behind the plan, was still somewhat uneasy about the idea. It was all very well for the British government to press Raglan for an attack on Sevastopol but Saint-Arnaud remained unconvinced that even if successful it would bring about an end to the war. He said:

> To land in the Crimea, and besiege Sevastopol is in itself a whole campaign. It is not a *coup de main*; it requires enormous resources and a certainty of success . . . Supposing us landed, we should require, perhaps, more than a month's siege to capture Sevastopol, if well defended. During that time, succours arrive, and I have two or even three battles to fight . . . Nevertheless, despite all difficulties, all obstacles, and the lack of means and of time, Sevastopol tempts me to

> such a degree, that I should not hesitate, should there be even an appearance of success; and I prepare myself accordingly.[13]

One wonders what Saint-Arnaud would have thought of the venture had he known that it would take not just a month, but almost a year to take Sevastopol.

But the more disturbing opinions were to be found amongst Raglan's own officers. On the very day that the *Fury* steamed off to the Crimea, the British Army's chief engineer in Turkey, General Tylden, wrote to Sir John Burgoyne, the veteran Royal Engineer, expressing doubts as to the wisdom of attacking Sevastopol so late in the campaigning season. 'I think it very late in the season to commence the siege of Sevastopol, even if the generals are mad enough to undertake it.'[14] Interestingly enough, and by way of emphasising the opinion that Raglan was too influenced by the press, Tylden added, 'but as Marshal St. Arnaud [sic] is independent of the English press, I hope he will not be goaded to undertake so hazardous an affair at this late period.' Tylden was to be disappointed however, for the French commander decided to support Raglan.

Meanwhile, the *Fury* continued its reconnaissance along the Crimean coast with the Allied fleet steaming off Sevastopol to draw attention away from the real object of the exercise. The *Fury* cruised within a mile of the shore, observing the locals going about their business. Word evidently spread amongst them, for crowds could be seen along the shore, gazing out at the 'enemy' flotilla. At one point, some Russian guns opened fire on the ships, but caused no real damage. The Allied fleet meanwhile kept Russian ships at bay and prevented any interference in the business of discovering a suitable landing place. Seven miles north of Sevastopol runs the Katcha river, and at its confluence with the sea was the sort of beach the Allies were looking for. After a lengthy survey of the coast Canrobert and Brown decided that this was just the place. Thus satisfied, Lyons put the *Fury* about and the reconnaissance party steamed happily off back to Varna.

The return of the reconnaissance party on 28 July prompted another meeting on 29 July, at which its findings were discussed. The meeting also gave the French another chance to air their fears about the proposed expedition. Once again the French trotted out the old case for remaining in Bulgaria to face any threat from the north by Russian troops. Raglan would have none of it, however, and with his quiet but firm manner brushed aside the French arguments. There was no more time for dissension otherwise the already late campaign season would be virtually over. 'The theory that it was the duty of the Allied commanders to abandon the enterprise was never put down by argument, but left to die away uncontested.'[15] And so, despite an almost total lack of credible information about the Russians and Sevastopol, Raglan fixed the date for embarkation. It would be either 31 July or 1 August.

The day after the conference General Tylden wrote again to Burgoyne calling the coming venture, 'a very rash undertaking'. Burgoyne himself was none too impressed either. The 72 year-old engineer was a veteran of many a bloody siege in the Peninsular War. Indeed, there was nobody more qualified than Burgoyne to comment on the projected plan to besiege Sevastopol, and when the reconnaissance party returned from their outing along the Crimean coast, their report was passed to the Duke of Newcastle and copied to Burgoyne. The latter's comments so alarmed the government that on 11 August he was asked by the duke to join the army in the east.

During his journey Burgoyne spent much of his time 'forming projects' for the invasion of the Crimea. 'I have done so,' he wrote, 'because I think the manner of commencing which we understood when in England to be contemplated, very injudicious.' And no sooner had he arrived at Varna than he was writing again. 'An attack on Sevastopol at the present time [29 August] must be considered a most desperate undertaking'.[16] The army's concerns extended down even to junior officers, one of whom was Henry Clifford, who was to win a Victoria Cross during the war.

> Everyone is convinced of one thing and that is, that if an attack is made upon Sevastopol, with the best possible management and under the most favourable circumstances the loss of life will be very great on our side. The least sanguine look upon the plan as that of a madman and the taking of the place as impossible.[17]

But even as thoughts turned to the impending invasion, the Allied troops were attacked by another more deadly and invisible enemy that swept through the camps, 'like the sword of a destroying angel'. Cholera had struck. The plague is said to have been brought into Varna from Marseilles in a transport ship. Whatever the source, it spread quickly and silently through the Allies' camps. The French had been suffering for a while before the British troops began to be struck down. Up until that point Raglan's men had been suffering from cases of diarrhoea but nothing more serious. Even so, diarrhoea was bad enough, particularly given the heat and unpleasant conditions within the British camps. William Russell was correspondent for *The Times* and would become famous for his vivid dispatches from the theatre of war. Commenting on the diarrhoea, Russell wrote:

> The quantity of apricots ('kill Johns') and hard crude fruit which were devoured by the men, might in some degree account for the prevalence of this debilitating malady. The commissariat bread was not so good at first, and speedily turned sour; but the officers took steps to remedy the evil by the erection of ovens in the camp. As the

> intensity of the sun's rays increased, the bread served out to us from the Varna bakeries became darker, more sour, and less baked. As a general rule, the French bread was lighter and better than our own, and yet they suffered as much from diarrhoea as our troops.[18]

Cholera, on the other hand, was something quite different. The Allies' conference on 18 July had barely ended when the plague began spreading through their camps. It began slowly, the Light Division recording just over a hundred cases on 19 July, for example. But by the end of the first week in August there were almost 2,000 British troops lying sick and incapacitated in hospital at Scutari, of which 112 died, a figure which rose to 345 by 9 August. Sickness in the army was nothing new of course. For example, almost 800 men of the 1st Foot Guards died from sickness within a month of landing in Spain at the end of 1812. The regiment was consequently sent to Oporto to recover, which prevented the spread of the sickness. But in 1854 even by dispersing the regiments the plague refused to be halted. It even spread to the ships, with the *Britannia*, for example, losing 139 men dead out of a company of 985. The outbreak of cholera, combined with diarrhoea and other illnesses, only served to shed more doubt on the wisdom of the decision to invade the Crimea. In a memorandum of 29 August, Burgoyne, writing with the benefit of his experience in Spain and Portugal, cited two 'casual circumstances' that might prove great impediments to the success of the coming campaign. The first was the advance of the season, and with it the coming storms which might prevent communications between ship and shore. The other factor was sickness amongst the troops.

> Magnificent as the troops were on coming out, they are now enfeebled and much shaken in body, as well as, it may be feared, in *morale*, by climate, disorder, and the want of excitement created by engaging with the enemy. The diminution of bodily power, and consequent ill-effects of a moderate degree of fatigue, will be a positive evil, and tend to renewed sickness; while the loss of spirits that there is every reason to fear exists, will prevent the exertions necessary to reduce the effect of the other. The disadvantages under which they will labour, if the above remarks be true, will soon be perceived by them, and create a loss of *morale* that will greatly affect every proceeding.[19]

The effect that cholera had on the troops was not lost on Raglan, who was forced to postpone the embarkation. This, combined with a continued shortage of intelligence about the Russian Army, convinced Raglan to put things off until the situation improved. The only comfort for Raglan, not that it was terribly important to him, came when he received a letter from

Newcastle who acknowledged the fact that Raglan had made the decision to attack Sevastopol against his better judgement and in deference to the government's wishes. It was too late now, of course, but at least Newcastle agreed to send reinforcements to the east.

The cholera continued, as did the discussions about the proposed landing site in the Crimea, for despite the recommendations made by Sir George Brown in his report following the reconnaissance, Raglan remained unconvinced. Perhaps it was for this reason that Brown's report found its way into the hands of his old friend, Burgoyne, who was both critical and sceptical of many of its conclusions. Burgoyne's main criticism of the report was reserved for the recommended landing site. In the report Brown stated:

> The first landing place between Eupatoria and Sevastopol, which is on the river Alma, is too far from Sevastopol. The second, on the river Katcha, about three leagues from Sevastopol, is favourable. The third, on the river Belbec, is too close, being only 3,000 metres or more from Fort Constantine.[20]

Burgoyne disagreed. 'I do not understand or concur in this apparent argument,' he wrote, 'except as to the river Belbec being too close; but so is, I apprehend, the second landing place on the Katcha.' He went on to say that the Katcha site appeared to be, 'anything but desirable.' In his proposed plan of campaign for the Crimea – written at Piraeus on his way to Varna, Burgoyne considered Eupatoria as the most favourable landing site. It was an opinion expressed once again during the first council of war at which Burgoyne was present after having arrived at Varna. After considering and rejecting the various proposed landing sites in another memorandum he wrote: 'The most practicable and advantageous place, then, would probably be on the north at Eupatoria.' He then went on to point out the advantages it had to offer, such as a fine shallow bay and some jetties, in addition to which he thought it likely to be undefended. It is not known whether Burgoyne's views were made known to Raglan, for they only appear in his memoranda. Indeed, on 29 August Burgoyne himself wrote that he did not expect to have any opportunity of 'expressing any opinion on the great project'. However, given the relationship between the two old comrades, and the fact that they dined together at Varna, it is hard to believe that Burgoyne did not venture to put forward his views on the various landing sites.

By 19 August the number of British deaths from cholera had risen to 532, but the figure appeared to be levelling off. The French had suffered dreadfully however, with the column that had marched north into the Dobrudscha suffering an estimated 10,000 casualties from sickness. But, just as the plague threatened to derail the whole expedition, it suddenly receded and disappeared, largely from the British troops, leaving the Allied commanders to breathe a sigh of relief. They could now get on with the business of embarkation for the Crimea.

But what about the Crimea itself? It is true that the Allies knew much about Sevastopol and its role as a powerful naval base in the Black Sea. But of the Crimean peninsula, far less was known. It was all somewhat mysterious. The history of the Taurida (Crimea) peninsula, its inhabitants, and its towns can be traced back thousands of years. Centuries before Russia and the Allies became locked in their struggle in 1854 various tribes and civilisations had fought for possession of the peninsula. When the Russian empress Catherine the Great first visited the Crimea in 1787, she was taken aback by its great beauty. Indeed, she went on to say, with great enthusiasm, that the Crimea was, 'the best pearl in my crown!' The Crimean peninsula, soon to be the scene of the main struggle between Russia and the Allies, is indeed a charming place. It has a warm, mild and salubrious climate, a marvellous sea, and picturesque mountains, while the beautiful vegetation makes it very attractive place indeed. It is also a place steeped in history.

Three thousand years before the Crimean War began the peninsula was inhabited by wild and austere people called the Taurs, hence the original name of the peninsula, Taurida. The Taurs were idolaters and offered captured foreign navigators as sacrifice to their virgin-priestess, Iphigenia, a cold-hearted but beautiful priestess who lived in a grove on the Cape Partenitum. But the Taurs were soon forced to fight for their homeland. The convenient location and rich natural beauty attracted other, stronger, peoples. The Greeks came from across the sea, and after establishing reasonably friendly relations with the Taurs, pushed them aside and began to build their own fortified towns along the shore. It was at this time that Chersonesus was built. From the north came the Scythians. They also built their own fortifications and fought with the Taurs.

Before the birth of Christ Chersonesus, the outlying villages and the surrounding area, belonged to the Chersonesus republic, which was beginning to expand and prosper. It continued in this way for a few more centuries before it fell under the control of the Byzantine Empire. The empire ruled over a further period of prosperity until 987, when the Russian Prince Vladimir arrived with a large army, supported by ships, and conquered Chersonesus. In order to consolidate his triumph, Vladimir married Anna, a sister of one of the Byzantine emperors, but before the wedding he had to convert from paganism to Christianity. Vladimir was duly baptised in Chersonesus where a beautiful cathedral is now situated. After his conversion and wedding, Vladimir gave Chersonesus back to the Greeks. But if he thought this move would lead to stability and continued prosperity he was mistaken. Indeed, his move initiated a long period of turmoil, during which the people became exhausted by the constant fighting with various invading forces which sought to control their lives and their lands.

In the 12th century the Tartars came to the Taurida peninsula and called it 'Crimea'. And it was these same Tartars who, between two picturesque harbours just to the west of Chersonesus, built a small village for their fish-works and called it 'Ahtiar'. Today we call it 'Sevastopol'. The Tartars remained in the Crimea for centuries. Indeed, they are still there today. But in 1782 Admiral Potemkin, a favourite of Empress Catherine the Great, conquered the Crimea. In her manifesto of 1783 the Russian empress declared to Europe that the last Tartar khan Shagin-Girey had abdicated and that the Crimea was now part of her great empire.

Soon afterwards, construction was begun on a port, intended to give the Russian fleet a safe and secure base in the Black Sea. The port was built on the site of the original Tartar village and in 1784 was called by Catherine the Great 'Sevastopol', which in Greek meant 'famous, glorious town'. Little did she know that seventy years afterwards, Sevastopol was to become more famous and glorious than she ever could have imagined. The town soon began to grow, largely under the supervision of Admiral Thomas Mackenzie (or Mekenzy, a Russian admiral of Scottish origin). But the development of the port of Sevastopol was not just for the benefit of Russia's navy, for the Russian government declared the port a free trade zone for the foreign and local merchants in Sevastopol.

By way of political demonstration against anti-Russian propaganda and in order to show that Russia was strong enough for war, Catherine visited the Crimea in May 1787. It was with a great sense of pride that she and her retinue looked out along the Sevastopol roadstead and saw the majestic array of twenty ships and eight transports. The Black Sea Fleet added many glorious pages to the naval history of Russia; the campaign in the Mediterranean under Admiral Ushakov in 1799, the Battle of Navarino in 1827, and the heroic deed of the brig *Mercury* in 1828 under Captain-lieutenant Kazarsky, who was attacked by two large Turkish ships and eventually blew up his ship rather than give in to the more powerful enemy, an episode commemorated in 1839 by the erection of the first monument in Sevastopol.

The development of Sevastopol as a naval and mercantile base did not go unnoticed by Russia's neighbours, however, who began to see the move as a threat to the stability of Black Sea trade and to the region in general. Turkey, in particular, viewed with suspicion the joining of the Crimea to Russia and the foundation of the Sevastopol naval base. Britain and France also took a dim view of the development of the port. They feared the Black Sea might one day become a 'Russian lake'. There was no hint whatsoever of any future conflict between the various disputants but the construction and development of Sevastopol certainly sowed the seeds of the so-called 'Eastern question'. Although deep-rooted religious causes set in motion the long chain of events that ended with the outbreak of the Crimean War, the development of the Russian naval base on the site of the small Tartar fishing village would cause a serious rupture in relations between Russia, her neighbours and Britain and France, and become a major factor in the outbreak of war in 1854.

On 24 August 1854 thousands of British, French and Turkish troops began to concentrate in the Varna area, ready to board the transports which would take them across the Black Sea to the Crimea. Saint-Arnaud earmarked some 24,000 infantry and seventy guns, along with around 5,000 Turks, who would be transported in their own ships. Very few cavalry were to be taken across initially, to be used for patrol and reconnaissance work. Raglan's force numbered roughly the same, with 22,000 infantry and sixty guns. But unlike the French, Raglan embarked around 1,000 cavalry from Lord Cardigan's Light Brigade. In theory this was a wise move. The undulating, barren terrain in the Crimea was most suitable for cavalry, particularly light cavalry. Unfortunately, Raglan seemed to harbour the same fears that his former great leader had in the Peninsula, with the result that he was loath to use them even when the situation cried out for them. He wasn't helped either by the fact that the brigade was commanded by Cardigan, one of the most infamous men in the army. Indeed, his perpetual feud with his superior, Lord Lucan, was to have dire consequences for the cavalry. The embarkation was painfully slow. Burgoyne wrote:

> Everything is in a state of great activity and bustle here . . . the great slowness of the operation and embarking, even when at work with *six* piers here in the bay, shows what a formidable operation it is, and how even disembarkations, except for the men alone, must be long.[21]

After having witnessed the time it was taking for the embarkation, doubts as to the wisdom of going ahead with the invasion obviously began to creep into Burgoyne's mind, although he realised it was rather late in the day to begin 'rocking the boat'. Indeed, he wrote, somewhat ominously:

> This is not the time for discouraging anybody, and consequently I do not hold to a soul, opinions that I may give to you at a distance, confidentially. It appears to me to be the most desperate enterprise ever attempted . . . On the whole, I shall really not be sorry, under my views, if circumstances of weather (which seems to be breaking), or other accidental circumstance, should cause the proceeding to be deferred for this season.[22]

Unfavourable winds did indeed cause problems with the embarkation, particularly of the horses, but the departure for the Crimea was only delayed, not postponed. Admiral Sir Edmund Lyons worked tirelessly to get the British troops aboard their ships, whilst Saint-Arnaud's lieutenants struggled to find enough steamers to carry the French. ('Des difficultés! – des difficultés!! according to Saint-Arnaud). But by 5 September, and with the year entering its final third, the Allied ships steamed out into the open sea from Varna, bound for their rendezvous point off the Crimean coast. 'The great expedition,' as Raglan put it, was finally underway.

The morning of 8 September found the Allied flotilla well out into a very choppy Black Sea, the last vessels having departed Varna the previous day. The sea was so rough, in fact, that it prevented Lord Raglan – with his one arm – from boarding the French ship, the *Ville de Paris,* in order to attend a conference of Allied commanders being held on board. Saint-Arnaud himself was soon forced to leave the meeting because of his increasingly poor health. Otherwise, Admiral Dundas, Colonel Sir Thomas Steele, Raglan's military secretary, and Colonel Hugh Rose, the liaison officer, were present from the British side, whilst the French representatives were Admirals Hamelin and Bruat, and Colonel Trochu. The main topic of discussion was, naturally, the choice of landing site. Given that neither Raglan nor Saint-Arnaud, who had returned to his sick bed, were now present at the meeting it is not surprising that no decision was taken. Opinions varied, although all seemed to agree that Katcha, the original choice, was unsuitable. The meeting broke up with Colonel Trochu and Admiral Hamelin joining Raglan on board his ship, the *Caradoc,* whereupon Raglan suggested that another reconnaissance be made of the coast the following day.

At 6 am on the morning of 9 September, Admiral Lyons' ship, the *Agamemnon,* with Sir George Brown on board, steamed alongside the *Caradoc,* with Raglan and Burgoyne, and was joined soon after by the French steamer, *Primoguet,* carrying Colonel Rose, Admiral Bruat, Colonels Trochu and Leboeuf, and Generals Canrobert, Tiry, Bizot and Martimprey. The *Sampson* joined the reconnaissance to cover the other three ships. The small flotilla arrived off Sevastopol at daylight on 10 September, running close to the shore, so close in fact that Admiral Lyons exchanged greetings with a Russian officer who bowed in return. The flotilla cruised along the coast as far as the harbour of Balaklava before returning north, round Cape Chersonesus, and past Sevastopol for a second time. It then continued north, passing and reconnoitring the mouths of the Belbec, Katcha, Alma and Bulganak rivers, with opinions being expressed as to their various merits and drawbacks. General Canrobert continued to favour the Katcha as the landing site, whilst the British officers argued against it. At length, Burgoyne was introduced to the French officers, upon which he proceeded to explain why the Katcha was a bad choice. Not only was it too narrow, but Russian troops had been seen encamped there and on the Alma river, but none north of the latter.

There was little doubt also that garrisons would be found at Simferopol and Batchki Serai, which could threaten the Allied rear if they landed at the Katcha and got into difficulties. Canrobert, on the other hand, said that if the Allies landed north of the Alma they would most likely have to fight three battles, on the Alma, Katcha and Belbec rivers, before they could approach Sevastopol. This was true, stated Burgoyne, but, 'if we beat them well in the first, they will hardly fight two others so immediately'. It would take just a month for Burgoyne to be proved correct, but in the meantime Raglan made his final decision as to the landing site. It would be a fair distance north of the Alma, on a wide expansive beach that lay just south of Eupatoria. The generals leaned over and peered at the map in order to find out its name. Strangely, no one in that crowded room on the *Caradoc* chose to comment on the unusual and ominous name of the landing site. It was Kalamita Bay.

The Allied fleets anchored off Kalamita Bay during 12 and 13 September, ready for the landing the following morning. The mixture of steam and sailing ships presented a magnificent spectacle that night, creating a veritable forest of masts. The French historian, Bazancourt, thought his pen was powerless to portray the magical picture but certainly did his best.

> It seemed some vast fantastic city, which had sprung from the bosom of the waves. The sun had set; the air was pure; the sea smooth as a mirror. The numerous signals and flags of the vessels could still be distinguished, and the camp fires, faint amid the dying rays of the twilight, began to shine in all directions. On the horizon, the town of Eupatoria was buried in deep shade, while the mills which crown the surrounding heights stood sharply defined against the still luminous blue of the heavens.[23]

The landing site itself was four miles long. The French and Turks were to land to the south, or the right, with the British troops landing to the north, on the left of their allies, at a place called the Old Fort. A buoy was to be placed out at sea as the demarcation point between the two armies. The British beach was flat, and was a mixture of sand and shingle, 'cast up by the violence of the surf, and forming a sort of causeway between the sea and a stagnant salt-water lake, about a mile long and half a mile broad'. The lake, in fact, was virtually midway between the two landing beaches, with another much larger lake, Kamishlu, to the north. The French site was a broad, flat, sandy beach, ideal for landing troops. But, not content with the suitability of their site, the French apparently moved the demarcation buoy farther north, thus allowing themselves more room to manoeuvre, and consequently cramping the British somewhat. This was done at night, prompting Kinglake to suggest that the buoy might have been moved 'to bring the harmony between the French and the English forces into grievous jeopardy'. It was either moved by mistake, by plain French greed, or, as he ventured to suggest, 'from a scheme more profoundly designed . . . by those French officers who had been labouring to bring the enterprise to a stop'.[24] Whatever the reason for the 'mistake' it was to cause some confusion the next morning when Admiral Dundas discovered what had happened. Raglan took a pragmatic approach to the matter, deciding to land his men to the north of the buoy, rather than try to move it back and cause even more confusion. It simply meant that there would be about a mile between the two Allied armies when they landed. Other than that, Raglan saw no great reason to get upset.

At 2.30 am two rockets were fired from the French flagship, the *Ville de Paris*, as a signal to Admiral Dundas for the fleets to get underway for the final push towards the beaches. Dundas duly acknowledged the signal and soon the whole fleet, both steam and sail, was puffing and heaving towards the landing sites. The French had devised a most elaborate scheme for their landings. The *Ville de Paris*, being towed by the *Napoleon*, led the main convoy of ships, three other French ships, the *Primoguet*, the *Caton* and the *Mouette*, having already sailed ahead in order to place buoys of different colours to designate the anchorage of the three French columns. Then, at 7 am Admiral Hamelin gave the order for the ships to anchor according to their plan. The first line of ships transported the 1st Division of the French Army, their landing site being designated by a red flag. The second line of ships was to transport the 2nd Division, theirs being a white flag, and the third line of ships transporting the 3rd Division of the French Army, their landing site being marked by a blue flag. Bazancourt wrote:

> There are long files of ships of all sizes, extending over the waters of the sea. All are filled with soldiers, whose bayonets shine in the first rays of dawn. It is a town, floating and animated, which transports a human exodus from one shore to the other. The coast is before us; the beach, silent and deserted, appears to await these thousands of beings, to receive from them life, movement, and tumult.[25]

There were some 250 Allied ships waiting anxiously off shore for the small landing boats to be dropped into the sea. Then, at around 7 am the *Ville de Paris* began dropping its boats into the water, whilst large barges, which were towed behind the ships all the way from Varna, were brought alongside. These barges had been built at Constantinople for the use of the French artillery. Each one was capable of carrying two guns and their carriages, with one piece being placed at the front and one at the rear. Between them stood twelve horses with their equipment and drivers, numbering eighteen men. Each gun could be made ready for firing within ten minutes of landing on the beach. The British did not use barges but instead tied two boats together and laid a platform across the two on which they placed their guns.

Once the boats were dropped over the side, the French troops clambered into them before being rowed to the beach. It was ten minutes past eight. The British troops, however, were late on account of having to move to their new landing site. Twenty minutes later the first French boat hit the beach, and no sooner had it ground to a halt than General Canrobert leapt on to the sand to unfurl the tricolour. As the French historian proudly remarked, 'Forty-two years before, day for day, – on the 14th of September, 1812, – the Grand Army commanded by the Emperor Napoleon, entered Moscow.' Elsewhere on the French beaches the three divisional flags were hoisted and before long the troops began to muster at their respective stations.

Meanwhile, Raglan's men had begun to land, the time varying between 9 and 10 am The men of Sir George Brown's Light Division were first ashore, their large, flat-bottomed boats towed by brawny sailors who heaved at the oars to get them from ship to shore. The graphic descriptions of William Russell, the correspondent from *The Times*, were to gain for him great fame as one of the first war correspondents. His description of the landings at Kalamita Bay is typical of his vivid but informative style.

> A gig or cutter, pulled by eight or twelve sailors, with a paddle-box boat, flat or Turkish pinnace in tow (the latter purchased for the service), would come alongside a steamer or transport in which troops were ready for disembarkation. The officers of each company first descended, each man in full dress. Over his shoulder was slung his haversack, containing what had been, ere it underwent the process of cooking, four pounds and a half of salt meat, and a bulky mass of biscuit of the same weight. This was his ration for three days. Besides this, each officer carried his greatcoat, rolled up and fastened in a hoop round his body, a wooden canteen to hold water, a small ration of spirits, whatever change of underclothing he could manage to stow away, his forage-cap, and, in most instances, a revolver. Each private carried his blanket and greatcoat strapped up into a kind of knapsack, inside of which was a pair of boots, a pair of socks, a shirt, and, at the request of the men themselves, a forage-cap; he also carried his water canteen, and the same rations as the officer, a portion of the mess cooking apparatus, firelock and bayonet of course, cartouch box and fifty rounds of ball-cartridge for Minié, sixty rounds for the smooth-bore arms.[26]

By about noon the British landing beach was swarming with red-coated infantry, dragging themselves ashore and looking to their officers and muster stations. 'By twelve o'clock,' Russell wrote,

> that barren and desolate beach, inhabited but a short time before only by the seagull and wild-fowl, was swarming with life. From one extremity to the other, bayonets glistened, and redcoats and brass-mounted shakos gleamed in solid masses. The air was filled with our English speech, and the hum of voices mingled with loud notes of command, cries of comrades to each other, the familiar address of 'Bill' to 'Tom,' or of 'Pat' to 'Sandy,' and an occasional shout of laughter.[27]

About eight miles to the south three British frigates, the *Sampson*, *Fury* and *Vesuvius*, and two French steamers, the *Caffarelli* and *Coligny*, shelled a Russian camp of around 6,000 troops, knocking over some of the tents and sending their evidently reluctant occupants hurrying off to the rear. Otherwise, apart from a few inquisitive Cossacks and a Russian officer taking notes, the Allies encountered no opposition whatsoever. There were, however, many locals, mainly Tartars, who were bold enough to come and greet the invaders, bringing sheep, cattle and vegetables for sale. They also fed the Allies useful information regarding the size of the Russian armies in and around Sevastopol, and of their movements. Otherwise, those pessimistic Allied officers who had expected opposition were sadly disappointed. In fact, the bigger danger to the disembarkation came from the weather, which began to worsen as the day wore on. Indeed, towards the close of the day the sea had got up to such an extent that the order was given to suspend the disembarkation of the artillery and horses. This was not before a large portion of the French troops had been landed, however, as Lieutenant Garnault, on board *Ville de Paris*, wrote in his journal:

> When the order to suspend the landing was signalled, the fleet had already landed three divisions, completely furnished with provisions for four days, and their baggage and horses; the companies of engineers and all their tools; the horses of the Spahis, and the horses of the Marshal [Saint-Arnaud] and the Staff.[28]

By the close of the day the British troops had got themselves sorted out and had taken up their respective posts, with the Light Division pushing farthest inland. Two miles behind them was the 1st Division, whilst the 2nd and 3rd Divisions took post on the hills and cliffs near the beach. The 4th Division remained close to the beach. It was barren landscape, with no shelter whatsoever for the troops. Their tents had not been landed and consequently the British troops had to spend the night wrapped in their blankets and greatcoats beneath the open Crimean sky. The French, on the other hand, brought with them their *tentes d'abri*, which were distributed in pieces amongst several men, and when assembled were capable of sheltering them. It appears that only Sir De Lacy Evans, commanding the 2nd Division, was provided with a tent, which was good fortune for him, as it turned out to be an extremely unpleasant night. It was so bad that William Russell was moved to write that 'seldom or never were 27,000 Englishmen more miserable'.

The night sky on 14 September grew darker, 'black and lowering', the wind got up and before long the rain was falling in torrents. 'The showers increased in violence about midnight,' wrote Russell, 'and early in the morning fell in drenching sheets, which pierced through the blankets and greatcoats of the houseless and tentless soldiers'.[29] The weather paid little respect to rank, and senior officers – unless they were lucky, like Sir De Lacy Evans – endured much the same miseries as their men. Sir George Brown spent the night under a cart, whilst even the Duke of Cambridge, Queen Victoria's cousin, had little joy in finding shelter, choosing instead to spend the night wrapped in a waterproof coat, riding about his men in an effort to cheer them up. An officer with the 4th Division, Lieutenant Peard, described their situation up on the beach:

> We took up our position for the night just before dusk, and piled our arms. At dusk our men lay down under them for the first night's campaign in the Crimea. Before our first hour's sleep had passed over, however, we were aroused by a drenching rain, and, before long, were wet to the skin. So there was nothing left for us but to congregate round the huge bonfires the men had made out of the barrels and planks they had picked up. Of all miserable nights I ever spent in my life this was the most wretched.[30]

The men of the 4th Division could at least console themselves with the fact that, being on the beach itself, they had been able to find wood to burn for fuel. Elsewhere, the men were not so fortunate, and thus the British passed an extremely unpleasant night. The French, on the other hand, with their 'little scraps of tents' were more fortunate, whilst the Turks, with their much lighter tents, 'were lying snugly under cover'.

It was indeed a thoroughly filthy night, and on the morning of the 15th the older generation of officers, like Raglan himself – who remained on board the *Caradoc* until the 15th – probably cast their minds back to the morning of Waterloo when a similar uncomfortable situation presented itself. Russell went on:

> Let the reader imagine old generals and young gentlemen exposed to the violence of pitiless storms, with no bed but the reeking puddle under the saturated blankets, or bits of useless waterproof wrappers, and the twenty-odd thousand poor fellows who could not get 'dry bits' of ground, and had to sleep or try to sleep, in little lochs and

> watercourses – no fires to cheer them, no hot grog, and the prospect of no breakfast; – let him imagine this, and add to it that the nice 'change of linen' had become a wet abomination, which weighed the poor men's kits down, and he will admit that this 'seasoning' was of rather a violent character – particularly as it came after all the luxuries of a dry ship stowage.[31]

On 15 September both the cavalry and artillery were landed. The horses of the cavalry were by now accustomed to being cooped up aboard ship in slings and berths and were brought ashore without too much trouble, although one or two were drowned. Lord Raglan himself saw one of his chargers jump overboard but it was rescued and brought safely ashore. The greatest problem facing the British army was an almost total lack of transport. It seems remarkable that the problem that most had troubled Wellington's army in the Peninsula had still to be resolved even forty years on. The problem was one that plagued Wellington continually and was only really resolved towards the end of the Peninsular War when a system of transportation was 'perfected'. Lessons were not learned, however, nor was the importance of having suitable and sufficient numbers of vehicles appreciated, otherwise the army would surely have ensured that transport was available. It should not have been good enough simply to assume that transport would be available locally. The first consequence was that the tents that would have given the troops shelter on that terrible first night could not be landed and brought forward. In fact, they were landed on the 15th but when no transport could be found to move them they were loaded back aboard ship. Nevertheless, the disembarkation continued and by the evening of 18 September the entire Allied force, of 61,400 infantry, 1,200 cavalry and 137 guns, was ashore, and with no loss through enemy action. In all, it had gone very well indeed, and hopes were high for a rapid advance on Sevastopol.

Despite the fact that few Russians had been seen during the disembarkation, the Allies knew it would not be too long before they encountered them. British estimates had put the Russian army at between 45,000 and 75,000. There were, in fact, 24,000 Russian infantry and 3,200 cavalry in front of the Allies, commanded by Prince Menshikov, as well as an estimated 20,000 Cossacks. They would be met soon enough. The Allies themselves began their advance on 19 September, although the French had wanted to move south two days earlier but claimed they had been prevented from doing so because of the tardiness of the British. 'The English are not ready to march, an enormous quantity of impedimenta retards their operations indefinitely. The departure is therefore postponed, perforce, until the following day'.[32] These ungenerous remarks take no account of the fact that the British army had to disembark its cavalry and attendant equipage, so it was only natural that they would take longer to disembark than the French who had no cavalry. Nevertheless, when the Allied advance did eventually get underway on the 19th it formed a very impressive and colourful sight.

The Allied armies formed, as Kinglake put it, 'a moveable column'. The French army marched south with its right flank resting on the sea. Thus, it had the protection of the fleet. The French 1st Division marched by battalion, in columns by petelon, with the artillery in the centre. The 2nd Division covered its right, each of the two brigades marching in column. The 3rd Division covered the left flank. The 4th Division, along with the Turks, formed the rearguard. The formation was 'an immense lozenge' at the salient angle of which was the 1st Division; at the lateral angles, the 2nd and 3rd, and in the rear the 4th Division, preceded by the Turkish division. The baggage was in the centre.

The British army marched with the infantry formed into two great columns; the left column consisted of the Light Division, leading, behind which came the 1st and 4th Divisions. The right-hand column consisted of the 2nd and 3rd Divisions. The formation and direction of march naturally meant that the left flank of the British army was open to attack by Russian troops, although by marching in column the British were able to face left and form line relatively quickly in order to meet such a threat. The baggage followed behind. Out in front of the whole rode Lord Cardigan, resplendent at the head of two regiments of his light cavalry, the 11th Hussars and 13th Light Dragoons. The 8th Hussars and 17th Lancers protected the left flank of the infantry whilst Lord George Paget and the 4th Light Dragoons brought up the rear. The march south by the Allied armies on that hot, sunny summer's day presented a wonderful sight. It was also a day that found Kinglake at his descriptive best:

> Thus marched the strength of the Western Powers. The sun shone hotly, as on a summer's day in England; but breezes springing fresh from the sea floated briskly along the hills. The ground was an undulating steppe alluring to cavalry. It was rankly covered with herb like southernwood; and when the stems were crushed under foot by the advancing columns, the whole air became laden with bitter fragrance. The aroma was new to some. To men of the western counties of England it was so familiar that it carried them back to childhood and the village church; they remembered the nosegay of 'boy's love' that used to be set by the Prayer-Book of the Sunday maiden too demure for the vanity of flowers.
>
> In each of the close-massed columns which were formed by our four complete divisions there were more than 5,000 foot-soldiers. The colours were flying; the bands at first were playing; and once more the time had come round when in all this armed pride there was

> nothing of false majesty; for already vedettes could be seen on the hillocks, and (except at the spots where our horsemen were marching) there was nothing but air and sunshine, and at intervals the dark form of a single rifleman, to divide our columns from the enemy. But more warlike than trumpet and drum was the grave quiet which followed the ceasing of the bands. The pain of weariness had begun.[33]

It was all too true. The march might well have looked spectacular but it did not take long for men to start falling by the wayside through sickness. It was a scene superbly captured in the 1968 feature film, *The Charge of the Light Brigade*, which captured the spirit of the march – and its agonies – superbly. The uplifting beat of the regimental bands soon gave way to the wearied, muffled groans of men falling out, suffering from cholera which now returned with a vengeance. Kinglake again:

> Yet now, before the first hour of march was over, the men began to fall out from the ranks. Some of these were in the agonies of cholera. Their faces had a dark, choked look; they threw themselves on the ground and writhed, but often without speaking and without a cry. Many more dropped out from mere weakness. These the officers tried to inspirit, and sometimes they succeeded; but more often the sufferer was left upon the ground. It was vain to tell him, though so it was believed at the time, that he would fall into the hands of the Cossacks. The tall stately men of the Guards dropped from their ranks in good numbers. It was believed at the time that the men who fell out would be taken by the enemy; but the number of stragglers at length became very great, and in the evening a force was sent back to bring them in.[34]

The march continued throughout the 19th, south towards Sevastopol across the barren landscape, with just the odd burning farmhouse dotted here and there. Otherwise there was little to interrupt the view across the vast, grassy plain, save for one or two Russian cavalrymen who disappeared as fast as they had appeared, and who were obviously out scouting and keeping a watchful eye on the invaders. But, as yet, there was still no sign of any large bodies of Russian troops to impede the Allies' march which continued south along the road to Sevastopol. By the early afternoon the Allies had reached the Bulganak river – more correctly a stream – the first of four barriers between Kalamita Bay and Sevastopol, and it was here that the Russian army first showed itself in any great strength.

Cardigan's cavalry reported a group of Cossacks, estimated to be around 2,000, sitting on the brow of a hill on the south bank of the Bulganak. In fact, not only was there a body of Cossacks but also two hussar regiments and a brigade of infantry were present, the whole force being commanded by Lieutenant General V Kir'iakov. Both the 11th Hussars and the 13th Light Dragoons pushed forward, with Cardigan and Lord Lucan in attendance. Skirmishers were then sent out in front at intervals of ten to twelve yards as the Cossacks, 'rough-looking fellows, mounted on sturdy little horses', moved forward. The British cavalry were wheeled into line, ready for action, when Raglan and Airey saw in the valley beyond, the glint of bayonets, whilst dark masses of cavalry were spotted also. Mindful perhaps of several mishandled cavalry charges during the Peninsular War Raglan immediately ordered the cavalry to halt and retire, whilst at the same time ordering forward the 2nd and Light Divisions, as well as the 8th Hussars and the 17th Lancers. No sooner had the cavalry begun to draw back than some Russian guns appeared and opened fire, causing light casualties of two men wounded and five horses killed. However, these Russian guns were in turn fired upon from the 6-pounder guns attached to the cavalry, C Troop and I Troop, and by the divisional 9-pounder guns of the 2nd Division. The fire from these guns, commanded by Captains Brandling, Maude and Henry, settled the business, for the shot from their guns sent the obviously reluctant Russians hurrying to limber up and move off, their infantry and cavalry following likewise. In all, it was a satisfying end to the Allies' first encounter with the Russian army in the Crimea.

The two Allied armies camped on the 19th on the banks of the Bulganak, reflecting on a hard day's march but a good afternoon's work in the field. Rations of rum and meat were served out, after which the casks were broken up and the staves used to make fires for cooking, helped by nettles and long grass. The first barrier on the road to Sevastopol had been passed with little effort, although the real test would come the following day on the banks of the second barrier, the Alma river.

NOTES

1 Fortescue, The Hon. J W. *A History of the British Army* (London 1899), XIII, 36.
2 Bazancourt, the Baron de (trans. by Robert Howe Gould). *The Crimean Expedition, to the Capture of Sebastopol. Chronicles of the War in the East* (London 1856), I, 34.
3 Ibid, I, 139.
4 Ibid, I, 144.
5 Ibid, I, 146.
6 Russell, William Howard. *The British Expedition to the Crimea* (London 1877), 57.
7 Kinglake, Alexander William. *The Invasion of the Crimea: Its Origin, and An Account of its Progress down to the Death of Lord Raglan* (London 1863), II, 106–7.
8 Ibid, II, 107–8.
9 Ibid, II, 108.
10 Ibid, II, 114.

11 Ibid, II, 114–15.
12 Bazancourt, *The Crimean Expedition,* I, 123.
13 Ibid, I, 126–7.
14 Wrottesley, The Hon. George (ed.). *Life and Correspondence of Field Marshal Sir John Burgoyne* (London 1873), II, 51.
15 Kinglake, *The Invasion of the Crimea*, II, 150.
16 Wrottesley, *Sir John Burgoyne,* II, 69.
17 Clifford, Henry. *His Letters and Sketches from the Crimea* (London 1955), 40.
18 Russell, *The British Expedition to the Crimea,* 50.
19 Wrottesley, *Sir John Burgoyne,* II, 72.
20 Ibid, II, 59.
21 Ibid, II, 73.
22 Ibid, II, 73–4.
23 Bazancourt, *The Crimean Expedition,* I, 195.
24 Kinglake, *The Invasion of the Crimea*, II, 168.
25 Bazancourt, *The Crimean Expedition,* I, 199.
26 Russell, *The British Expedition to the Crimea,* 86.
27 Ibid, 87.
28 Bazancourt, *The Crimean Expedition,* I, 201.
29 Russell, *The British Expedition to the Crimea,* 89.
30 Tyrell, Henry. *History of the War with Russia* (London n.d.), I, 292.
31 Russell, *The British Expedition to the Crimea,* 89.
32 Bazancourt, *The Crimean Expedition,* I, 217.
33 Kinglake, *The Invasion of the Crimea*, II, 207–8.
34 Ibid, II, 209.

# CHAPTER FIVE
## 'Bulldog Courage . . .'

The skirmish on the Bulganak river had been nothing more than that, a small and very minor skirmish. Nevertheless, it was a good start for the Allies and it had given them cause to be optimistic. The Allied landings had been made unopposed, whilst the first resistance – feeble as it was – had been easily brushed aside. Furthermore, reports suggested that even Sevastopol was in a state of some disrepair, with defences yet to be completed and the defenders in a state of some alarm. Perhaps it was to be a walkover after all, and that the destruction of the great Russian naval base in the Black Sea would prove to be nothing more than a formality. Sadly, the Allies' optimism was misplaced.

Although Russian opposition to the Allies' advance had been virtually non-existent the Russians were, nevertheless, well aware of the arrival of the Allied fleet off the Crimean coast. Indeed, the smoking funnels of the British and French steamers had been spotted as early as 13 September, although Menshikov did little to retard their operations once they had landed. The Russian commander is frequently criticised for not opposing the landings but his actions – or rather the lack of them – owed more to caution on his part and to the advantages the Allies enjoyed with their fast moving steamships. Menshikov may well have moved his troops north to Eupatoria to oppose the landings, but suppose it was only a feint, designed to lure the Russian troops out of Sevastopol? With the Russians on the march north the Allied ships would have little difficulty in steaming to the south, catching Sevastopol without an effective garrison.[1] Instead the Russian commander contented himself with sending riders and Cossack patrols to keep an eye on the Allies and report back on their strengths and movements. These reconnoitring forces varied in strength and it was one such patrol, commanded by Kir'iakov, that had first encountered the Allies on the Bulganak river on 19 September. Meanwhile, Menshikov himself set about preparing his troops to meet the Allies in what would be the first major engagement in the Crimea.

Even as the Allies were coming ashore at Kalamita Bay the Russian army was beginning to take up positions on the southern bank of the Alma river, and by the evening of 14 September almost 20,000 Russian troops had arrived there, including the 1st Brigade of the 16th Infantry Division and the 1st and the 2nd batteries of the 16th Artillery Brigade who had arrived previously. They were joined on the evening of 13 September by the 4th battalion of the 2nd Brigade of the 17th Infantry Division and the Minsk Regiment with the 4th light battery of the 4th Artillery Brigade, who came from Sevastopol. The next day from Sevastopol came the last battalions of the regiments of the 2nd Brigade of the 17th Infantry Division with the light No.4 and No.5 batteries of the 17th Artillery Brigade, the Volyn Regiment with the light No.3 battery of the 14th Artillery Brigade, and the 5th and the 6th reserve battalions of the Belostok and Brest regiments. On 14 September itself two regiments came from Simferopol, the regiment of Grand Prince Mikhail Nikolaevitch with six guns of the light No.2 battery of the 16th Artillery Brigade and the Hussar regiment of Grand Duke Saxe-Weimar. On 15 September the Hussar regiment of Prince Nikolay Maximilianovitch, along with the light cavalry No.12 battery came up from the Katcha river. On 18 September one of the newly formed naval battalions was sent from Sevastopol. From Perekop in the north came the Uglitch Chasseur Regiment with six guns of the light No.2 battery of the 16th Artillery Brigade and Cossack Regiment No.60. By the evening of 19 September the 1st echelon of the Moscow Regiment came from the detachment of General Khomutov. On the morning of the battle came the 2nd echelon of the same regiment, with the Don horse-battery No.3 and the Cossack *sotnias* (hundreds) of the 57th Regiment. On these last two days two companies of the 6th Field Engineer Battalion arrived piecemeal from Sevastopol.

By the morning of 20 September Menshikov's force numbered 33,600 troops, consisting of forty-two infantry battalions, sixteen squadrons of cavalry, 1,100 Cossacks, eight troops of horse artillery and sixteen batteries of other artillery, totalling eighty-four guns. In Sevastopol, meanwhile, the Commander-in-Chief left behind as a garrison the sailors and four reserve battalions.

The position chosen by Menshikov to block the Allies' march towards Sevastopol was a strong one. Nearly six miles in length from west to east, it blocked the only road to Sevastopol, the old post road, and covered the wooden bridge over which the road ran across the Alma river, close to the Tartar village of Burliuk. The river itself was deep but fordable along most of its length, but its southern banks were steep in many places, particularly to the east of the Sevastopol road. The northern approaches were planted with vineyards, making it difficult for the attacking troops to maintain their formation, whilst low stone walls likewise hindered progress. At the mouth of the river, on the Russian left, there were steep, cliff-like hills, rising to a height of around 150 feet, dominating both the river itself and the northern approaches to it. Although the cliffs themselves were inaccessible there were at least five tracks or paths which

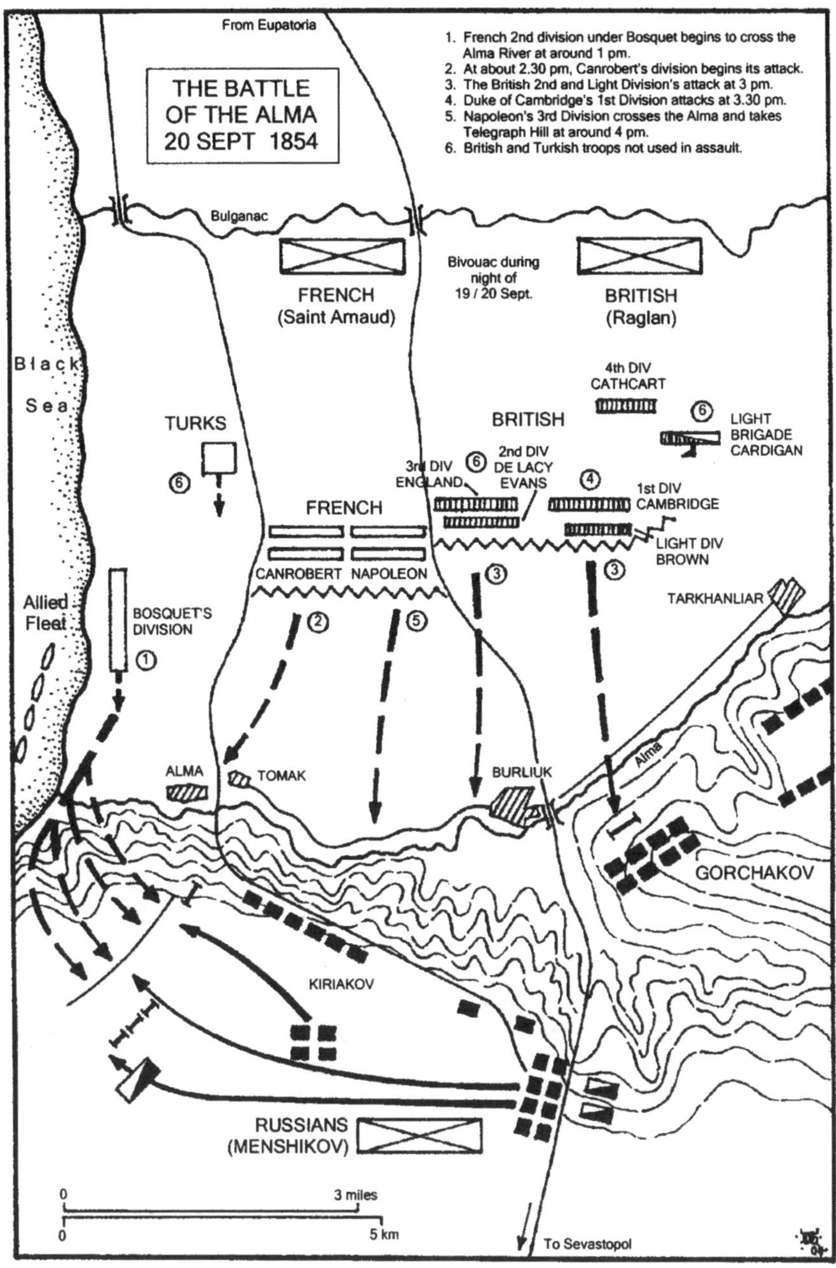

THE BATTLE OF THE ALMA 20 SEPT 1854
From Eupatoria
1. French 2nd division under Bosquet begins to cross the Alma River at around 1 pm.
2. At about 2.30 pm, Canrobert's division begins its attack.
3. The British 2nd and Light Division's attack at 3 pm.
4. Duke of Cambridge's 1st Division attacks at 3.30 pm.
5. Napoleon's 3rd Division crosses the Alma and takes Telegraph Hill at around 4 pm.
6. British and Turkish troops not used in assault.
Bulganac
Bivouac during night of 19 / 20 Sept.
FRENCH (Saint Amaud)
BRITISH (Raglan)
Black Sea
4th DIV CATHCART
BRITISH
LIGHT BRIGADE CARDIGAN
TURKS
3rd DIV ENGLAND
2nd DIV DE LACY EVANS
1st DIV CAMBRIDGE
FRENCH
LIGHT DIV BROWN
CANROBERT NAPOLEON
Allied Fleet
BOSQUET'S DIVISION
TARKHANLIAR
Alma
ALMA
TOMAK
BURLIUK
GORCHAKOV
KIRIAKOV
RUSSIANS (MENSHIKOV)
0
3 miles
0
5 km
To Sevastopol

wound their way through them. These tracks were found, from west to east, close to the coast, at the village of Almatamack, and opposite a place known as the White Homestead, with two others issuing from or close to the village of Burliuk. Apart from these last two tracks, none of them were guarded by Russian troops, nor had they been broken up. Thus, any enterprising Allied troops would find it possible to gain the heights on the Russian left without too much difficulty. The plateau, extending east from the coast, and bordered by the heights, ran as far inland to a hill known as Telegraph Hill, which lay about 1,500 yards to the south of the Alma river, opposite Burliuk. From here, the plateau dropped away to the Sevastopol road, before rising again on the east of the road, culminating in a commanding height called the Kourgane Hill, the summit of which was about 1,500 yards south of the river. From here, the land rolled away to the east and to the south. Apart from Almatamack and Burliuk, there were three other villages, all of which lay on the southern bank of the Alma at around 1,500 to 2,000 yards distance from the river. These were Orta-Kisek, Aklez (or Akles) and Adzgi-Bulat (or Ulukul).

Although the Russian position was a strong one, and well-chosen, it did have a major disadvantage. It was vulnerable to attack from the west, along the coast, for although the steep cliffs gave the Russian left flank immense strength, the terrain alone would not be enough to prevent the Allies from turning the flank. The two tracks that cut through the hills allowed Allied troops to gain the plateau, something which should have been easy to prevent with just a few battalions of infantry and artillery. However, any Russian troops positioned close to the coast would immediately come under fire from the Allied ships situated offshore. It was a great problem for Menshikov. The position was also too great in length for the number of troops available to the Russian commander, although this problem was solved – somewhat ironically – by the presence of the Allied ships. For although the six-mile long position was too long to defend in any great depth, Menshikov decided that, rather than expose his men on his left flank to the deadly fire from the Allied ships, he would trust instead to the lie of the land, and to the steep cliffs in particular, to thwart the Allies. This allowed him to concentrate the overwhelming bulk of his force to the east and west of the Sevastopol road. The plan was fatally flawed.

Menshikov placed far too much faith in the topography of the battlefield, and in the cliff-like face of the hills at the mouth of the Alma river. If he had taken a close look at the ground, or at least sent his staff to take a look, he would have seen that any half-decent troops would find it relatively easy to ascend the cliffs and establish themselves on the south bank of the river. Sadly, the Russian commander, wary of the expected fire from the Allied fleet, and trusting in the lie of the land, chose to keep his men well away from the coast and thus exposed his left flank to a direct threat from the Allies. Furthermore, not a single spade of earth was turned to dig entrenchments along the Russian position, save for the crude earthworks thrown up around the Great Redoubt on the forward slope of the Kourgane Hill which mounted twelve guns, and the Lesser Redoubt, away to the east. Given the amount of time the Russian troops had been in position on the Alma the oversight is all the more puzzling. Not only would earthworks have afforded the Russian troops on their left flank some degree of protection from the guns of the Allied fleet, but they would have allowed the defenders to dispute the possession of the heights there far more effectively than they were to do. Good, sound field works occupied by both infantry and artillery, and sited behind the river obstacle, would have made the task of fording the river extremely difficult for the Allies. In the event it was difficult enough but the task would have been immense had Menshikov put his men to work turning over the soil.

Instead, Menshikov simply placed skirmishers along the south bank, near the village of Burliuk and in the vineyards to the north. Occupying the heights to the west of the post road were the Brest, Belostock and Borodin regiments, with the Tarutin Regiment behind them. To the east of the road, on and to the west of the Kourgane Hill, were placed the Kazan, Vladimir and Sousdal regiments. The Volyn, Minsk and Moscow infantry regiments, along with two light foot batteries, were placed in reserve in the centre of position, whilst the Ouglitz Regiment was positioned behind the right wing. One battalion of the Minsk Regiment was then detached from the reserve to occupy the village of Ulukul whilst hordes of Cossacks covered the Russian right flank. Commanding the Russian left flank was Lieutenant-General V Kir'iakov, said to be a man of no great intelligence, and lacking any real military abilities. He is reputedly to have been rarely sober. Despite this – or rather because of it – Kir'iakov declared before the battle that he would emerge victorious by sheer numbers alone. Commanding the right flank was General P D Gorchakov, brother of the Commander-in-Chief of the Russian Army on the Danube. Undeniably brave, Gorchakov was not exactly tactically astute, although his men were to give the attacking British troops a real test.

Preparations for battle could not have been more different amongst the men who were destined to fight the Battle of the Alma. 20 September was an orthodox religious holiday in Russia, marking the birth of the Blessed Virgin, and prayers were said amongst the Russian regiments. And so, whilst British and French troops cooked their breakfasts and drank their coffee, priests went amongst the Russian troops holding aloft the sign of the cross and casting consecrated water, praying to God to deliver them victory against the western invaders.

But what of these invaders from the west? The Allies themselves were present in overwhelming strength. Saint-Arnaud could call upon some

30,000 French infantry, supported by sixty-eight guns. There were also around 7,000 Turkish troops attached to the French army. The British contingent under Lord Raglan numbered 25,000 infantry and 1,000 cavalry, and like the French had sixty-eight guns. In other words, the Allies enjoyed an advantage of two to one in personnel, and had nearly forty more guns than the Russians. How they would make this advantage count was soon to be seen.

If the Russian plan for the defence of the Alma river was lacking in any sort of imagination, the Allies' own plan can hardly have laid claim to be anything other than ordinary or predictable. Lord Raglan and the increasingly ill-looking Saint-Arnaud, accompanied by Colonel Trochu, had met on the night of 19 September in the small house on the Bulganak which Raglan used for his headquarters. Remarkably, no reconnaissance of the Russian position appears to have been carried out, save for a distant view from the French fleet. Thus, the Allied commanders discussed the coming battle on little more than a rough map. As one historian put it, 'no enterprising young officers on lean, well-bred horses had been sent over those few miles of grass down, to dodge the Cossacks as they would have dodged the French forty years before'.[2]

Despite his illness Saint-Arnaud was able to give full vent to his optimism for the coming fight. He informed Raglan of how the battle would be fought, with the French attacking the heights on the Russian left whilst the British went straight for the centre and right. His plans were delivered with typical Gallic gusto and animation, and with typical British nonchalance Raglan nodded politely, appearing to agree with everything his French comrade suggested, and yet agreed to nothing, save that an advance and attack would be made upon the Russian position the next day. Raglan's approach to his dealings with the French was understandable, if a little harmful to the Allied cause. His active military career in the Peninsular and Waterloo campaigns had been spent fighting the French. Indeed, they had cost him an arm at the latter battle. Schooled firmly in the cautious views of the late Duke of Wellington, he was reluctant to relinquish any control of his army to anyone, nor was he about to allow his former enemies to dictate to him. Nevertheless, he fully appreciated the delicate balance to be struck with his French allies and his grasp of the situation allowed him enough tolerance of them to be able to maintain a good if sometimes shaky working relationship. And so, while Saint-Arnaud rode off into the night with his staff, satisfied that his British allies apparently understood and agreed to 'his' plan, Raglan went to bed, happy that the French commander had been kept outside the narrow limits of his own thinking.

The day of battle, 20 September 1854, dawned fine and bright. For Saint-Arnaud and the French army it was as if the years were rolling back. Almost forty years had passed since the end of the Napoleonic Wars, when the great Emperor Napoleon led his armies to countless great victories. True, they were now fighting alongside their old, traditional and most dogged opponents, but the spirits of countless old warriors were with them, and the sight of row upon row of dark blue coats and fluttering tricolours was enough to make the breast of every Frenchman swell with pride. With so many memories and traditions thus evoked, Saint-Arnaud's men needed little else to inspire them. There was also the bitter memory of 1812 and the ill-fated Moscow campaign. At 5.30 am the French troops began to quit their camps. There was no great blaring of bugles or beat of drums, but a silent, grim determination to succeed. By 6.30 am they began forming to the north of the Alma river. It all did not bode well. But as they began to deploy for their forward movement in concert with their British allies, they realised that the latter had yet to stir from their camps.

This British inactivity so astonished the French that both General Canrobert and Prince Napoleon, commanding the French divisions closest to the British right, rode quickly over to try to discover the reason. They found Sir De Lacy Evans, whose 2nd Division was to attack on the left flank of Canrobert, still in his tent. 'I have received no orders,' the British general replied to his bewildered French colleagues. Evidently, Raglan had kept not only Saint-Arnaud from knowing his plans, but also his own commanders. The point was, of course, that General Bosquet, who had been assigned the task of scaling the heights close to the mouth of the Alma river, had already begun his forward movement, at which the rest of the Allies would move forward. Bosquet's division, unsupported, and although some way from the Russian position, nevertheless risked being destroyed unless it was halted. The order was duly despatched and Bosquet thankfully halted, after which Colonel Trochu rode over to see Raglan and ask why his men had yet to break camp. It was 7 am when Trochu reached Raglan's headquarters, by which time the British commander was in the saddle. The exchange between the two was duly recorded in the French history of the war:

> 'My Lord,' said the latter [Trochu], 'the Marshal thought, after what you did me the honour of saying, last night, that your troops forming the left wing of the line of battle, were to have marched forward at six o'clock'.
>
> 'I am now giving my orders', replied Lord Raglan. 'We are preparing and are about to march; a part of my troops did not reach the camp until very late in the night'.
>
> 'For Heaven's sake, my Lord', asked the Colonel, 'be speedy; every minute of delay takes from us a chance of success.'
>
> 'Go and say to the Marshal', answered Lord Raglan, 'that at this moment orders are despatched along the whole line'.[3]

The delays had been caused by faulty staff work and by wheeling two divisions which had been posted to cover the open British flank into line. There were further delays while the British brought up the ammunition wagons, and the other divisions wheeled into line, ready for the advance. Meanwhile, the French settled down and waited, drinking coffee amidst fields of reaped corn with some using it to light fires, whilst others used it to lie on. By 10.30 am Raglan's men were finally and belatedly ready to advance, by which time the sun was well and truly up and beginning to beat down on the battlefield. At around 11.30 am the left flank of the French army and the right flank of the British finally came into touch with each other, and soon afterwards they topped a low rise, beyond which, at a distance of about two miles, rose the heights on the south bank of the Alma river. It was a spectacular sight for the Allied troops, the heights presenting a mass of sparkling and flashing along the entire length of the position as thousands of swords and bayonets caught the sunlight. Once within a mile and a half of the river the Allies halted.

The halt in front of the river afforded Lord Raglan his first opportunity of studying the Russian position. It was soon clear to him that although the Russian right flank appeared to be open, with no significant topographical feature on which to anchor it, it would be dangerous to try to attempt an outflanking move, particularly as Menshikov had almost three times the number of cavalry possessed by Raglan. There was nothing for it but to allow Saint-Arnaud to attack the Russian left, after which Raglan would launch his British divisions against the Russian right and right centre. It would be a hard fight but there was little other option. The French, too, expected a hard fight, but at least they would be covered by the guns of the Allied fleet hovering out at sea against the Russian left flank.

During the lull, an eerie silence descended over the battlefield, broken only by the cheers of the British as they greeted Saint-Arnaud who rode over to see Raglan. Then, as if to bring the men to their senses, the order to load ball cartridge was barked out along the line. After so many years of inactivity, save for far-off colonial scrapes and training camps in England, the men suddenly realised this was the real thing, and the effect of the order is said to have turned many men white. Finally, at some time after noon, Bosquet's division, supported by the Turks, began its move along the shore towards the Russian left. Once on the move, the rest of the Allies lumbered into motion and followed suit.

Prince Menshikov and his Russian army watched the initial Allied movements – or rather the lack of them – with an uninterested air. Russian outposts noticed a movement to the north by the Allies at around 7 am, after which they began to take a greater interest in proceedings and prepare for battle. Menshikov himself had no actual headquarters, although Telegraph Hill seems to have been his main position during the day. More alarmingly, however, was the apparent absence of a plan.

Menshikov appears to have had no actual battle plan, other than to stop the Allies. His generals had no idea of his strategy or of his intentions. Instead, they relied only on themselves, on the memories of 1812 and on God's will.

Although French ships had opened fire at long range earlier in the morning, the first real shots were fired at around 1 pm, after which Bosquet moved forward once again with his division and the battle began in earnest. Bosquet himself had taken advantage of Saint-Arnaud's earlier order to halt and had ridden forward with his staff and with the heads of the artillery and engineers, under cover of some sharpshooters, to reconnoitre the cliffs. Two passes were clearly marked, one close to the sea and the other just over half a mile farther inland, close to the burned village of Almatamack. Both were accessible to infantry, if a little difficult, but what concerned Bosquet was the difficult accessibility for his artillery. Nevertheless, Bosquet assumed command of D'Autemarre's brigade and sent it forward to the pass close to the village of Almatamack, whilst Bouat's brigade and the Turks headed for the pass close to the sea.

Bosquet's column had little difficulty in passing the village of Almatamack, and his Zouaves quickly threw themselves into the river, heading for the south bank.

> They were speedily seen, spreading to right and left, on the side of the mountain, clinging with their hands to the irregularities and accidental protuberances of the ground, and assisting each other up the ascent. Often, these fragile supports would suddenly give way, and the soldiers roll from top to bottom of the slope.[4]

But despite the difficulties it took just five minutes or so before the first troops were standing on the summit of the cliffs, from where they opened fire upon a body of Cossacks who retired without offering much resistance. At this, Bosquet himself rode forward, accompanied by his staff, and he too was quickly on the summit with his men. Here, Commandant Barral told him it was possible to get his artillery across and up, and so orders were despatched for this to be done. Some fifteen minutes or so later Captain Fiévet's battery was splashing its way across the Alma, after which it ploughed its way to the top of the cliffs, the guns being helped on their way by dozens of infantrymen who had left their packs and equipment at the foot of the hills. Once on the summit, Fiévet had his guns moved forward a hundred yards and immediately they opened fire. 'It was the French artillery who fired the first cannon-shot upon that memorable day.'[5] Farther to the west, the river was full of French and Turkish infantry under Bouat who plunged waist-deep into the water, making for the south bank with a little difficulty.[6] Once across, the troops began ascending the steep and difficult cliffs, but before long they too were on the summit, whilst a second battery of artillery, under Captain Marcy, also came up using the path at Almatamack. The Russians watched and waited in silence, much to the surprise of Bosquet who is said to have remarked, 'Obviously these gentlemen don't want to fight'. The silence did not last long, however.

The news that the French were deploying upon the heights, which were considered to be unassailable, took Menshikov aback. He immediately despatched three batteries, each of eight guns, forward to try to dislodge Bosquet, following these shortly afterwards with a further two batteries. Some forty Russian guns were now turned against the French and a fierce exchange of shot ensued. The unequal contest between the twelve French guns and the forty Russian guns continued for almost ninety minutes, Bosquet growing increasingly anxious about his isolation, whilst Saint-Arnaud also worried. There were no other French troops on the plateau, save for Bouat's brigade half a mile away to the west. Their British allies still sat – or in most cases lay – motionless in the fields and vineyards to the north of the Alma. They were not the only ones, for both Canrobert and Prince Napoleon also sat waiting for orders.

Meanwhile, the struggle on the cliffs continued with Menshikov sending some hussars to join the artillery opposing Bosquet. He also sent forward four battalions of the Moscow and three of the Minsk regiments, but these too failed to make any impression on the French. Bosquet's men fought hard to maintain possession of the heights and, despite the efforts of the Russians to dislodge the enemy at bayonet point, the French held on and began to consolidate their position. The disadvantages under which the Russians fought soon became obvious as the power and accuracy of the French rifles proved far superior to the old Russian smoothbore muskets. Indeed, Menshikov's men trusted far too much to the power of the bayonet over the bullet, but in the event were unable even to close with their enemies. It is true that some Russian troops were armed with rifles, but this may have been as few as 2,000. The vast majority of the Allied troops, on the other hand, were armed with modern Minié rifles. These, with a range of around 1,200 yards, easily outranged the Russian muskets, limited to just 300 yards' range. The problem was noted in the memoirs of one of the Russian soldiers, V Beytner, who wrote:

> The reserve battalions of the Brest regiment had nothing to do on the ledges they occupied. They were armed with old firelocks, which couldn't fire more than 250 paces. The Brests suffered many casualties without causing any damage to the enemy at all.[7]

The same problem was noted in the memoirs of another Russian officer, positioned on the left flank of the Russian position at the very moment when General Bosquet arrived on the plateau.

> On 20 September the enemy, with its terrible fleet and huge army, began to approach us. Our hearts wavered when we saw well-shaped, endless mass of troops moving towards us. But our artillery managed to occupy a favourable position and prepared to meet the enemy. But it began to fire too early so that the balls fell shot of the enemy and the charges were wasted . . . Ours set a garden near the sea and the village of Burliuk on fire. Smoke – straight in our direction, a bad omen . . . It had to be done beforehand, as the experienced people say, in order not to give the enemy the opportunity of seeking shelter behind the buildings and of firing at us without suffering any losses. The enemy was approaching closer and closer to us, so that our bullets were now reaching them and claiming victims. As soon as they got within cannon-shot our artillery began to annihilate them but they continued approaching as if they didn't see their comrades being killed. At last they came within range of us but soon they began to use their deadly rifles, whilst a shower of cannon balls began to fall from the direction of the sea and in a few minutes almost destroyed the Minsk regiment which was placed near the sea under the guns of the enemy. God knows for what. I say 'the deadly rifled guns' because each bullet hit its mark. Many officers and staff-officers were wounded, especially the generals, and all those who were on horse-back. But that was not all. Our artillery was smashing the enemy, its ranks thinned out, but there was a lack of shells! Two ammunition-wagons for each gun were put out of range, that is, two versts [c. 1.3 miles] from them. They were afraid of the explosions, and our artillery fire, which began so brilliantly, had to be stopped at the very beginning! We went in with bayonets but the enemy case shot killed our soldiers by the ranks. In spite of this, it was not only Russian bayonets that worked a lot but also Russian butts. However, the Russians had to cede their position to the enemy, not having any real command, not getting help from anywhere else and being afraid to be outflanked by the enemy and cut off from the others.[8]

With the situation worsening away to the left, Menshikov sent his Chief-of-Staff, Colonel V Vunsh, to the left flank to try to rally the men of the Minsk Regiment, many of whom had begun to fall back towards the village of Orta-Kisek, almost a mile south of the Alma. Soon afterwards, Menshikov himself arrived on the left to see what needed to be done. He was greeted with a brisk fire from French skirmishers, one of the bullets apparently hitting the hoof of Menshikov's horse. The 2nd battalion of the Minsk Regiment, under the command of Lieutenant Colonel A Rakovitch, together with the battery under the command of Lieutenant Colonel Kondratiev, were brought forward to try and stem the French tide. Rakovitch's battalion was fighting against a whole brigade but despite their superior numbers the French had difficulty in halting the Russian assault, which they carried out with the bayonet. A furious fight ensued with the colours of the Minsk battalion changing hands many times. Indeed, on one occasion Rakovitch saved it himself, bayoneting the Zouave who tried to capture it. But in spite of their gallant efforts to halt the French they were unsuccessful, suffered great losses and were forced to retreat.[9]

The fighting on the western flank of the battlefield had been in progress for almost ninety minutes, and still there was little sign of any activity from either the British or, indeed, from Canrobert and Prince Napoleon. Finally, an understandably anxious Saint-Arnaud ordered his two divisions forward to cross the Alma in support of Bosquet who himself must have wondered where on earth the rest of the Allied army had got to. Canrobert's division crossed the Alma at the White Homestead, the 1st and 9th Chasseurs leading the way with the 7th Ligne. Behind them were the 7th Zouaves. The men went up with typical French élan, crying 'Vive l'Empereur!' Despite opposition from the Moscow Regiment the French made good progress, although they found it impossible to get their guns across, forcing them to turn to the west and cross at Almatamack, using the same path by which Bosquet had got his guns across.

At the same time Prince Napoleon's 3rd Division advanced on the left of Canrobert. As they approached the village of Burliuk, which lay to their left, they noticed hordes of Cossacks, darting in between the houses, setting them on fire, and soon clouds of thick smoke hung over the battlefield. Fortunately, the smoke afforded a measure of cover to the advancing French, the Russian gunners on the heights being unable to see them. Having passed the burning village, the 1st Brigade, under General de Monet, crossed the river, with Colonel Cler leading at the head of his Zouaves, with the marines, under Colonel Duchateau, close behind. But as soon as they began to debouch on the south bank and on the heights above, Prince Napoleon's men came under intense fire from Russian artillery, as did Canrobert's men. A severe fight now broke out along the heights where the French frantically deployed to meet the oncoming Russian counter-attacks, all the time being showered with shot from Russian artillery. Fortunately, Canrobert received timely assistance from Commandant Barral who sent forward Fiévet's battery of artillery, which had an immediate effect on the Russian columns, particularly at such close range.

Prince Napoleon's situation could have been made worse save for the conduct of General Kir'iakov who, with his 2nd Brigade of the 17th Division and the reserve battalions of the 13th Division, left his position to the west of the Sevastopol road and the heights above that road without any fighting. At this very moment the French placed their artillery on Kir'iakov's former position and began to smash the Russian left wing from there. Kir'iakov's conduct continues to be the cause of some debate even today. He defended himself, claiming he withdrew only when the battle was as good as lost. However, many believe him to have retreated far too early, and without orders from Menshikov. Whatever the reason, it left a gap for the French to take advantage of, which was duly done. Saint-Arnaud watched as his troops fought their way up the cliffs and established themselves on the plateau. 'Oh! My brave soldiers,' he said, 'worthy sons of Austerlitz and Friedland!'[10]

There does indeed remain a great deal of confusion about the progress of the French attack at this point, and it concerns eight battalions of Russian infantry which Menshikov had handed over to Kir'iakov earlier in the afternoon. According to Kir'iakov himself, he took the eight battalions and threw back Canrobert before the latter's artillery had come up. This is a version accepted by Kinglake in his history of the war.[11] According to Kinglake, Kir'iakov massed the great column of eight battalions with a frontage of two battalions and a depth of four after which he moved against Canrobert. According to Kir'iakov's own version the French were completely driven back. 'Canrobert's division,' he wrote, 'could not resist our charge. Hastily taking off their batteries they began to descend the hilly bank.'[12] The French, however, make no mention of this reverse whatsoever. Even allowing for national pride, it is unlikely that they would have failed to mention it in some way. Kinglake was almost certainly correct when he said that the truth probably lay between the two versions. Namely, that Canrobert, without artillery, was unwilling to attack such a strong Russian force and so simply fell back until his guns came up, remembering that they had been forced to turn west in order to get up on to the plateau.

But while Saint-Arnaud's troops had fought their way onto the plateau, Raglan's British infantry remained frustrated and motionless, watching their allies stealing the glory in front of their eyes. Raglan's plan was based on whether or not the French would be able to make headway against the cliffs away to the west. At around 1 pm his men had advanced to within a short distance of the village of Burliuk, close enough for them to feel the heat and smoke of the burning houses. But there they were ordered to lie down and wait once more while Raglan watched the progress of the French in front of him. Then, and only when he was satisfied, would he order his men into the attack on the left of their French allies.

Not only was it a frustrating wait for the red-coated British infantry but it was a trial also. As they lay down in the fields and vineyards they had to endure a galling fire from the Russian guns placed in the Great Redoubt. They looked on inquisitively as, every now and then, small black dots emerged from the grey smoke, flying towards them. Bouncing across the fields, these solid iron balls dealt death to anyone unlucky enough to be in the way, tearing off limbs, and ploughing men into the ground. It was a real ordeal. Finally, Raglan, seeing that the French were establishing themselves on the plateau, turned to his staff and gave orders for the men to advance, orders which had an immediate and transforming effect on those around him. 'Every man, whether he had heard the words or not, saw in the gladness of his neighbour's face that the moment long-awaited had come.'[13] The British Army was about to fight its first major land battle in Europe since Waterloo.

The word flew back and forth along the long, red lines waiting in the fields to the north of the Alma river. They were to attack immediately. Staff officers galloped back and forth whilst regimental officers looked to their men and ordered them to their feet. De Lacy Evans' 2nd Division would advance against the bridge over the Alma, attacking the centre of the Russian position, whilst the Light Division advanced on their left. Behind the 2nd Division came Sir Richard England's 3rd Division, and on their left, following the Light Division, came the Duke of Cambridge with the 1st Division of the army, including the Brigade of Guards. The order from Raglan was delivered to De Lacy Evans by an excitable young cavalry officer, a certain Captain Louis Nolan. Evans, a veteran of the Peninsular and Carlist Wars, got his men into line in the traditional manner, and with Sir George Brown's Light Division on its left, the entire two-deep British line presented a front of almost two miles. Cathcart's 4th Division was incomplete on the day, owing to the fact that it had been on outpost duty the night before covering the flank of the army. Nevertheless, three of his battalions were up in time to form a reserve to the left rear of the 1st Division. And then, with the men of the Rifle Brigade out in front, and with colours flying and bugles blaring, the line moved forward towards the Alma and the waiting Russians beyond it. Not since the days of the Peninsular War forty years before had such long, red lines been seen on an European battlefield, and the sight of them must have stirred vivid and cherished memories in the minds of men like Raglan, who had seen them at their greatest. How his old chief would have been proud of them.

The British infantry had not gone far before they came under the increasing fire of the Russian guns. Initially they came under fire from round shot, but as the range decreased common shell was hurled amongst the men, the hot, jagged iron ripping holes through the ranks. Then, as the range reduced further, shrapnel shells began to explode above the men, followed by canister. Russian sharpshooters positioned on both banks of the river also took their toll. Despite this, the British lines rolled on and when they came within range of the Russians they were able to hit back, as one Russian NCO recalled:

> At about midday English rifle bullets, with their characteristic ricocheting 'ping', began to fly overhead – a sound not heard before

> by our troops who had never been under fire and knew little of rifles. It filled most of the men with alarm so that they kept asking each other in frightened tones what the sound was, though in reality they must have known. The first to be hit was a man named Cherenov, and the news of his fall went up and down the ranks. A Russian battery on our right, just below the Commander-in-Chief's tent, engaged the English and, as Burliuk was not yet aflame, we could see how its shots were falling short. Then the English guns opened up and straightaway caused havoc among our troops.[14]

Another Russian officer who also watched the ominous British advance from the west of the post road admitted that the firing of the village of Burliuk actually hampered the Russians rather than the British:

> Our hearts pounded at the sight of the endless mass of troops marching steadily towards us, but when our artillery, which occupied good commanding positions, opened fire, the shells fell short as the enemy was still out of range. Our troops then set alight the village of Burliuk and we became blinded by the smoke which drifted back on us. It would have been wiser, as those with battle experience said at the time, not to have created a smoke screen for the enemy's benefit since this enabled him to fire on us without any loss on his side; but these mistakes were not the last. As the enemy got closer our shells began to blow great holes in his ranks; but the many gaps were immediately closed up and the enemy strode on, apparently indifferent to his losses. Soon afterwards we began to feel the terrible effects of his rifle fire.[15]

But despite the pessimism of these two Russian officers the British were indeed beginning to suffer. Their situation was not made any easier by the fact that Sir George Brown had not allowed himself enough space to deploy and thus when the 2nd Division came forward, they discovered there was not enough room for them to pass to the left of the burning village of Burliuk, and so Evans detached General Adams to his right, taking the 41st and 49th Regiments with him, along with Turner's battery of artillery. It was all very cramped, and space tight. Nevertheless, they pressed on, coming under intensive fire as they pushed on towards the river. Norcott's green-jacketed men of the Rifle Brigade drove the Russian skirmishers back across the river, leaving the way for the main British lines to come forward and cross. Also, they could draw some comfort from the fact that eighteen British guns were now in action, firing on the Russian position. But the trial was only just about to begin for Raglan's infantry, for as they approached the bridge over the river the ground was swept by grapeshot and canister from the Russian batteries.

At last the British approached the river. From the 47th Regiment, on the right of the main attacking line, right along to the regiments of Buller's brigade of the Light Division, out on the left, British infantry hurried through the vineyards and over walls, making for the river bank. Many of the men had discarded their knapsacks and even their shakos, mistakenly regarding them as superfluous items. Others snatched bunches of grapes from the vines and went into action with them hanging from their lips. With Adams' brigade having been split in two the task of anchoring the British line fell to Brigadier General John Pennefather's brigade, the 95th, 55th and 30th, but as they reached the last hundred yards or so before the river Russian artillery fire brought the red lines lurching to a halt, sending the men running for cover behind walls and damaged buildings. The confusion was intense, caused by a combination of a lack of space and, of course, a heavy fire brought upon them by the Russian guns. Nevertheless, they worked their way towards the river, advancing whenever a lull afforded them the opportunity to do so. It was simple fire and movement stuff. Pennefather's three regiments worked their way towards the partially destroyed bridge and towards the ground either side of it around the post road, drawing fire from the Russian batteries which began to take their toll. Grape shot and canister were at their most destructive at such relatively short range. Indeed, Pennefather's brigade lost about a quarter of its strength at the Alma. Even the divisional commander himself, Evans, was wounded, as were several members of his staff. With such a storm of shot and shell pouring down into them it was inevitable that Pennefather was brought to a halt, his regiments being forced to seek cover as best they could, whilst above them the intensity of the Russian artillery fire increased, as did that from the clouds of Russian skirmishers that covered the road.

But even as Evans' attack stalled Sir George Brown's Light Division came storming forward on his left, making for the river and, beyond that, the Great Redoubt. This was no Light Division in the old sense of the word. Gone were the famous light infantry regiments that formed the Light Division in the Peninsula forty years earlier, save for the Rifle Brigade, who displayed the same fire and dash as their illustrious green-jacketed forebears. Indeed, two regiments of the Light Division from Codrington's brigade, the 23rd and 7th, had fought side by side at the Battle of Albuera in 1811, when they formed part of the famous Fusilier Brigade. Nevertheless, the Battle of the Alma was shaping into something resembling the bloodbath that their ancestors had come through over forty years before. 'Nothing could stop that astonishing infantry,' wrote the historian of the Peninsular War when referring to the conduct of these two great regiments at Albuera, and their descendants were determined to uphold their noble tradition.

Whilst Pennefather's men had to clear away the Russians from the vineyards and buildings themselves, Buller's brigade of the Light Division had the benefit of four companies of Colonel Norcott's riflemen, who did the job for them.[16] Codrington's men were without such protection, but once across the river Norcott had his men extend to their right to cover them. On the right of Codrington' brigade were the 7th Fusiliers under their firebrand colonel, Lacy Yea, a hard swearing, hard fighting soldier, who brought his men storming past the 95th who were halted on the south bank of the river under heavy fire from the Russian guns. The 95th, under Colonel Webber Smith, were the left hand battalion of Pennefather's brigade, and such was the shortage of space that the 7th actually passed through the ranks of the 95th to get to the river. As Lacy Yea's men hurried forward, the Derbyshire men looked on with dismay. They could not conceive of the idea of anyone fighting in their front and in their anxiety to get forward many of them, including the Colour Party, simply abandoned the idea of remaining with Pennefather but instead set off after the 7th.

Meanwhile, Codrington's brigade reached the Alma river. Codrington himself was one of the first to reach the river, spurring his horse down the bank and into the water, which was not a particularly difficult obstacle to pass. The men of the 7th followed close behind him, with his other two regiments, the 23rd and the 33rd, plunging into the water on their left. The three other regiments of the Light Division, from Buller's brigade, being the 19th, 88th and 77th, followed suit farther to the left, and before long both brigades of the division were scrambling on to the southern bank of the Alma. Brown's men were just sorting themselves out on the river bank when suddenly, behind them, came the 95th, one of their officers, Hume, splashing through the river proudly carrying one of the regiment's colours in his arms. Keen not to let the Light Division have all the fun the men from Derbyshire had parted company with their own division and had followed Codrington across the river, coming up in the rear of the 23rd.

The shortage of space naturally ensured that a great deal of confusion ensued in the ranks of the red-coated battalions now crowded together on the south bank of the Alma. Things were not improved either by the knots of Russian skirmishers that lined the top of the steep bank hanging above the heads of both Codrington's and Buller's men. There was no point in dallying too long on the river bank, otherwise both men risked losing their brigades. Codrington himself was 50 years old, and had joined the army at the age of 17, but had yet to savour the smell of powder in action. Nevertheless, he realised the folly of remaining where he was and so spurred his small white Arab up the bank and on to the foot of the long, sloping glacis that led all the way to the Great Redoubt. As he emerged from the confines of the river bank he saw hordes of Russian skirmishers pulling back, which allowed the Russian guns to fire without fear of hitting their own men. Away to Codrington's right came the 7th Fusiliers, who also emerged from the shelter of the bank, with their commanding officer, Lacy Yea, driving them on relentlessly. Yea, 'a man of an onward, fiery, violent nature, not likely to suffer his cherished regiment to stand helpless under muzzles pointed down on him and his people by the skirmishers overhead',[17] didn't bother to wait for the order to advance. Nor did he wait for his men to deploy into smart, long lines. Instead, he sat upon his horses, roaring, 'Never mind forming! Come on, men! Come on, anyhow!' The order had the desired effect, not that his men needed any encouragement to scramble out from the confines of their sheltered position. Up they went, clambering out on to the glacis, crying, 'Forward! Forward!', sending the Russian skirmishers scattering in all directions, whilst on their left, Codrington's other two regiments, the 33rd and 23rd, came forward with fixed bayonets, determined to get to grips with the Russians. And they were not alone. We have already seen how the 95th had detached themselves from Pennefather's brigade in order to join the Light Division's attack. The four regiments were now joined by a fifth, the 19th, who left Buller's brigade and came forward also to join Codrington, Buller having halted his other two regiments, the 77th and 88th, away to the left, after having first formed the latter into square, believing the left flank of the British attack to be under threat from a large force of Russian cavalry that sat menacingly away to the east. Fortunately for the British, the Russian cavalry did just that for the remainder of the day. They sat there.

The British infantry at the foot of the glacis leading up to the Great Redoubt were now formed in a 'knotted chain,' with the 19th on the left, continuing with the 23rd, 33rd and 95th, with the 7th slightly more detached farther to the right. The 77th and 88th, meanwhile, remained motionless away to the left or to the east. The expected storm of shot and shell failed to materialise, but if the British thought they were to be spared they were sadly mistaken, for instead, coming down towards them at a good pace were two battalions of Russian infantry from the Kazan Regiment. There were some 1,500 men in their column, which made directly for the junction between the 19th and 23rd Regiments. It was immediately hit by a stiff fire from Norcott's riflemen who had been sent out earlier to skirmish in front of the Light Division. But this thin green line was unlikely to stop the mass of grey coming down the slope at speed. Instead it fell to the men of the 19th and 23rd whose brisk firing into the dense ranks of Russians brought them first to a halt, and then sent them retiring slowly back up the hill towards the Great Redoubt.

Meanwhile, a second Russian column, away to the west, engaged Yea's Fusiliers, advancing from the cover of the river bank. But unlike their comrades retreating back towards the Great Redoubt, this second column of the Kazan Regiment was not to be easily beaten. In fact, the fight between them and the 7th Fusiliers was destined to become one of the epic actions of the Battle of the Alma. As the Kazan came down the slope towards them Yea, said to be 'the most detested commanding officer in the army',[18] struggled to get his men into line, trying to form some semblance of order from the confused state the regiment was in after it emerged from the cover of the river bank. The Kazan was too close, however, and for a while the 7th fought as best they could, pouring a withering fire into the dense Russian column, bringing it slowly but surely to a halt. But it was not easy. Yea himself was in the thick of the action, swearing and cursing, barking orders and cheering his men. At one point Yea called out to one of his subalterns who was lying on the ground, unable to move. 'Come on!' shouted Yea, 'Why the hell don't you come on?' The subaltern replied, 'I am very sorry, Colonel, but I'm shot through the ankle and can't walk.' 'Why, damn your eyes!' replied Yea, 'I've got a bullet through my guts, and I'm going on!'[19] In fact, although Yea had indeed been struck by a spent bullet in the stomach, it had hit his belt buckle and had done no real damage. Eventually, Yea got his men into line, the traditional British fighting formation, after which the Fusiliers turned back the clock, meeting the Russian column much in the same way that their ancestors had done at Albuera when they met the French columns. The effect was much the same. The British line overlapped the Russian column, allowing every fusilier to fire his rifle, whereas the Russians, hampered by their formation, could only bring to bear a fraction of their firepower, the vast majority of them being locked away inside their tightly-packed column. But despite their formation the Russians could not be easily swept aside. A thick cloud of skirmishers was thrown out on either side of the Russian column, extending their formation right and left, compensating for their original lack of firepower and drawing Yea's men into a deadly close-range duel that was to last for almost the remainder of the battle. At some point during the fight the range was as close as fifty yards, as both sides unloaded volley after volley into each other. It was as if the spirits of Albuera were with them as the Fusiliers traded volleys with their Russian adversaries, but in spite of the dreadful casualties neither side was willing to give an inch of ground. And so the killing continued.

Whilst Lacy Yea and his men were engaged in their struggle with the Kazan, Codrington's men began the long advance up the glacis towards the Great Redoubt. With the first column of the Kazan having been driven back, and with the Russian skirmishers now grouped around the redoubt, the way was clear for the twelve guns in the redoubt to open fire on the advancing British lines. The British formation presented a long mass of green-jacketed riflemen along with the red-coated men of the 19th, 95th, 23rd and 33rd. With colours flying and with their officers mounted in front, the men from the shires of England and from the Welsh valleys began to move slowly forward, over the open ground towards the Great Redoubt. Ahead of them, up on the slopes of the Kourgane Hill, the Russian guns waited, primed for action. The barrels of the guns could clearly be seen in the crudely cut embrasures, but as yet not a single shot had been fired. But every man in the British host advancing up the slope knew that when the Russians did give fire it would be very unpleasant indeed. At such a relatively short range, grape and canister was at its deadliest.

Finally, when Codrington's men had got to within three hundred yards of it, the Great Redoubt became a blaze of smoke and flame as the guns opened fire. 'Death loves a crowd,' wrote Kinglake, and how right he was. Russian round shot came first, the solid iron balls ploughing their way through the ranks of the British infantry, bowling men over like skittles, and smashing their bodies into a bloody pulp. Then, as the range shortened, grape shot and canister burst from the barrels of the guns, sweeping away whole groups of men like grain before the wind. The men were seen to lean forward, as they do when walking into the teeth of a strong wind. They bunched together, as if there was safety in numbers, not realising they were making it even easier for the Russian gunners, who sponged away furiously, loading and firing as fast as they possibly could.

But despite the storm of iron flying through their ranks, Codrington's men could not be stopped. They had crossed the Alma river under fire having driven the Russian skirmishers from the vineyards. They had then cleared the way of more Russian skirmishers lining the southern bank, and had seen off a column of the Kazan Regiment. All of this had been achieved whilst advancing uphill, over ground devoid of any natural cover, and in the teeth of a devastating fire from the Great Redoubt. The men must have been exhausted, but they could not be stopped. Even the watching Russians could not help but admire the determined advance of their enemies. General OA Kvitsinsky, commanding 16 Infantry Division, wrote:

> The mass of English troops, notwithstanding our devastating fire of shot and shell that made bloody furrows through their ranks, closed up once more and, with new forces, protected by swarms of skirmishing riflemen and supported by a battery firing from behind the smoking ruins of Burliuk, crossed the river and drove back the brave Kazan, forcing our field battery to limber up and depart.[20]

As Codrington's men approached the final few yards before the Great Redoubt it seemed as though every Russian gun belched forth at the same time, tearing bloody lanes through them. But as the smoke cleared Codrington and his men looked on and saw, not hordes of waiting Russian infantry, but instead the Russian gun teams desperately trying to limber up and draw off their guns. It was just the kind of boost to morale

Codrington's hard-pressed men needed to get them over the last few yards and into the redoubt itself. This unexpected turn of events brought hoots of derision from the oncoming British infantry. 'Stole away! Stole away!' they cried. 'He's carrying off his guns!'[21] It was true. As Codrington's men approached the parapet of the redoubt the Russian gun teams were seen retreating with their guns, although some were not quick enough. Indeed, it was impossible for the teams of horses to be moved at anything other than a slow pace and not all of the guns could be got away. Amongst the first to reach the parapet of the redoubt was 18 year-old Henry Anstruther, of the 23rd Royal Welsh Fusiliers. He was also one of the first to die, for as this brave, young officer stood and planted the bullet-ridden Queen's colour of his regiment on the rampart, he was sent backwards by a Russian bullet that struck him in the heart. As Anstruther fell, so did the colour, but not for long, for it was picked up by one of his men, William Evans, who waved it proudly above his head amidst the cheers of his comrades who followed close behind him.

By now scores of British infantry were pouring over the ramparts of the Great Redoubt. Codrington was amongst them, waving his hat in the air and cheering his men who brushed aside the few remaining Russian infantry. One Russian gun remained inside the redoubt, apparently a huge 24-pounder, and the sight of it sitting there unguarded was enough to spur Captain Heyland, of the 95th, on towards it, the exhausted British officer scratching the number of his regiment on the barrel. It was quite an achievement for Heyland, who had lost an arm during the advance. Not to be outdone, Captain Bell, of the 23rd Fusiliers, dashed after a Russian gun team as it was drawing its gun away from the rear of the redoubt. Despite being totally exhausted by the advance, Bell had enough puff left in him to chase after the gun team and, drawing his pistol and aiming it directly at the head of the driver, managed to stop the team and lay claim to the gun, which was quickly engraved with the number '23'. Bell was later awarded the Victoria Cross for his action.

The men of the Light Division, and in particular Codrington's mixed bunch of the 19th, 23rd, 33rd and 95th, had performed heroics in taking the Great Redoubt. But as they gazed back over the open slopes towards the Alma river they saw the heavy price they had paid for their success. For along with the green-jacketed riflemen who had advanced under Norcott they saw hundreds of their dead and wounded comrades, stretched out on the grass. Limbs, torn off by Russian guns, were scattered here and there, as were the shattered remains of many a brave man. The Russians too lay thickly about, killed whilst they retired from the river to the redoubt, and scores lay in the redoubt itself. It was a tremendous achievement for the British but their troubles were only just about to begin.

As Codrington looked away to the western slopes of the Kourgane he could see Lacy Yea and his fusiliers, still locked in a fierce struggle with the left hand column of the Kazan Regiment. Beyond them Pennefather's brigade held its position around the damaged bridge and on the post road, whilst even farther to the west the French were heavily engaged on the plateau where they were supported by Turkish troops. But where, he wondered, were his own supports? When the Light Division advanced it did so supported by the 1st Division under the Duke of Cambridge. But now, at this critical moment, and with his men exhausted and running short of ammunition, Codrington realised he was alone in the Great Redoubt, with no supports other than the 77th and 88th of Buller's brigade, which had been halted and formed into squares away to the east. There was not even any indication of the whereabouts of the Commander-in-Chief, Lord Raglan.

Raglan himself had done what his old chief, Wellington, would never have done. He put himself in a position from where he could neither influence nor direct the battle. Wellington once said that he got greater effort from his men when he was on the spot, which is one of the reasons he could always be found at the hottest spots on any battlefield. He simply could not afford to be static during a fight. Raglan, on the other hand, had been extremely brave but very foolish in crossing the Alma river, some way to the west of the post road, and had galloped up with just a handful of his staff and some artillery, and had taken up residence on a knoll with the French on his right and the Russians on his left. He was oblivious to the shot and shell flying around him, and in fact appeared to be enjoying himself enormously, tugging at the empty sleeve of his right arm and laughing whenever a shell flew close by. However, the knoll – some way inside the Russian lines – was not a good position for an army commander to be in, particularly if he wished to exercise full control over it.

Codrington, meanwhile, clung on to his prize, hoping for support from the 1st Division. And he needed it. Away to his right the two battalions of the Kazan Regiment continued their fight with the 7th Fusiliers, whilst on his left were the two other battalions of the same regiment which had yet to be engaged. Along with these were four battalions of the Sousdal Regiment and, in a hollow directly in front of him, four battalions of the crack Vladimir Regiment, who in turn were supported by four battalions of the Ouglitz Regiment. Added to this there were 3,000 Russian cavalry hovering away to the east, there was a battery of artillery in the Lesser Redoubt, and two battalions of sailors for good measure. In all, the 2,000 or so British infantry found themselves relatively isolated in the presence of around 14,000 Russian troops. In a word, Codrington was in a perilous position and in dire need of help. Unfortunately, the 37 year-old Duke of Cambridge, devoid of any military experience, had halted his division some way short of the Alma river, leaving the Light Division isolated – save for the distant and somewhat hard-pressed 2nd Division – and exhausted on the south bank. The 1st Division of the British Army consisted of two brigades, being Sir Colin Campbell's Highland Brigade and the Brigade of Guards, and it was these particular bear-skinned gentlemen who now drew the attention of the Russian guns up on the heights in front of them.

NOTES

1 With such an antiquated transport system, it is little wonder that Menshikov was very cautious about marching away from Sevastopol. The effect of a lack of good communications is reflected in some of the huge marches undertaken by Russian troops to get to the Crimea. For example, the Tarutin Regiment had left its base at Nizhnii-Novgorod on 2 December 1853, intending to fight the Turks, only to be rerouted to the Crimea following the declaration of war by the Allies in March 1854. Albert Seaton, *The Crimean War: a Russian Chronicle* (London 1977), 56. The regiment finally arrived in the Crimea in April 1854. It was all typical in a country where railway systems had yet to be developed.
2 Sir George MacMunn, *The Crimea in Perspective* (London 1935), 56.
3 Bazancourt, the Baron de (trans. by Robert Howe Gould). *The Crimean Expedition, to the Capture of Sebastopol. Chronicles of the War in the East* (London 1856), I, 226–7.
4 Ibid, I, 232.
5 Ibid, I, 235. As always, nationalistic pride tends to cloud judgements as to who did and did not fire the first shots of any battle. The timings of the various events at the Battle of the Alma vary by degrees, depending upon which account is read. For example, Russian accounts have Bosquet reaching the plateau at around 11am, over two hours before Allied accounts have him even beginning his advance. We have tended to use Allied timings rather than Russian for our account of the battle.
6 Ibid, I, 230.
7 'Intendantstvo: iznanka kampanii', *Rodina*, 1995, No.3–4, 92.
8 Tarle E V *Krymskaya voina* (Moscow, 1941–1944), II, 108–9.
9 Zayonchkovsky A M *Oborona Sevastopolya. Podvigi zashchitnikov* (St Petersburg, 1904).
10 Bazancourt, *The Crimean Expedition*, I, 248.
11 Kinglake, Alexander William, *The Invasion of the Crimea: Its Origin, and An Account of its Progress down to the Death of Lord Raglan* (London 1863), 398–401.
12 Ibid, II, 400.
13 Ibid, II, 297.
14 Seaton, *The Crimean War*, 82.
15 Ibid, 83.
16 Norcott himself was suitably irritated by Kinglake's version of events at the Alma that he wrote a letter to *The Times*. According to Kinglake, II, 307, Codrington was left without any cover at all, a fact disputed by Norcott. See Fortescue, *History of the British Army*, XIII, 62, for his version of events.
17 Kinglake, *Invasion of the Crimea*, II, 321.
18 Fortescue, The Hon. J W *A History of the British Army* (London 1899), XIII, 63.
19 Ibid, 64.
20 Kvitsinsky, quoted in Seaton, *The Crimean War, a Russian Chronicle*, 92.
21 Kinglake, *Invasion of the Crimea*, II, 332.

# CHAPTER SIX
## *'. . . and go-ahead bravery'*

During the Peninsular War, the 1st Division of the army was nicknamed 'The Gentlemen's Sons', on account of the fact that it consisted largely of the Foot Guards. The name derived from the very high percentage of titled officers and the sons of the landed gentry to be found within their ranks. Indeed, of all the titled officers in the British Army at the time of the Peninsular War, a third were to be found concentrated in the three regiments of Foot Guards.[1] The tradition was continued by the three regiments of Foot Guards now serving in the Crimea. The Guards were an elite body of men; they were the Household Troops, the royal bodyguards. They were the truly the 'Soldiers of the Queen.' And now, as they were halted short of the enclosures on the northern bank of the Alma, they came under sustained artillery fire for the first time since they had endured Bonaparte's 'unremitting shower of death' at Waterloo almost forty years before. Thus, when it was suggested that they be withdrawn lest they be destroyed by Russian artillery fire, Sir Colin Campbell retorted, 'It is better, sir, that every man of Her Majesty's Guards should lie dead upon the field than that they should now turn their backs upon the enemy!'[2]

The Guards were not allowed to remain stationary for too long, however, for soon afterwards General Airey, the quartermaster general, came galloping up with orders for the Duke of Cambridge to get forward in support of the Light Division. De Lacy Evans also rode over, urging an immediate advance, and soon the Brigade of Guards was on the move again, advancing towards the river and plunging through the water, with Campbell's Highland Brigade on their left. What a sight it must have been, with the tall, bear-skinned Guards, resplendent in their scarlet coats, moving forward with the kilted Highlanders on their left, pipes skirling. The contrast could not have been greater. The question now for Codrington, still struggling at the Great Redoubt, was 'who would arrive first, the Russians or the 1st Division?' He was about to find out.

In the Great Redoubt up on the Kourgane Hill, the tired but victorious men of Codrington's mixed force were resting, seeing to their wounded and preparing the position for defence in anticipation of a Russian counter-attack. They were also looking round anxiously for support. Then, on the slopes above them a large force of infantry appeared, stirring the British from their labours and causing the officers to call their men to arms once more. At first there was some confusion, then a tense wait while the men levelled their rifles and prepared to open fire. The large mass continued coming down towards them at a good pace, the front ranks with charged bayonets. And then, with hundreds of British fingers twitching on the triggers of their rifles, and with the men of the Light Division ready to blaze away, someone, somewhere, shouted, 'The column is French! The column is French! Don't fire, men! For God's sake, don't fire!' Despite this, a ragged fire opened up from the British ranks, but as the word flew back and forth a bugler from the 19th sounded the ceasefire, a call that was picked up by other buglers who then sounded the call to retire, much to the mystification of the majority of both officers and men in the redoubt. Any doubts were removed, however, when the call 'Retire' was sounded again, at which the confused but obedient British troops began to fall back, leaving the Great Redoubt to the mass of infantry approaching it. Unfortunately, the column wasn't French; it was Russian.

The four battalions of the Vladimir Regiment had been waiting patiently in the hollow, its mounted officers watching the fight on the slopes below them. The men themselves stood all this time in battle order, under fire from stray British bullets. Soon afterwards a shell exploded beneath regimental aide-de-camp Lieutenant N Gorbunov's horse, sending him crashing to the ground. As he lay on the there he saw another officer, Colonel Kovalyov, hit by a British bullet which smashed into his Cross of St George. A brother officer, N A Naumov, carried his commander away from the battlefield but the wound was a mortal one. The officers and men of the Vladimir Regiment were curious to examine the Minié bullets – they called them 'thimbles' – which were taking such a toll of them. Gorbunov later recalled:

> During our long stay in battle order it was evident that the order of our columns of attack must have been known to the enemy because the battalions' flanks were shelled. We didn't fire a single shot in reply, but many of our officers, mainly company commanders, were killed. Our blood began to run quicker; there was the horror of the endless victims, and, finally, the approaching enemy – all these electrified us so much that as soon as we heard the order the battalions began to advance immediately as if on parade.[3]

The attack by the Vladimir Regiment was destined to become one of the great feats of Russian arms, but arguments raged as to who actually led it. General Kvitsinsky claimed he was responsible, although General

Gorchakov also claimed the credit. It mattered little at the time, of course. What was important was that the British had to be driven from the redoubt, and driven from it quickly. The Russians advanced slowly and steadily, with their front ranks charging their bayonets. Codrington's men were already pulling back, although many remained to open fire on the Russians.

The British fire from the redoubt was answered by the Vladimir Regiment, with the 33rd in particular suffering. Here and there small groups of British soldiers, convinced that the call to retire had been sounded in error, held their ground and returned fire but the momentum was well and truly with the Vladimir Regiment which swept forward and retook the Great Redoubt, killing, wounding or capturing all those who attempted to dispute the position with them. Once the redoubt had been secured the Vladimir halted. It is said that a lack of artillery support forced them to do so. After all, there was just a single gun remaining in the redoubt, the one which had been taken by Heyland of the 95th. The gun captured by Captain Bell had already been removed. Perhaps it was the lack of guns that caused the halt or, possibly, it was the sight that greeted them upon their arrival at the Great Redoubt. For, coming up at pace from the river was the Brigade of Guards, and on their left rear, Sir Colin Campbell's Highland Brigade.

The Brigade of Guards was commanded by Major General Henry Bentinck, and consisted of the 1st battalions of the Coldstream Guards, under Colonel Arthur Upton, and the Scots Fusilier Guards, under Colonel Sir Charles Hamilton, and the 3rd Battalion Grenadier Guards, under Colonel Frederick Hood. All three battalions were deployed in line, from left to right in that order. The order to advance was, naturally enough, greeted with cheers by the Guards who had been subjected to long-range Russian artillery fire since halting at the enclosures on the north bank. The advance of the Grenadier Guards on the right took them towards the bridge over the Alma, whilst the Coldstreamers, away to the left, were forced to cross the Alma three times, on account of the bends in the river. The Scots Fusiliers occupied the centre of the Guards' line, and it was they who were the first to feel the blast of the Russian guns. Russian round shot came bouncing in thick and fast, knocking over Guardsmen like skittles and reducing the bodies in most cases to a bloody pulp. And yet, even at times such as these, the officers of the Guards could still find time to enjoy a joke or two, as Lieutenant John Astley later recalled.

> A big shot came bounding along and passed through the centre. A capital chap, named George Duff, who was our best wicket-keeper, was just in front of me, and I sang out to him, 'Duff! You are keeping wicket, you ought to have taken that.' He turned, and, smiling quietly, said, 'No, sir! It had a bit too much pace on. I thought you

> were long stop, so I left it for you.' ... the shot and shell kept whizzing and whistling over our heads, and the dirt sent flying every now and again as the shot struck, and some poor fellow to the right or left would be carried to the rear. Now we got up for the last time and marched down to the corner wall – no running for its shelter, mind, but as cool as lettuces. By this time the skirmishers were nearly through the vineyards, and we got the order to advance, and over the wall we went. I gave one or two fellows a hand up, and the balls did whistle like 'old Billy.' We were now in the vineyards, and pushing our way through the tangled vines. Few stooped to pick the grapes; but the grape and canister made many a poor fellow double up. We reached the edge of the stream – already tinged with blood – and I saw poor Charlie Baring, who was with the right flank of the Coldstreams, tumble over. I ran up to him for a second and saw that his arm was broken. I cut back to my company and went into the river, but it was only up to my knees.[4]

The Scots Fusiliers crossed the river under fire, although casualties were fairly light. But the situation changed dramatically once they reached the south bank. Indeed, they had barely begun to emerge from the cover of the river bank than they began to come under heavy fire from Russian artillery situated on either side of the post road. One of the first up was Lieutenant the Hon. Hugh Annesley, whose cry of, 'Forward, the Guards!' had barely left his lips when he was struck in the mouth by a bullet from a canister shell. The bullet passed through his jaw and shattered his teeth, but he survived his terrible wound. John Astley didn't get much farther before he too was struck down.

> Immediately in front of us was one of those infernal earthworks armed with eight or nine big guns, well served with grape and canister, also a regiment of Russian riflemen, some lying full length, others kneeling, and the rest standing; but one and all taking pot shots at us as we came up the hill, and they must have been bitter bad marksmen, or else our line of two deep ought to have been annihilated. We had fixed bayonets, and I verily believe we should have driven the Ruskies out of their battery; but just at the critical moment the 23rd Welsh Fusiliers – who had been terribly cut up, and had gathered round their colours at the corner of the battery – got the order to retire, and they came down the hill in a body, right through the centre of our line, and carried a lot of our men with them.
>
> This caused our line to waver and retire, leaving the officers in front, and just as I was yelling to our company to come back, I got a fearful 'whack' and felt as if some one had hit me hard with a bludgeon on the neck. Fortunately, I did not fall, but turned and went

> down the hill, feeling awfully queer and dizzy. How I got there I don't know; but I found myself standing in the river and sousing my face with water, which somewhat revived me; then one of our drummers came running up and gave me a go of brandy, and helped me through the vineyard, and there I lay down behind the wall which we had crossed so lately.[5]

Astley was out of the battle for the time being. His comrades were likewise in a bad way. Their advance up the slope towards the Great Redoubt was carried out in the best tradition, in line, as if they were on parade. And this despite the intense Russian fire, and despite the fact that they were unsupported, being several minutes ahead of both the Grenadiers and Coldstreamers. Leading the way was the Scots Fusiliers' colour party, consisting of Lieutenant Robert Lindsay, carrying the Queen's Colour, Lieutenant Arthur Thistlethwayte, with the Regimental Colour, and Sergeants Bryce, McLeod, McKechnie and Lane. Their main problem came when Codrington's retiring men came charging down towards them. The Guards could not return fire, of course, as Codrington's men masked the Russians, whilst they in turn received the fire aimed at the retiring British infantry as well as that intended for themselves. A group from the retiring 23rd Welsh Fusiliers hit the Guards so hard, in fact, that several men were bowled over. One man even suffered several broken ribs when he was clattered into by a fleeing Welshman. The 5th and 6th companies of the Scots Fusiliers were swept backwards whilst the others were thrown into confusion. Captain Reginald Gipps takes up the story:

> Our formation already imperfect was more broken by the rush of the Light Division breaking through our ranks, nevertheless we advanced to within I should say twenty yards of the Russian Redoubt, in our progress bayoneting those Russians who had left the shelter of the Redoubt in pursuit of the Light Division. Up to this moment we had continued to advance but now finding our flanks unsupported and masses of the enemy in our front, we halted and commenced firing, as yet we had not fired a shot, waiting for the Grenadiers and Coldstreams to arrive, well knowing their eagerness to be with us, and that a few minutes at the most would see them at our side.[6]

Taking heart from this, two battalions of the Vladimir Regiment began a slow advance from the Great Redoubt, intent on engaging the Scots Fusiliers. Both sides were preparing to get stuck into each other when suddenly a shout rang out, 'Fusiliers retire!' It remains a mystery who gave the order, and who it was intended for. There is every possibility that it was intended either for Lacy Yea's fusiliers, still fighting the Kazan away to the right of the Guards, or perhaps even the 23rd Fusiliers. Nevertheless, it was repeated and picked up by the Scots Fusiliers, the left companies of which were in total confusion, and with the Vladimir battalions almost upon them the Guards suddenly turned and gave way, as Gipps later recalled. 'At this moment some one (alas, who was it?) rode or came to our commanding officer and told him to give the word for us to retire and then and then only did we give way to the overwhelming masses in our front – this order was repeatedly given and retire we did.'[7] The Scots Fusiliers fell back in some disorder, much to the amusement of the other two battalions of Foot Guards, who hooted with derision, crying out, 'who's the Queen's favourites now?' a reference to the fact that Queen Victoria is said to have favoured the regiment.

But not all of the Scots Fusilier Guards retreated, for as the Vladimir Regiment advanced they found a small group of bear-skinned Guardsmen standing firm, in the middle of whom were Lieutenants Lindsay and Thistlethwayte, proudly and defiantly holding the regiment's two colours. The Russians stepped forward to engage them and some severe close-quarter fighting ensued. Lord Chewton, commanding the 3rd Company, was in the thick of it, waving his bearskin above his head, crying, 'Come on, lads, we'll beat them yet and gain the battle', before he was struck down, his leg shattered by a ball. He was quickly surrounded by a group of Russians who bayoneted him mercilessly. Lieutenant-Colonel Francis Haygarth attacked two Russians himself, trying to save Chewton. He later wrote:

> I was horribly distressed on looking back for my company to find them going down the hill, and I rushed after them shouting to them to come back as I had never heard the order to retire given. As I was cutting along I saw Chewton fall and immediately afterwards received a blow in my left thigh from a bullet, which broke my thigh and brought me down. The next thing I saw was a Russian about to bayonet Chewton, when another brute came at me and fired his musket at my head. The bullet entered my bearskin, grazed my head and made a most awful wound in my shoulder. I feared that I should bleed to death but could do nothing as I was at the mercy of the Russians. Our fellows however rallied at once and came back again and right glad was I when they marched over me.[8]

Chewton was left wounded on the ground to be horribly mauled by the Russians when they passed over him. 'Poor Lord Chewton,' wrote Astley, 'was most awfully cut about, five wounds in arms, head and leg; he was bayoneted and beat about the head as he lay on the ground with a broken thigh, and his life only saved by a Russian officer during the momentary retreat we made'.[9] Elsewhere, a fierce struggle began for the colours being proudly held aloft by Lindsay and Thistlethwayte. Lindsay, who was to become Lord Wantage, described the fight.

> The Russians, seeing what they considered a renewed success, sprang out of their earthworks and came forward, hoping to capture the colours. The desperate fire from the redoubt must have ceased on account of the risk to their own men, for I remember a lull in the fire at that time . . . The colours were well protected by a strong escort, four non-commissioned officers and eight or ten privates; one amongst them I especially remember on account of his cheery face and perfect confidence-inspiring, trustworthy demeanour. Sergeant Major Edwards always afterwards took the credit for having selected Reynolds as one of the escorts to the colours, but he chose him on account of his size . . . When the colours were attacked Reynolds did some execution with the bayonet, and Hughie Drummond, who had scrambled to his legs after his horse was killed, shot three Russians with his revolver. Berkeley was knocked over at this time, and all the non-commissioned officers with the colours excepting one sergeant. The colours I carried were shot through in a dozen places, and the colour staff cut in two. Poor old Thistlethwayte had a bullet through his bearskin cap. As is frequently the case with troops in their first engagement, the elevation given to the Russian fire was, fortunately for us, too high for the deadly execution which might have been given to it. In my own case I neither drew my sword nor fired my revolver, my great object being to plant the standard on the Russian redoubt, and my impression was that nobody was into the earthworks before I was.[10]

Much confusion surrounds this particular phase of the battle. Indeed, Kinglake, the British historian of the war, completely overlooks the stand made by Lindsay and the men of the centre companies of the Scots Fusilier Guards. Lindsay himself always maintained the men on either side of him never gave way. Furthermore, the historian of the Scots Guards claimed it was a vital stand, for if the entire regiment had been thrown back there was every possibility that the Kazan Regiment on their right would have almost certainly swept back Yea and the 7th Fusiliers, with the result that a huge breach would have been made in the British line.[11] There was also one final piece of evidence to support Lindsay; he was awarded the Victoria Cross.[12]

While Lindsay, Chewton and Thistlethwayte made their stand with men of the centre companies the rest of the Scots Fusilier Guards were driven back almost all the way to the river. Nevertheless, the check was only momentary, for coming up on the right of the Scots Fusiliers were the Grenadier Guards, whilst away to their left came the Coldstream Guards.

With them came Major Hume, of the 95th, with a small group of Derbyshire men, bringing with them their colours. These men received permission to join the Grenadiers, and so took part in the advance, as did other groups of men from the Light Division who rallied, turned and then began advancing once more towards the Great Redoubt. One of the decisive moments of the Battle of the Alma was now at hand, and Kinglake was at his descriptive best when he wrote of the advance, particularly that of the Coldstream Guards.

> What the best of battalions is, when, in some Royal Park at home, it manoeuvres before a great princess, that the Coldstream was now on the banks of the Alma when it came to show its graces to the enemy. And it was no ignoble pride which caused the battalion to maintain all this ceremonious exactness; for though it be true that the precision of a line in peace-time is only a success in mechanics, the precision of a line on a hill-side with the enemy close in front is the result and the proof of a warlike composure.[13]

The retirement of the Scots Fusilier Guards had left a yawning gap, however, between the Coldstream on the left and the Grenadiers on the right. Beyond the Grenadiers, the 7th Fusiliers were still locked with the two battalions of the Kazan Regiment, whilst down towards the river bank Codrington's men, the 19th, 23rd, 33rd and 95th, began to reform, as did the Scots Fusiliers. Away to the left of the Coldstream Guards Sir Colin Campbell's Highland Brigade was advancing – passing by Buller's two battalions, the 77th and 88th, who still remained static – the 42nd on the right, the 93rd in the centre and the 79th on the left, the three battalions advancing in echelon, right in front. It was a great sight as the long lines of British infantry went forward, and by now they were supported by Sir Richard England and the 3rd Division, and by Cathcart's 4th Division.

Sir Colin Campbell had seen it all before. As a young ensign he had fought at the Battle of Vimeiro on 21 August 1808, after which he had served throughout the Peninsular War, fighting at Corunna and continuing right through to the invasion of France. Those great days must have seemed an age away as he watched the fighting up at the Great Redoubt. Or perhaps it brought them vividly back to life. Campbell was also mindful of the number of men lost during a battle as a result of them falling out to carry off the wounded. Earlier in the morning he had addressed his men, leaving them in no doubt as to what he expected of them once the battle began. Sitting on his horse, he said:

> Now, men, you are going into action. Remember this: whoever is wounded – I don't care what his rank is – whoever is wounded must lie where he falls till the bandsmen come to attend to him. No soldiers

> must go carrying off wounded men. If any soldier does such a thing, his name shall be stuck up in his parish church. Don't be in a hurry about firing. Your officers will tell you when it is time to open fire. Be steady. Keep silence. Fire low . . . Now men, the army will watch us; make me proud of the Highland brigade.[14]

Then, turning to the 42nd, Campbell said simply, 'Forward, 42nd'. And with that the Highlanders began their advance on the left of the Coldstream Guards. Waiting for them at and on either side of the Great Redoubt were four battalions of the Sousdal Regiment, four of the Ouglitz, and four of the Vladimir Regiment. The Vladimir battalions had been buoyed by their success against both Codrington and the Scots Fusiliers, and no doubt looked to another success. But there was something more imposing about the advance of the British infantry now coming on to meet them. 'We were all astonished,' wrote Captain Hodasevich, a Pole serving with the Tarutin Regiment, 'at the extraordinary firmness with which the red jackets, having crossed the river, opened a heavy fire in line upon the redoubt'. He added:

> This was the most extraordinary thing to us, as we had never before seen troops fight in lines of two deep, nor did we think it possible for men to be found with sufficient firmness of morale to be able to attack in this apparently weak formation our massive columns.[15]

The newly-appointed Flag Lieutenant to Admiral Kornilov, Prince Bariatinsky, was another admiring Russian observer of the British advance. His horse had been wounded in the fighting on the plateau, and he watched the oncoming columns on foot. He wrote:

> In the centre, a huge mass of English troops in their red tunics had already crossed the river and I could hear their blood-curdling screams as they advanced up the hill; and somewhere, far away, the sound of bagpipes. To their front and flanks their 'black riflemen' were going forward at the run. And all round the bridge were the heaps of red-uniformed English, the dead and wounded.[16]

It is likely that the 'blood-curdling screams' were, in fact, the screams of those British soldiers being hit by Russian shells, the British infantry usually coming on in a deathly silence.

As the Grenadier Guards advanced, Lacy Yea's fusiliers finally got the better of the two left battalions of the Kazan Regiment. He had been engaged with them for some time, until the intervention of the 55th, who had been brought forward – belatedly – by Lacy Evans, along with the remaining regiments of the 2nd Division, finally turned the fight in favour of the British. The two beaten battalions of the Kazan rallied, however, and faced up to the oncoming Grenadiers, threatening their right, whilst into the gap on their left between them and the Coldstream, Gorchakov advanced leading the two left-hand battalions of the Vladimir Regiment.

At 64 years old Gorchakov was a veteran of the Napoleonic Wars and had fought during the great campaign in 1812. He was the brother of the commander-in-chief of the Army of the Danube and was regarded as being as bad a tactician as the hapless Kir'iakov. But there was no denying his bravery and when he joined the Vladimir Regiment, he did so with his coat full of bullet holes. He also arrived on foot, his own horse having already been shot from under him. 'When I reached the Vladimir battalions,' he later wrote,

> which were left and forward of the epaulement, most of my staff had been wounded. My horse had been shot from under me and I had to send my aide, Major Durnov, to bring the first troops he came across. Meanwhile, in order to hold back the English, I took command of a battalion of the Vladimir – not having met any commanders as they were all wounded. The battalion started its advance, myself in front, no shot being fired. The enemy stood waiting. We had only to cover another 150 paces to close with him when again my horse was shot down; the Vladimir at once opened battalion fire.[17]

The Vladimir battalions tried to close with the Grenadiers but the latter's well drilled and destructive Minié volleys kept them at arm's length, as one of its officers, Gorbunov, later described.

> The troops of the former 6th Corps [the Vladimir] were real parade troops, famed for their military bearing, recruitment, their smartness and deep knowledge of all regulations. Our battalions, a moving iron mass, were ready to fulfil their purpose – to plunge a bayonet up to the musket's barrel, but each time we met with the deadly killing fire, and our soldiers failed to get to grips with the enemy. The failure of the repeated attacks brought our soldiers to a state of frenzy. The soldiers rushed to the attack without an order and perished needlessly.[18]

The left Vladimir battalions charged their bayonets once more and advanced towards the gap between the Grenadiers and Coldstreamers, but Colonel the Hon. Henry Percy, commanding the 8th company on the left of the Grenadiers' line, quickly wheeled his company to the left and opened fire into the left flank of the advancing Russians. Percy had already been shot through the arm, but didn't consider the wound particularly dangerous, and, after bandaging it up himself, simply got on with his job.[19]

Although the rolling fire of Percy's men brought the Vladimir to a halt, the two remaining battalions of the Vladimir, along with the two right battalions of the Kazan, now joined the fight. Thus, the two battalions of British Guards were taking on six battalions of Russians. However, the latter were encumbered by their formation, the overwhelming bulk of their firepower being locked away inside their column, unlike the British, whose two-deep lines repeated the dose given out to the French on numerous occasions forty years earlier in the Peninsula.

Soon afterwards, the Grenadiers and the Coldstream were joined in the centre by the re-formed Scots Fusiliers, and together the three battalions of Her Majesty's Guards drove on towards the Great Redoubt, firing volley after volley into the mass ranks of grey trying desperately to return the fire. Campbell's Highlanders were also coming upon the scene on the left of the Guards, with the re-formed men of Codrington's brigade – along with their additions – and with Yea's fusiliers. It was an unstoppable host. But still the Vladimir stood. There were numerous instances of bravery on both sides, particularly when the two sides closed with each other. Gorchakov himself fought as a private soldier. Indeed, for his bravery at the Alma he was made a patron of the Vladimir Regiment. Elsewhere, Gorbunov recalled the bravery of a grenadier from the Vladimir who fought like blazes in front of the Great Redoubt. 'In the hand-to-hand fighting,' he wrote, 'a tall, brave corporal of the 1st grenadier company, Bastrykin, distinguished himself. He was a native of the Yaroslv province. I saw how he was surrounded on all sides, but took his musket by the barrel and hit his enemies' heads with the butt, defending himself and clearing the way.'[20] The commanding officer of 16 Division, Kvitsinsky, was himself wounded in the leg. As he ordered the troops in the second line to move in support of the Vladimir he was struck again by a rifle bullet in the same leg, whilst a third wounded him in the arm. It was a critical moment, as Kvitsinsky himself later wrote.

> The English advanced in three columns and threatened to turn my right flank, and the French were coming up on my left; the French battery deployed against my left wing [presumably Toussaint's battery, of which more later] began to rake the Vladimir. I then decided that my aim must be to save the regiment and its colours and not the guns ... I put out a screen of skirmishers under Lieutenant Bresmovsky, but then my horse was struck down and I was wounded in the leg. As I was being carried off on a stretcher made of rifles I was hit yet again by a bullet which smashed my arm and rib.[21]

Once again, the colours being proudly borne by the British regiments came in for special attention from the Russian infantry. Lieutenant Colonel A Rogozin, later recalled:

> Many people saw the desperate, or rather the frantic, bravery of a soldier of the 1st grenadier company, called Zverkovsky, among a group who were running forward during the battle to try and seize an English flag. I can still see now his tall, strong figure as, having thrown away his musket and broken bayonet, he snatched a musket from the hands of a dead enemy soldier and began lashing out with the butt at those English troops who were attacking him until his lion strength at last finished. He fell after being struck down by a blow to the head. I was a witness to that frightful but grand scene and I pitied from my heart that this courageous man would never receive a much-deserved Cross of St George. How surprised we were when, three days later, Zverkovsky suddenly returned to the regiment, not alone but with some lightly wounded comrades. Zverkovsky explained that at night, after the battle of 20 September, and being refreshed by cold dew, he regained consciousness and found himself in captivity. He incited the other wounded, which were able to stand, to escape. They took advantage of the drunken state of some English soldiers and broke through their line. Of course, he was awarded with the Cross of St George.[22]

Whilst the fight raged in front of the Great Redoubt, the Highland Brigade came up on the left of the Guards, the 42nd leading the way, with the 93rd and 79th in echelon away to their left. Ahead of these three battalions were no fewer than twelve Russian battalions: the two right battalions of the Kazan, four of the Sousdal, and four battalions of the Ouglitz Regiment which lay in wait higher up on the slopes above the Great Redoubt. In addition to these battalions, the two right battalions of the Vladimir Regiment peeled away from the Great Redoubt, bringing themselves up on the left of the two Kazan battalions who lay directly in the path of the advancing 42nd. The problem was, of course, that the twelve Russian battalions were still in column, whereas Campbell's Highlanders were deployed in their two-deep line, in which formation every rifle could be brought to bear.

The 42nd, under Colonel Cameron, were just about to open fire when for the umpteenth time in the day, a staff officer suddenly appeared, crying, 'Don't fire! They're French!' Fortunately, the wily Highlanders chose to ignore this ridiculous order. 'Na, na, there's na misstakin thone deevil,' one Highlander is reputed to have said as he sent a Minié ball flying into the Russian column. The 42nd opened fire on the two right battalions of the Kazan and the right Vladimir battalions without halting. The fire ripped into the Russians who, in their confined formation, could reply only with a fraction of the firepower being unloaded into them. But as Campbell, whose horse had been hit twice, peered through the smoke he could see another Russian column heading towards him from his left. It was the two left battalions of the Sousdal Regiment who were coming on at pace heading directly for the 42nd's exposed left flank. But then, right on cue, the 93rd, 'mad with warlike joy', came storming forward to the left of the 42nd. The 93rd, not one of Wellington's old regiments, but one which had been given a good drubbing at New Orleans on their last major outing, were eager to get into the action and Campbell was forced to ride over and see to their dressing which had become somewhat disorganised. Campbell calmly got the 93rd to dress its ranks whilst under fire from the Russians. In fact, a third shot brought his horse down, and he was forced to mount the horse offered to him by his aide-de-camp, Shadwell, although a groom brought Campbell his second horse soon afterwards.

Once the 93rd were correctly formed Campbell returned to the 42nd – who had also halted – and together they continued their advance, firing as they went. Finally, the two battalions of Highlanders reached the slope where the Kazan, Vladimir and now the Sousdal battalions waited for them. A tremendous firefight ensued, with Russian officers and NCOs being forced to manhandle their men in order to make them stand firm in the face of the storm of British lead being fired into them. Indeed, both the 93rd and 42nd were enjoying the better of the fight until, once again, yet another Russian column was seen approaching towards the open left flank of the 93rd. This column consisted of the two right battalions of the Sousdal Regiment who came pushing on in order to join their left battalions, now engaged with Campbell. It was a critical moment for Campbell, and the Russians were coming on, relishing the prospect of catching the two Highland battalions in the flank. 'But, some witchcraft, the doomed men might fancy, was causing the earth to bear giants.'[23] And so it seemed. For, just as the 93rd had come up in time to cover the left of the 42nd, so it was the 93rd's time to be saved, this time by the 79th, who came driving forward against the right flank of the Sousdal as it passed their front heading towards the 93rd.

Caught whilst moving across the front of the 79th, the two Sousdal battalions were hit by a tremendous fire unleashed into their flank by the Camerons who had little trouble in dispersing the Russians. Caught by such a devastating fire, the two right battalions of the Sousdal soon melted away in disorder, whilst almost at the same time, the two left battalions of the same regiment finally broke under pressure from the 93rd. With no friends fighting on their right, the two battalions of the Kazan and the two Vladimir battalions had little option but to fall back. 'Then . . . there was heard the sorrowful wail that bursts from the heart of the brave Russian infantry when they have to suffer defeat; but this time the wail was the wail of eight battalions; and the warlike grief of the soldiery could no longer kindle the fierce intent which, only a little before, had spurred forward the Vladimir battalions. Hope had fled.'[24]

All three Highland battalions were now up, abreast of each other, rolling over the ground held previously by the Russians. They had put in a tremendous effort to clear away a vastly superior number of Russian infantry, their task being made easier by the unwieldy formation which hampered the Russian battalions. But what an effort it had been, and now, standing triumphant upon the slopes of the Kourgane they allowed themselves the loud, deserved cheers which rang out along the hillside. Their supports, Cathcart's division, were still some way off but the experienced Campbell knew the job was done. Even so, there still remained four battalions of the Ouglitz Regiment that had watched the fight from the upper slopes of the hill. They watched, frustrated as their comrades ran back in disorder, many of them even trying to halt the flight, but to no avail. Finally, and rather belatedly, the Ouglitz themselves tried to enter the fray, advancing downhill a little distance to attack Campbell. But it was no use. Shaken and astonished by the sight of the dense Russian columns being flung back by two thin red lines, their advance was little more than a token gesture, and when Campbell's men opened fire again the Sousdal quickly turned and began making their way from the field. The Ouglitz also suffered from the fire of Maude's and Brandling's horse artillery, six guns in all, which came up courtesy of Lord Lucan to support Campbell. The triumph by Sir Colin Campbell's Highland Brigade completed the victory on the British left and centre, for the battered and bruised Brigade of Guards had finally got the better of the Russians at the Great Redoubt. It had been an extremely hard fight but between them the Guards, along with Codrington's men, the 19th and 95th, had driven the Russians from the area in and around the Great Redoubt and now stood cheering themselves hoarse on the slopes of the Kourgane, cheers that, it is claimed, could be heard over a mile away.

The retreat of the Russians from the Kourgane forced General Kvitsinsky into pulling back the guns covering the post road, and thus the way was then left open for Pennefather and Adams, still fighting on either side of the road to continue their advance. This was made easier by the support given to them by two guns from Turner's battery that Lord Raglan had brought forward to join him on the knoll from where he had watched, somewhat dangerously exposed, most of the fighting. Turner's gunners disabled one Russian gun and blew up an ammunition wagon, which was scattered to the winds in spectacular fashion. Lacy Evans' 2nd Division, less those who had gone off with Codrington, were now pouring up the lower slopes on the eastern side of Telegraph Hill, covered by Turner's guns, whilst away to their right the French continued to drive home the Allies' advantage.

The French, it will be remembered, had kicked off the battle by scaling the heights on the south bank of the Alma, close to its mouth at the sea, after which they had made great efforts to establish themselves on the plateau in the face of stiff Russian resistance. Saint-Arnaud had watched

Raglan's men struggle to get up to the Great Redoubt, and had ordered Prince Napoleon to move his division to the east to try to support the right of the British attack. Saint-Arnaud, in fact, was doing quite a remarkable job considering just how ill he was. In fact, he had barely a few days to live, but he was all activity on the afternoon of 20 September, organising his troops and sending them into action. General Forey was sent to support Canrobert with one of his brigades, the other being despatched to fight on the extreme right of the French attack. He then sent General d'Aurelle to support also, and after a brief reconnaissance of the river Colonel Beuret was splashing across the Alma at the head of the 39th Ligne. Once across, the men threw off their packs and set off in double quick time, heading towards the telegraph station. All along the heights French troops had struggled to establish themselves in the face of heavy Russian fire, but as more and more of them gained the plateau, and with the eventual success of the British to the east, Russian resistance had began to crumble. The 1st Zouaves and 1st Chasseurs, along with the 2nd Zouaves, were exposed to a particularly heavy fire, forcing them to take shelter, until two batteries of artillery under Commandant Boussinière came up to support them. But the fire of four Russian guns continued to cause casualties amongst them, whilst a heavy column of Russian cavalry suddenly appeared, hovering menacingly.

And then there was still Kir'iakov's mysterious column of eight infantry battalions. Despite some accounts that have them disappear along with Kir'iakov at an early stage of the battle, it appears that the column was, nevertheless, still present and very threatening during the latter stages of the battle. Indeed, these eight battalions were brought forward against the advancing head of Canrobert's division once again, as they had apparently been earlier in the afternoon. However, on this occasion they had not bargained for French artillery which quickly began to pour shot and shell into their confused ranks. Indeed, Kir'iakov himself claimed he was shelled by French ships as he could not see where the firing was coming from. In fact, the guns had been deployed in some dead ground from where it was difficult for the Russians to see them. Whatever the case, the columns were sent reeling backwards in retreat, allowing Canrobert to continue his advance.

With the Russians in the part of the battlefield now pulling back, Colonel Cler, commanding the 2nd Zouaves, took it upon himself to charge the telegraph station. Cler raised himself in his saddle and, turning to his men, cried, 'Follow me, my Zouaves! To the tower! To the tower!'[25] The 2nd Zouaves were followed instantly by the 1st Zouaves, the Foot Chasseurs and the 39th Ligne, under Beuret and d'Aurelle. The French surged on towards the unfinished telegraph station and swept the Russians out at bayonet point. Cler himself seized the eagle of his regiment and planted it proudly on the tower, shouting 'Vive l'Empereur!' Sergeant Fleury, of the 1st Zouaves, dashed forward to place the flag of his regiment on the tower also, but he was struck down soon afterwards by a grape shot that smashed into his forehead. And as if to make a point a Russian shot smashed the staff of the flag soon afterwards. Not to be outdone, Lieutenant Poitevin, of the 39th Ligne, placed the eagle of his regiment on the tower also, but he too was struck down, hit in the chest by a musket ball.

The fighting intensified, and even Canrobert was knocked down by the fragment of a Russian ball that struck him in the shoulder. He was carried to the telegraph station unconscious, but was revived soon afterwards. By now, the French army was well and truly established on the plateau, pressing on despite the receding Russian fire. The Turks were up also, supporting them. Even Saint-Arnaud was on the plateau, congratulating his generals for their efforts. Boussinière's artillery had moved to support them also, with Toussaint's battery opening fire on the left flank of the Russians directly opposing the British attack at a range of about 400 yards. Indeed, this artillery fire frequently goes overlooked in the majority of British histories of the Alma battle, but there is little doubt it gave De Lacy Evans' division and, in fact, the whole of the right of the British attack, vital cover during the latter stages of the battle.

Saint-Arnaud's troops were on the plateau in strength and in possession of Telegraph Hill, their artillery pounding away at the left of the Russian army, whilst the British in their turn occupied the Kourgane. There was no option for Menshikov but retreat. It was, as Kir'iakov later wrote,

> impossible to leave the left wing thus exposed to a cross-fire, and I could not send or wait for orders from the Commander-in-Chief. The right wing having already begun a very decisive retreat, I commanded the march towards the main road, on either side of which I ranged the troops. This road was beyond the height where our principal reserve had stood. Then I became aware that our right wing was indeed retreating; and, wishing to conform as much as possible with their movements, I ordered a second march towards a height beyond the road . . . The enemy did not follow us.[26]

As soon as the general retreat began, the commander of the Volyn Regiment, Colonel A Khrushchov, was ordered to cover the retreating army. The commander of artillery, Major General L Kishinsky, placed thirty guns ahead of the Volyn, its right flank being protected by the Hussar brigade and its left by the Cossacks. All these were fresh troops, who had taken no part in the battle. After Kishinsky's guns opened fire, the Allied pursuit stopped. It was a painful retreat for the Russians, not only from a morale point of view, but from a human perspective also. One Russian eyewitness wrote:

> The sight was so painful and distressing that a man of a weak and nervous disposition could easily go mad. Indeed, it was impossible to watch with indifference the hundreds of mutilated soldiers, gasping for breath, who dragged themselves almost unconsciously after their comrades, letting out terrible, unbearable cries at each step. But it was an inevitable consequence of the war. Some soldiers had several wounds, six or seven, in all the parts of body, mainly from rifle bullets. Fatal inflammations and infections quickly set in. Also, the soldiers were parched with thirst, but there was neither water nor help. A retreating army doesn't leave behind it doctors, medical attendants and carriages. The wounded had to take care of themselves. The flaps of coats and ragged shirts were used as bandages. They were pleading with the passing soldiers for help but they used the last spark of life to reach their friends.[27]

Here again there is much conflict and confusion regarding the course of events from the Russian point of view. Kir'iakov was and still is alleged to have abandoned the position on the left of the Russian army without orders and at a premature stage of the battle. Menshikov's chief of staff, Vunsh, accused Kir'iakov of performing a disappearing act shortly after the French attack on Telegraph Hill, adding that he was not seen again until the army reached Sevastopol, to which Kir'iakov responded somewhat unconvincingly in the Russian press. Captain M I Enisherlov, of the Ouglitz Regiment, writing about the battle four years later, said that only Kir'iakov himself could throw any light on the 'strange withdrawal'.[28] Whatever Kir'iakov's conduct – and it is not our intention here to examine it in any great depth – the situation for the Russians was now dire. British and French artillery were pouring shot and shell into the retreating ranks of Menshikov's army. Indeed, the Ouglitz Regiment, covering the retreat of both the Vladimir and Kazan regiments, suffered terrible casualties from British artillery fire as they melted away to the south. All was confusion in the Russian ranks. They had been driven from a strong position by troops they had considered to be vastly inferior to themselves, whilst many of their officers were, according to some Russian accounts, by now drunk and incapable of maintaining discipline. In all, it was a desperate situation that needed to be exploited by British cavalry. Indeed, one Russian officer (actually Polish) wrote of the ten minutes of 'fear and trembling' when he saw British cavalry coming over the hill, cutting off stragglers. And yet, just at the moment when Lucan's cavalry ought to have been sent off in pursuit of the retreating Russians, Lord Raglan decided that 'the cavalry were not to attack'.

Initially the British cavalry had in fact been sent forward. Lord Cardigan went off with half of his cavalry escorting the British guns on the right, whilst Lord Lucan advanced with the remainder to escort the guns on the left. Lucan, riding in front with a squadron of the 17th Lancers, actually managed to cut off a sizeable number of Russian stragglers, whilst a troop of the 11th Hussars did likewise. Among the latter was RSM George Loy Smith, who wrote about the brief pursuit in his diary.

> On arriving at the brow of the opposite hill, before us was a vast plain. In the distance could be seen the Russian Army in full retreat, with many stragglers. We now sent out pursuers to make prisoners of all that could be overtaken. A number were brought back – most of them unwounded. One (a Pole, not wounded) appeared rather glad he was taken. The ball part of the grenade of his helmet had been shot through, which I appropriated and now have in my possession. Sergeant Bond, during the pursuit, received a bayonet wound in the face from a prisoner he had taken who pretended to surrender, then treacherously made a point at him. Bond would have cut him down, but an officer galloped up and told him to spare the scoundrel. At this moment it was perceived that a swarm of Cossacks were rapidly approaching, so that the pursuers had to retreat and this Russian escaped. It is singular that Bond was the only man of the cavalry that was wounded, and not a single horse – although we had, during the day, at three different times been exposed to a cannonade – and once been under rifle fire.[29]

There were, in fact, easy pickings to be had by Lucan's cavalry if they had been allowed to press on. Indeed, some Russian officers thought that, had the pursuit been pressed home with the vigour it demanded barely 15,000 of them would have made it back to Sevastopol. In the event, Lord Raglan decided not to risk his cavalry, but keep them instead in his now famous 'bandbox'. Naturally, both Cardigan and Lucan, already enraged by their lack of activity during the day, were astonished by the recall, which also involved freeing their prisoners. It was too much for them. Not only had they watched, motionless, whilst the infantry held sway all day, but now they were being denied the opportunity to turn a hard-earned victory into a fully-fledged rout. One can almost feel the hand of Wellington again here. We know just how much Raglan looked to Wellington during their long years of working together. Like Wellington, Raglan had seen for himself how British cavalry had come to grief on a few high profile occasions in the Peninsular War. Indeed, Wellington developed a great distrust of his cavalry between 1808 and 1815. Now, forty years on, was that same distrust put upon his old, faithful servant, Raglan? Perhaps.[30]

Despite the failure to follow up and pursue the retreating Russian Army the Battle of the Alma was a resounding victory for the Allies. The position which Menshikov bragged could be held for weeks had been taken within a few hours. But it had been taken at a great cost to both British and

French, to which the countless dead and wounded bodies lying about the field testified. Indeed, the last time the British Army had slumped down exhausted after such an action in Europe was the night of 18 June 1815. British losses were put at twenty-five officers and nineteen sergeants killed, and eighty-one officers and 102 sergeants wounded. Of the rank and file, 318 were killed and 1,438 wounded. French losses are not so easy to determine. Indeed, when Lord Raglan read Saint-Arnaud's despatch and accompanying casualty list he was more than a little surprised. Officially, the French suffered 1,343 killed and wounded. Raglan, however, thought that sixty killed and 500 wounded was nearer the mark, based upon Saint-Arnaud's own figure of just three officers killed.[31] One is tempted to suggest that, with the fighting on the plateau being nowhere near as bitter as on the Kourgane, Raglan may well have had a point. After all, he had spent six years in the Peninsula with Wellington reading exaggerated and often absurd casualty reports. The battle highlighted the problems that existed between the French and British command. For although the French appeared willing to act in a spirit of comradeship Raglan was still very suspicious and uneasy about his French allies. The intervening years between the end of the Napoleonic Wars – and certainly since the death of Napoleon Bonaparte in 1821 – and the Crimean War had gone some way towards smoothing the way for Anglo–French cooperation, but he could never forget that it was these very same allies who had taken his right arm off at Waterloo. Whilst he was willing to entertain their ideas and plans, and go to great pains to keep them happy, he was, nevertheless, careful to play his cards as close to his chest as possible. The British army was his to command, and he would do so as he saw fit, and not how the French wanted him to.

The battlefield itself was a shocking sight. The killed and wounded lay thick about the Great Redoubt and on the slopes leading to it, testifying to the bitterness of the fighting. 'The quantity of firelocks, great coats, bearskin caps, shakos, helmets and flat forage caps, knapsacks (English and Russian), belts, bayonets, cartouch-boxes, cartridges, swords, exceeded belief; and round shot, fragments of shell smeared with blood and hair, grape and bullets, were under the foot and eye at every step.'[32] The dead were buried in pits, close to where they had fallen, after all re-useable equipment had been removed. The Russians were buried together in their own mass graves, as were the British and French, separated in death as they had been in life.

The British soldier at the Alma had shown himself a worthy successor to those who had gone before. Indeed, the men of Albuera would have been more than satisfied by the conduct of their descendants. There was a great deal of inexperience amongst both the commanders and the men themselves, and mistakes were undoubtedly made. But when the time came for them to get stuck into their enemies they were not found wanting. The French too showed they lacked nothing of the passion and élan that had swept their ancestors across Europe decades before. And, it should not be forgotten, it was barely six days since the Allies had set foot in the Crimea. It was still an extremely early stage of the war. Both British and French were still feeling their way, and the victory at the Alma put them both in good spirits. Optimism was high for the advance on Sevastopol and a possible early end to the war.

As for the Russians, things were more serious. Their losses were tremendous – 145 officers and 5,600 other ranks were recorded as casualties. The newspaper *Russian Invalid* put the figure at 1,752 killed, 2,315 wounded, and 405 'shell-shocked'. Among the killed there were forty-five staff and chief officers, among whom were four wounded generals: the commander of the 16th Infantry Division, Lieutenant General Kvitsinsky, and one of its brigade commanders, Major General Shchelkanov, the commander of the 17th Regiment, Major General Goginov, and the commander of the Moscow Regiment, Major General Kut'anov. But, more harmful to the Russian cause was the damage done to the soldiers' morale. Their confidence in their commanders and in their own abilities to send the invaders back into the sea was severely shaken. Furthermore, there was little now between the Allies and Sevastopol, the defences of which were far from ready to withstand a siege. The next few days would see whether the Russians' worst fears would be realised.

NOTES

1 For a study of the Foot Guards between 1808 and 1815 see Ian Fletcher's *Gentlemen's Sons: The Foot Guards in the Peninsula and at Waterloo, 1808–1815* (Speldhurst 1992).

2 Kinglake, Alexander William, *The Invasion of the Crimea: Its Origin, and An Account of its Progress down to the Death of Lord Raglan* (London 1863), II, 351. Others, such as Baring Pemberton, *Battles of the Crimean War* (London 1962), 58, have Campbell passing this memorable comment at a later time, during the heavy fighting in front of the Great Redoubt. We are inclined to believe Kinglake's timing.

3 'Vospominaniya N A Gorbunova.' *Collection of manuscripts, introduced to His Imperial Highness Crown Prince (Cesarevitch) about defence of Sebastopol by its defenders* (St Petersburg 1872) I, 57–8.

4 Sir John Dugdale Astley, *Fifty Years of My Life* (London 1894), I, 213–14.

5 Ibid, I, 215–16.

6 Gipps, quoted in Sir F Maurice, *The History of the Scots Guards* (London 1934), II, 81.

7 Ibid, II, 81–2.

8 Ibid, II, 80.

9 Astley, *Fifty Years of My Life*, I, 222. Kinglake, *Invasion of the Crimea*, II, 423, would have us believe that Chewton was killed at the Alma. In fact, he died on 8 October.

10 Lord Wantage (Lindsay), quoted in Maurice, *Scots Guards*, II, 83–4.

11 Although regimental pride should never be discounted, it is difficult to argue with the evidence in Maurice's *History of the Scots Guards* (II, 73–5), and with eye-witnesses themselves, including Lindsay (by then Lord Wantage).
12 Arthur Thistlethwayte, who carried the regimental colour, died of disease at Scutari afterwards. Had he lived he might well have been awarded the Victoria Cross like Lindsay.
13 Kinglake, *Invasion of the Crimea*, II, 427.
14 Ibid, II, 450.
15 Hodasevich, Captain R *A Voice from Within the Walls of Sebastopol* (London 1856), 70.
16 Seaton, Albert, *The Crimean War: a Russian Chronicle* (London 1977), 93–4.
17 Ibid, 92.
18 'Vospominaniya N A Gorbunova' *Collection of manuscripts*, I, 57–8.
19 Henry Percy was later to win a Victoria Cross at Inkerman. He was one of the famous Percy family, from Alnwick Castle, Northumberland. Another member of the Percy family had brought back Wellington's Waterloo despatch, along with the two captured French eagles.
20 Gorbunova, *Collection of manuscripts, introduced to His Imperial Highness Crown Prince (Cesarevitch) About defence of Sebastopol by its defenders* (St Petersburg 1872), I, 59.
21 Seaton, *The Crimean War*, 93.
22 'Vospominaniya N A Gorbunova' *Collection of manuscripts*, I, 204–5.
23 Kinglake, *Invasion of the Crimea*, II, 461.
24 Ibid, II, 462.
25 Bazancourt, the Baron de (trans. by Robert Howe Gould). *The Crimean Expedition, to the Capture of Sebastopol. Chronicles of the War in the East* (London 1856), I, 252.
26 Kinglake, *Invasion of the Crimea*, II, 485–486.
27 Dubrovin N F *Materialy dlya istorii Krymskoy voinyi oborony Sevastopolya* (St Petersburg, 1871–1874), 184.
28 Seaton, *The Crimean War*, 87.
29 George Loy Smith, *A Victorian RSM: From India to the Crimea* (Tunbridge Wells, 1987), 106.
30 For an in-depth study of Wellington's cavalry, see Ian Fletcher's *Galloping at Everything: The British Cavalry in the Peninsular War and at Waterloo, 1808–1815* (Staplehurst 2000).
31 Kinglake, *Invasion of the Crimea* (II, 503), quotes a conversation with a French soldier who suggested their (the French) loss to be at around fifty. Kinglake naturally discounted this but used it as an indication of just how light the French considered their initial losses to have been.
32 William Russell, *The British Expedition to the Crimea* (London 1877), 126–7.

# CHAPTER SEVEN
# *Sevastopol*

After the victory at the Alma it was essential that the Allies follow it up as quickly as possible. Menshikov's army had not been scattered, or even routed, but it had been thoroughly demoralised and was in a state of mild panic. Furthermore, the fortifications on the Severnaia, the suburb on the northern side of Sevastopol, were considered to be virtually non-existent, save for a large star fort, and it was believed that even that had yet to be armed by the Russians. A swift move south by the Allies would surely bring about the capture – possibly – of Sevastopol and with it a swift end to the war. After all, the destruction of Russia's great naval base on the Black Sea was the object of the game.

The need to move south, and move fast, was appreciated even by Raglan, but when, the day after the battle, he urged upon Saint-Arnaud the need for a rapid advance on Sevastopol he found his French allies unwilling to move. Saint-Arnaud claimed his men were exhausted, that their packs had been left behind in the rear, and that the French soldier went nowhere without them. Raglan's profound sense of frustration only increased on 22 September when Saint-Arnaud, by now extremely ill, again declined to move his army in pursuit of the beaten Russians. It was all too much. Now was the time for rapid pursuit, regardless of how tired the men were. Some, however, were not unduly worried by the delay, and thought it unlikely that they would see the Russian army again. Indeed, when George Paget, of the 4th Light Dragoons, was inspecting the battlefield afterwards with Sir George Cathcart, the latter commented, 'Ah! Those fellows have had such a dressing, that they will never meet us in the open again.'[1]

As well as the need for a hasty pursuit, it was also of the utmost importance that the British army secure a base for their forthcoming operations. After all, it would be impossible for the army to conduct any sort of operation if they were unable to land supplies, assuming that Sevastopol did not fall immediately. It was this latter problem, of supply and transport, which surfaced immediately after the Battle of the Alma. Hundreds of British wounded lay scattered round the battlefield and these had to be attended to before the army moved off. Needless to say, it was a great problem, for like Wellington forty years earlier, Raglan possessed nowhere near the number of wheeled vehicles necessary for conveying the wounded from the battlefield. It must have seemed like *déjà vu* to Raglan. It wasn't so much a problem for the French, as their wounded numbered far less than the British. Furthermore, they were a lot closer to their fleet than were the British. Many of the British wounded had to be taken a distance of four miles across the battlefield to boats waiting to take them out to the ships lying at anchor. It was a task that was only accomplished through the efforts of the officers and men of the Royal Navy. It was also a task that took a full two days to complete. Nor was it made any easier by the reappearance in the British ranks of the dreaded cholera, which took up where it had left off in Varna, striking down scores of soldiers every day.

The delay caused by the removal of the wounded now gave the French cause to complain. Whilst most histories of the Crimean War blame the dithering, reluctant Saint-Arnaud for the delayed pursuit, Saint-Arnaud himself claimed it was the fault of the British. Writing to his brother on 22 September, he said, 'The English are not yet ready; and I am detained here,' although he did admit that the British had more wounded than the French and that they were farther from the sea.[2] They were sentiments echoed by the French historian of the war, Bazancourt:

> The English, intrepid and indefatigable in action, appear not to understand the vast importance of a day, or an hour of delay, in warlike operation. They either know not how to hurry themselves, or they will not do it. 'I have lost fewer men than they,' writes the Marshal [Saint-Arnaud], 'because I have been more rapid. My soldiers run; theirs march.' . . . the English army . . . was completely wanting in pliability (mobility). The 22nd was another lost day.[3]

But on the morning of 23 September both Raglan and Saint-Arnaud finally decided to march south towards Sevastopol, and after eight miles both armies bivouacked in the valley of the Katcha, whilst Lucan's cavalry division halted farther to the south on the line of the Belbec. The Allies had been reinforced this day, the British by the arrival of the Scots Greys and the 57th Regiment, who landed at the mouth of the Alma, and the French by around 7,000 troops. The sun rose early on 24 September, a day that saw a marked increase in temperatures and in the number of cholera cases. It was also a day when one of the most significant decisions of the war was made. A reconnaissance carried out earlier suggested that the Star Fort on the Severnaia was much stronger than had at first been realised. With a circumference of around 700 yards it was certainly a large work. It was also protected by a ditch twelve feet deep and eighteen wide. Furthermore, a new battery had been thrown up close by, threatening the

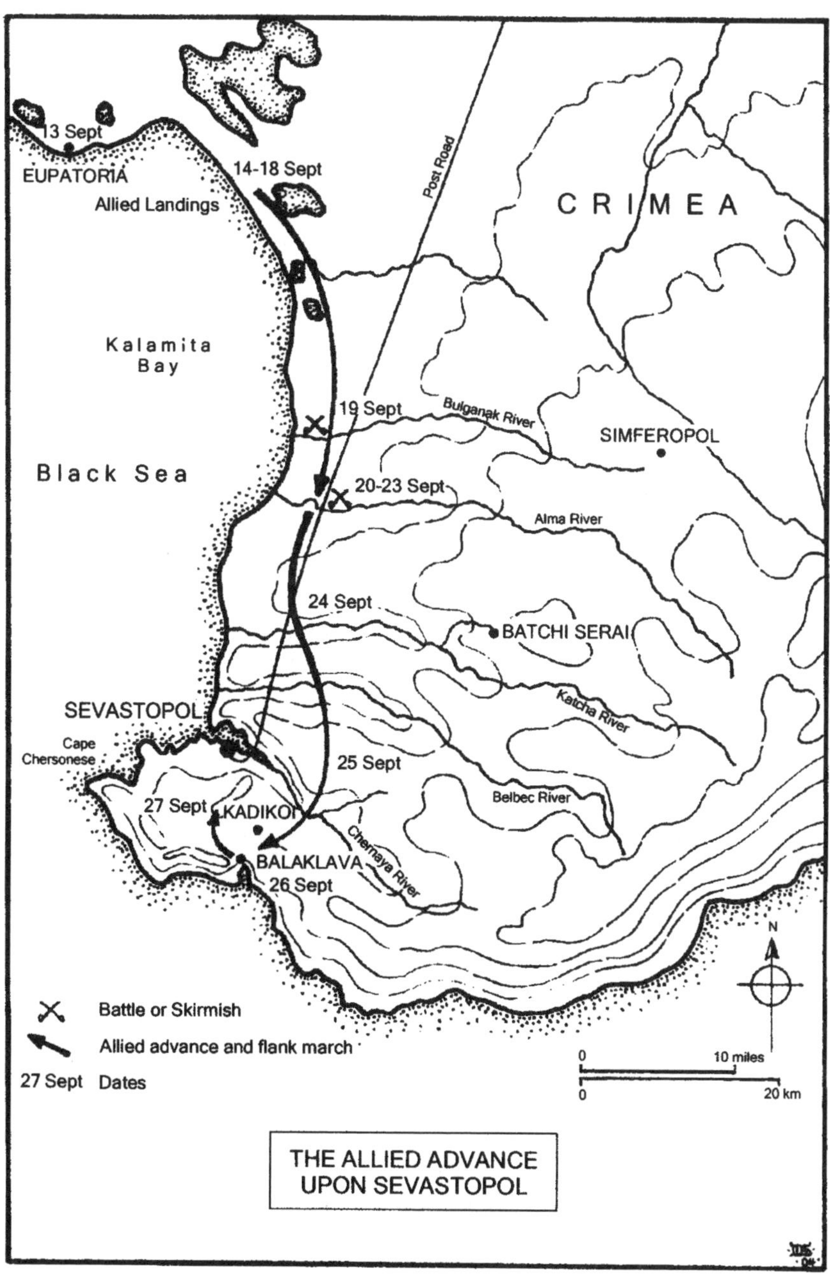
13 Sept
EUPATORIA
14-18 Sept
Allied Landings
Post Road
CRIMEA
Kalamita Bay
19 Sept
Bulganak River
SIMFEROPOL
Black Sea
20-23 Sept
Alma River
24 Sept
BATCHI SERAI
Katcha River
SEVASTOPOL
Cape Chersonese
25 Sept
Belbec River
27 Sept
KADIKOI
BALAKLAVA
Chernaya River
26 Sept
N
Battle or Skirmish
Allied advance and flank march
27 Sept Dates
0
10 miles
0
20 km
THE ALLIED ADVANCE UPON SEVASTOPOL

Allies' line of march and causing them to think hard about their next course of action.

Whilst many, including Raglan and Sir Edmund Lyons, commanding the Royal Navy's inshore squadron, advocated a quick advance directly upon the so-called weak defences of the Severnaia, Sir John Burgoyne, the most experienced engineer in the army, advocated an attack from the south. It was a view shared by the French and, in particular, Saint-Arnaud, who would not counsel an attack on the northern defences of Sevastopol on account of the heavy casualties he expected to sustain in the attempt. The decision to avoid the northern defences and march inland, to the east of Sevastopol, and approach the place from the south remains a point of some debate. Certainly Kinglake states quite clearly that both Raglan and Lyons were of the opinion that the victorious Allied army, numbering around 50,000 men, was more than capable of taking the Star Fort, the only real work on the Severnaia. And, writing with the benefit of hindsight, added, 'Time, at last, has apparently proved that the inferences of Lord Raglan and Sir Edmund Lyons were sound.'[4]

Saint-Arnaud thought otherwise, however. The French were understandably concerned about possible heavy losses, particularly as reports had been received suggesting that new Russian works had been thrown up, in addition to which reports of large concentrations of Russian troops were received also. They also said that the guns of the Star Fort covered the mouth of the Belbec river, the obvious landing place for siege guns and material, and so when Sir John Burgoyne presented his plan for the so-called 'flank march' around Sevastopol, avoiding the Star Fort, the decision was as good as made. In fact, Raglan's most recent biographer claims that both he and Burgoyne were committed to an assault from the south all along. Whether he was simply expressing support for the decision is not clear, but on 28 September Raglan wrote to the Duke of Newcastle, stating, 'I have always been disposed to consider that Sevastopol should be attacked on the south side, and Sir John Burgoyne leant strongly to the same opinion.'[5] There is no doubt that the Star Fort on the Severnaia had indeed been strengthened in recent days, but the man who was to emerge as one of the great heroes of the siege on the Russian side, the 36 year-old Lieutenant Colonel Francis Totleben, thought – somewhat ironically – that an Allied attack on the Star Fort would have been successful.[6] But whatever the arguments, Saint-Arnaud and the French, supported by Burgoyne, had their way, and so Raglan agreed to the flank march.

It is interesting again to consider how much influence Raglan's and Burgoyne's experiences of the terrible sieges in the Peninsular War had on the decision-making process in September 1854. Both men had seen at first hand how such operations could become long, drawn-out and very costly affairs. Was Raglan's wish to push on quickly and attack the Star Fort based upon his desire to avoid a long siege operation, attended with the inevitable casualties? After all, many considered the Star Fort to be the key to Sevastopol. Once it had fallen, the Severnaia would fall with it. It would have been impossible for the town to survive for much longer afterwards. Burgoyne, on the other hand, an experienced Royal Engineer, had also seen the costly assaults on fortresses, and perhaps wanted to avoid such repetitions, believing that a regular siege operation would succeed, hopefully without the bloody assaults that attended the sieges in Spain.

The march from the Belbec continued, the Allies moving away to the east so as to avoid any contact with the Star Fort and the new battery that had apparently been thrown up close to it. By moving farther inland, however, the Allies were gambling for they were distancing themselves from their fleets and putting at risk their communications. Nevertheless, they were heartened by the sight, every now and then as they crested a hill here and there on the line of march, of the white houses in distant Sevastopol. Optimism was, therefore, high despite the delay in pursuing the Russians and the dithering over the strategy to be employed against Sevastopol. With the decision to attack Sevastopol from the south having been made it became even more essential for the Allies to secure bases where they could land supplies. Maps indicated the possibility of a suitable port to the south of Sevastopol, at a place called Balaklava.

The Russians, meanwhile, were still coming to terms with their defeat on the Alma. Russian reaction to the battle was one of dismay. It was also one of shock, for Czar Nicholas had every confidence in Menshikov's abilities and when the latter declared that he could hold the position for days the czar doubted him for not a single minute. Thus, it came as a great blow when news of the battle arrived at St Petersburg. The Battle of the Alma was coming to an unfortunate end for the Russians when Menshikov sent one of his aides-de-camp, Captain S Greig, off to Czar Nicholas with a report of the battle. It is said that when Greig asked Menshikov what he was to report to the emperor, Menshikov simply pointed at the retreating detachments of Russian troops, saying, 'Report what you see yourself.' The young officer was so affected by the unpleasant sight of retreating troops and large numbers of wounded, that when he arrived at St Petersburg on 27 September to deliver the report, he was still shaking with emotion. Having listened to Greig's report, a stunned Nicholas cried bitterly and, seizing him by the shoulders, began to shake him repeatedly, asking him, 'Do you understand what you are saying?'[7] An official from the Russian ministry for war, D Milyutin, later recalled:

> 27 September was a very sad day for our society. Captain Greig came as a courier from Prince Menshikov with a sorrowful message of an unlucky end to the battle. His brief report didn't have any details of

> the battle's progress. Prince Menshikov left his aide-de-camp to tell his own story, for he was an eyewitness of the battle. It was clear that the Czar was eager to hear the details of the first meeting between his army and the Allies. But the impressionable aide-de-camp was so shocked with images of battle, in which he took part for the first time, that even after the seven days' galloping he couldn't get rid of the impression and described the battle in such an unattractive and offensive light that the Czar grew angry, rebuked him and sent him off to bed to sleep.[8]

News of the defeat was kept from the Russian people for days. In fact, it wasn't until the first week in October that word of the disaster began to filter out on to the streets. When it did, it hit hard. Indeed, the great Russian historian of the war, Eugene Tarle, considered the news of the defeat at the Alma to have produced a far worse reaction in Russia than anything else during the entire war. 'Neither Inkerman nor the Chernaia Rechka nor even the final assault and the fall of Sevastopol, though this latter event was far more important than the Alma, produced a more depressing effect.'[9] Soon after Greig's arrival in St Petersburg, Menshikov's couriers had delivered his own account of the battle, in which he intimated that his men had not fought well, a version that was initially believed by the czar. It is a sad reflection of Menshikov's own abilities as a commander that he should have to try and put the blame for the defeat on the Russian soldiers in order to cover up his own short-comings. Fortunately, his chief of staff, Vunsh, later presented the czar with a more accurate account of the battle, but not before Nicholas was writing of the 'want of courage on the part of the troops'.[10]

Russian reaction can almost be gauged by the changes in the mood of Admiral Kornilov, which went from one of optimism prior to the battle, to one of a more despondent nature afterwards. Before the Battle of the Alma, Kornilov was in good spirits, though he was more aware than most of the bad condition of the Sevastopol fortifications. Although many of the inhabitants had left the town, many more had arrived and were working hard to improve the defences. Indeed, the work progressed as such a rate that on 17 September Kornilov wrote to his wife in Nikolaev, telling her that everything was progressing well, that the people were quiet but busy, and that they were going about their work with great enthusiasm. He was, however, realistic enough to know that, in spite of the good work being done, the fortifications were far from adequate. Indeed, he hoped that a Russian victory on the Alma river would mean they would not be needed. On 18 September he rode out to visit the Russian position on the Alma and was cheered by Menshikov's infectious optimism and by the sight of more Russian troops arriving every hour. And so came the day of battle itself, 20 September. After one o'clock the sound of distant artillery fire was reported to Kornilov, at which he immediately set off for the Russian camp on the Alma.

> I soon met the first of the detachments withdrawing from the battlefield, and although these were all moving in good order the picture was a sad one. But God's will be done! The enemy, after a bloody error drove us off by turning our left flank using his superiority in artillery.[11]

From the moment they saw the retreating Russian army, Kornilov, his staff and friends understood that they were going to have to rely only on themselves and that the aloof Menshikov was obviously not fitted for such a task as the defence of Sevastopol. Even so, when the retreating troops arrived at Sevastopol they found that no preparations had been made to receive them. There were hardly any hospitals, no dressing stations, and not enough stretchers, all of which partly explains the great number of Russian wounded that were left on the battlefield. Indeed, it was a desperate situation after the battle. Even the men of the gallant Vladimir Regiment, which lost the greater part of its staff, were unable to carry away their wounded.

There were few finer places to build a naval base than Sevastopol. The base was situated on the south bank of Sevastopol Bay, which itself was four miles long and about half a mile wide. The bay was known as the roadstead, or Sevastopol road, the south side of which was marked by a series of inlets or bays, one of which, the Iuznhia (or South Bay) was a mile long and during the Crimean War was capable of accommodating virtually the whole of the Black Sea Fleet. The Iuznhia effectively divided the town of Sevastopol, with the Gorodskaia (old or main town) to the west and the Korabel'naia faubourg (Karabel Faubourg) to the east. Another small bay, the Korabel'naia (or Dockyard Creek) flowed to the east of the Iuznhia, close to the roadstead. The other large bays, from west to east were the Karantinnaia (Quarantine Bay), the Artilleriiskaia (Artillery Bay), and the Kilen-bukhta (known as the Keeling or Careenage Bay or Bight).

The beginning of the nineteenth century saw much development of industry in Sevastopol. In 1812 and 1813 several plants and factories were built including saltpetre and lime plants, brickyards, bakeries and so on. In addition, there were 202 shops and two markets, with two major fairs being held every year. At the beginning of the second quarter of the nineteenth century Sevastopol was the largest city in the Crimea with a population of 30,000. The largest proportion of these were, of course, naval and military personnel, most of whom endured severe drilling, strict discipline, hard work, bad food and beatings, all of which were common for the sailors and soldiers. The civilian population fared little better, which gave rise to much discontent. In June 1830 the first mass demonstration of working class people and sailors against the government took place. In fact, Sevastopol was in the hands of the insurgents for four days before the czar's government finally regained control, putting down the demonstration with great cruelty.

In 1834 Admiral M P Lazarev was appointed commander of the fleet and the Black Sea ports. Under his leadership five stone fort-batteries, which defended Sevastopol from the sea, were built. He also undertook the task of refitting and reorganising the Russian fleet. Although Lazarev was himself an outstanding naval officer, he was fortunate in having round him a group of similarly gifted and honest men, including admirals, Nakhimov, Kornilov and Istomin, who were to emerge as three of the great heroes of the siege of Sevastopol. During Lazarev's tenure as commander of the Black Sea ports, trade continued to increase in Sevastopol. In 1838, for example, 170 vessels laden with different goods came to the port. The number of merchants increased also. In 1831 there were twenty merchants in the town, which by 1848 had risen to eighty-three. Most of these provided the fleet with flour, meat, cereals, salt and firewood. There were also some 280 different shops, including forty-six 'pottery establishments'. Naturally, the construction of sea fortifications, the Admiralty, sea fronts, the new docks, and numerous other buildings in the centre of the town helped swell the population, with thousands of people arriving looking for work. Indeed, by 1853 the population of Sevastopol had increased to 47,000, and the number of houses to 2,810, all of which were built in forty-three streets and four squares.

In the 1820s two pipelines supplied Sevastopol with its water, although only one supplied the people, the other being used strictly for the Admiralty and the fleet. The pipes fed from natural springs, however, and failed to supply the town with sufficient water. By 1846 the situation had improved to the extent that Sevastopol boasted forty-eight wells. The water supply was to prove an important factor during the siege which took place during the Crimean War. The first medical establishment in Sevastopol was the Naval Hospital, built between 1790 and 1791, and capable of housing 200 patients. However, it served only the naval and military officers and their families, and the Sevastopol aristocracy, the overwhelming mass of the population in the town having to call upon the services of just one other doctor who was also responsible for the condition of the markets, bakeries and shops. It was a thoroughly unsatisfactory state of affairs.

The quality of education was not much better, although efforts to improve the situation were made during the second half of the nineteenth century. In 1826 a School of Sea Cadets for a hundred pupils was opened and two years later, the Civil District (*uyezd*) opened a specialised school for forty pupils. During the following eight years other schools were opened, including schools for sailors' daughters, a parish school, and a private finishing school. In 1846 it is recorded that there were only thirteen teachers and 404 pupils, of whom seventy-four were girls. The arts and sciences were not neglected. In addition to it being the premier naval base in the Black Sea, Sevastopol was second only to St Petersburg as the centre of naval sciences in Russia. In 1842 the navigational charts of the Black and Azov Seas were published, whilst on land important excavations were made of ancient Chersonesus. In 1822 one of the first naval libraries was opened in Sevastopol. The town also enjoyed visits from troupes of actors from countries such as Italy and Spain, who performed in the theatre, built in 1843 at the bottom of Boulevard Height.

But what of the defences of Sevastopol? Although several batteries had been constructed under Admiral Lazarev between 1835 and 1837, it was not until the outbreak of the Crimean War that any real consideration was given to the city's defensive batteries. On the northern side of Sevastopol, the Severnaia, were built the Constantinovskaya (Constantin) and Mikhailovskaya (Mikhail) batteries, and on the southern part the Alexandrovskaya (Alexander), Nikolaevskaya (Nicholas) and Pavlovskaya (Pavel) batteries. Simple earthwork batteries were constructed also – the No.5 Battery in Appolonova (Appolon) ravine, No.8 and No.10 near Alexandrovskaya Bay, and No.4 on Severnaia. The batteries in Sevastopol were named after their commanders or builders, and were numbered according to the order of construction. At the time of Turkey's declaration of war, the batteries were armed with some 533 guns, each battery consisting of between thirty-four and 105 guns, the calibres of the guns ranging from 12-pounders, right up to heavy 36-pounders, in addition to which there were various calibre howitzers and mortars.

The first real fortifications had been built between 1807 and 1811 under the supervision of the engineer, Major-General Garting, and were constructed on the Severnaia. The walled fortification housed forty-seven guns and could accommodate a garrison of almost 4,000 men. These were hardly likely to thwart an enemy attack, however, and so plans were drawn up for the construction of more fortifications in 1834 by the Engineer Department and revised in 1837 following an inspection by Czar Nicholas himself. The plans involved the building of eight bastions connected by a defensive wall and ditch, and extending from the Kilenbukhta (Careenage Bay), south to Bastion No.3 and then north, running to the west of Gorodskaia and up as far as the Sevastopol Road. This would protect Sevastopol from attack from the south. Seven of the bastions were known simply by numbers, the eighth being the Malakhov Hill.[12]

The defences looked all well and good on paper, but actual construction was another matter. Indeed, very little work was carried out, and even as the Allied fleet came gliding towards Sevastopol in September 1854 frantic efforts were underway to try to improve – and in some cases even start –

the fortifications. The construction of Bastion 7 had only just begun, whilst only a defensive wall had been erected on the ground laid out for Bastion 5. On the site where it had been intended to build Bastions 1, 5 and 6 only barracks had been constructed, whilst on Malakhov Hill there was just a fortified tower. In some places the fortifications were connected with simply a thin and unstable defensive wall. The plan of the Engineer Department was far from perfect. For example, although Malakhov Hill, some ninety-seven metres high, rose above the height of Bastions 1, 2, 3 and 4, it was nevertheless lower than some of the heights which surrounded those bastions, such as Vorontsov's Hill and the Careenage Heights.

The worsening situation and the likelihood of war with Britain and France prompted the Russians to begin improving the works. In January 1854 the Svyatoslavskaya (Svyatoslav) battery for seventeen guns was built on the western side of Careenage Bay and was named after the ship *Svyatoslav* on account of the fact that its crew had built it. At the same time were erected the Dvenadtsatiapostolskaya (Twelve Apostles) battery between the Panaitova ravine and Hollandia Bay, and the Parizhskaya (Paris) battery on the nameless cape, which separated Sukharnaya Bay and Hollandia Bay. Behind Constantinivsky fort a new battery, called after its builder, Colonel Kartashevsky, was built, as was Volokhov's tower. This tower, along with its battery, was built by Daniil Volokhov in twenty-one days and at his own expense.

With the appearance of the Allied fleets off Sevastopol, the construction of the fortifications took on a more vigorous and urgent nature. Everyone, both civilian and military, toiled furiously to finish the works. Sailors, soldiers, workmen, women and even the children of Sevastopol helped build the fortifications. The people worked tirelessly, day and night, carrying logs, turfs and sacks filled with soil. The soil itself was hard and the digging of the ditches around the bastions proved to be particularly onerous work. The barrels and mounts of guns and the shells themselves were brought together at three wharfs, Grafskaya (Count's), Pavlovskaya and Gospitalnaya (Hospital), from where they were hauled up into their respective batteries and bastions. During the days following the Battle of the Alma, Sevastopol resembled a busy ant hill, with thousands of people working frantically by day and night to improve the defences. Yet there was neither panic nor chaos, nor were there any outward signs of despair or fear. In a remarkably short period of time a deep defensive system was built, and although it was not finished by the time of the Allies' landings it did at least give the people some cause for optimism. The eight bastions extended in a semi-circle from Careenage Ravine to Alexandrovskaya Bay. Significantly, the fortifications around Sevastopol differed greatly from the traditional star-shaped type fortifications used in Europe. The irregularity of defence lines, instead of giving the Allied engineers the opportunity to apply their skill, only served to cause them great problems. It was one thing to lay siege to regularly fortified European fortresses but the Russian defenders deviated so far from the accepted principles of siege warfare that they gave the Allies tremendous problems.

Indeed, siege operations had never been one of the British Army's favourite pastimes. During the Peninsular War, they had proved to be the most disappointing aspect of what was otherwise an extremely successful campaign. Unfortunately, some of the very same engineers who had conducted Wellington's sieges were on hand again to supervise the operations around Sevastopol. Forty long years had passed since they had last experienced siege warfare on any significant scale. They were to enjoy little change in their fortunes.

One of the most important tasks facing any besieging army was to cut off and isolate the town or fortress they were besieging. It was no good laying siege to a place if the garrison was able to come and go as it pleased, and to receive supplies and reinforcements. It was absolutely vital that the town or fortress in question was completely cut off and the failure of the Allies to achieve this at Sevastopol would cost them dear. The Russians' ability to feed into Sevastopol supplies and reinforcements was all due to the 6 Corps sapper battalion which constructed a road from the Korabel'naia suburb, passed the Careenage Ravine and east towards Inkerman. This road, called Sapper Road, proved to be vital artery in the town's fight for survival. From the very beginning the construction of fortifications was carried out according to the advanced principles and ideas of the skilled Russian military engineer, A Teplyakovsky, 'the grandfather of Russian fortification'. He wrote one of the first Russian textbooks on the subject, *Field Fortification*, in 1839. In his book he emphasised the importance of combining the science of fortification with the strategy and tactics of the army, taking into account the state of the artillery and the means by which the enemy undertook their siege operations.

The construction of these new works and batteries at least gave the Russian commanders some hope that Sevastopol would at least be in some sort of condition – albeit a poor one – to defend itself. Hopefully, the Allies would delay their attack long enough for the defenders to improve and even finish the defences. It was all a matter of time. Ironically, the Allies' decision to embark upon their flank march to the east of Sevastopol rather than attack immediately probably saved the town. But there still remained the problem of securing it against a seaborne attack. There may well have been nearly 600 guns, primed and ready to blast any Allied ships that might try and enter the harbour, but that did not guarantee total security from attack. The solution to the dilemma was a pretty straightforward one, which involved sinking a number of ships at the entrance to the port. It was not an easy decision to make, but with the

Allies having defeated the Russians at the Battle of the Alma on 20 September it was a course of action that could not be avoided and was one that had to be made quickly.

But before the idea was even put forward, Admiral Kornilov assembled the fleet commanders on 21 September and informed them that he intended to put to sea and attack the Allied squadron near Cape Lukull. At the very least he wanted to die with honour, blowing up both his and Allied ships if necessary. His commanders fully understood his sentiments, but nevertheless would not agree to allow him to sacrifice himself in this manner. Instead, the commander of the ship *Selafail,* Captain Zorin, suggested sinking a number of old ships across the harbour entrance and sending the sailors to the bastions to defend Sevastopol. Once the meeting was over Kornilov went to see Prince Menshikov to try to gain support for his original plan, but he was overruled. Instead, an order was issued on 23 September 1854 whereby the commander-in-chief decided to sink five old ships across the mouth of the harbour to block it and deny the Allies access.

Reflecting on the decision to sink the ships, Kornilov said, 'It's very sad to destroy one's own work; we made great efforts to keep the ships, which are now condemned to be sacrificed in perfect order. But we have to resign ourselves to cruel necessity.' He also drew a comparison with an earlier and much more dramatic sacrifice which Russia made in order to defend itself. In 1812, 'Moscow was in flames but Russia didn't perish. Quite the contrary – it became stronger. God is gracious! And no doubt he is preparing the same destiny for the faithful Russian people.' Hopefully, the sacrificing of the Russian ships would prove as significant as the torching of Moscow had been forty-two years earlier. Eventually, seven ships were sunk between the Constantinovskay and Alexandrovskaya batteries: the frigates *Sizopol* and *Flora,* and the ships *Uriil, Three Consecrators, Selafail, Silistria* and *Varna,* the operation being carried out on 23 September. In February 1855 eight more vessels were sunk.[13] These measures, once undertaken, made Sevastopol practically unassailable from the sea, and although only time would tell whether or not the defences were capable of withstanding the coming Allied attack, they could at least take some comfort from the knowledge that the fortifications which had previously been virtually non-existent had been raised to a level sufficient to afford some degree of protection. What that protection would be, would soon be discovered. Much depended upon the speed and direction of the Allies' attack. But for now, there was little more for the people and the garrison to do, except continue to work.

But not all was harmony within the confines of Sevastopol. Indeed, 23 and 24 September saw a great deal of looting and disorder by drunken Russian soldiers, convinced of the hopelessness of the task facing them, and convinced also that Menshikov had betrayed them and was not fit to command them. Menshikov's radical solution to the problem was to remove the army from Sevastopol and decant to the interior of the Crimea, leaving the town to be defended by a garrison made up largely of sailors and marines. Thus, on the evening of 24 September Major General I P Zhabokritsky, with an advanced guard of 13,000 troops, marched out of the town, followed by Prince P D Gorchakov and 6 Corps, with Kir'iakov's 17 Infantry Division leading the way.

So, what of the defenders left behind in Sevastopol? When Prince Menshikov marched out of Sevastopol on the evening of 24 September he left a problem for his garrison commanders. In effect, there was a three-way split in command, something that initially caused problems for the Russians. According to Menshikov's orders Admiral Kornilov was to assume command of all defences on the northern side of Sevastopol, the Severnaia, whilst Admiral Nakhimov, the victor of Sinope and the senior of the two admirals, was to command all troops in the old town and in the suburb of Korabel'naia, on the eastern side of the Iuznhnia (South Bay). This divided command was bad enough, but things were further complicated by the appointment by Menshikov of Lieutenant General F F Moller as commander of the army forces in Sevastopol. Menshikov had left a situation where three commanders held different commands, the latter two effectively overlapping. Technically speaking, both Nakhimov and Moller were ordered to command the same troops. It was a situation which left Nakhimov none too pleased. He was a sailor and an admiral, and he certainly did not consider it his business – nor did he think he had the qualifications – to command Russian soldiers. His protests to Menshikov went unheeded, however, and two days later Nakhimov himself, taking the initiative, relinquished his command and placed himself under Kornilov who, despite being junior in rank to Nakhimov, was fast becoming the dynamic force behind the reorganisation of the Sevastopol defences. Moller followed suit, although Kornilov, uncertain of his ability to command infantry, wisely appointed Moller as his chief-of-staff. Both Nakhimov and Kornilov, along with Admiral Istomin, would prove to be three of the great heroes of the siege of Sevastopol, as would Totleben, the head of engineers of the Sevastopol garrison. Totleben, who was to survive the siege, proved to be a master of fortification and fieldcraft and it was largely as a result of his efforts that the Allies' attempts to storm Sevastopol would be bloodily frustrated.

Although reinforcements were received throughout the siege of Sevastopol, the garrison at the outset numbered around 18,000 men, most of whom were sailors and marines. However, there were still a number of infantry from the Brest, Belostosky, Vilen and Litov battalions of the 13th Infantry Division, as well as a battalion of riflemen and another of sappers. The bulk of the force consisted of seventeen battalions of sailors, and it is these men who are traditionally viewed as being the real defenders of Sevastopol. On the face of it, these 18,000 men hardly represented much of a threat to the Allies, but it should be remembered that in the Peninsular War, garrisons as small as 5,000 men had thwarted Wellington's army. The main difference was that unlike the strong walls of the fortresses in Spain, the defences at Sevastopol were in such an awful condition that it would take a lot more than 18,000 men to keep the Allied armies from walking into the town. Hence the apprehension felt by the garrison and the population on the approach of the Allies and the urgency of the work being carried out on the fortifications. The question now was, would the fortifications be completed to a reasonably satisfactory standard before the Allies attacked? Kornilov, his garrison and the people of Sevastopol were about to find out.

But even before the Allies could test the mettle of the garrison of Sevastopol there was drama just a mile or two outside the town. When Menshikov and his main field army left Sevastopol on 24 September it marched via the road to Batchki Serai which ran across the Mackenzie Heights to the east. The Russian army was well on its way on the 25th, but on the same day, and with the rearguard of Menshikov's army still lingering on the Mackenzie Heights, the advance guard of the British army came marching merrily down upon them. In fact, it was – amazingly – the commander-in-chief of the British army himself, Lord Raglan, along with his staff. This remarkable piece of blundering had come about as a result of Lord Lucan, his cavalry and a battery of horse artillery having lost their way. It left Raglan and his staff out in front and alone in the presence of a large number of completely unsuspecting Russian troops.

Raglan, in fact, had been off on a reconnaissance, leaving the road to Sevastopol and heading off to the west, towards two lighthouses that stood at the head of Sevastopol Bay. From there, Raglan and his staff gazed down, untroubled, at the great prize, Sevastopol, that lay invitingly before them. He was able to take a good look at the town, its defences and the harbour. He could also see the protruding masts of the Russian ships that had been sunk in order to block the mouth of the harbour. It was a great sight. Having satisfied himself Raglan set off back towards the road where he expected to meet Lord Lucan and his cavalry. However, only Maude's horse artillery were waiting there, the cavalry having lost their way. This left Raglan with just his staff and some horse artillery, alone, and way out in front of the main army coming up behind. The mistake was largely due to the dense undergrowth that characterised the area. Thick, thorny bushes made visibility and movement difficult, which was just as well, for lurking unsuspectingly ahead of Raglan was part of Menshikov's rearguard. Raglan reacted in typical fashion, quietly ordering an officer to go and find Lucan, whilst he and his escort withdrew carefully in silence. Eventually, Lucan's cavalry arrived, Lucan himself being greeted sternly by Raglan with the words, 'Lord Lucan, you are late!' Lucan himself said nothing but simply galloped on with his men, whilst Maude unlimbered his guns and opened fire. The Russians quickly made off, leaving behind them several wagons belonging to the Weimar Hussars, the contents of which were quickly distributed amongst the British troops. Several prisoners were taken also. It was a fortuitous outcome for the British, but it was very tiresome. The heat was oppressive, and the men's tempers frayed. This sort of incident was the last thing they needed. It was, in fact, a serious situation, or at least it could have been if the Russians had reacted to it in the proper manner.

> Had the Russian infantry by chance entered the wood, they would have found at their mercy the Commander-in-chief and his staff, a long train of thirty guns without supports, and the rest of the army in hopeless disorder . . . A single battalion of sharpshooters, skilled in forest fighting and with knowledge of the country, could have made havoc of them.[14]

But such are the fortunes of war. The Russians failed to appreciate the situation, and thus missed their chance to inflict a major and very embarrassing reverse on the British. However, it wasn't only the Russians who were guilty of spilling such an opportunity, for the following day it was the turn of the British.

For now, though, the Allies contented themselves in halting for the night, the British in the valley of the Chernaya and the French on the Mackenzie Heights themselves. 25 September had been a real trial for the Allies. True, there had been no Russian activity, save for the brush with the Russian rearguard close to Mackenzie's Farm, but the conditions under which the day's march was done were tiresome to say the least. The weather was extremely hot, and the lack of water brought on a rapid increase in the number of cases of cholera. It was a real trial. It had also been an ordeal for the fast-fading Saint-Arnaud who was being ravaged by cholera. Indeed, at 4 am on the morning of 26 September, Saint-Arnaud ordered his secretary, Colonel Trochu, to send for General Canrobert. An hour later Canrobert ducked into Saint-Arnaud's tent to find his commander-in-chief exhausted, weak and barely able to speak, and it was only with great effort that Saint-Arnaud said:

> You have made me acquainted, General, with the instructions of His Majesty, which confide to you the Command-in-Chief of the army, in case my health should force me to abandon it. From today, take that command. In surrendering it into your hands, General, I feel less regret at resigning it.[15]

Later that same morning, Raglan and his army were on the move again towards Balaklava, snaking their way slowly along the Chernaya river. After crossing the Tractir bridge they passed through a low series of hills known as the Fedioukine. When the army emerged from the hills they crossed a long valley running across their front, bordered to the south by the Vorontsov Road, one of the few metalled roads in the area. Few could have known that this valley would, within a month, become the scene of one of the most famous – or infamous – fights in British military history. Beyond the valley and the low heights, the Causeway Heights, along which ran the Vorontsov Road, lay the small village of Kadikoi. From here the shining waters of Balaklava could clearly be seen, but there was no indication that the place was defended. Riding into Kadikoi with his staff, Raglan was assured by the people that there were no Russians in Balaklava, upon which he continued, relieved, until at around midday he finally arrived at the water's edge.

> A bend in the road brought him to the edge of what seemed to be only a small inland pool with a rivulet trickling into it; for the rest of the sheet of water to which he had come lay hidden behind the fold of the hill. Beyond the pool, but still very close at hand, there rose a barrier of steep, lofty hills; and one of them was crowned, as it seemed, with an antique castle in ruins.[16]

A short distance on brought the harbour into full view. It looked ideal. The harbour, almost half a mile long, the width varying between 150 and 250 yards, was surrounded by high cliffs, whilst its narrow entrance from the sea must have reminded Raglan of Passages, the vital base for Wellington's army in northern Spain. Both Passages and Balaklava were real tests for captains bringing their ships into port.

While Raglan and his staff surveyed the dark waters of Balaklava a shot was fired at them from the ruined castle on the hill above, prompting Raglan to despatch some of the Light Division to climb up and flush the offending troops out. In the event, the 'defenders' of Balaklava turned out to be no more menacing a unit than a mob of local militia, numbering about sixty, mainly Greeks, under the command of a Colonel Monto. Even as the men of the Light Division were bringing off their prisoners a small British vessel sailed into the harbour, apparently taking soundings, and a few minutes afterwards came the happy sight of Sir Edmond Lyons' own ship, the *Agamemnon*, gliding majestically into the harbour.

The question now arose; who should occupy Balaklava, the British or the French? The other ports available to the Allies were Kazatch and Kamiesh, which lay about ten miles to the west of Balaklava and five to the south-west of Sevastopol. Balaklava was far too small for both the Allied armies to use. In fact, many argued it was too small for either of them.

Already Balaklava 'was thick crowded with masts . . . the landing place swarmed with busied men, and the little street overflowed with the red-coated soldiery.'[17] By rights, the French should have occupied Balaklava. After all, they had claimed the honour of holding the right of the line ever since the Allies had landed in the Crimea. Once the Allies had completed their flank march to the south of Sevastopol they should have wheeled to the right (i.e. towards the west and the coast) and thus, the British should have occupied the ports of Kazatch and Kamiesh. The French would then, naturally, have the honour of continuing to hold the right of the line during the siege operations and, consequently, the port of Balaklava. The shrewd French, however, didn't see it this way. Indeed, they were quick to realise that whoever occupied Balaklava would not only have to manhandle and transport their supplies miles uphill to the Chersonese and the Sapoune Ridge, but they would have to ensure the security of both Allied armies against the threat posed by Menshikov's army which still lurked away to the east.

This is exactly how the wily Canrobert, now in command of the French, saw it. There was much honour in holding the right of the line. But there was also a point at which it was better to relinquish this in favour of an easier life. That point was now at hand. And so, realising the advantages which both Kazatch and Kamiesh offered above Balaklava, Canrobert now turned 'with delicacy and tact' and offered Raglan the pick of the ports available to the Allies. Raglan then consulted with Admiral Lyons who strongly urged him to take Balaklava as it afforded the only real communication between the fleet and the army. Only time would tell just how wrong he was. Raglan and Canrobert met on 27 September on what was to become known as 'Canrobert's Hill' and it was during this meeting that Raglan declared himself for Balaklava as his preferred port. Thus it was that Lord Raglan 'with the best of intentions in the world, signed unwittingly the death-warrant of the British Army'.[18] The decision was undoubtedly a bad one and the responsibility lies heavily with Sir Edmond Lyons. It was also a decision that would come back to haunt the British.

In his defence, of course, it should be said that in September 1854 no one envisaged spending the coming winter on the bleak, open Chersonese. Indeed, with the main Russian field army having retreated towards Batchki Serai, leaving Sevastopol apparently defended by a motley garrison of sailors and marines, supported by a few regular infantry, the Allies had high hopes of a swift end to the campaign. Ironically, this might well have happened had Sir George Cathcart's pleas not fallen on deaf ears. Once Cathcart, commanding the 4th Division, had completed the flank march he was moved up from the Chernaya to a position on some heights to the south of Sevastopol, overlooking the town. From here he could see just how weak the defences were. Indeed, he wrote a letter to

Raglan on 28 September saying that he considered the Russian defences of Sevastopol at the north-east angle of the town to be virtually non-existent. It would, he suggested, be advisable to attack without delay. He went so far as to say that, with a few guns, he could probably take Sevastopol with his division alone, so confident of success was he.

> I am in the strongest and most perfect position I ever saw. Twenty thousand Russians could not disturb me in it with my division . . . the place is only enclosed by a thing like a low park wall, not in good repair. I am sure I could walk into it, with scarcely the loss of a man, at night, or an hour before daybreak, if all the rest of the force was up between the sea and the hill I am upon. We could leave our packs, and run into it even in open day.[19]

Sadly, he was to be denied the opportunity. Raglan was firmly of the old school and was bent on conducting a regular siege along traditional lines, the sort which he had conducted along with his old chief in the Peninsula. But back then fortresses had been protected by strong, masonry walls and elaborate defences. Sevastopol, by all accounts, was protected by little more than a rudimentary earthwork or wall linking several bastions, all of which were growing stronger by the hour. In fact, when Raglan told Cathcart that nothing would happen until the Allied siege trains had been landed the latter, obviously irritated, said in astonishment, 'Land the siege trains! But, my dear Lord Raglan, what the devil is there to knock down?'[20] The opportunity was therefore lost, and the Allies committed themselves to the long, drawn out and, as it would turn out, painful process of a regular siege. Whether or not a swift assault on Sevastopol, as urged by Cathcart, would have succeeded, is not known. Certainly, Cathcart himself later expressed doubts, adding that such an attempt would have been a gamble. *The Times* correspondent, William Russell, was another who thought Sevastopol might have been taken early on but, like Cathcart, added 'who knows?' Indeed, we will never know.

NOTES

1 Paget, Lord George, *The Light Cavalry Brigade in the Crimea* (London 1881), 24.
2 Bazancourt, the Baron de (trans. by Robert Howe Gould). *The Crimean Expedition, to the Capture of Sebastopol. Chronicles of the War in the East* (London, 1856), I, 270.
3 Ibid, I, 270–2.
4 Kinglake, Alexander William, *The Invasion of the Crimea: Its Origin, and An Account of its Progress down to the Death of Lord Raglan* (London 1863), III, 23.
5 Sweetman, John, *Raglan: From the Peninsula to the Crimea* (London 1993), 230.
6 Totleben E I *Opisanie oborony goroda Sevastopolya* (St Petersburg 1863–1872), I, 230–3.

7 *Russkiy Arhiv*, 1892, π 8, 479.
8 Tarle E V *Krymskaya voina* (Moscow 1941–1944) II, 116.
9 Seaton, Albert, *The Crimean War: a Russian Chronicle* (London 1977), 103.
10 Ibid, 103.
11 Ibid, 95.
12 The name 'Malakhov Hill' first appeared on the general map of Sevastopol in 1851 and was named after a Russian sailor, Mikhail Mikhailovitch Malakhov. He began his military services in 1789 in Kherson as a cabin-boy on one of the ships of the Black Sea fleet. He was a boatswain, a skipper, a rigging-master. By 1827 he was a captain, after which he went to Sevastopol where he commanded a company of sailors working in the town. He made his home in the Korabel'naia. Malakhov was greatly respected by the lower ranks and by the poor people for his honesty and justice. The people often went to his house, which was situated at the bottom of the hill, with their requests or simply asking for advice, and soon the hill was called the 'Malakhov Hill'. Malakhov had two sons, Afanasy and Iliya, and six daughters. His sons also became sailors and both took part in the defence of Sevastopol from 1854 to1855. Afanasy fought on the 5th bastion, and was badly wounded and died in March of 1855. Iliya fought on the 6th bastion, and was also wounded but survived the war. *Nikolaevsky Vestnik*. February 9, 1868, No.11.
13 On the 50th anniversary of this episode, a monument in the form of a Corinthian column, crowned with a bronze eagle was erected on a rock, several metres out in the harbour of Sevastopol. The sculptor was A Adamson, the architect V Feldman, and the military engineer O Enberg.
14 Fortescue, The Hon. J W. *A History of the British Army* (London 1899), XIII, 81.
15 Bazancourt, *The Crimean Expedition*, I, 290.
16 Kinglake, *Invasion of the Crimea*, III, 97–8.
17 Ibid, III, 102.
18 MacMunn, Sir George, *The Crimea in Perspective* (London 1935), 76.
19 Kinglake, *Invasion of the Crimea*, III, 238–9.
20 Ibid, III, 252n.

# CHAPTER EIGHT
## *'Monstrous Difficulties'*

Having decided upon which army should occupy which port, the Allies began to deploy their forces. Canrobert allotted two of his four divisions to undertake the siege operations themselves, the two divisions being supervised by General Forey. The left of the French siege operation rested on the Black Sea, their line extending east as far as the ground opposite Dockyard Creek. Although French siege operations would eventually extend beyond the British right their initial operation benefited enormously from the close proximity of their base at Kamiesh, barely three miles away. In addition, the ground here was much softer and easier than the area taken by the British. The other two divisions, under Bosquet, would act as a covering force, being deployed on the southern end of the Sapoune Ridge.

The British Army faced far more difficult problems. The distance from Balaklava to the area from where they would begin their own siege lines was almost six miles, twice as far as the French had to travel. It was bad enough during late September and October when supplies began to come ashore, transporting them to the siege lines, but when winter set in things took a turn for the worse. Initially, the British had the benefit of the Vorontsov Road, but when that was lost to the Russians everything, every nut, bolt, bullet and shell had to be taken via the infamous Col de Balaklava at the very southern end of the Sapoune Ridge. Security of the base was a problem also. True, the compact nature of the port itself rendered it relatively safe from Russian attack, but its isolated position, situated as it was outside the Allied lines on the Sapoune, gave it a degree of vulnerability to attack from both north and east. Defence of the base was given over to Sir Colin Campbell and the 93rd Highlanders, along with about 1,000 marines and 3,000 Turkish troops. The main British field army, meanwhile, took up its positions on the Chersonese with, from west to east, the 3rd and 4th Divisions, the Light Division, and the 2nd Division all facing Sevastopol with the Foot Guards in reserve. Once the men had begun to take up their stations it soon became clear that, not only had the shrewd French taken possession of the more accessible ports, but they were also turning over softer earth, the ground taken by the British troops being extremely hard, rocky and very difficult to excavate. As Burgoyne was forced to admit, 'these are monstrous difficulties before us'.[1]

The French Army had by now begun to establish itself at Kazatch and Kamiesh but their former commander-in-chief was not among them. Saint-Arnaud was so weak he had been placed in a carriage, and soon after the British had begun to take up residence at Balaklava the old man arrived there. He was taken to a house by the sea where, remarkably, his illness appeared to subside. But it was a false hope. By the night of 28 September it was obvious to everyone that he had very few hours to live. Even so, Saint-Arnaud mustered enough strength to order the ship *Berthollet* to Balaklava, adding that he wished to embark as soon as it arrived. At 8 am on 29 September Lord Raglan, accompanied by Admiral Lyons visited Saint-Arnaud at his house in Balaklava. Saint-Arnaud shook their hands and thanked them for their visit. Then, in a voice no more than a whisper, the ever-optimistic Frenchman said, 'I am better, my Lord; the sea air and the care of my wife will soon re-establish my health. My good wishes will ever follow you.'[2] And with that, the two Englishmen left, apparently with tears running down their cheeks. Soon afterwards, sailors from the *Berthollet* came to carry Saint-Arnaud to their ship. They were escorted by a company of Zouaves and, with Saint-Arnaud covered by a tricolour to shield him from the sun's rays, he was put on board a waiting boat and ferried out to the waiting *Berthollet*, whilst every soldier watching on the harbour bared and lowered his head as a mark of respect. At 4 pm that same afternoon it was all over. Surrounded by General Yusuf, Monsieurs de Puységur and de Grammont, the Commandant de Place, his aide-de-camp, the Commandant Henry, and his doctor, Cabrol, Saint-Arnaud 'seemed to fall asleep in death'.[3]

Meanwhile, the business of landing the siege trains began. The French laboured under few of the disadvantages that so dogged their allies' operations and things went off relatively smoothly. Lieutenant Colonel Raoult, on the staff of the French 2nd Division, was put in command of the battalions covering the French siege operations and assisting in the digging and construction of their works. Whilst a thorough reconnaissance of the defences in front of Sevastopol was carried out by Canrobert's engineers, others traced out works, gabions and bundles of fascines were brought up by the men, and entrenching tools gathered in the engineers' park. Forty guns were landed also, along with thirty naval guns and 1,000 sailors who were to man them and assist in the works. These were commanded by Captain Rigaud de Genouilly, of the *Ville de Paris*.

The British also began to land their siege train, and a difficult business it was, particularly as they had to transport everything the best part of six miles up to the Chersonese. Indeed, it didn't take too long for the British to realise the folly of their decision to make Balaklava their base. There

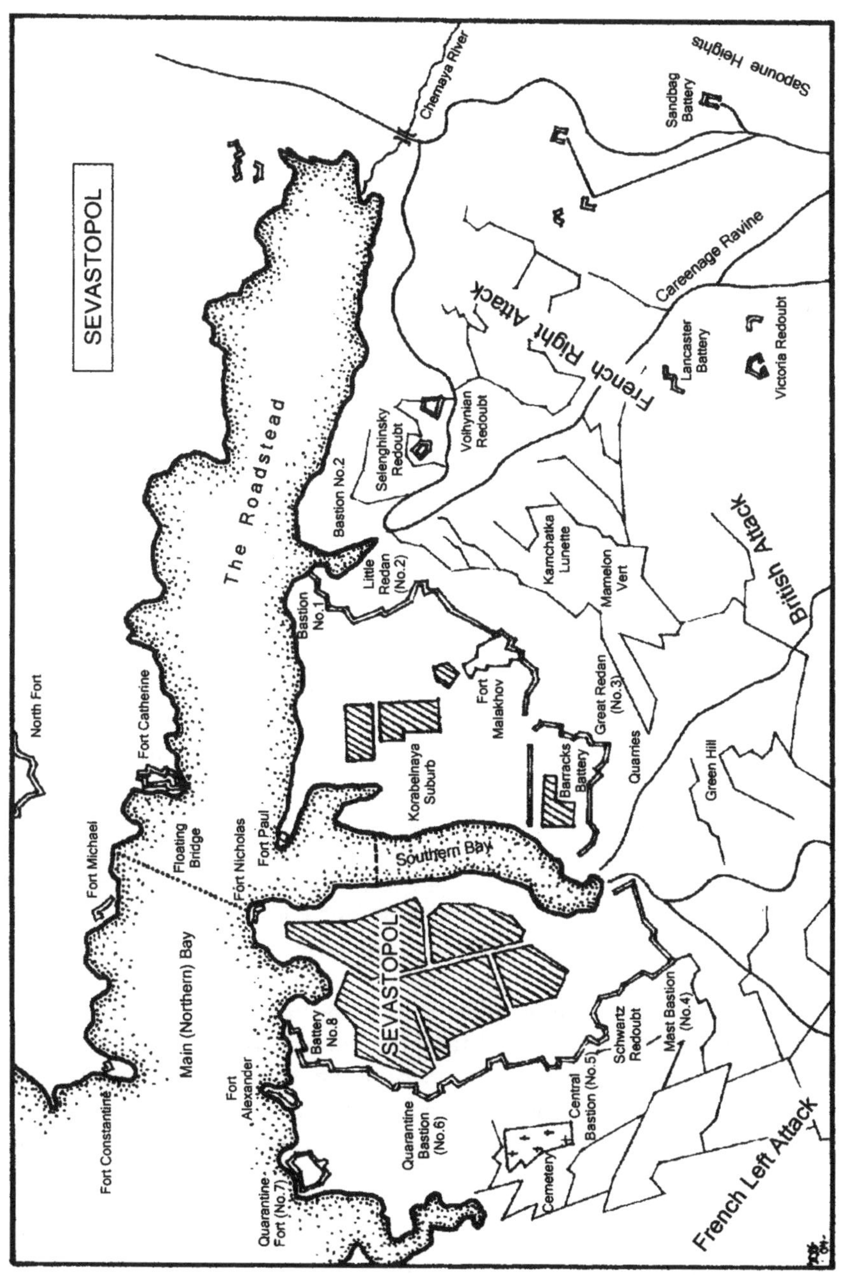
SEVASTOPOL
The Roadstead
Main (Northern) Bay
North Fort
Fort Catherine
Fort Michael
Floating Bridge
Fort Constantine
Fort Alexander
Quarantine Fort (No.7)
Fort Nicholas
Fort Paul
Southern Bay
SEVASTOPOL
Battery No.8
Quarantine Bastion (No.6)
Central Bastion (No.5)
Schwartz Redoubt
Mast Bastion (No.4)
Cemetery
French Left Attack
Korabelnaya Suburb
Barracks Battery
Fort Malakhov
Great Redan (No.3)
Quarries
Green Hill
British Attack
Mamelon Vert
Kamchatka Lunette
Little Redan (No.2)
Bastion No.1
Bastion No.2
Selenghinsky Redoubt
Volhynian Redoubt
French Right Attack
Lancaster Battery
Victoria Redoubt
Careenage Ravine
Chernaya River
Sandbag Battery
Sapoune Heights

was also the problem of manpower. The business of siege warfare not only involves having trained sappers and miners, tools to do the job, and means of transport, but it also requires the services of a large number of other men. Not only was it necessary for a besieging army to have men available in order to undertake the construction of the works and to ensure their security, but it required a similarly large force to protect the entire operation and to prevent any enemy force from interfering with the operations. Raglan himself knew only too well the dangers of undertaking a siege without sufficient numbers. At Badajoz, in May and June 1811, Wellington's siege operations had ended in failure as a result of insufficient numbers. When French relieving troops arrived in the vicinity of Badajoz Wellington – who did not have enough troops to form a covering force – had to abandon the siege and make off to the north.[4] However, when he returned in March 1812 he made sure that he had enough troops to undertake the siege operation itself and to provide a covering force. In the event, the operation was a success. Indeed, Raglan himself – then Fitzroy Somerset – personally took the surrender of the French commander the day after the town's capture. Nevertheless, when Raglan approached Sevastopol to begin his own siege operation he did so without the strength to provide sufficient cover for the troops working in the trenches, nor could he prevent the Russians from feeding in men and supplies as and when they wanted.

One of the main principles of siege warfare was the need to completely seal off a besieged fortress. After all, there was little point in undertaking a siege operation – where one option open to the besiegers was always that of starving out the garrison – if the besieged were able to receive supplies on a regular basis. But if the besiegers lacked sufficient manpower to achieve this, the siege was flawed from the start. Indeed, as early as 3 October, Raglan was writing to the Duke of Newcastle about the woefully inadequate number of men at his disposal.

> I enclose a statement of the effectives of the infantry, by which you will see that the rank and file little exceed 16,000; and when these have furnished the guards and working parties for the trenches, there remain in camp available for the support of those in advance in case of a sortie, and for the maintenance of our position, which is assailable on our extreme right, and right rear, something under 8,000 men.[5]

A little over two weeks later, the French could boast 46,000 men. The problem was also noted by Sir John Burgoyne, now the senior engineer, following the death from cholera of the head Royal Engineer, Colonel Tylden, on 22 September. Writing to Colonel Matson, RE, in England, Burgoyne noted, 'Our forces (British) are immensely reduced by cholera, &. Our infantry [are] not more now than 16,000 or 17,000, and no reinforcements to look to.'[6] Indeed, he was forced to admit the following day that, 'the difficulties we have to face here are far greater than I could have anticipated'.[7]

Burgoyne, it will be remembered, had been a strong advocate of the flank march, and whilst he had not been the one to favour Balaklava as a base for the British army he was soon beginning to rue the decision.

> On our British side of this attack on Sebastopol [sic], we are beset with very great difficulties, and shall hardly be able with every effort to make much progress; the French, however, seem more confident on theirs, and if a good opening can be made there, we will join them in the assault, and back their progress previously; moreover, we have half the front of the fortress to attack, and under the most disadvantages, while we have not one-half of their force! We have a little mountain to get our guns and siege equipment up, while they are on a plain.[8]

But it was too late to do anything about it now. Only a massive injection of manpower could alleviate the British problems in the short term. To contemplate a major siege operation with just 16,000 men was simply ridiculous. Not even Wellington, during his most anxious days in the Peninsula, ever fought a battle with fewer men, save for his very first battle, Roliça, and even that was considered to be little more than a skirmish. Raglan, on the other hand, was expected to conduct one half of a major siege operation.

Despite the difficulties the Allies soon agreed a plan for the siege and bombardment of Sevastopol. The defences of Sevastopol have already been described, but if we consider them to resemble a triangle, with the Roadstead or harbour of Balaklava along the top edge, and the Flagstaff Bastion at the bottom angle of the triangle, we begin to get a rough idea of the shape and extent of the defences. From the mouth of the harbour, the western side of the Russian defences, or of the triangle, ran down from the Sea Quarantine Fort, through the Land Quarantine Bastion, on to the Central Bastion and, finally, to the Flagstaff Bastion. This, the western side of Sevastopol, was the sector to be assaulted by the French. From the Flagstaff Bastion the defences ran north-east, through the Redan, up to the Malakhov Hill and on to the Little Redan. This eastern side was to be the British area of attack.

With the plan having been decided upon, Raglan moved his headquarters up on to the Chersonese plateau, to a large abandoned farmhouse at Khutor, not far from the Col, and about two miles from Sevastopol. The move was carried out on 5 October, Raglan's staff moving along with him, and before long the house was a hive of activity, as it would remain over the coming twelve months as riders came and went in succession, bringing and taking delivery of despatches and orders. Despite its initial dilapidated condition Raglan could at least brag about being one of the few officers in the British army not under canvas, not that the commander-in-chief shouldn't have a house anyway. The house proved a happy home for Raglan. It also proved to be the house in which he would die.

On 9 October the Allies finally began to dig their trenches or, to give it its technical term, they broke ground. The construction of the trenches, or parallels, was not as simple as it seemed. Indeed, it was not just a question of digging a long hole in the ground, for the lives of the besiegers depended upon there being enough earth to protect them from incoming fire. The usual process was for a line of men to do the actual digging whilst a second line, standing above them, piled up the spoil and formed it into a kind of rampart. It was the same method that had been adopted for centuries. The trick was to make sure the earth was pounded into a solid bank, capable of withstanding enemy cannon shot. Wet weather proved a nightmare, as Raglan himself knew all too well. As a young man in the Peninsula, he had seen the ramparts of the British trenches at Badajoz reduced to streams of liquid mud, rendering them all but useless. The problem at Sevastopol was rather different. The French, occupying decent ground, where the depth of the earth was substantial, found no problem at all in constructing good, effective trenches. The British, however, occupied hard, rocky ground which proved extremely difficult to excavate, forcing them to make extensive use of gabions – baskets fall of earth and stones – as makeshift ramparts. In fact, a line of gabions was thrown out first of all, each man having carried one to the designated area. These were the only defences for the men who would otherwise be totally exposed to the fire of the defenders. Once the first trench had been completed the besiegers would then sap forward before constructing a second trench. By this method they would gradually be able to approach the walls of the besieged town, constructing batteries as they went. It was then the job of the artillery to begin breaching the walls. It all seems very simple, but it was actually a very precise science, which would either save or cost lives, depending upon how effective the besiegers were.

It was important that the first trenches be constructed out of range of the guns of the defenders. This wasn't a problem during the Napoleonic Wars but the advent of long-range and more accurate guns ensured it was now a difficult and dangerous task. Hence, the French started to dig their trenches under cover of darkness, beginning their works along the top of Mount Rudolph, about 1,000 yards from the Central Bastion and 1,300 yards from the Flagstaff Bastion. 800 French troops were detailed to begin the first shift, being replaced three hours later by another detachment of 800. The work of digging trenches represented the unglamorous, inglorious side of soldiering, but it was no less important. Indeed, it was a very significant, and even emotional, moment for the French as the first pick-axe struck the earth amidst the howling of a fierce north-westerly wind.[9] The signal given, 800 pick-axes struck at the 'rocky and rebellious ground'. The siege of Sevastopol had begun.

The good people of Sevastopol had retired to their beds on the night of 9 October in a state of some apprehension. They had good reason, given the fact that Menshikov's army had left the town days before, leaving them in the hands of Admiral Kornilov and his motley garrison of sailors, marines and a few battalions of infantry. Outside the walls of Sevastopol a large Allied army waited, poised, so they believed, for an assault on their beloved town, an assault that few believed could be repulsed. And everybody knew what a successful assault would mean for the town's inhabitants. It usually left them at the mercy of an army, loosed from discipline and hell bent on destruction and debauchery. It had always been the way. It may easily be imagined, therefore, with what relief the inhabitants of the unfortunate town woke on the morning of 10 October to see, up on the top of Mount Rudolph, a long bank of earth, thrown up for a length of over a thousands yards. It could mean only one thing; there was to be no assault. The Allies were digging in for a siege.

Inside Sevastopol, Totleben looked out from behind the flimsy defences and could hardly believe his good fortune. An engineer himself, Totleben knew exactly what the siege meant. It meant long days and nights, even weeks – almost a year as it would turn out – of toiling in harsh conditions, probably with insufficient tools, under fire and in the open at the mercy of the elements. He wrote:

> If only men chance to know what siege warfare is, they can imagine the joyful impression which we must have experienced at the sight of those works . . . Every man in Sevastopol rejoiced at this happy event. People congratulated each other upon it; for each man saw in it a guarantee of success, and the hope that the town might be saved.[10]

It says much for the optimism of the people and the garrison of Sevastopol that they were happy to see the Allies open up siege lines even though thousands of them would die as a result of Allied artillery fire and through sickness.

When Totleben wrote of the difficulties accompanying siege warfare he was only stating fact. For, up on the heights facing the Redan and the Malakhov – the two great bastions that would be the centre of the battle for Sevastopol – the British scratched their heads in frustration. Away to the west they could see that the French had already completed the first thousand yards of the siege works, whereas they themselves had yet to achieve anything more than a mere scrapping away of the topsoil. Nevertheless, they tried again and on the night of 10 October managed to open trenches on Green Hill and on Victoria Ridge. A relieved Burgoyne wrote on 13 October:

> Chapman opened 1200 yards of trench, and by great exertion sufficient cover was obtained for occupying it in the morning; and Gordon opened about 500 yards on the succeeding night. The soil is tremendous, and we have not enough gabions to do more than line the spots meant for batteries.[11]

The trenches that opened on Green Hill were to accommodate a forty-one gun battery, known as Chapman's battery, whilst to the east, or right, across the Vorontsov Ravine, a second battery, consisting of thirty-six guns, known as Gordon's battery, was begun. But it was not easy. The problems were made worse by the ravines that ran through the British siege lines. Whereas under normal conditions the besiegers would have been able to cut communication trenches laterally behind their front line trenches, these ravines meant it was impossible to

> run across the chords, as is usual in cases of emergency, on account of the long deep precipitous ravines that cut through all the ground in front of the British part, being one-half of the whole; thus they [the Russians] can bring the great bulk of the garrison against any one part, and have, perhaps, two hours work at it, before it can be effectively supported.[12]

It was all rather unsatisfactory for the British. The French had secured the better two ports and had landed themselves the easier ground to construct their trenches and batteries. They also had ample troops to man and protect them. Their British allies, on the other hand, had the ordeal of the long, tortuous and exhausting trek from Balaklava to the Chersonese, and they had extremely hard ground ahead of them and insufficient men to construct the works and ensure their security, notwithstanding the fact that they also had the responsibility of protecting the open flank of the siege operation against the threat of Russian attack from the east. The situation was best summed up by Fortescue, in his masterly work on the British Army. 'The truth is,' he wrote, 'that those who enter upon a campaign of this kind must be eternally drawing and renewing bills upon fortune; and fortune is an usurious goddess.'[13]

Conditions in both French and British trenches were not helped when, on 10 October, the Russians turned every available gun on them, materially damaging the works and making it impossible for anyone to remain there any length of time. In fact, Admiral Kornilov was doing what any good garrison commander would have done, and for a naval man he was doing a very good job, as would the other admirals who would follow him. A garrison commander can do two things; he can sit and wait for relief to come or he can save himself by conducting an aggressive defence. Any time that can be bought by a garrison commander or saved by an attacking commander can often be the difference between success and failure. Every day that can be bought by a garrison can often lead to their being saved by a relieving force, and this time is usually bought by being aggressive, by conducting sorties and by doing everything that can be done to retard the operations of a besieging force. A garrison commander who does nothing but sit and hope for salvation does nothing to help himself. There are good examples from the Peninsular War. Dubreton at Burgos and Phillipon at Badajoz were superb examples of aggressive defenders. The former saved himself and his garrison and caused Wellington untold problems. Phillipon only just failed, though not through want of trying, but he did manage to inflict terrible casualties on Wellington's army before he succumbed. But perhaps the best example is Charles Gordon, later of Khartoum fame. Gordon, present in the Crimea, did everything he could to save himself from the clutches of the Mahdi's fanatics in the Sudan. He failed, of course, but only just, the relieving force turning up just two painful but fatal days later. It was all about buying time, and Kornilov was determined to do everything he could to upset the Allies' efforts.

The Russian guns continued night and day, wrecking the French works and causing casualties amongst the troops crowded together in the trenches.

> Balls whistle in the air, or bound along the ground; shells traverse the sky with their fiery trails. Like those meteors which fitfully illumine the obscurity of the night, they bury themselves in the soil, tearing it up, and bursting with a terrible noise, striking down, senseless, the soldier who watches or who works. But nothing stops, nothing disturbs these courageous men, already inured to these new and unknown dangers.[14]

In an attempt to keep down the fire of the Russians the French had organised a company of sharpshooters, consisting of a captain, a lieutenant, two sub-lieutenants, four sergeants, eight corporals and 150 men, selected from the best marksmen in the battalions of Zouaves and chasseurs. The company sent out seventy-five men each day positioned in front of the French siege works at around 900 yards in front of the Flagstaff Bastion. Operating each day from rifle pits in groups of five or six, from 4 am to 6 pm, these marksmen were to keep watch for any Russian sortie and to keep up a harassing fire on the gunners in the embrasures. A second company was added later.

By 13 October the first five French batteries had been completed and work begun on the sixth. The British works also progressed, and despite his 'monstrous forces and difficulties' Burgoyne was able to report that batteries for fifty or sixty pieces were under construction, adding that three small batteries had been completed and armed with two Lancaster guns and four 68-pounder naval guns. The fire from the Russian guns in Sevastopol continued during the next few days, but despite its intensity – no fewer than 845 shells were fired in the first hour of 14 October – the Allied works continued. At last, on 16 October, the guns in the batteries – fifty-three French and seventy-three British – were unmasked, ready to be fired.

In addition to the land bombardment the Allied plan also involved a naval bombardment to be directed by the fleets against the forts protecting the harbour mouth and on the ships in the harbour itself. Admiral Hamelin, the French naval commander, had every faith in the attack, although his British counterpart, Admiral Dundas, had grave doubts. Dundas, a lukewarm supporter of the war in any case, proved a difficult man to get on with. Indeed, the relationship between himself and Raglan was so frosty that the latter was forced to resort to using Sir Edmund Lyons as a sort of go-between. Nevertheless, the plan was adopted and it was agreed that the Allied navies should time their attack to co-ordinate with the land bombardment. One feels as though the army was trying desperately to involve the navy in the operation. Many thought there was every chance that a successful bombardment would lead to a swift assault, the success of which they never doubted for a moment. Should not the navy have their share of the glory?

So, all was set. The bombardment was scheduled for 6.30 am on 17 October, the signal being the firing of three guns from the No.3 battery in the French lines. Final inspections were carried out, with General Thiry and Colonel Leboeuf checking the batteries and General Bizot and Colonel Tripier touring the trenches and examining the works for any damage caused during the day that had yet to be repaired. And when the moon rose above the Chersonese plateau on 16 October the Allies settled down for the night, looking forward to the morrow and the long-awaited opening of the attack on Sevastopol.

The Russian defenders of Sevastopol were on the alert way before dawn on 17 October, and when the first grey streaks of light dawned overhead they peered through the mist and saw with some alarm that scores of embrasures had been cut in the Allies' earthworks, revealing the protruding barrels of heavy guns. Their reaction was immediate. Without waiting for the Allies to open the firing the Russians took to their guns, loaded them and, before long, the first of their guns opened fire, followed soon afterwards by others in succession, opening up a desultory fire on the Allies' batteries. Despite claims that the Allied bombardment opened as planned at 6.30, there is every indication that the Russian fire prompted an earlier start, certainly from the French. Nevertheless, the signal guns were duly fired at 6.30 am – how the rest of the waiting Allied gunners could tell the difference between the signal guns and those already firing is not clear – whereupon a mighty roar burst forth from the hills to the south of Sevastopol as a semi-circle of fire opened up on its defences.

By the time dawn had given way to morning Sevastopol was shrouded in clouds of dirty, white smoke, from which bursts of stabbing flame erupted as the guns fired away. For the majority of the Allied soldiers and sailors manning the guns the experience was a new one. But for men such as Raglan and Burgoyne the sight of heavy guns pounding away at enemy defences was a familiar one, that brought back distant memories of bloody sieges in the Peninsula. How they must have hoped the siege of Sevastopol would be a quick and less bloody affair than those they had witnessed all those years ago. But although they had been accustomed to such bombardments there was something different about this one. In Spain the Royal Artillery had directed their fire against the walls of French-held fortresses in order to breach them. True, there was much misdirected fire which damaged houses in the rear of the target areas. But, on the whole, it was an accurate fire. It had to be in order to create the breaches. After all, the attackers' lives depended on it. But here, at Sevastopol, the fire seemed almost indiscriminate. Not only did the Allied guns fire upon the bastions but they shelled the town itself. Indeed, when the Allies finally entered the town a year later they found the town in a terrible, ruined condition. The effects of the bombardment and consequential loss of life amongst the civilian population can well be imagined.

But whereas the Allied guns continued to pour shot and shell against Sevastopol from the land to the south, there was no sign or sound of activity from the Allied fleets. In fact, the French had altered the plan at the last minute. Instead of bringing in their ships to open fire on the forts Admiral Hamelin decided to anchor them out at sea from where they would fire upon the forts at extreme range. This was the second time he had changed the plan without any consultation with his British allies; for at 10.30 pm on 16 October he had informed Admiral Dundas that his ships would not be able to open fire at 6.30 the following morning in concert with the land-based batteries on account of the fact that he did not have enough ammunition. With the limited quantity of shot available to him Hamelin said his ships would be able to fire only for a short time, after which they would have to retire. Conscious of not wanting to appear to have been beaten off Hamelin thought it better to delay the opening of his bombardment in order to try to co-ordinate his bombardment at least with the latter phases of the land operation.

Meanwhile, the artillery duel continued. The batteries on the French left were really suffering. No.5 battery, in particular, came in for some severe punishment, with guns disabled and men horribly mutilated by Russian artillery fire that ploughed into it. Then at around 8.40 am, a shell burst inside No.4 battery, the extreme right-hand end of the French line. A powder magazine exploded, sending about thirty blackened bodies flying into the air, and killing and wounding scores of others. A huge cheer rose from the Russian batteries as they watched the dust settle over the smouldering wreckage of the battery. The Flagstaff Bastion, in particular, suffered as a result of being at the salient angle of the town's defences.

After about two hours' firing the guns slackened off somewhat, for although the French were taking a pounding on their left the Russians too were feeling the full force of the weight of iron being sent crashing into their defences. Once the shelling had started Admiral Kornilov, along with Totleben and Prince V I Bariatinsky, rode off to the Flagstaff Bastion. It was a desperate scene that greeted them, as Bariatinsky later recalled.

> Inside No.4 Bastion the scene was frightful for the destruction was enormous, whole gun teams having been struck down by shellfire; the wounded and dead were removed by stretcher-bearers, but they were still lying around in heaps. In particular the naval infantry battalion under Alexander Petrovich Spitsyn, had been formed up in close order inside the bastion awaiting the enemy assault, but, as there had been no time to build the protecting traverses, the men were exposed to the enemy fire and had suffered great loss; yet still they stood stoutly waiting, motionless and silent.[15]

Displaying no outward signs of panic or fear Kornilov, conscious of the need to show a brave face, went amongst his men, moving from gun to gun, talking to the gunners and encouraging them. There was always the danger that an assault by the Allies might be imminent, and the men knew it, but Kornilov was undaunted by the prospect. 'Calm and stern was the expression of his face,' wrote Admiral Likhatcheff, an officer on his staff, 'yet a slight smile played on his lips. His eyes – those wonderful, intelligent, and piercing eyes – shone brighter than was their wont. His cheeks were flushed. He carried his head loftily. His thin and slightly bent form had become erect. He seemed to grow in size.'[16] After leaving the Flagstaff Bastion Kornilov rode over to the Central Bastion, passing through a storm of fire that swept the ravine separating them. Here he found Admiral Nakhimov, his cheek already bleeding from a wound he had sustained earlier. Nakhimov well knew the dangers of appearing in full view of the French wearing his medals and orders. Indeed, they were bound to draw the unwanted attention of French guns and sharpshooters. But he refused to remove them. Bariatinsky noticed that the white ribbon of one such order, the Cross of St George, awarded to Nakhimov for his victory at Sinope, had already been stained red. In fact, at one point Bariatinsky was forced to push both admirals to one side having spotted an incoming shell which crashed into the bastion a few yards from them, showering them both with stones. When the dust had cleared, Bariatinsky looked up and saw Admiral Likhatcheff coming towards him, his face a mass of bloody flesh. The admiral had been extremely lucky, however, for the crimson mess smeared round his face and body was, in fact, the remains of a sailor who had been blown to atoms by the shell. A somewhat dazed Likhatcheff then asked for a cigarette which he lit from the burning portfire of a gun and calmly began to smoke, leaning against the rampart of the bastion.

At around 10.30 am there was another explosion in the French lines as an ammunition wagon blew up in battery No.1. Coupled with the continued heavy fire from the Russian batteries, the explosion only served to 'increase the discouragement in the French batteries,' and shortly afterwards Canrobert ordered his batteries to cease firing. 'The place [Sevastopol] has borne our fire better than expected,' he was forced to admit, adding, 'The English batteries are in the best possible condition.'[17] This was just as well, for with the French batteries having now ceased for the day, the full responsibility for the bombardment fell upon them.

The firing continued during the afternoon and intensified at around 1 pm when the ships of the French fleet sailed into view. They immediately opened fire on Fort Constantine, Fort Alexander and the Quarantine Fort, finding their targets very quickly and sparking off a brisk response from the Russian guns inside. Fort Constantine, on the north bank, mounted ninety-seven guns, Fort Alexander, on the south bank, fifty-six guns, whilst the Quarantine Fort mounted fifty-eight. Soon afterwards, British ships joined them, the *Agamemnon* leading the way, anchoring at the mouth of the harbour and opening up at a range of 800 yards. Within an hour virtually the entire Allied fleet was in action against the forts, bringing some 1,100 guns to bear on them. It was a tremendous sight. But the Russian guns in the forts made a good reply, and certainly the *Ville de Paris*, *Arethusa*, *Albion* and *London*, in particular, sustained heavy damage. By the end of the afternoon virtually every Russian gun that had not been protected by casemates had been knocked out, although it had taken much effort on the part of the Allies to achieve this. Indeed, the 1,100 guns of the Allied fleet had taken on three forts armed with just over 200 guns, and had disabled the unprotected guns at a cost of 520 killed and wounded, the Russians losing just 138 men. This was over and above the damage to the Allied ships themselves.

But elsewhere the firing from the British guns continued into the afternoon, and there were further explosions in the Redan and in Sevastopol itself. The Malakhov, too, was very badly damaged. Meanwhile, Kornilov had resumed his tour of the defences. On his way to visit the heavily shelled Malakhov he received a message from Admiral Istomin, who said it would not be advisable for him to visit the bastion on account of the heavy fire being put down upon it. The British guns had found their range and their targets by now and were laying down a very destructive fire on the Flagstaff, Redan and Malakhov Bastions. Kornilov was not to be discouraged, however, and was cheered by his men as he made his way to the ruined Malakhov bastion, accompanied by his aide-de-camp, Lieutenant Zhandr, and a single Cossack horseman. Kornilov found Istomin busy organising the Russian guns still returning the British fire. The two men had a brief discussion about the day's events before Kornilov turned to visit the wounded who had been laid inside the tower inside the bastion. The tower, which would soon become a battlefield magnet for the British and French gunners, was already an extremely dangerous place and it was only the pleadings of Istomin himself that prevented Kornilov from climbing to the top of the tower for a better view of the area. Then, having done all he could in the Malakhov, he turned to leave, moving along a breastwork that shielded his horse from enemy fire. Kornilov had barely walked a few yards when suddenly he was sent sprawling to the ground by a round shot that struck him at the top of his leg, inflicting a terrible wound upon him.

When Zhandr recovered from the shock of seeing his chief lying unconscious he dashed to him, followed by a crowd of sailors and Istomin himself. He was immediately carried to an ambulance and taken to the naval hospital where he recovered consciousness. He was in terrible pain. His leg had been smashed and he had a bad wound in the lower body. Later on Istomin came to the hospital to see his friend, expressing hope that he would recover soon. Kornilov was no fool, however, and knew the wound was mortal. Indeed, he told the doctors not to waste any time with him and told Istomin to return to the Malakhov. Towards the end of the afternoon he was given some anodyne which sent him into a sleep for a while, but he later woke. The story goes that an officer came to visit him with the news that the British guns had virtually been silenced. Sadly, it wasn't true, but it was, apparently enough to make Kornilov raise his head and cry out, 'Hurrah! Hurrah!' after which he lost consciousness again. He died soon afterwards. Admiral Kornilov, mourned by the entire garrison, was wrapped in a St Andrew's flag and buried on a hill next to his old chief, Admiral Lazarev. He followed Saint-Arnaud as the second major figure of the war to die in the campaign. He would not be the last.

The barking of the guns before and inside Sevastopol marked the beginning of a siege that was to last almost a year. And yet it all could have ended much sooner. The Allies had already spurned the chance to attack Sevastopol after their march from the Alma. Many thought they passed up a similar chance on 17 October. By 3 pm the Redan was crushed into a ruin, whilst even the Malakhov was silenced and the Russians unable to return fire. Casualties were also severe. Indeed, those Russian infantry battalions that had remained in Sevastopol had, through necessity, to remain close to the bastions to prepare for any possible assault. Drawn up in dense ranks they suffered at the hands of Allied artillery, and so it was found necessary for them be withdrawn and ordered to the rear. The effect on the defenders, of course, was to cause a great deal of nervousness and anxiety. The explosion of a magazine in the Redan led to much cheering in the British lines, cheers that could be heard inside the Redan itself. To the Russians this could mean only one thing; the assault was about to begin.

The defences were down and the guns silenced. Indeed, so bad was the situation that even the normally optimistic Totleben decided to don his orders and medals in order that his dead body be recognised after the Allied assault, which everybody knew must now come. He wrote:

> Thenceforth, there disappeared all possibility of replying to the English artillery. The defence in that part of the lines was completely paralysed; and in the Korabel'naia men expected to see the enemy avail himself of the advantage he had gained, and at once advance to the assault.[18]

And so the Russians waited. But nothing happened. There was no assault. Instead, the Russians took the opportunity to reorganise and move troops to the Redan. And even when another magazine blew up in the Malakhov the assault still failed to materialise. Instead, the British and Russians resumed their artillery duel, which lasted until shortly after dark when silence descended once more on Sevastopol.

The day ended with some 1,100 casualties on the Russian side, whilst the French lost ninety-six killed and wounded, and the British 144. In addition, the Russians had fired over 20,000 rounds, the French expending some 4,000 rounds and the British 4,700. But the question remained; should the Allies have made an assault upon Sevastopol? Certainly the Russians thought so. Indeed, after the peace treaty of 1856 Totleben told Canrobert that of the various mistakes made by the Allies during the war, the decision not to assault Sevastopol on the late afternoon of 17 October 'was undoubtedly the greatest'.[19] With the Redan a ruin, the Malakhov silenced and wrecked, and with the defences of Sevastopol ripped open the situation called for storming columns of the calibre that a young Raglan had seen thrown into the fiery breaches of Badajoz forty-two years before. The problem was that Raglan was now an old man, and a cautious one, and he well remembered what had happened to those storming columns. The defences of Sevastopol were undeniably weaker than those he had seen in his youth, but dare he risk such casualties and a possible setback, with all the dreadful consequences? Airey later claimed that

Raglan did indeed want to storm Sevastopol on 17 October, but without the support of the French – Canrobert apparently refused to move – he dare not risk it.[20] Nakhimov's reaction perhaps summed it up best. 'Raglan and Canrobert were,' he said, 'donkeys.'[21]

The guns that had fallen silent on the night of 17 October were back in action shortly after daylight the next morning. Once again the Redan and Malakhov were pummelled and pounded and Russian casualties high. Indeed, during the next three days they totalled more than 2,000. The bombardment continued but still no assault came, and day by day the defenders were able to adjust to life under siege and under fire. Allied siege works were improved and progressed, moving closer towards Sevastopol. There were the inevitable sorties and clashes between piquets and patrols, but the immediate threat to Sevastopol seemed to have passed.

With the first week of the siege of Sevastopol over, and with little indication that the Allies intended to launch an assault on the town, the Russians, growing in confidence, decided to take the offensive themselves. It did not take a military genius to see that the open flank of the Allies offered the greatest prospect of success, and the opportunity to inflict real damage on their operations. With this in mind the Russians looked beyond Sevastopol and turned their attention towards Raglan, the British and their base camp, Balaklava.

NOTES

1 Wrottesley, The Hon. George (ed), *Life and Correspondence of Field Marshal Sir John Burgoyne* (London 1873), II, 99.
2 Bazancourt, the Baron de (trans. by Robert Howe Gould). *The Crimean Expedition, to the Capture of Sebastopol. Chronicles of the War in the East* (London 1856), I, 306.
3 Ibid, I, 309.
4 The Battle of Albuera, fought on 16 May 1811, and one of the bloodiest battles of the Peninsular War, was fought when Beresford, at the time superintending the siege operation at Badajoz, had to lift the siege and march south to meet the oncoming relieving French force under Marshal Soult.
5 Kinglake, Alexander William, The *Invasion of the Crimea*: *Its Origin, and An Account of its Progress down to the Death of Lord Raglan* (London 1863), III, 504.
6 Wrottesley, *Burgoyne* (London 1873), II, 99.
7 Ibid, II, 99.
8 Ibid, II, 100.
9 Bazancourt, the French historian, said it was a north-westerly wind, whereas Kinglake claimed it was a north-easterly. We do not intend labouring the point. Suffice to say it was a fierce wind blowing in a northerly direction!
10 Kinglake, *Invasion of the Crimea*, III, 340.
11 Wrottesley, *Burgoyne*, II, 104.
12 Ibid, II, 101–2.
13 Fortescue, The Hon. J W *A History of the British Army* (London 1899), XIII, 88.

14 Bazancourt, *The Crimean Expedition*, I, 350.
15 Seaton, Albert, *The Crimean War: a Russian Chronicle* (London 1977), 126.
16 Kinglake, *Invasion of the Crimea*, III, 363.
17 Bazancourt, *The Crimean Expedition*, I, 363.
18 Kinglake, *Invasion of the Crimea*, III, 475.
19 Seaton, *The Crimean War*, 133.
20 Sweetman, John, *Raglan: From the Peninsula to the Crimea* (London 1993), 242.
21 Ibid. 133.

# CHAPTER NINE
## *'Valiant Lunatics'*

Even as the Allied siege guns began to pound away at Sevastopol Russian reserves were being rushed to the Crimea. This was not an easy thing to do given the lack of rail transport available to them. Nevertheless, it had to be done and if it called for exhausting forced marches then so be it. At the forefront of these Russian reinforcements was 12 Infantry Division, part of the Russian 4th Corps, under the command of General Pavel Petrovitch Liprandi. This division, consisting of the Azovsky, Dnieper, Ukraine and Odessa regiments, along with four batteries of artillery, had been marching hard to the Crimea all the way from Bessarabia, just as the great Marshal Suvorov had done the previous century. By the time he arrived Menshikov had reinforced the garrison of Sevastopol and had decided to use the Liprandi's division to attack the Allies' rear from Chorgun, the object of the attack being the British base at Balaklava.

The vulnerability of Balaklava was well known, not only to the Allies but to the Russians also. There was simply far too much being asked of the British Army. From undertaking the siege operations up on the Chersonese to ensuring the security of the Allies' eastern flank, was a tall order given the already dwindling numbers available to Raglan. The problem was noted by Totleben, who wrote:

> To protect Balaklava he [the Allies] established a spacious fortified camp, which was too large considering the number of troops carrying out the siege of Sevastopol, protecting the chain of heights from Inkerman to Balaklava and defending Balaklava itself at the same time.[1]

Cholera still drifted amongst his men, whilst many more simply fell sick as a result of the burden of heavy work. The shortage of manpower had already resulted in the failure of the Allies to sever the road from the interior into Sevastopol, allowing the Russians to drip feed supplies into the place, and much as Raglan would have liked to occupy the heights at Inkerman, overlooking the western end of the Chernaya valley, he simply lacked the men to do it. There was, in effect, no covering force, a vital ingredient for a successful siege. Instead, to protect his eastern flank Raglan could call only upon the service of a battalion of the 93rd Highlanders, under Sir Colin Campbell, and around 3,000 Turks, supported by artillery.

Whilst the port of Balaklava itself was relatively easy to defend – a high, almost mountainous ridge, occupied by 1,200 marines with artillery, covered its eastern approaches – the area farther to the north and east gave Raglan cause for concern. Immediately to the north of Balaklava lay the village of Kadikoi, effectively securing the entrance to the port. Beyond this lay a long, sweeping valley running almost four miles east to west, and the best part of one mile wide at its widest point. The valley was bordered in the west by the southern end of the Sapoune Ridge and the Col de Balaklava, and in the east by a distinctive, round hill, soon to be known as Canrobert's Hill. Beyond this lay the village of Kamara. The northern boundary of the valley was marked by the Vorontsov Road, a metalled road which ran east–west along a narrow causeway before running in a north-westerly direction, ascending the mid point of the Sapoune Ridge. Beyond the road there lay yet another valley, slightly shorter in length – about three miles long – and narrower than its more southerly counterpart. The eastern end of the more northerly valley was relatively open and ran through to the Chernaya river, and the village of Chorgun, whilst the western end was again marked by the Sapoune Ridge. The northern boundary of the valley was marked by a series of rounded heights called the Fedioukine Heights. Being divided by the causeway, the valleys naturally became known as North Valley and South Valley, with the heights along which ran the Vorontsov Road becoming known as the Causeway Heights. The area was soon to become the scene of arguably the most famous exploit in British military history.

The terrain itself was well suited for the defence of Balaklava, and six redoubts were established along the length of the important Vorontsov Road. The more easterly redoubt, No.1, was sited on Canrobert's Hill, whilst the other five were spread at regular intervals of about 500 yards from each other – although there were 800 yards between numbers 3 and 4 – with No.6 redoubt being thrown up about 800 yards from the Sapoune Ridge. It should not be imagined that these redoubts were anything other than rudimentary fieldworks and at least half of them had an open back so that they were, in effect, glorified batteries. Indeed, the haste in which they were constructed meant that the sort of elaborate fieldworks seen in the Napoleonic era were sadly absent. Earth was dug, the spoil piled up and hammered into ramparts, but little else was done. Nevertheless, the redoubts did provide mutual support – theoretically – and did provide Balaklava with a defensive line. The redoubts also housed artillery. In fact, they contained a total of nine guns, all 12-pounders; three in No.1 redoubt and two each in redoubts 2, 3 and 4. Redoubts 5 and 6, the two at the

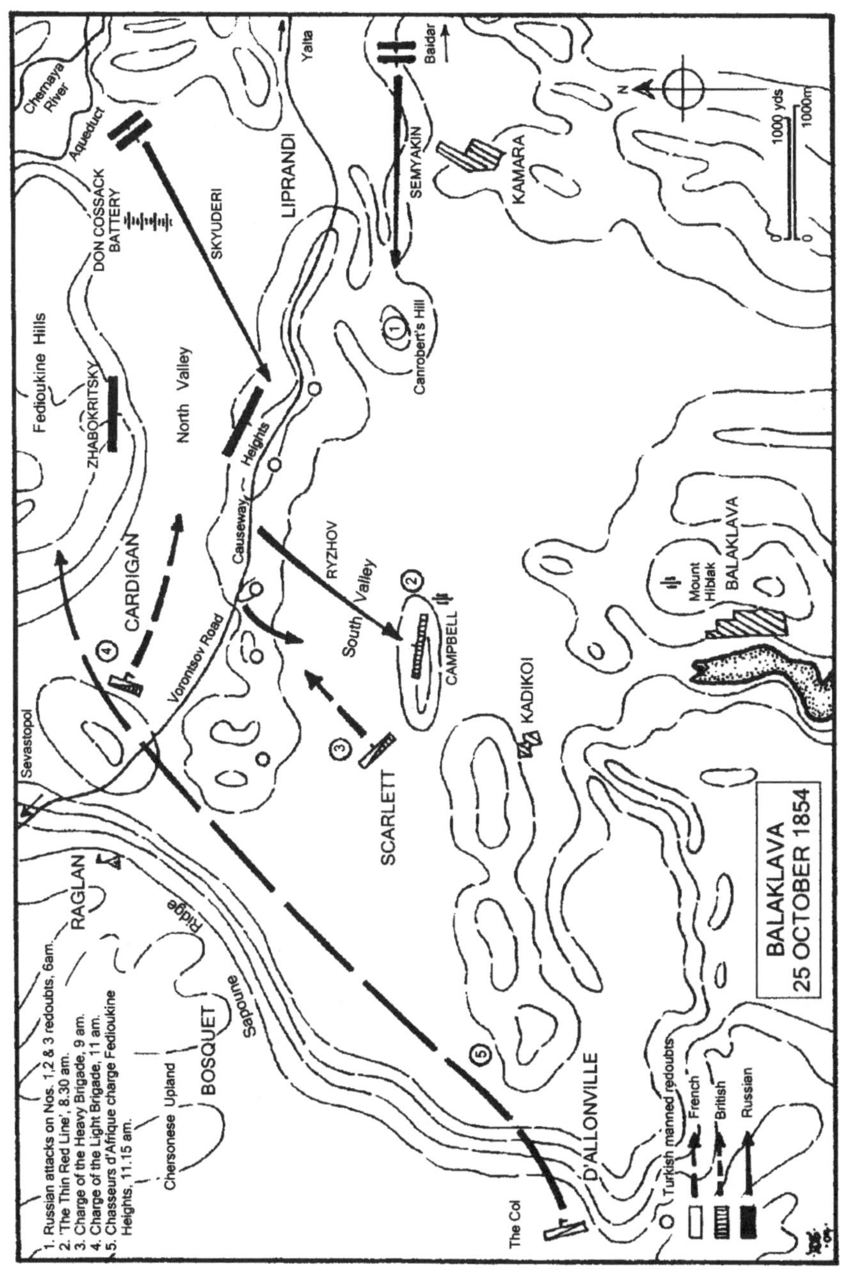
1. Russian attacks on Nos. 1,2 & 3 redoubts, 6am.
2. 'The Thin Red Line', 8.30 am.
3. Charge of the Heavy Brigade, 9 am.
4. Charge of the Light Brigade, 11 am.
5. Chasseurs d'Afrique charge Fedioukine Heights, 11.15 am.
Sevastopol
RAGLAN
BOSQUET
Chersonese Upland
Sapoune
Ridge
The Col
D'ALLONVILLE
Turkish manned redoubts
French
British
Russian
SCARLETT
KADIKOI
CAMPBELL
South Valley
RYZHOV
Causeway Heights
Vorontsov Road
CARDIGAN
North Valley
ZHABOKRITSKY
Fedioukine Hills
DON COSSACK BATTERY
SKYUDERI
LIPRANDI
Aqueduct
Chernaya River
Yalta
Baidar
SEMYAKIN
KAMARA
Canrobert's Hill
Mount Hiblak
BALAKLAVA
N
0
1000 yds
1000m
BALAKLAVA
25 OCTOBER 1854

western end of the Causeway Heights, were still unfinished and without any guns when the last week of October began. Despite their condition, the redoubts were not small works. Indeed, No.1 had a garrison of 600 Turks inside the redoubt itself and around it, whilst redoubts 2, 3 and 4 each had garrisons of 300 Turks. In addition to these, Raglan could call upon the two brigades of British cavalry, 1,500 in all under Lord Lucan, which were encamped at the western end of the south valley, along with a troop of Royal Horse Artillery.

In all, the garrisons in the redoubts plus the British cavalry, the marines and the 93rd Highlanders gave Raglan a total force of around 4,500 men supported by twenty-six guns in and around Balaklava. The problem was, of course, that this was too few to provide an adequate defence in depth for such an extended position of some three miles. Indeed, Wellington had occupied a position three miles in length at Waterloo, but he had almost 70,000 men to do it. There was also the question of how well the Turks would fight if the Russians attacked. True, the Turks had artillery but they had no British officers to give them confidence. Indeed, Kinglake was at his jingoistic and arrogant best when he wrote, 'What is wanted for converting a herd of Turks into a formidable body of warriors is the presence of a resolute man or of a higher station in life, who will undertake to lead them.' In other words, he was referring to the 'singular power that can be exerted over a Turkish force by a fearless English gentleman'.[2] Campbell himself, commanding at Balaklava, certainly thought himself strong enough to withstand any Russian attack but had no real idea of how the Turks would fight. He also knew just how important his task was. After all, if the Russians broke through his thinly-held defences there was little to stop them bearing down upon Balaklava, where they would find an even thinner line, and if Russian infantry and cavalry came storming into the port itself the consequences for the Allies would be tremendous.

With Liprandi and his division having arrived in the theatre of war Menshikov's force numbered around 65,000. For in addition to 12 Infantry Division, Menshikov had also been boosted by the arrival of the Butyr Regiment, a rifle battalion, six reserve battalions of the Minsk and Volynsky regiments, and a battalion of Black Sea Cossack infantry, plus a further battery of artillery. His cavalry force, commanded by Lieutenant General Ryzhov, had likewise been strengthened by the arrival of two hussar and two uhlan regiments, the Ural Cossack Regiment and 53 Don Cossack Regiment. Furthermore, the two remaining divisions of 4 Corps, 10 and 11, were making great efforts to reach Sevastopol. Although the strength of the Russian Army in the vicinity of Sevastopol was around 10,000 fewer than the French and British armies, it was certainly more than sufficient to deal the Allies a great blow. The arrival of 10 and 11 Divisions, on the other hand, would raise numbers to around 85,000, thus giving Menshikov a numerical superiority, but he decided not to wait for these two divisions but to attack as soon as possible. The reasons for this were twofold.

On the one hand Menshikov, who apparently entertained few prospects of success, was coming under increased pressure from Czar Nicholas, who was anxious that Menshikov hit back as soon as possible, reminding him once more of the great victories of the Russian Army over Napoleon some forty-two years earlier. 'I hope that you will find an opportunity,' he said, 'to attack the enemy and uphold the honour of our arms when the 10th and the 11th Divisions reach you. It is extremely desirable to prove to our foreign enemy, and even Russia itself, that we are still the same Russians of 1812 – Borodino and Paris Russians! God will help you, amen!'[3] He was also boosted by reconnaissance reports that indicated that the British defensive line outside Balaklava was held largely by Turkish troops, and poorly trained second line ones at that. They were not of the same calibre that had inflicted defeats on the Russians on the Danube but were a mixture of Tunisians, raw recruits and militia. Given this news, and with the czar demanding results Menshikov decided to attack and not wait for 10 and 11 Infantry Divisions to arrive.

The attack on the Balaklava forts was to be led by one of the best generals in the Russian Army, Pavel Petrovitch Liprandi, a man with a distinguished military career. He had fought against Napoleon during the French invasion of 1812, and was a friend of the great Russian poet Alexander Pushkin and of many Decembrists. He was known as a man who held progressive views, and his great military experience, the care he showed to his men, both on and off the battlefield, made him very popular and respected among both his officers and his men. Indeed, when he despatched 12 Infantry Division from the Danube to the Crimea, Gorchakov wrote to Menshikov, urging him to talk to Liprandi and listen to his views not only on strategy but also on his methods for caring for the welfare of his troops.[4]

The first move by the Russians came at dawn on 18 October when Lieutenant Colonel A E Rakovitch, who had fought with great distinction at the Alma, moved against the village of Chorgun with three infantry battalions, 200 Cossacks and four guns. From here, Rakovitch and Liprandi, along with Major General K R Semyakin were able to reconnoitre the Turkish-held redoubts along the Causeway Heights. It was clear to them that the redoubts were too far forward of the inner defensive line around Balaklava to be adequately and quickly supported, which was noted somewhat belatedly by some officers of the Royal Engineers themselves. A swift strike against the redoubts was certain of success, after which they could turn their attention to Balaklava itself.

By 23 October Liprandi had gathered together a strong force, to become known as the 'Detachment of Chorgun', consisting of seventeen battalions of infantry and thirty squadrons of cavalry, supported by forty-eight guns and sixteen horse artillery guns. The total force numbered around 16,000 men and was divided into three columns. The left column was to be commanded by Major General Gribbe, and consisted of four battalions of the Dnieper Regiment, four squadrons of ulhans, 100 Cossacks and ten guns. Moving south from the Chernaya river, Gribbe was then to march directly west, his objective being the village of Kamara which lay to the east of Canrobert's Hill and in which were positioned some Allied piquets. The centre column, commanded by Major General Semyakin, was in turn divided into two wings; the left wing, under Semyakin himself, consisted of four battalions of the Azovsky Regiment, one battalion of the Dnieper, and ten guns, and the right wing, under Major General Levutsky, of three battalions of the Ukraine Regiment and eight guns. Semyakin's job was to advance south from Chorgun and, skirting the eastern end of the Fedioukine Heights, was to move against Canrobert's Hill and No.1 redoubt. Levutsky, meanwhile, was to follow him before peeling off to his right in order to attack No.2 redoubt, farther to the west. The right column, commanded by Colonel Skyuderi, of the Odessa Regiment, consisted of four battalions of his own regiment, 300 men of 53 Don Cossack Regiment and eight guns. Crossing the Chernaya river via Tractir Bridge, Skyuderi was take the track running south through the Fedioukine Heights and cross North Valley to attack No.3 redoubt. The attacks were to be supported by sixteen squadrons of Ryzhov's cavalry, consisting of the Kiev, Ingermanland and Ural Cossack regiments, supported by a Don Cossack battery and a battery of horse artillery. Liprandi's reserve, held back at the Tractir Bridge, consisted of a single battalion of the Ukraine Regiment, a company of the 4th Infantry Regiment, and a battery of artillery. Liprandi's attacking force was to be supported on its right by a further force, numbering around 4,500, under the command of Major General Zhabokritsky, consisting of seven battalions of infantry from the Vladimir and Sousdal regiments, and the 6 Rifle battalion, two squadrons of the Ingermanland Hussars, 300 cossacks from 60 Don Cossack Regiment, and fourteen guns. Zhabokritsky was positioned on the right of Liprandi to prevent the Allies from interfering in the attack on the redoubts. Once the redoubts had been taken Zhabokritsky was to advance and occupy the Fedioukine Heights. In total, and including Zhabokritsky's force, Liprandi had at his disposal around 25,000 men, not enough to seriously threaten the Allied siege lines, but more than enough to compromise the defences at Balaklava. The orders having been given, the attack was scheduled to begin just before dawn on 25 October.

It was inevitable that such a large Russian force would not go undetected by the Allies. In fact, Liprandi's force had been spotted on 18 October during its advance upon Chorgun, and the intelligence was duly passed on to Lord Raglan who reacted by sending over 1,000 men of the 4th Division marching down from the Sapoune Ridge into the valley of

Balaklava, only to be sent marching all the way back again when it was discovered that the Russians were not about to threaten the British base but were obviously on some sort of reconnaissance. This in itself was not particularly important at the time but it did, nevertheless, have a significant bearing on the outcome of the fight about to break out on 25 October. For, on the evening of 24 October, the Turkish commander, the diligent Rustam Pasha, brought in a Tartar spy bearing positive information on Liprandi's planned attack scheduled for the next morning. After he had been questioned by Lord Lucan and Sir Colin Campbell it was decided to send a letter to Raglan, the letter and intelligence arriving at his headquarters in the middle of a conference the British commander was having with Canrobert. Raglan read the letter before sending a reply, requesting any further information be sent straight to him. Then, mindful perhaps of the wasted and tiresome march of the 4th Division a few days earlier, Raglan did nothing. No orders were despatched and no troops moved. Thus the Russian attack was able to proceed the next morning without any immediate threat from any British infantry.

The evening of 24 October was quiet, and the weather warm. Lieutenant Koribut-Kubitovitch, commander of the 2nd squadron of the composite Uhlan regiment, wrote:

> The campfires were seen around the whole valley. The officers in groups were sitting around them, mainly with their 'samovars', the eternal companions of camp life. Loud laughter was heard everywhere. Some of them, not so light-hearted, were talking quietly and preparing for the next day, burning letters they didn't want to see fall into the enemy's hands in the case of death, and writing wills. It's rather strange now to recollect so many things which were quite natural at that time and amazed nobody. What, you can ask, does the will mean for a man who has nothing but a tent, two great coats and a samovar? But still the wills were being written anyway.[5]

Elsewhere, soldiers bade farewell to each other, asking their comrades to send their relatives family relics and money in the case of their death. The young soldiers listened to the stories of the older ones about their first impressions of the noise and smell of battle. Cavalrymen saw to their horses. The camp of the Uhlan regiment was situated near Chorgun on the right bank of Chernaya river. One of the old soldiers of that regiment, respected by his squadron, was standing in front of his horse and crying bitterly. The commander came and asked the reason for his tears. The soldier answered:

> How can I not cry, sir? My Yunona will be killed tomorrow; she is not eating and it's very sad. I have been riding her for eight years, she is

> attached to me, and she understands what I say to her and doesn't allow anybody to clean her but me. Tomorrow I'll become an orphan and will have nobody to love!

The premonition of the old soldier came true: Yunona was killed.[6] Early on the morning of 25 October, when everything was ready for the attack, Liprandi went amongst his troops, asking them to fight as bravely as they had done on the Danube. He told them he was confident of a victory for Russian arms, adding, 'a bayonet is the main instrument to achieve certain and quick success.'[7] Then, just before 5 am, the troops of the Chorgun detachment left their camp and marched off in absolute silence towards the Balaklava valleys. The momentous Battle of Balaklava was about to begin.

A few miles to the west of Chorgun Lord Lucan and his staff were preparing for their daily morning ride. It had become something of a routine for the diligent Lucan to parade his men before dawn before taking himself off to tour the outposts around Balaklava. The men of the British cavalry brigades saw things differently, of course. It was so tiresome to rise every dark, cold morning, just to parade for his lordship. Standing there, half asleep, hungry and tired, just as a precaution against some imaginary enemy, was not their idea of soldiering. It was a real pain. And to make matters worse for the men of the Light Cavalry their brigade commander, Lord Cardigan, was spared the chore. Instead, 'the Noble Yachtsman', as he had become known, was to be found each morning snug aboard his yacht, *Dryad*, moored in the overcrowded port of Balaklava.

The village of Kamara was home to the most easterly of all the soldiers in the Allied army. Situated to the east of Canrobert's Hill it provided a useful observation point for Lucan's vedettes – effectively, mounted guards – watching for signs of any Russian activity to the east. On the morning of 25 October Kamara was occupied by a drowsy, snoozing piquet formed by about thirty NCOs and men, who had little idea of the impending storm about to break over their sleepy heads. Even as the vedettes blinked wearily into the dark dawn a *sotnia* (squadron) of Russian Cossacks, followed by a host of uhlans, was riding slowly towards Kamara and was within a mile of the village before they were spotted. These were the leading elements of Gribbe's force, their objective being the very village in which the unwary British piquets were sleeping. In fact, it was only when a visiting field officer, Major Alexander Low, of the 4th Light Dragoons, rode in that they were detected, pouring up the slopes to the south-east of the village. There was little time to lose as Low roused the piquets and had them fall in, the men tumbling out of the village as fast as they could. It was a close call but everyone managed to scramble off into the gloom leaving Kamara in the hands of a grateful

Gribbe. Behind the Cossacks and uhlans came the Dnieper Regiment, along with the artillery. Immediately, Gribbe began deploying his ten guns on the slopes to the west of Kamara, leaving his gunners with a clear view of No.1 redoubt on Canrobert's Hill.

While the Russians made themselves at home in front of Kamara, Lucan and his staff came slowly forward towards Canrobert Hill. It was about 6 am and the grey dawn was just beginning to give up vague shapes in the distance, one of which was a flagpole, standing erect inside No.1 redoubt. One of Lucan's retinue was the Assistant Adjutant General, Lord William Paulet, who evidently had his wits about him. Lord George Paget, commanding officer of the 4th Light Dragoons, was another of the group, and he later recalled the moment when Lucan and his friends realised something was very wrong.

> We rode on at a walk across the plain, in the direction of the left of Canrobert's Hill, in happy ignorance of the day's work in store for us; and by the time we had approached to within about three hundred yards of the Turkish redoubts in our front, the first faint streaks of daylight (for the sun had not yet appeared on the horizon), showed us that from the flag-staff which had, I believe, only the day before been erected on the redoubt, flew two flags, only just discernable in the grey twilight.
>
> The conversation which ensued will ever be vividly impressed in my memory. 'Holloa,' said Lord William, 'there are two flags flying; what does that mean?' 'Why, that surely is the signal that the enemy is approaching,' said Major McMahon. 'Are you quite sure?' we replied. We were not kept long in doubt! Hardly were the words out of McMahon's mouth, when bang went a cannon from the redoubt in question, fired on the advancing masses of the enemy.[8]

The Battle of Balaklava began at around 6 am when a gun was fired by the Turks from No.1 redoubt on Canrobert's Hill. The round had barely whizzed from the mouth of the barrel of the 12-pounder when Lucan turned and despatched Captain Charteris to ride the five miles to British headquarters and inform Raglan that the redoubts were under attack. The British commander-in-chief was informed by Charteris of the attack at about 7 am, but the sound of the gun had already disturbed those at headquarters. Indeed, it was enough to make 'The Noble Yachtsman', Lord Cardigan, stir in his bed. Lucan, meanwhile, reacted to the sudden crisis by ordering forward both Light and Heavy brigades of cavalry, whilst Campbell, already alerted by the sound of gunfire, was informed of the attack also. Other than that, there was little Lucan could do until his cavalry came forward. Even then, he knew there would be small chance of him thwarting the Russian attack, coming on as it was in strength, and consisting of all arms including a large number of guns. He assumed, correctly, that Raglan would send him infantry support, but knew also that it would be hours before they arrived. Any support from the French would likewise take time to arrive. Canrobert himself had been informed of the Russian attack at about 7.30 am and had immediately ridden over to join Raglan on the Sapoune Ridge from where they watched while the Russian masses flooding into the North Valley. Bosquet, having been roused by cannon fire, was on the spot immediately, and had ordered the 2nd Brigade of the 1st Division of the French Army, commanded by General Vinoy, to march towards Balaklava to support their allies, whilst the 1st Brigade, under General Espinasse, was set in motion also, along with the divisional artillery and the Chasseurs d'Afrique. The French 3rd Division was put on the alert and the horse artillery of the reserve harnessed, ready to move at the first signal.[9]

Raglan, meanwhile, had ordered Cathcart's 4th Division, and the 1st Division, under the Duke of Cambridge, to move down into the plain of Balaklava, marching via the Col. Unfortunately, the false alarms of the past few days were to cause a delay in getting the divisions to march, at least the 4th Division. Raglan's aide-de-camp, Captain Ewart, was taken aback somewhat when, upon asking Cathcart to move his division into the plain of Balaklava, Cathcart flatly refused, saying that his men had only just finished their shift in the trenches before Sevastopol. It was impossible for them to move, he said, and suggested that Ewart join him for breakfast. When the young officer declined, Cathcart told him he might as well ride off and tell Raglan. There had simply been too many alarms for Cathcart. Raglan – or at least the piquets – had cried wolf once too often. This time Cathcart wasn't moving. Yet, this time the alarm was very real. Ewart rode off but, to his eternal credit, stopped and turned back, determined to confront Cathcart again. After all, when a messenger arrived bearing an order from the commander-in-chief, it had to be treated by the recipient as if the commander-in-chief himself was delivering it. It simply wasn't done to disobey such an order. Fortunately, Cathcart changed his tune, and by 8.30 his division was beginning to stir once again, preparing to march down into the plain. The Duke of Cambridge, meanwhile, had got his division into marching order immediately. But it would still take them at least two hours to reach the plain.

Meanwhile, Lucan was doing his best to stabilise the situation at the redoubts, but without either artillery or infantry support had little chance of success. Away to his left, coming across the North Valley, were the Russian columns under Levutsky, Semyakin and Skyuderi, whilst Gribbe's artillery continued to shell No.1 redoubt on Canrobert's Hill. In fact, the Turks in the redoubt were putting up a good show, returning fire with the few guns at their disposal, but it was obvious to Lucan that there was little to stop the Russians taking the redoubt, along with Nos 2 and 3 unless infantry and artillery support arrived soon. In the meantime, he was joined by his cavalry division, the Heavy Brigade on the right and the Light Brigade, still minus Cardigan, on the left. The division halted about 300 yards away from No.2 redoubt, close enough for them to come under fire from stray shots flying over from the direction of Kamara.

In addition to the cavalry division, help had arrived in the form of Captain George Maude's troop of horse artillery, I Troop, which unlimbered its four 6-pounder and two 12-pounder guns between redoubts 1 and 2, opening up soon afterwards at the oncoming Russians. The problem was that the Russians' guns were heavier, had greater range and, unlike Maude, they had a plentiful supply of ammunition. It was just as well that Campbell had sent forward Captain Barker's battery, W Battery, of the Royal Artillery, from Balaklava to engage the Russians. Barker's battery was armed with four 9-pounder guns and two 24-pounders, although it seems likely that only the 9-pounders were sent forward. The battle then became an artillery duel between the British batteries and the Turks in the redoubts on one side, and the Russians in the North Valley and on the hill in front of Kamara on the other. Unfortunately for the Allies it was a very one-sided duel, the heavier Russian guns, particularly battery No.4 under the command of Lieutenant Postnikov and the riflemen of the Ukraine regiment, beginning to take their toll on both men and ordnance, and when a shell exploded in the midst of Maude's battery, sending pieces of men and horses, guns and wagons spinning into the air, Lucan realised it was time for Maude to retire. The men were quite happy to continue the fight but their ammunition was running short and so they were forced to withdraw. Maude himself was carried off the field with a terrible wound to his left shoulder. With I Troop having retired, their place was taken by two guns from Barker's W Battery.

As the British artillery fire slackened, Semyakin made final preparations for the assault on the redoubts. Leading the way against No.1 redoubt were three battalions of the Azovsky Regiment, under Colonel V M Krudener, who formed his men into 'two lines in company column, not more than 100 paces between the lines, with a battalion of the Azovsky and one of the Dnieper in battalion attack formation in the third line'.[10] Semyakin was in the midst of the attacking columns as they scrambled up the slopes of Canrobert's Hill. He later recalled: 'On 25 October I didn't take my sabre from the scabbard. I only crossed myself and waved my hat on both sides. Everybody rushed after me and I was protected by the stern Azovs.'[11] The Azovs, with their seemingly fearless commander, Krudener, were attacking

> without paying any attention to the shower of bullets and shells. Neither the great steepness [of the ground], nor the well-aimed fire

> could stop the brave Azovs. In any loss they closed their lines until they came to the bottom of the hill in good order. The drawling 'Hurrah!' rang out and all at once the slope was covered with the crowd. The Azovs, as only they could, charged the fortification like a swarm of bees; some ran round the rear and others went through the embrasures, and then the bayonet work of the Russian soldier began.[12]

Some controversy surrounds the next phase of the action. Most sources agree that, in the ensuing fight, 170 Turks were killed, a very high death rate considering the redoubt and the surrounding ground were held by no more than 600 Turks. Many histories – and even many eye-witnesses – would have us believe the Turks ran at the first sign of the oncoming Russians. A death toll of 170 would certainly seem to put paid to this argument, and would suggest, rather, that they did in fact put up one hell of a fight to save themselves and the redoubt. The more sinister explanation offered is that many were simply slaughtered by the Russians during the frenzied assault, either during the fight itself or when they had been taken prisoner afterwards. Whatever the reason, the Turks had offered fierce resistance but it had been enough to stop the Russians surging into the redoubt, and by 8 am the colours of the Azovsky Regiment were fluttering proudly on the redoubt. The losses to the Azovsky were two officers and 149 men.

No sooner had the Russians taken possession of the rampart than Colonel Afanasyev brought up four guns of the light 6th battery which began to fire on the retreating enemy. It's a long way from Canrobert's Hill to Balaklava. It's very open too, and the pursuing Cossack cavalrymen had little trouble in despatching any straying, isolated Turks running away from the redoubt. The Turks did themselves no favours either, by insisting on taking their possessions with them. Indeed, rather than a retreating force they looked more like 'a tribe in a state of migration'.[13] Shortly after the capture of No.1 redoubt, General Liprandi himself arrived to congratulate Semyakin on his success, adding that he would recommend him for the Cross of St George. Towards midday, Menshikov arrived with his staff. He thanked 'the hero of the victory' and said, 'You have pleased the Czar and I will send a courier to him with an account of your great deeds.'[14]

No.1 redoubt had been the anchor upon which the entire outer line of defences around Balaklava was based. It was the right of the line, and with it now in the possession of the Russians the remaining redoubts were in grave danger of falling too. In fact, Gunners Jenkins, McGarry and Barrett, serving with W Battery, were despatched to spike the guns in redoubts numbers 2, 3 and 4, to prevent them falling into the hands of the oncoming Russians. They were not long in coming. The battalions of the Ukraine

Regiment under command of Colonel P N Dudnitsky-Lishin attacked redoubts Nos. 2 and 3, whilst the Odessa Regiment, under its experienced commander Colonel Skyuderi, was advancing upon redoubt No. 4. The Turks, having already witnessed the capture of their main fortification, and keen to avoid the same fate as their compatriots, left their tents, guns, powder and shells and rushed down to Balaklava. No. 4 redoubt was considered by Liprandi to be too close to the enemy and so he had it razed to the ground. The guns were smashed and the wheels of gun-carriages broken up before his men abandoned the redoubt.

The situation at Balaklava just after 8 am saw Liprandi's men occupying redoubts 1, 2 and 3, whilst they had destroyed redoubt No.4. Possession of the redoubts gave the Russians control of the vital Vorontsov Road. Meanwhile, the two French brigades under Vinoy and Espinasse were making great efforts to reach the Col to get down into the plain. Cathcart's 4th Division and the Duke of Cambridge's 1st Division were likewise making their way across the Sapoune Ridge in order to get down into the plain, but they were some way behind the French. The British cavalry division, which had at last been joined by Lord Cardigan, had been forced to pull back towards their own camps and sat waiting and watching, receiving the occasional shot, close to redoubts 5 and 6. Both Maude's and Barker's batteries had also been forced to pull back, and drew up to the right and right rear of the cavalry. The last of the Turks – frustrated by the lack of support from Lucan – had yet to reach sanctuary at Balaklava. Raglan, meanwhile, watched with growing anxiety from his position up on the Sapoune Ridge.

From Liprandi's point of view all had gone according to plan. By capturing the first four redoubts along the Vorontsov Road, and by driving back both the British cavalry and artillery, he had, in effect, swung open the door leading to Balaklava. At least, it was almost open, for there still remained a motley combination of a hundred invalids under Colonel Daveney, about 1,000 reluctant Turks, Barker's W Battery and 550 men of the 93rd Highlanders, commanded by Colonel Ainslie. There were even two young officers of the Grenadier Guards, Hamilton and Verschoyle, who had taken it upon themselves to join the defenders. There were, therefore, around 1,700 men standing between Liprandi and a great Russian success. Or, to put it another way, they were all that stood between Liprandi and a massive British disaster. Fortunately for Raglan the defence of Balaklava was in good hands. Sir Colin Campbell, the old Peninsula veteran, and one of the many heroes of the Alma, was completely undaunted and calmly had his Highlanders file out to a low hillock to the north of Kadikoi. Here, after taking some casualties from fire at long range from the guns on the distant Causeway Heights, he had his men lie down. The Turks, too, lay down, having joined their kilt-clad comrades on the hillock. The Turks, in fact, rarely warrant a mention in traditional accounts of the 'thin red line' story. The Russians had already enjoyed a pretty field day against the Turks who had retreated from No.1 redoubt, but the sight of another thousand of them, standing with the 93rd, no matter how inferior the Russians considered them to be, was something that could not be ignored.

Liprandi surveyed the satisfying scene before him from a good vantage point on the Vorontsov Road, somewhere between redoubts 2 and 3. Now was the time to bring forward Ryzhov's cavalry in order to press home his advantage. Initially, Ryzhov's force consisted of eight squadrons of the 11th Kiev Hussars, six of the 12th Ingermanland Hussars, and three of 53 Don Cossack Regiment. The 1st Ural Cossacks were to remain behind as a reserve, although Liprandi later decided to add them to Ryzhov's attacking force, giving it a strength of about 2,000 men, in addition to which he had sixteen guns. Ryzhov's cavalry filed over the Tractir Bridge and began streaming into the North Valley, riding south-west. It was about 9 am.

At about the same time that Ryzhov's cavalry were crossing the Chernaya river, Lord Lucan's cavalry division was on the move, or at least it would have been if he could work out just exactly what it was that Raglan was ordering him to do. The first order, issued earlier by Raglan at 8.30 am, called for Lucan to 'take ground to the left of the second line of redoubts occupied by the Turks'. The problem was that Raglan was dictating his orders from his lofty position on the Sapoune Ridge. Whether or not his decisions were good ones is neither here nor there. The trouble was that the recipient, that is to say Lucan, had no idea what the word 'left' meant or what the 'second line' referred to. The two men had entirely different viewpoints, and the word 'left' could mean something entirely different to a man looking in a different direction from the person who had issued the order. The safer bet would have been to use either the word 'west' or 'east'. Hence, Lucan was completely mystified – not for the last time on 25 October – by the order, and it fell to Captain Wetherall, Raglan's aide and the bearer of the message, to position the cavalry, placing them between No.6 redoubt and the foot of the Sapoune Ridge.

The problem was that the capture of the redoubts by Liprandi opened up a huge gap between Balaklava and the nearest British troops, Lucan's cavalry division. Realising this, Raglan issued the second order shortly afterwards: 'Eight squadrons of Heavy Dragoons to be detached towards Balaklava to support the Turks, who are wavering.' By the time Raglan's aide, Captain Hardinge, reached Lucan fifteen minutes later the situation had begun to change dramatically with the arrival in the North Valley of Ryzhov's cavalry. In fact, this was only the second in a series of largely confusing orders issued by Raglan that would culminate in one of the great disasters in British military history. Thus, at the same time that Lucan was moving his eight squadrons of heavy cavalry south-east in the direction of Balaklava, Ryzhov's 2,000 cavalry were trotting in the opposite direction, west, along the North Valley. Raglan's two orders were, of course, to culminate in the famous charge of the Heavy Brigade and in the stand made by Sir Colin Campbell in front of Balaklava. The question is, did they happen at the same time? Many authors since 1854 have treated the two incidents as if they were separate actions whereas it is clear they were part of the same, Ryzhov-led operation, albeit slightly staggered.

Ryzhov's cavalry continued moving west along the North Valley until it reached a point almost level with No.4 redoubt, whereupon they wheeled to the left and crested the Causeway Heights. Before him, Ryzhov could see Lucan's heavies moving east across his front, whilst away to the south he could make out red-jacketed infantry, Turkish refugees from the redoubts, and some British artillery. Ryzhov immediately detached about 400 men of the Ingermanland Hussars to turn slightly to their left in order to make for Balaklava and this small force of British and Turkish infantry that were defending it at Kadikoi. The bulk of his force, meanwhile, came to a halt on the southern slopes of the Causeway Heights, barely 800 yards or so from the British heavy cavalry.

The detachment of the Ingermanland Hussars was quickly picked up by Campbell and by the marines on the heights overlooking Balaklava, on the eastern slopes of which they had deployed their guns. These guns opened up at long range, but soon began to cause the Russians some discomfort as they continued to close. Campbell, meanwhile, had the 93rd Highlanders and the Turks get to their feet and brought them forward of the hillock where they had been sheltering from Russian artillery fire. With nothing but Balaklava and the Black Sea at their backs, Campbell told his men, 'Remember, there is no retreat from here men. You must die where we stand!'[15] Unfortunately, the sight of these 400 hussars bearing down on them, even from hundreds of yards away, was too much for many of the already shattered Turks who simply turned and fled towards Balaklava crying, 'Ship! Ship!' Many stayed put, however, encouraged, no doubt, by the steady stream of fire being opened upon the Russian cavalry not only by the marines' artillery, but also by Barker's guns. Canister was loaded when the range grew shorter, upon which the 93rd began to show signs of wanting to advance, which brought an immediate admonishment from Campbell. 'Ninety-third! Ninety-third!' he shouted, 'Damn all that eagerness!'[16]

He need not have worried. The Russian hussars were already beginning to feel the heat of British artillery, and when the 93rd opened fire with a volley at extreme range they were brought almost to a halt. Captain Ross, commanding the 93rd's grenadier company, wheeled his men to their right before sending another volley towards the Russians. Although very few saddles were emptied, the combination of British – and presumably

Turkish – infantry and artillery fire was enough to cause discomfort amongst the Ingermanland Hussars and barely five minutes after they had entered the South Valley they were retreating towards the Causeway Heights having achieved nothing, save for helping to immortalise what is probably one of the most insignificant skirmishes in British military history, for when William Russell wrote his despatch on the battle, he referred to the Highlanders as a, 'thin red streak, tipped with a line of steel'. Thus was born the myth and legend of the oft-misquoted 'Thin Red Line'. But while Campbell was shooing away the Ingermanland Hussars, a much greater action was taking place not far away to the north-west.

The remaining 1,600 men of Ryzhov's cavalry – the 400 Ingermanland Hussars driven off by Campbell played no further part in the battle – continued to stall on the slopes of the Causeway Heights. Meanwhile, the British Heavy Brigade, under Brigadier General the Hon. Sir James Scarlett, was still moving south-east in the South Valley, having been ordered by Raglan to support 'the Turks who are wavering'. It was all quite amazing. There was Ryzhov, with a strong force of cavalry, just sitting there, hesitating, whilst Scarlett's brigade blundered their way across his front. Scarlett, notoriously short-sighted, had no idea the Russians were even there. Furthermore, he had neglected to send out scouts on his flanks. It was literally a case of the blind leading the blind. Coincidentally, Ryzhov appears to have made the same mistake and had not sent out any scouts on his flanks. Indeed, he appears to have been completely unaware of Scarlett's presence until he topped the Causeway Heights. The eight squadrons of the Heavy Brigade consisted of two each from the Scots Greys, the 6th (Inniskilling) Dragoons, 4th Dragoon Guards and the 5th Dragoon Guards. The remaining two squadrons of the Heavy Brigade, the 1st (Royal) Dragoons, were left in their original position to the west of No.6 redoubt.

The advance of the Heavy Brigade was not without its problems thanks to a vineyard that lay irritatingly in its path, and to the sprawling encampment of the Light Brigade. They were, therefore, in a state of some disorganisation when they emerged from behind the obstacles. Although Scarlett had yet to see the Russians the French certainly had. Two guns booming out from the top of the Sapoune Ridge was testament to that. Lucan also had seen what was coming, and immediately galloped over to warn Scarlett, still oblivious to the Russians away to his left. But before he rode off, he gave Lord Cardigan specific orders to 'attack anything and everything that should come within your reach'. Cardigan naturally stated later that Lucan had ordered him not to move on any account, and that he was to remain with his brigade and to defend it against any Russian attack. Whatever the order, Lucan rode away to warn Scarlett of the threat to his left.

He need not have worried, however, for Scarlett had by now been warned by one of his aides of the close proximity of the Russian cavalry. Before long orders were being shouted to 'left wheel into line', but finding himself cramped for room he continued advancing in columns until he emerged into more suitable ground. Then, as Lucan arrived with his staff, the order was given again to wheel left into line which was, on this occasion, duly accomplished. Still Ryzhov and his men waited, walking slowly forward. Perhaps they were simply amazed by the sight of hundreds of British cavalrymen blustering about in their front, seemingly oblivious to the threat they posed, or maybe they were just slightly wary of their opponents. Had Ryzhov charged whilst Scarlett was forming his men he would have caught them completely disorganised, and with the momentum of a downhill charge in his favour the odds were that his cavalry would have been successful. But he let the chance slip, and Scarlett continued to dress his lines. In fact, so impatient was Lucan that he had his own bugler sound the charge. Nothing happened. His bugler sounded the charge a second time. And still nothing. Instead the officers of the Scots Greys and the Inniskillings sat there with their backs to the Russians, calmly watching as the NCOs got their men into the correct order. Then, when they were finally satisfied that all was ready they turned round to face the astonished Russians. Scarlett at last signalled to his trumpeter, Monks, to sound the charge. This time the response was instantaneous. The Heavy Brigade was on the move.

At least part of it was, for when Scarlett led his men forward, with himself and his staff some fifty yards ahead of the main British cavalry line, only three squadrons, two of the Scots Greys and one of the Inniskillings, were actually with him. The other squadron of the Inniskillings was coming forward away to the right, whilst the remaining squadrons of the 4th and 5th Dragoon Guards were only just finishing negotiating the obstacles of the vineyard and the Light Brigade camp. The Royals, meanwhile, determined not to let their comrades have all the fun, were coming up without orders. But, for now, barely 300 heavy British dragoons found themselves charging a large, grey mass of Russians, around 1,600-strong. The regiments in question, however, had a long and very distinguished history. Indeed, the Scots Greys had charged alongside the Inniskillings and the Royal Dragoons at Waterloo, where all three had captured French 'eagles', those much-prized gilded birds that had been touched by the hand of Napoleon, although the Inniskillings had sadly been forced to relinquish theirs during the fight. But here they were again, the old Union Brigade of Waterloo fame. And coming up behind them were the 5th Dragoon Guards who, under the guiding hand of John Gaspard Le Marchant, had smashed the centre of the French at Salamanca on that hot and dusty day back in July 1812. They were about to gain more glory for their regiments.

The charge of the Heavy Brigade was, actually, anything but a charge, for Scarlett had launched his men uphill and from a standing start. One is almost reminded of the famous comment made by Captain Mercer at Waterloo when describing the French cavalry charges. 'There was none of your furious galloping,' he said, and the same thing almost certainly occurred here. Indeed, it says much for the prowess of Scarlett and his men that they were able to cut their way through a far denser mass of Russians without sustaining particularly heavy casualties. Scarlett was first into the Russians, his odd looking helmet disappearing into the midst of a mass of grey. His staff followed close behind. Then, coming up behind them, came the three squadrons of the Scots Greys and Inniskillings who bludgeoned their way into the centre of the Russian mass. Soon afterwards, the second squadron of the Inniskillings crashed into the left flank of the Russians, followed soon afterwards by the 5th Dragoon Guards who followed the Greys into the middle of the Russians. Then came the 4th Dragoon Guards, frustrated at having to clear the vineyard and camp, attacking the right rear of Ryzhov's cavalry. Finally there were the Royals, casting to the wind their orders to remain behind and attacking on their own initiative, striking at the right front of the Russians. It was, therefore, a 'staggered' attack which hit Ryzhov on all sides, and at intervals. 800 British were taking on twice there own number, but the odds of two against one daunted them not one minute. Furthermore, Ryzhov was caught flat-footed and static, although some accounts suggest he extended his flanks by throwing out the Cossacks of 53 Don Cossack Regiment in an attempt to encircle the British. In fact, if he did so he certainly made it easier for the British to cut their way through. As it was, Scarlett's men had a tough enough time, and observers on the Sapoune Ridge watched with a mixture of shock and awe as the Heavy Brigade disappeared into the midst of the Russians. For a fleeting moment it looked for all the world as if they had been swallowed up, but then, suddenly, Scarlett emerged, followed by his staff, from the rear of the Russian mass.

Following hard on the heels of Scarlett came the Scots Greys and then the Inniskillings, who had cut and hacked their way through, scattering the Russians and forcing them to give way. They literally knocked them aside in some cases. Surprisingly, casualties were relatively light on both sides, largely due to the ineffectiveness of both swordsmanship and of the swords themselves. There had long been two different schools of thought about the most effective use of the sword, particularly in the British Army. Many advocated the use of the point, whereas others considered the edge to be more useful. It was a debate that had stretched back to the Napoleonic Wars and beyond. The 1821- and 1853-pattern Heavy Cavalry swords were suited to both cut and point but it appears that the point was more effective then the edge.[17] Commenting on the problem after the British cavalry's fight at Sahagun in 1808, Dr Adam Neale said, 'for every four Frenchman we put in hospital they put one of ours in the grave'. (The

French used the point whereas the British preferred to cut.) The problem at Balaklava for the British cavalry was exacerbated by the fact that the Russians wore heavy grey overcoats which often proved impossible to penetrate. The sword cuts simply bounced off. It was imperative, therefore, that the point was used, at least on the body. To achieve anything with the cut, it was necessary to strike at the head.

By now battle was well and truly joined between Russian and British cavalry, with the heavier British driving their way into and through the Russians, whose Cossacks went forward, whooping and screaming at the top of their voices. The first to feel the force of the British attack were the Ingermanland Hussars, under the command of Major General I A Khaletsky. Among them was Staff-captain Eugeny Arbuzov who later described how his Ingermanland Hussars (Saxe-Weimar) regiment,

> had to fight with the regiment of Queen Victoria's Dragoon Guards in their red coats. At once the fire against us stopped and a hand-to-hand battle began. Neither we nor the English wanted to yield. In the battle, which lasted eight or ten minutes, with the constant 'hurrah', neither orders nor trumpeters were heard. Our Hussars said they charged into the English. When we rushed at the dragoons, the 2nd squadron of our regiment was pressed from the left side and moved to the right at a full gallop. They pressed the 1st squadron and made them do the same, so that the 1st platoon of the squadron, which was under my command, didn't have an enemy facing them during the minute of their clash with the English because the left flank of the enemy ended opposite to the right flank of the 2nd platoon of our squadron. I used this opportunity and my platoon immediately attacked the left flank and rear of English squadron and greatly damaged their lines. Frankly speaking, I can't say what I did there; I only remember that I hit a dragoon in his shoulder so that my sabre cut into him and I could hardly pull it out. At the same time the sabred dragoon, while falling from his horse, caught the curb of my horse with his spurs, broke it and my horse reared and nearly overturned.[18]

In the confusion, the commander of the 3rd squadron of the Ingermanland Hussars, Captain P P Marin, was thrown to the ground along with his horse after colliding with a British dragoon. Keeping his head, he jumped back on to his horse and cut his way through the British line before emerging without his shako and with three wounds in his head. Major General Khaletsky himself was wounded in the arm and neck in the fight and his sabre knocked from his hands. His batman, 65 year-old Corporal Karp Pivenko, gave him his own sabre before dismounting in order to retrieve his master's lost sabre. He then jumped on to his horse in time to parry a blow aimed at Khaletsky. Corporal Pivenko was decorated for his action.[19]

Scarlett's dragoons continued pushing, heaving and hacking their way through Ryzhov's cavalry. Scarlett, who went through the action whirling and twirling his sword about him, led a charmed life and came through unscathed, unlike his ADC, Elliot, who was struck no fewer than fourteen times, several times about the head. It was just as well that Russian swords seemed to be as blunt as those wielded by the British. Scarlett himself had the benefit of a bodyguard, a huge Irishman called Shegog, in addition to which he was wearing an odd-looking brass helmet, which probably drew nothing but curiosity from the Russians. Elliot, on the other hand, went into action wearing the cocked hat of a staff officer. The trouble was that the chin strap was loose and, having no time to make repairs to it he simply stuffed a silk handkerchief into it to make it fit tighter. The cocked hat naturally drew the unwanted attention of the Russians, and when Elliot emerged dazed and blackened from the scrimmage he found it cut through in several places. Indeed, Elliot had suffered fourteen sabre wounds but the silk handkerchief had saved his life by absorbing the blows.

Ten minutes after the two sides had come together – some say it was eight – the fight was over. The bear-skinned hats of the Scots Greys, and the brass helmets of the dragoon guards had made a magnificent sight as they cut their way into the large Russian formation, slowly but steadily getting the better of Ryzhov's Russians until the latter, shaken and making no progress, turned and broke. They wheeled away their horses and made off in the direction of the Causeway Heights where they were pounded by the guns of Captain Brandling's 'C' Troop, Royal Horse Artillery. If they had any ideas of re-forming and charging again, the forty-nine shells thrown into them changed their minds and they made off along the Causeway Heights before halting at the eastern end of the North Valley. The repulse of the Russian cavalry by Campbell at Kadikoi had lasted barely five minutes. The charge of the Heavy Brigade had lasted slightly longer, perhaps ten minutes. It had, therefore, taken just fifteen minutes to create two of the greatest mythical achievements in the history of the British Army. A third was yet to come.

Casualties among Ryzhov's cavalry were put at forty to fifty killed and over 200 wounded. This equates to one man in six being a casualty, a high rate considering there had been twice as many Russians as British. Nearly all the officers of the four squadrons of the Ingermanland Hussars – Matveevsky, Svetchin, Marin and Aleshchenko – were wounded, as well as Lieutenants Khanzaev and Belyavsky. Captain Khitrovo, Lieutenant Stavitsky and Cornet Gorelov were also sabered. Khitrovo, in fact, was very badly wounded and was picked up after the battle by British troops and taken to one of their ships along with a lieutenant of the Kiev Hussar regiment, Obukhov. When Obuhov returned from captivity he said that Khitrovo died not more than three hours after he was brought to the ship.[20]

The British Heavy Brigade suffered ten killed and ninety-eight wounded. It had been a short but nevertheless important action. It was also, from the British point of view, a successful one. And yet it could have been far more so. Cardigan, it will be remembered, had been ordered by Lucan – apparently – to take advantage of any Russian disorder and charge at the most favourable opportunity. If ever one presented itself it was now. Ryzhov's cavalry had been flung back in some disorder by Scarlett and had been further shattered by British artillery fire. The Heavy Brigade was in no mood to follow up its success but the Light Brigade, itching to be let loose from its bandbox, certainly was. Why it never attacked remains a mystery. Cardigan himself later claimed that Lucan had given him implicit orders not to move on any account, something which Lucan naturally denied. In defence of the fiery Cardigan we have his own reaction to the successful action made by the Heavy Brigade. Sitting on his horse, 'Ronald', a frustrated Cardigan said simply, 'Those damned Heavies. They have the laugh of us this day.' Were these the words of a man who had failed to execute Lucan's orders to attack, or were they the words of a man angered by the shackles placed upon him by his superior?

The men of the Light Brigade certainly knew what was required. Indeed, Captain Morris, of the 17th Lancers, could not believe what was happening. His exchange with Lord Cardigan is well documented. He pressed his brigade commander so hard that he drew a strong rebuke upon himself. He even went so far as to request to be allowed to charge with just his own regiment, but this again was denied by a blustering Cardigan. 'No, no, sir, we must not stir from here.' And so a great opportunity to finish off what Scarlett had started was lost. Morris himself rode back to his regiment, desolated and in a state of some distress, knowing full well what a golden opportunity had been allowed to slip away. 'We all felt certain,' wrote Albert Mitchell of the 13th Light Dragoons, 'that if we had been sent in pursuit we should have cut up many of them.'[21] Interestingly enough, George Paget thought otherwise. Morris was undoubtedly justified in urging Cardigan to follow up and take advantage of Ryzhov's disorder. Mitchell, however, was writing with the benefit of hindsight. Paget, supporting Cardigan's decision not to move, said, 'clearly such a step [i.e. an attack by the Light Brigade] would have been unjustifiable, until the result of the combat [i.e. Scarlett's attack] was known, and certainly the probabilities were against the actual result; added to which, they [the Russians] were in expectation of, or rather on the watch for, an attack from another direction.'[22] Although Paget later added that, following subsequent information 'gained by conversations with some who were in the first line [Paget was in the second line], have tended to shake my confidence in my own opinion.' True, it is almost certain that Morris was correct in urging Cardigan to attack, but if officers like Paget were not so sure, who are we to cast doubts? Perhaps Paget summed it up best when he wrote, 'But all this is but an ex post facto argument, and as unanswerable as most of such arguments are and as easy of proof when the whole thing is over.'[23]

Lucan himself was livid, and demanded to know why Cardigan had not followed up Scarlett's success. Cardigan simply reminded Lucan of the orders he had been given by Lucan himself only minutes before, orders that, according to Cardigan, instructed him to remain where he was and not move. Well, the arguments raged and will, no doubt, continue over Cardigan's refusal to move. Even if Cardigan had been instructed not to move there were, of course, occasions when commanders simply had to use their initiative and discard orders if the opportunity to achieve something positive arose. But then we come back to Paget's comment on hindsight, which is, after all, a wonderful thing.

It was approaching 9.30 am, and so far Liprandi had enjoyed mixed fortunes. His attack on the redoubts had been a success and he now occupied Nos 1 to 3, having destroyed No.4. Possession of the redoubts also gave him control of the Vorontsov Road. His subsequent operations had not fared so well, however. Not only had Ryzhov's cavalry been repulsed by Campbell, but also by Scarlett. Nevertheless, it had been a relatively good morning for the Russians. Lucan, on the other hand, had been reduced somewhat to a toothless wonder. He had reacted well to the initial attack on Canrobert's Hill, but with no infantry support there was little more he could do but demonstrate and watch the redoubts fall. Thereafter, Raglan had interfered with his command of the cavalry by moving the Heavy Brigade forward, and although Scarlett's attack had been a success Lucan can hardly have claimed any credit for it. Finally, when he wanted the Light Brigade to act and follow up Scarlett's success he found Cardigan at his belligerent best. So we find him riding here and there, without exercising any real influence over the battle. His great chance was soon to come.

Scarlett, meanwhile, had returned to camp where he received the congratulations of Lord Raglan. Indeed, up on the Sapoune Ridge the Allied staffs were in jubilant mood having witnessed the short, but very well handled attack of the Heavy Brigade. There was much clapping and polite cheering, as if Scarlett had just completed a century at Lords. It had all gone very well. But one of Raglan's staff was not so enthusiastic. Louis Nolan was a 36 year-old captain in the 15th Hussars. He had seen extensive service in India and had very pointed views on, amongst other things, how the cavalry should be used in battle. Two years before the war he had written a book, *The Training of Cavalry Remount Horses*, which he followed the next year with *Cavalry: Its History and Tactics*. He was, therefore, someone, in the opinion of a man like Cardigan, who should be kept at arm's length. It is not surprising that, with such views on the cavalry he had been reduced to utter rage, not only by Cardigan's performance so far that morning at Balaklava but also by Raglan's refusal to use the cavalry at the Alma. Opportunities had been scorned by men whom he considered ignorant in the effective use of cavalry. Like Lucan, his chance to influence the battle would soon come. And how.

With Ryzhov's cavalry now drawn up across the eastern end of the North Valley, a quiet calm descended on the battlefield. So far that morning, Liprandi had achieved much with the capture of the redoubts, although he was somewhat disappointed not to have accomplished more with his cavalry. So, what was he to do next? The Allies had long since been roused from their slumbers and the surprises of the early morning were now at an end. He knew full well that Raglan would be despatching infantry into the valley and that, once there, he would be looking to his own defences. In the meantime he did nothing but wait and redeploy his forces.

Zhabokritsky's force, it will be remembered, consisted of 4,500 of infantry and cavalry, as well as fourteen guns. Earlier that morning they had occupied the Fedioukine Heights that bordered the northern side of North Valley. Liprandi, meanwhile, still had with him his main force, the troops under Gribbe, Semyakin, Levutsky and Skyuderi, who had taken the redoubts earlier on. These were still on and around the Causeway Heights. The link between Liprandi and Zhabokritsky was provided by the eight guns of 3 Don Cossack Battery, commanded by Colonel Prince A V Obolensky. The eight guns – some say there were as many as twelve – four 6-pounders and four 9-pounders, were served by 200 men who had drawn up their guns according to their manuals with a frontage of about 150 yards. The guns stared west, straight down North Valley, with Zhabokritsky's guns on their right, Liprandi's on their left and had Ryzhov's cavalry behind them. At the rear of the mass of cavalry there was a section of the Lazarev water pipe or aqueduct, which was built in 1853 to fill the dry docks of the Sevastopol Admiralty.

They also had a clear field of fire as far as the dog-leg that jutted out slightly from the Fedioukine Heights about half way along the valley. This prevented them from seeing the extreme western end of the valley where they knew the Allies to be. It is generally given that for every pound weight of shot a gun had a range of 100 yards, giving the 6-pounders a range of about 600 yards and the 9-pounders 900 yards. Added to this, however, was the yardage gained by ricochet, the solid iron balls being able to bounce along like deadly cricket balls, often hundreds of yards farther than the accepted range. Obolensky could, therefore, consider himself fairly safe on that dreary, late morning of 25 October 1854.

With no sign of any British activity Liprandi decided not to commit troops to any further attacks but instead began removing the British 12-pounder guns from the redoubts. They would make very nice trophies to present to Menshikov and, hopefully, the czar. He was now in a position to push home his advantage and with British and French infantry descending into the valley it was time to think about retiring. The work of removing the British guns from the redoubts had been in progress for some time when, just after 11 am, dust clouds could be seen rising from the western end of the North Valley. Liprandi then noticed the Odessa Regiment, still up on the Causeway Heights, shifting and drawing back a little. There was activity also on the Fedioukine Heights where Zhabokritsky's men were positioned. Then, as he gazed down the valley, Liprandi saw the incredible sight of lines of British cavalry galloping towards him. Obolensky and his men could hardly believe what they were seeing. In fact, very few of the Russians at Balaklava could believe it. For, moving along the North Valley in good order, there were indeed lines of British cavalry, apparently alone and unsupported, obviously making for 3 Don Cossack Battery at the end of the North Valley.

The British cavalry now charging up the North Valley was, of course, the Light Brigade under Lord Cardigan, sent on their ride to destruction by a series of misunderstandings and blunders emanating from Raglan himself. The sequence of events that led to the now-famous Charge of the Light Brigade is well known and it is not our intention to add to the hundreds and hundreds of pages which have tried – without success – to determine whose fault it all actually was. Suffice to say that, to use the words of the poet Tennyson, someone had indeed blundered.

Raglan, watching from the Sapoune Ridge with a growing sense of both impatience and anxiety, had felt the shadow of Wellington descend upon him once more. He knew all too well that Wellington had never lost a gun in the Peninsula, which was in itself a remarkable achievement considering the war lasted for six years. Indeed it had almost become a point of honour not to lose one's guns in battle. But here, at Balaklava, Raglan watched helpless while in the distance he saw the Russians beginning to carry off the guns from the redoubts. Feeling the weight of history upon him Raglan reacted by ordering Lucan to advance and prevent the Russians from carrying them off. It was as simple as that. Or so it seemed.

Lucan had already received one order from Raglan, at 9.30 am, ordering him to advance with the cavalry and 'take advantage of any opportunity to recover the Heights. They will be supported by infantry which have been ordered.' Lucan was mystified. There were no infantry. Did Raglan really expect him to advance unsupported against Russian infantry, cavalry and artillery? Raglan himself surely must have cast his mind back thirty-nine years to the day he lost his arm. On that occasion he had witnessed for himself the folly of sending cavalry unsupported against infantry, cavalry and artillery. He was now asking Lucan, who naturally refused to move, to do the same. Just before 11 am, and with Raglan growing ever more anxious at the lack of movement by his cavalry, he had Airey write out another order for Lucan. 'Lord Raglan wishes the cavalry to advance rapidly to the front – follow the enemy and try to prevent the enemy carrying away the guns. Troop Horse Artillery may accompany – French cavalry is on your left.' The order, to which the word 'immediate' had been added, was signed R Airey.

Raglan and his staff and the excitable cavalryman, Louis Nolan, had watched incredulous Lucan's inactivity which had prompted this latest order. The need for swift action was essential, and so Raglan called for Nolan to be given the job of delivering the order, knowing he would complete the task more quickly than anybody else on the staff. He was right, for Nolan, snatching up the order and leaping upon his horse, rode not via the Col but directly down the steep, broken side of the Sapoune Ridge. Nolan found Lucan sitting with his staff on the Causeway Heights between redoubts 4 and 5. The commander of the cavalry turned as Nolan reared up in front of him, his hand bearing the order stretched towards him. Lucan read the order carefully. He read it a second time. Nolan remembered that Raglan had called out after him, 'Tell Lord Lucan the cavalry is to attack immediately.' One can well imagine Nolan's thoughts, therefore, as the minutes ticked away with no action being taken to prevent the Russians carrying off the guns and with Lucan, whom Nolan detested, taking an eternity to fathom what, on the surface, was a simple and clear order. 'Lord Raglan's orders are that the cavalry are to attack immediately,' he said. This was all very well, but where in the order did it mention the word 'attack'? At length an exasperated Lucan looked at Nolan and said, 'Attack, sir! Attack what? What guns?' To which Nolan, in a thoroughly insubordinate manner, replied, 'There, my lord, is your enemy, there are your guns!' and as he did so he flung out his arm and pointed east to the head of the North Valley where 3 Don Cossack Battery sat waiting.[24]

Lucan read the order again in stunned silence. It made no sense to him and seemed to contravene all accepted laws of military practice. At best one wonders whether he should have sent Nolan back for clarification, but Nolan would only have clarified it himself on the spot no doubt. There was nothing for it but to carry it out. Nolan then left to join the 17th Lancers – Captain Morris, commanding, was an old friend – whilst Lucan trotted over to Lord Cardigan with the order. Cardigan was as stunned as Lucan had been. 'Certainly, sir;' was Cardigan's response to the order, 'but allow me to point out to you that the Russians have a battery in the valley in our front, and batteries and riflemen on each flank.' 'I know it,' replied Lucan,' but Lord Raglan will have it. We have no choice but to obey.' And he was right. Thus, the Light Brigade was committed to its date with destiny.

Lord Cardigan duly formed his brigade with the 13th Light Dragoons on the right of the first line, and the 17th Lancers on their left. In the second line, there were the 11th Hussars, and in the third line came the 4th Light Dragoons and on their left the 8th Hussars. Apart from this last regiment, which fielded just a squadron and a half, the other four regiments consisted of two squadrons each. Thus, the brigade, with a total strength of 664 officers and men, effectively equated to a slightly under-strength regiment. They did, however, have the support of the Heavy Brigade which Lucan himself led, riding out in front at quite a distance in order to maintain contact with the Light Brigade. Despite the rigours of the earlier combat with Ryzhov's cavalry the Heavy Brigade was still in good shape and formed up, uncomplaining, in order to support Cardigan. And so, at around 11 am, Cardigan and his men began to walk slowly forward down the valley, breaking into a trot soon afterwards.

By now there was quite a gathering up on the Sapoune Ridge, where an anxious Raglan had been joined by several other staff officers, both British and French. He knew full well that he was sending cavalry to do what in effect was infantry work. But he knew also there were sufficient numbers, and that his cavalry had already been buoyed by their earlier success over Ryzhov's cavalry in the South Valley. But as he watched, pensive, from his lofty position, he saw with shock that Cardigan, instead of moving to his right to attack the redoubts, was trotting straight up the North Valley and into a three-sided Russian trap. But it was too late to do anything.

At the eastern end of the North Valley the Russian gunners prepared for action, as did those on the Fedioukine Heights and on the Causeway Heights. The Light Brigade continued advancing, Cardigan out in front and his men keeping nice neat lines behind him. Suddenly, the guns on the Fedioukine Heights away to their left opened up and a shell exploded in front of the first line. Ironically, it struck down Nolan, who went to his death uttering a terrible, piercing scream which was heard and noted by dozens of survivors. The guns on the Fedioukine Heights were followed by those away to the right on the Causeway Heights, and when the Light Brigade came within range of Obolensky's guns they too opened up. Thus, the brigade was caught in a deadly arc of fire which soon began to rip great gaps in the British lines. By now, the Light Brigade was alone, for Lucan had suddenly realised what going on, and so ordered the Heavy Brigade to halt. He could do nothing to stop the Light Brigade but he could at least save the Heavies from disaster.

The Light Brigade continued 'into the mouth of hell', and seven minutes after they had moved forward they reached the Don Cossack Battery. Now it was their turn to hit back, and scores of Russian gunners were hacked down, sabred or lanced by Cardigan's battle-crazed men. But they also had another problem to contend with, for Ryzhov's cavalry sat waiting behind the guns, eager to finish off what the Don Cossack battery had begun. However, seeing the determination of the Light Brigade – and no doubt remembering the beating they had already received earlier that same morning – they turned tail and began to retreat towards the Chernaya river that ran at the exit of the valley. There was, in fact, a good deal of killing done here, particularly by the 4th Light Dragoons who rode a good way beyond the guns before they turned to look for home. In fact, once the Light Brigade had finished lingering at the guns they all began to think of the return ride back to their own lines, and once more the ordeal began.

The ride back up the valley was made slightly easier by a charge by the 4th Chasseurs d'Afrique, commanded by Major Abdelal, who swept up on to the Fedioukine Heights, completely overwhelming the Russian gunners there and silencing the guns. Thus, the Light Brigade was spared the fire from at least one direction. But they still had the problem of Russian cavalry to contend with, for General Eropkin's lancers had ridden down from the Causeway Heights to bar the way home. The ensuing fight produced scores of incidents as the British fought desperately to cut their way through. Eropkin himself had a narrow escape when he was attacked by a British officer and two troopers. Eropkin shot one of his assailants himself, the second was sabred by his orderly, a corporal of the Burgsky uhlan regiment, Denis Mukha, the third was stunned with two heavy blows in the face and temple by Eropkin.

Cardigan himself may well have been a bit of a text-book soldier but there was no doubting his bravery. He had led his men, unflinching, right to the mouths of the Russian guns. He was even assaulted by a pair of Cossack lancers who tried to capture him. One of them thrust a lance into Cardigan's thigh, slightly wounding him, but 'The Noble Yachtsman' refused even to draw his sword, considering it unworthy of a commanding officer to be seen brawling with private soldiers. After having led his men to the guns, and considering his work done, he turned and began the ride back to the British lines. One by one his men followed, many on horse and even more on foot, having lost their horses in the charge. In fact, it was the horses that suffered more than anyone. 497 horses were lost, against some 298 men, of whom 110 were killed, 130 wounded and fifty-eight taken prisoner.[25] The majority returned safe and sound, albeit somewhat dazed. Perhaps the true picture of the charge can best be summed up in the most recent book on the episode.

> When the prisoners [British] were released a year later the number of men who had lived to tell the tale was the astounding figure of 540 (allowing for about ten who died in captivity). Discounting those who died of wounds or as prisoners only 103, or fifteen per cent, were killed on the battlefield. Looked at another way, only one man in six of those who rode down the valley, and up it again, died while doing so. Not quite the picture so often painted.[26]

It's all a question of perspective. It is a shame that so many of the Russian officers who fought at Balaklava thought the British cavalry were drunk, and said so in their reports. Given the circumstances they could be forgiven for thinking so. After all, who but a madman would send his cavalry unsupported into a valley of death, with guns on three sides? But the British soldier needed no such liquid courage to guide him on his way. He never had, and it was only when real madmen got to work in the trenches of the Western Front some sixty years later, that they began looking for some sort of 'Dutch courage' to get them through their nightmare. Balaklava, however, was simply a case of the ordinary British soldier at his best. Indeed, even the Russians were amazed by their bravery. 'The true quality of the Light Cavalry,' wrote Lieutenant Kubitovitch,

> could really be appreciated during the retreat after their attack in full view of the enemy. We must give the English their due: they presented the height of perfection in this respect and were riding at a trot in order as if on manoeuvres. Some Uhlans fell upon a group of the retreating English and engaged them in hand-to-hand fighting. English Hussars and Light Dragoons cut their way through to their lines, having mixed it with the Russian cavalrymen. They were violently defending themselves against Uhlan lances, and even the dismounted and wounded would not surrender but were fighting to the end. The Russian infantry and artillery were firing, not differentiating between friend or foe.[27]

One other Russian officer, S Kozhukhov of 12 Artillery Brigade, paid tribute to the fighting qualities of the British cavalry. 'It is difficult,' he wrote,

> if not impossible, to do justice to the feat of these mad cavalry, for, having lost a quarter of their number and being apparently impervious to new dangers and further losses, they quickly re-formed their squadrons to return over the same ground littered with their dead and dying. With such desperate courage these valiant lunatics set off again, and not one of the living – even the wounded – surrendered.[28]

Remarkably, when Cardigan reached the safety of the British lines he was more consumed with anger at Nolan, who had ridden across his front during the initial stages of the charge, rather than at the loss of his brigade. We will never know why Nolan did so, and it is certainly something we are not about to hypothesise upon here. Cardigan's men, however, were not put off by their ordeal and in fact, in true British tradition, wanted to 'go again'. Cardigan wisely told them they had done enough already. The repercussions began almost immediately, with Raglan blaming first Cardigan then Lucan, who in turn stated he was just following orders. There is today in Britain an almost unhealthy obsession with the charge and whose fault it was. Despite the arguments put forward we suspect the blame can never really be laid at any one person's feet, and if one person alone was to blame, well, the jury is still out. One thing we can safely say for sure, and that is that the name of the guilty person ends in the letters 'an'.

The Charge of the Light Brigade may well be one of the most famous exploits in British military history but to the Russian people it means very little. It is of no great importance and barely rates a mention in Russian accounts of the war. Had it not been for the famous poem by Alfred, Lord Tennyson, one suspects the charge would certainly be less famous even in Britain. It was, after all, little more than a cavalry skirmish lasting no more than twenty minutes at most. Britain, however, has a seemingly insatiable appetite for military disaster, and loves its Dunkirks, Ishandlwanas, Sommes and Maiwands. The 'Charge of the Light Brigade' fits very nicely into this category; a glorious, bungled disaster.

Strategically, Balaklava was a Russian victory, albeit a partial one, for despite Ryzhov's setback against Scarlett's Heavy Brigade, Liprandi had taken the British redoubts, captured their artillery and had gained control of the Vorontsov Road. The loss of the outer ring of defences was a blow to the Allies, for it severely restricted their movements and confined them and tucked them up to a very narrow area between Balaklava and Sevastopol. The Russian Army was now able to move up and pose a far more serious threat to Allied operations. Indeed, they would grow increasingly bold, as the events of the next ten days were to demonstrate. For the Russians, Balaklava came as a huge morale lift. In both Sevastopol and in Menshikov's camp the Russians were in a state of great excitement with stories of how the 'English' cavalry forced its way through the rifle and canister fire, overthrew the Hussars and Cossacks and threw them back to the Chorgun ravine, after which they were rescued by the French and managed to dash away with great loss. Some of the Cossacks caught the horses of the 'crazy cavalry' and sold them for 15–20 roubles, and those who bought them resold those expensive thoroughbred trotters at once for 300–400 roubles.[29]

Amongst many Russian officers and men, eager to write home with the news of the Russian 'victory' at Balaklava was General Constantine Romanovitch Semyakin, who had led one of the detachments against the redoubts. In a letter to his wife written in camp at Kamara the day after the battle, he conveyed something of the feeling of joy at what he considered to be a Russian victory.

> Let us thank our God for the 26th [the letter actually referred to the 13th, this being the Russian date], a hard day of effort and danger and a glorious day for the Russian army and, especially, for the Azovsky Regiment. On the 26th it was decided to attack the enemy's line of fortifications, which defended the Balaklava roads, the base camp of the English. According to the plan, which I wrote myself, I was appointed to the middle column, consisting of two detachments. I carried out the attack with God's help. At 5.30 I started from Chorgun, went nearly 5 *versts* along the mountains and at 7.30 the banners of the Azovskys were raised on the main fortified hill [Canrobert's Hill] and the two nearest fortifications were cleared of the enemy. The captured equipment included eight heavy guns, all the soldiers' rifles, ammunition, clothes, much powder and a lot of English stuff. At this point the English took alarm and the real fighting started. First of all there was an infantry battle and at midday the cavalry battle, which I observed as if from the clouds [from the Causeway Heights]. I write this while sitting on an English cartridge box, while a powder one I use for my table. I spent a night under a Turkish tent on the grass without any straw, but all this passed away by God's mercy and I'm well. In memory of this day I send a Turkish watch which I bought from a corporal. Many Turks and English were killed by our Russian bayonets, and many English were pierced with lances of our Uhlans and Cossacks, and by the sabres of our Hussars. I lost one officer and forty-four other ranks killed and four officers, and 132 other ranks wounded. The main losses are in the Azovsky regiment: two officers and 149 soldiers. Krudener [the commander of the Azovsky regiment] is very brave! General Liprandi came galloping over and embraced and kissed me and declared that the St George Medal of the 3rd degree would be awarded to me. At midday His Serenity [Prince Menshikov] came. He gave me his hand and said: 'I congratulate you, – you'll make the Emperor happy and I'll send an eyewitness report of your efforts and deeds by a courier. [Baron Villebrant – Menshikov's aide-de-camp]'. God grant the heart of the Czar rejoices. I have no time to write any more, besides which the unceasing sound of the cannonade hampered me. All our efforts are directed to the defence of honour and duty. Farewell then. Pray.[30]

Czar Nicholas I was quick to lavish awards on those who had taken part in the Battle of Balaklava. Lieutenant Captain Baron Von-Villenbrandt, an aide-de-camp of Prince Menshikov, who brought the emperor the news of the Russian 'victory', was promoted to the rank of colonel, leapfrogging one rank, and aide-de-camp to the emperor. Pavel Liprandi, meanwhile, was awarded a golden sabre encrusted with diamonds and inscribed 'For Bravery'. His daughter Maria was appointed a Maid of Honour to the empress. General K R Semyakin received the Order of St George of the 3rd degree, which had been promised to him by Menshikov. General Gribbe and Major General Levutsky became the cavaliers of the Order of St Stanislav of the 1st degree, and Colonel Krudener was promoted to Major General. In fact, nearly all the officers received awards. The other ranks were not forgotten either. The military Order of St George (it was called the Georgy, Egory or Georgievsky Cross) was given to forty-eight soldiers and corporals of the Azovskys Regiment and thirty-six to the Dnieper Regiment, who became known as 'the Georgievsky cavaliers'.[32]

The Charge of the Heavy Brigade, the Thin Red Line, and, more famously, the Charge of the Light Brigade, had all ensured that 25 October 1854 was destined to become one of the most famous days in the long and very distinguished history of the British Army. This is all the more remarkable considering the actual fighting during these three episodes combined lasted no more than an hour. For Menshikov and the Russians it was to be a day that started well, promised much but ultimately ended in disappointment. It was also a day when the frailties of an already fragile Allied position were dangerously exposed. No more would they have the run of the plain of Balaklava. Now, they would have to conduct the siege of Sevastopol while continually looking over their right shoulders.

NOTES

1 Totleben E I *Opisanie oborony goroda Sevastopolya* (St Petersburg 1863–1872), 1, 235).
2 Kinglake, Alexander William, *The Invasion of the Crimea: Its Origin, and An Account of its Progress down to the Death of Lord Raglan* (London 1863), IV, 91.
3 Dubrovin N F *Istoriya Krymskoy voiny i oborony Sevastopolya* (St Petersburg 1900), II, 114.
4 Ibid, II, 121.
5 Koribut-Kubitovitch 'Vospominaniya o Balaklavskom dele 13 oktyabrya 1854 goda', *Voenniy sbornik*, 1859, No.5, 153.
6 Ibid, No.5, 153.
7 Ibid, No.5, 156.
8 Paget, Lord George, *The Light Cavalry Brigade in the Crimea* (London 1881), 161–2.
9 Bazancourt, the Baron de (trans. by Robert Howe Gould). *The Crimean Expedition, to the Capture of Sebastopol. Chronicles of the War in the East* (London 1856), II, 26–7.
10 Seaton, Albert, *The Crimean War: a Russian Chronicle* (London 1977), 143.
11 'Hero of the Only Victory', *Rodina*, 1995, No.3–4, 58.
12 Dubrovin, *Istoriya Krymskoy voiny*, II, 129–30.
13 Kinglake, *Invasion of the Crimea*, III, 110.
14 'Hero of the Only Victory', *Rodina*, 1995, No.3–4, 59.
15 Kinglake, *Invasion of the Crimea*, III, 124.
16 Ibid, III, 125.

17 It appears that both British Light and Heavy Brigades were armed with both 1821-pattern swords and the new 1853-pattern swords. See Brian Robson, *Swords of the British Army* (London, 1996) 30–2.
18 Arbuzov E 'Vospominaniya o kampanii na Krymskom poluostrove v 1854 i 1855 godah, *Voenniy sbornik*, April 1874, No.4, 400–1.
19 Ibid, 402. This was Pivenko's second award. He received his first during the Hungarian campaign. Pivenko was personally known by the czar who invited him to join his bodyguard at the palace in St Petersburg, an invitation which was declined by Pivenko who said that he was ready to serve his emperor anywhere but asked to be allowed to die as a Hussar. He died of typhus in spring of 1855 and was buried in the Petrovskoye cemetery in Simferopol.
20 Ibid. 403.
21 Mitchell, quoted in Adkin, *The Charge* (London 1996), 113.
22 Paget, *Light Cavalry*, 177.
23 Ibid, 177.
24 It is astonishing that, given the amount of literature on the Charge of the Light Brigade, and on the exchange between Lucan and Nolan, that some authors have still found it impossible to distinguish east from west. For example, Alan Palmer, in his *Banner of Battle* (129), Saul David, in *The Homicidal Earl* (298) and even Trevor Royle in *Crimea* (273) all have Nolan pointing westwards, that is, back towards Raglan. Now, there would have been a charge!
25 These numbers are based upon the figures given in Mark Adkin's book, *The Charge* (London 1996), 217.
26 Adkin, *The Charge*, 217.
27 Koribut-Kubitovitch 'Vospominaniya o Balaklavskom', *Voenniy sbornik*, 1859, No.5, 153.
28 Kozhukhov, quoted in Seaton, *The Crimean War*, 151.
29 Tarle E V *Krymskaya voina* (Moscow 1959), II, 165–6.
30 'Pis'ma K R Semyakin', *Sbornik rukopisey . . . o Sevastopol'skoy oborone* (St Petersburg 1876), III, 88–9.
31 Shavshin V.G. *Nad 'Dolinoy Smerti' (Balaklavskoe srazhenie)* (Simferopol 2002), 76–7.

# CHAPTER TEN
# *Inkerman Prelude*

Despite the limited success of Liprandi's attack at Balaklava on 25 October the Russians were encouraged to make further offensive operations, but this time they would not come from the interior but from the garrison of Sevastopol itself. Despite Menshikov's doubts as to a successful outcome to the war he had ordered Liprandi to attack on 25 October ostensibly to placate an increasingly frustrated Czar Nicholas who was naturally anxious that his armies be seen to be taking the offensive. Despite the partial success of the attack at Balaklava it was enough to give the people and garrison of Sevastopol a great lift. It also served to prompt Menshikov, still under pressure from the czar, into another attack. There was little point in directing his efforts against the main Allied siege lines. After all, any Russian force that sallied out in strength would march straight into the waiting arms of the Allies, whose front extended from the sea, inland as far as the Careenage Ravine. That is, unless they could identify a weak point in the Allied line, and to Menshikov that weak point seemed to be on the extreme right flank of the Allied line, on the Inkerman Heights overlooking the Chernaya river.

When the Allies took up their positions it was agreed that both British and French would occupy an equal share of the frontage, from the sea to the Careenage Ravine. The problem was, of course, that the British were vastly under strength as a result of both the action at Balaklava and through the effects of cholera that still dogged their camps. There were simply not enough troops to man the trenches adequately to the required depth. There were barely enough to maintain a covering force, the consequences of which had been seen on 25 October. Thus, the extreme right of the Allied line, on the Inkerman Heights, was weakly held. This, of course, was not only due to a lack of manpower but also to the fact that Raglan had no wish to expose his men to the fire of two Russian warships, *Vladimir* and *Chersonese*, moored in the Sevastopol Roads, that could bring their guns to bear on the position and sweep the ground. An indication of the weakness of the position is that the Russians were still able to feed into Sevastopol both troops and supplies and these entered via Sapper Road, the route from the interior that passed right beneath the Inkerman

Heights. The British were simply unable to sever the road. Part of the blame for this must be put down to the British staff and their refusal to use the 6,000 Turkish troops at their disposal. It was a great mistake.

The Inkerman position itself was marked by a series of ravines and gullies, it was covered in scrub and bushes, and there was no real open ground on which to deploy troops in any great number. It was difficult ground on which to fight. The Chersonese Plateau, on which the Allied siege lines were positioned, was lacerated by a series of five ravines that ran south and south-east from Sevastopol. This in itself caused great problems for the British in particular, as four of the ravines – the Picquet (often called the valley of the shadow of death) Vorontsov, Karabel and Careenage – ran through their sector, whilst the fifth, the Great Ravine, effectively provided a demarcation between the British and French lines. It was, however, the Careenage Ravine that would feature in the action of 26 October and in the Battle of Inkerman on 5 November. It ran south-east from Sevastopol, running out from Careenage Creek. To the east of it lay the Inkerman Heights and to the south-west Victoria Ridge. The ravine culminated in a ridge, known as Home Ridge, which ran in a sort of north-east south-west direction across the head of the ravine. Extending north-west from the eastern end of Home Ridge was yet another, called Fore Ridge. The main British position was sited upon these two ridges. About a mile to the north-west of Home Ridge lay Shell Hill, a distinctive height level with Home Ridge. Running up beneath Shell Hill, to the east, was Quarry Ravine, which came in from the north-east and carried the old Post Road. There were actually two Post Roads in 1854, the one running in the bed of the ravine being little more than a track, whilst the more recently constructed Post Road ran along the western slope of Quarry Ravine, looking down on its older namesake. The two joined at the head of Quarry Ravine where the British had constructed a low breastwork called The Barrier. Finally, there were two other prominent features of the Inkerman battlefield, the first being Inkerman Tusk, a spur which extended north on the eastern side of Quarry Ravine, and the second being the Kitspur, which was separated from Inkerman Tusk by yet another ravine, a minor but very steep one, called St Clements Ravine. Situated on the forward edge of the Kitspur was an abandoned gun position called the Sandbag Battery. Originally constructed for just two guns to fire on some Russian artillery across the Chernaya river it had been disarmed and abandoned. It would be the scene of some of the most savage fighting at Inkerman on 5 November. The battlefield was a remarkably small one, no more than two miles from east to west and the same distance north to south. Not only was it a small battlefield but the amount of ground suitable for effectively deploying troops was small also, owing to the very broken nature of the battlefield, the consequence being that large numbers of troops were necessarily bunched together, which in part accounted for the high casualties.

Situated on the reverse slope of Home Ridge was the camp of De Lacy Evans' 2nd Division. The camp of the Brigade of Guards lay a mile down the road to the south, whilst the camp of the Light Division lay just over half a mile to the west of the Guards' camp. The camps of the 3rd and 4th Divisions lay about three miles to the west. Therefore, the 2nd Division, in the case of emergency, would have to depend upon the Guards Brigade and the Light Division, as the remaining British divisions were occupied with the siege itself and the security of the open right flank. It was late October and already the problem of a lack of manpower was becoming all too apparent. It was this reason, apparently, that Evans cited as his excuse for not constructing any fieldworks on the position. The 2nd Division were not taking part in the actual siege operation itself but were to protect the right flank of the line. To secure their position it was important that field works should have been constructed, particularly given the amount of broken – and, to the Russians, advantageous – ground in front of them. Indeed, the ravines and gullies would provide wonderful cover for the attacking Russians. Good field works constructed in salient positions would have been of great advantage to Evans but apart from The Barrier, sited at the head of the Post Road, and a low stone wall constructed across the front of the 2nd Division's camp, none were. Instead, Evans simply entrusted the security of his position to the abilities of his piquets. It was a dangerous policy. Each of the piquets, in theory of company strength but rarely more than seventy men in each, worked in shifts twenty-four hours long. Their duty was, of course, to maintain a screen well in front of the Allied camps, but not so far out in front that they could be easily isolated and cut off. There was one field officer to each four piquets and it was his job to inspect them at regular intervals, making sure they were on the alert for anything unusual. In the Peninsula Wellington's piquets were rarely surprised and, indeed, the Light Division, for example, were so adept that in the summer of 1810 they held down an area of almost 400 square miles, yet never once was their chain of outposts pierced. In fact, it was said that the chain of outposts 'quivered at the merest touch'. But this only came with experience, and it was this kind of experience that was sadly lacking at this early stage of the Crimean War.

The Russians, meanwhile, were planning another attack. A reluctant Menshikov still remained unconvinced of the abilities of his troops, but he was under pressure from the czar to deliver a victory. Furthermore, the people of Sevastopol, buoyed by what they perceived as a victory at Balaklava, were in good spirits and demanded further success. This combination prompted Menshikov to launch, not so much an attack, but rather a reconnaissance in force or a strong sally against the thinly-held Allied position on the Inkerman Heights. The assault was designed, not only to reconnoitre the British position but also to distract the Allies' attention away from Liprandi and to further retard the siege operations. It was also a prelude for the Battle of Inkerman itself a week later. The attack on 26 October was to be made by around 4,500 men of the Buytrsky and Borodinsky Regiments, supported by artillery and led by the commanding officer of the Buytrsky, Colonel Dimitry Petrovich Federov. The bulk of the force was to leave Sevastopol via Sapper Road and begin crossing Careenage Ravine before making its way up on to the northern slopes of Shell Hill where they were to form up. In order to cover Federov's right flank a column of 700 sailors, acting as infantry, was detailed to make its way directly up the Careenage Ravine itself. Thus, just after midday on the warm and sunny afternoon of 26 October, some 5,000 Russian troops, supported by four light guns, began snaking their way up towards the British position on the Inkerman Heights.

Up on the Inkerman Heights themselves, the British piquets were enjoying the sun, listening to the sound of numerous bells that still tolled in Sevastopol, celebrating the Russian 'victory' of the previous day. Their arms were piled and some even lay on the ground, idling away the time. At around 1 pm the piquets of the 49th Regiment on Shell Hill, under Lieutenant John Connolly, were suddenly aware of a large number of troops beginning to appear in front of them. Initially, they thought they were British, after all, they wore the same sort of grey coat, and there were no signs of the tall, leather helmets habitually worn by Russian infantry. Instead they were wearing squat shaped flat hats, not dissimilar to those worn by the British. But when the mysterious troops opened fire Connolly and his men were soon left in no doubt as to their intentions. Once they had overcome their initial surprise the men of the 49th began returning the Russians' fire, with Connolly himself in the thick of the action, throwing aside his greatcoat and revealing his scarlet jacket in order that his men should recognise him. When the Borodinsky Regiment closed with his men Connolly waded into them brandishing his sword, and cutting down anyone within reach. And when his sword broke he took his telescope and set about his adversaries with it, knocking down more than a few of them. It was an action that won him a Victoria Cross. But a combination of a lack of ammunition and overwhelming Russian numbers began to force his men back. Fortunately, the four piquets away to the right of the British position, some 240 men of the 95th under Major Champion, came rushing up to support the 49th. They too became heavily engaged, with the normally pious and deeply religious Champion famously shouting, 'Slate 'em! Slate 'em, boys!' And slate them they certainly did. The problem was, they were actually doing the wrong thing by putting up such a strong resistance to Federov's attack.

The British piquets around Shell Hill were there specifically to keep watch and provide cover for the camp of the 2nd Division and for the Allies in general. At the first sign of Russian activity they were to buy time for the main force and allow them to get organised before they themselves withdrew. Connolly and Champion, in fact, by staying and slugging it out with the overwhelming Russian force coming up against them, were not acting as piquets should. Experienced troops knew exactly when to retire, but the men fighting at Inkerman on the afternoon of 26 October were not experienced. Instead, they fought with typical British spirit, unwilling to give an inch, but this was not what was required at the time. De Lacy Evans had long since been informed of the escalation of the fighting at Shell Hill and his men were ready to face Federov. It was, therefore, high time that Champion and Connolly withdrew. More important was the fact that Evans' eighteen 18-pounder guns on Home Ridge were unable to fire, as the British piquets fighting out in front effectively masked the Russians from their fire. Evans was furious, and when the 2nd Division's senior staff officer, Colonel Percy Herbert, rode to Evans to request re-inforcements the divisional commander famously replied, 'Not a man.'[1] Eventually Connolly was forced to give ground, but Champion and his men continued to stand fast until they were informed of the advance of a Russian column emerging behind their right rear, out of the Quarry Ravine. Threatened with being cut off from the main British position, therefore, Champion and his men scrambled at speed, over the scrub and back to The Barrier, where they formed up.[2] By now, the full Russian force had deployed on and in front of Shell Hill, and were coming on in force, in spite of the very best efforts of Champion and his men.

Meanwhile, away to the west the 700-strong column of sailors had been advancing along the Careenage Ravine. Unfortunately for them they had the misfortune to hit the sixty-strong detachment of handpicked sharp-shooters from the Brigade of Guards under Captain Gerald Goodlake, of the Coldstream Guards. This band of men had an unusual role, particularly for Guardsmen, for it fell to them to make as much of a nuisance of themselves as was possible, sniping at the Russian gunners, undertaking armed raids into the Russian lines, and providing extra cover for the British piquets. They operated largely in the area of the Careenage Ravine, and were there when the column of Russian sailors suddenly came along. Goodlake was not there, however, for along with one of his men, Sergeant Ashton, he was exploring some caves above the ravine when the Russians passed beneath them, effectively cutting them off from their comrades. They were quickly spotted and were forced to open fire. This worried Ashton somewhat and he reminded his captain of a recent foray into Russian lines during which they had captured a Russian officer and several men. 'They would kill us over that piquet job,' suggested Ashton.[3] Nevertheless, they couldn't remain where they were or they'd be taken. Goodlake decided they should make a run for it and after a brief scuffle with a handful of Russians both he and Ashton ran down the side of the ravine to join the advancing Russian column that, amazingly, failed to notice the two interlopers. This was almost certainly because they wore the same sort of greatcoats as the Russians, whilst their caps were similar also. The two British Guardsmen elbowed their way to the front of the column unnoticed, until they came to the junction of the Miriakov Glen and the Wellway, two smaller ravines that branched off to the east of the Careenage Ravine. Here, Goodlake's men had formed up behind a trench and no sooner had Goodlake come in sight of them than he shouted a warning to them before he and Ashton dashed out from the Russian column, turning and firing as they did so. It was a remarkable escape. Goodlake later received the Victoria Cross for his heroics. More important was the fact that Goodlake and his small band brought the column to a halt. The Russians might well have had numerical superiority but they were unable to make numbers tell in the narrow, cramped confines of the ravine, and when a number of men from the 2nd Rifle Brigade under Captain Markham appeared at the top of the western side of the ravine, the Russians were left with little choice but to retreat.

Back up at The Barrier, meanwhile, Champion's men were running low on ammunition. Fortunately, they had been joined by a company of the 41st and one from the 30th, and between them their steady volleys of Minié bullets began to stem the Russian tide. Evans himself had actually handled the situation well, refusing to allow hundreds of men to be drawn into what was essentially an action at the piquets, but instead waited for them to retire in order to allow his guns to finally open fire. As soon as the British guns opened up the Russians began to waver, the British round shot causing severe casualties amongst the densely packed Russian ranks. And when they tried to take cover in Quarry Ravine they came under fire from across the ravine from where the fire of the British troops was as accurate as it was deadly. Federov himself was badly wounded, and when his men saw him carried from the field they began to tumble backwards, at which the British piquets suddenly charged, driving the Russians completely from the Inkerman Heights. It was 2.45 pm.

'Little Inkerman', as the battle became known, was a successful action for the British, 'an hour of the most wholesome training that any good troops could well have',[4] which cost them just twelve men killed and seventy-two wounded. But although the Russians had been repulsed with losses estimated to have been around 270, it was they who almost certainly gained more from the day's fight. They now knew all they needed to know about the nature of the Inkerman position, its strengths and dangers, and of the British dispositions there. Although many Russian troops carried entrenching tools on 26 October it is extremely doubtful whether they actually intended remaining there. It was essentially an armed reconnaissance. The fight also lured the British into a false sense of security. The Russians had tried to attack the Inkerman position once and had been driven back. Why should they attack there a second time? The British were to find out exactly why just over a week later.

Meanwhile, the siege pressed on. All hopes of a swift and successful end had long since passed. 'Events have turned out so different from all the bright anticipations of the speedy fall of Sevastopol', wrote Burgoyne on 21 October. 'The ground round Sevastopol is prodigiously strong, and well adapted to defence. The defences of the enemy, as we found them, would by no means justify an assault at the moment, knowing that we had a battering train at hand.'[5] And yet, just thirteen days later he was criticising the French for their apparent lack of haste in the siege.

> It appears to me that the French are over-cautious, and too much bound by system and ordinary method for our pressing circumstances. They have their approaches within 300 or 400 yards of the front of attack, the front works of which are greatly ruined, the guns silenced, the parapet a heap of rubbish, no ditch or obstacle to it or the adjoining line, which has itself great openings in it; and yet they hesitate to storm, or rather take possession of it, while the enemy's interior line is distant.[6]

Perhaps Burgoyne would have been wise to be mindful of the vicious and bloody stormings he had witnessed in the Peninsula and the extremely high casualty rate amongst the British stormers that resulted from a lack of proper preparation. But Burgoyne was right in one respect. Time was now an issue. The majority of sieges pose time problems for the besiegers, usually as a result of having to take their objective before relieving troops could intervene. The problem for the Allies in front of Sevastopol, however, was of a different nature altogether. The Crimea at this stage of the year was notoriously prone to very bad weather, particularly up on the Chersonese plateau. Indeed, Raglan himself had been warned about this by one of his interpreters, Charles Cattley, the former British consul at Kerch, who, realising that the siege was likely to take some time, was very apprehensive about remaining on the Chersonese. 'Does Lord Raglan know what a winter here is likely to be?' he asked.

> The army would have to encounter bleak winds, heavy rains, sleet, snow, bitter cold. But cold like the cold in England is not the worst of what may come. Once in some few years it happens that there comes a fortnight or so of Russian cold. When I speak of 'Russian cold', I mean cold of such a degree that if a man touches metal with an uncovered hand the skin adheres. I am not a strong man, and I feel certain that a winter here under canvas would kill me.[7]

The Chersonese plateau would indeed prove a most unpleasant and uncomfortable place to be during the coming winter, and would kill off stronger men than Cattley.

But it was not just the need to avoid spending the winter on the exposed Chersonese that was reason enough for certain British officers to be advocating a swift assault on Sevastopol. It was also because they genuinely believed an assault in strength on the correct part of the defences would succeed. Cathcart himself was one advocate of such a course of action. His argument was based not only on the fact that he believed the Russian defences to be in a poor state but also that for every day that passed without an assault, the defences grew stronger. We will never know what might have happened if Cathcart had been allowed to attack Sevastopol on 28 September, but it is almost certain that he would have failed in November. Indeed, when he himself wrote of his plans to Burgoyne on 2 November, he began by admitting that, 'I know little about the scientific part of the business', basing his arguments purely on what he had seen with his own eyes over the previous five weeks.[8] Sadly, Cathcart would not live to see any Allied troops inside Sevastopol.

The British success of 26 October at Inkerman had perhaps lured them into a false sense of security. Federov's armed reconnaissance had, on the surface, resulted in failure, but the lessons of the day were evidently absorbed better by the Russians than by the British. The Russian attack had certainly succeeded in identifying a weak point in the British position, something which should have been corrected by the construction of simple earthwork fortifications here and there on the heights. Even rudimentary works can often prove vital in retarding or even repulsing an enemy attack, but there were simply not enough men to build them. Already the strain of conducting the siege of Sevastopol, whilst at the same time providing cover for the operation, was proving a drain on Allied – and particularly British – resources. Thus, not a spadeful of earth was turned and, save for certain improvements made to the Barrier and to the work around the 2nd Division camp, the important Inkerman position remained the same as it had been on 26 October.

Having thwarted the Russians at Inkerman once the British had little reason to think the enemy would try again, but try they did. In fact, Menshikov ordered an attack to be made just over one week later. The problem was that, despite the lessons learned and information gained by the Russians on 26 October, Menshikov threw away his advantage by deciding to employ troops that had yet to arrive in the theatre of war. General P A Dannenberg's 10 and 11 Divisions, part of the Russian 4 Corps, had been marching hard from Bessarabia to reach Sevastopol and only arrived on 3 and 4 November. They were, naturally enough, in some need of rest. They were also completely unfamiliar with the ground over which they were being asked to attack. Nevertheless, Menshikov was determined to press on with his attack, conscious once more of the pressure being put upon him by the czar. He was also aware that French reinforcements were on their way to the Crimea. With 10 and 11 Divisions arriving before them, however, Menshikov would have numerical superiority for a while at least, and he intended to make it count.

Menshikov originally intended to attack on 4 November but such was the superstitious nature of Dannenberg's men that they asked for the attack to be postponed on the grounds that 4 November was the first anniversary of the Russian defeat at Oltenitsa. Menshikov duly postponed the attack and re-scheduled it for the early morning of 5 November. The Russian plan involved Soimonov's 10 Division, along with 16 Division and the Buytrsky Regiment, under Zhabokritsky, the latter being detached from 17 Division. Soimonov's force, which had actually entered Sevastopol via Sapper Road, numbered around 19,000 men with thirty-eight guns. Soimonov was ordered to begin his attack at 6 am, advancing up and to the east of Careenage Ravine. Lieutenant General P Pavlov, meanwhile, was to take command of 11 Division and a brigade of 17 Division, some 16,000 men in all, along with ninety-six guns. Pavlov was to take his corps and, after repairing the Inkerman bridge at 6 am, would join Soimonov. Dannenberg himself would ride with Pavlov and would assume command of the two columns once they had joined together. While Dannenberg was attacking at Inkerman himself, Prince P D Gorchakov was to make a demonstration from the east, moving against the Sapoune Ridge from the Balaklava plain. This, hopefully, would occupy the attention of Bosquet's French, who might otherwise move north to support their Allies at Inkerman. Gorchakov's force was essentially the Chorgun force, and consisted of 22,000 men and eighty-eight guns, being Liprandi and his 12 Division, along with fifty-two squadrons of cavalry and ten Cossack squadrons. Finally, a further demonstration was to be made by the garrison commander, Lieutenant General F F Moller, who was to sally out and cover the right of the main attack and prevent any interference from the Allied left.

On the face of it, Menshikov's attack, to be made by some 60,000 men and 234 guns, appeared to be based upon a sound plan. Menshikov, however, could never be accused of being tactically astute. Indeed, his plan was already beset by doubt, confusion and internal dispute. First there was the decision to postpone the attack one day because of the Oltenitsa anniversary; there was confusion, with Dannenberg, who it will be remembered, had only just arrived in the area and had little knowledge of the ground, not receiving his orders until the afternoon prior to the attack. Furthermore, Menshikov's order of battle resulted in many units fighting under commanders whom they regarded as complete strangers. Finally, there was the strange situation of Dannenberg, who had barely received his own orders from Menshikov, re-writing them and setting off real confusion within the Russian camp.

Soimonov, for example, had originally been ordered by Menshikov to proceed up the Careenage Ravine, before attacking the British.

Dannenberg, however, altered the order to the effect that three regiments of Soimonov's command, the Kolyvansky and Tomsky, with the Ekaterinburgsky in reserve, should instead cross the Careenage Ravine and continue on to Inkerman bridge, with the remaining units of Soimonov's command following suit soon afterwards. Pavlov, meanwhile, instead of repairing the bridge and proceeding to join Soimonov, was now ordered to pass over the bridge and move along Sapper Road before turning to his left, attacking with Soimonov's units on either side of him. It was all rather confusing, particularly as Dannenberg's orders contained no timings. In the event, the new orders were largely ignored. Certainly, Soimonov stuck to the original plan as given to him by Menshikov. Things, therefore, did not bode well for the coming Russian attack. Nevertheless, the men began to move forward into their positions prior to the attack. Thirty-year-old Pyotr Alabin served as part of the Sevastopol garrison with a rank of staff-captain and held the post of chief aide-de-camp of the staff of 11 Division. On 4 November he was riding with Pavlov's column, and later recalled the advance towards Inkerman. His account perhaps illustrates some of the confusion surrounding the Russian advance.

> Yesterday [3 November] it was a typical autumnal day. The rain clouds rushed around the sky and a heavy and piercing wind made us wrap ourselves in our warm greatcoats. We waited impatiently for dawn. The rumours flew everywhere. The majority were saying that we would march to Sevastopol and from there would attack the French breaching battery, which they were erecting in front of our 4th bastion. They said it was very important to destroy it before it was built, because the southern part of Sevastopol would not be able withstand its fire.
>
> Dawn came. Without any noise we stood to arms and moved one after the other down the valley of the river Chernaya. The wind became stronger and when we began to climb up the Mackenzie Height we could hardly keep in our saddles. Cossack artillery was gliding past us and added to the dimly-lit picture of our advance. All those soldiers and Cossacks, moving in the moonlight, seemed to us to be the shadows of our friends who had perished exactly one year ago in the Oltenitsa battle and whose blood was not yet avenged.
>
> We had hardly reached our position when it started to drizzle. There were no tents and the fires went out. The second issue of rum warmed me but not for long. Everything was wet; the ground, my clothes, and even my leather coat – what could I do, where could I go? In the morning I saw with delight a view of Sevastopol and the choppy sea, the mountains to the left and the sea shore to the right. What a strange coincidence: we planned to attack today but

remembered that it was the anniversary of the Oltenitsa battle and postponed the attack because the men saw this as an evil omen. The battle was put off till tomorrow.

During a reconnaissance I heard some unusual cries in Iakutsky regiment, which waited near our headquarters near a road. Was it possible that the enemy had used the fog and had attacked us in a weak moment? If so, it would be a disaster; there were no commanders – we would be killed. I rushed towards the cries with my sabre, but there were only crowds of our soldiers throwing their hats in the air. The 'hurrahs' became louder. A carriage stood among the excited crowd. There were the Grand Dukes! 'We will fight, lads,' they said. 'Aye-aye, Your Highness!' came the reply. 'We are ready to die!' the others cried, throwing up their hats. 'Czar Emperor ordered us to bow low to you, lads.' 'Hurrah! Hurrah!' and the soldiers ran alongside the carriage of the Grand Dukes regardless of the mud and spray.

Death to the enemy or death to us! Tomorrow it will be a decisive battle. The reconnaissance was finished successfully. Ironically, the day after the Inkerman battle a special map of the place, on which the battle took place, was sent from headquarters. It is incredible! The battle began with us not having a plan of the place, because General Dannenberg declared that he didn't need any plans for he knew the area like his own pockets. There were plans of the area surrounding Sevastopol but they were left in Odessa. There was also a really detailed map with the General Staff but the Minister of War dared not give it to us without permission. Menshikov had no time to ask for such permission for he was in a hurry to give battle in order to prevent an assault on Sevastopol.

The great distance to the battlefield, the foggy and drizzly weather, the great number of troops – all these were reasons why the regimental commanders lacked information even after the reconnaissance. The only thing left for it tomorrow was to act according to each person's circumstances.

It grew dark. Our friend Kleingauz brought us an order for the morrow's battle . . . Two hours later we received the order from General Dannenberg. We also devised our own plan, not having in our mind Dannenberg's. There was one more plan, worked out by General Soimonov . . . Two or three hours after receiving General Dannenberg's first order we received his second, to be at the Inkerman bridge by 5 o'clock in the morning and advance not in the order indicated in his first order.[9]

Soon after midnight Soimonov's men began to muster close to No.2 bastion in Sevastopol. Menshikov's orders bade them begin their march at

4 am but, with final preparations for the advance having been made Soimonov began his march at 2 am, his columns led by Lieutenant Colonel Zalesky and Captains Iakovlev and Andreianov. Half an hour later Pavlov too began to move, marching down towards the Chernaya river and the Inkerman bridge. Pyotr Alabin was with them:

> It was a dark night. Although the rain had stopped, there was much sticky mud, which would make it difficult for us to climb the mountain. There was another strange omen. Before the Oltenitsa battle it was also raining, and the soaked earth made it difficult for us to move. But the time past and soon the regiment began to move. We saddled the horses. We boiled a samovar and drank some tea. Who knows, it may have been for the last time! The regiments drew up. Our horses danced impatiently. It was time for me to shut my diary.[10]

Meanwhile, up on the Inkerman Heights the British piquets were enduring a thoroughly unpleasant and wet night. The task of mounting a piquet was never a job that the British soldier could muster much enthusiasm for. The ever-present danger of enemy attack and the lack of sleep made it an uncomfortable and tense time, something made worse on the early morning of 5 November by the steady drizzle that gave them all a good, gradual soaking. Nevertheless, the piquets were not completely unprepared for what was about to hit them. Indeed, Brigadier General Pennefather had already suspected something was afoot. Pennefather was in temporary command of the 2nd Division, as De Lacy Evans was still recovering from a serious fall from his horse, and one can well imagine how serious this might have been for a man of 67. Pennefather, a good, solid soldier, was touring the piquets on 4 November when he saw across the Chernaya river a very smart-looking carriage and an assemblage of Russian troops. He did not know it, of course, but the carriage actually carried the two Russian princes, and was the same carriage described by Alabin. This, together with the sight of flocks of sheep being gathered and various troop movements, convinced Pennefather that something was brewing, probably an attack. He therefore sent Lieutenant Carmichael forward to reconnoitre the front edge of the British position and report any unusual activity. The piquets were almost certainly spoken to and told to be on the alert. Pennefather then returned with his staff to the 2nd Division camp.

General Pavlov, meanwhile, prepared to move forward. His men greeted him with cheers, 'a sure sign that they had woken from the drowsy state in which they had been up until now'.[11] Soon after this, however, an aide from General Dannenberg arrived with an order for Pavlov reminding him of the need for silence lest his men be heard by the Allies. The regiments then stood to in silence in their positions, in columns. The Okhotsky regiment was at the head of the column. Its commander, Colonel Bibikov, 'sat on the edge of a ditch, complaining of the disturbance to his natural habits caused by the early morning start, although he was feeling even sorrier for the poor Englishmen who were about to be woken by our bayonets'.[12] Pavlov was ready to move but could not do so until he knew for certain that the construction of the bridge over the Chernaya was finished. Alabin was summoned by one of his staff to go and find out whether the work had been completed.

> The corps commander told General Pavlov that we had to send a man to the bridge to see what was happening there. The general called me. The corps commander ordered me personally to go to the bridge to see if it was ready and to examine the position of the Okhotsks. Pavlov gave me two Cossacks to show me the way. While we were riding I was afraid the enemy sentries would hear the clatter of our horses' hooves. It was very dark and I could only make out the gloomy surface of the harbour, which was to the right of me. But soon I heard some vague sounds, a real hue-and-cry. I was extremely surprised when I approached a crowd of men who were building the bridge as they made much noise at the very bottom of the heights occupied by the enemy. The prisoners and sailors were working together on the bridge reconstruction. Nobody noticed me. Where is your officer? I asked. But nobody answered me; they continued to work, to swear or to laugh with their comrades or to shout droningly in the usual way of workers when they are working together. At last I found an officer, Lieutenant Tveritinov. I made my way to him. 'Are you building the bridge?' I asked. 'Yes,' he replied. 'The commander of the detachment sent me to know if it is ready.' 'No, it is not,' he told me. I told him to let me know when he thought it would be finished. 'I don't know,' was the reply. 'It will be ready when we finish our work.' This was not helpful. 'So, is this what I have to report?' I asked. 'Yes, it is. You see, we are not sleeping, we are working.' I asked him to give me a boat in order to cross the river and to examine the situation of the Okhotsks. They were all okay. On our way back I ran up against our front line sentries but did not know the reply to the password. Fortunately, the sentry did not fire. Half an hour later I was sent to the bridge again. Dawn was very near. The bridge was still not ready but the officer promised that it would be done in about half an hour. When I reported this to the corps commander he decided not to wait any more but to advance.[13]

And so Pavlov's men lurched into motion, making their way down to the bridge over the Chernaya, whilst away to the west Soimonov's column was heading out of Sevastopol in the direction of the Careenage Ravine.

The events of 26 October had demonstrated that while the British had succeeded in throwing back Federov's attack, the fight had, nevertheless, exposed their lack of experience. But would they learn from it or had their success merely cast the shadow of complacency over them? They were soon to find out, for even as they continued their drowsy, uncomfortable watch some 35,000 Russian troops were slowly but steadily making their way through the darkness and drizzle, up the northern side of the Inkerman position. One of the bloodiest and most savage battles ever fought by the British Army was about to begin.

NOTES

1 Kinglake, Alexander William. *The Invasion of the Crimea: Its Origin, and An Account of its Progress down to the Death of Lord Raglan* (London 1863), IV, 9.
2 This hasty retirement later gave rise to the story, at least according to Totleben, that Champion had been driven back helter-skelter by the Russians, rather than was the case, that is, that they withdrew out of necessity.
3 Kinglake, *Invasion of the Crimea*, IV, 11.
4 Ibid, IV, 18.
5 Wrottesley, The Hon. George (Ed). *Life and Correspondence of Field Marshal Sir John Burgoyne* (London 1873), II, 111–12.
6 Ibid, II, 114.
7 Kinglake, *Invasion of the Crimea*, IV, 5. Cattley survived the winter but died, ironically, during the summer the following year. For more of Cattley's services and, indeed, British intelligence in the Crimea see Stephen Harris's, *British Military Intelligence in the Crimean War, 1854–1856* (London 1999).
8 Wrottesley, *Burgoyne*, II, 115.
9 Alabin P V *Chetyre voiny. Pohodnye zapiski v 1849, 1853, 1854–1856 i 1877–78 godah* (Moscow 1892), 91.
10 Ibid, 91.
11 Ibid, 92.
12 Ibid, 93.
13 Ibid, 94–5.

# CHAPTER ELEVEN
# *'Remember, remember . . .'*

They say the hour before dawn is the time when a man's spirits are at their lowest ebb. Possibly with this in mind, it was at this exact time that the British piquets were changed on the Inkerman Heights. Sunday 5 November began much like any other day for the British piquets. Or maybe it was worse than usual, for the weather had begun to deteriorate as autumn gave way to the early signs of winter. The rain fell in a steady drizzle, making an already dark and misty morning even gloomier. Piquet and patrol work was an important task in any army, but it was also the unglamorous side of soldiering, particularly the night watch when nerves were wound tight, or when staying awake could prove difficult. And here at Inkerman the British piquets were indeed weary. They were also very damp, not through any torrential downpour but through a steady drizzle that gradually seeped into the men's greatcoats, leaving them cold and uncomfortable, and looking forward to coming off duty at daylight for a well earned cup of hot chocolate. The incoming piquet would arrive an hour before dawn but the outgoing piquets would not march off immediately but would remain in their positions until daylight, whereupon they would return to their camp.[1] The phased changeover of piquets was important, as it allowed the incoming piquet to know the state of affairs in their front; were there any listening posts out front? Were there any passwords and what were they? Had anything unusual occurred? There were all manner of things to be passed on. Also, the phased changeover allowed the incoming piquets to get their 'night sight'. In camp they would have been accustomed to a degree of light, thrown out from pipes, fires, lanterns, etc. Out on the piquet line, however, it was completely black and it would take time for the incoming men's eyesight to become adjusted. Overall, it was just common sense for the incoming and outgoing piquets to remain with each other for a while in order to ensure a smooth and effective changeover. After all, it was sheer folly to change over immediately between one piquet and another without the new piquet being informed of the situation.[2]

But by the first week in November arrangements in the British lines had already become somewhat sloppy. The pressure on the men had increased, largely as a result of the need to maintain a strong presence in the siege lines, to undertake the siege itself, and yet still maintain an effective covering force. But things were slightly different on 5 November. The situation was made worse by the weather, which left the piquets in no mood to hang around any longer than they had to. 'Sound tactical practices were beginning to be ignored and corners were starting to be cut.'[3] Although there is no evidence of it, it may be that the Russian attack was timed to coincide with the changeover of the British piquets. After all, as surely as the British had been watching the Russians it is almost certainly the case that they had, in turn, been watching us. The British had been in their positions for some weeks now, and it is impossible to believe that the Russians had not made careful observations of British operational movements.

Several incidents had occurred during the late afternoon of 4 November, and throughout the same night and during the early morning of 5 November which, although unimportant individually, together indicated that something was stirring in the Russian lines. The rumbling of guns and wheeled vehicles was heard down in the valley below, there had already been the sight of the smart-looking carriage, whilst flocks of sheep had been seen being herded forward, the traditional sign that an army was on the march. There was even the pealing of church bells in Sevastopol, heard by the piquets as early as 4 am. It all gave cause for concern amongst the British piquets. The tension was heightened further when Captain Sargent, of the 95th, aware that something might well be afoot, ordered his men to load their rifles, not an easy task given the rain that was falling at the time. Such an order only served to put the piquets further on edge. Indeed, Private Simmonds, of the 95th, was so nervous that he accidentally shot himself through the hand, an action that brought others rapidly standing to. But nothing worried the British more than the thick, swirling fog that began to descend during the night.

At about one hour before dawn the crunching of boots coming up from the rear duly indicated that the new piquets were coming on duty. Those on the right of the British position were made up of the 55th Regiment, under Lieutenant Colonel Carpenter, whilst those on the left consisted of men from the 41st, 47th and 49th Regiments, under Lieutenant Colonel Haly. It had been such a miserable night that, instead of remaining on the ground until daylight with the incoming piquets and ensuring a phased changeover, the outgoing piquets marched off in small groups almost straight away, and returned to camp for some hot food and drink, although they were not to be allowed much time to enjoy it. The new piquets were left to themselves, gazing out into the wet, foggy darkness, unaware of what was heading towards them.

Normally, dawn was indicated by streaks of grey light away to the east, but not on this morning. The fog swirled round and hung low over the

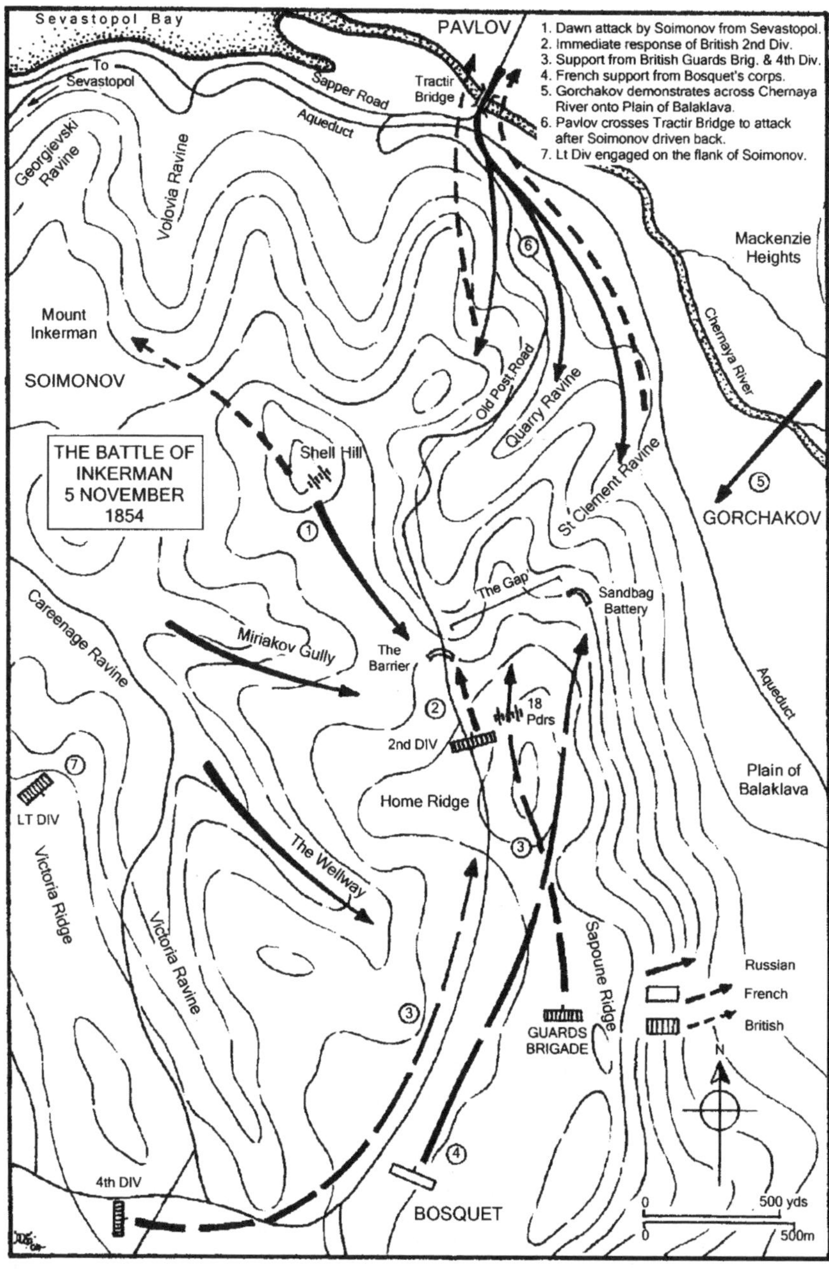
Sevastopol Bay
PAVLOV
1. Dawn attack by Soimonov from Sevastopol.
2. Immediate response of British 2nd Div.
3. Support from British Guards Brig. & 4th Div.
4. French support from Bosquet's corps.
5. Gorchakov demonstrates across Chernaya River onto Plain of Balaklava.
6. Pavlov crosses Tractir Bridge to attack after Soimonov driven back.
7. Lt Div engaged on the flank of Soimonov.
To Sevastopol
Sapper Road
Tractir Bridge
Aqueduct
Georgievski Ravine
Volovia Ravine
Mackenzie Heights
Chernaya River
Mount Inkerman
SOIMONOV
Old Post Road
Quarry Ravine
THE BATTLE OF INKERMAN 5 NOVEMBER 1854
Shell Hill
St Clement Ravine
GORCHAKOV
The Gap
Sandbag Battery
Careenage Ravine
Miriakov Gully
The Barrier
18 Pdrs
2nd DIV
Aqueduct
Plain of Balaklava
LT DIV
Home Ridge
Victoria Ridge
The Wellway
Victoria Ravine
Sapoune Ridge
Russian
French
British
GUARDS BRIGADE
N
4th DIV
BOSQUET
500 yds
500m

scrubby, broken ground in front of the British camps, making it difficult to see very far, even after the light had improved. Nevertheless, Captain Hugh Rowlands, of the 41st, had diligently gone about his duty, placing piquets 150 yards down the northern slope of Shell Hill (Rowlands himself called it Cossack Hill, the name used by the 2nd Division). He had barely returned to the rest of the company, who had piled arms and begun to take off their packs, when a brisk firing was heard coming from the sentries. Rowlands immediately hurried back to discover that a sharp-eyed sentry of the 41st, standing in advance of Shell Hill, had picked up a movement in front of him which he thought was a Russian column. The firing continued until Rowlands arrived, the officer peering down the northern slopes of the hill. Fortunately, the mist cleared long enough for him to be able to see a good distance, and there, sure enough, coming slowly up the hill towards him were 'very truly, thousands of Russians'.[4]

Realising that it was obviously no sortie Rowlands gave the order to retire 200 yards, whereupon he had his men lie down to wait for the oncoming Russians. He was joined shortly afterwards by the 41st's light company, and together they waited for the Russian columns to crest the hill in front of them. The leading Russian troops were from the 6th Rifle Battalion, with no fewer than eight battalions of the Tomsky and Kolyvansky Regiments following behind them. These in turn were supported by four battalions of the Ekaterinburgsky Regiment. Immediately they came into view Rowland's men opened up with their Minié rifles, inflicting heavy casualties on the Russians now coming down from Shell Hill in their densely packed columns. Initially, many of the men's rifles refused to fire, being wet through, but soon they were in action, warming to their task and sending bullets whizzing into the Russian columns. It was impossible for Rowlands to hold back this surging mass, however, and after a short while he gave the order to retire towards Home Ridge.

The British reaction to the Russian attack was swift. It was also very different to 26 October. On that occasion, it will be remembered, Lacy Evans had refused to reinforce the piquets, but waited until they had retreated whereupon he was able to bring his guns to bear on the Russians. Evans, however, was still recovering from his fall and command of the 2nd Division rested with Brigadier General John Pennefather, 'Old Blood and 'Ounds' as his men liked to call him. Pennefather, the hard-swearing, hard-fighting soldier, decided upon totally different tactics from Evans, and determined to fight it out with the Russians out in front. After all, with little or no ground behind Home Ridge upon which to form his men, it was dangerous to simply fall back to the ridge and try to thwart the Russians there. Once over The Barrier and across Home Ridge the Russians would almost certainly have had a clear run into the depths of the British positions. The consequences for the Allies would have been dire. The decision to throw every man forward from the 2nd Division's camp also deprived the Russian guns of lucrative firing into the British rear, where they fully expected Pennefather's reserves to be drawn up. But with almost every man out in front on Home Ridge, there were no such rich pickings to be had.

Even as Rowlands and his men were falling back, Pennefather was starting to feed in units to bolster the main firing line. First of all, the 30th Regiment was divided into two wings, one, under Lieutenant Colonel Mauleverer, being sent to reinforce The Barrier, and the other, under Major Patullo, being sent to support Haly's piquets. Then, the remainder of the 41st, under General Adams, the brigade commander, were sent to the right side of Home Ridge, along with the one wing of the 49th under Captain Bellairs. The other wing of the 49th, under Major Dalton, along with a wing of the 47th under Major Fordyce, was sent to the left to defend the head of the Mikriakov Glen. This left the 95th as Pennefather's only reserve, although they were not to remain so for very long. With the rest of the 2nd Division's regiments having been flung forward it just remained for the 95th to go forward likewise, with one wing, under the god-fearing Major Champion, taking off towards the Sandbag Battery, and the other, under Major Hume, heading off to reinforce The Barrier. Thus, when all troops had been despatched to their positions Pennefather was left with just a few companies of the 47th and 55th Regiments, probably no more than 500 men. It was essentially Pennefather's only reserve.

Meanwhile, Haly's piquets, including Hugh Rowlands and his men, were retiring towards Home Ridge, but on their way back they met Major Patullo, who was doubling forward with four companies of the 30th Regiment. Some of the 55th were with them also. This combined force was still massively outnumbered by the Russian troops now pouring up to and over Shell Hill, but it did not stop them turning and charging with their bayonets, a charge which initially drove the Russians back about 500 yards after which another Russian column, coming up from below, forced them to turn and retreat. During the fight Haly was dragged from his horse and wounded by a bayonet thrust. He lay there for a few moments, surrounded by Russians, until Rowlands himself, along with Privates Kelly and McDermond, dashed in to rescue him, dragging him away to safety. Both Rowlands and McDermond were later awarded the Victoria Cross for their action. Kelly, sadly, paid for his efforts with his life.

Having swept back the British piquets from Shell Hill, Soimonov was now poised to strike at the very centre of the British position itself. There was still some confusion in the British camps as units hurried here and there in the misty conditions, following their officers and rushing to their posts. Soimonov, on the other hand, was in full control of his men who knew what was expected of them. But despite this, he was still prevented from launching an all-out attack as there was still no sign of Pavlov's columns which, unknown to him, had become delayed at the Inkerman bridge. In the meantime, he detached a column of the Ekaterinburgsky to test the left flank of Pennefather's position. Whether by accident or by intention, the column veered far to its right and crossed the head of the Mikriakov Glen where Major Dalton's wing of the 49th had been positioned, along with Fordyce and his wing of the 47th. By now, the men of the 49th were commanded by Major Thornton Grant, Dalton having been mortally wounded early on in the fight. Grant was apparently sitting unconcerned upon his horse when suddenly the Russian column came surging through the mist in front of him. Without so much as a hint of panic or alarm, Grant turned to his men and nonchalantly uttered the immortal words 'Give them a volley and charge!'[5] His men duly obeyed, and after unloading a volley of lead into the Russian apparition they charged their bayonets and, with a cheer, drove the Russians back beyond their own gun line on Shell Hill. It was a fine achievement. It was also one that convinced Soimonov of the folly of waiting for Pavlov any longer. Rather than wait for him to arrive he would attack with his own columns.

Lord Raglan, meanwhile, had been informed of the situation early on by Captain Ewart, one of his staff officers. Quick to grasp the situation, Raglan sent orders to Sir Richard England, asking him to watch out for the British left, whilst ordering Cathcart and the Duke of Cambridge to march in support of Pennefather. He also ordered two 18-pounder guns to be brought forward from the siege lines, and despite being told initially that it would be 'impossible', he sent a second order, and this time it was obeyed. It was a significant move.[6] Raglan arrived at the scene of the action at around 7 am, and found Pennefather more than capable of fighting the battle. He was, however, none too pleased to learn that both Sir George Brown and Cathcart had declined the help offered to them by Bosquet. This was no time for bravado and English arrogance, and a staff officer was immediately despatched by Raglan to Bosquet informing him that any French assistance would be more than welcome.

Back on Shell Hill the Russians had established their gun batteries. So far, Soimonov's attack had been relatively successful. Covered by the 6th Rifle Battalion, the battalions of the Tomsky and Kolyvansky regiments had swept over Shell Hill, driving back Haly's piquets, but only after a hard fight against the tenacious British. Twenty-two Russian 12-pounder guns were now beginning to pound Home Ridge and under cover of these Soimonov ordered forward all twelve of his battalions, save one of the Ekaterinburgsky which had veered off slightly towards Quarry Ravine, to advance against Home Ridge. The mist still hung low over the battlefield but visibility was good enough for Pennefather's men to see the 9,000 Russian troops lurching towards them. Pennefather's own artillery now came into action with a vengeance. There were already two guns in position – taken from the Sandbag Battery when it had been disarmed – and these had been joined by Captain Pennecuik's battery, to the right of the post road, and by Captain Turner's battery, on the left. Twelve guns were in action, blasting away at the approaching Russian columns and causing them to veer slightly to the west, their right. This took them in the direction of the head of the Mikriakov Glen once more where Major Grant and his wing of the 49th still loitered after their earlier successful charge. This time the numbers were too much for Grant's merry band and they fell slowly back, firing as they went, carefully shepherding with them the prisoners taken in their earlier charge.

While Soimonov was making headway along the tongue of ground between Shell Hill and Home Ridge another Russian column was feeling its way along Careenage Ravine itself, ostensibly to protect Soimonov's right flank. However, the direction of this column, the so-called 'under-road column,' was taking it directly up the Careenage Ravine and into the Wellway, a sort of narrow extension of the ravine that emerged well behind the left rear of the 2nd Division's camp. The under-road column, consisting largely of sailors and marines, was acting in much the same way as Federov's column had done on 26 October. And once again it was met by Captain Gerald Goodlake and his 'roving band' of Guardsmen, numbering about thirty men. While Soimonov was making his way up to Shell Hill with his main force the under-road column had been snaking its way along the bed of the Careenage Ravine until its movements were picked up in the fog by Goodlake who had not only opened fire but had sent a runner back to the British camp to warn Pennefather. Unfortunately, the runner was captured by the Russians. However, the noise of rifle fire had been picked up by Rowland's piquets and thus the camp was warned of the Russian attack. Goodlake, meanwhile, had roused Codrington, who quickly got those of his brigade of the Light Division who were not in the trenches to stand to. The other brigade of the Light Division, Buller's, was also alerted and he too began to muster his men in order to move towards Home Ridge.

So far, the only Russian troops engaged at Inkerman had been Soimonov's battalions and the under-road column, but at around 7.30 am, and with the British fighting hard to maintain their left and centre, Pavlov's columns finally began to appear. They had been delayed by the building of the bridge over the Chernaya river and in fact had not begun crossing it until 7 am, by which time it was already light. Now, the Battle of Inkerman was well under way, and the sounds of gunfire and artillery from the heights only served to increase the anxiety of Pavlov's men, who were desperate to get forward. Pyotr Alabin recalled the events of the morning.

> General Pavlov rode at the head of column. We followed him and went with the vanguard of the Okhotsky regiment. It was still dark

> and quiet. We stepped on to the long and narrow log-path and heard a cannonade from Sevastopol. The day was just dawning but the bridge was still not ready. They were throwing the last boards across and we began to hurry to the battlefield. Having passed the bridge, General Pavlov stopped. It was 7 o'clock. We forgot about the close proximity of the enemy, and thought only about how we were to get to the battlefield as quickly as possible.
>
> General Pavlov allowed the Okhotsky regiment and two companies of the 4th infantry battalion to pass, and he joined us as we presented arms to his staff. The rifle skirmishers of the Tarutinsky and Borodinsky regiments went ahead of the Borodinsky regiment while the Tarutinsky regiment turned to the left from the bridge along the old post road. We moved slowly along the narrow road on the left bank of the harbour and turned to the left into the second ravine. The skirmishers were like wild cats as they began to climb up the vertical rocks of the left side of the ravine and in a short time came to the very top. We, meanwhile, began to climb up the right side of the ravine; we had not gone far before the first cannon-ball of the day flashed by and ricochet from stone to stone.[7]

Pavlov, it will be remembered, had received orders to march west along Sapper Road before turning off and heading up St George's Ravine which lay to the north-west of Shell Hill. From here he would be able to advance and bring up his men directly behind Soimonov and support the attack on Pennefather's line. However, his two light infantry regiments, the Tarutinsky and the Borodinsky, decided there was a quicker way to the top and cut off to their left, straight up the Volovia Ravine, which would bring them on to the ground directly behind Shell Hill. Emerging from the Volovia Ravine the Tarutinsky and the Borodinsky immediately fell in with the battalion of the Ekaterinburgsky which had veered off towards Quarry Ravine, leaving its sister battalions to continue moving directly towards Home Ridge. This single battalion increased the strength of the new Russian column to around 6,000 men, who began to move against Pennefather's right. Alabin takes up the story again.

> We climbed up and up. At last we reached the top, which seemed to be inaccessible. The skirmishers rushed forward to the left; the enemy poured case-shot, balls and rifle fire on us as if it was boiling water. I was sent to order our Tarutinsky and Borodinsky skirmishers to extend. During this heated exchange of fire Lieutenant Colonel Totleben with a young sailor came from the left flank. We learned from him that, although our forces had beaten the English and entered their camp, the regiments of the 10th Division were in disorder, and Soimonov badly wounded. We had to hold our

> positions. General Pavlov noticed that we urgently needed artillery, at least one battery. Totleben added, 'You see how they are firing; it seems that their forces are increasing. We have to hurry before the arrival of the French.'
>
> I was sent to find a corps commander to order him to send a battery. I took one Cossack with me and rushed in the direction of Inkerman Bridge. I had difficulty finding the commander in the smoke of battle but I gave him the general's request and was told that the artillery batteries were already on the top. I was sent across the bridge to order the rest of the artillery to go there. Near the bridge I overtook crowds of wounded. On the bridge I met the Grand Dukes and the C-in-C, who asked me, 'What is happening on the mountain?' I answered that we had suffered much but had taken two earthworks and the English camp and that the battle was moving forward in our favour. Every man crossed himself.
>
> I found the general to the left of the bridge, the place I left him, not far from the enemy. The battlefield was covered with the killed and wounded. Our troops were mixed up and in great disorder. The regiments were losing heavily, which would make it impossible to hold our positions. There were no reinforcements. The general was again left alone with his Cossacks. All the other aide-de-camps and orderlies were running about with orders from one part of the battle to another.[8]

When they reached the top of the Volovia Ravine the leading elements of the Tarutinsky Regiment caught sight of the single Ekaterinburgsky battalion, making its way east. It would, in fact, be passing across the front of the Tarutinsky within a few minutes. Without waiting the Tarutinsky turned to their left and descended into the Quarry Ravine, crossing the head of it and emerging on top of the eastern side. When the first companies gained the top they looked away to their left and, through the clearing mist, saw an earthwork, some distance in front of the right of the British line. The earthwork looked abandoned and was, in fact, defended by just a handful of British troops, a sergeant and six men of the 55th. These in turn were supported by a piquet of the 55th commanded by 22 year-old Lieutenant William Barnston, who later described the Russian advance.

> On the day of the 5th, and before I was wounded, I very nearly got into a mess. I commanded a piquet that morning, part of which I sent out in front about 100 yards; after we had been firing a short time I thought it time my advanced party should come in, and I went down to call them in. I got up to within fifteen yards of the place when I was fired at, and then I discovered for the first time Russians were there, and not my own men; luckily they missed me. The Russians are awful

> savages; if they come across a wounded man (not one of their own) they would kill him at once, so you have no chance if you get into their hands.[9]

In a second letter to his brother Harry, Barnston elaborated on his experiences at Inkerman:

> Presently over the hills I saw swarms of Russians advancing, bringing with them a number of artillery. My piquet stopped out for about two hours, when we had a chance of being surrounded I retired it. The shots came about very thick. At last we got to the main body of the piquet, where I was forming up mine again, when I musket ball took me in the front – a side shot which struck my watch, which I at first thought saved me, but I have come to the conclusion it turned it in again, and it came out just above the right thigh bone.[10]

Barnston had resisted as long as possible, but the Tarutinsky were coming on in such numbers as to make it almost suicidal to remain out in front. Barnston therefore gave the order to retire, which was duly accomplished, but not before his men had inflicted a good few casualties on the Russians. The men inside the earthwork were also driven out, and so the Russians were left in possession of it, the men cheering and waving their hats in the air. The earthwork was, of course, the Sandbag Battery, and despite its utter worthlessness – it had long since been disarmed – it was about to provide the everlasting image of the extremely savage hand-to-hand fighting that so marked out Inkerman as one of history's bloodiest battles.

The possession of the Sandbag Battery meant that the Russians had an almost complete arc of infantry from the battery on their left, right across to the Careenage Ravine and the Wellway to their right, the centre being held back slightly. 16,000 Russians, supported by artillery, were therefore hammering away at the front door of the British position on Home Ridge. The British right had been compromised by the capture of the Sandbag Battery and the men on Fore Ridge behind it were struggling to hold back the Russians, whilst all the time they looked nervously over their left shoulders as Soimonov's columns pressed in against Home Ridge and the centre of the British position. It was desperate stuff. All over the broken, scrubby field, groups of British and Russian soldiers could be seen fighting it out with each other in the swirling mist that cleared every now and then, long enough for the combatants to see each other clearly and to get good aimed shots away. Trying to hold back this mass of Russians were just 3,000 British troops, for Pennefather had as yet received few reinforcements from other divisions. But help was about to arrive in the form of P Battery (Townsend's) and in the forward elements of Buller's brigade of the Light Division.

In fact, only three of Townsend's guns were actually making their way forward through the scrub, under Lieutenant Miller. In effect, it was a half-battery, and it began to deploy to the left of Home Ridge on the ground overlooking the very head of the Mikriakov Glen. Buller was very short-handed, as the majority of the men in his brigade were still in the trenches before Sevastopol. Nevertheless, he sent forward four companies of the 88th, about 390 men in all, who marched off to the left of Home Ridge and into the mist at the head of the Mikriakov Glen. Unfortunately, they blundered straight into two Russian columns that were emerging from the other side, and after a brief exchange of fire were driven back, scrambling over the rocky ground as they did so. As the 88th fell back they came into contact with Grant and the 49th who themselves were giving up ground after their earlier successful charge. Together, the two units fell back, passing through Miller's guns and leaving the way clear for them to open fire. The two attacking Russian columns were the 2nd and 3rd battalions of the Ekaterinburgsky Regiment, and after driving back the 88th they came upon Miller's three guns, drawn up in the open. Miller had barely time to get one round of canister away before the Russians were upon him. Worse still, the limbers had been taken off to the rear, leaving the gunners with no means of getting their guns away. A gunner without his gun is, of course, like a cavalryman without his horse. They are prized possessions. Unfortunately, they were also prized by the Ekaterinburgsky as trophies of war, and the Russians came surging out of the fog to claim them. Miller had no option, therefore, but to order his gunners to stand and fight for them and in no time at all he was riding into the head of the Russian column, twirling his sword above his head like a demented Dervish.

> As though bewildered by the novelty of the challenge and the sudden necessity of having to encounter a horseman, these men [the Russians] for a moment stopped short in their onset; and then there followed a conflict of a singular kind between, on the one hand, a great weight of advancing infantry, and, on the other, a few score of artillerymen, finding vent in some part of their rage in curses and shouts of defiance, but wildly striving besides to beat back the throng from their beloved guns with swords, with rammers, with sponge-staves, nay even, one may say, with clenched fists – for the story of the mighty Clitheroe bruiser felling man after man with his blows, and then standing a while unmolested and seemingly admired by the enemy, is not altogether a fable.[11]

The fight – one might almost call it a brawl – was sadly a little too one-sided, and Miller's brave band were parted from their guns, at least for the time being, and retreated towards the rear. Miller was later awarded the

Victoria Cross for his attempts to save the guns. The Ekaterinburgsky, meanwhile, rolled over the position, cheering as they claimed the spoils of battle. They were not, however, allowed to enjoy them for long.

With Miller's guns having been overrun the British left, as well as the right, was now being severely tried by Soimonov's columns. The word column is, however, to be used with caution, because they were not columns in the true sense of the word. Military manuals and text books had long been filled with neatly engraved diagrams illustrating the various evolutions of armies of their respective periods. But what is rarely taken into account are the conditions on the ground. It was all very well for the manuals to demand ranks of a certain width and depth, but when officers attempted to apply these rules in the heat of battle they were often found wanting, particularly when the ground was bad. The Battle of Inkerman was just one of those occasions where not only was the ground bad, and the weather poor, but the intensity of the struggle was extremely fierce. Consequently, it was virtually impossible for Russian officers to deploy their battalions into the nice, neat stuff of the drill manual. It simply wasn't on. One of Wellington's men perhaps coined one of the best and most effective descriptions of columns advancing over broken ground in battle whilst watching French columns attacking at Busaco in 1810. There were no elaborate columns of companies or columns of battalions. No, at Busaco the French, he claimed, came on in 'column of mass'. And this is exactly what the Russians were doing at Inkerman. As anyone who has ever visited the battlefield will know, it simply isn't possible to deploy large formations into neat columns. What more effective way of describing them is there then, than 'column of mass'? But what masses they were. Soimonov's men were everywhere across the narrow saddle of land between the Quarry Ravine and the Careenage Ravine, lapping against Pennefather's thinly held defences and threatening to break through at any moment.

Pennefather's problems were not confined to the saddle either, for out of the Wellway, deep in the left rear of the British position, the Under-Road column suddenly began to emerge. It was just as well that, at this very moment, Buller himself arrived with reinforcements. But there were no battalions or brigades with him, for Buller, with the pressure of having to maintain the siege lines, had brought with him just 260 men, four companies of the 77th Regiment under Lieutenant Colonel Thomas Egerton. That was all. It perhaps sums up the nature of the fight at Inkerman – at least from the British perspective – with reinforcements being fed in wherever and whenever they became available. It really was hand to mouth stuff. But it was working, at least so far. The four companies of the 77th were pitched into the action between Home Ridge and the Wellway, with the left of their line overlooking the latter. Riding alongside Buller was his aide-de-camp, 28 year-old Lieutenant Henry

Clifford. Buller himself was very short sighted and it was left to Clifford to inform his chief, with some alarm, that a column of Russians was suddenly looming out of the fog just fifteen yards ahead of him. 'It was a moment or two before I could make General Buller believe that they were Russians,' wrote Clifford later.[12] But Russians they were, and crying out, 'In God's name, fix bayonets and charge,' the men of the 77th went surging into the densely packed Russians. Not all of the 77th went forward, however, nor did Clifford, for at the very moment that Egerton's men went forward with their bayonets the men of the Under-Road column suddenly began to emerge from the Wellway in their left rear. No more than twelve men remained with Clifford but the small group was undeterred, and when Clifford shouted 'Come on, my lads', they turned and charged right into the Russian column, cutting their way through it, completely severing the top, cutting through it, and leaving around fifteen Russians to throw up their hands in surrender.[13] Clifford's little enterprise – for which he was awarded a Victoria Cross – came at a price, however, for no fewer than six of his gallant band were killed and three others wounded.

Having already been dealt a blow by Clifford and his small band, the Under-Road column was now hit hard for a second time, this time by a company of the Grenadier Guards under Prince Edward of Saxe Weimar. Prince Edward came from a family with a noble tradition of military exploits. Indeed, the 18 year-old Prince Bernhard of Saxe Weimar had fought with great distinction at Waterloo almost forty years before. The company of Grenadiers had been on forward piquet duty on the edge of Careenage Ravine when the battle began but were withdrawn slightly soon afterwards. When they saw the Under-Road column being driven back down the ravine in front of them it was too good an opportunity to miss. Prince Edward ordered his men to lie down and wait until the Russians were right underneath them, before they suddenly unleashed a storm of Minié bullets into the left flank of the Russians as they headed north back the way they had come. Prince Edward had his men pursue the column for a short distance, scooping up prisoners and effectively rendering the Under-Road column inoperative. Thus, between them, the 77th – and in particular Clifford's men – and Prince Edward's company of Guardsmen had secured Pennefather's extreme left flank, at least for the time being.

The position on the British left was further strengthened following actions by Major Fordyce and his 300-strong unit of the 47th, and by Egerton's equally small band of the 77th, less those who had been struck down during Clifford's charge into the Wellway. Fordyce was still holding his position at the head of the Mikriakov Glen when the 1st Battalion of the Ekaterinburgsky Regiment came looming noisily out of the fog from the forward slopes of Shell Hill, firing wildly as they advanced. Despite being outnumbered by almost three to one Fordyce had two distinct advantages over the Russians: first of all, the 47th were armed with rifles, with greater range and accuracy. Second, Fordyce deployed his men in a traditional line against the oncoming column, which enabled him to bring every rifle to bear, unlike the Ekaterinburgsky, the greater part of whose firepower was locked away deep inside their column. As only the front ranks of the Russians and those on the flanks could fire it did not take a military genius to predict the outcome. It was a simple mathematical equation that dictated that in a fire fight, a line will always triumph over a column, provided it is carefully handled. Fordyce certainly handled his men with care and attention, forming them up and having them unleash a dreadful fire into the stunned Russian ranks. The men of the Ekaterinburgsky were not accustomed to meeting their enemies drawn up in line, and appear to have assumed that Fordyce and his 300 or so men were just the front of a very deep column. After all, they could barely see the actual British line, lit up as it was by flashes of rifle fire, let alone determine whether or not there were others behind. The Ekaterinburgsky duly broke after a brief exchange of fire upon which Fordyce advanced about a hundred yards or so before halting beneath a crest on the western forward slope of Shell Hill. His men then lay down in the fog, awaiting developments and wondering who would be next to emerge from the fog, friend or foe.

It is quite remarkable, or perhaps not given the weather conditions, just how many of this ripple of small but significant actions took place in isolation, with British units attacking larger Russian formations whilst being completely unaware of the whereabouts of other Russian units. British units simply charged into the mist against the Russians completely ignorant of the dangers and the risks they were taking, for if the mist had suddenly lifted it would have revealed a battlefield littered with small, odd groups of redcoats fighting for their lives, passing larger Russians formations which remained in their rear. It was just as well for them that the mist remained swirling across the battlefield. It is also almost certainly the case that, had certain British officers known their true situation, it is likely that most of them would have thought very hard before launching themselves against the Russians.

A perfect example of this was Thomas Egerton and the remains of his four companies of the 77th, whom we last saw in action with Buller close to the Wellway and beyond. Away to Egerton's left front was Grant, and his wing of the 49th, along with the five companies of the 88th, all of whom had been driven back by the advance of the 2nd and 3rd Ekaterinburgsky. These troops, however, were invisible to Egerton, who could only see – apparently – two battalions of the Tomsky Regiment, 1,500-strong, advancing in the mist towards him. Egerton immediately adopted the same aggressive stance and tactics as Fordyce, and formed his men into line. Then, turning to Buller, who was still with him, declared 'There are the Russians, General, what shall we do?' The answer was simple. 'Charge them!', at which Egerton turned to his men and shouted 'Halt, then fire a volley, and charge!'[14] The Middlesex men needed no encouragement to do so and within seconds they were firing away like mad into the ghostly, grey figures shrouded in the mist before them. Like the 1st Ekaterinburgsky, the Tomsky battalions were shocked rigid by the sudden apparition, of a long line of British infantry, their rifles spewing fire at them. Once again they could not be sure whether the long line was exactly that, or whether it was the front of a much larger, denser column. But they were not given much time to think about it, for after delivering a deadly volley into the packed ranks of the Tomsky the 77th charged and were upon the Russians in no time, bayoneting, firing and clubbing away with their rifles like men possessed. During the Peninsular War, actual bayonet fighting had been extremely rare; it was the mere sight of 'the white weapon' that caused men to flee, but at Inkerman the weapon was used with a vengeance. It was real bloody, hand-to-hand stuff. After having piled into the midst of the Russian columns there was no time for Egerton's men to heed the niceties of war. It was simply time to drive the bayonet home and drive it deep. Butts were smashed into men's faces, punches were thrown, men kicked and bit each other, and if a man lost his weapon he picked up a rock and threw that instead. The 77th were outnumbered by as many as five to one but they carved a huge slice into the Tomsky who, unnerved by Egerton's very aggressive attack and not knowing just how many more redcoats were about to come down upon them, began to fall slowly back.

Egerton's attack completely threw back the two Tomsky battalions but it left him in quite a serious situation. Not only was he driving deep into the Russian position but he was slowly being surrounded, both by those overlapping his flanks and by scores of Russians who, having thrown themselves on the ground to feign death, now rose up to threaten Egerton's rear.[15] Fortunately, the fog was shielding his movements from the surrounding Russian units, which was just as well for he was, in fact, attacking the right wing of Soimonov's main attacking force, which numbered about 8,000 men. Egerton pressed on until he reached the lower slopes of Shell Hill, whereupon he and his exhausted but triumphant men were able to recover and reflect momentarily upon a job well done which had driven the Tomsky right back beyond the main Russian gun line. It is highly likely that, by now, Egerton's instincts told him that he was far in advance of the British line on Home Ridge and that, for all he knew, he was isolated. In fact, not far away in the mist to his left, was Fordyce and the 47th, still lying down on the soaked ground after their efforts against the 1st Ekaterinburgsky.

Apart from having driven back the two Tomsky battalions, one of the significant effects of Egerton's charge was that it left the 2nd and 3rd battalions of the Ekaterinburgsky Regiment out on a limb and somewhat exposed. These two battalions, it will be remembered, had overrun Miller's guns but had proceeded no farther, faced as they were by Grant and the 47th and by the remains of the five companies of the 88th, all of whom had passed through the battery before the guns were abandoned. But with both Fordyce and Egerton having driven back the 1st Ekaterinburgsky and the 1st and 2nd Tomsky, the two battalions of the Ekaterinburgsky grew increasingly isolated. The mist unnerved them, not knowing whether British troops would be upon them at any moment, whilst the sounds of battle close to them had drifted away to the north. Every now and then a ghostly rider would pass in and out of the fog, the odd round shot bounced into their ranks, and small units of men could be discerned running to and fro in the brushwood around them. But still no attack came. Finally, their commanding officers, their nerves taught and frayed, decided to retreat back towards their own line around Shell Hill.

The rearward movement by the 2nd and 3rd Ekaterinburgsky was picked up by both Grant and his wing of the 49th, and by Colonel Jeffreys, commanding the five companies of the 88th who followed the retreating Russians until they came within range of the Russian guns on West Just, whereupon they halted to await developments. The Russian retirement was also noted, of course, by Miller and his fellow gunners who dashed back to their guns to discover, to their relief, that not one of them had been spiked. Remarkable as it seems, not one of the Russian soldiers who had overrun P Battery had considered spiking the guns, which was a very easy thing to do. All it took was a single headless nail, driven into the touch hole of the gun, and the gun was effectively out of action. Every cavalryman carried – or should have carried – headless nails in his pouch; infantry needed only to stick a bayonet into the touch hole and break it off. It is possible that the Russians intended to carry off the guns as trophies, much in the same way as Liprandi had done at Balaklava. The problem for the Ekaterinburgsky was that they had no means, save simply man-handling them, of getting them away, and with the tide of battle flowing around them they decided upon a hurried retreat, leaving their trophies behind them. Thus, the three guns of P Battery were now safe and sound in the hands of their rightful owners.

It was not yet 7.30 am, but so far Pennefather's strategy of fighting out in front of Home Ridge was holding good. But it had been one hell of a struggle for the vastly outnumbered and isolated groups of British troops fighting desperately in the fog. Nowhere along the British front had the Russians been able to achieve any sort of penetration, their attacks being flung back by individual regimental groups, often led by junior officers, fighting by instinct rather than by the heady demands dictated by any official drill manual. The Russians themselves, after some initial success, had suffered badly. Their unwieldy columns, attacking on very narrow fronts, had felt the full fury of the British soldier and his well aimed and very effective rifle fire. But it did not deter them from coming on and trying again. Nor were they deterred by the death of their commander himself, Soimonov, for it was somewhere around the time of Egerton's charge that he was mortally wounded, struck down by a British rifle. It was, in fact, a bad day for Russian commanders, for no sooner had Soimonov's place been taken by Major General Vil'boi than he himself was wounded. Command then devolved upon Colonel Pristovoitov, who was wounded, and then Colonel Uvazhnov-Alcksandrov, who was killed. The immediate impact of Soimonov's death was felt on the British left and left centre, where the Russian attacks seemed to fade, although they did not cease altogether.

Pennefather's left flank was secure for the time being, but in the centre the Russians continued their attacks. The fog still hung low over the scrub when two battalions of the Tomsky Regiment and four of the Kolyvansky began moving across the front of Shell Hill, and, turning south-east began advancing directly upon Home Ridge where it bars the Post Road. One battalion of the Kolyvansky turned to its left and headed off in an easterly direction, but the other five Russian battalions continued on advancing over the open ground to the west of the Post Road, driving the British piquets back as they went. Waiting with his battery – albeit only half of it – on Home Ridge was Captain Turner, whose three guns of G Battery were primed and ready for action. Unfortunately, a similar situation to that which had occurred on 26 October arose, in that the retiring British piquets masked the Russian approach, and Turner dared not fire for fear of blasting away his own people. The Russians continued forward, a low, moaning howl coming from within their ranks as they advanced. With a potentially dangerous situation arising one of Turner's sergeants, named Conway, suddenly dashed forward and called out as loudly as he could to the retreating British piquets, telling them to lie down. As if hit by invisible shot the British piquets, realising what was about to happen to them if they didn't heed Conway's advice, dived to the ground as two rounds of canister came spewing out of the guns, tearing great gaps in the oncoming Russian columns. Such was the impact at very close range of the two rounds, poured into the densely packed ranks of the Kolyvansky and Tomsky battalions that they were brought, first to a halt, and then running to the rear, pursued by some very relieved British piquets who scrambled to their feet and chased the Russians back to the foot of Shell Hill, passing as they did Egerton and the 77th who lay on the ground, hidden and unnoticed in the fog. Once again, a small British unit, backed by artillery, had come out on top against massively overwhelming Russian forces.

The single battalion of the Kolyvansky, meanwhile, had reappeared to the east of the Post Road advancing towards Home Ridge. In front of them were scattered groups of British piquets whose fire was becoming increasingly slack due to a shortage of ammunition. Indeed, as men fell their comrades would rush to their ammunition pouches and fumble around in them for spare bullets. Even the artillery here, Pennecuik's guns, were silent, having either run out of ammunition themselves or having been put out of action by the Russian guns on Shell Hill. It was desperate stuff once again. All that remained standing in front of the Kolyvansky were three companies, just 183 men, of the 49th Regiment under Captain Bellairs who watched intently from his position on Home Ridge. Suddenly, Captain Adams, aide-de-camp to his father, General Adams, came riding up to Bellairs and, after surveying the situation for a short time, said nonchalantly, 'I think you had better advance, Bellairs.'[16] The Kolyvansky were within eighty yards of the main British position on Home Ridge when Bellairs ordered his men to fix bayonets, after which they scrambled over the breastwork in front of them and headed down towards the heavy undergrowth through which the Kolyvansky were struggling. By the time the head of the Russian column had begun to emerge from the scrub, Bellairs and his men were just forty yards from them, their bayonets charged and a look of grim determination on their faces. A British cheer rang out from the men of the 49th before they launched themselves at the surprised Russians who were evidently in no mood to taste cold steel. They simply turned and tumbled backwards in the direction of Shell Hill, leaving Bellairs and his small band in their wake, the 49th not having had to fire, it is said, a single shot.

The repulse of the Kolyvansky battalion effectively put paid to the attacks by Soimonov's front line troops of the 10th Division. The Ekaterinburgsky, Kolyvansky and Tomsky regiments had all tried in vain to force the thin line of British troops back over Home Ridge and now hundreds of them lay dead, including Soimonov himself, along with at least one of his successors. The attack on the right of Pennefather's position had come to grief also. After ascending the Volovia Ravine and crossing the Quarry Ravine, the Tarutinsky and Borodinsky regiments, along with the single Ekaterinburgsky battalion, had driven back Barnston's piquet of the 55th and had taken the empty Sandbag Battery. This left over 6,000 Russian infantry hovering threateningly on the British right, poised to strike at the thinly held defences. Once again, there was just a small British unit available to face them. It is difficult to believe just how many times this happened at Inkerman, but happen it did. Indeed, there can be few battles in history where so many small bands of men had launched themselves unflinchingly against massive superior numbers without the slightest fear of destruction. But such were the circumstances at Inkerman that Pennefather's men had little choice.

Facing this 6,000-strong host were just 200 men of the 30th Regiment under Colonel Mauleverer and away to their right some 500 men of the

41st under Major Eman, the senior field officer, although General Adams himself was with the regiment at the time. Coming up against the 30th were four battalions, around 2,000 men, of the Borodinsky Regiment, whose evidently reluctant advance was almost certainly born out of a wariness of the British Minié rifle, whose tongue had lashed them both at the Alma and at Little Inkerman. Unfortunately, very few of Mauleverer's Miniés were able to hand out a similar lashing this morning as the majority of them were soaked by rain. As the men fumbled anxiously with their rifles Mauleverer realised there was nothing for it but to use the 'white weapon' instead and so led them hurriedly down to The Barrier, where he ordered them to take cover and fix bayonets. Then, with the Borodinsky advancing upon them, he and his fellow officers sprang over the wall and flung themselves at the Russians, followed by their men who ripped into the Borodinsky, driving them back upon their supports and sending them reeling backwards. Mauleverer himself was badly wounded, whilst scores of his men fell also. But the charge had the desired effect, and with Mauleverer down Captain Mark Waller took up the reins and led the men on, winning for himself – on Mauleverer's recommendation – the Victoria Cross. The two leading battalions of the Borodinsky had thus been torn apart by the 30th but there were still two more battalions of the regiment coming up from the rear. However, when they saw their two sister battalions reeling backwards they too turned and retired to the relative safety of the Quarry Ravine.

It only remained now for the 41st to deal with the four battalions of the Tarutinsky and the single battalion of the Ekaterinburgsky which were massed farther east close to the Sandbag Battery. When General Adams brought forward Eman and the 41st to face the Russian mass he was embarking upon an attack in which his men would be outnumbered by eight to one. For, although the 41st could boast 500 men, the largest force as yet to attack the Russians, there were still around 4,000 Russians to be dealt with. Undeterred, Adams formed the 41st in line and advanced from the northern slope of Fore Ridge. In the centre of the line, flying above the men's heads, were the regimental colours which were proudly borne by Lieutenants Lowry and Stirling, the latter having risen from his sick bed to take part in the fighting. The sight of the long line coming towards them, blazing away with their rifles, was too much for the Tarutinsky who, like the Borodinsky, had already experienced the power of the Minié at the Alma. Eman was at the head of the 41st as they flushed the Russians from the Sandbag Battery – not for the last time – and began slowly driving them back. At such a short range the Minié was deadly, and the combination of well-aimed, steady fire and effective use of the bayonet sent the Tarutinsky and the Ekaterinburgsky tumbling down the steep slopes of the Kitspur to the east with British bullets whistling after them. In fact, so steep was the Kitspur that the Russians, 'dropped quickly out of their reach'.[17]

It was barely 7.30 am and the initial phase of the battle had thrown up numerous heroes all along the British line. Some of the Russian units had fought with extreme bravery but, it should be said, many had not. Indeed, given the overwhelming numbers they could call upon compared with the piecemeal feeding in of troops by Pennefather, it is remarkable that Soimonov was unable to break through. The opening stages of the battle had demonstrated once again the superiority of the line against the column and of rifles over smooth bore muskets. The fog had certainly been an important factor, although this had assisted both sides at various times. The sheer audacious courage of 3,500 or so British troops had thrown back numerous attacks by over 15,000 Russians along the length of Pennefather's position, but there was to be little respite. The British had performed incredibly well so far, but worse was yet to come.

For the next hour or so the fighting was concentrated in and around the Sandbag Battery, the relatively useless and empty earthwork that was to typify the nature of the fighting at Inkerman. The battery had no strategic importance whatsoever, but its mere possession by one side seems to have galvanised the other side into outbursts of extremely violent behaviour. The battery simply had to be taken and held at all costs, so the combatants seemed to think, and yet it was completely useless. But such is war. The prize simply far outweighed its importance, and was out of all proportion to the losses sustained by both sides and to the savage nature of the fighting itself.

The remnants of Soimonov's 1st and 2nd Brigades of 10 Division may well have been sent limping away from the battlefield, but there still remained some sixteen battalions of fresh infantry waiting on the reverse slopes of Shell Hill. These battalions were the Vladimirsky, Sousdal, Ouglitz and Bourtirsky Regiments from the 1st and 2nd Brigades of Zhabokritsky's 16th Division. These troops had come up via St George's Ravine and were, in effect, Soimonov's second line troops. Although they had yet to be engaged on 5 November they had, nevertheless, faced the British at the Alma. Whether it was for this reason is not clear, but Dannenberg, who had by now arrived on the battlefield, chose not to use them, but instead decided to attack with Pavlov's 10,000 troops who had only just arrived before Sevastopol a couple of days earlier. They must have been very exhausted, and one can well imagine their feelings when they were ordered to climb the steep slopes of the Inkerman Heights in order to attack the British. Indeed, they had already had a long march that very morning. Orders were orders, however. Dannenberg was not the only luminary on the battlefield, for Menshikov himself had arrived, bringing with him the two royal princes, taking up a position at the head of St George's Ravine, about half a mile north-west of Shell Hill. But if the czar's sons had come forward expecting to see their troops defeat the invaders they were to be disappointed, for the fog still clung to the battlefield.

It is doubtful whether Menshikov and the princes could even see Shell Hill, but if they could they would have seen an extensive gun line, stretching from East Jut, across Shell Hill and on to West Jut, for while the battle had been raging above him Pavlov had been busy bringing forward no fewer than ninety-seven guns, eighty-six of which Dannenberg directed against Home Ridge and the British position. It was a massive array of guns, the total number being just twenty short of the total number of guns which Wellington had at Waterloo. Thus, Pennefather's line, held by little more than 3,000 men, was about to be assailed once more, not only by Pavlov's 10,000 troops, but pounded by what could truly be called a 'grand battery', largely made up of 12-pounders, to which the British could reply with no more than eighteen guns; six from Townsend's battery and twelve from Fitzmayer's. As for the infantry, well, they were tired and in desperate need of reinforcements. They were also in need of food and drink, their ammunition was low, and with units mixed up and many officers down there was, naturally, a degree of disorganisation. The word went round that the Guards were on their way, but many wondered who would arrive first, the Guards or the Russians.

At about 7.45 am Pavlov's 11 Division finally began to move against the British right, cutting south-east from Shell Hill, across the head of Quarry Ravine and making for the Sandbag Battery, to which they appear to have attached some misplaced sense of importance. The Russian mass was fronted by four battalions of the Okhotsky Regiment with a single battalion of sappers. Behind them came four more battalions of the Iakoutsky Regiment, who were in turn followed by four of the Selenghinsky. Many of these troops had already seen much fighting against the Turks on the Danube. Indeed, it will be remembered that Pavlov had requested a postponement of the original date of attack, 4 November, as it was the anniversary of the Battle of Oltenitsa, a Russian defeat. They were, therefore, experienced troops. They had also yet to face British troops and so, unlike Soimonov's men, were not deterred by the prospect of facing British Minié bullets.

Over at the Sandbag Battery General Adams, Eman and the 41st were still recovering after their repulse of the Tarutinsky and Borodinsky regiments when rifle bullets suddenly began to whiz around them. A cloud of Russian riflemen was scattered out in front of the battery, taking cover in the bushes and behind rocks, whilst behind them came the lumbering masses of the Okhotsky Regiment, some 4,000 men in all. Although Adams was joined by Bellairs and his three companies of the 49th, there were no more than 700 British at best in and around the Sandbag Battery. Adams' first decision was whether to stand and fight or pull back. He considered the position – erroneously as it happened – to be an important and integral part of the British line, which made all thoughts of a retreat impossible. On the other hand, the mist had cleared long enough for him to appreciate the size of the Russian mass coming against him. He quickly despatched his brigade major, Captain Armstrong, to go and find out whether any reinforcements were on their way. In the meantime he would stand and fight.

The first thing to do was to try to clear away the Russian skirmishers from in front of the position, and so two companies of the 41st were sent dashing off into the scrub, only to be overwhelmed by the Russians. Three British officers, Captain Edwin Richards, and Lieutenants Swaby and Taylor, were killed during this fight, all three of them refusing to surrender when called upon to do so by the encircling Russians who were left with no choice but to bayonet or shoot the three brave young men. The remnants of the two companies fell back towards the Sandbag Battery leaving the way clear for their comrades to open fire on the oncoming Russians who displayed none of the reluctance shown by the Borodinsky earlier in the morning. The men of the Okhotsky Regiment were experienced fighters, and a gradual clearing of the mist revealed to them just how small the British force was. Scores of Russians were shot down but their places were simply taken by any number of men who stepped forward from the thronging mass coming up across the head of the St Clements Ravine. At this moment, Captain Armstrong returned with news that the Guards were on their way, news that was conveyed to the cheering defenders by Adams himself. The fighting continued.

Colonel Carpenter, commanding officer of the 41st, having shed his duties as a field officer, joined his men but no sooner had he done so than he was dragged from his horse and set upon viciously by a group of Russians who began bayoneting him ruthlessly and knocking him about the face with the butts of their muskets. This was too much to bear for Private Thomas Beach who earned for himself a Victoria Cross after wading into the Russians, flaying away with both ends of his rifle, to save his wounded colonel. Sadly, Carpenter died of his wounds. The commanding officer of the Okhotsky, Colonel Bibikov, was mortally wounded also. Elsewhere, the colour party of the 41st was assailed, and Lieutenant John Stirling, carrying the regimental colour, shot and killed. Fortunately, one of the escorts, Sergeant Ford, picked it up and carried it safely to the rear, but not before he had been forced to run through with his bayonet one Russian soldier and punch another who had dared to lay their hands upon the colour. Despite their efforts, and the fire brought down upon the Russians by three guns which had been brought forward by Captain Hamley, Adams' men could not stem the Russian tide and when Dannenberg's guns, finally able to see their target from East Jut and from the east of Shell Hill, began shelling them there was no option but to retreat slowly back to Home Ridge. As they fell back, Adams was wounded in the ankle by a Russian bullet, and although innocuous at first it was to prove fatal. The Okhotsky meanwhile continued to pour forward, leaving the 41st and 49th to make their retreat back to the main British line. The Sandbag Battery was back in Russian hands.

While the Okhotsky consolidated at the Sandbag Battery the four battalions of the Iakoutsky came forward on their right, heading straight towards The Barrier, whilst the four battalions of the Selenghinsky edged their way round the back of the Okhotsky, skirting the top of the eastern slopes of the Kitspur. There was, therefore, a mass of around 13,000 Russian infantry, including the battalion of sappers, now occupying the ground on Pennefather's right as well as the northern approach to The Barrier. Only the northern edge of Fore Ridge, between the two, was clear of Russians. Now, more than ever, reinforcements were needed to fling them back.

At last, the Brigade of Guards began to arrive, the 3rd Grenadier Guards leading, with the 1st Scots Fusilier Guards close behind them. The 1st Coldstream Guards was still some way to the rear having only just got off piquet duty. The brigade was commanded by Brigadier General Bentinck who, along with the Duke of Cambridge, quickly surveyed the scene before deciding what to do next. The Duke, lacking any military experience save for the Alma a few weeks before, was not the best man in a crisis, and this certainly was one. He did have enough presence of mind, however, to send an order to General Bosquet, asking him to march to the assistance of their British allies. This was in stark contrast to the arrogant behaviour of Cathcart and Brown, both of whom – having met Bosquet on his way forward earlier on – declined the Frenchman's original offer of help, adding, astonishingly, that they were well in control of everything. Between them, Cambridge and Bentinck decided to use their men against the Sandbag Battery, now in Russian hands, 'and whilst there was no tactical sense in trying to recover it, honour demanded that the British should do just that.'[18] Thus was instigated the bloody struggle for the Sandbag Battery.

The task of recapturing the battery fell to the seven companies of the Grenadier Guards, around 500 men in all, who formed line on the eastern slope of Fore Ridge under the command of Colonel Reynardson, commanding the regiment since the previous commander, Colonel Hood, was decapitated by a cannon ball in the trenches before Sevastopol. The Grenadiers then marched forward, with Reynardson out in front and the colours in the centre. There was none of the pomp and ceremony that usually accompanied their marches in London and Windsor but few would have failed to recognise Her Majesty's Foot Guards as they advanced steadily towards the Sandbag Battery, swathed in their heavy greatcoats, their tall bearskins giving them a sinister appearance. The Russians certainly recognised them as they came down through the mist, their bearskins making them appear as giants. Reynardson then gave the word to fire but, like the rifles of so many other regiments that damp morning, many of them misfired. Instead, it was left to their trusty bayonets again to flush the Okhotsky from the battery, driving them out and flinging them over the edge of the Kitspur before halting and taking possession of the position. The problem was that, by not pursuing them down the Kitspur the Okhotsky were allowed to re-form and advance again. On the other hand, any pursuit by the Grenadiers would have exposed their left flank to attack. And so Reynardson's men remained where they were, preparing to face the expected onslaught, which was not long in coming. Indeed, barely had the Grenadiers sorted themselves out than the Russians returned to the attack, swarming over the lip of the Kitspur and breaking against the high parapet of the Sandbag Battery which, although affording good protection against artillery, actually hindered the defenders in as much as there were no firesteps and the men were unable to fire over it. Even the Russians found it difficult, for although they could point their muskets and rifles over the parapet they could not depress them sufficiently to be able to hit any defenders who kept close beneath it, whilst any who ventured through one of the two narrow embrasures was quickly shot or bayoneted from within.

While the Grenadier Guards were recapturing the Sandbag Battery the Scots Fusilier Guards, numbering around 400, were hurrying to support them. It was obvious to their commanding officer, Colonel Walker, that the Fusiliers should form up across the head of St Clements Ravine in order to block the Russians now coming up it. The Duke of Cambridge saw things differently, however, and barking out 'where the devil are you going to sir?' he ordered Walker to form on the left of the Grenadiers, a move which would have exposed the Fusiliers' left flank to the Russian troops emerging from St Clements Ravine. Reluctantly, Walker obeyed the order, coming as it did from the Queen's cousin, but Bentinck had no such qualms about ignoring it and he had Walker counter-march to their position at the head of the St Clements Ravine, forming an 'upside down L shape' with the Fusiliers at the top facing north and the Grenadiers facing east over the Kitspur, the Sandbag Battery being at the hinge of the two regiments. It was a timely move for no sooner had they completed their evolution than the Russians surged forward, getting to within fifty yards of Walker's men before the latter opened up with their Miniés, bringing the Russians shuddering to a halt. This was followed by a swift bayonet charge that sent the Russians tumbling back. At this point the Grenadiers, frustrated at not being able to fire over the top of the parapet of the Sandbag Battery decided to leave the 'paralysing shelter of the work', and charged the men of the Okhotsky coming over the lip of the Kitspur. The Grenadiers set about their adversaries with a vengeance, but it left the Battery open and undefended and soon the Russians were in again, cheering and waving. Fortunately, Walker saw this and led his men against them, losing his horse in the process. Once again the Russians were flushed out and so the Battery remained in British hands. The problem was that each Russian attack left an increasing number of Guardsmen dead or wounded. It was okay for the Russians as there were so many of them, but the British could ill afford to take such a pounding. Cambridge, aware of the problem, rode frantically here and there, desperately trying to find reinforcements.

And reinforcements were urgently needed, for a dangerous gap had opened up between the area round the Sandbag Battery and The Barrier, leaving about four hundred yards of broken but open ground between the two, a gap that went unnoticed by the British troops, consumed as they were by events immediately around them. The Iakoutsky were pouring forward from the head of Quarry Ravine and surely it would not be long before they discovered it. Only the fog seemed to prevent them from doing so. The first person Cambridge met was Sir George Cathcart, but he could not be swayed by the Duke's arguments. Certainly, he had seen what was happening at the Sandbag Battery but he had also spotted through breaks in the fog the Selenghinsky snaking their way along the Chernaya valley, round the right flank of the Guards. Here, Cathcart decided, was the danger and the Duke went away empty-handed. Fortunately, some reinforcements were available, for not all of the 4th Division came under Cathcart's personal command. Pennefather was able, therefore, to call upon the 1st Rifle Brigade, the 95th and, following a miserable night in the trenches, the 20th. The three regiments themselves numbered barely a thousand men, which was grossly under strength, but was nevertheless an extremely welcome and strong reinforcement, particularly by Inkerman standards. However, rather than use them as single battalions Pennefather further reduced their effectiveness by dividing each of them into wings, thus creating six relatively small units. He therefore despatched one wing from each of the three regiments, numbering 521 in all, to try to plug The Gap, as it became known. Although only half of these three regiments were sent forward the reinforcement was sorely needed and, given the numbers of other units, was a relatively strong force. However, they too soon became almost entranced by the fighting at the Sandbag Battery and were likewise sucked into its consuming fire. Thus, The Gap remained open.

Even as these reinforcements were making their way towards the Sandbag Battery the Russians were launching another attack upon it, with the Okhotsky and the sappers attacking from the northern end of the Kitspur while the Selenghinsky swarmed over the top of the eastern side. At the same time, the Iakoutsky advanced from the Quarry Ravine to put pressure on the left of the Fusiliers. The Grenadiers and Fusiliers were thus hit in great strength from two sides and once again the position fell into the hands of the Russians after a furious assault that left the commanding officer of the Scots Fusiliers, Walker, seriously wounded after being shot in the jaw. He had already been wounded twice and this third wound forced him to the rear, leaving his regiment in the hands of Colonel Seymour. Elsewhere, British and Russians exchanged fire at point blank range, and when bullets ran out rocks and stones were hurled, fists flew and boots lashed out. And then, of course, there was the bayonet, used viciously by both sides, most effectively by thrusting into the face or throat, the heavy greatcoats worn by both sides proving to afford some degree of protection against them. It was bloody stuff.

The Grenadiers and Fusiliers might well have been forced out again, but they were in no mood to allow the Russians to remain there for long. The Grenadier Guards, in particular, were anxious to flush them out. Having been the first of the Guards to fight for the Sandbag Battery, they appear to have regarded the capture of the position as 'their fight', and they were going to do it on their own, without the assistance of the other Guards battalions. Such was regimental pride and rivalry. So, when the long line of bearskinned Coldstreamers appeared coming up from behind them they determined to form and charge at once. This was their fight. They were going to drive the Russians out, and they were going to do it on their own. 'Charge again, Grenadiers!' was the call as Captain Burnaby broke to the front, and with a huge cheer and bayonets charged, the Grenadiers stormed forward against the battery, driving the Russians out and pitching them over the eastern side of the Kitspur. It had been a hard fight, during which Colonel Henry Percy, of the famous Northumberland family, who had been wounded at the Alma, was struck on the head by a rock thrown by a Russian whilst standing on top of the ten-foot high parapet to get a better view of what was happening. He was knocked back but, undeterred, he got up again but was struck a second time, this time by a fragment of rock hurled by 'some Russian Ajax', a blow which this time sent him tumbling back unconscious inside the battery.

The Okhotsky, who had attacked from the northern slope of the Kitspur was driven back at the same time by Seymour and the Scots Fusiliers, thus clearing the area of the Sandbag Battery of Russian troops. But the Okhotsky and Selenghinsky had not retreated far, and a few of them still lingered below the Kitspur making a nuisance of themselves. It was just as well that, at this point, the reinforcements sent by Pennefather, as well as the Coldstream Guards, finally arrived to bolster the defences. The Coldstreamers themselves formed on the right of the Grenadiers, with the wing of the 20th, under Crofton, continuing the line to the right. The wing of the Rifle Brigade, under Colonel Horsford, meanwhile, formed up across the head of St Clements Ravine, whilst Champion and the wing of the 95th formed behind the Guards as support. There were now well over a thousand British troops in and around the Sandbag Battery, watching both the eastern and northern approaches to it. But this still left a relatively thin line against the overwhelming masses of the Okhotsky and

Selenghinsky, not to mention the Iakoutsky, who still lingered threatening around the head of the Quarry Ravine. These troops now began to push forward in earnest, but each time their efforts to break into the Sandbag Battery were met with a blaze of rifle fire, the 20th too pitching in with their smooth bore muskets. There were so few defenders that they dared not pursue the Russians down the Kitspur after each repulsed charge, which allowed the defeated Russians to re-form and try again. Each attack by the Russians was flung back leaving scores of dead and wounded behind them. The problem was, the British line, the 'long, knotted string of English',[19] was dwindling too. And so the battle continued to surge back and forth around the blood-soaked position. One can only imagine the horror of the fighting, the cheering, the smoke, the shouts and cries of the combatants, the furious firing and bayoneting, the hand-to-hand struggle with fists, rocks, boots, swords, revolvers, and anything that could be employed usefully as a weapon. At one point, some men of Captain Wilson's company of the Coldstream Guards, enraged by the fury of the Russian assaults, pursued the beaten Russians down the Kitspur and even went as far as the valley floor where they were brought to a halt by Russian fire. It was that sort of fight where the men's passions, regardless of their training and discipline, simply got the better of them.

In addition to the British reinforcements now fighting it out in the Sandbag Battery French troops were also hastening to the battlefield to prop up the ailing defences. General Bosquet, in fact, had been active since the first shots had been reported earlier in the morning. His natural instincts told him that his men should march north to the sound of the guns, and, indeed, he had received a request from Lord Raglan to do so. Before long, Bosquet was on his way with General Bourbaki, bringing with him a battalion of the 7th Léger and a battalion of the 6th Ligne, as well as four companies of Foot Chasseurs and two batteries of horse artillery under Commandant Boussinière. It is unfortunate that on the way he had the misfortune to meet both Cathcart and Brown who very arrogantly declined his offers of help and suggested he watch the Russians under Gorchakov now approaching from the south-east. Turning his men round deprived Pennefather and his men of valuable assistance. Shortly afterwards, however, one of Raglan's staff, Colonel Steele, came galloping up, his horse 'covered in foam'. Steele's report was precise and to the point. The real battle was at Inkerman after all. Gorchakov's advance was just a feint. 'I was certain of it!' cried General Bosquet, turning towards Colonel Steele; and he added 'go and say to our allies, that the French are coming at full speed.'[20]

Bosquet ordered his chief of staff, Cissey, to tell Bourbaki to move all his troops back towards Inkerman. Bourbaki, however, had already done so. In fact, so quickly had Boussinière's guns moved that they were almost back at Inkerman before they had even received orders. Meanwhile,

Bosquet ordered a battalion of Zouaves and a battalion of Algerian riflemen to hasten to the battlefield too, whilst General D'Autemarre began moving a second battalion of Zouaves and two battalions of the 39th Ligne, Commandant Barral also moving one of his batteries. At last, substantial reinforcements were on their way.

Back at Inkerman the savagery continued unabated. The Okhotsky were throwing hundreds against the Sandbag Battery but without success, each cheering surge being greeted by blasts of Minié fire. The attacks were relentless, however, and it seemed only a matter of time until even the Guards would be forced out. Then, right on cue at about 8 am, the sound of bugles and drums was heard as the first French troops began to arrive in the rear of Home Ridge. Finally, a decent sized reinforcement of around 1,600 men was at hand. Unfortunately for the hard-pressed British the leading French battalions, the 7th Léger and 6th Ligne, advanced no farther than Home Ridge itself, the troops forming up on the eastern side of the Post Road, and despite the urgings and pleas from Pennefather they simply could not be induced to go any farther, arguing that they were waiting for their brigade commander, Bourbaki, to arrive. Pennefather tried labouring his argument with Colonel Filliol de Camas, of the 6th Ligne, but the French colonel 'had death on his face', as if he was expecting to die.[21] Thus, the French remained static at a time when The Gap was yawning as large as ever.

The French had arrived at Inkerman shortly after Sir George Cathcart and his 4th Division. Upon being asked by Cathcart where his men were wanted, Pennefather simply replied, 'everywhere'.[22] The problem was, that such was the distribution of Cathcart's men, from the brigades of both Brigadier Generals Goldie and Torrens, that Cathcart himself was left with no troops to command. The situation was that bad. Fortunately, Torrens arrived with six more companies, four of the 68th and two of the 46th, but these still numbered just 400 men, which was hardly the kind of force that Cathcart, regarded as one of the most gifted soldiers in the British Army, imagined he would lead in a major battle. But use them he would, in one of the most controversial episodes of the day.

Sixty year-old Sir George Cathcart served in the Crimea under pressure imposed upon him by the so-called 'dormant commission', an arrangement whereby he would assume command of the British army should anything happen to Raglan. Sir George Brown was, of course, senior to Cathcart, but such was Cathcart's reputation – he had recently served in the Kaffir Wars – that he was deemed by Horse Guards to be the man best suited for the job. In order to remove any friction that might have existed between Cathcart and Brown the commission was kept secret. Thus, from the moment Cathcart set foot on Crimean soil at Kalamita Bay he did so labouring under his secret. When Cathcart arrived on the battlefield the Guards and the Okhotsky were engaged in slaughtering each other at the

Sandbag Battery. Cathcart, however, was drawn to the Chernaya valley where the Selenghinsky were slowly making their way up and along the eastern slopes of the Kitspur, attempting to get round the right flank of the Guards. Nevertheless, Raglan, watching from Home Ridge, could see the increasing danger as pressure mounted on The Gap and wanted Cathcart to move his small force to across and support the left flank of the Guards and plug it. Cathcart, who had already seen his troops taken and scattered across the battlefield to plug gaps and reinforce thinly held positions, had other ideas.

Cathcart was notoriously short-sighted and was a habitual user of field glasses. It was through such glasses that he spied the Selenghinsky skirting the Kitspur and trying to get up round the Guards' right flank. He knew instantly what was required and gave the order for Torrens to advance with his small force of six weak companies of his brigade. The men of the 4th Division, armed with smoothbore muskets, immediately opened fire downhill against the approaching Selenghinsky. Small pockets of mist still hung down the hillside but visibility was improving all the time, and despite the inaccuracy of their muskets Torrens' men began to take a toll of the Russians. Suddenly, the Quartermaster General, Airey, arrived bringing an order from Raglan for Cathcart to move back and support the left flank of the Guards. The firing ceased while Cathcart conferred with Airey. When such an order arrived, coming as it did directly from the commander-in-chief, it simply had to be obeyed. It was not as though the order was coming from its bearer. No, such an order had to be treated as if it were being delivered by the C-in-C himself. Despite this, Cathcart seemed to think he knew better. He knew full well of the mounting danger at The Gap but appears to have considered the threat to the Guards' right flank as more serious. Thus, Raglan's order was disobeyed. Instead Cathcart ordered Torrens to resume his advance. Cathcart's advance, 'an evil moment',[23] was to have tragic consequences.

There were at least 800 men of the Selenghinsky making their way slowly uphill through the scrub below the Sandbag Battery, whilst at the top Cathcart had barely 400 men. Considering the odds faced by other British units earlier that morning, it was almost an equal fight. The four companies of the 68th, under Colonel Henry Smyth, formed line with the two companies of the 46th, under Captain Hardy, formed on their right. Most of the men had discarded their greatcoats and there was no mistaking this thin red line as it began to make its way down into the scrub with Torrens himself riding at their head. It was a steep and treacherous descent, with rocks strewn everywhere and thorny bushes making any sort of order difficult to maintain. No sooner had they come into view of East Jut than the Russian guns there began to fire, whilst the men of the Selenghinsky halted and likewise opened fire. It was a severe test for Cathcart's men who were now under heavy fire. Officers were struck down everywhere. Smyth, leading the 68th, was brought down when his horse was killed, whilst Captain Wynne was shot through the head. Torrens, too, had not gone far before he was badly wounded. 'Well and gallantly done!' was Cathcart's remarkable comment to his chief lieutenant as he rode past.[24] Torrens would die of his wound several months later.

The problem now was that Cathcart had unwittingly set off a chain reaction along the line of British troops fighting on and to the south of the Sandbag Battery. For while Cathcart's men continued pushing north along the slopes of the Kitspur, they came into contact with Wilson's company of the Coldstream who were returning after their pursuit down to the valley floor a few minutes before. On their right was Crofton's wing of the 20th, now under Lieutenant Dowling; Crofton himself had been wounded. When approached by Colonel Cunyngham, a staff officer and an old 20th man himself, Dowling asked what he and his men were to do, adding that all the mounted officers were down. Cunyngham had them advance to the forward slope of the Kitspur where they opened fire into the right flank of the oncoming Selenghinsky. However, as soon as Cunyngham had left them the 20th forgot themselves and they too advanced to link up with Cathcart's men. Thus, Cathcart, who had originally gone forward with his six companies of the 46th and 68th, now had part of a company of Coldstreamers and a company of the 20th going forward with him against the Selenghinsky. To make matters worse, the defenders at and around the Sandbag Battery, maddened by the fury of the fighting and unable to control themselves, decided to join in the advance also. It was a fatal move.

It was vital that the British retained possession of the high ground. The slopes of the Kitspur and the St Clements Ravine were extremely steep and troops pursuing too far down would quickly exhaust themselves. Indeed, it is a testament to the prowess of the Russians attacking here that they were able to persist in their attacks for so long. It was dangerous too, for any British troops advancing too far down the slopes risked being cut off by Russian troops coming across from Quarry Ravine. They also risked being cut off by any Russians who managed to get through The Gap. It was a recipe for disaster, but the invitation offered by retreating Russians was too great for them to resist. The Grenadier Guards, in particular, had been involved in some truly vicious hand-to-hand fighting with no quarter being asked and none given. It was a nightmare of a battle. It was only natural, therefore, that when the Russians began to fall back the Guards piled forward with their bayonets in an explosion of fury and anger. Indeed, it is easy to criticise them for overreaching themselves but it is equally difficult to imagine that they could have simply switched off and returned calmly to their positions. To criticise the Guards for their advance is to misunderstand the nature of the fighting in the Sandbag Battery.

The Duke of Cambridge may not have been the greatest of tacticians, but even he knew the folly of abandoning the battery in favour of a pursuit of the Russians. He was powerless, however, to prevent the Grenadier Guards from advancing down the Kitspur although he did manage to retain control of about a hundred men including the Colour party. The remainder went down cheering in pursuit of the Russians, joined by men of the Coldstream Guards and the Scots Fusiliers. Champion and his wing of the 95th went too, cheering and shouting, as did a group of the 20th who had just arrived at the position. It was mayhem, and it had all been caused by the impetuosity of Sir George Cathcart. Champion himself had not gone too far down – some say he was attempting to restrain his men – before he was forced to dismount in order to negotiate some boulders. Sadly, he was hit by a bullet and mortally wounded. The consequences of the advance were as predictable as they were fatal, for while Cathcart and Torrens continued to drive north into the masses of the Selenghinsky they failed to realise they were marching into a death trap, not that it was caused by design or by any Russian planning, it was just that the Russians were taking advantage of the situation created by Cathcart's decision to ignore Raglan's order to plug The Gap.

The British troops were already convinced that the battle was won, even before they approached the valley of the Chernaya. Russian troops were tumbling back before them, unwilling suddenly to face the line of steel being wielded by hundreds of angry British soldiers. But there were other British who suddenly became very aware of a feeling of great vulnerability, among them Lieutenant Carmichael and Captain MacDonald of the 95th who were drawn by shouts of 'Come back, you are cut off!' coming from above them. Carmichael later wrote of the moment when he realised something very wrong was happening.

> I noticed just at this time, and the men near me also remarked it, that those following us but a good deal in the rear, were turning back, and soon after cries were raised, 'Come back, you are cut off!' I could see no cause to retreat and stopped those near me who began to retire thinking it was a false alarm, but the smoke and mist rolling away for a minute, a heavy Russian column became visible forming to our left on the high ground covered by a strong fringe of skirmishers . . . three or four of their companies were already formed and in order and the officers were busy marshalling the remainder . . . Not a moment was to be lost and it seemed to me more than doubtful if we could reach the Sandbag Battery before them.[25]

On the face of it, the Guards and the other small bands of British infantry now pursuing the Russians down the Kitspur and the St Clements Ravine had achieved a great success, but with so many Russians now threatening

The Gap – some were already pouring through it – it is little wonder that the success is usually referred to as the 'false victory'. For that is exactly what it was, and when Carmichael, his comrades, and the Guards realised the Russians were about to cut them off they turned and began to hurry back as fast as they possibly could. This wasn't easy, of course, given the nature of the ground and the fact that they were nigh on exhausted by their efforts at the battery and in the pursuit. Nevertheless, if they stayed where they were they were doomed. It also left the Duke of Cambridge stranded back at the Sandbag Battery with no more than about a hundred men, including the Colour party of the Grenadier Guards. Indeed, the colours of the Grenadiers quickly came to the attention of the Russian troops now swarming into The Gap.

The Russian columns consisted of four battalions of the Iakoutsky and two battalions of the Okhotsky, who surged forward from the direction of the Quarry Ravine, towards the very gap which, if Cathcart had obeyed his order, would have been holding. It was also a gap which, if De Camas and his French troops had used their initiative, rather than wait for their brigadier to arrive, could have held. It would certainly have prevented the disaster which was now unfolding. The capture – or even death – of the Duke of Cambridge would have been a massive blow to British prestige and a great coup for the Russians, and it was imperative that he got out and back to Home Ridge before the net closed. Gathering a small group of men about him he began to hurry to the rear and was fortunate in brushing past and through the front of the Iakoutsky before the column could get to grips with them in strength, although some were cut down in the scramble to safety. Meanwhile, the colours of the Grenadier Guards were being held proudly aloft by Verschoyle and Turner as they carried them back towards Home Ridge. The trouble was they were in great danger of being engulfed by the oncoming Russians who must have been licking their lips at the prospect of seizing the colours of the first regiment of Queen Victoria's own bodyguards. 'Carry high the colours!' was the shout as the small bearskinned group trod steadily to the south and safety, keeping to the lip of the Kitspur but it would be a close call. The fire of the Grenadiers seemed to push the leading Russian column, the Iakoutsky, to their right, away from the Guards, thus leaving the Colour party and those on the left of the Guards, to get back by skirting along the top of the Kitspur. Those on the right, closest to the Iakoutsky, had to fight it out and cut their way through. At the same time, another small group of British from the 20th and Coldstream, and led by Assistant Surgeon Wolseley of the 20th, appeared from the direction of the Sandbag Battery, slicing their way through the astonished Iakoutsky with Wolseley, sword in hand, at their head crying, 'Fix bayonets, charge, and keep up the hill!'[26] About half of Wolseley's men failed to make it through the 700-strong Iakoutsky column, although he himself made it to safety with the other half of his band of heroes.

The Colour party of the Grenadiers continued skirting along the top ledge of the Kitspur, marching rapidly to the south, surrounded by about sixty or so others. Although the Iakoutsky had drawn back somewhat they still threatened the colours. Indeed, by the simple expedient of a rapid march to their left the Iakoutsky would have had little difficulty in cutting them off from the main British position on Home Ridge. Already, the two sides had closed with each other and the Guards were forced to fight desperately to fend off their assailants trying to cut them off. Worse still, the two battalions of the Okhotsky were fast coming up in the rear of the Iakoutsky. Then, right on cue, Captain Burnaby, breathless after his pursuit with his men down the Kitspur, appeared with a small group of no more than twenty men, from the Guards and the Line, who appeared as if from nowhere to bring the Okhotsky to a halt. Burnaby had gathered his men together after breaking back into the Sandbag Battery, explaining to them that if the colours were to be saved they would have to buy time for them by acting as a sort of rearguard. Burnaby knew this course of action would probably end in most of them being killed or wounded but he saw no other choice. His men knew it too, but none flinched. Turning to his men, Burnaby said simply, 'Are you ready?' before springing forward into the massed ranks of the Okhotsky.

The attack by Burnaby and his small band of men is the stuff of pure legend. Their heroic sacrifice stands out on a day littered with acts of tremendous bravery by men on both sides. After all, who but a battle-crazed English captain would lead twenty men against 700 Russians? Burnaby's men tore into the Russians who were taken aback by the audacious charge. Burnaby's men fired, bayoneted, kicked, punched and hacked at the Russians but there were simply too many of them. Burnaby himself escaped when a Russian bayonet caught in the folds of his cloak. Others were not so lucky, however, and one by one they fell at the point of Russian bayonets or were shot down at close quarters. Remarkably, seven men including Burnaby survived, all but Burnaby himself suffering bayonet wounds.[27] Burnaby had a second close shave after slipping on the wet barrel of a musket that had been dropped on the ground. He lay there, helpless, whilst his men were knocked down and overcome, leaving the heartless Russians to move amongst the dead and wounded, stabbing at them with their bayonets. Burnaby knew instantly what his fate would be, and noticed a wounded Russian officer lying close by him who appeared to be on the verge of attracting the attention of his comrades to the fallen Englishman. Without any fuss, the quick-thinking Burnaby drew his pistol and held it at the Russian's head, whispering in his limited Russian that if he so much as uttered a word he would find himself in the next world. But then, to his amazement and utter relief, the Russians suddenly began to melt away. The French had finally arrived.

NOTES

1 For a good account of the piquet system and the state of the British piquets on the morning of 5 November 1854, one can do no better than consult Patrick Mercer's *Give Them a Volley and Charge!* (Staplehurst 1998). The author writes not only as an historian but with the benefit of personal experience, having been a regular officer for twenty-five years.
2 Little has changed today, and the authors have had the benefit of an interesting discussion on this with James Falkner, an ex-regular officer. James afforded us a very useful insight into the problems of piquet work, particularly at night.
3 Mercer, 74.
4 Ibid, 78.
5 Kinglake, Alexander William. *The Invasion of the Crimea: Its Origin, and An Account of its Progress down to the Death of Lord Raglan* (London 1863), V, 130. This memorable phrase forms the title of Patrick Mercer's classic account of Inkerman.
6 Ibid, V, 129.
7 Alabin P V *Chetyre voiny. Pohodnye zapiski v 1849, 1853, 1854–1856 i 1877–78 godah* (Moscow 1892), 96.
8 Ibid, 97–8.
9 Trevor-Barnston, Michael (Ed). *Letters from the Crimea and India* (Chester 1998), 8.
10 Ibid, 9.
11 Kinglake, *Invasion of the Crimea*, V, 140–1.
12 Clifford, Henry, *His Letters and Sketches from the Crimea* (London 1955), 88.
13 There is some confusion here as to the direction taken by Clifford. Although Clifford himself gives no indication of the direction in which he charged, save that it was to his left, Kinglake describes him as attacking the Russian column 'defiling before him', although his map would seem to indicate that Clifford had to turn and charge down *behind* himself in order to sever the column. (See Kinglake, V, 143, and Clifford, 88.)
14 Kinglake, *Invasion of the Crimea*, V, 152.
15 The British troops referred to these skulking Russians as 'the Resurrection Boys'.
16 Kinglake, *Invasion of the Crimea*, V, 162.
17 Ibid, V, 167.
18 Mercer, *Give Them a Volley*, 102.
19 Kinglake, *Invasion of the Crimea*, V, 228.
20 Bazancourt, the Baron de (trans. by Robert Howe Gould). *The Crimean Expedition, to the Capture of Sebastopol. Chronicles of the War in the East* (London 1856), II, 66.
21 Kinglake, *Invasion of the Crimea*, V, 213.
22 Ibid, V, 236.
23 Ibid, V, 244.
24 Ibid, V, 245.
25 Carmichael quoted in Mercer, *Give Them a Volley*, 115–16.
26 Kinglake, *Invasion of the Crimea*, V, 277.
27 The magnificent seven were Burnaby, James Bancroft, Issac Archer, Joseph Troy, John Pullen, Edward Hill, and William Turner.

## CHAPTER TWELVE

# '. . . the Fifth of November'

From the moment of their arrival at Inkerman the French had done nothing but sit and wait for their brigade commander, General Bourbaki, to arrive. For, in spite of the butchery going on in front of them and the perilous situation in which their British allies found themselves, the French simply would not move without orders. But now, with Bourbaki's arrival, they finally began to lumber into motion, moving down against the right flank of the Okhotsky who, in their efforts to cut off the small groups of British troops now trying to regain their own lines, had failed to notice the oncoming French. With De Camas at their head, the 6th Ligne drove the Okhotsky back to the head of the St Clements Ravine, avoiding the temptation to become embroiled in fighting for the Sandbag Battery. In fact, the presence of Russian troops in the position brought about a temporary halt to the French advance, and it was only the implorings of British officers – some verbal and many others physical – that got them moving again. Once at the ravine Bourbaki linked up with Colonel Horsford and his riflemen who had been busy engaging the Russians throughout the last half hour or so. Indeed, Horsford and his men had led a charmed existence, remaining well out in front of The Barrier whilst large Russian columns passed by on both sides of him without ever seriously threatening him. Bourbaki greeted Horsford and after a short exchange the French general turned to his men before leading them off, for some strange reason, to the north-east along the narrow ridge that separated the Quarry and St Clements Ravines and culminated in the Inkerman Tusk.

Unfortunately, the arrival of the French came too late to save Sir George Cathcart and his small band of no more than 400 men fighting down the eastern slope of the Kitspur. Cathcart, it will be remembered, having ignored Raglan's order to return to The Barrier and plug The Gap next to it, had begun to advance northwards against the Selenghinsky, but quickly found himself being attacked by no fewer than 800 Russians. Even when the Russians were flung back Cathcart's men were not out of danger, for they began to receive a strong fire from above, causing many of them to begin shouting angrily that they were being fired upon by their own troops. What they did not know was that it was, in fact, the fire of the battalion of the Iakoutsky that had got through The Gap at exactly the spot where Cathcart should have been standing had he obeyed Raglan's order. The situation was now extremely serious for Cathcart, for not only was he confronted by about 800 Russians but most of his men – he had gone into action with the 46th and 68th – had been either scattered into the scrub during the fighting or had simply been cut down. In fact, when Cathcart looked round there were barely fifty men with him, the remains of Crofton's company of the 20th, led by Dowling, who had since been killed, who had made the fatal charge down the Kitspur during the so-called 'false victory'. Nevertheless, Cathcart decided to attack, despite being massively outnumbered. The result was predictable. The survivors of the attack fell back and took cover amidst the rocks and bushes whilst Cathcart himself, still in the saddle, looked around, unable to see a way out. It is little wonder, therefore, that he turned to one of his staff officers, Major Maitland, and uttered the massively memorable understatement, 'I fear we are in a mess.'[1]

Maitland now rode off farther down the Kitspur to try to bring back the 46th and 68th but they were out of ammunition. Maitland rode back to Cathcart with the bad news, but barely had the words left his lips than a volley rang out from the Russian ranks, mortally wounding him and killing another staff officer, Colonel Charles Seymour, while several other men were brought down also. But the most important casualty, and the most senior British casualty of the day, was Cathcart himself, who fell from the saddle mortally wounded after being shot by a Russian bullet. In disobeying Raglan's order he had unwittingly signed his own death warrant. His impetuosity and misjudgement had cost him his life. Thus, the man who claimed he could have taken Sevastopol even before the siege began, and the man of whom such good things were expected, and who carried the controversial 'dormant commission', was now dead. 'His last act was one of ill-judgement in a long series of mistakes and petty jealousies. Death in such romantic, even heroic, circumstances was the only thing that saved his reputation from being tarnished forever.'[2]

It should not be thought that the battle died down whilst the fight at the Sandbag Battery raged. Far from it, in fact, for while the Guards and their supports were fighting like devils at the battery the defenders at The Barrier were equally hard-pressed. But, as there were about 400 yards between the two positions, in addition to which was the northern end of Fore Ridge, the men at The Barrier fought on completely oblivious to what was happening at the Sandbag Battery and vice versa. The attacks on The Barrier had been unrelenting and had been difficult to contain. The Barrier itself was aptly named for it was a simple, crude and not very high earthwork which barred the way to Home Ridge, the main British position about 500 yards to the south. Defending it against great odds was

Lieutenant Colonel Mauleverer's wing of the 30th, now commanded by Mark Waller – Mauleverer had been wounded – no more than 200 men in all. The 30th had been in the thick of the fighting since the battle began and the men were tired and hungry. They were low on ammunition too. But they still proved a match for the two fresh battalions of the Iakoutsky that came marching steadily down from Shell Hill before turning to their left in order to form in Quarry Ravine. The 30th reloaded and fired, after which they charged down the slope into the oncoming Russians, only to be thrown back. They repeated the exercise time and again until, with their ammunition almost expended, they retreated back to Home Ridge where they rejoined the other wing of the 30th under Major Patullo. The men then lay down, completely knocked up, many of them falling asleep.[3] The enforced withdrawal of the 30th left The Barrier in the hands of the Iakoutsky, although they were not allowed to linger there for long once the British guns, now free to fire on the position, opened up.

The mist continued to swirl about over the battlefield revealing large Russian formations here and hiding others there. British troops likewise continued to appear and disappear in the fog, but overall it seemed to be clearing somewhat and Pennefather was able to get a better appreciation of his position. It was not yet 8.30 am and the battle had been raging bloodily backwards and forwards for the best part of three hours. But still there appeared to be no let up in the determined Russian assaults. The Barrier was unoccupied and The Gap continued to concern him. The defenders on Home Ridge were hard pressed, not through any immediate Russian assault, but because of their efforts during the morning so far, and through the unwanted attentions of the massed batteries of Russian guns on Shell Hill. But reinforcements continued to dribble in. Major Horsford's 140 riflemen had by now returned to Shell Hill, but unlike Waller and the 30th they were not allowed to get any rest. Instead Pennefather ordered them to form up and charge the Iakoutsky and drive them back from The Barrier.

Without any fuss, Horsford's riflemen scrambled over the breastwork at Home Ridge and charged down the slope towards The Barrier, driving the Iakoutsky back towards Quarry Ravine which was by now beginning to become clogged with wounded and skulking Russians. The Iakoutsky re-formed once again and turned to face Horsford's men, but just at that moment Major Hume and his wing of the 95th came forward behind them and deployed to their right. Yet another clash ensued between column and line which, as usual, resulted in the triumph of the latter over the former. During the clash Hume was unhorsed and badly wounded but his men fought on, side by side with the Rifles, preventing them from penetrating the fatal gap between the Sandbag Battery and The Barrier. There was still one other Russian column, however, that skirted to the left of the Rifles and 95th, by now inextricably mixed. The column bore down on the left of Home Ridge but a few rounds from Turner's battery left them shattered, reeling and staggering back the way they had come.

Despite these setbacks Dannenberg still seemed to have limitless resources and the Russian attacks continued unabated. No sooner had Pennefather's men thrown back an attack on one part of the field than they were called upon to face another elsewhere. Even while Horsford and Hume were repulsing the Iakoutsky from in front of The Gap another Russian column came gliding through the ever-thinning fog to attack the centre of Home Ridge where the weary 30th lay resting and snoozing. No sooner had the spectre-like figures loomed out of the fog than the 30th were on their feet and, leaping over the breastwork, were firing into the Russians, driving them back down the slope up which they had come. On the right of the 30th two more columns of the Iakoutsky came on, only to be repulsed by two companies of the Coldstream under Colonel Upton. It was relentless. Pyotr Alabin, serving on Pavlov's staff, later described the nature of the fighting, the Russians attacking time and time again without any real orders or direction from their commanders.

> Soimonov's detachment attacked the point which was to be attacked by our forces. Of course, we annihilated the English we met, but the two detachments were crowded together on the small space. Not seeing or knowing anything, not receiving any orders about what we had to do, we stood and were killed in great numbers until the battle turned into a series of uncoordinated skirmishes and fisticuffs. On one side some of our troops rushed to the enemy fortification, took it and stayed in it, not knowing what to do next, all the time being fired on by the enemy artillery. The enemy then took the fortification from us but we retook it again when help came. At one point one of the commanders saw the enemy line firing at our riflemen; he sent one of his units to destroy it; the unit achieved its object and the enemy line was overthrown; but what were we to do next? And our battery was under terrible rifle and artillery fire. Men were falling on both sides. At one point our troops advanced and defeated the English, who not only threw away their rifles but even their ammunition, which helped them to run at top speed. On another occasion, our unit retreated in disorder in confusion towards a steep ravine. Some were still returning fire, the others were already going down, and some just jumping down the steep slope. There were no general orders at all.[4]

Undeterred by their setbacks, the Iakoutsky tried again, this time attacking the eastern end of Home Ridge where just a small mixture of odd British units under Colonel Percy Herbert held the line. Fortunately, a wing of the 20th, under Colonel Horn, came rushing forward and, forming into line, advanced against the Russians. The 20th formed part of

Brigadier General Goldie's brigade of the 4th Division and were armed not with rifles but with smooth bore muskets. They may have been slow to load and inaccurate but they were still dangerous weapons in the hands of men like the 20th, who loaded and fired as they went, driving the Iakoutsky back once again to the Quarry Ravine, which by now was acting as a sort of rallying point for the Russians as well as providing a safe haven for their wounded and for the many shirkers who simply weren't up to facing the British again. Horn and the 20th had driven back two columns of the Iakoutsky, but there remained a third, lurking on the slope in front of Home Ridge. At that moment, Captain Stanley and 200 men of the 57th Regiment appeared, coming up behind the 20th. These 200 men were faced with overwhelming odds and it was only natural that some of the men appeared to baulk at the sight of the dark, grey column in front of it. Detecting signs of wavering the young captain called to his men, using the memorable exhortation of a previous commander, Colonel William Inglis, who, at Albuera, the bloodiest battle of the Peninsular War, had urged his men to, 'Die hard, 57th! Die hard!' Hearing these cherished words, the men of the 57th straightened up and flew at the Iakoutsky, exchanging volleys before tearing into them to engage in hand-to-hand combat. It was a tough fight, with bayonets and butts being used freely, and with men being slaughtered at point-blank range. Stanley himself was mortally wounded whilst crying, 'Men, remember Albuera!'[5] It is fitting that upon Stanley's being wounded, command of the regiment passed to Captain Inglis, the son of the very man who had so inspired his men to earn their nickname way back in May 1811. In true die-hard fashion, Inglis led his men forward, slowly driving the Iakoutsky back until they halted, having driven them down into Quarry Ravine. Having achieved their objective and with yet another Russian column looming close by, the 57th returned to Home Ridge, firing as they did so.

The fighting so far had been bloody, savage and unrelenting all along the thinly held British position. The Russians, admittedly in great strength, had come forward time after time but had yet to enjoy any real success in terms of captured ground. Pavlov's men, in particular, had fought extremely bravely, whilst Soimonov's men had shown less enthusiasm to meet British bullet and bayonet. And yet, remarkably, barely three hours had lapsed since the initial Russian attack. Indeed, it was only just gone 8.30 am. The British line had held, but only after desperate counter-attacks, their ranks thinning all the time. In fact, of no more than 4,500 British troops engaged so far that morning, around half had been put out of action. But at least the French had begun to arrive. So too had further British reinforcements, although they were still relatively low in number. Dannenberg, meanwhile, still had around 9,000 men sitting behind Shell Hill, ready to exploit any gains won by the Russians on the battlefield. These sixteen battalions were from Soimonov's command. In the event, they were not to see any real action at Inkerman. And there were, of course, the men from Gorchakov's force, now skirting along the valley of the Chernaya. In fact, his artillery had already shelled Cathcart's men earlier in the morning. It was, therefore, a satisfied but nevertheless anxious Pennefather who sat with his staff on Home Ridge, waiting to see where the next Russian attacks would come from.

Pennefather did not have to wait long for the next Russian attack to develop, for at around 8.45 more grey-clad Russian infantry began to spill down the side of Shell Hill and form in Quarry Ravine. Soon, a massive column had formed along the line of the Post Road, consisting of the remnants of the four battalions of the Iakoutsky Regiment. It was, in effect, the entire regiment, advancing with its huge regimental flag – some say there was a religious icon also – being held aloft in the centre. Some British officers on Fore Ridge claimed to have seen as many as twelve Russian battalions advancing, the other eight consisting of the Tomsky and Kolyvansky Regiments. No matter how many battalions there actually were it was an extremely large force. This great column, called 'the great trunk column' by Kinglake, was covered on both flanks and in advance by battalion and company columns as well as clouds of skirmishers, all of whom moved well ahead of the main column. This 'vanguard' was to shield the Iakoutsky from British fire until it hit Home Ridge, whereupon Dannenberg hoped it would break through and drive the British back from the Inkerman position, the Russians linking up, hopefully, with Gorchakov's men who had advanced from the Balaklava plain.

This great Russian force numbered around 6,000, against which the British and French directly in its path could muster no more than 3,000. Indeed, the total Allied force at this time was no more than 5,000 with forty-eight guns, the Allied artillery having been increased since the arrival of Boussinière's twelve guns. The British troops holding the front line consisted of wings and small detachments of various regiments who would have to pull together an act like one tight-knit unit if they were going to be able to withstand this latest Russian attack.

The first British troops to feel the force of the attack were the men of Turner's battery, away on the west of Home Ridge. In fact, it was a half battery, just three guns, commanded by Lieutenant Boothby. The guns were able to fire off just one round of canister before they were overwhelmed and taken, but not before Sergeant Major Henry won for himself a Victoria Cross for defending his gun within an inch of his life, suffering fifteen bayonet wounds. Although Henry survived, the guns didn't, for they fell into the hands of the Russians, but not for long. Earlier on that morning Miller's guns of P Battery had been overrun but, for some strange reason, not spiked. The same was about to happen to Boothby's guns, for the Russians just stood around congratulating themselves instead of putting the guns out of action. In the meantime a small unit of

**1.** Napoleon III, 1808-1873.
Emperor of the French.

**2.** Nicholas I, 1796-1855.
Czar of Russia.

**3.** Raglan's reluctant successor,
General James Simpson, 1792-1868.

**4.** Commander-in-Chief of the British Army
in the Crimea, Lord Raglan, 1788-1855.

**5.** Marshal Pierre Joseph Francois Bosquet, 1810-1861.

**6.** Marshal Francois Antoine Certain Canrobert, 1809-1895.

**7.** Marshal Amiable Jean Jacques Pélissier, 1794-1864.

**8.** Marshal Leroy de Saint-Arnaud, 1801-1854.

**9.** Prince M.D. Gorchakov, 1795-1861.

**10.** Alexander Sergeivitch Menchikov, 1787-1869.

**11.** Omar Pasha, 1806-1871, commander of the Turkish Army in the Crimea.

**12.** Alexander II, 1818-1881. Became Czar of Russia on the death of Nicholas I in 1855.

**13.** Admiral Vladimir Istomin, 1809-1855.

**14.** Admiral Pavel Stepanovitch Nakhimov, 1802-1855.

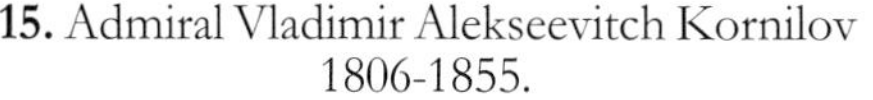

**15.** Admiral Vladimir Alekseevitch Kornilov 1806-1855.

**16.** General Francis Eduard Totleben, 1818-1884.

**17.** The Battle of the Alma, 20 September 1854. British Foot Guards move forward to begin crossing the Alma river before attacking the heights beyond. After a print by Dupray.

**18.** A view of the Alma river looking east from the right of the Russian position. The river, photographed here by Klembowsky in 1904, is barely more than a wide stream today.

**19.** The Charge of the Light Brigade, 25 October 1854. After a print by Dupray.

**20.** The Light Brigade's view of the Valley of Death, looking east towards the Russian gun position. After a photograph taken in 1904 by Klembowsky. Vineyards cover the valley today.

**21.** The Battle of Inkerman, 5 November 1854. Pennefather and the British fight desperately to hold back the Russian onslaught. After a print by Dupray.

**22.** A view of the British position at Inkerman, as seen from Quarry Ravine. The main British position is on the skyline. From a photograph taken by Klembowsky in 1904.

**23.** The sinking of the ships in the mouth of Sevastopol harbour on 23 September 1854.
After a painting by I. Vladimirov.

**24.** Angels of Mercy; The Sisters of Mercy of the Community of the Cross.
After a painting by V. Timm.

**25.** 'The Gale off the Port of Balaklava.' The great storm of 14 November 1854. The ship about to come to grief in the centre is the *Prince*. After a print by Simpson.

**26.** Another view of the great storm of 14 November 1854. Note the British officers huddled together behind the windmill. After a print from *The Officer's Portfolio*.

**27.** British light troops skirmishing in the snow during the winter of 1854-55. After a print from *The Officer's Portfolio.*

**28.** Seaman Ignati Shevchenko saves the life of Lieutenant Birulev during a sortie on 19 January 1855. Sadly, Shevchenko was killed during the episode. After a painting by V. Makovsky.

**29.** 'Sentinel of the Zouaves in front of Sevastopol.' After a print by Simpson.

**30.** 'Embarkation of the Sick at Balaklava.' After a print by Simpson.

**31.** An all-too familiar occurence during the siege of Sevastopol; a funeral on the Severnaia side of Sevastopol. After a painting by V. Timm.

**32.** Despite the siege the children of Sevastopol still manage to play amidst the rubble-strewn streets of the town. After a painting by V. Makovsky.

**33.** The view from the Malakhov looking east towards the Mamelon. In 1855 the ground here was covered in trenches. From a photograph by Klembowsky taken in 1904.

**34.** A view towards the town cemetery from the Central Bastion, showing pocked marked terrain, the result of French shelling, even in 1904, when this photograph by Klembowsky was taken.

**35.** Seaman Trofim Alexandrov extinguishes an Allied shell in the Russian defences at Sevastopol. After a painting by V. Makovsky.

**36.** British, Turkish and French prisoners are questioned by Russian officers inside Sevastopol in February 1855.

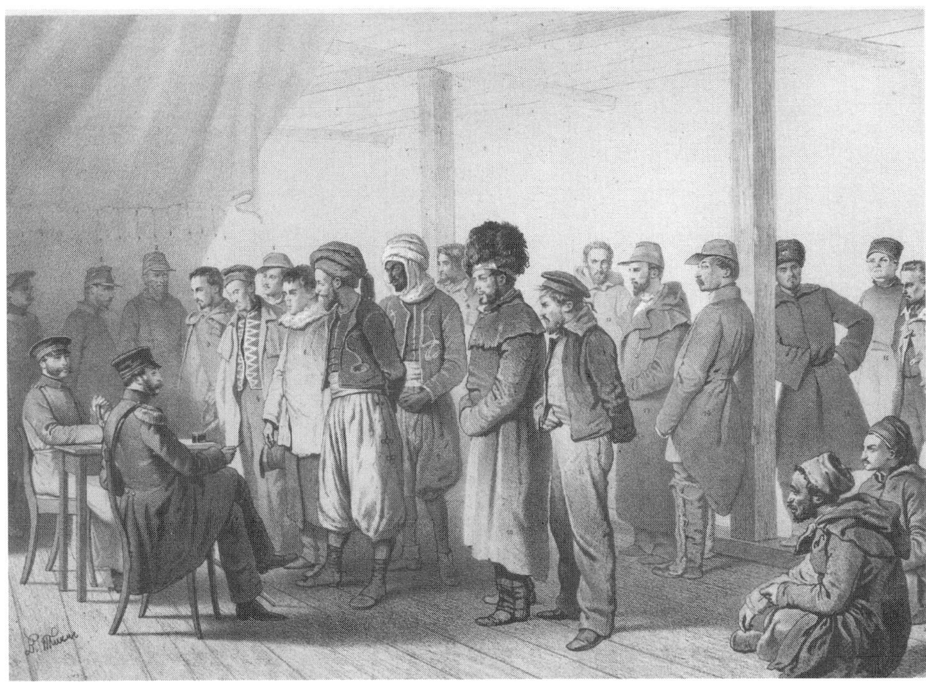

**37.** Admiral P. Nakhimov in his dugout in the Redan on 10 July 1855. He was killed shortly afterwards by an Allied sharpshooter. After a painting by I. Pryanishnikov.

**38.** A party of Russian scouts on the prowl at night before Sevastopol. After a painting by V. Perov.

**39.** The ill-fated British attack on the Redan, 8 September 1855. After a print by Dupray.

**40.** 'The Last Glance.' A Russian soldier and one of Sevastopol's citizens take a last look back as the old town is abandoned on 9 September 1855. After a painting by F. Rubo.

French Zouaves, about sixty strong, appeared – nobody has quite explained where they had come from, although it is possible they had left their camp without orders to join in the fight – and fell upon the Russians with their bayonets, recapturing the guns and putting the Russians to flight, aided by 466 men of the 63rd under Colonel Swyney and 201 of the 21st under Colonel Ainslie. These British troops continued their advance as far as the lower slopes of Shell Hill, where they halted.

The fighting, meanwhile, was still affected by the patches of fog that hung around the battlefield. Not far to the right of Turner's guns Colonel Warren and his small band of the 55th, no more than a hundred men, were suddenly surprised by a large force of Russians that loomed out of the mist. At first Warren thought they might be British troops but realised his error too late. His men were overwhelmed, most being killed, wounded or captured, although many managed to get away. Boothby's three guns having been captured and recaptured, it was now the turn of the three guns commanded by Turner himself to come under threat. Turner had sufficient warning, however, and kept his guns firing until the very last moment, whereupon the guns were limbered up and brought away to the rear.

By now the vanguard of Dannenberg's force was almost upon the crest of Home Ridge, whilst the main column itself surged up towards The Barrier. Watching the fight behind Home Ridge was Lord Raglan himself, sitting with his staff around him. It was a perilous position because Russian shot continued to pepper the British line. Before long the Russian vanguard began to break through at Home Ridge, leaving nothing in their front save for the French 7th Léger which formed to the east of the Post Road, just in front of the 2nd Division's camp. The French hurried forward, causing the Russians to stop, but the French then halted themselves and, after some hesitation, began to fall back much to the consternation and annoyance of Raglan. The Russians continued and, in fact, were now able to see almost a mile to the south beyond the British camp. There was simply nothing between them and Gorchakov's force in the valley north of Balaklava. It was a serious situation for Raglan and it was just as well that, at that very crucial moment, Egerton and his unit of the 77th, withdrawn from their position away to the west of Home Ridge, came charging up. They were helped somewhat by the artillery of the Russians themselves which came crashing down upon their own men, bringing them to a halt. Then, when the French 7th Léger had finally re-formed, the 77th and their French allies went charging up the hill to drive the Russian vanguard back. At the same time the re-formed remnants of the 55th, surprised only minutes before and determined to avenge themselves, charged the flank of the Russians and helped drive them back, much to the satisfaction of Colonel Warren, still seething after being embarrassed earlier on.

It is remarkable that while the vanguard of the Russian attack had reached the breastwork on Home Ridge there still remained about 200 men from the 49th, 20th and the 95th, positioned at The Barrier. The two officers, Bellairs and Vaughan, had watched in amazement as the vanguard of the Russian attack had surged forward on both sides and yet had paid little attention to them. Perhaps the mist and smoke of battle obscured the Russians' view. They were not to be left alone for much longer, however, and when the great column of the Iakoutsky came up to The Barrier, Bellairs received an order from a staff officer to retire. It was a sensible thing to do, for there was no way that this small mixed bunch of British troops could have halted the Russians. The men fell back slowly, firing as they went for as long as their ever-diminishing supply of ammunition lasted. The problem was that Bellairs and his men effectively masked the advance of the Iakoutsky, which prevented the British and French on Home Ridge from firing.

Eventually, frantic shouts from the French commander, Vaissier, of 'Mais retirez vous. Nous allons ouvrir!'[6] sent them darting round the left flank of the French 7th Léger, leaving them free to open fire. The trouble was that the 7th's fire had been delayed so long that the Iakoutsky were almost upon them when they got their first volley away. The young soldiers of the 7th fumbled at their ramrods as the Russians continued to close and, soon enough, a ripple effect was set in motion when one of the companies gave way. The French wavered and were only prevented from running by Bellairs and Vaughan who had drawn up their men behind them. A bayonet charge might well have halted the Russians but the French simply weren't up to it. Despite appeals from Pennefather and other British officers they would not stand, leaving the Iakoutsky with a clear run upon the reverse slope of Home Ridge. But at the very moment when it seemed as though the Russians would roll over the 7th Léger along with Bellairs and Vaughan they ground to a halt whilst a wild commotion broke out behind them. Pennefather was not alone in wondering what on earth had caused the halt, but he soon had his answer, for as he gazed through the smoke and mist he saw a flurry of punches being exchanged, rifle butts heaved left and right, bayonets were thrust and shots fired. And then, suddenly, from the midst of the Russian column, a small group of British soldiers staggered from it, their coats bloodied and torn.

Lieutenant Colonel Daubeney, of the 55th, had watched the progress of the Russian attack from behind the breastwork on Home Ridge. He and his men were about fifty yards or so to the west of the Iakoutsky column when a staff officer arrived and suggested he charge. There were no more than thirty men of the 55th but they were itching to hit back at the Russians after being compromised minutes earlier. Daubeney and his men knew they were up against it but not a man flinched as they went scrambling and cheering over the breastwork to lay into the right of the second Iakoutsky battalion, about 600-strong. It was almost certainly a combination of British determination and Russian surprise that caused the Iakoutsky to grind to a halt. After all, there were almost 6,000 Russians heaving up towards Home Ridge. What on earth were these mad Englishmen doing? What they were doing was bringing the column to an astonished halt.

Daubeney set about the Iakoutsky with a wild charge that sliced through the grey-coated ranks after a savage hand-to-hand fight. The Russians were so tightly packed and astonished by the audacity of the charge that they had difficulty in fighting back. But once they recovered themselves they did so with a vengeance and it was only after an immense struggle that Daubeney and his men were able to emerge, bursting from the midst of the Russian column on its eastern side, suffering several killed and wounded. Remarkably, Daubeney himself emerged completely unscathed. Despite their losses – they were relatively light considering the odds against them – the men of the 55th had brought the Russians to a halt. Furthermore, their assault restored confidence throughout the ranks of the 7th Léger who were galvanised and inspired to turn and charge. The Russians, meanwhile, in disarray, wondering what was going on behind them, began to fall back slowly. Unfortunately, those in the front ranks, hemmed in by the mass behind them, couldn't move and were simply shot down by the French. Gradually, the rear of the leading Iakoutsky battalion began to melt away, followed soon afterwards by those at the front, precipitating a sudden flight to the rear by the great Russian column which was pursued with great gusto by the now confident French, and by Bellairs and Vaughan, whose men joined in the chase, as did Inglis and the men of the 57th who had returned from their foray into Quarry Ravine.

There still remained the covering columns, however. The eastern Russian column was effectively dealt with by the guns of Pennecuik's battery and by the recently arrived horse artillery of Boussinière. Between them the Allied guns took a heavy toll of the Russians, firing canister into their left flank at relatively short range. There was no reply to this devastating fire and the Russians were left with no option but to retreat once more to the sanctuary of Quarry Ravine, pounded all the way by Allied shot and shell. However, it was the western-most column which posed the greater threat, pressing in as it was against the western end of Home Ridge. Here, the line was held by men representing the two extremes of the British soldier. On the left there were the highly trained 21st Fusiliers, under Ainslie. These good quality troops were supported on their right by Swyney and the 63rd, 'a body which owed its main strength to lads newly and hastily recruited in the city of Dublin; and, until it moved down to the port for embarkation, the battalion thus rawly constituted had never executed so much as even one march.'[7] These 600 or so men formed line, loaded and prepared to meet the oncoming Russian battalions.

The 21st and 63rd were still armed with old smooth bore muskets which, like the Minié rifles wielded elsewhere on the battlefield, were plagued by the wet weather. Nevertheless, the muskets were soon 'warmed into life' and a rolling fire poured out from the line against the dark mass moving towards them. A few volleys followed after which the men fixed bayonets and slowly began to move forward. Smooth bore muskets, charged bayonets, cheers; it was like the good old days of the Peninsular War as the British line went forward to drive back the columns approaching them. The unwieldy Russian column was simply outgunned and slowly began to fall back in the direction of Quarry Ravine with the 21st and 63rd coming after it. Eventually, the two British units halted astride the Post Road. Their advance brought them into contact with the retreating elements of the great Russian column which the 7th Léger had flung back, leaving them with a second fight on their hands. This time, the Iakoutsky decided to stand and hold their ground and a severe and murderous firefight ensued between the two sides. Indeed, Swyney was shot from his horse and killed, whilst his successor, Dalzell, had his own horse shot from under him. The two young officers carrying the colours, Clutterbuck and Twysden, were shot also, the former being killed outright and the latter mortally wounded. Nevertheless, the 21st and 63rd gave as good as they received and gradually began to push forward, steadily driving the Iakoutsky back. Colonel Ainslie now being wounded, Lieutenant Colonel Frederick Haines assumed command of the 21st, leading them and the 63rd in the pursuit as far as a trench which the British had dug across the Post Road north of The Barrier. Haines evidently considered the position to be too isolated, however, and he pulled the 21st and 63rd back to The Barrier where he joined other isolated groups of British troops.

It was now past 9 am and all Russian attacks had somehow been beaten back. One feels that Dannenberg's chances had passed him by. The thinly-held British line had buckled but had not broken and re-inforcements were coming up, piecemeal perhaps, but they were arriving. The French, too, were arriving along with their artillery. If Dannenberg could not succeed when up against Pennefather's thin line what chance did he have against the Allies' growing forces? But there was still much fighting to come and more close calls for the Allies despite their numbers.

The 6th Ligne, it will be remembered, had advanced from Home Ridge, driving the Russians back before continuing on to the Inkerman Tusk, effectively the high ground on the eastern side of Quarry Ravine. By remaining out on the Inkerman Tusk, however, De Camas and his men were in serious danger of being cut off by any Russian force that turned on them from the Quarry Ravine as there was no way back other than to the south, by the same way they had come. The situation De Camas feared now arose when, at about 9.15 am, five battalions of Russian infantry suddenly began working their way up the ravine to attack the French who were left with no option but to fight their way out through the Russian column. Sadly, the 47 year-old De Camas fell, shot in the chest by a Russian bullet, but his men continued advancing against the overwhelming Russian mass, firing as they went and dragging their wounded leader with them. The regimental 'eagle' that topped their colour fell to the ground also when the standard bearer was killed, and it was only through the efforts of Lieutenant Colonel Goze that the precious symbol of regimental pride did not fall into the hands of the Russians. Goze himself was wounded shortly afterwards and he was forced to give the flag to Lieutenant Bigotte. It was a severe struggle for the French and as the Russians closed they were even forced to leave behind their commanding officer, De Camas, who was near death in any case. De Camas fell into the hands of the Russians and died soon afterwards. The battalion finally reached the relative safety of the forward slopes of Home Ridge where it formed alongside the 7th Léger.

With the 6th Ligne having been driven back from Inkerman Tusk, the prospects for Haines and the defenders of The Barrier looked fairly desperate. The men were tired, ammunition was low and numbers were dwindling with each successive Russian attack or barrage. By now, Brigadier General Goldie was at The Barrier, assuming command of the troops there from Haines. Goldie was not to remain for long, however. He had already had his horse shot from under him and not long after arriving at The Barrier he too was shot in the head by a Russian marksman. It was a blow, but the fight went on. Meanwhile, an officer was sent back to Pennefather requesting both men and ammunition, both of which were rapidly diminishing. In the event, ammunition was sent forward along with a single company of the 77th under Lieutenant Acton, followed shortly afterwards by a company of the 49th. Thus, the number of British troops at The Barrier was increased. The question was, would they be enough to withstand the next Russian attack?

The Russians themselves had shown enormous courage and bravery, particularly Pavlov's men, in advancing time after time against the withering fire of the British and French Minié rifles. Their losses had been far greater than the Allies although their columns, being so much larger, had naturally presented a better target than the thin British and French lines. When Pyotr Alabin returned to Quarry Ravine he was appalled by what he saw there.

> In the Quarry Ravine I saw a terrible picture. The whole ravine was full of dead and wounded. The French skirmishers were sitting in

> many places behind the rocks on the opposite side of the ravine and were exchanging fire with our skirmishers. There were many killed and wounded under the arches of the aqueduct. I rode farther and found many of our soldiers on the old Post road and on the bank of the Tchernaya river, waiting for the enemy's advance from the Quarry Ravine. It was a terrible mess. The officers were trying to sort out the soldiers into their regiments but in vain. I gathered together the soldiers of the Okhotsky regiment, and ordered them to be on guard on the bridge and not to allow any soldier in good health to escort the wounded. After that I rushed to the dressing station and, with the help of a paymaster of the Iakoutsky regiment, Efimov, assembled 200 men and led them beyond the bridge to the ravine where I saw thousands of miserable soldiers. I also took more than ten carriages and loaded them with the wounded under the aqueduct. What bloodcurdling scenes I witnessed! The medical attendant of the Okhotsky regiment, Danilov, was dressing the wounded under a rock. Having sent the bloodstained transport, I galloped to find my general to inform him about the crowds of soldiers at the bottom of the mountain on the river bank; what would he order them to do? By that time everything was finished for us: the French overthrew us totally and only our reinforcements could renew the battle. Every minute we expected the French to follow our troops to the Quarry ravine and cut off our retreat. In that case a terrible disaster would happen! There was no order at all among our troops thronging on the river bank; the voices of the commanders were not heard; there was neither place to turn around nor to form to fight. Each shot of the enemy caused tremendous casualties, having plunged into the thronging crowd. There was no place to advance artillery to cover our retreat. So, if the Allies advanced it would be absolutely disastrous for us![8]

Although Raglan was present with his staff on the reverse slope of Home Ridge he had done little to interfere with the control of the battle, not that much control was possible anyway in the dense fog in which the battle had begun. Instead, he was content to let Pennefather run the show. Raglan did, however, manage to influence the outcome of the battle by ordering up two 18-pounder guns. Raglan, it will be remembered, had ordered up the guns as soon as news of the fighting had reached him earlier that morning. It was to prove a crucial move. With almost ninety Russian guns pounding away at Home Ridge Dannenberg certainly had the upper hand during the first two or three hours of the battle. The Allied reply was not insignificant but, outnumbered by about two to one, there was more iron being dropped on to the Allied positions than was dropped on Shell Hill. That all changed, however, with the arrival of the two 18-

pounders under Colonel Gambier that were manhandled with immense effort up to the firing line, taking up a position at the angle of Fore Ridge and Home Ridge where a low breastwork, protected by gabions, had been constructed for three lighter guns, all of which were withdrawn upon the arrival of Gambier's beasts.

During the Napoleonic Wars, 18-pounder guns were rarely seen on the battlefield. They were essentially siege guns. Capable of firing at a rate of about one shot per minute, these great guns could smash masonry and bring down whole sections of walls with great effect. It is easy to imagine, therefore, the effect they had on a battlefield. Although there were several mighty 32-pounders on Shell Hill, the majority of the Russian guns were 12-pounders. Thus, these two British 18-pounders enjoyed good advantage over the Russians. The problem was there were only two of them and they were sure to attract the immediate and unwanted attention of the Russian guns. Despite Gambier's great efforts in getting the guns up to Home Ridge, he did not remain long to see them in action for he was wounded by a round shot soon afterwards. Fortunately, the Royal Artillery was blessed with several capable officers, amongst whom was Colonel Collingwood Dickson, son of the great Alexander Dickson, Wellington's artillery chief in the Peninsula. Dickson soon had his guns in action, commanded by Sinclair and D'Aguillar. The Russian response was predictable. Shell after shell came flying towards the two British guns but, amazingly, none of them hit home. Instead, they either hit the earth bank behind, or landed in front and smashed into the groups of unfortunate gunners that served the guns. They led a remarkably charmed existence. The effect of Dickson's guns was soon felt by the Russian gunners away on Shell Hill. Within easy range and silhouetted against the grey sky on the slightly higher hill the Russian guns began to fall silent as a result of the accuracy of the British guns. On the face of it the duel between the two was terribly one-sided but slowly but steadily the two 18-pounders, supported by the other Allied guns, began to gain the upper hand, and when Boussinière brought forward twelve more French 12-pounders the situation really did begin to improve for the Allies. It was a turning point in the battle.

Despite having some sixteen battalions of relatively fresh infantry waiting behind Shell Hill, Dannenberg appears to have sensed that his chance had gone. He had thrown overwhelming numbers of Russian infantry against the sorely tried and thinly held British line, but apart from inflicting casualties on the British he had failed to achieve anything worthwhile. The Iakoutsky in particular had shown incredible fortitude in persisting with their attacks despite grievous losses and despite the fact that, even to them, it must have been obvious that they were never going to break what was, certainly by 9.30 am, a line which was increasing in strength by the minute. The French and British guns were now dominating the Russian guns, in addition to which they were effectively covering the exit from the Quarry Ravine as well as the St Clements Ravine, from where the most persistent and dangerous Russian attacks had come. But the battle was still far from over.

Indeed, even as the two British 18-pounders were beginning to make their fire tell on the Russian guns on Shell Hill, another Russian attack was beginning, not up on the heights but emerging from Sevastopol itself. Part of Menshikov's 'plan' involved a sortie in strength from Sevastopol, with four battalions of the Minsky Regiment and four light guns from 14 Artillery Brigade. Commanding the 5,000-strong column was Major General N D Timofeev, a veteran of the Russo–Turkish War of 1828. The garrison commander, Moller, had despatched Timofeev in accordance with Menshikov's overall plan, the sortie's objective being two-fold. First, the sortie was to fix the French and prevent them from assisting their British allies struggling to cope with Dannenberg on the Inkerman Heights. Second, Timofeev's men were to destroy as much of the Allied siege works and put out as many of their guns as possible.

The sortie was launched at around 9.30 am, when Timofeev and his men issued from Sevastopol to the right of Bastion No.6, which was situated on the western side of the town, well away from the fighting at Inkerman. Covered by the fog the Minsky were able to penetrate the French siege lines, the leading battalion under Major Evspalev managing to break into the trenches and spike fifteen guns. Timofeev's attack was preceded by a clouds of skirmishers who exchanged fire with the French 39th and 19th Ligne, who drew back in the face of the heavy Russian attack. Two companies of the 19th Chasseurs were brought forward also as the French struggled to hold on. General La Motte-Rouge was commanding in the trenches that morning and he managed to bring up a few companies of the 20th Léger, but by the time they had got forward they discovered that the Russians had already withdrawn. La Motte-Rouge pursued them through the trenches but was brought up by the sight of Russian reinforcements in the form of six battalions of the Bretsky Regiment and one of the Vilensky, along with six guns. The fighting escalated with the arrival of General de Lourmel's brigade whilst General d'Aurelle's brigade marched by the sea road in order to try to cut off the Russian columns. General Forey, meanwhile, in overall command of the French siege corps, marched with the 5th Chasseurs to try to cut off any Russian retreat on the eastern side of Sevastopol. Aware that the French were now moving against him in overwhelming strength, the wily Timofeev began to withdraw his men, which was achieved despite pressure from the French. During the latter phase of the sortie Lourmel was mortally wounded and died two days later. In retrospect, the sortie was launched too far away from the scene of the main fighting to have had any real and effective bearing on the battle, but it did nevertheless delay and prevent French reinforcements from moving to help the British. Also, French casualties were heavy whilst the loss of as many as fifteen guns was a blow in itself.

The British and French struggling to cope with the grey tide of Russians on the Inkerman Heights had little knowledge of what was happening away to the west around Sevastopol. They were consumed by the fighting around them and had little time for events elsewhere. Haines, now in sole command at The Barrier, certainly had no idea that a sortie had taken place. Instead, he watched, no doubt with growing pleasure, as the British and French guns began to get the upper hand in their duel with Dannenberg's guns. By 10 am the tide of battle appeared to have swung distinctly in the Allies' favour, for not only had their artillery wrested the advantage from the Russians but French reinforcements were now beginning to arrive in good numbers.

General Bosquet, whose help, it will be remembered, had originally been declined by Cathcart and Brown, had ordered D'Autemarre's two brigades forward earlier in the morning. At around 10 am the first of these two brigades, consisting of the 2nd Battalion of the 3rd Zouaves, the 2nd Battalion of Algerians, began arriving on the battlefield. D'Autemarre's second brigade, consisting of the 50th Ligne and the 1st Battalion 3rd Zouaves, was marching hard towards the battlefield also. They had been preceded by four companies of Foot Chasseurs from Bourbaki's brigade and with D'Autemarre's first brigade almost 3,000 French troops were added to those already engaged in fighting the Russians. No sooner had Bosquet surveyed the scene before him than he ordered the Chasseurs, some 450 in all, to charge and retake the Sandbag Battery which still lay intimidating and full of Russians away to the right of the Allied line. But just at the very moment that the Chasseurs were advancing towards the battery, two columns of Russians began to emerge once more from Quarry Ravine. Showing remarkable resilience, the Iakoutsky were attacking yet again. Despite their mauling at the hands of the disparate bands of British infantry and their artillery the Iakoutsky simply refused to lie down. They emerged from the ravine driving before them a scattered bunch of the 20th Foot under Colonel Horn, whose men came back turning and firing as they did so. Seeing these Russian columns in front of them the Chasseurs turned away from the Sandbag Battery and continued on towards the head of Quarry Ravine which was boiling over with advancing Russians. Between them, the 20th and the Chasseurs managed to stop the Iakoutsky for a short time but when the Russians regrouped and advanced once more the French pulled back towards the Kitspur, leaving Horn, who was wounded shortly afterwards, to fend for himself. Their ammunition dwindling, the 20th continued to fire into the Iakoutsky, hoping that help would arrive before it was too late.

Fortunately, help did indeed arrive in the shape of some 3,000 French troops of the 2nd Battalion of Zouaves, under Dubos, and the 2nd

Algerian Battalion under Colonel Wimpfen. These were supported by twenty-four guns. Bosquet formed the Zouaves and the Algerians on the east of the Post Road where they were joined by the Chasseurs who had fallen back after their clash with the Iakoutsky. Thus, just over 3,000 French infantry were now ready to be flung against the oncoming Russians. But, for some bizarre reason, Bourbaki led his men past the 20th, still fighting at the head of the ravine, and took them out on to Inkerman Tusk, the narrow spur that juts out to the north-east, with Quarry Ravine on one side and St Clements Ravine on the other. It was the same piece of ground where the 6th Ligne had almost come to grief earlier on. Bourbaki was about to find himself in a similarly difficult situation.

Bosquet then rode forward with some of his staff to the head of Quarry Ravine to see the situation for himself. But instead of finding British troops hard at it with the Russians he saw nothing but Russians coming on once more. He immediately sent for artillery, two of Toussaint's guns arriving a few minutes later. The guns were just being unlimbered when a cry went up, 'General, here are the Russians!'[9] It was true. Russian skirmishers were pouring up on to the Tusk, taking one of the French guns before Toussaint had time to get it away. Whilst Bosquet scanned for British troops – the nearest to him were the isolated 20th down beyond The Barrier, and Haines and his men at The Barrier itself – scores of Russian skirmishers were clambering up the side of Inkerman Tusk, with a battalion of the Iakoutsky following hard on their heels. In fact, even as Bosquet sat there on his horse Russian skirmishers were within fifty yards of him but for some strange reason they held fire. Considering how many British officers were shot down and killed Bosquet can consider himself fortunate that he was able to ride off unharmed.[10] Meanwhile, the Iakoutsky battalion reached the top of Quarry Ravine and, looking to their left, saw with some astonishment that they had managed to emerge in the left rear of the French troops on the Tusk. They could scarce believe their luck. In fact, so surprised were they at this unintentional success that they seemed unable to take advantage of it. Victory was there for the taking, for all they had to do was to turn to their left and they would leave the French with no option but to fight their way back through them or risk being driven over the steep sides of the Tusk or be taken prisoner. The perilous position for the French increased dramatically soon afterwards when a battalion of the Selenghinsky that had been clinging to the eastern side of the Kitspur emerged in the right rear of the French on the Tusk.

Between them, the Iakoutsky and Selenghinsky had it in their power to virtually wipe out the French troops stranded on Inkerman Tusk but they were simply unable to grasp the situation and the opportunity went begging. The French, suddenly aware of the danger, turned, and with the Zouaves leading the way they dashed at the Selenghinsky, fending them off long enough for the French to slip between the two Russian columns before the jaws of this unintentional trap closed. It was a very close shave. The flight from Inkerman Tusk also precipitated a rearward movement by the 6th Ligne and the 7th Léger who, gripped by a degree of panic, retreated to Home Ridge. The Zouaves, Algerians and Chasseurs, meanwhile, returned to the relative safety of Fore Ridge but were soon under artillery fire from the Russian guns on East Jut and Shell Hill. In fact, the Russian guns began to hit back after their mauling by the British 18-pounders. The fire of the two British guns began to slacken as a result of a shortage of ammunition and this, coupled with a degree of mobility amongst the Russian guns as they sought positions which afforded them some protection against the Allied guns allowed the Russian artillery to claw their way back into the fight. Boussinière's guns and gun teams suffered in particular, with tumbrels exploding, men being blown apart and knocked down, and guns being knocked out of action. 'We are getting massacred,' a worried but philosophical Boussinière said to Dickson, adding, 'Well, after all, this is war.'[11]

By now the French commander-in-chief, General Canrobert, was present, nursing a slight shrapnel wound in the arm and peering through the smoke and mist to see just how bad the situation was. Away to his right Boussinière's guns continued to take a pounding, whilst out in front he saw nothing but isolated pockets of British troops. Apart from his own troops there appeared to be no large units of Allies anywhere. But if he thought the situation serious, it was just as well he had not been present three hours earlier during the really desperate fighting. Despite Raglan's forebodings – 'I believe we are in a bad situation,' he told Canrobert – the French commander remained optimistic. 'Not so very, my Lord; let us hope for the best,' he replied.[12] Canrobert might well have appeared confident but his first move was called by Kinglake, 'half despairing.'[13] It was his decision to bring forward cavalry.

Inkerman could never be described as a battlefield suited to cavalry. Indeed, many mounted infantry officers had already come to grief on the broken, treacherous ground, and to expect cavalry to achieve something useful was hoping against hope. The 4th Chasseurs d'Afrique had already demonstrated their prowess when coming to the aid of the Light Brigade at Balaklava, attacking the Russian guns on the Fedioukine Heights. The ground at Inkerman was something completely different, however. It was a strange decision and was one that yielded few benefits for the Allies. Indeed, it took just a single Russian shell, bursting in front of the regiment, to cause them all to turn about and ride to the rear, finally halting about a mile to the south. During their retreat they passed the sorry remains of the Light Brigade under Lord George Paget, Lord Cardigan having apparently overslept on his yacht. They too were called into action by Canrobert but immediately came under artillery fire from the guns on Shell Hill. This was no place for cavalry, and when the brigade had suffered its first ten casualties Paget had them turn about and withdraw from the field.

Coming on to the battlefield late in the morning appears to have given the French a false impression of what was happening. Bosquet had already come to grief on the Inkerman Tusk, charging in without really knowing the ground or the true situation there, and now the optimistic but obviously anxious Canrobert had seen fit to throw in cavalry in a mark of desperation. Furthermore, he had seen his columns flung back, they had retreated, his artillery were being smashed and there remained thousands of Russian troops on Shell Hill, poised, so he thought, to strike. On top of all that, he was still concerned about events in the trenches and about the sortie made by Timofeev against his siege lines. The fact that Pennefather's men had been literally hanging on by their eyelids without ever considering retreat as an option appears to have escaped him. Instead, his officers began to consider retreat as inevitable. Indeed, Collingwood Dickson was still supervising the fire of the two 18-pounders when a French officer galloped up to him, urging him to draw off his guns, crying, 'Save your guns! All is lost!'[14]

The battle might well have appeared lost to the French but it had, in some ways, reached stalemate. The British were simply exhausted. Superhuman efforts alone had prevented the Russians from steam-rollering over both The Barrier and Home Ridge, to which hundreds of shattered and broken British bodies testified. They were certainly in no position to consider an attack. The French, on the other hand, were now on the field in good numbers but had obviously been affected both by what they had seen so far and by the failure of their own attacks, not to mention the fact that their artillery had taken a savage mauling at the hands of the Russian guns. Dannenberg, meanwhile, sat there with virtually the whole of Soimonov's battalions waiting up on Shell Hill, whilst even the battered and bruised Iakoutsky and Selenghinsky were still capable of a renewed offensive. His artillery, despite their losses, remained strong also. An attack in strength by these combined corps would surely break the back of the Allied resistance and with Gorchakov still hovering in the valley of the Chernaya the consequences for the Allies would be dire to say the least. Now, surely, was the time to strike. And yet, poised though he was in such a wonderful position, Dannenberg failed to take advantage of it. He simply couldn't see just how precarious the Allies' situation was and just how good his own was. His caution was understandable, however, for despite the massive and prolonged attacks on the British position and his successes, however marginal, over the French, he had yet to achieve anything really tangible. Only one gun had been captured from the Allies whilst the possession of a tract of ground above the Kitspur and around the Sandbag Battery remained scant reward for his men's efforts which had cost him several thousand casualties. The simple truth was that the two sides had fought themselves to a standstill and it was time to see whose nerve would hold best.

The hesitation on Dannenberg's part brought about a slight lull in the fighting. Haines' men continued firing away in a desultory manner, using their bullets as economically as possible, as did other small British units here and there along what might be termed the 'front line'. The Russian guns continued to bark away also, with the Allies' guns returning their fire with interest. But still neither side advanced. It was as if each side was taking stock of the situation, waiting to see who would make the next significant move. The stalemate was finally broken with the arrival of D'Autemarre's brigade, consisting of the 1st Battalion of the 3rd Zouaves and the two battalions of the 50th Ligne. The arrival of these new units brought about a marked change in the hitherto hesitant French ranks. It gave them a real boost, and coupled with the evident reluctance on the part of Dannenberg to attack, it gave the French a new impetus. Bosquet seized the moment immediately and ordered Dubos' Zouaves and Wimpfen's Algerians to form up in readiness for a fresh attack on the Sandbag Battery which was still occupied by the Selenghinsky, and the ground on either side of it. The men formed, Bosquet rode along the front ranks, shouting in Arabic, 'Come on, my valiant Zouaves! Come on my brave Chasseurs! . . . show yourselves sons of fire!'[15] His words were greeted by a mighty roar, and all at once his men began to move down from Fore Ridge to deliver Bosquet's 'supreme effort'.[16]

The Selenghinsky, hovering to the south of the battery, were taken aback by the French who turned to their right to attack them. Such was the fury of the assault that the Selenghinsky were pursued almost to the valley of the Chernaya below. Not only did the onslaught clear the Kitspur of Russians but it resulted in the happy re-emergence of some isolated pockets of British troops who had been sheltering in the thick brush since being cut off during Cathcart's so-called 'false victory'. Amongst them were about a hundred men of the 95th under Vialls and Sargent, who had been cut off at the bottom of St Clements Ravine. The Derbyshire men had listened anxiously to the sound of hundreds of pairs of boots as they came thudding down the hillside, and prepared for the worse. But when they heard 'the cry of the Zouaves, and the howling of the African soldiery', they rose and joined in the pursuit.[17] And then there was the eerie sight of scores of bearskins rising from the bushes as Wilson and his Coldstreamers also emerged from their hiding place, they too having concealed themselves since being cut off during the 'false victory'. The blood-soaked Sandbag Battery was taken during the same attack by the Zouaves and Algerians who piled into it, driving out the defenders and spilling them over the edge of the Kitspur and down the eastern side of the hill along with the rest of the Selenghinsky. The battery was finally back in Allied hands and would remain so. The Selenghinsky were chased completely from the battlefield, Bosquet's men hunting them down over the same ground where Cathcart and the 'false victory' had taken place. This time, however, there was no false victory.

While the Zouaves and Algerians took themselves off to the east Bosquet ordered the 6th Ligne and 7th Léger to advance also, but these two regiments did nothing more than bring themselves up on the right flank of Haines and the defenders at The Barrier who continued to hold on in the face of Russian attacks. Meanwhile, Monet's brigade of the French 3rd Division had arrived, further bolstering the defences and by the time the bells in Sevastopol were tolling eleven, there were some 7,000 French infantry on the ground alongside the much tried and tested British, bringing the total Allied infantry strength up to around 12,000. With Dannenberg evidently showing no sign of any further major offensive Raglan sensed there was finally light at the end of a very dark and difficult tunnel. The battle had been a supreme trial for the British soldier but now, with Canrobert present in force and with the Russians apparently lacking ideas, it seemed as though the final stage of the battle was at hand. Pennefather too sensed that things were coming to a head, and when an aide-de-camp arrived from Raglan asking him for a report on his situation he found 'old blood an 'ounds' in good spirits. Pennefather, known for his liberal use of expletives, apparently bit hard on his tongue when replying to Raglan's messenger, saying that if he were reinforced he would 'lick them [the Russians] to the devil!'[18]

Both Raglan and Canrobert were so delighted with Pennefather's response that Raglan sent for him in order to present him to the French commander-in-chief. One can well imagine Pennefather's thoughts at this moment. There he was in the middle of a bloody battle, when he was suddenly summoned to appear before his commander-in-chief so he could simply say hello to Canrobert. It was all rather ridiculous. The exchange also brought about a notable change in Canrobert's hitherto optimism, for when he informed the two commanders that he had just 750 men the French commander baulked, surprised at what he considered to be Pennefather's gross over-confidence. After all, he had seen his own infantry embarrassed on at least two occasions and his artillery had taken an awful battering, whilst his cavalry had turned tail at the first shot fired into them. No, he thought, the British were simply being ridiculous if they thought they could go on and win the battle with such a small force available to them. And with that all further hope of a French offensive ended.

Dannenberg's inactivity at least allowed some attention to be paid to the hundreds of Russian wounded choking Quarry Ravine. Our friend Pyotr Alabin was sent to see what he could do for them but it was a thankless task, as he later recalled:

> Colonel Byaliy sent a battalion of the Iakoutsky under command of Major Novashyn with me. We moved towards the corner of the ravine; on this side of the ravine there was only one weak battalion, which consisted of not more than 200 men. The skirmishers rushed with me into the ravine, I drew them up behind the rocks and placed them behind the aqueduct and, returning the enemy's fire, began to carry away the wounded and the killed. The same carriages, which had not previously stopped to carry the wounded, were now loaded with the sorrowful cargo. The French bullet, thank God, did not reach us. The most active among the other soldiers was a soldier of the Tarutinsky regiment, Fyodor Netchaev. He carried out fifteen wounded from the aqueduct on his own shoulders. Soon the number of the French against us increased. They opened a very strong fire and soon it was time for us to retreat.[19]

Alabin went on to say:

> Netchaev asked me, 'Sir, let me go there; two soldiers are sitting under the rock behind the bridge. Allow me to bring them in.' 'But what if they kill you', I asked. 'They are too weak for me! Even ten like them are not enough.' 'But what if the French hit you?' 'So be it, Sir. It matters not where you die, here or any other place.' 'Let it be so, dear friend, but go and come back quickly. We'll wait for you.' Netchaev ran and I ordered my men to lie down. The Iakoutsky lay under cover behind the hewn stones around them. Novashyn, who had already begun to retreat, paused. We had been waiting for ten minutes when we suddenly we saw Netchaev, rushing two soldiers along with his butt and carrying their two rifles. The French paid special attention to this small group but all three lived. 'Why did you remain there, rogues? Why?' I asked. 'We were tired, Sir, so we sat down to have a rest.' 'But the others are also tired', I said, 'but they do not rest! Give them their rifles and make them carry them to the position. See that you appoint them to be on duty today.' I gave Netchaev all the coins that were in my purse as his reward. We were retreating. I wondered how many men we were leaving on the battlefield. How many of them would die today because they could not be taken in time to hospital. The others might be saved with just one drink of water but there would not be anybody to give it to them! But what could we do? Such is the course of a battle.[20]

While Alabin was busy removing some of the wounded from Quarry Ravine other Russian troops began to batter away once more at Haines at The Barrier. Indeed, Dannenberg might well have known his chance had gone but it did not stop him ordering the Iakoutsky to continue their attacks. The firing had slackened off for a while at around 11 am as the opposing sides paused for breath and weighed up their situation. For Dickson's 18-pounders the lull came about largely as a result of a shortage of ammunition, and it was with some alarm that he realised that he could only maintain his advantage over the Russian guns for a short while longer. The two mighty guns had come into action with one hundred rounds per gun but the fire they had poured on the Russians had reduced this enormously. Fortunately, Captain Chermside made a tremendous, back-breaking effort and succeeded in bringing up a further 200 rounds, enabling Dickson to maintain the pressure on Shell Hill.

As Dickson's guns began tearing once more into the Russian guns on Shell Hill there came a gradual shift in the balance of the battle. For the last few hours The Barrier had been a forward defensive position for the British, breaking up the Russian attacks directed against Home Ridge and proving a massive irritant to first Soimonov and then Pavlov and Dannenberg. But now, with the Russian attacks seemingly losing impetus, The Barrier shifted from being a forward defensive position protecting Home Ridge to assuming a far more crucial role, certainly as far as Dannenberg was concerned. Indeed, Kinglake made the important point when he wrote:

> Our soldiery, whether combating at The Barrier or on its left front, passed gradually and almost unconsciously from the task of defence to the task of attack, for in truth the same kind of acts which before would have been acts of defence had now an aggressive force. To fight for The Barrier in the hours when Dannenberg was an assailant had been to defend the Home Ridge by fighting half a mile in its front. To fight for The Barrier now was, as it were, to hold open by force the gate of the enemy's castle, and grievously embarrass his defence. It was rather as a consequence of the enemy's having abandoned the offensive than from any abrupt change yet made in their own measures that the efforts of our people acquired an aggressive character.[21]

Thus, the Russians were fighting not to take The Barrier and break through to Home Ridge but to take and hold it in order to maintain the security of their own increasingly fragile position. It was a shift sensed by Haines himself, who had been holding on valiantly at The Barrier with his small band of men. Indeed, such was his growing confidence that he appealed to Pennefather to be allowed to take the offensive himself, at least by troops on his left front. Pennefather, it will be remembered, was himself growing in confidence but was not yet that confident that he would allow Haines to leave The Barrier without first receiving reinforcements from either Raglan or Canrobert. And while no such reinforcements were forthcoming Pennefather denied Haines' request. This left an increasingly frustrated and confident Haines to take matters into his own hands. It was a bold move – possibly a risky one – but Haines had been in the thick of it for some time now and gauged the temper of his men and that of the Russians to be ripe for an offensive move.

Haines' first move was to send forward Captain Astley, of the 49th, with all those carrying Minié rifles into a position away to his left front, far enough forward to be able to make life extremely uncomfortable for the Russian gunners who were already being ploughed into the ground by Dickson's mighty 18-pounders. Those armed with muskets would, in the meantime, remain at The Barrier. The next part of the story is rather confused, although the outcome is not in doubt. According to Haines he moved across to Lieutenant William Acton who was standing off to his left with about fifty or sixty men of the 77th. Haines ordered Acton to take his men and act in much the same way as Astley's party, annoying the Russian gunners on Shell Hill. Kinglake, on the other hand, wrote that it was Lord West, a fellow officer of the 21st in position watching the head of the Mikriakov Glen, who ordered Acton to advance.[22] There was even more confusion to come, for Acton apparently thought he was being ordered to advance directly upon Shell Hill and capture the Russian battery there, whereas he was really supposed just to join Astley and bring his rifles to bear on the guns. Whatever the orders, Acton was certainly clear in his own mind about what he was being asked to do. He was to lead his small group of Middlesex up a slope, over a distance of around 800 yards and attack a Russian battery.

Even as Acton turned to address his men round shot was continuing to come bounding in from the very battery which he was about to attack. The reaction of his men can well be imagined as, turning towards the battery, they weighed up the prospects before them. There were no more than sixty dirty, exhausted and severely tested men of the 77th who were being asked to advance uphill over this great distance to attack a Russian battery. It is little wonder, therefore, that when Acton gave the order to advance not a man stirred behind him. Acton, however, was the sort of man upon whom empires were built and, undaunted and in one of the most famous moments of the battle of Inkerman, he drew his sword and set off alone, saying to his men, 'Then I'll go by myself.'

One wonders what went through Acton's mind as he trudged alone for some fifty yards, heading towards Shell Hill. Round shot flew overhead as he pushed his way through the low scrub whilst way behind him his men continued to stand, no doubt wondering what sort of so-and-so Acton thought he was. Finally, James Tyrell, a private in the 77th, came forward saying, one suspects with a sense of great reluctance, 'Sir, I'll stand by you.' One by one, in the true tradition of such stories, the remaining members of the 77th followed, first another private, then an officer, two here, two there, until all were suddenly following behind a no-doubt relieved Acton. As they closed on the Russian battery Acton divided his tiny force into three, with two sergeants each taking a wing to move round the flanks of the battery whilst Acton continued to lead in the centre. It was as well that the 77th spread out for as they got closer the Russian guns changed from round shot to canister. Several men were knocked down by the blistering fire but most pressed on. Whether or not this bold and dramatic advance was observed by those back on Home Ridge is not clear, but if it was the British must have been holding their breath as they watched Acton close in on the guns. Perhaps the advance was seen, for suddenly Dickson's 18-pounders began to fire over the heads of Acton's men, dropping their shots in amongst the Russian battery, much in the style of a creeping barrage of later years. And when Major Horsford and his riflemen, under orders from Haines, along with Astley's men, were seen coming forward in support, the Russian gunners knew it was time to be off. One gun had already been dismounted by Dickson's 18-pounders and there was no sense in allowing the remaining guns to fall into the hands of the British. Hence, in an instant, the hillside was a flurry of horses and limbers as the Russians tried desperately to draw away their guns. It says much for the quality of the Russians that, despite the intense pressure they were under they managed to haul away not only their remaining operational guns but the dismounted gun also. Thus, when Acton and his men dashed onto the ground where the battery had stood they were allowed the satisfaction of capturing just a single carriage and two limbers. More important, however, was the fact that around 300 British infantrymen now stood, exhausted but triumphant on Shell Hill.

It was fast approaching 1 pm and the tide of battle had swung dramatically towards the Allies. Dannenberg, on the other hand, now found himself with a huge crisis on his hands. And yet, it was not a crisis that was impossible to surmount. Indeed, he still had Soimonov's troops, the Vladimirsky, Sousdal, Ouglitz and Bourtirsky Regiments at hand, and a counter-attack even now might yet have reversed the tide. But Dannenberg's nerve failed him. He had seen successive attacks by the Iakoutsky and Okhotsky flung back, his artillery had been pounded by the unrelenting fire of Dickson's 18-pounders, thousands of French troops were now in position on and in front of Home Ridge, and, worst of all, British troops now stood on Shell Hill. Of course, he was not to know that the French were in no mood for an advance but their presence alone was enough to make him wary. There was no prospect of Gorchakov coming up on the Allies' right rear either, and with his guns now under threat Dannenberg decided there was nothing for it but to order a withdrawal.

Despite the presence of Menshikov not 500 yards away to the north-west at the head of St George's Ravine, Dannenberg made no attempt to consult with his commander-in-chief, who himself did little to influence the outcome of the battle nor had he even exercised personal control of any Russian troops at any stage of the day. Instead, he had contented himself with sitting alongside the two royal princes, probably in the expectation of them seeing their troops achieve a great victory. He had also been happy to leave the fighting to Soimonov, Pavlov and Dannenberg. But now, as he watched the guns being limbered up, the awful truth suddenly dawned upon him; Dannenberg was retreating. Only now did he attempt to do something to try to stop the retreat. He galloped over to Dannenberg and demanded to know what he thought he was doing. 'Is it you who have ordered the retreat?' he asked, adding, 'It is impossible for us to fall back.' Dannenberg might have lacked real tactical ability and nerve at Inkerman but he was no fool and knew when it was time to call a halt to things. His men had fought themselves to a standstill, suffering horrendous casualties in trying to force a position held throughout the day by a small, disparate but tenacious British force. He pointed out the failure of Gorchakov to support him and to the fact that with the French present in good numbers there was little likelihood of a Russian success. Undeterred, Menshikov ordered Dannenberg to stop the retreat, but Dannenberg would not be swayed. 'Highness,' he said, 'to stop the troops here would be to let them be destroyed to the last man. If your Highness thinks otherwise, have the goodness to give the orders yourself, and take from me the command.'[23] Menshikov said nothing but turned his horse around and rode off towards Sevastopol.

Dannenberg meanwhile began the supervision of the retreat by ordering the most hard-pressed guns to move off first, leaving the lighter guns to cover the retreat for as long as possible. In the meantime, the Vladimirsky battalions were to remain and cover the retreat of the infantry. Unfortunately, the Vladimirsky, who had performed heroically at the Alma, seem to have misunderstood their orders for instead of simply remaining to cover the retreat they began advancing down Shell Hill as if to attack the position occupied by Dickson's 18-pounders. It was a fatal mistake.

It was now past 1 pm and a light wind parted the mist for a while, revealing to Captain Chermside, who had brought up the ammunition for Dickson, a huge column of Russian infantry. Colonel Fitzmayer was with him at the time and a swift glance through their field glasses was all the confirmation they needed. The information was passed on quickly to Dickson who immediately got Sinclair and D'Aguilar, still faithfully serving the two 18-pounders, to depress the barrels of their guns in order to pound the Russians into the dust. The Vladimirsky had, unfortunately, adopted the worse type of formation to employ against such powerful guns and one by huge, solid iron balls came smashing into their densely packed ranks, squelching the brave but helpless Russians into a bloody mess, and sending them hurrying back in disorder. While the Vladimirsky struggled to get back with round shot flying into them the Russian guns drew off in a relatively orderly manner, four at a time, making off down St George's Ravine and Sapper Road before continuing west alongside the Roadstead and into Sevastopol, covered by the guns of the town.

The Russian retreat was not marked by any real sign of disorder or confusion. Instead, the guns were limbered up and withdrawn whilst the infantry likewise retired in relatively good order. But it could have been far worse if Canrobert had launched his troops in pursuit. But Pennefather and other British officers, exhausted and unable to conduct any really effective pursuit, looked in vain for signs of any French offensive moves. In fact, the only aggressive move made by Canrobert came at about 3 pm when two battalions of Zouaves and Lainsecq's battery of artillery managed to get forward on to East Jut from where they opened fire upon the retreating Russians. Other than that the French, who were the only Allied troops capable of carrying out a pursuit, did nothing and thus the Russians were able to withdraw unhindered and covered by the guns of the two warships, the *Chersonese* and *Vladimir*, which lay moored in the Roadstead. Pyotr Alabin recalled the retreat:

> The enemy placed their guns on the highest point on the Sapoune Ridge (it was a battery of La Carrier de Lainsecq – Prince Napoleon's division) and began to fire at the bridge and the log-path we were going to retreat along. Not far from the bridge the sailors had made a temporary wharf from which they took many of the wounded in their boats and launches. Gradually, they brought them back to Sevastopol and to their ships. One shell fell near the wharf and, of course, caused turmoil. Another shell fell just near the log-path. One more hit the dressing station full of the wounded. This last shell caused terrible scenes. Many doctors and priests took to their heels. The wounded that could move followed them, among them one man from the operation table with a partially amputated leg. It was a very sad picture. There were heart-rending cries and howls of despair instead of prayers and consolations. Every minute we expected the enemy's fire to increase and, as a result, increased the turmoil. But at last we saw a blue smoke on the ridge of our bank of harbour. The second, third, and fourth shots from our battery swept away the enemy battery and saved the retreating troops from a more serious danger.[24]

The fighting at Inkerman was almost over. But there was still some sporadic fighting. Throughout the day Codrington and his brigade of the Light Division had occupied a position on Victoria Ridge, overlooking Careenage Ravine and across to West Jut where the westernmost end of the Russian gun line was situated. The guns were well within rifle range of his men who, though they had never become engaged to the same degree as the British troops fighting it out in front of Home Ridge, had, nevertheless, done their best to annoy the Russian gunners with a desultory fire which they maintained throughout the morning. The Russian artillery responded in kind, causing 180 casualties amongst Codrington's men. Now, at around 4 pm, just when the battle appeared to be dying down, the fifty-six-strong No.7 Company of the 50th Royal West Kent Regiment, under Colonel Waddy, came hurrying forward to join Codrington on Victoria Ridge. The 50th, part of Sir Richard England's 3rd Division, had been doing duty in the trenches before Sevastopol but had been sent over to reinforce Codrington. Keen not to miss out on the fighting Waddy led his men across Careenage Ravine and down across the slopes that led towards the Roadstead. As Waddy and his men pushed their way through the scrub they saw before them the Russian guns and their limbers as they retreated back into Sevastopol. It was the perfect chance to inflict some serious and belated damage on them. The 50th duly opened fire, their bullets whizzing out of the darkening gloom to cause panic in the ranks of the retreating Russian artillery. Fortunately for them Totleben was present to assume command, and taking a company of the nearest available infantry, the Ouglitz, he sent them forward into the brushwood to disperse the 50th, who duly retired back up the slopes, firing as they went. Thus, it fell to the 'Dirty Half Hundred', the old 'Black Cuffs', to fire the last shots of the Battle of Inkerman.[25]

Not since Waterloo had the British Army experienced such fearful scenes on a battlefield as those on the morning after Inkerman. Casualties had been high at the Alma, but not as high as at Inkerman. Furthermore, the casualties from the first battle were spread over a wider area. At Inkerman, however, hundreds of bodies lay around the Sandbag Battery, in front of The Barrier and choking up the exit of Quarry Ravine, whilst others lay scattered far and wide in the bushes and scrub. Difficult as it was to put an accurate figure on the total numbers of British soldiers who fought at Inkerman, Kinglake nevertheless suggested 7,464 infantry, in addition to which there were around 1,200 gunners and 200 cavalry. The butcher's bill amongst these troops was 632 killed and 1,878 wounded. Sixty-three were reported missing. No fewer than 144 officers were casualties, including some very senior officers such as Cathcart, Strangways and Goldie. In other words, almost every fourth British soldier who fought at Inkerman became a casualty. The French, who by the end of the battle had managed to get about 8,000 troops to the field, claimed 175 killed and 1,530 wounded. The heaviest casualties, of course, fell upon the Russians who, of 35,000 put into the field, lost an astonishing 3,286 killed and 7,673 wounded or captured. Their casualty figure, therefore, equalled the total number of British who actually fought at Inkerman.

Inkerman is often referred to as 'the soldiers' battle', largely on account of the absence of control from the higher command. It is true that Raglan himself exercised little control over affairs on 5 November but he did make one telling decision, to bring forward the two 18-pounders guns, whose contribution to the battle was as crucial as it was deadly. Other than that Raglan was unable to contribute anything of real significance. The only real command exercised at Inkerman was by Pennefather, a truly inspiring leader, who did his very best despite dreadful odds and faced with immense problems. But even Pennefather cannot claim to have done anything other than plug the gaps and despatch units when and where they were needed. There were none of the brilliant text-book manoeuvres which the men had been trained to carry out. Instead, it was simply a case of 'all hands to the pumps'. The real heroes, of course, were the rank and file and their officers, men like Burnaby, Daubeney, Acton, Egerton, and Haines, to name just a few. The men fought like lions in a most savage way, with their muskets, rifles and bayonets, with their swords and revolvers, and with fists, feet, rocks and boulders, anything, in fact, that came to hand.

The French saw themselves as the saviours of the British, and there is little doubt that Pennefather and his dwindling forces would indeed have struggled to hold back the Russian tide without them. If Brown and Cathcart had not, very arrogantly, declined Bosquet's offer of assistance early on, the British situation, perhaps, might not have been so perilous. But even when the French did arrive they immediately got themselves into trouble on the Inkerman Tusk, something which they did on two occasions on 5 November. The Brigade of Guards fought tremendously at Inkerman, disputing the Sandbag Battery with the Iakoutsky and Selenghinsky, but even they would have admitted receiving very timely assistance from their French allies. The great criticism levelled against the French was their blank refusal to follow up the victory during the Russian withdrawal. If ever there was a time when relatively fresh troops should have been launched against an opponent who was exhausted and thoroughly demoralised by his own inability to win, that time was 4 pm on the afternoon of 5 November. The only possible explanation was that Canrobert feared losing men to the guns of Sevastopol itself, something which, interestingly enough, Totleben recognised. In fact, Totleben bemoaned the fact that the Allies did not pursue the Russians as he thought he could have given them a real dusting down. He later wrote:

> I would have desired nothing better. I honestly think you would have incurred disaster. The batteries – our works – the forts – the ships and an army of 40,000 men would have inflicted tremendous losses on you. A retreat in front of us then might have lost you your trenches. Though Gorchakov was incompetent, he must have come up from the Chernaya on your flank with 20,000 excellent troops. No, you did very well – too well. I only wish you had come on.[26]

So, perhaps the French were being wise after all. Who knows? The Russians themselves fought heroically, to which their heavy losses testify. However, the losses also bear testament to a lack of good leadership from the higher command. Menshikov played no real part in the battle and was content to allow Soimonov, Pavlov and Dannenberg to carry out the attack, with the latter coming in for most criticism afterwards. Like their British opponents it was the ordinary Russian soldier who emerged as the real hero, particularly the men of the Iakoutsky and Selenghinsky Regiments who, despite tremendous losses, never flinched from the attack. Considering the numerical advantages enjoyed by the Russians it seems incredible that they failed to break through Home Ridge, which in itself was proof of both British tenacity and Russian incompetence. But it was not for want of trying on the part of the Russian soldier.

Pyotr Alabin survived the battle but feared an Allied pursuit. He was also stunned by the number of casualties. In fact, Russian losses were so high, particularly amongst officers and NCOs, that hardly any were left to call the muster rolls afterwards.

> Our army became very despondent. The regimental aides-de-camp could not count the men. Sergeant majors were killed and wounded; many company commanders, battalion aides-de-camp, some corporals and lance corporals were out of action. I worked the whole day, counting the men with the regimental aides-de-camp. Many wounded and shell shocked still remained in the ranks. The regiments were in disorder. I wondered, what would happen if the Allies decided to advance? We were absolutely without artillery. They could kill us or throw us back under the guns of the Severnaia or scatter us, some of us to one side, some to the other and then defeat us piece by piece. But have they got fresh forces for this? Those forces they used yesterday suffered no less that we did. The whole Allied army is suffering greatly, so the prisoners say, from cholera![27]

The fallout from Inkerman fell heaviest on the Russians who had been confident of victory and who now realised they had a great struggle on their hands if they were to save Sevastopol. As the Russian historian of the war put it 'Only after Alma did the higher authorities begin to realise the terrible error they had made – and only after Inkerman did they begin to understand the seriousness of that error.'[28] The czar himself was naturally disappointed but refused to blame anybody for the failure of the attack. A week after the battle he wrote to Menshikov, asking him to keep faith with his men.

> Do not give up, dear Menshikov, because you are the commander of 80,000 Sevastopol heroes, who proved that anything is possible for them if they are led the right way. With such heroes it would be

> shameful to think about further failure. Tell everybody that I am pleased with them and thank them for their true Russian spirit. If there was no good luck before, I hope it will be so in future.[29]

The czar's son, Grand Duke Nikolai Nikolaevitch, was rather more critical of Menshikov in a letter to his brother.

> In spite of the fact that the regiments got mixed up, they advanced and chased everybody who was before them. They took two lines of breastworks and began to retreat only after four large enemy columns had advanced against them. There were troops of three nations; the English, the French and the Turks, and before them there was a thick line of riflemen which opened a terrible and deadly fire. There was one more cause of our disorder; the superiority of the Allies' artillery was very great. But all the troops fought like heroes. Dannenberg himself told me how they continued to advance despite the deadly fire. After the action, we returned from Sevastopol, and went to the Prince [Menshikov] and saw that he had absolutely lost heart and continued repeating that the troops had not fought well. Then I said to him, 'Your Serenity, you yourself have not spoken to the troops today but we have been visiting the battalions and talking to the men. It was very good to hear them in a good mood.' Menshikov then changed his opinion of the soldiers, knowing that nobody believed him anyway, because they had seen the battle with their own eyes.[30]

Colonel Men'kov was another who was critical of Menshikov and the higher command at Inkerman.

> Menshikov ordered General Dannenberg with the 10th and 11th infantry divisions to attack the right flank of the English positions. To strengthen the troops the chasseurs of the 16th and 17th divisions were also put at General Dannenberg's disposal. But the story of the Alma was repeated. Nobody knew either the aim of the attack or the order in which the troops were to advance. The columns became confused; the artillery of one column became mixed up with another. Infantry were taking the enemy positions without artillery support but was losing thousands, and had to yield to the Allies' great numbers. We failed to use our advantages in field artillery and cavalry, which did not take part in this action at all. Our massed artillery, having crowded on a small piece of ground, was losing the horses and gunners. Our loss was, as they say, up to twelve thousand. Nearly all the regimental and battalion commanders and the senior officers became casualties, and this without any result at all. During the battle neither Dannenberg nor Menshikov did anything right.[31]

But while the senior commanders played the blame game with each other, the junior officers were left stunned by the size of the defeat. Not only did it come as a great shock in terms of the campaign, but the sheer number of casualties sustained in what was a relatively small area left a vivid impression on them, as one officer later recalled.

> As an eyewitness of the battle, I will retain the impressions of those terrible hours for the rest of my life. There were many among us whose coats were like sieves. Everybody would remember the tremendous deed of a skirmisher of the 2nd Battalion of the Ekaterinburgsky regiment, named Polenov, who, having exhausted himself in his efforts against the enemy, threw himself down a steep cliff and smashed himself up, in order to avoid being taken prisoner.[32]

Another officer, reflecting on the sudden lack of faith in their commanders, wrote:

> The consequences of the disaster were tremendous, not so much in material as in morale. That seven or eight thousand men became casualties unnecessarily is, of course, a great misfortune, but it can be put right. What cannot be righted is the troops' faith in their commanders, which was undermined on the Inkerman Heights. The troops didn't lose heart but they stopped believing they could be successful and instead expected only failure. This manifested itself in the great number of anecdotes and stories in which there was great criticism of our plans and a kind of mischievous self-condemnation.[33]

But perhaps the main culprit of the Russian failure at Inkerman was their system itself. All armies had their fair share of incompetent generals but most at least had the benefit of a well founded system, maintained and improved as new developments evolved, that allowed them to fight on good terms with an enemy. The Russians, largely through complacency, had allowed their army to fall behind, particularly in the development of modern weapons and in certain areas now seen as vital in modern armies.

> It also becomes clear that the whole military system, with its emphasis on massed bayonet attacks, its scorn of accurate musketry, its distrust of military scholarship and reliance on practical experience, as well as its training the cavalry for glittering parades and reviews rather than for scouting and outpost duty, was to blame. The Russians' artillery was very good and their engineers were excellent in siegecraft, mining and fortification, but in the main the Russian army used tactics and weapons that were out of date, and it was this antiquated system that produced the incompetent

> commanders and the inferior weapons that caused the defeat at the battle of Inkerman.[34]

The in-fighting amongst the Russian generals did little to comfort their hundreds of dying and wounded soldiers who still lay out on the battlefield. Although Pyotr Alabin had come through the battle unscathed he remained on the battlefield trying to do as much as possible to remove the wounded. It was a thankless task, with hundreds of Russian troops choking the ravines.

> But what could we do in the dressing station? My heart was torn at the sight of so many wounded lying everywhere in their own blood. The paymaster of the Iakoutsky Regiment, Efimov, along with the paymaster of the Okhotsky regiment, Lieutenant Loginov, helped me try and catch some passing carriages and turn them back to the dressing station, load them with the wounded and send them away. I will never forget the scene when I rushed after the carriages to try and stop them in the ravine. But they did not hear my voice. I stood in the middle of the road to block their way but it was in vain. I could not do it alone against fifty carriages. But, just at this moment Captain Den came to help me. He drew his sabre and threatened to kill the first man that dared to move farther without orders. The convoy stopped. Within a minute we unloaded the fascines and gabions, and replaced them with the wounded. Only the dead and the heaps of weapons were left at the dressing station.
>
> Our troops returned to the places they began their advance from. They were extremely exhausted. They had not slept the previous night. They spent the night from 3rd to 4th November on the move, and the whole of 5th November fighting a battle without food. As soon as we reached the camp we lit the campfires. All throughout the night the tired and wounded from the different regiments gathered round them and to share their stories about that day.[35]

An indication of the size of the problem facing the Russians and, in particular, their medical services, can be gauged from a letter written by the great Russian surgeon, Nikolai Pirogov, who arrived in Sevastopol some eighteen days after the battle but still found hundreds of wounded untreated and in a terrible state. Writing to his wife, Pirogov said:

> Having come to Sevastopol on 23 November, eighteen days after the affair, I found 2,000 wounded, congested together, and lying on dirty mattresses, soaked with blood. I sorted through them and during ten days from morning till night was operating on those who should have been operated on just after the battle. What motivation has a

> man to fight bravely if he knows he'll be treated like a dog afterwards if he's wounded? The C-I-C asked about the Sisters of Mercy. 'Will you be able to make use of them?' he asked. 'I don't know, Your Serenity, everything will depend on the personalities of the women, who are chosen.' 'Yes, you are right.' We have now a Daria [Dasha: see chapter XV *Angels of Mercy*], they say she helped a lot and even dressed the wounded at the Alma ... Time will show whether Menshikov is a military leader. But even if he defends Sevastopol I would not put this achievement down to him. He cannot and does not want to sympathise with the soldiers. He is a bad Caesar . . . The naval hospital is now empty of the sick. The shells were falling on it during the bombardment despite the red flag. One shell fell between two beds and burst but did no harm. They say that there was an interesting incident; during the evacuation of the sick the shells falling in the yard didn't hurt any of the sick or the doctors. But at the dressing station, which was opposite to the hospital in the house of Unten, one shell came through the roof into the operating room and tore the arms off the man being operated on.[36]

Overall, Inkerman was an Allied victory and, given the difficult circumstances under which the battle began, was very much a British victory despite the undoubted vital contribution from the French. But in the days that followed the British could not be sure they had actually won a victory. It was true that they had fought off a large Russian force and had maintained their position but it had come at such a frighteningly high price that many doubted whether it was a victory at all. Indeed, when the first reports reached England both government and public were shocked. The general public, of course, were mainly concerned with the tremendous losses, particularly as they came so soon after the Alma and Balaklava. The government, however, naturally looked at the bigger picture and the extent of the casualties at Inkerman and the possibility of a retreat evoked some very bad recent and not so recent memories. Some politicians could still recall the ill-fated Peninsular campaign of Sir John Moore in the winter of 1808–9 when, in an early nineteenth-century version of Dunkirk, he led his bedraggled army through the bleak Galician mountains in order to escape the clutches of the pursuing French under Marshal Soult. And in far more recent times the British Army had experienced a similarly traumatic retreat from Kabul in Afghanistan. Now, with the British Army so reduced in numbers, politicians feared another Russian offensive might lead to a retreat from the Crimea, accompanied by a repetition of the experiences of 1808 and 1842. 'Everyone is downbeat about the victory (if it was one),' wrote Lord Cowley, 'and feels that another such triumph, or another such attack, would finally smash us, and then will come the monster catastrophe – a horrible compound of Afghanistan and Corunna.'[37]

After Inkerman a sense of realism seems to have set in amongst both sides. The Russians, initially confident of bringing about a swift and successful conclusion to the campaign, had now fought three battles, but apart from limited success at Balaklava had enjoyed little else. Indeed, their infantry had sustained heavy casualties at the hands of British and French infantry whose rifles completely outperformed the old smoothbore muskets wielded by the vast majority of Russians, whilst Allied artillery also appeared to dominate. After Inkerman, the Russians' confidence in their leaders was severely shaken and whilst their resolve to get to grips with the invaders remained as firm as ever hopes of a decisive victory in the field faded. Instead, they retired to within the walls of Sevastopol. It was here, they decided, that the battle for the Crimea would be won or lost. The Allies, too, appear to have realised that their initial optimism was, perhaps, misplaced. Maybe Cathcart was right all along when he had advocated an immediate assault on Sevastopol at the time of the flank march. Had the Allies' greatest opportunity passed them by after all? Sir John Burgoyne was certainly of the opinion now that more might have been accomplished had the Allies been rather more direct in their approach. Writing to Colonel Matson RE after Inkerman, Burgoyne said, 'Speaking confidentially, I think we have lost many advantages by over-caution, and not pressing harder upon the enemy, and that it could have been done without risk.'[38] Of course, this was being wise after the event, as Burgoyne had earlier been wary of attacking Sevastopol without first having gone through the laborious and, one might say, the traditional process of approach by way of sapping and entrenching.

The Allied commanders held a council of war on 6 November. There were, no doubt, guarded congratulations following their victory the previous day at Inkerman. Raglan himself had experienced a very close run thing on 18 June 1815 but Inkerman had been every bit as close. The defeat of the Russians had been a tremendous achievement but none of the Allied leaders present at the meeting was under any illusions as to just how close the victory had been and just how dire the consequences would have been had Dannenberg been rather more tactically astute. They were also very aware now of having to commit to a long, drawn-out siege operation which nobody really wanted. The defences of Sevastopol had stood up to the first bombardment whilst a Russian army still hovered menacingly in the interior. Inkerman had demonstrated just how fragile the Allies' position was. It was even worse now, with casualties having reduced the British to fewer than 15,000 fit men. Indeed, from now on Raglan's army would be the junior partner in the enterprise, the main burden of responsibility falling heavily upon the more numerous French. By far the most disturbing prospect for the Allies, however, was spending a winter on the exposed Chersonese plateau. Raglan must have cast his mind back to the advice given to him by Cattley, one of his interpreters, who had warned him about the extremely cold winters that often descended on the Crimea. Raglan was not the only Allied commander to harbour concerns about the weather. Indeed, such was De Lacy Evans' despondency that he went so far as to advocate abandoning the campaign and an evacuation of the Crimea. Raglan had heard it all before, however. After all, his old chief had experienced the same pessimism during the Peninsular War when, in the summer of 1810, the 'croakers', as they were called, cried out for the same course of action and an end to the war in Spain. Wellington, of course, simply bided his time and ignored their pleadings, going on to win the war four years later. Raglan and Canrobert would have to bide their time also, and continue with the siege. But how difficult that would be would largely depend upon whether or not the winter would bite as hard as many feared or whether they would get off lightly with a mild winter. Naturally, the Allies hoped for the best whilst the Russians prayed for the kind of severe winter that would so cripple the Allies' cause. The question was; whose prayers would the Almighty answer?

NOTES

1 Kinglake, Alexander William. *The Invasion of the Crimea: Its Origin, and An Account of its Progress down to the Death of Lord Raglan* (London 1863), V, 270.
2 Mercer, Patrick, *Give Them a Volley and Charge! The Battle of Inkerman* (Staplehurst 1998), 118.
3 One is reminded here of the British troops on the reverse slope at Waterloo, where, despite the 'unremitting shower of death' being poured on them, many, exhausted after their efforts, simply fell asleep.
4 Alabin, P V *Chetyre voiny. Pohodnye zapiski v 1849, 1853, 1854–1856 i 1877–78 godah* (Moscow, 1892), 105–6.
5 Kinglake, *Invasion of the Crimea,* V, 310.
6 'Come, do retire. We are going to open.' Ibid. V, 344.
7 Ibid. V, 354.
8 Alabin, *Chetyre voiny.*
9 Kinglake, *Invasion of the Crimea,* V, 392.
10 Bosquet later said, 'You see, they look as if they were about to present arms to us.' Bazancourt, the Baron de (trans. by Robert Howe Gould). *The Crimean Expedition, to the Capture of Sebastopol. Chronicles of the War in the East* (London 1856). II, 82.
11 Kinglake, *Invasion of the Crimea,* V, 396.
12 Bazancourt, *The Crimean Expedition,* II, 84.
13 Kinglake, *Invasion of the Crimea,* V, 397.
14 Ibid. V, 397.
15 Bazancourt, *The Crimean Expedition,* II, 86.
16 Kinglake, *Invasion of the Crimea,* V, 405.
17 Ibid. V, 402.
18 Ibid. V, 409.

19 Alabin, *Chetyre voiny*, III, 102–3.
20 Ibid. III, 103.
21 Kinglake, *Invasion of the Crimea*, V, 420.
22 See Barthorp, *Heroes of the Crimea*, n117, for an explanation of how this confusion came about.
23 Kinglake, *Invasion of the Crimea*, V, 434. The exchange is based upon the respective aides-de-camp of Menshikov and Dannenberg, Urosov and Tchaplinsky.
24 Alabin, *Chetyre voiny*, III, 104.
25 The 'Dirty Half Hundred' and 'the Black Cuffs' were nicknames given to the 50th on account of their black facings. In the Peninsula, Rowland Hill memorably described them as, 'not a good looking regiment, but devilishly steady.'
26 Totleben, quoted in Mercer, *Give Them a Volley and Charge!*, 165.
27 Alabin, *Chetyre voiny*, III, 92.
28 Tarle E V *Krymskaya voina* (Moscow 1959), II, 191.
29 *Archives of the Sevastopol Museum of Defence*, No. 5154, VII.
30 'Na Severnoy storone u 4 batarei, Nikolay Nikolaevitch Alexandru Nikolaevitchu, 26 oktyabrya 1854', *Central State Historical Archives, Moscow*.
31 *M E Saltykov-Shchedrin State Public Library*, Department of Manuscripts, Q.IV, 365/1, sh.161–2.
32 Major Kurpikov. 'Epizod iz Inkermanskogo dela', *Collection of the manuscripts . . . about the Sevastopol defence*, St Petersburg, 1872, I, 118–19.
33 'Iz pohodnyh vospominaniy o Krymskoy voine', *Russian Archives*, 1870, No.11, 2044–2045.
34 Curtiss, John Shelton. *Russia's Crimean War* (Durham NC 1979), 333–4.
35 Alabin, *Chetyre voiny*, III, 105.
36 'Sevastopol'skie pis'ma N.I. Pirogova. 1854–1855', *Sevastopol* (Sevastopol, 2002), I, 321–4.
37 Cowley, Henry Richard Charles Wellesley, First Earl of. *The Paris Embassy during the Second Empire* (London 1928), 63.
38 Wrottesley, The Hon. George (Ed). *Life and Correspondence of Field Marshal Sir John Burgoyne* (London 1873), II, 123.

# CHAPTER THIRTEEN
## *The Great Storm*

With the prospect of having to spend the winter on the Chersonese plateau looming ever closer the Allies' thoughts began to turn to the problem of trying to improve the accommodation for their men. With clothing already in a bad way new supplies were deemed essential, whilst huts, similar to those being used by the French, were also being considered. Indeed, Burgoyne himself was now advocating the timber framed huts, 'lined with plank, and the roof tarpaulin stretched over rafters . . . a kind of emigrant's house of the most temporary construction', and that large quantities of them should be sent out from England as soon as possible.[1]

The Allies were just coming to terms with the consequences of Inkerman and the prospects of a long, cold winter when they were given a nasty insight into what they could expect during the next few months. On the night of 13 November the wind began to get up and stir into life across the Chersonese plateau. The sea grew rougher by the hour and waves began to batter the shore. The Allied troops on duty in the trenches before Sevastopol certainly noticed the worsening weather, as did the people inside the town. But at least they would have the benefit of shelter, unlike the poor souls out on the plateau in their flimsy tents and huts. 'The Great Storm', as it was to become known, was about to break. In his diary, Pyotr Alabin recalled the storm as it began to unfold.

> Early morning. Camp. A terrible Black Sea storm has broken out and is raging now with unbelievable fury. The gale – our only ally, which was sent us by God – can do us a good turn. I climbed the nearest height and watched the turbulent sea; the Allies' ships had lost their steadiness as if they had come alive, preparing for a decisive battle with the elements! Our inquisitive auditor, Galaynitsky, constantly watches the position of the enemy's fleet and has been sitting since dawn on a rock and has not taken his eyes from the sea despite a terrible cold wind and rain. I have to go to a height on the right bank of the Belbec river and report to Colonel Golev; he is there with his Kamchatsky regiment; he has an excellent warm tent with a stove.

> The other day they captured an Englishman and a Tartar. The Tartar took his new friend to some gardens on the banks of Katcha to get fresh cabbages and grapes, and the Cossacks seized them. Before being taken to the colonel the Tartar was flogged with whips as much as was possible. The Englishman, of course, was treated properly and was presented to the commanders, not having been beaten but relieved of his extra weight! [i.e. the cabbages and grapes!][2]

For the Allied troops on the Chersonese plateau, the storm meant disaster. There was little shelter and the tents and flimsy huts which had been constructed were no match for the violence of the elements. Although the majority of them had small tents d'abri – small dog tents – the French troops, habitually better equipped than the British soldier when it came to campaigning, at least had the benefit of some wooden huts which had been constructed in time, although many of these were blown away like matchwood. The British, however, had no chance in their canvas bell tents. The weather during the last week of October had been fairly warm, although cold at night, but after Inkerman the days became colder and the nights bitter. Even at this early stage of the war the men's clothes had become threadbare whilst even the officers were finding it difficult to stay warm. The men had worked hard in the trenches, digging, fetching and carrying and with few supplies of clothing having reached the men since they had left England the condition of the uniforms can well be imagined. Indeed, many a ragged British soldier resorted to using sandbags, spirited away from the engineers' stores, to repair their clothes. Footwear was equally difficult to maintain. For example, the future General Sir Evelyn Wood, then a young officer serving in the Crimea, wore out his only pair of shoes after just one week's duty as a messenger, and would have remained barefoot had it not been for a marine who kindly loaned him his spare pair.[3]

The wind had got up well before dawn on 14 November and was soon blowing a gale. To make matters worse it began to pour with icy rain, which lashed down upon the tents. The men struggled to keep hold of their precious coverings, the tents tugging violently at the guide ropes as the wind roared overhead. Evelyn Wood shared his tent with Lieutenants Partridge and Douglas who, realising they were about to lose everything they possessed to the wind, quickly donned every item of clothing they owned. The two officers then took it in turns to hold on to the tent pole for an hour until at 6 am a huge blast of wind sent it spiralling into the air, leaving the three young men to watch as their shelter sped off across the plateau along with scores of other tents, blankets, chests, furniture, papers and all sorts of items of equipment. 'It pours in torrents,' recorded Sir George Bell,

> the poles shoot through the old decayed canvas tops, and down they come by the run. Anything and everything exposed is blown away

> out of sight; barrels or casks, full or empty, once set in motion away they go never to return – clothes, hats, caps, blankets, rugs, buffalo robes. It was a terrible night, and lucky was the soldier or sailor who kept his house standing over his head till morning. I had hard work to weather the gale myself, but my external mud wall, and my servants hammering down the pegs every now and then, while I held the pole inside, kept all up upright . . . Had I opened my door for the reception of strangers, one gush of such a hurricane might have whirled my tent into the air. I still held the pole tight, to keep it steady, fearing every moment it would shoot through the top, and descend upon me like a wet blanket. The whole town was now down, church and all, the General, Sir Richard England, under the ruins of the last edifice (a marquee). He scrambled out with a blanket about him, and made for an old wall, where he lay for shelter. The hospital tent lay upon the dead! Horses were blown from their picket posts. Weakly men were whirled off their legs, or could not resist the violence of the wind until they were far away down from their lines.[4]

George Higginson, with the Grenadier Guards, wrote:

> Every tent in our exposed position was laid low; such was the force of the wind that to stand upright without the support was impossible, and we crouched as best we could under improvised parapets or any hollow of the ground which afforded shelter. The bearskin caps of our men, according to invariable custom, stood on short posts or pegs outside the tents; such was the successive blasts of the south-westerly gale that the whole of the bearskin caps of the battalion were blown into a ravine nearly a quarter of a mile off! Camp kettles and drums from the Light Division on our left, flew in like manner over our heads, lodging finally in the bushy scrub of the same ravine.[5]

There are scores of accounts of the Great Storm. It remains one of the great unwanted episodes of the war. Lieutenant Edward Hamley left one of the most graphic accounts, in his famous *Campaign of Sebastopol*.

> About daybreak on the 14th, a strong wind from the south drove before it a flood of rain; the tents, swelling inward beneath the blast, left no slant sufficient to repel the water, which was caught in the hollows, and filtered through. I was awoke by it dripping on my face, which I covered with my cloak, and slept again. Again I was awoke, and this time more rudely. The wind had increased to a hurricane, in which the canvas flapped and fluttered, and the tent-pole quivered like a vibrating harp-string. At the opening of the tent, my servant appeared uttering some words, which were blown away, and never reached me

till, putting his head within, he told me I must get up, – adding, that the tents were nearly all blown away. As he spoke, the pegs that held mine to the ground parted – the canvas was driven against the pole, and the whole structure fell with a crash across my bed.

Sitting up and grasping my fluttering blankets, I beheld such as my effects as had not weight enough to keep them stationary, dispersed in the air, and borne on the wings of the wind into a distant valley. Half-written letters clung for a moment, in places, to the muddy ground before pursuing their airy flight, and garments of every description strewed the plain. My servant was in full pursuit of a cocked-hat which was whirled onward at a tremendous pace, till its course was arrested by a low wall; and on the muddy wheel of a cart hung a scarlet waistcoat grievously bemired. All round me were figures like my own, of half-clad men sitting amid the ruins of their beds, and watching, with intense interest, the dispersion of their property, while those tents which had continued to resist the gale, fell over, one after the other, like inverted parachutes. Horses, turning their scattered tails to the blast, leaned against it with slanting legs, blinded by their clothing, which, retained by the surcingles, was blown over their heads; and all around were seen men struggling up, with frequent loss of ground, each holding some recovered article. Whatever could be collected in this way was placed beneath the fallen tents, the edges of which were then loaded with heavy stones. In the distance other encampments were seen in familiar flight, and everywhere the rows of tents which had dotted the plain had disappeared. Hard as it seemed to be stripped of shelter by the storm, those who had passed the night in the trenches had still greater reason to complain. There they had consoled themselves during the watches of the wet, gusty night, by the promise of warmth and rest in the morning; and hastening chilled and weary, to their camp for the comforting hot coffee, and pleasant well-earned sleep, officers and men found their temporary homes level as a row of Persians worshipping the rising sun, and the space they had kept dry in the midst of mire, became a puddle. No fires could be lit, no breakfast warmed, for the blast extinguished the flame and scattered the fuel; and all that could be done was, to gather the blankets out of the mud, and to try to raise again the fallen tents.[6]

The storm was bad enough for the men on land, but for the sailors and those still out at sea the situation was far worse. All along the coast of the southern Crimea, from Eupatoria, along to the Katcha, around to Kamiesh and on to Balaklava, Allied ships struggled in vain against the hurricane. Outside Balaklava in particular, the storm wreaked absolute havoc against the British ships which, owing to a lack of common sense, had been forced to remain anchored off shore. The Russian attack on 25 October had exposed the weakness of the Balaklava position and fearing another Russian attack it was decided that all British merchant and transport ships should leave the harbour and, with very few exceptions, none had been allowed to return. The senior officer in charge of the harbour was Captain Dacres, of the *Sanspareil*. Dacres obviously lacked any common sense and enforced the order to the letter, with few ships being allowed into the harbour. This included all new arrivals, as well as those vessels that had been forced to leave the harbour already. This ludicrous situation became all too evident on the morning of 8 November when the *Prince*, a great screw steamer on its maiden voyage, came steaming up to the entrance of the harbour where it was forced to drop anchor and wait for permission to enter. The point was, of course, that, not only was the *Prince* carrying the 46th Regiment, but it was carrying a vital cargo of virtually all the army's warm clothing for the coming winter. There were 57,000 woollen frocks, 35,700 woollen socks, 2,500 watch-coats, 17,000 pairs of flannel drawers, 3,700 rugs, 16,000 blankets, and numerous boxes full of medical supplies and equipment. It also carried boxes of specie for the Commissariat. Unfortunately, when the *Prince* dropped anchor, it did so in thirty-five fathoms of water and the first anchor was lost when the cable ran out. Remarkably, a second anchor was lost in the same way. Apparently, the cause of the loss of the anchors was the omission to 'clinch' the cables, which was a common thing in recently built ships. Nevertheless, the *Prince* was secured by tying it to the *Jason* by means of a hawser whilst yet another anchor and cable were prepared. In the afternoon, two tugs, *Minna* and *Brenda*, were sent out to bring off the 46th and the boxes of specie, but Dacres refused permission for the *Prince* to enter the harbour. Instead, it remained out at sea, despite the problem with its anchor. The condition of the ship gave great cause for concern and Captain Christie, on board the *Melbourne*, tried on several occasions to request that the *Prince* be allowed in, but each time Dacres refused, saying there was simply no room for the ship in the overcrowded harbour. At one point, Christie even sailed into the harbour himself in a small boat and actually pointed out to Dacres a space where the *Prince* could dock, but again Dacres refused to let the ship in. On 10 November a gale blew up, giving the Quartermaster General great cause for concern, and not without reason either. The *Prince* was carrying such an immense cargo of stores that the prospect of anything happening to her in a storm was unthinkable. But not even the Quartermaster General could persuade Dacres to allow the ship in. Instead, he was told that, if the weather calmed down the *Prince* would be allowed into the harbour, but not before, as it would be impossible to unload the cargo in such bad weather. Given the importance of the *Prince*'s load it seems incredible that it was not allowed to dock in the harbour. Moreover, several other vessels were admitted but still Christie's requests were denied on the grounds that, with over two hundred ships already inside there was simply insufficient room. Thus it was that when the Great Storm began on the early morning of 14 November, the *Prince,* laden with its priceless cargo, was still waiting out at sea off the entrance to Balaklava.

A large slice of the blame for the wreck of the *Prince* was laid at the feet of Christie, who took it badly. The matter was later raised at the Roebuck Enquiry into the administration of the army in the Crimea. At the enquiry, Dacres admitted that Christie should not get the blame. The *Prince* was soon joined by the *Trent* and the *Bride,* both of which were forced to remain outside the harbour. It was particularly hard for the captain of the *Trent,* Captain Ponsonby, as he was carrying horses. On being informed by Captain Christie's secretary that he should get into the harbour as soon as possible, Ponsonby found himself on the end of a reprimand from Dacres for ignoring his order to remain outside. This, despite being loaded down with horses who needed to get ashore as soon as possible. The *Resolute* had arrived also, bearing a cargo of over ten million rounds of Minié ammunition. But even this vital cargo was not deemed important enough to get the ship into the harbour. Indeed, the *Resolute*'s captain, Lewis, went so far as to petition Admiral Lyons. 'It is very hard that I am compelled to lay outside, and lots of room in here, and with my ship deep with the very sinews of war. Captain Christie would let me come in, were he not overruled by a higher authority.'[7] That higher authority was, of course, Captain Dacres, and he should bear a great deal of the blame for the loss of so much equipment during the storm of 14 November. It is true that, with the harbour crammed full of shipping, dozens of ships, both large and small, were unable to get inside and were forced to remain at anchor off the coast, but when such precious cargoes arrived from England the greatest efforts should have been made to unload them. Instead, they were refused admittance with fatal consequences, as Sir George Bell later wrote:

> No coast could be more fatal in a storm. There rode our ships, under craggy and perpendicular cliffs, to be battered to staves, without remedy, within a few lengths of the harbour, where they were refused admittance the day before. The red-tape system, it was said, caused the loss of eight fine ships and their unhappy crews. The *Prince,* screw steamer, a noble ship, laden with clothing for the famishing army, provisions, powder, shot, shell and stores, was all in pieces, scattered along the coast next morning, the bodies of the poor crew being battered against the rocks.[8]

When the great hurricane of 14 November blew, therefore, these ships soon found themselves at the mercy of the elements. No fewer than twenty-one British ships, loaded with their invaluable cargoes of supplies and munitions, were lost, along with the majority of their crews. Eight more lost their masts. The Duke of Cambridge can consider himself fortunate. He was ill aboard the *Retribution* at the time of the storm, the ship losing its rudder and two of her anchors. Captain Drummond only managed to save the ship by throwing the upper deck guns overboard. And while the ships were being dashed against the high cliffs outside the harbour those inside suffered also. 'Even in the land-locked pool of Balaklava,' wrote Kinglake,

> the shipping there huddled were grasped, as it were, and confounded and rudely battered together, by the whirling tornado; whilst, moreover, the captains of vessels which had been lying outside, seized the one hope of saving their crafts which seemed to be left them, and lawlessly drove their way in, carrying yet more confusion and havoc into a crashing thicket of bulwarks, and masts, and spars.[9]

The ships outside Balaklava that decided to make a dash for the port had little choice. The captains either risked seeing their ships smashed upon the rocks or they incurred the wrath of the port authorities. The choice was simple, though it heaped more confusion upon the turmoil in the port. Even so, the narrow entrance to the harbour, difficult enough in calm waters, proved the downfall of many a captain whose ship was dashed upon the rocks as it tried to get inside.[10] The greatest loss by far suffered by the British was the *Prince*, with its immense quantity of supplies, including warm clothing, thousands of blankets, shoes, boots, shirts, drawers and surgical equipment. The *Resolute* was lost also, carrying with it to the bottom of the sea the ten million rounds of Minié bullets that should have been unloaded days earlier. And when the *Progress* went down it took with it enough hay to feed all the horses and mules in the British Army for a period of twenty days. No one knew better than Raglan just how vital the supplies being carried by the *Prince* were, and its loss was a severe blow to the army.

Despite their obvious antagonism, the Russians nevertheless did what they could to try and help the crews of the many floundering ships, particularly those off the mouth of the Katcha and off Eupatoria. This humane work, of course, met with mixed fortunes as some of the Allies, understandably suspicious of the Russians' motives, opened fire on their would-be rescuers. Indeed, whilst genuine efforts were made by the Russians to help the crews of the Allied ships others simply took advantage of the storm to take prizes or to carry out reconnaissance work. Under cover of the storm, General Korv moved with his corps against Eupatoria, which was garrisoned by a Turkish force. A half-hearted attack followed which was easily repulsed in about an hour or so, after which

Korv's men turned to trying to save the crews of the ships offshore. Major Jolinsky, with some Cossacks, tried to rescue the crew of a merchantman which had been driven ashore by the ferocious waves, but no sooner had he neared it than the ship opened fire with its few guns, Jolinsky himself receiving a severe head wound. They were rather more successful with an Italian ship, however, the crew of twelve being picked up without any trouble. Elsewhere, Major Terpilewsky, commanding a unit of lancers, boarded a beached vessel to try to save the crew only to find there was nobody on board. With no crew to assist, he instead set fire to the ship!

Colonel Roslavlew, of the Novoarkhangelsky Regiment, was another Russian officer to move against a beached British ship. His story, recounted in Totleben's *Defence of Sevastopol,* is perhaps typical of the incidents that happened during the storm, although it was received with great scepticism by the correspondent of *The Times,* William Russell, when he read it. Taking with him some of his lancers, Roslavlew found a large transport ship, the *Culloden,* beached on shore, with the sea crashing against it. He waited until his artillery had come up, whereupon he went forward with a white flag. The crew nervously responded by lowering the Union Jack and raising a white flag themselves, although they hoisted their boats which had previously been lowered over the side, possibly hoping that a friendly ship might yet come and throw them a rope. After a delay of about half an hour, Roslavlew ordered his guns to open fire and two shots were sent straight through the bows of the ship. With no sign of any response from the crew the guns fired two more shots that smashed away the ship's bulwark. These two shots had the desired effect and soon afterwards the boats were launched into the sea carrying the captain, two mates, seven Turks and twenty-eight British sailors. The captain of the *Culloden* then explained that there were still twenty-five Turks on board along with 700lbs of powder and 32,000 rounds of shot and shell. There were also some twenty-five Arab horses. Naturally, Roslavlew was keen to get the Turks off and, if possible, take the ship, but the captain refused, saying that the sea was too rough and it was too great a risk to try to save the Turks. While the two men argued a British man-of-war apparently came steaming towards the *Culloden* at which the watching commander of the 2nd Brigade of Lancers, Prince Radzivill, ordered his own guns to open fire. The Russian guns quickly set the *Culloden* ablaze but the huge waves extinguished the flames. At length the ship sank and Roslavlew was left to escort his prisoners to Sevastopol.[11]

Pyotr Alabin was in no doubt as to what the Russian reaction should be towards the stricken Allied ships. Here was a golden opportunity to bring about wholesale destruction of the Allied fleet as it floundered off shore in the Black Sea. The ships were in no condition to respond and so, in his opinion, it should have been possible for the Russians to bring forward their own artillery to wreak havoc of a human kind. However, little was done. Instead, the Allied ships were left alone to battle nature and the elements which did enough in any case to inflict great damage on their war effort. Alabin later claimed that Dannenberg was more criticised for not taking advantage of the situation than he was for his handling of the Battle of Inkerman. His account of the storm continued:

> Evening. Today a terrible storm began which soon turned into a hurricane. At 2 pm a Cossack came to the corps commander with a dispatch informing us that the enemy ships at the mouth of the Katcha river were being dashed against the coast. You could hardly imagine our delight as we rushed to the place. During our march the corps commander called for me and ordered eight guns from our battery and the Kamchatsky regiment to march to the Katcha. It was a terrible storm, but I was happy because our enemy was suffering. I reached the river and climbed up on to a height. What a spectacle! Even in my dreams I had never seen anything like it! The sea was black now not only in name but also in colour. The sky was black also. It seemed as if a monster of extraordinary size had opened its mouth, in which many of the enemy's ships were floundering in a life or death struggle. Some vessels were lying on the coast like dead bodies, others were floundering without masts. To the right only the masts of some vessels were visible above the water. The furious roar of the sea could be heard from a great distance. Our battalions marched one after another towards the coast, which was very difficult against the strong wind. The artillery followed them, being drawn by horses which quickly became exhausted. One staff-officer, a sturdily built man, climbed the highest point of the height and was blown right off his feet! You can well imagine what happened to the tents and flimsy shelters of the Kamchatsky regiments! The wind smashed and destroyed everything!
>
> The corps commander came with his staff. From the last height he observed the enemy's position and had a conversation with some English, French and Italian sailors who were cast ashore and captured by the Cossacks. He ordered the artillery and infantry to withdraw and left only one company to help the Cossacks because, as he explained, the enemy ships were just merchant ships and it would not do to open a fire against them. The Cossacks captured fifteen foreign sailors. They were mainly from the merchant vessels, which were chartered by the French and English governments to transport different kinds of military goods. They were mainly from the ship *Mogador*, which had sent some members of its crew to help the other sinking vessels. The Cossacks said that the crews of two more ships also wanted to get to the coast, but there was absolutely no opportunity to take them away. The corps commander left. We stayed to see what would happen.

> We prayed to the heavens to prolong the storm in order that it might achieve greater results than just the wreck of some vessels! We hoped the storm would grow stronger and drive these floating fortresses to the brink of disaster! Perhaps we would realise that fortune was smiling upon us and that we should take advantage of it. The stormy day began to calm down but still we did not profit from the favourable conditions. It was clear that Providence was offering us a substantial part of the enemy's military might as a sacrifice and we should take it. As soon as the storm subsides the Allies will use all the strength to rescue their vessels or, at least, the crews. We wondered why we did not take advantage of the conditions to capture enemy ships, prizes, prisoners and flags. Why did we not take the opportunity to lift Russia's spirits and make the people happy with stories of successes over the enemy, or at least, of the damage caused to them?
>
> The hatches of the enemy ships were closed; fighting the storm, the fleet could not fire against us. If our artillery had opened fire it would have increased the chaos in the fleet and brought about its destruction. Why did we not take two or three guns from the nearest batteries? It was possible to use the horse artillery horse and to make temporary platforms. If we could position the guns in several different places it would have been possible to wreak great devastation. But nothing was done.[12]

Whilst the British struggled against the elements in Balaklava and up on the Chersonese plateau the French fared little better to the west at Kamiesh. 'Day breaks,' wrote Bazancourt,

> and with it comes not an attack from the hostile army, but a most fearful tempest. The rain falls in torrents, and a furious wind, whose howling resembles the gloomy roll of thunder, ravages the plains, and tears up the tents, throwing them in confusion, one upon the other. Many of them are carried up in the air, and the tempest plays with them as it would with feathers torn from a bird; others are swept away with such violence that they overturn everything they encounter in their passage. The horses are half drowned in the pits which have been hollowed to shelter them; the soldiers and officers, to resist this torrent suddenly let loose upon them, cling fast to anything their hands can grasp. Tables and chairs are spun about in space, and garments of all sorts darken the air with their insane whirlings; for this sudden storm has fallen upon us just at the dawn, and surprised, in their sleep, some quarters of the camp.[13]

But, like their British allies, the French were hit hardest of all out at sea where their ships lay helpless at anchor. Even those moored within the port of Kamiesh itself were not safe from the hurricane which dashed the ships against the rocks, exploding them like so much matchwood and casting both their crews and cargoes into the raging sea. 'The wind,' Bazancourt continued,

> coming from the South with extreme violence, changed the torrents of rain into whirlwinds. At the beginning the sea was disturbed, and rolled its waves with a heavy sound, while it took, in the distance, that sombre tint which announces the tempest. The harbour of Kamiesh, though sheltered, became rough and foamy; the wind, lashing the waves, raised them into crests of whitened spray; the vessels at the bottom of the bay bowed their naked masts over the billows, and threatened, every moment, to break from their anchors; while torn fragments of sails passed noisily through the air. For a moment the storm seemed to lull; but suddenly the wind, turning from South-east to West, redoubled its fury. The vessels were dashed against one another; the yards and the cordage of the different ships, for an instant entangled with each other, broke loose with a fatal crash. Some of them overturned and sank.[14]

Once the hurricane had shifted from south-east to west the French ships really began to suffer, the gales blowing the ships hard against the coast and causing mayhem in the port. At Kamiesh most of the damage was suffered by the fleet of merchantmen and transports, with the men-of-war surviving the onslaught. But off the coast of Eupatoria it was a different story. Despite great efforts to save them both the *Henry IV* and the *Pluto* were lost, being dashed to pieces on the shore.

In addition to the disastrous state of affairs out at sea and in the camps, the Allies' siege lines suffered materially also. The torrential rain caused the trenches to collapse in on themselves in places, whilst in others the parapets ran away in streams of liquid mud, thus affording the besiegers no protection whatsoever against Russian fire. The trenches filled with water and prevented passage here and there, whilst in most places the men found themselves up to their knees in muddy water. Indeed, it must have been similar to the conditions experienced by the besiegers' descendants, sixty years later on the Western Front. The clayey soil formed very quickly into a thick, clingy and heavy mud, which proved extremely difficult to scrape off. More often than not, the men's boots were simply sucked off instead. But despite these extreme difficulties the besiegers still maintained their vigilance, watching for any offensive moves from the garrison inside Sevastopol. Fortunately, none were made. Instead, the Russian defenders, inspired by Nakhimov, stepped up their work rate and pressed on with new defensive works, whilst at the same time maintaining and improving the existing defences.

In fact, conditions inside Sevastopol were far from good. Like the Allies, the garrison badly needed warm clothing and suffered from a lack of decent shelter. It is true that the houses in the town were much better than the tents and huts being used by the Allies but there were simply not enough of them to shelter both the population and the garrison. Ironically, both sides thought the other was better off. The truth was that both sides were suffering. 'Their condition was most trying,' wrote Totleben of the garrison of Sevastopol.

> They wanted altogether shelter and warm clothing. They had for the most part remained night and day in the line of defence since the opening of the siege, and had not been relieved as the troops of the Allies had been. Wounds or death alone had put a term to their sufferings and privations. Cholera began to rage with violence, and dysentery and fevers of various kinds made many victims . . . The Russians could only permit the general reserve to go under cover in the houses of the city, and in expectation of an assault, were compelled to keep the greater part of their force in the open works. Notwithstanding the more favourable condition of the Allies, however, deserters began to arrive inside the lines in considerable numbers. The Russians learned from them that the morale of the besiegers was singularly affected, that they were harassed by fatigue and suffered from cold, that the hospitals were filled with sick, and that the deplorable state of the roads rendered it exceedingly difficult to supply the batteries.[15]

The Great Storm of 14 November hit the Allies extremely hard and put back all prospect of a swift resumption of the bombardment. It certainly removed all thoughts – if any were ever entertained – of an assault on Sevastopol. Supplies of warm clothing and of equipment and ammunition had been lost, and it would take weeks to replace them. Fortunately, the weather improved during the few days following the storm, but it had been enough to send shivers – literally – through Raglan and Canrobert, who were now painfully and acutely aware of what the coming winter would bring. However, it is doubtful whether even they really knew just how bad things were going to get. Inside Sevastopol, meanwhile, both garrison and population continued to suffer whilst believing at the same time that the Allies were having a better time of it. 'The besiegers had less to suffer, for they were only obliged to keep two or three brigades at furthest in the trenches at a time, while those in camp were sheltered in tents.'[16] If only they had known just how bad things were they might have taken a different view. The Great Storm had been bad enough but the coming winter on the Chersonese would push the Allies to breaking point.

NOTES

1 Wrottesley, The Hon. George (Ed). *Life and Correspondence of Field Marshal Sir John Burgoyne* (London 1873), II, 118–19.
2 Alabin P V *Chetyre voiny. Pohodnye zapiski v voinu 1853–1856 godov* (Moscow 1892), 144.
3 Wood, General Sir Evelyn. *The Crimea in 1854 and 1894* (London 1896), 168.
4 Bell, Sir George. *Soldier's Glory; being Rough Notes of an Old Soldier* (London 1856), 252–3.
5 Higginson, Sir George. *Seventy-One Years of a Guardsman's Life* (London 1916), 210.
6 Hamley, E Bruce. *The Story of the Campaign of Sebastopol* (London 1855), 111–13.
7 Tyrell, Henry. *History of the War with Russia* (London n.d.), I, 373.
8 Bell, *Soldier's Glory*, 253.
9 Kinglake, Alexander William. *The Invasion of the Crimea: Its Origin, and An Account of its Progress down to the Death of Lord Raglan* (London 1863), VI, 161.
10 The *Journal of the Operations Conducted by the Corps of Royal Engineers* lists the following ships lost on 14 November 1854:
*Off Balaklava:*
A Maltese merchant brig: totally lost.
The Progress, bark; totally lost, containing hay and barley.
The Pultown, bark; totally lost, containing biscuits.
The Wanderer, bark; totally lost, containing oats.
The Resolute, ship, totally lost, magazine ship.
The Kenilworth, ship, totally lost.
The Rip Van Winkle, ship; totally lost.
The Wild Wave, ship; totally lost.
The Prince, screw steamer; totally lost, containing winter clothing and Engineer stores.
The Mary Anne; totally lost.
The Marquis; totally lost.
The Melbourne, steam ship; lost fore and main mast.
The Mercia, ship; dismasted.
The Lady Valiant, ship; dismasted.
The Caduceus, ship; dismasted.
The Pride of the Ocean, ship; dismasted.
Medora, ship; dismasted.
The Sir R. Sale, ship; dismasted.
*Off the Katcha:*
The Pyrenees, ship; wrecked.
The Ganges, ship; wrecked.
The Rodsley, ship; wrecked.
The Tyrone, ship; wrecked.
The Lord Raglan, ship; wrecked.
HMS Simpson; dismasted.
*Off Eupatoria;*
Her Majesty, ship; wrecked.
The Asia, ship; wrecked.
The Glendalough, ship; wrecked.
The Harbinger, ship; wrecked.
The Georgiana, ship; wrecked.
11 Russell, William Howard. *General Totleben's History of the Defence of Sevastopol*

*1854–5, A Review* (London 1865), 213–17. Interestingly enough, the *Culloden* does not appear on the list of sunken ships that appeared in the *Journal of the Operations Conducted by the Corps of Royal Engineers*.

12 Alabin. *Chetyre voiny*, 148–9.

13 Bazancourt, the Baron de (trans. by Robert Howe Gould). *The Crimean Expedition, to the Capture of Sebastopol. Chronicles of the War in the East* (London 1856), II, 127–8.

14 Ibid, II, 129–30.

15 Russell, *Totleben's Defence of Sebastopol*, 218–19.

16 Ibid, 218.

# CHAPTER FOURTEEN
## *'Nightmares for a Lifetime'*

When the Allies arrived before Sevastopol in late September 1854, Raglan had been warned of the dangers of spending a winter on the exposed Chersonese plateau. The failure to launch an attack on the town back then and, indeed, following the first bombardment, was about to have serious consequences for the Allies. Crimean winters can be terribly harsh at the best of times, but the winter weather between late November 1854 and January 1855 was far worse than normal. Furthermore, the problems and the miseries were compounded by massive problems of supply, particularly amongst the British army which suffered an almost total breakdown in its administration.

The problems for Raglan had begun as early as 6 November when he was confronted with a huge number of casualties from the Battle of Inkerman, fought the previous day. This problem would have an enormous impact on the medical services, the hospitals at Scutari finding themselves overrun and ill-prepared to handle them. The Great Storm of 14 November didn't help matters either, and when the *Prince* went down, taking with it the army's supply of warm winter clothing, the signs must have been very ominous indeed for the British troops. The seeds of discontent were sown, therefore, and affairs were already in a bad way when the first signs of winter began to appear in the Crimea.

A day or two of fine weather had followed the storm of 14 November but this had proved a false dawn, for shortly afterwards the rain began to pour in torrents, reducing the Allied camps to miserable, muddy shanty towns. The British base camp at Balaklava was a real cesspit. Wracked by storms and overcrowded with shipping, the harbour was choked with debris and rubbish that floated on the surface of the water, added to which was the odd dead body or two. The town, small in itself, was piled high with rubbish and discarded equipment, soldiers skulked in street corners, whilst wagons and carts choked the narrow streets. It was all quite disgusting. William Russell, of *The Times*, said 'words could not describe its filth, its horrors, its hospitals, its burials, its dead and dying Turks, its crowded lanes, its noisome sheds, its beastly purlieus, or its decay.'[1] Nevertheless, he had a very good go at it.

> All the pictures ever drawn of plague or pestilence, from the work of the inspired writer who chronicled the woes of infidel Egypt, down to the narratives of Boccacio, De Foe, or Moltke, fall short of individual 'bits' of disease and death, which anyone might see in half-a-dozen places during half an hour's walk in Balaklava. In spite of all our efforts the dying Turks made of every lane and street a *cloaca,* and the forms of human suffering which met the eye at every turn, and once were wont to shock us, ceased to attract even passing attention. By raising up the piece of matting or coarse rug which hung across the doorway of some miserable house, from within which you heard the wailings and cries of pain and prayers to the Prophet, you saw in one spot and in one instant a mass of accumulated woes that would serve you with nightmares for a lifetime. The dead, laid as they died, were side by side with the living. The commonest accessories were wanting; there was not the least attention paid to decency or cleanliness – the stench was appalling – the foetid air could barely struggle out to taint the atmosphere, through the chinks in the walls and roofs. The sick appeared to be tended by the sick, and the dying by the dying.[2]

The small port of Balaklava was bad enough at the best of times, but the storm of 14 November had left it in a terrible state. The dreadful winter rains did little to improve matters, and by the following month Balaklava, the main port of entry for all men and supplies sent out to the British army in the Crimea, had become a place of unimaginable filth. Fanny Duberley was the wife of Captain Henry Duberley, an officer in the 8th Hussars. This energetic and adventurous 24 year-old lady had travelled to the Crimea with her husband and kept a diary of her experiences there. On 12 December she left directions in her diary for anybody wishing to make a model of Balaklava.

> Take a village of ruined hovels and houses in the extremest state of all imaginable dirt. Allow the rain to pour into and outside them, until the whole place is a swamp of filth and ankle deep; catch about, on an average, 1000 sick Turks with the plague, and cram them into the houses indiscriminately; kill about 100 a day, and bury them so as to be scarcely covered with earth, leaving them to rot at leisure. On to one part of the beach drive all the exhausted *bat* ponies, dying bullocks and worn-out camels, and leave them to die of starvation. They will generally do so in about three days. Collect together from the water of the harbour all the offal of the animals slaughtered for the use of about 100 ships, to say nothing of the inhabitants of the town – which together with an occasional floating human body, whole or in parts, and the driftwood of wrecks, pretty well covers the water – and

> stew them altogether in a narrow harbour, and you will have imitation of the real essence of Balaklava. If this is not *piquante* enough, let some men be instructed to sit and smoke on the powder-barrels landing on the quay, which I myself saw two men doing today.[3]

If things were bad in Balaclava, they were every bit as bad elsewhere. After just a few days of heavy rain the various camps became quagmires, whilst the trenches were flooded and almost impossible to man. Indeed, they were not dissimilar to the conditions to be found on the Western Front some sixty years later. 'By the first week in December,' wrote George Higginson of the Scots Guards,

> snow to the depth of eighteen inches had fallen, often thawing as it fell. I need not dwell upon the imperfect protection afforded by a tent, which could neither be warmed by a fire within nor protected from the downpour without. Narrow causeways of stone (of which plenty lay in easy reach) were made from tent to tent; walls four or five feet high sheltered the enclosures within which the cooking kitchens were constructed, and fires were with difficulty maintained day and night. I say with difficulty, for we could obtain no fuel save from the roots of the oak scrub which grew to the height of three or four feet in the rocky ravines. Extracted from the half-frozen ground by pick-axe and mattock, the green roots were kindled with difficulty; the result being smouldering embers, rather than the welcome blaze which would have served to dry the drenched and tattered great coats of the working parties, returning from their six-and-thirty hours in the trenches.[4]

It is little wonder, therefore, that the British troops, finding it difficult even to light a fire, took such pains each morning to get a little breakfast. Higginson again.

> My own early breakfast was as follows; two navy biscuits were placed overnight in a tin inside my tent, and sufficient water poured upon them to soften their toughness by a night's soaking. As soon as my servant had succeeded in making a fire in my little enclosure outside the tent, the biscuit was broken up into a frying-pan, a thick slice or two of the fat of salt pork was added. While it was still hot and frizzling, I extracted bit by bit, not daring to remove the frying-pan lest it should harden again so as to be uneatable. Under the ashes of the fire I was in the habit of laying an 18lb shot, which gradually accumulated heat, so that in the evening it was transferred to the foot of my camp bed under my blankets, my damp clothes were heaped

> on the outside, and by this means I secured a certain amount of warmth for myself, and immunity from the danger of damp garments.[5]

Sergeant Timothy Gowing, of the 7th (Royal) Fusiliers, was another to comment on the difficulties of procuring fuel for fire and on the appalling conditions in the camps.

> The cavalry horses, that had cost an enormous amount, sank up to their knees in mud at every step, until they dropped exhausted; and all the way from the camp to Balaklava were to be seen, dead horses, mules and bullocks in every stage of decomposition. And our poor fellows, who had fought so well at the Alma, Balaklava and the two Inkermans, were now dying by hundreds daily. The army was put upon half rations, viz: – half-a-pound of mouldy biscuit, and half-a-pound of salt junk (beef or pork); coffee was served out, but in its raw green state, with no means of roasting it. No wood or firing was to be had, except a few roots that were dug up. Men would come staggering into the camp from the trenches soaked to the skin and ravenously hungry, when a half-pound of mouldy biscuit would be issued, with the same quantity of salt junk, so hard that one almost wanted a good hatchet to break it. The scenes were heartrending. The whole camp was one vast sheet of mud, the trenches in many places knee deep; men died at their posts from sheer exhaustion or starvation rather than complain, for if they reported themselves sick the medical chests were empty.[6]

It is not surprising, given the terrible conditions in the Crimea, that the men's uniforms quickly deteriorated. It was always the same for the army on campaign. In the Peninsula, for example, Wellington had become so used to seeing his men looking threadbare and patched that he simply gave up on the idea of trying to keep them looking smart. So long as they turned out well appointed and with sixty rounds of ball cartridge, he later said, he didn't care what his men looked like. In the Crimea it was even worse, for apart from the retreat to Corunna and the retreat from Burgos Wellington's men had never suffered the sort of privations now being experienced by Raglan's men before Sevastopol. In fact, the uniforms had started to deteriorate the moment they landed. A shower of rain would quickly start to work away at the colour of the uniform whilst the hot sun that followed would distort helmets and further discolour the cloth. Trousers and jackets would catch on thorn bushes, dust would dirty the smart red tunics, whilst fording streams had the same effect as rain. The effects of a battle were even worse. The simple act of kneeling or lying down continued the process of general wear and tear and with the onset of winter things took a massive turn for the worse. Timothy Gowing again:

> Men were positively forbidden to take off their boots, as it was found impossible to get them on again; while some might be seen limping about the camp in the snow (two or three feet deep) with no boots of any sort; others with boots up to their knees, which they had borrowed from some dead Russians. Some of our critics (newspaper correspondents) were at a loss to find out to what regiment a man really belonged, or even what nation, as during the worst part of the winter no two men were dressed alike. Some had hay bands round their legs, others had long stockings outside their rags or trousers, some had garters made from old knapsacks, others had leggings made from sheep skins, bullocks' hides, buffalo hides – anything to keep the extreme cold out. Some had got hold of a Russian officer's overcoat, which was almost a load to carry. As for Joseph's coat of many colours, I do not think it would have taken a prize for patchwork by the side of some of our men's clothing. They say patch beside patch looks neighbourly, but our men's coats were nothing but rags tacked together. As for head dress, some had mess tin covers that could be pulled down well over the ears; others had coverings for the head made out of old blankets four or five times doubled.[7]

Richard Temple Godman served with the 5th Dragoon Guards and was evidently more concerned with the impression the appearance he and his fellow officers might have had upon admiring young ladies. 'You would not recognise the British soldier again were you to see him here,' he wrote,

> unwashed and unshaven, covered with mud from head to foot, some clothed partly in Russian garments, an old sack, or some original dress made out of an old blanket, tied on with bits of string. Then alas! The Heavy Dragoon and smart Hussar, what if some of our lady friends could see us now; I don't think they would ever care much about us soldiers again, with uniforms torn, and hardly to be recognised, legs bound up with hay and straw bands, some without shoes or socks, etc.[8]

It is remarkable just how similar the observations were of British officers in the Peninsula and the Crimea. An officer in Wellington's army had remarked upon the fact that the martinets who came out from England were horrified by the army's 'fancy dress', as a result of the necessary adoption of the many items of non-regulation uniform. Forty years later, the same sentiments were being echoed by Captain Robert Hawley, of the 89th Regiment.

> You would be amused were you to see the dress of the Army just now. To say there is any prevailing dress would be wrong. I think the costumes are about as numerous as our chiefs' ideas are small and unfeeling. Guards, hussars and infantry or gunners in blankets, buffaloes' skins, sheep-coats, all flannel and worsted, or Greek gragoes [a coarse hooded jacket], long boots and tarpaulin leggings, fur caps of every sort, smashed helmets, once brass now verdigris, or canteen covers as a last substitute, now form our uniform. Ah, pipe clay! That is gone – only temporarily perhaps: its substitute soot and mud. There is no doubt a fearful want of energy exists. Look at the arms. They are coated with rust. Look at our soldiers. I have men in my own draft who have never bit off the end of a Minié cartridge, possibly even a smooth one. I don't mention this for any reason save to show how totally unprepared we attacked a large military power. It reminds me of a fly dashing against a light and thinking that by sacrificing itself it can be put out.[9]

Even when the weather improved in the spring of 1855 the problem of non-regulation uniform continued to exist. As late as 30 March, the secretary for war was writing:

> I wish to direct your attention to one point which is reported to me, viz. the licence adopted by Regimental Officers as to costume. Depend on it that this betokens a loose discipline, and the sooner you strike it the better. Give any relaxation you please, but let it be given by superior authority in an official way, and don't let young gents, or old gents, be the judges of their own dress.[10]

Although the winter was intensely cold, many writers actually stated in their diaries that some of the days were bright and fine. There was even the odd warm day. But overall there was no let up in the atrocious conditions in the camps and in the trenches. Surgeon George Lawson wrote:

> For two days after writing my last letter to you, there was continued rain and sleet, varied now and then with a little hail. Last night this changed to snow and this morning, on getting or rather waking up, we found inside the door of the tent and extending two or three feet inwards a quantity of snow. On looking out we discovered the ground well covered . . . Imagine the condition of the poor fellows in the trenches, their clothing first getting wet thro' and then freezing on them, they have now to sit up to their knees in snow . . . Russ, with this state of affairs, has taken to fire more than ever.
>
> This morning in the middle of a heavy snow storm . . . the French

> brought their mules to convey about a hundred of our fellows, many of them too ill to walk, lifted into the easy chairs slung on each side of the animal's back, and others placed in couches hung in the same manner, to be carried nearly seven miles on a bitter cold morning, snow the greater part of the way beating into their faces . . . So severe is the frost that, from your breath during the night, we find icicles all over our blankets in the morning, and many men who have long beards awake with them frozen.[11]

Colonel Edward Hodge, of the 4th Dragoon Guards, was powerless to prevent the sufferings of the regiment's precious horses. They moved camp but little changed. 'We have moved away from our very exposed, cold camp,' he wrote,

> and I have got the regiment in a snug valley near Balaklava. The truth was that we could not any longer feed the horses where we were. The animals were so weak they would not struggle up the hill with the sacks of corn. The condition of everything is awful; weather makes no difference, the horses are always out. They stand knee deep in mud, and frequently die from being suffocated in it. Some 12 a night generally die in the Brigade, and you cannot form any conception of what the men are. Their clothing is nothing but mud-stained rags. They have not time to wash, and are so far from water that they cannot go to it, and having no utensils to convey water in, their condition is horrible. I assure you that I am obliged sometimes to go two days without washing, even my hands. The violence of the rain and wind has sometimes been such as to prevent my sending for water beyond a sufficiency for my coffee, or to boil our ration of pork in.[12]

Twenty-one year-old Captain William Rous served in the Crimea with the 90th Foot, arriving in November 1854. His father and uncle had both fought under Wellington in the Peninsula. What they would have made of the conditions in the Crimea is anyone's guess, but certainly William found it very hard going at times. Writing to his mother on 23 February 1855, Rous said:

> It is so bitterly cold that I can scarcely hold the pen. But the worst day we have had since the middle of January was last Tuesday, the 20th. At three o'clock on that morning in the trenches, where I had passed the night, the thermometer was at 2 degrees below freezing point, with a driving north wind, and snow. As the snow fell on the face it froze, and my hair was matted with ice, and icicles formed on my eyelashes. So intense was the cold that whenever I was compelled in

> visiting the sentries or otherwise to face the blast, my nose burst out bleeding, which with the exposure exhausted one so much, that it was only the certainty of never rising again that prevented me throwing myself down in the snow. The soldiers have become so apathetic that they yield and lie down in despair, and of course morning brings its tale of frozen and frostbitten.[13]

Central to the problem of supplies for the army was, naturally, the Commissary General, James Filder, an elderly, well meaning gentleman who did his best but found himself completely overwhelmed following the loss of so great a quantity of his precious supplies during the storm of 14 November and by the harsh winter that followed immediately afterwards. The frustrating fact was that Filder served not only the British Army but was a servant answerable to the Treasury and as such could only provide the army with whatever the government in London authorised him to. His hands were effectively tied. The problem was not a new one and in fact dated back to the creation of the modern British Army following the restoration of the monarchy in 1660. Marlborough had experienced great problems during his campaigns in the early eighteenth century and only managed to overcome them with great difficulty. Wellington, too, experienced great problems one hundred years later, but at least had the benefit of a prolonged campaign during which he transformed what was in effect a blunt instrument into a finely honed blade. But even he felt the frustration of working with a department which did not come under the auspices of Horse Guards but was answerable to the Treasury. Indeed, Wellington's hand was upon everything except the commissariat, over which he could extend only limited influence.

Despite this problem nothing was done to rectify the situation and thus when the British Army went to war in 1854 it still remained. Unlike Marlborough and Wellington, Raglan did not have the luxury of being able to procure supplies from the interior. Instead, everything had to come from England in the ships of the Royal Navy or hired specifically by the government. This was no bad thing, of course. With no Russian fleet to hinder or harass the British and French fleets the lines of communication were relatively secure. There was certainly no danger of the Russians interfering within the Crimea itself as the Allies had no such lines of communications there. Filder himself initially did a good job and set out to ensure that the coming campaign – which he quickly realised would involve at least one winter – ran as smoothly as possible, at least from his own point of view. Sadly, his hopes were blown away with the storm of 14 November, after which his problems became almost insurmountable. But the blame did not lie entirely with him and his department. Even after the storm and with the onset of winter, Filder managed to procure supplies but these simply accumulated by the harbour at Balaklava, nobody having the means or will to transport them to the camps up on the Chersonese. Supplies even accumulated back in England, particularly forage for horses. Indeed, whilst horses sank up to their knees in the mud in the camps to the north-west of Balaklava, starving and weak, tons of hay were simply left standing on the dockside at Southampton owing to a lack of transport. The whole unhappy situation ran, in the words of one historian, like the house that Jack built.

> The Army starved because there was no transport. There was no transport because the Government would not organise it, but such transport as there was could not work in the rain because there was no road, and it could not live because there was no fodder, and there was no fodder because the storm wrecked the fodder ships, and there was no reserve of fodder because the Government at Home would not send it . . . And so the British Army died in its tracks.[14]

In addition to the mounting problems in the Crimea and with criticism growing in England, Raglan now had the French to put up with. The French army had suffered few of the horrors experienced by the British during the winter. True, it had been extremely hard for them, and, indeed, they had sent off almost 7,000 sick to Constantinople in January alone. Frostbite in particular had hospitalised thousands during the winter months but their numbers were great enough for this loss to be absorbed. Their supplies had arrived in good quantities, and with their camps within easy reach of their supply ports of Kamiesh and Kazatch there existed none of the supply problems that had bedevilled the British. Furthermore, the large numbers of French troops at hand enabled them to get supplies forward to the camps. It was a simple case of having sufficient manpower. Perhaps an indication of the French success in supplying their men can be gauged by the fact that Raglan, through no fault of his own – arguably – had failed to adequately provision fewer than 20,000 men, whereas Canrobert had maintained an army of almost 65,000 in December, the number rising to 75,000 by January. This was indeed a sad reflection of British misadministration.

The difference between the British and French was noted by Sir John Burgoyne. Shortly to be recalled by London – he was replaced by Sir Harry Jones – Burgoyne had written: 'When I compare our army with theirs [the French], I see much to admire and to follow among them in matters of organisation, and much to envy in their habits, and knowledge how to make themselves comparatively comfortable, when our poor helpless creatures are full of miseries.'[15] This was nothing new, of course. Forty years earlier, one Peninsula veteran had written of the way in which the French had not only constructed huts made from trees and branches, but had formed them into avenues. The British soldier, he said, simply sat on a log and lit his pipe. Burgoyne went on. 'We find our allies, even as circumstanced here, frequently singing and gay, while for months I have not witnessed so much as a smile on the face of a British soldier – who, although suffering and serious, make no complaints!'[16]

Naturally, conditions for the Russians inside Sevastopol were far from good but they were far better than conditions on the Chersonese plateau. Two days into 1855 Surgeon Pirogov wrote to his wife from Sevastopol, describing how he passed New Year's Day.

> Happy New Year, My Dear! Would you like to know how we saw in the year of 1855? Here is a description. The day before, we heated our stove thoroughly with coal. Kalashnikov [a doctor] decided to surprise us and, for want of champagne, gave us Donskoe [a sparkling wine] to drink. Six more doctors came with cigarettes and cigars as well to see out the Old Year. A severe intoxication was its effect and even a hard night's firing at the batteries couldn't drive it away. I woke up with a splitting headache and at first thought about staying at home for the day but, fortunately, didn't do such a foolish thing. I went to the hospital and felt a bit better, not expecting, however to greet the New Year so merrily.
>
> But everything has turned out all right. A field-doctor from the position, one of my former students, came with an invitation from his regimental commander to celebrate the New Year Eve at their place. I'd just come back from the hospital and refused at first, but then I agreed. Two of us went there in a carriage; me and a field-doctor. Our position is five *versts* from Sevastopol between the mountains not far from the Chernaya river. We found a lot of small piles of snow and under these heaps the dugouts are hidden. We went down five steps, we found ourselves in a rather large room with a table laid for the guests of the commander of the Odessky regiment, Colonel Skyuderi. The walls were upholstered with shabby cloaks; one window dug into the ground above lit the dugout; a stove, made of stones, was heating the room without any smoke despite the snowstorm. A chimney from it went out through the ground as well. The table was set for twenty people or so. Among the guests there was a brigade general, a regimental priest, a quartermaster, commissary, and two field-doctors, we three and some field officers.
>
> Our dinner began and what a dinner! There were jellied meat, kulebyaka [pie with meat, fish or vegetable], game with truffles, pâtés, jellies and champagne! Not bad! If the French and the English could see such a dinner, they would leave, knowing they had not a hope of taking Sevastopol. At the dinner the divisional quartermaster, a witty fellow, made us laugh. The brigade general, a fat and good-natured person, was chewing away thoughtfully; all the other

> guests were completely relaxed. Our host, a handsome man, a hero with a wounded arm, treated us first-rate. When we were drinking to the czar's health, music began to play and a choir of choristers struck up: God save the czar!
>
> At the end of the dinner we heard a hue-and-cry in the yard; it was the other officers from the neighbouring tent, proposing loud toasts. We went outside. The snow was falling in large snowflakes; we were surrounded by white mountains, and in the distance an enemy camp was seen on them. The musicians, choristers and officers formed a circle in the middle of which dancing began, in the ankle-deep mud. The regimental field-doctor, my student, and a virtuoso at pulling faces, in a soldier's coat and a mutton hat was dancing a can-can with an ensign, representing a Saint Petersburg ball dandy. The other guests also couldn't help dancing and a mazurka began. Our host the colonel, with his tied up arm, and the battalion commander joined the dancers. A sumptuous feast began. I was dying of laughter; it was impossible not to be merry, seeing just how merrily and light-heartedly a Russian man lives. In the distance, behind a mountain, gunfire was heard. There was shooting in the trenches as well but out here they were dancing *trepak* [a Russian folk dance] and one soldier, having turned his sheepskin coat inside out, was even walking head over heels. At last they began to raise the guests and lift them up, drinking champagne after each lifting. I was also lifted up three times and I was afraid I might fall down into the mud but at least my headache had disappeared and I was in a very merry mood. We returned home late at night. And what do you think happened at our headquarters? In the morning Menshikov locked his gate, didn't receive anybody and didn't visit anybody. He hasn't stood a treat to anybody; the headquarters were dull and gloomy on the New Year Eve; it was not very Russian.[17]

The bad winter weather naturally meant that the Allies were unable to prosecute the siege of Sevastopol with the sort of vigour they would have liked. Instead, the siege lapsed into rather more of a blockade, with none of the intensity of bombardment that had been seen before the onset of winter. For the Russians, on the other hand, little had changed. Conditions might well have been bad inside Sevastopol but the Russians were determined to keep up the pressure and take advantage of the bad situation in the trenches, particularly the shambolic British sectors. This was done by carrying out sorties and raids on the Allied trenches, which we will look at in greater detail later. With things not going too well for the British the French, somewhat understandably, had begun to look upon their British allies as dead wood, and talked of 'galvanising' the English sloth. 'The English are altogether in the background; they have neither horses nor workmen; it is an army no longer existing except in name,' wrote one French officer.[18] Harsh though this seems, the verdict was not far from the truth. The British army, barely the size of a French division, was simply too weak and incapable of manning the right of the Allied trenches before Sevastopol.

As early as 26 December Burgoyne had a meeting with Airey and General Bizot, the chief French engineer, at which it was suggested that the French take over the right of the Allied trenches on Victoria Ridge from the British. It was a simple plea for help. Burgoyne had always considered the Malakhov to be the key to Sevastopol's defences, but with the British occupied with approaching the Redan they were not strong enough in manpower to carry out attacks on the two. The French, with their greater numbers, would therefore have to come and take over the British trenches opposite the Malakhov and carry out the attack in this sector themselves. Canrobert initially resisted, but when he too realised that the Malakhov was indeed the key he began to relent. Unfortunately, before Canrobert agreed to Burgoyne's request he bowed to pressure from his own staff who had begun to grow weary of British lethargy and apathy. As a result, Canrobert was forced to write to Raglan a spiky letter calling for assurances of future co-operation from the British. In effect, he was demanding to know whether the British army was capable of continuing or not. Naturally, Raglan's feathers were somewhat ruffled and it needed all of his diplomatic acumen to keep the apparently fragile alliance from falling apart.

One can almost feel Raglan's exasperation at receiving Canrobert's note, written on 28 December, for he was beset not only by problems in the Crimea but by severe criticisms at home. For a man of Raglan's age, under such pressure and with his army experiencing the very worst of conditions in the field, the strain must have been intense. Furthermore, he must have cast his mind back to his decision to accept Balaklava as the British base and the additional responsibility of protecting the right of the Allies' position around Sevastopol. This decision, it will be remembered, had been rather cleverly engineered by the wily French who, although they held the right of the line during the march from the Alma, suddenly relinquished it once they realised the difficulties the possession of Balaklava entailed. If Raglan had given any thought to New Year's resolutions he surely must have wished for an end to the problems both at home and in the Crimea. On 1 January he responded to Canrobert's note, described by Burgoyne as 'very distressing', by sending Airey to defuse a situation which threatened to boil over into a serious fallout between the two Allied armies. In the event Airey, himself under even more pressure at home than Raglan, carried out his master's errand with great aplomb, reducing the French commander to a state of some unease and embarrassment, to the extent that he apparently regretted sending Raglan the note in the first place. More important, however, was the decision taken to revert to the plan suggested by Burgoyne a few days earlier, which involved the French taking over the British trenches on the Inkerman Heights and the Victoria Ridge. From now on, the Malakhov would be their object, allowing the much weaker British to concentrate on the Redan. The only drawback was the French could not take up their new posts until the first week in February.

In the meantime, the British continued to man their trenches, but in a less than effective manner. The neglect shown by the guards in the British trenches was so bad that Canrobert was forced to send the 17th Chasseurs to give them cover against the Russian marksmen who took a heavy toll of the careless British who would take little care when walking through the trenches, exposing themselves unnecessarily and fatally to the Russians. Often, men would look over the parapet or through embrasures and fall to the skilful marksmanship of the Russian snipers. They simply didn't exercise enough care. Much of this has to do with the quality of the men who were now manning the trenches. Gone were the men of the Alma and Inkerman, the men who had fought to the bloody death from September to November. The great regiments who had come out in September were pale shadows of their former selves. Instead, the skeleton battalions had been filled with raw recruits from England, many of whom were little more than boys. Indeed, Burgoyne was moved to write: 'The reinforcements we are getting consist of a vast number of recruits – lads who have not been six months in the service, and many have not fired a musket in their lives.'[19] Not only were these boys careless, they were mischievous too. Bored, perhaps, with the tedium of duty in the trenches they set about amusing themselves in a very irresponsible way. 'The covering parties and others,' complained Burgoyne, 'in the trenches, are regularly every night pulling the fascines and gabions out of the facings of embrasures, and of parapets of the batteries, and have occasionally attacked the platforms. This is for self enjoyment, and so it is when those in charge of horses sell the corn to buy liquor, but what will be said to numbers parting with their *new warm clothing* to the French, to get liquor from their vivandières!'[20] The selling of equipment by British soldiers to buy drink was nothing new, of course. During the Peninsular War the practice was rife, with the exception of the cavalry of the King's German Legion who actually shared their rations with their horses! In the Crimea, however, it was unforgivable. To think of the efforts being made to improve the lot of the soldiers, apparently in dire need of warm clothing, and then to read of them selling their new kit for drink is beyond comprehension. What Raglan commanded was an army not only weak in number but also consisting of inexperienced men, raw recruits and young boys, with the battalions stiffened by a few old sweats. It is little wonder, therefore, that the French viewed the British with such dismay and contempt.

Raglan's problems were exacerbated by his army having to manhandle every item of siege equipment and each round of ammunition from the base camp at Balaklava up to the Chersonese plateau and the siege lines. This in itself required a superhuman effort on the part of the men bringing the supplies forward. Indeed, as is frequently pointed out by various writers, the 4,000 miles from England to Balaklava was the easy bit; the few miles from Balaklava to the Chersonese were pure hell. Needless to say it took a bit of Victorian ingenuity to solve the problem of getting supplies from Balaklava to the camps. Messrs. Peto, Betts and Brassey sailed for the Crimea in December 1854 with instructions to build a railway between Balaklava and the Chersonese. Remarkably, the railway was in operation by March the following year upon which the life of many a miserable and exhausted redcoat was made immeasurably easier.

The construction of the railway came as a blessed relief for the British army, but it was too late to save the government in London. As early as November, reports had been appearing in the press giving accounts of the bad state of affairs in the Crimea. *The Times* was particular hostile to the government. William Russell, the newspaper's correspondent, took every opportunity to attack arrangements – or rather the lack of them – in the Crimea, whilst the uncensored letters of officers and men that appeared in the press did little to help matters either. Forty years earlier Wellington had complained about the amount of information leaked out in the press by British officers. The Crimean War demonstrated that little had changed. Indeed, just as the French had claimed forty years earlier that they gleaned more from the English press than they did from their own intelligence services, so the Russians did likewise now. And how they must have relished the accounts of the sufferings of the British troops at the front. Along with their other favourite generals, December, January and February, the czar now had a fourth ally, the British press.

William Russell was not unaware of the difficult position in which he and his fellow correspondents found themselves. On the one hand, he had a duty to inform an avid readership of how the campaign was faring. On the other hand, he had no wish to divulge important information to the Russians. Whilst admitting the dangers of communicating important information to the enemy he argued that the same information could have been easily got by normal methods anyway, and defended the correspondents' actions. 'During the winter,' wrote Russell,

> newspaper correspondents in the Crimea were placed in a difficult position. In common with generals and chiefs, and men-at-arms, they wrote home accounts of all we were doing to take Sevastopol . . . It mattered little, therefore, if we pointed out the losses of our men, the number and position of our guns, the site of our quarters, the position of our magazines, or the range of the Russian cannon. How much

> knowledge of this sort the enemy gleaned through their spies, or by actual observation, it is not needful to inquire; but it may be inferred that much of the information conveyed to them, or said to have been conveyed to them, by the English press, could have been ascertained through those very ordinary channels of communication, the eye and ear, long ere our letters had been forwarded to Sevastopol and translated.[21]

Russell could certainly argue his case against him having possibly divulged sensitive information in the British press, although there were probably few in the British army itself who would agree with him. The reports of the conditions in the trenches and camps before Sevastopol, however, were a different matter altogether and whilst not perhaps overly damaging to the army certainly had an enormous impact on the British people and, consequently, did great damage to the government. Russell himself recognised this and wrote: 'Although it might be dangerous to communicate facts likely to be of service to the Russians, it was certainly hazardous to conceal the truth from the English people.'[22]

They say the truth hurts, and for the good people of England, eagerly anticipating reports of the fall of Sevastopol and the defeat of the czar's armies, Russell's despatches, along with the condemnations that appeared with painful regularity in *The Times* – written by its editor, John Thadeus Delane – came as a great shock. Britannia might well have ruled the waves but she was faring very badly on land in the Crimea. During the sabre-rattling and lead up to war in 1853 and 1854 *The Times* had not exactly roared out its approval for war, but it had generally supported Aberdeen's government. Now, with reports coming not only from Russell but also from Thomas Chenery, *The Times* correspondent in Constantinople, who first reported the condition of the hospitals at Scutari, public pulses began to race. The great British public had read with pride news of the Allied victory at the Alma. Even the reports that followed of the large number of casualties failed to open their eyes to the realities of war. Indeed, they were blinded by the expectation of victory and by the reawakening of the power and glory of British martial power. But successive reports of the conditions at Scutari and of the apparent lack of care of the sick and wounded, combined with the non-appearance of the longed for and expected report of the capture of Sevastopol, had only served to fuel public disquiet. These reports were soon followed by accounts, both by correspondents and by serving officers, of the lack of progress and of the dreadful conditions, and with the onset of winter and the accompanying reports of the troubles public disquiet turned first to shock and then to anger. The call for war against Russia had been supported with gusto by the great British public, particularly following Sinope, and indeed, public opinion had been an important factor in swaying the government towards war. Waterloo might well have been a distant memory but many still remembered it with pride; it was high time to emblazon more honours on British regimental colours. Thus, the Crimean War was popular, and Queen Victoria's regiments sailed off to war on a sea of frenzied expectation. Scutari, Inkerman and winter changed all that. The British army was now wasting away in the snows of a Russian winter and nobody was doing anything about it. It simply wouldn't do.

As the sense of outrage and despair at both the treatment of the British soldiers in the Crimea and the apparent lack of any progress grew, so the vitriolic leaders that appeared in *The Times* became more personal, with Raglan as Delane's main target. On the penultimate day of 1854 the newspaper thundered out its disapproval of Raglan and, in particular, what they considered to be his haughty and uncaring attitude.

> There are people who think it is a less happy consummation of affairs that the Commander-in-Chief and his staff should survive alone on the heights of Sevastopol, decorated, ennobled, duly named in despatch after despatch, and ready to return home to enjoy pensions and honours amid the bones of fifty thousand British soldiers, than that the equanimity of office and the good humour of society should be disturbed by a single recall or a new appointment over the heads now in command.[23]

This sort of leader was bound to annoy the public, particularly the working classes, who viewed Raglan's aristocratic bearing as just typical of those managing – or rather mismanaging – the army in the Crimea. The public clamour for something to be done grew in intensity, as did their demands for heads to roll. After all, rarely has a government been allowed so much time to prepare for war, and yet accomplished so little. Somebody was to blame, and something had to be done. Enter one John Arthur Roebuck, Member of Parliament for Sheffield. At 54 years old, John Roebuck was a diligent, hard-working and relatively anonymous backbench MP. There was nothing particularly spectacular about his career to date and, indeed, he was typical of scores of jobbing back-benchers. In an age which bred men of the calibre of Palmerston, Gladstone and Disraeli, men like John Roebuck could look forward to nothing more than playing a very minor role in the running of the British Empire, but the scandalous conditions in the Crimea and at Scutari being reported in the press suddenly brought Roebuck to prominence. On 23 January 1855 he presented a motion to the House of Commons calling for an enquiry into the management of the army in the Crimea. It was duly debated in the House on 28 January, during which Roebuck made a very impassioned and effective speech in support of his motion, a speech that was cut short on account of him falling ill. It was well past midnight when the members filed off to cast their votes, of which 305 of the 453 cast were in favour of the motion. It was a rather unexpected result and when the members trundled off wearily into the dark, January morning – it was 1.45 am when the House adjourned – they realised that Aberdeen's government was in its death throes.

On 30 January Queen Victoria accepted the resignation of Aberdeen's ministry, whereupon she was saddled with the problem of finding a new man to take up the reins. Lord Derby declined the post, whilst Lord John Russell, who had so recently turned his back on his government colleagues following Roebuck's motion, was unable to accept when it was found impossible to find anyone who would serve under him. The queen was now faced with appealing to the one man she disliked above all, the man whom she considered to be 'a trial'. Henry John Temple, 3rd Viscount Palmerston, was one of the greatest men of Victorian England. His experience and knowledge of foreign affairs was second to none and, indeed, he had been Queen Victoria's foreign secretary during the crisis in the late autumn and early winter of 1853 before he was removed from office in December that year following the latest in a series of clashes with the queen and Prince Albert. The trouble with Palmerston was that he was fiercely independent, and in an age when respect for the monarchy was placed above all others – save perhaps for the Almighty – his flippant attitude towards the young royals, who were over twenty years his junior, caused great offence to the queen and her consort. His experience and qualifications were not in doubt, but his manner still rankled with the queen who was loath to ask him to become prime minister. The problem was that the series of refusals by others left her with little choice, and so on 6 February 1855 'Pam', as he was known, was back in office as head of Her Majesty's government.

Palmerston's appointment was a step in the right direction, especially as far as the public were concerned, but it was the appointment of Lord Panmure in place of the Duke of Newcastle as secretary for war that would have a greater effect on affairs in the Crimea. Panmure, a straight talking Scot, possessed little of the eloquence of other more noted politicians of the day, but he at least had the benefit of some twelve years' military experience with the 79th (Cameron) Highlanders. Panmure and Palmerston proved popular with the British public who expected quick results and an improvement in their army's lot in the Crimea. Panmure certainly wasted no time in irritating Raglan, whom he accused of hiding away in his headquarters while his men starved and froze to death all round him. Indeed, Panmure didn't mince his words, and he strongly criticised Raglan for not keeping the queen or the government informed of the true state of affairs in the Crimea, and for allowing things to degenerate to such a level of despair. He singled out for particular criticism Airey and Estcourt, whom he considered to be complete blockheads, recommending that they be replaced. Barely a week into office, Panmure wrote:

> I have to observe that on assuming the charge of the War Department, I cannot find that your Lordship has been in the habit of keeping Her Majesty's Government acquainted, in a clear and succinct manner, with the operations with which you are engaged, the progress which you have made in them, and the results likely to attend them.
>
> Your notices of the condition of your Army are brief and unsatisfactory, and convey little more than is to be gathered from the gloomy characters of the 'morning states'; while, on the other hand, elaborate statements reach us from quarters which you denominate as unauthentic, but to which it is impossible for the Government not, to some considerable extent at least, to attach credit.
>
> We know that the communications between the Army and the port to which all its stores are shipped, have never been in a fit state for the transport of those stores, but from yourself we have had no satisfactory explanation how this came to be originally overlooked, and why the error has not even been attempted to be repaired.
>
> We learn from sources the truth of which cannot be impeached, that while clothing and medical stores are in abundance at Balaklava, your troops have been suffering all the miseries of cold, and your sick all those melancholy consequences which the want of medicines occasions.[24]

Panmure, evidently well informed or simply acting on gossip, went on to say how the men suffered from a want of fresh vegetables despite there being large stocks of 'fresh juicy onions' at Eupatoria. The tents of the men were wet and filthy, he claimed, despite there being a type of felt available to the men, again at Eupatoria. 'It would appear,' he went on, 'that your visits to the camp were few and far between, and your staff seem to have known as little as yourself of the condition of your gallant men.'

Panmure said he had great difficulty in believing the stories coming out of the Crimea, but eventually gave in to the inevitable, saying that 'concurrent and indisputable testimony from diverse sources has forced the truth upon me'.[25] But despite his criticism, Panmure went on to blame the quartermaster general, Airey, who he said had 'totally failed', for the sufferings of the men and for misleading Raglan by not informing him of the true state of the men and the stores. 'It seems to me that after all that has passed Generals Airey and Estcourt might perform more efficient service in some other department of the Army than those which they now occupy.'[26]

The criticisms did not stop there, for Panmure's stinging rebuke went on to inform Raglan that an officer would be sent out from England to act as chief of staff, in order to 'superintend the whole routine of staff duties, and who will test the capabilities of any officer on the general staff of the Army, and report to your Lordship such as in his opinion are unfit for the positions which they occupy'.[27] The officer in question was 63 year-old General James Simpson, a veteran of the Peninsular and Waterloo campaigns, and, more recently, the Sind campaign. Perhaps by way of softening the blow of his despatch, and possibly realising he had been rather too aggressive, Panmure followed his initial despatch with a more subtle one, placing before Raglan the difficult position he [Panmure] found himself in.

> The public are roused and the House of Commons has already sacrificed two victims to their disappointment in the persons of Lord Aberdeen and the Duke of Newcastle. I have most reluctantly come here – not that I expect to do any better than my predecessor, but because I wish to protect, as far as possible, the interests of the Army, and to stand between you and those who are so angry at all that has happened.[28]

Panmure went on to explain the political situation at home, and the 'curious position' of almost all the members of the new government having been members of the old one. He also praised the way Raglan had kept up friendly relations with the French. However, Panmure could not resist repeating his suggestion that Airey and Estcourt be replaced. The implication was that Roebuck's enquiry into the management of the Army would take place unless Raglan himself demonstrated his willingness to change things. 'Your Staff must be changed at least,' he wrote, 'that will satisfy the public, and that radically, and I would strongly advise both Airey and Estcourt to go either to Divisions or come home.'[29]

What must have irked Raglan as much as the criticisms, the suggestions that he should change his staff, and the news that Simpson was coming out to report on them, was the fact that Panmure seemed to be advising him – or at least Airey – on how to do his job. Referring specifically to the absence of a road from Balaklava to the British camps, Panmure said, 'With plenty of stone, he might have laid a thick bottoming first, and a causeway on top of this.'[30] For somebody sitting in the comfort of his London office to be preaching the obvious must have grated at Raglan's headquarters. But it was not only Panmure, the government and the British public who were dismayed at affairs in the Crimea. Queen Victoria herself had become exasperated by the lack of information contained in Raglan's despatches and welcomed Panmure's direct reproach. 'His [Raglan's] letters are as usual not very full of information, and the Morning State shows an unfavourable condition of the Army.' And referring to Panmure's letter she wrote: 'The Queen was much pleased with the despatch which Lord Panmure has addressed to Lord Raglan – painful as it must be to have to write or to receive it.'[31]

It was indeed painful for Raglan, a man who had dedicated his life to the service of his country, and who had given a limb for it at Waterloo, to receive such criticism, especially when it came from such high circles. One can well imagine the normally placid Raglan's feelings of dismay and hurt when he read the despatches from London. It was all very well dealing with the tremendous problems in the Crimea, where everything was at least close at hand – even his fraught dealings with the French were handled subtly and successfully – but he must have experienced great frustration at not being able to answer immediately his critics, thousands of miles away. Nevertheless, he responded in his typical, quiet manner, in a despatch that exudes the pain and the sense of injustice he felt at what he considered to be unwarranted criticism. In response to the allegation that he rarely left his headquarters to visit the British camps Raglan wrote:

> I have visited the camps as frequently as the constant business in which I am engaged . . . will permit; and though I have made no note of these visits, I find one of my aides-de-camp who keeps a journal, and who frequently, though not always, attends me has accompanied me above forty times in the last two months. A ride is not taken for pleasure on this ridge and in this weather.[32]

And as to the criticism generally, an obviously hurt Raglan wrote:

> I have passed a life of honour. I have served the crown for above fifty years; I have for the greater portion of that time been connected with the business of the Army. I have served under the greatest man of the age more than half my life; have enjoyed his confidence, and have, I am proud to say, been regarded by him as a man of truth and some judgement as to the qualification of officers; and yet, having been placed in the most difficult position in which an officer was ever called upon to serve, and having successfully carried out most difficult operations, with the entire approbation of the Queen, which is now my only solace, I am charged with every species of neglect.[33]

Given Raglan's last comment, it is just as well that he never knew that even Queen Victoria had turned against him. It would have been a crushing blow to his pride.

The flurry of letters from London might well have got Raglan's back up, but they also proved a catalyst for improvement in the Crimea, helped in no small way by the appointment of various commissions, and by a gradual change in the weather. In fact, on the very day that Panmure sent off his hostile despatch to Raglan, a Memorandum, written by Palmerston, was drawn up incorporating measures to be taken for the improvement of the Army in the Crimea. The document, entitled, 'Memorandum of measures taken to establish a better order of things in the Crimea' ran:

1. A Land-Transport Corps has been formed under the orders of Colonel McMurdo: the duties of this Corps will be to undertake the whole of the transport for the Army, and will be carried out on a much greater scale than the Royal Waggon train was under the Duke of Wellington. Agents will be sent to all parts of Asia Minor to purchase animals of burden.
2. Instructions have been sent to Lord Raglan to procure immediately from Constantinople a Corps of Scavengers to remove all the filth which exists in the camps.
3. Sanitary Commissions are to be sent out to suggest to Lord Raglan the measures necessary for keeping the camp in a good state, and their attention will also be directed to the sanitary conditions of our hospitals.
4. A Commission, of which Sir J. McNeill is to be the head, is to be sent out to inquire into the working of the Commissariat in all its branches of supply and issue, and every other detail.
5. Civil medical men are to be sent out to the East, and a hospital at Smyrna is to be formed entirely under their direction.
6. Major-General Simpson is to proceed to the Crimea as Chief of the Staff. His duty will be to convey Lord Raglan's orders to the Staff, and through them to the Army, and see their orders quickly and implicitly obeyed; to inquire into the manner in which the Staff Officers perform their duties, and to report fully thereon to Lord Raglan and otherwise to the Secretary of State. He will recommend to Lord Raglan any change which the result of his inspection may prove to be necessary.
7. A Sea-Transport Board is to be formed at the Admiralty, which will, so far as regards Military Transport, communicate duly with the War Office.[34]

There was also to be a general reform of all civil departments. There is a saying amongst British soldiers that the British Army always trains for the last war. In other words, reforms are made following a conflict but are outdated by the time a new one arises. It was the same in the Crimea. The sad thing was that, given the amount of time both government and army had to prepare for the Crimean War it is astonishing that nothing had been done. The sense of betrayal was felt so acutely at home that Lord Lyndhurst proposed a motion of censure, indicting the government for going to war without the necessary means to do so and that this neglect had led to the disastrous state of the British army in the Crimea. The motion was, however, introduced largely to goad Palmerston into agreeing to set up the Committee of Enquiry proposed by Roebuck. Indeed, Lyndhurst, along with many others, felt strongly about the unacceptable 'gung-ho' attitude of the government that had so swept the nation to war without first having prepared adequately for the conflict. But he had no wish to damage the new ministry and when Palmerston agreed to the Committee the motion was withdrawn.

Whilst the upheavals were taking place at home, the state of affairs in the Crimea improved somewhat. It was as if the storm and the winter had brought the Allies to their senses. The criticisms at home seem to have forced them into a re-appraisal of their situation. Looking around at the dreadful conditions the Allies, and particularly the British, quickly accepted that things could not continue in this way. Something had to be done. Somewhat belatedly, supplies of warm clothing arrived, as did the *Erminia* loaded with over a thousand tons of much needed stores and clothing sent out from England by various charities. The government might well have dithered over supplying their men but the people of England would be damned if their army was allowed to waste away. Admiral Boxer, meanwhile, had somehow managed to get a grip of Balaklava and transform it from an overcrowded and watery refuse tip into something resembling a proper port of supply. Corpses were scooped out of the water, as were scores of dead horses, and buried properly elsewhere; rubbish was collected, the narrow streets cleared and a more efficient system of harbour traffic introduced. Gradually, a sense of order descended upon the previously chaotic port, and whereas before captains vied and argued with each other as they struggled with their vessels, boats now glided in and out in a much more orderly manner. It was still overcrowded but it was a definite improvement. A metalled road was also constructed between Balaklava and Kadikoi, allowing supplies to be transported from the harbour. From here, French troops, brought in to assist their allies, carried the supplies up the road leading to the Col and from there to the British camps. By the end of March the railway would be in use. The lack of provisions and supplies was certainly a problem that was beyond the scope of most soldiers but their personal appearance was not. No longer was it acceptable for the men to walk round like so many vagabonds. General Orders were issued impressing on the officers the need to keep their men in good order and to ensure that proper uniforms were worn. It all helped raise the morale of the men.

It was just as well that supplies of warm clothing were getting up to the British camps, for the weather was still extremely cold. Severe frosts and heavy snows fell in the middle of January. Major Gordon, of the Royal Engineers, wrote:

> The thermometer was seen as low as 10 degrees, and in a double tent it stood, between 8 and 9 pm, at 17 degrees, the tent being well closed,

> and two people sleeping in it. There was also a good deal of wind during the cold days, and this made the cold more severely felt. The army suffered greatly. One regiment, at one parade, exclusive of officers, mustered 1 sergeant and 7 men. Three companies of another regiment mustered 8 files between them. Many companies are reduced to 7 and 8 files effective each.[35]

At least he had the comfort of noting an increase in the issuing of warm clothing.

> A great quantity of warm clothing has been got up, and the men have enough of this to keep them warm, but their feet are poorly covered. These swell after long being wet and cold, and the men have no boots but regulation ones, and they will not stretch, nor keep out wet, and the men cut them to get them on, and they have wet feet for days together. The Artillery, with their long boots, fur caps and waterproof great-coats are the envy of many . . . Buffalo robes have been issued as flooring for the men's tents, and sheepskin coats have been issued to officers and men.[36]

An improvement in the weather also helped. Indeed, by early March horse racing resumed and things seemed to be slowly turning round for the Allies. At home, Roebuck's Committee began to hear evidence from scores of witnesses, amongst them several senior officers who had returned or been recalled from the Crimea, including the Duke of Cambridge, De Lacy Evans, Lords Lucan and Cardigan, Admiral Dundas, and Sir John Burgoyne. Of course, the Committee was too late to achieve anything by way of improving the soldier's lot in the Crimea in the short term, but the root causes of the problems were identified and it did provide the stimulus for an improvement in the months to come. The change of government and the setting up of the Committee of Enquiry seemed to have exorcised many ghosts and partly, but not entirely, soothed the frayed tempers of many of the hardened critics who appreciated that finally something was being done. Even Delane and *The Times*, hitherto one of the government's greatest and most influential critics, ceased their tirade of criticisms, realising that with something at last being done there was little to be achieved in continually attacking the government. A watchful eye was kept on things instead.

In the meantime General Simpson arrived in the Crimea, having been appointed chief of staff by Panmure. He was armed with instructions from his masters which were clearly intended to lead to the removal from office – or even the Crimea itself – of Airey and Estcourt. In the event, Simpson found little wrong with the two men, nor did he have much to say by way of criticism of Raglan or any of his staff. 'I consider him the worst used man I ever heard of!' wrote Simpson of Raglan on 16 April, whilst of the staff he said, 'The Staff at headquarters have, I am convinced, been very much vilified. They are a very good set of fellows – civil and very obliging to every one who comes . . . Nor have I any fault to find with Airey and Estcourt . . . As far as I can judge, the Officers of the Staff of the Divisions are excellent, some of them first rate.'[37] The pressure was in some measure taken off Raglan, therefore, and Panmure let it be known that he would no longer be interfering in matters relating to Raglan's choice of staff.

The improvement in relations between London and the Crimea coincided with an improvement in the weather, and, as we have seen, the problem of supply was being dealt with, whilst Florence Nightingale and her nurses – about whom more later – were setting about the massive problems at Scutari. The situation for the British Army was, on the face of it, improving. There seemed to be light at the end of the very long tunnel. In reality, however, Raglan and his men were just about keeping their heads above water. The worst of the winter troubles might well have passed but there was still a siege to be prosecuted and the British army emerged from the winter far from capable of playing their part.

NOTES

1 Russell, William. *The British Expedition to the Crimea* (London 1877), 192.
2 Ibid, 192.
3 Tidsall, E E P. *Mrs Duberley's Campaigns; An Englishwoman's Experiences in the Crimean War and Indian Mutiny* (London 1963), 115.
4 Higginson, Sir George. *Seventy-One Years of a Guardsman's Life* (London 1916), 211.
5 Ibid, 211–12.
6 Gowing, Timothy. *A Soldier's Experience, or A Voice from the Ranks* (Nottingham 1903), 101–2.
7 Ibid, 104–5.
8 Warner, Philip (Ed). *The Fields of War; A young cavalryman's Crimea Campaign* (London 1977), 110.
9 Ward, S G P (Ed). 'The Hawley Letters: The Letters of Captain R B Hawley, 89th from the Crimea, December 1854 to August 1856,' in *The Journal of the Society for Army Historical Research*, Special Publication No.10 (London 1970), 23.
10 Douglas, Sir George, and Ramsay, Sir George Dalhousie (Eds), *The Panmure Papers; being a selection from the correspondence of Fox Maule, second Baron Panmure, afterwards eleventh Earl of Dalhousie, KT, GCB* (London 1908), I, 136.
11 Bonham-Carter, Victor (Ed). *Surgeon in the Crimea, The Experience of George Lawson, recorded in letters to his family, 1854–1855* (London 1968), 113–14.
12 Anglesey, The Marquess of (Ed). *'Little Hodge.' Being extracts from the diaries and letters of Colonel Edward Cooper Hodge written during the Crimean War 1854–1856* (London 1971), 62.
13 William Rous to his mother, 23 February 1855. MSS.
14 MacMunn, Sir George. *The Crimea in Perspective* (London 1935), 149.

15 Wrottesley, The Hon. George (Ed). *Life and Correspondence of Field Marshal Sir John Burgoyne* (London 1873), II, 170.
16 Ibid. II, 170.
17 'Sevastopol'skie pis'ma N.I. Pirogova. 1854–1855', *Sevastopol*, (Sevastopol 2002), I, 336–8.
18 Vulliamy, C E *Crimea; The Campaign of 1854–56* (London 1939), 132.
19 Wrottesley, *Burgoyne*, II, 206.
20 Ibid, II, 187.
21 Bentley, Nicolas (Ed). *Russell's Despatches from the Crimea 1854–1856* (London 1966), 150.
22 Ibid, 151.
23 Hibbert, Christopher. *The Destruction of Lord Raglan* (London 1964), 222.
24 Panmure to Raglan, *The Panmure Papers*, II, 521.
25 Ibid, II, 522.
26 Ibid, II, 522.
27 Ibid, II, 523.
28 Ibid, I, 58.
29 Ibid, I, 59.
30 Ibid, I, 58.
31 Ibid, I, 60–1.
32 Hibbert, *The Destruction of Lord Raglan*, 254–5.
33 Ibid, 255.
34 *Panmure Papers*, I, 53–4.
35 Gordon, quoted in Wrottesley, *Burgoyne*, II, 195.
36 Ibid, II, 196.
37 Ibid, II, 152.

# CHAPTER FIFTEEN
## *Angels of Mercy*

The Crimean War was a war of firsts, such as the first war photographers and newspaper reporters. It also saw for the first time, at least in the British Army, an attempt at proper nursing of the sick and wounded. Women serving at the front and, indeed, on the battlefield was nothing new and went back centuries. But never before had such a determined effort been made to look to the care of the sick and wounded. The most famous angel of mercy was, at least from the British viewpoint, Florence Nightingale, of whom more later. But she was not the only one. True, she had far greater influence on the future subject of sick and wounded soldiers, of sanitation and hospitals, but there were others who preferred a more 'hands on' approach to nursing.

At the beginning of the Battle of the Alma a young sailor, a mere boy, and mounted on a shaggy Tartar horse, appeared in a hollow behind the Russian position. He tied his horse to a bush, took off his knapsack and took out some bandages, lint, linen and scissors from it. When the battle began many of the wounded were brought to the hollow. The wounds were of a terrible nature, some of the men having no arms and some no legs. Some had serious chest wounds, others head wounds. There was blood and suffering everywhere. It was certainly no place for a boy, but he quickly began to put dressings on the men's wounds, and bandage the broken bones as best he could with makeshift splints, and to help generally in whatever way he could. Soon afterwards, a medical officer came over to help with the wounded and between them the unlikely couple established the first Russian dressing station on the battlefield to which scores of men were later brought. The work of the young boy did not go unnoticed, of course, and those soldiers whom he helped thanked him for the care he showed in the absence of more experienced Russian doctors. Little did they know, however, that the 'boy' was, in fact, a girl.

The girl in question was 18 year-old Dasha Sevastopolskaya, the first Russian nurse. Dasha was an orphan whose mother had died long before, whilst her father, a sailor, was killed in action at Sinope. She then lived alone in a small house in the Sevastopol shipyard, going in each day to do needlework and general work. Naturally, the life of an orphan girl – and indeed orphan boys – was a harsh one. The sailors' wives offended and rebuked young Dasha, often unfairly. Fortunately, the older sailors took Dasha to their hearts, and often sat her on a bench and told her stories and jokes whilst they smoked their pipes. Dasha called them 'nunkies' and was happy whenever she was with them. The men of the Black Sea fleet reminded her of her own father. The sailors felt sorry for her and brought her the presents and things she needed, such as honey-cakes, or baranka, or headscarves. Dasha would repay her 'nunkies' for their compassion and kindness by doing what she could for them when the war began.

When the Allied fleet appeared off the Crimean coast everybody began to talk about how the war would go, about the coming battles and how things might change. Dasha immediately sold all her possessions to a Jew for nineteen roubles, and cut her long hair. She then asked the Jew for an old sailor suit and some white linen and, after filling her knapsack, she followed the army during its advance to the Alma. None of the Russian soldiers gave her a second thought, most of them thinking that this was a ship's boy, following his father. But it was only after the battle that they discovered the truth. At that time Dasha was only 18 but during the eleven months of the siege the young girl worked in the barracks, in the sick quarters of the naval hospital, and in the various dressing stations. Despite the Allied bombardment and the horrors of the war Dasha remained in Sevastopol. Indeed, Russian legend has it that when Czar Nicholas's brothers (the grand dukes) departed for the Crimea he asked them to find Dasha and to give her a fatherly kiss in recognition of her great deeds.

Naturally, the Russian wounded liked the young nurse very much and took her to their hearts. Often, the mortally wounded Russians would leave Dasha money, a watch or some other item. She was the first woman in the Crimea to be awarded the gold medal 'For Eagerness' on the Vladimir ribbon in addition to which, on 16 October 1854 and by order of Nicholas himself, she was granted five hundred silver roubles. She even assisted the famous surgeon N Pirogov. Indeed, he wrote, 'Dasha now wears a medal on her chest. She assists in the operations.'

During the siege of Sevastopol Dasha lived in a small house in the Dry Ravine, not far from No.4 battery on the southern side of the town. In July 1855, she opened a tavern on the Belbec river and married a soldier, M Khvorostov. The empress sent her a thousand roubles as a wedding gift. After the war she continued to live at the shipyard and in 1911 she even acted in a film *The Defence of Sebastopol*. Unfortunately the exact date of her death is not known but it is thought to have been some time in 1911. She was buried in the cemetery in Dockyard Ravine. The monument on her grave existed until the 1960s but after that it was destroyed along with the cemetery.[1]

In October 1954, on the 100th anniversary of the Crimean War, one of the Sevastopol streets in the Nakhimov district changed its name from Fourth Street to Dasha Sevastopolskaya Street. Since 1986 an annual competition for the best nurse traditionally takes place in the naval hospital of the Black Sea fleet named after Pirogov. The winner of the competition is awarded the memorial medal named after Dasha Sevastopolskaya. The names of the two outstanding figures in Russian military medicine, surgeon Nickolay Pirogov and nurse Dasha Sevastopolskaya, are thus united to this day. Dasha is usually referred to as 'the Russian Florence Nightingale', although this is not strictly appropriate. The fact is that Florence and her nurses were far from the front, in the Scutari hospital, unlike Dasha who was on the battlefields themselves and in the Sevastopol hospitals. A more accurate comparison would be between Florence Nightingale and Surgeon Pirogov. They would not only influence the fate of sick and wounded soldiers during the war, but would also change the practice of military medicine forever. Like Nightingale, Pirogov was renowned for his sheer energy, but, unlike her, he was literally up to his elbows in blood.

Of course, Dasha was not the only Russian woman to serve in the war. For the British nurses it was difficult to get to the Crimea, even given the improvements in travel. Indeed, Florence Nightingale and her colleagues deserve great credit not only for their work but for getting to the theatre of war in the first place. For Russian women, however, it was a different story. For them, playing a part in helping the Russian war effort was second nature. Every day they saw not only wounded soldiers and sailors, but civilians too, including hundreds of women and children. The work of the Russian women paved the way for the Sisters of Mercy of the Community of the Cross, but it was largely the Allies who had inspired them. Indeed, Ekaterina Bakunina wrote: 'I read that French nurses had set off to the military hospitals; then, that Miss Nightingale, with some ladies and sisters, had set off for the English hospitals. And what about us? Surely we were not going to sit and do nothing?' Grand Duchess Elena Pavlovna founded the Community of the Cross, an organisation intended to send female assistance to the sick and wounded on the battlefield. She proposed that Pirogov select the medical personnel and take charge of its direction.

Russian women from all backgrounds – rich, poor, noble, simple – went to the theatre of war. We know about the work of the Community of the Cross from the notes of one of its members, Ekaterina Bakunina. She was born into a rich and noble family. She was brought up as a prim young lady of the mid-Victorian period; she learned foreign languages, music, drawing, attended balls and wore beautiful dresses. Then, at the outbreak of the Crimean War, she suddenly announced, much to her parents' dismay, that she wanted to serve the people and that she would go to the theatre of war to nurse the wounded.

On 22 December 1854 a group of eight nurses, led by Bakunina, was sent to the Crimea and before long were spending long days and nights in the hospitals and dressing stations, tending the wounded. Bakunina wrote to her sister:

> If I described to you all the terrible wounds and the sufferings I've seen this night, you would not sleep for several nights. At 10 o'clock in the evening it was as if lightning had struck. The crash was heard everywhere and the glasses were tinkling in the frames. It was impossible to hear each blow as everything merged into one continuous roar. It was the enemy firing on the 4th and 5th bastions. We were sitting and listening in twilight. Nearly half an hour passed. Then they began to bring the stretchers in and people began to fuss. Soon, the entire floor in the main hall was covered with the wounded. Such shouting! Such a noise! Absolute hell![2]

Of the 140 Sisters of Mercy who went to the Crimea half worked in the Sevastopol hospitals from January 1855 under the direction of Pirogov who organised them and allocated them their duties. There were matrons, chemists and nurses, who not only looked after the wounded but assisted with operations. Seventeen nurses were killed whilst on duty.[3] Nearly all the nurses became ill at some stage with typhus or fever, many of them dying. Bakunina herself contracted typhus but recovered, and was soon back on duty working shifts of twenty-four hours at a go. Surgeon Pirogov had nothing but praise for the Sisters of Mercy and knew just how much they had contributed to the Russian cause in Sevastopol. On 6 December he wrote:

> Five days ago thirty nurses of the Community of the Cross under Elena Pavlovna came here and began to work at once. There is no doubt they will bring much needed help to us. They work in the hospitals during both day and night, helping with the dressings and operations, giving out tea and wine to the sick and watching the attendants, keepers and even the doctors. The presence of these women, neatly dressed and sympathetic, lifts the veil of tears and sufferings. Very soon we expect a group of widows from the Empress to arrive also and be placed at my disposal.[4]

It was not only the nurses who tended the wounded in Sevastopol, but also the women of the town. After each of the battles and engagements scores of women hurried to the dressing stations to do what they could. The wives of the officers and sailors brought linen, sheets, lint, bandages, tea and bread. They helped to clean the wounds, to bandage them, to look after and feed the men, and to give water to the wounded. Often, the women would take the walking wounded back to their own homes where they took care of them until they recovered. One such woman who went to the bastions each day to see to the wounded was the wife of Captain Reunov, who commanded the men in the 8th Bastion. The wives of the soldiers even gave up their underwear and their skirts to be used for dressings for the wounded. Indeed, it is said that by the end of siege the women of Sevastopol had no underwear at all!

Another legendary Russian woman was the laundress, nicknamed Red Dun'ka, who lived in the 3rd Bastion, the Redan, during the siege. Her tiny hut was in full view of the Allies and was not protected by any earthwork, gabion or any other defensive means, but it did not deter her. Indeed, she was an extremely brave woman who was afraid of nothing. On one occasion, Red Dun'ka was hanging out the washed linen to dry it and was happily singing a song when suddenly a shell fell upon the bastion, sending the soldiers scattering in all directions. It seemed to those around that, following the explosion neither laundress nor her hut would be left. But when the smoke and dust cleared Red Dun'ka was still alive, roaring with laughter and baiting the soldiers who had run. The only reason she was angry was because the explosion had dirtied her linen with sand and soil. Apparently, it was extremely difficult to wash it in the bay whilst under rifle fire! Red Dun'ka led a charmed life, for during the eleven months she spent in the bastion she was not even injured.

During the siege, Sevastopol was a town full of heroes, mostly anonymous. Dun'ka, Dasha, Pirigov and Bakunina were just four of the more famous ones, but there were hundreds of men, women and even children who emerged as the real heroes of the siege. The children who lived in Sevastopol would rush to the bastions several times each day in order to bring their fathers, grandfathers and brothers the things they needed, and to clean shirts, coats, mend their boots and carry food and water. Then there were the many 13 to 15 year-old sea cadets who worked tirelessly alongside the older sailors and who were afterwards awarded medals, some of them even the Cross of St George.

One of the most remarkable – but probably typical – stories concerns 10 year-old Nikolay Pashchenko, the son of a gunner fighting in the 5th Bastion. Young Nikolay served beside his father, helping to load and even aim his gun, and when the boy's father was killed he took his place. He was awarded the Cross of St George. Another young hero was 12 year-old Maxim Pybachenko, the son of a sailor. Each day Maxim, along with several other boys, would gather up the spent Allied shells from around the bastions and in the ravines and streets and fetch them to the bastions. He plagued the officers with requests to be allowed to remain inside the bastion and, in fact, was later allowed to do so, helping the gunners to load and aim the guns. Like young Nikolay Pashchenko, Maxim was awarded the Cross of St George.

The failure of the Allies to cut the road from Sevastopol to the interior of the Crimea should have allowed the civilian population to leave the town, but few appear to have done so. Not even children were sent away. Indeed, as we have seen, many took an active part in the siege, helping in the bastions or in the hospitals. Others, meanwhile, adapted pretty quickly to life under siege. A favourite game amongst the children during the siege was a kind of 'little war', where children acted out their own miniature siege. Red rags doubled as flags, beams of wood as guns, whilst stones served as shells and bombs. The children acted out the siege, the battles and the explosions and even the wounds and their treatment at the dressing stations. The re-enactments of Sinope and Inkerman were apparently especially popular. The bravest boy was always given the name Nakhimov. Often such battles ended in real fighting. Indeed, police were called to one such affair when a boy was hurt during the re-enactment of Sinope. 'Nakhimov' and some other boys quickly ran away when the police appeared, whilst four 'Turks' and an 8 year-old girl were caught. The 'Turks' were apparently punished, although the girl claimed she took no part in the fighting but was playing the part of 'Kornilov' and was thus forgiven! The long siege produced many a young hero in Sevastopol but it also produced hundreds of orphans, and many children themselves were either killed or wounded.

In the British Army, women had long since been allowed to march with the army. Six women per company accompanied Wellington's army during the six-year war in Spain and Portugal, for example, and the same number accompanied their men to the Crimea, Fanny Duberley being probably the most famous. The main difference, however, was that no women nurses served in the Peninsula, the work being carried out by orderlies and medical staff. Death through sickness was common during the Peninsular War but at no time did it ever reach the terrible proportions which ravaged the British army in the Crimea. Indeed, it did not take long before reports of the conditions in the Crimea began to filter through to Britain by way of soldiers' letters, and through the reports of men such as William Russell. The reports prompted whole groups of nurses to sail from England to see to the sick and wounded British soldiers, most of whom were sent to the base hospitals in Scutari, which lay on the Asian side of the Bosphorus at Constantinople.

Amongst those who brought nurses to the Crimea was Miss Mary Stanley, who arrived after Florence Nightingale and immediately found herself at odds with the somewhat egotistical nurse, so much so that she did not remain long at Scutari but took her group of twenty nurses to work in the hospital at Kulali, also on the Bosphorus. Elizabeth Davis was another nurse who clashed with Nightingale after applying to work in the Crimea itself, where she thought she would better serve the men. Theirs was very much a 'hands-on' approach to nursing, unlike Florence

Nightingale's, whose main work lay in the organisation and administration of the hospital at Scutari, and in the general reform of army health and hygiene afterwards.[5]

The story of Florence Nightingale is well known, and hardly needs telling in any great detail here. A personal friend of the secretary of state for war, Sidney Herbert, she arrived at Scutari on 4 November at the head of a group of nuns and nurses. They immediately took residence in Scutari Barracks, soon to become the most notorious hospital for the sick and wounded British soldiers coming from the Crimea. Popular myth and legend depicts Nightingale as the saviour of the British soldier, coming out to the Crimea to reorganise the previously chaotic and disgusting conditions in the hospitals at Scutari. While there is little doubt that she made immense strides to right the many wrongs that prevailed within the army system at the time, with varying degrees of success, the truth is somewhat different. Indeed, she had been at work for just over a week even before the winter troubles really began. The enormous problems were no fault of hers, of course, and were largely to do with the tremendous number of casualties that resulted from the Battle of Inkerman. Notwithstanding the deluge of wounded from the battle, the problems were compounded soon afterwards following the Great Storm, after which floods of men began to arrive at Scutari, sick with fever or starving. The hospital was simply swamped and was in no state to handle the influx of patients.

Despite Florence's efforts at Scutari the men continued to die in droves. During the first six months following her arrival some 12,000 British soldiers were admitted – one could almost say sentenced – to the base hospitals at Scutari, the overwhelming majority through sickness. Most were moved there from the primitive regimental hospitals in the Crimea itself where the death rate was considered high at one man in eight. The decision to get them away from the Crimea was seen as a solution to the high mortality rate. Surely they would be better cared for by British nurses under Nightingale in the larger hospital at Scutari? Not so. In fact, the death rate amongst patients at Scutari in Nightingale's own hospital was actually three in eight. Indeed, with no fewer than 5,000 British soldiers dying during the winter of 1854–5, Nightingale's own hospital rated as the worst of all the base hospitals in Scutari. 'In the five months before the Sanitary Commission arrived, between November 1854 and March 1855, Nightingale had not been running a hospital. She had been running a death camp.'[6] Many men died even before they reached Scutari as a result of being taken there aboard ships ill-equipped to handle sick and wounded men, but 'her hospital was easily twice as lethal even without the voyage'.[7]

The problem was a combination of a total lack of decent sanitation and of bad hygiene. Nightingale and, indeed, many of the doctors were blinkered to the extent that they could not see beyond the actual wounds the men had sustained or the fevers or illnesses from which they suffered. What they failed to recognise was that many of the men were dying not because of their wounds but because of the dreadful conditions in the hospital. They were packed close together, there was little ventilation, whilst germs and diseases bred and multiplied easily in the overcrowded corridors. Some wards were even formed above sewers. But all of this went unnoticed, as did the low number of men who returned from Scutari, having been sent there from the Crimea to recover from wounds. Some soldiers, discharged from the army because of serious wounds, even made the fatal mistake of staying over at the hospital en route to England. It was only following the various government commissions of enquiry into the conditions at Scutari that the awful truth finally dawned upon Nightingale who suddenly realised just why the men had been dying in such terrible numbers. The government, of course, appeared to know this anyway following the commission and attempted to shift the blame on to the Army. But when Nightingale realised the situation at Scutari had been caused by government neglect and not Army incompetence she attempted to expose the government for what it was, even though it would undoubtedly tarnish her own reputation in the eyes of an adoring public. To her great credit she set about her cause with a vengeance and when she died in 1910 at the ripe old age of 90, she could reflect with some satisfaction on the reforms not only in Army hygiene but in public hygiene also.

A totally different character from Florence Nightingale was Mary Seacole, or 'Mother Seacole', as she was known to the British soldiers. Born in Jamaica in 1805, Seacole had grown to know the officers and men of the British Army garrison, particularly the 97th Regiment, in Jamaica, where her mother ran a hotel. When news of the outbreak of war in the Crimea reached her she decided to go there and see what she could do to help. Mary stopped at Scutari en route with a letter of introduction to Florence Nightingale who naturally but incorrectly assumed she was applying for a job. Mary was, in fact, just stopping to see the state of affairs for herself. She continued on to the Crimea, arriving at Balaklava in early March 1855 to be welcomed by several officers of the army, including Sir Colin Campbell and officers who knew her from their days in Jamaica. Her initial stay was spent aboard ship by night whilst by day she sold tea from a stall in the harbour. Before long she was selling her goods from a tent and later on established the British Hotel, a glorified coffee house, situated by the road at the top of the Col.

Mary Seacole was not a nurse but she certainly made a name for herself, providing the troops with a few home comforts, much in the same way that the numerous regimental sutlers did in the French Army. Mary, however, was not attached to any particular regiment but literally set up shop to sell her goods. She was also to be seen amongst the men during the fighting itself. Indeed, during the attack on Redan in September 1855, she was seen in the rear areas handing out refreshments to the men. One British officer, serving with the Turkish army, wrote:

> So extremely rare was it for one of the other sex to be seen amongst the Allied troops engaged in the siege, that the appearance of a female was something of an event. One such I saw on this day – 'Mother' Seacole, a dark sutler from the West Indies, who kept a store at Kadikoi two or three miles from British Headquarters, where we could on emergency obtain some kind of meal. Mounted on a horse, and conspicuous by her costume, which was bright blue in colour relieved by yellow, she had made her way to the high ground overlooking the scene of action and, provided with a large basket of provisions and comforts, generously distributed refreshment to exhausted or wounded soldiers.[8]

Whilst the men were not expected to pay for their tea and coffee the officers certainly were and appear to have subsidised the men by paying high prices for the refreshments. Many of the officers left promissory notes which, sadly, were not honoured, and when Mary left the Crimea in July 1856 she was virtually bankrupt. Fortunately, her story had a happy ending for upon her return to England, public subscription raised enough money for her to pay off her debts.

One final word should be said of the surgeons in Sevastopol. The most famous was undoubtedly Nikolai Pirogov who, in October 1854, asked to go to Sevastopol where his experience and skill would be of undoubted use to both civilians and the army. He duly departed for Sevastopol with a group of other doctors, followed soon afterwards by three groups of nurses. He arrived in Sevastopol to find a poor state of affairs. The casualties from Inkerman in particular had stretched the already hard-pressed medical services to breaking point. Indeed, although three weeks had passed since the battle, there Pirogov found over 2,000 wounded Russian soldiers lying on bloody mattresses, still waiting to receive attention.

Pirogov was not only a great surgeon but he was a man of immense energy and within days of his arrival he had begun to reorganise the medical services. His efforts saved thousands of lives in Sevastopol, largely through the first large-scale mass use of anaesthesia, the antiseptic treatment of wounds, the use of plasters, etc. In his reports to the Russian Army High Command he demanded an improvement in the conditions for the wounded, and a greater provision for stretcher bearers and ambulances and for new hospitals and dressing stations. Pirogov personally took command of the main dressing station, which was situated in the centre of Sevastopol before it was moved first to the Mikhailovskaya battery on the Severnaia side and later to the Nikolaevskaya battery.

In addition to Pirogov and the Russian doctors, several American surgeons worked in Sevastopol, at the invitation of the Russian government. Some forty-three American doctors travelled to the Crimea, the majority serving in Sevastopol, whilst some worked in Kertch and others in Simferopol. Many of the American doctors, including King, Dreiper, Whitehead, Harris and Macmillan, were first accommodated on the Severnaia side of Sevastopol but later moved to the Nikolaevskaya battery. Sadly, many of them were taken ill with typhoid, Macmillan, Clark, Jones and Marshall all succumbing to the disease.

After the war the volunteer doctors were awarded medals inscribed 'For the defence of Sevastopol' and, 'In the memory of the Crimean War of 1853–1856'. Some of them were awarded the orders of St Stanislav and St Anna. Doctor Whitehead was proud of the fact that he had worked with the famous Pirogov and wrote that the awards would forever remind them of the time he 'was given the honour to help those officers and soldiers who had covered themselves with glory and won undying fame for Sevastopol'. The Russian doctors themselves ordered a silver medal to be struck for their American colleagues and engraved on it the inscription, 'Sevastopol. To our American colleagues, from the grateful Russian doctors in memory of their mutual work and hardships'.[9]

The suffering on both sides during the Crimean War was tremendous. For the Allies the winter of 1854–5 came as a cruel blow with thousands struck down by sickness and starvation. The Russians, on the other hand, whilst not experiencing the same sort of problems associated with exposure to the elements, nevertheless sustained thousands of casualties, both military and civilian, through sickness and through the constant fire of the British and French guns. The story of the failure of the medical services to cope with the great numbers of sick and wounded – particularly on the Allied side – is well known. But one wonders just how bad things might have got without the contribution made by the many men and women who volunteered their services to ease the suffering on both sides. [10]

NOTES

1 Remarkably, it was not until 1984 that the surname of Dasha was discovered in the Central State Military Historical Archives of the USSR (now the Russian state military historical archives) when historians came across some documents about her. Dasha was born in 1836. Following a report by General A I Filosofov (a cousin of famous Russian poet Mikhail Lermontov) it became clear that she was the daughter of a seaman of the 10th naval depot, Lavrenty Mikhaylov, who was killed at Sinope. On 19 November 1854 Czar Nicholas I

graciously deigned to award her a gold medal with the legend *For a Diligence* on the Vladimir ribbon. (The Russian state military historical archives. f.395, op. 101, 3 dep., unit of deposit 1, l.4. 1855).

2 Lukashevitch K *Oborona Sevastopolya i ego slavnye zashchitniki: iz istorii Krymskoy voyny 1853–1856* (Moscow 1995), 120–1.

3 Golikova L 'Syostry miloserdiya Krestovozdvizhenskoy obshchiny', *Sevastopol Encyclopaedic Directory* (Sevastopol 2000), 486.

4 'Sevastopol'skie pis'ma N I Pirogova. 1854–1855', *Sevastopol,* (Sevastopol 2002), I, 329–30.

5 Florence Nightingale, the subject of numerous biographies, continues to receive mixed reactions from historians today. Indeed, she remains a controversial character. One of the better modern accounts of her work and the myths and legends surrounding her reputation is Hugh Small's *Florence Nightingale; Avenging Angel* (London 1998).

6 Ibid, 88.

7 Ibid, 89.

8 Thomas Buzzard M D, *With the Turkish Army in the Crimea and Asia Minor* (London 1915), 179.

9 Shavshin V G *Bastiony Sevastopolya* (Simferopol 2000), 25–7.

10 Klavdia Lukashevitch *Oborona Sevastopolya i ego slavnye zashchitniki: iz istorii Krymskoy voyny 1853–1856* (Moscow 1995), 117–18. The first edition of this book was published in 1903, it was based on the memoirs of the eyewitnesses (e.g. Alabin, Bakunina, etc.). In an appendix to this book there is an amusing piece by T Tolycheva, *Rasskazy starushki ob osade Sevastopolya,* (Moscow 1881).

# CHAPTER SIXTEEN
# 'Changes of Mighty Magnitude'

The bitter Crimean winter had prevented the Allies from engaging in any real active operations for the time being, and whilst the town remained besieged from the south the mounting problems of maintaining their armies gave the Allies, and particularly the British, other things to think about. But matters did not come to a complete standstill. Indeed, despite the lull in military operations serious moves continued to be made on the political front. On 2 December Austria threw in its lot with Britain and France by signing an agreement which, although not providing for a declaration of war against Russia, left no doubts as to whose side had its backing. The following month Sardinia also joined the alliance against Russia. With the unwelcome prospect of Russia being attacked by this growing coalition on a wider front than the Crimea, the czar resorted once more to evoking the spirit of 1812 when his brother's armies had drawn in the invaders before defeating them decisively before Moscow. With the prospect of a similar invasion happening again in 1855, Nicholas drew up plans to meet the invaders in similar manner, calling upon the people to resist as they had done forty odd years before. The problem was, however, that the people's enthusiasm for war had waned dramatically since its outbreak. When Napoleon invaded Russia in 1812 he attacked the very heart of Mother Russia, whereas now the Allies were embroiled in a struggle in distant Crimea, at least it was distant as far as the majority of most Russians were concerned. Having read reports of the disasters at the Alma and Inkerman, with only relatively minor success at Balaklava, and faced with the prospect of a draining, long-drawn out siege at Sevastopol, enthusiasm for the war in the Crimea was at a low ebb. More alarming was the drop in the czar's popularity. After all, hadn't he been the moving force behind the whole business anyway, they asked? It was certainly no secret amongst the people that a change of leader might bring about peace. With powerful Austria now looking menacingly towards Russia it was time to make changes.

For the time being at least, things remained unchanged at St Petersburg. Nicholas, suffering from ill health brought about largely as a result of the tremendous strain that war had placed upon him, had no intention of standing down. But things certainly needed changing at the front. The first casualty was Dannenberg, whose inept performance at Inkerman finally led to his replacement as commander of 4 Corps by Baron von der Osten-Saken. The real change should have involved the removal of Menshikov himself, but he remained in command for the time being at least. Like Dannenberg, Menshikov had done very little to influence the outcome of the Battle of Inkerman. Indeed, he had simply sat and watched alongside the two royal princes, Nikolai Nikolaevich and Mikhail Nikolaevich, whilst his men battered away at the British positions on Home Ridge. The problem was that the two princes were able to see at first hand just how incompetent Menshikov actually was as a commander. They related their observations to their father in St Petersburg, which only served to confirm the stories the czar had already been hearing. By the beginning of 1855 virtually everyone at court in the Russian capital had come to accept that it was the Russian admirals and the navy who were the real heroes at Sevastopol. Menshikov was simply the field commander of an inactive army that was doing little to help the Russian cause. Instead of displaying the spirit of 1812 Menshikov contented himself with writing ridiculous and wildly optimistic despatches to the czar who, nevertheless, tolerated his eccentric commander and, rather than remove him from command, did his best to encourage him.

Menshikov rarely visited Sevastopol but remained instead with his army which sat impassive on the Belbec river. The terrible conditions in the Allied camps certainly afforded the Russians an opportunity of embarrassing them. The garrison in Sevastopol had never ceased maintaining the pressure on the Allies in the trenches, the sorties from the town keeping the besiegers ever on the alert. A concerted synchronised effort by both the garrison and Menshikov's field army might well have pushed the Allies to the limit but no such attack was ever carried out. Menshikov, in fact, was very much an advocate of abandoning Sevastopol anyway, considering the fall of the place inevitable. It showed just how much the Russian commander was out of touch with the defenders who considered, quite rightly, that the fate of the war depended upon a successful defence of Sevastopol. After all, the destruction of the Russian naval base at Sevastopol was the Allies' main war aim. Menshikov, on the other hand, seemed to believe that even if the town fell to the Allies the war could continue out in the field. As a result of Menshikov's obvious apathy Russian officers, from generals downwards, began to despair of their commander-in-chief. 'Prince Menshikov is a traitor,' wrote Colonel Prince Vasil'chikov, whilst General Semyakin was moved to complain of the lack of fortifications on the Belbec and Katcha rivers, adding with some irony that 'the only ones on the north side [of Sevastopol] are at No.4 Battery where Prince Menshikov and his parish live in a state of near-insensibility.'[1]

Needless to say, the rumours of disenchantment both in St Petersburg and, indeed, from within Sevastopol itself inevitably reached the somewhat impervious ears of Menshikov, finally forcing him to take the offensive. But the Russian offensive would not be against the Allies at Sevastopol but at the port of Eupatoria, the main port of entry for Omar Pasha's Turkish army and its reinforcements. Indeed, Omar Pasha's successful campaign against the Turks on the Danube had released thousands of Turkish troops from the region, troops who were now ferried across the Black Sea to Eupatoria. From a strategic point of view Eupatoria represented a great threat to Russian communications. A move east from Eupatoria by the Turks and any Allied reinforcements that might join them would have little trouble in severing communications and the vital artery which flowed between Perekop and Sevastopol. Considering all Russian supplies and reinforcements came in via Perekop and Kertch, such a move would have extremely dire consequences.

There already existed in the Eupatoria area a substantial Russian cavalry force which was commanded by Lieutenant General Baron K E Wrangel and when, in January 1855, he managed to round up over 10,000 head of cattle from the area without any interference from the Allies, Menshikov decided to take things a step further and attack Eupatoria itself. His own intelligence – or rather the information gleaned from the French press – and from information brought in by deserters and prisoners, suggested that the town was held by a sizeable garrison but Menshikov himself had been reinforced by the arrival of 18 Infantry Division and by the Reserve Brigades of 10 and 11 Divisions. The Reserve Brigade of 16 Division and four battalions of the Reserve Brigade of 17 Division were also expected. The arrival of these troops certainly encouraged Menshikov to attack Eupatoria, a move which would undoubtedly cause the Allies to take their eye off the ball (Sevastopol) for a while at least, whilst removing the threat to Russian lines of communication at the same time. Accordingly, the quartermaster general of the Russian Army in the Crimea, Staff Colonel N B Gersevanov, directed Wrangel's chief of staff, Lieutenant Colonel Batézatoul, to begin making preparations for an attack on the town.

Batézatoul's plan was presented to Menshikov on 1 February but it was not quite what the commander-in-chief expected nor wanted. Batézatoul did not consider it impossible to take Eupatoria but said it would be extremely difficult to re-form the troops inside the town afterwards where they would undoubtedly come under fire from the Allied ships. Wrangel himself was none too keen on the project and pressed his views at a conference with Menshikov, at which he said it would be difficult to take the town with the small number of troops available to him. Nevertheless, Menshikov ordered him to carry out a reconnaissance of the town to be made. Without waiting for Wrangel to return, Menshikov went ahead and ordered the concentration of Russian troops near Eupatoria. Accordingly, 8 Infantry Division advanced towards Eupatoria, along with its artillery, the 5th and 6th Reserve Battalions of Podoly's Chasseurs, with the 3rd and 4th batteries of light artillery, and four guns from the 3rd battery of 11 Artillery Brigade and the 4th battery of the 12 Artillery Brigade, these last guns coming down from Perekop and Baskai. Finally, there was the Azovsky Regiment, whose men had stormed Canrobert's Hill during the Battle of Balaklava. There were also a number of additional field and horse artillery as well as a large number of carriages, wagons and an ambulance. The men were ordered to draw twelve days' rations, whilst magazines were established at Orta-Ablam with rations for 16,000 men lasting four days. All in all, it was a serious undertaking by Menshikov, who had yet to receive Wrangel's report, and yet pressed ahead with his arrangements. On 8 February he ordered Wrangel to attack Eupatoria without delay, before the Allies could reinforce the place. Indeed, the seaborne traffic in and out of Eupatoria suggested to the Russians that, even as Wrangel was reconnoitring the place the Allies were shipping in substantial reinforcements. There was no time to lose.

On the very day that Menshikov ordered Wrangel to attack Eupatoria, Wrangel's own report arrived at Menshikov's headquarters, describing the town as having been fortified by 'the best European engineers', and that given the unlikelihood of a successful assault he would not accept responsibility for committing his men to an attack that was bound to result in heavy casualties. He would, however, order the attack to be made but only on condition that Menshikov give him a formal written order. In the meantime, Wrangel informed the commander-in-chief that he had made all necessary arrangements for the concentration of the troops, but even here the pessimistic baron could not resist adding that 'when mustered together, they would be without shelter, without water or firing, and, moreover, that thick and deep mud had rendered the roads almost impassable'.[2] This sort of attitude was no good to Menshikov who, despite his own apathetic showing so far, now demanded action partly to placate an increasingly irritable czar and partly because he had determined to make a show at Eupatoria and aggression was what was needed, not excuses. On 11 February Wrangel received Menshikov's reply to his report. If he was not going to attack the least he could do was to ensure the safety of the Russian lines of communication and to guard against any Allied sortie. Indeed, even before Menshikov's reply had arrived at Wrangel's headquarters, Allied reinforcements had arrived in Eupatoria.

Eupatoria was defended by 20,000 infantry under Omar Pasha, made up of the Turkish divisions of Mehamed Pasha and Ibrahim Pasha, and the Egyptian divisions of Selim Pasha, in addition to which there were a thousand armed tartars, a small detachment of 200 French infantry from the 3rd Regiment of Marines under Commandant Osmant, and 200

Turkish cavalry under Iskender Bey. These troops, most of whom had arrived on 9 February 1855, two days before Menshikov's reply to Wrangel and three days after Wrangel's own report reached Menshikov, sat behind strong defences mounting thirty-four guns, in addition to which there were the guns of the beached French ship, *Henry IV*, as well as the *Véloce*, and the Turkish ship *Shaffaer*. There were also four British ships, *Curaçao*, *Furiou*, *Valorous* and *Viper*, the detachment commanded by Captain Hastings. The guns of all of these ships were more than capable of laying down fire on the ground to the north of the town. Altogether, Omar Pasha could call upon around 23,000 Turkish troops and a small number – around 300 – French.

Eupatoria was not the most elegant of towns in the Crimea. In addition to the Allied troops, the overwhelming majority of whom were Turks, there was also a population of about 26,000 of whom, as Kinglake so nicely put it, 'some 5,500 were in easy circumstances, and the rest in a state of indigence'.[3] The town was situated with the Black Sea to the south and the large Lake Sasik – or the Putrid Lake, as the Russians called it – to the east, separated from the town by a strip of land about 900 yards wide. Any Russian attack would logically come in from the north, north-east and west and so a bank of earth had been thrown up to cover the town on these sides. It was a crude earthwork and was nothing like the sort of works of a more scientific nature that usually defended towns and fortresses, but it had been thrown up hurriedly and there was no time for the sort of elaborate sophistication one would expect. It did at least have the benefit of a ditch which, on the eastern side at least, was filled with water. When the Russians arrived in front of the town the works were still incomplete. On the eastern side of the town where the earthwork rampart had not yet been completed, rough stone walls were thrown up instead, and houses broken down or made into defensive positions. Houses were also turned into defensive positions on the western side of the town. All in all, the defences at Eupatoria were relatively weak and certainly incomplete, but they provided good cover for Omar Pasha's thirty-four heavy guns, and with a determined garrison of Turkish, French and Egyptian troops the town was certainly capable of providing stiff opposition to any Russian force that might threaten it.

Menshikov, meanwhile, had a change of heart, for just two hours after Wrangel had received his master's first order, to guard against any Allied sortie, a second despatch arrived, informing Wrangel that he had been relieved of his command, and that he had been replaced by his artillery chief, Lieutenant General S A Khrulev, who assured his chief that not only was an attack feasible but he would be successful also.[4] And so, whilst Wrangel was sidelined Khrulev made his preparations to attack Eupatoria. His force consisted of twenty-two battalions of infantry, twenty-four squadrons of cavalry, 500 Cossacks, and 108 guns, including twenty-four siege guns. In all, it was a strong force of around 20,000 men, who had come from Sevastopol, Perekop and Simferopol.[5] But despite its strength it would be attacking an Allied force at least as strong in number, possible stronger, sitting behind entrenchments, and in a good position. Mindful, perhaps, of Wrangel's warnings, Menshikov ordered further troops to be sent to Eupatoria, consisting of a regiment of dragoons with two batteries of artillery, a brigade of lancers, along with their artillery, and some Cossacks. Other Russian cavalry units were sent forward into villages in the surrounding areas to support the assaulting troops.

As the Allies suffered in the trenches in front of Sevastopol, so the Russians experienced bad conditions at Eupatoria. The troops that mustered before the town suffered in the open. The temperature dropped to freezing, and when it rose sufficiently to thaw the ground, everything was reduced to a muddy morass. The outlying villages had largely been destroyed and abandoned, so there was no shelter, nor was there any firewood. It was extremely unpleasant. Nevertheless, by 16 February Khrulev was ready to begin his preparations for the assault. That morning his men attended Divine Service before moving off at 8 pm to their positions out in front of Eupatoria. Just before midnight 420 Russian sappers from the regiments of Count Diebitsch, Alexopol, and from Podoly's reserve regiment crept out into the open protected by whole companies of skirmishers and Cossacks and began to construct crude earthworks in front of the town at about 600 yards distance as cover for some seventy-six guns that were expected to batter the town's defences the next day. Pits were also dug out front as cover for Russian marksmen. By dawn on the 17th all seventy-six of Scheidemann's guns were in position behind the earthworks.

Khrulev divided his troops into three columns of attack. The right Russian column, on the west of the town, was commanded by Major General Bobilov, and consisted of eight battalions of infantry and fourteen squadrons of cavalry, supported by two *sotnias* of Cossacks and thirty-six guns. The centre column, commanded by Major General Teterevnikov, consisted of just seven battalions of infantry and a single *sotnia* of Cossacks, and a further thirty-six guns. Finally, the left, or eastern column, consisted of seven battalions of infantry, ten squadrons of cavalry and two *sotnias* of Cossacks, with thirty-six guns, and was commanded by Major General Ogarov. Major General Prince Ouroussov was in overall command of the infantry, whilst Colonel Scheidemann took command of the artillery. Other units were positioned to the rear to watch for any enemy interference from outside, to cover the retreat and to ensure that the line of retreat towards Simferopol was kept open. The plan was simple enough. The attack by the right column was essentially diversionary, aimed at drawing the fire of the defenders, whilst the centre and left columns attacked shortly afterwards, moving against the north-east and east of the town. The assault was to be preceded by a bombardment by Khrulev's guns, after which it would be up to the ability of the infantry to brave the fire of the Turkish guns and break into the town.

The first streaks of dawn that broke through on 17 February revealed Scheidemann's guns arrayed out in front of the town, protected by the earthworks that had been thrown up during the night. There were also two batteries of Russian guns to the north-east of the town, the obvious intention being to enfilade the defences to the north of Eupatoria. But it was not the Russian guns that began the battle. Omar Pasha was no fool. Indeed, he had led his men with great success against the Russians on the Danube the previous year. His men had been on the alert throughout the night and had no doubt heard the noise out in front as the Russian sappers turned over the earth with their picks and shovels. As soon as the Russian guns became visible the Turkish guns opened fire, answered shortly afterwards by Scheidemann's seventy-six guns that opened up against the Turkish defences, pounding away and doing much damage to the town, its defenders and the earth entrenchments. While the guns blasted away at the defences, columns of Russian infantry waited patiently behind them, the leading files carrying bundles of fascines, grass bags and ladders that would be needed once they reached the ditch in front of the town. Omar Pasha's guns continued to fire but with little effect, thus encouraging Khrulev to move forward his guns to within 600 yards of the town. From here the Russian guns proved deadly, and with great damage being done to the Turkish defences and with the Turks' guns gradually falling silent, Khrulev ordered his columns to attack.

At 8 am the left column of Russian infantry began to lumber forward, moving by the so-called Lake Saisk and taking shelter behind the walls of the Jewish Cemetery which lay out to the north-east of the town, close to the shore of the lake. While they waited the Turkish guns, supported by the Allied ships, continued to fire, their shells and rockets raining in and over the waiting Russian troops. But after a while their fire began to slacken. Several ammunition wagons exploded and guns were knocked out, whilst the fire from the Russian marksmen in the pits before the guns proved exceptionally effective, plaguing the Turkish gun crews. At 9 am Scheidemann moved his guns even closer to the town and they were soon sweeping the entrenchments with grape shot. Nevertheless, Omar Pasha, ever the aggressive commander and not waiting for the Russian infantry to attack, launched some of his infantry against their right, but a swift counter-move by General Bobilov, who sent out the Novo-Arkhanghelsky lancers and some Cossacks, forced them back. Finally, the infantry assault began, with the 3rd and 4th Battalions of the Azovsky Regiment, under the command of Major General Ogarov, attacking in columns of companies from the Jewish Cemetery, with the Greek Volunteers under Lieutenant Colonel Panaev on their left with a dismounted battalion of dragoons in support. The right Russian column, meanwhile, advanced against the western side of Eupatoria.

It was apparent to Omar Pasha that the Russian attack against the western side of Eupatoria was only a diversion, intended to draw the Turks away from the defences in the centre and the east. The attack was beaten back in any case, by a combination of rifle fire from the ramparts and the guns of the British ships anchored offshore. In the centre the Russian guns continued to fire, but the real Russian attack was directed against the east of the town, the Russian columns moving past Lake Sasik before swinging to their right to attack the Turkish defences. The inactivity by the Russians in the centre, coupled with the repulse of the Russian attack on the other side of town, enabled Omar Pasha to reinforce his right and bring about a heavy fire against the attacking columns. As the Azovskys advanced towards the defences they came under fire not only from the land-based defences but also from the guns of the *Viper*, which had snaked its way across to the eastern side of the bay at the command of Captain Hastings. The *Viper* was followed soon afterwards by the *Véloce* and the *Shaffaer*, which came gliding across to join in the fight. The British ships were also able to fire upon the Russian guns themselves and thus the whole attacking Russian force was now under combined infantry and artillery fire.

Faced with such a heavy fire the Russians drew back, unable to make any headway whatsoever. Khrulev suddenly realised that the garrison in Eupatoria was greater than had been previously thought. Perhaps Wrangel was right after all? Khrulev then brought forward the 4th light battery of 11 artillery brigade and No. 23 Horse Artillery battery and positioned them close to the old Jewish Cemetery. The guns plied the Turkish defences with shot and shell under cover of which Ogarov sent forward two battalions of the Azovsky Regiment who advanced, bayonets to the fore and determined to break into the town. The Azovsky got to within twenty-five yards of the Turkish lines before they were flung back by the heavy fire poured out against them by the defenders. Undaunted, the Russians re-formed at the cemetery, turned and advanced a second time, only to be repulsed yet again, Major-General Krudener being wounded in the attack. A third attack was made, and this time the Azovsky reached the ditch before being forced to a halt by the water in it. It appears that they had no means of bridging the obstacle, unlike the other battalions that carried fascines, planks and ladders. With the attack having stalled the Turks brought every gun, rifle and musket to bear, forcing the Azovsky to turn and retreat for a third time. There would be no fourth attack. Instead, the Turks, sensing victory, leapt over the entrenchments and launched a bayonet attack against the retreating Russians, forcing them back in a northerly direction, away from the sanctuary of the cemetery. At this point the 1st and 2nd battalions of the

Azovsky Regiment came forward to cover the retreat of their comrades. Omar Pasha did not possess many cavalry but the small number he did have, about 200 under Iskender Bey, came forward between them and the cemetery, cutting them off and forcing them farther north in the direction of the main Russian force. The Russian infantry immediately formed square whilst the 4th light battery of 11 Artillery Brigade was brought forward, loaded with grape and canister. Faced with determined and steady infantry the Turkish cavalry halted and returned to the safety of their positions inside the town. The Austrian Archduke Leopold Lancer regiment and four hundred Cossacks were then sent forward to cover the retreat which was made in good order.[6]

The fighting had lasted about three hours, during which Khrulev realised, just as Wrangel had predicted, that Eupatoria could not be taken without serious loss of life. The fierce resistance put up by the Turks was bad enough but the covering fire from the Allied ships proved to be devastating to the Russians as they crossed the open ground, without any cover, to attack the entrenchments. There was little to be achieved by flinging more men at the defences and so Khrulev decided to halt the attack and withdraw. By 11 am the fighting was over and the Russians back in the positions they had originally occupied to the north of Eupatoria. The fighting had cost Khrulev 148 killed and 583 wounded. The Allies – mainly the Turks – suffered ninety-one killed and 286 wounded, amongst whom was the general of the Egyptian division, Salim Pasha, who was shot in the mouth and killed whilst looking over the parapet at the advancing Russians.[7] The action achieved little of significance. The threat to Russian communications between Sevastopol and Perekop remained, although Totleben claimed that the fight, and the continued Russian presence, forced the Allies into maintaining a heavy presence themselves at Eupatoria. Once again the Russian soldier demonstrated his bravery, whilst the shortcomings of the senior officers were exposed yet again. The attack had also been hampered by a lack of powder. In fact, so short of powder were the Russians that not all of their guns were allowed to be fired. Many of the Russian guns which had been aimed at the street along which the Turks moved their troops to protect the Turkish right, did not fire at all.[8] Apparently, this was done so that the shortage would not be known to the Russian gunners who would otherwise take a dim view of the situation. A regimental doctor, Genritsi, wrote: 'I knew . . . that the powder allowed for only one charge for each gun and it was not allowed to fire so as to give the impression to the gunners that there was enough powder.'[9]

Wrangel had predicted the outcome whilst the somewhat sycophantic Khrulev and his master, Menshikov, had paid the price for ignoring him. Menshikov's greatest mistake was in attacking in the first place. Indeed, ever since Eupatoria had been taken by the Allies in September 1854 there had been a very small garrison, and considering the size of the Russian field army, its capture should have been a foregone conclusion. That was, of course, provided the Russians attacked early on. Astonishingly, Menshikov waited until February before attacking, by which time a substantial garrison had arrived in the town. In Menshikov's defence it could be said that it was simply bad luck that the Turkish troops arrived at Eupatoria after his decision to attack and after Wrangel's reconnaissance, although given the flow of intelligence both by means of the press and by direct observation, the Russians would have known that a sizeable Turkish garrison had arrived in the town prior to the attack. It all added up to another Menshikov blunder.

Omar Pasha and his Turks, meanwhile, had emerged with great credit, demonstrating their fighting capabilities. They had been tremendously successful on the Danube and – contrary to popular belief – their scant, unsupported troops had fought well at Balaklava. Their showing at Eupatoria showed them as more than capable allies for their more renowned British and French comrades. The reputation of the Turks has taken an almighty battering since 1854. Indeed, their reputation compares with the treatment by the British of their Belgian allies at Waterloo, for example, a reputation which only recently has undergone some re-examination, much to the benefit of the Belgians. The Turks, too, appear to have enjoyed something of a renaissance in recent studies of the Crimean War but, overall, they continue to receive a mixed press.

Menshikov's despatch, bearing news of the Russian defeat at Eupatoria, reached the czar at St Petersburg on 24 February. It was the last straw. The czar had tolerated the often eccentric Menshikov throughout the war but with yet another defeat it was time for changes to be made. It is ironic that the czar was finally taking steps to replace his commander-in-chief only after the one action for which Menshikov was not directly responsible. True, he had instigated the move against Eupatoria but Khrulev was the man who had stated the attack was possible and who had carried it out. Nevertheless, the Court at St Petersburg had had enough of Menshikov and the reverse at Eupatoria finally gave them the excuse they needed. The czar was persuaded – if he ever needed it anyway – that a change had to be made, and three days after Menshikov's despatch reached him the czar decided to remove him from command. The letter was penned by Crown Prince Alexander, the future Alexander II, and read:

> The Sovereign, whose health is not too good, has ordered me, my dear Prince, to answer, in his name, your despatch of 19 February. His Majesty was most grieved by the unsuccessful attack on Eupatoria undertaken by General Khrulev at your order, and by the considerable losses which our brave troops have suffered yet again – without any profit whatsoever.

Alexander then went on to turn the knife by pointing out, somewhat with the benefit of hindsight, Menshikov's error in the timing of his attack.

> His Majesty could not be other than surprised that you let three months go by without attacking this point – at a time when its garrison was insignificant . . . but have waited till the present time when, according to all reports, there are considerable Turkish forces there under Omar Pasha. His Majesty cannot but remind you that he, unfortunately, foresaw this unhappy result.[10]

Czar Nicholas had supported Menshikov throughout his years of service to Russia both as soldier and diplomat, and it is difficult not to believe that the hand of others was upon the despatch that removed him from office. After all, it was Nicholas himself who encouraged Menshikov to do something to remove the threat to Russian interior communications. Furthermore, hindsight is a wonderful thing, and for Alexander to claim that Nicholas had foreseen the outcome of the fight at Eupatoria is somewhat fanciful. Menshikov undoubtedly mistimed his move against Eupatoria but to try to lay the failure of the whole sorry business at his feet is certainly unfair. It should also be remembered that Nicholas was very ill at the time the despatch was written. In fact, he did not survive his hapless lieutenant by long. On the very day that Khrulev's men were throwing themselves at the defences at Eupatoria Nicholas became very sick with flu, and despite the pleadings of his doctors for him to stay in bed he continued to carry out inspections of his troops in St Petersburg, braving sub-zero temperatures to do so. It was quite ridiculous and unnecessary. His condition continued to weaken and when he received news of the defeat at Eupatoria it drove him to the edge of existence. His last real act was to order the removal of Menshikov on 27 February, after which he finally took to his bed. Three days later he was dead. Thus, the two evil geniuses of the Crimean War pass from the scene of our story.

Remarkably – or perhaps not given the effect it was likely to have on the Russians in Sevastopol – news of the czar's death reached London well before Sevastopol. On 2 March, the very day of Nicholas' death, Panmure wrote to Raglan: 'We have this moment learnt by telegraph the death of the Emperor of Russia. This will paralyse all the efforts of his people, and make some changes of mighty magnitude in the complexion of affairs. I do not, however, feel justified in pointing to any relaxation of vigour in the conduct of the war.'[11] Eight days after the czar's death news had still to filter through to Sevastopol. Deserters brought in said they'd heard nothing about it, adding that the report was 'without foundation'.[12] Initially, the reports were hard to believe in Sevastopol, but even when they were confirmed little changed. The resolve of the defenders remained undiminished.

What did cause comment amongst the defenders of Sevastopol was the change of command, for this was something that directly affected their existence. Menshikov's replacement was to be Prince M D Gorchakov, the commander of the Army of Bessarabia. The advanced age of many of the British commanders has already been examined, and now it was the turn of the Russians to have placed at the head of their army someone of more than a mature age. Indeed, Gorchakov was a veteran of the Napoleonic Wars and could remember with pride the great campaign of 1812 when Russia and her army, with more than a little help from a severe Russian winter, had flung back and destroyed the Grande Armée of Napoleon Bonaparte. Gorchakov could at least call upon a great deal of experience, gained in the wars in Persia, Turkey and in Poland, although by the time of his appointment to command in the Crimea, his best years were well and truly behind him. In fact, when news of his appointment filtered through to the soldiers and sailors holding out in Sevastopol eyes were rolled, whilst many considered it the replacement of one bad general by another. His eyesight was bad, he was forgetful and was easily flustered by things, whilst his use of the Russian language was poor, owing to the fact that like most aristocrats at court he wrote and spoke French. Little wonder, therefore, that many of his men could not understand or grasp what he was saying to them. Nevertheless, there were those who thought the change was a good one. Like Menshikov, Gorchakov was rarely to be seen in any of the bastions or at the defences, but wary of the criticisms aimed at the cold and aloof Menshikov, he at least made the effort to come across as a likeable and approachable commander. With spring on the horizon, and with an improvement in the weather and in the condition of the Allied armies, Gorchakov would need more than just charisma to succeed in command.

NOTES

1 Albert Seaton. *The Crimean War: A Russian Chronicle* (London 1977), 182.
2 Russell, William Howard. *General Todleben's History of the Defence of Sevastopol 1854–5, A Review* (London 1865), 287.
3 Kinglake, Alexander William. *The Invasion of the Crimea: Its Origin, and An Account of its Progress down to the Death of Lord Raglan* (London 1863), VII, 50.
4 Seaton, *A Russian Chronicle*, 184, maintains that Wrangel was replaced and sent to Kerch, although Totleben has him down as commanding a unit of light artillery in front of Eupatoria on 17 February. We are inclined to go along with Totleben.
5 Report of Omar Pasha, in Bazancourt, the Baron de (trans. by Robert Howe Gould). *The Crimean Expedition, to the Capture of Sebastopol. Chronicles of the War in the East* (London 1856), II, 199.
6 Much of this comes from Khrulov's report, Central State Historical Archives in Moscow, f. 722, d. 213, l. 140. *Opisanie kanonady i shturma goroda Eupatorii 5 fevralya 1855 goda (Old style date).*

7 Salim Pasha commanded great respect amongst the Egyptian troops. His story was quite remarkable, and was noted in Bazancourt's *Expedition to the Crimea*, II, 201. 'They [the Egyptians] called him 'the last of the Mamelukes', because he alone escaped from the massacre at Cairo, which effected the destruction of that band. He was often pleased, himself, to relate the miracle to which he owed his life. Seeing all his companions in arms surrounded in the capital of Cairo, and falling under the fire of the viceroy, he took a desperate resolve; [he] caused his horse to mount the parapet of the fortress and leaped him into the space below. The animal crushed by his fall saved the life of his rider, who much injured, fell senseless. Mehemet Ali, astonished at so much resolution and good fortune, gave orders that he should be spared.

8 Tarle E V *Krymskaya voina* (Moscow 1959), II, 306–8.

9 'Zapiski doktora A Genritsi.' *Russkaya starina,* November 1877, 456.

10 Seaton, *A Russian Chronicle*, 185.

11 Panmure to Raglan, Sir George Douglas and Sir George Dalhousie Ramsay (Eds), *The Panmure Papers; being a selection from the correspondence of Fox Maule, second Baron Panmure, afterwards eleventh Earl of Dalhousie, KT, GCB* (London 1908), I, 92.

12 Raglan to Panmure, ibid. I, 102.

# CHAPTER SEVENTEEN
# *Midnight Battles*

The onset of spring brought about a serious resumption of siege operations at Sevastopol. Although the siege had never really ended the terrible winter weather had prevented any effective bombardment or any real offensive moves. Instead, the siege lapsed into rather more of an elaborate blockade. Nevertheless, fighting, at times heavy, had continued throughout the winter months, particularly in the French sectors. The Russians, keen to maintain an offensive spirit and to play on the nerves of the Allies, launched a series of sorties which frequently resulted in short but bitter bursts of frenzied fighting. It was important for the Russians to maintain some semblance of aggressive spirit otherwise they risked allowing the Allies, particularly the French, to dictate and dominate the fighting. It was also necessary for them to launch these sorties in order to cause as much damage as possible in the Allies' trenches and, wherever possible, to spike the Allied guns.

The sailors whom Nakhimov and Istomin, the two dominant admirals responsible for the defence of Sevastopol, positioned in the bastions played an essential and very often a leading role in the constant night-time sorties which the garrison launched against the Allied lines throughout the autumn and winter of 1854–5. In explaining the reason behind the raids, and in a damning indictment of British arrangements, General A K Baumgarten wrote:

> The sorties from Sevastopol were made in order to harass the enemy and tie down as many enemy troops as possible by keeping them in readiness in their trenches. The sorties were intended to exhaust the enemy and to attack them if the opportunity arose. Two or three companies were usually appointed to carry out the sorties. Nearly all the sorties which were made from the third bastion against the English were successful, as we found them very careless and their arrangements poor. Our sorties against the French were less successful, the French being far more careful.[1]

The Russians, in fact, developed a grudging respect for the French, whom they found to be tough opponents, always giving as good as they got. The

British, on the other hand, were viewed with disdain and frequently fell victim to the guile and craft of the skilful and stealthy Russians.

The Russian sorties started virtually as soon as the siege of Sevastopol began, but took on a more aggressive nature during November. On the night of 11–12 November, for example, a raiding party set out from the Flagstaff Bastion under cover of tempestuous weather that hid their approach. Once outside the bastion they divided into two groups, left and right, and made for the third parallel at a place where the trenches were apparently guarded by young French soldiers who had not long been in the Crimea and who had yet to acclimatise themselves to the conditions and to these sudden, night-time attacks. One of the Russian parties actually managed to haul forward with them two howitzers that suddenly opened up on the guards in the trenches with grape shot, after which they rushed into the trenches themselves, only to be thrown back by French troops. The other party, meanwhile, led by Major Golowinski, commanding some Black Sea infantry and a group of Cossacks, attacked the trenches which were guarded by the young, newly arrived French. Golowinski succeeded in driving the French back, allowing his men to begin wrecking the trenches and overturning the works. The French recovered, however, and led by their commanding officer, Captain Clement, made a bayonet charge at the Russians in the trenches. They were supported by a party of workmen from the 22nd Léger and between them they managed to drive the Russians completely out of the trenches, leaving behind some fifteen dead. Captain Clement was badly wounded by three bayonet thrusts, whilst Lieutenant Martin was captured, as were three small Turkish mortars. This was typical of the kind of fighting that took place frequently in the trenches before Sevastopol at night. It was not of any great significance taken in isolation, but over a period of time the sorties began to wear down the besiegers, both physically and mentally, keeping them ever on the alert.

These attacks continued into December, by which time the French were quickly adapting to the nocturnal mode of fighting. Measures were taken to guard against attack, including the lighting each night of a beacon in the Clock Tower, the headquarters of the major of the trenches.

> When night comes, the large beacon of the Clock Tower is lighted, in order to serve as a guide to the files which the Colonels on guard may have occasion to send to the depot of the trenches, and to the litters which pass by, carrying to the ambulance their melancholy burden. There, also, vigilant sentinels are incessantly on the watch, listening whether some distant shout may not announce an attack of the enemy upon some point of the trenches. In such case, the trumpeter on guard instantly gives the signal, composed of three progressive blasts, which respectively indicate the importance of the alarm; while at the

> same time signals, by rockets, point out the place of attack. In an instant the picket battalion hastens to the place of combat, whilst other battalions are formed in readiness to march, if the engagement takes any serious proportions.[2]

But despite these precautions the attacks continued to plague the Allies. On the night of 7 January some 400 Russians attacked the French trenches which were guarded by three companies of the 46th Ligne under Commandant Julien. A furious hand-to-hand struggle ensued during which every one of the Russians who managed to get into the trenches themselves were killed or wounded. The battalion's voltigeur company, which had been placed in reserve, came charging forward with 21 year-old Lieutenant Kerdudo at its head. The young man dashed, sword in hand, on to the parapet, and called for his men to follow him in pursuit of the retreating Russians who managed to reach the town under cover of their own guns which opened up with grape on the pursuing French. Kerdudo was awarded the Legion of Honour for his actions. Three days later, another attack was made, this time at 2 am, and once again some severe close-quarter fighting took place between the Russians and four companies of the French 80th Ligne. The Russians attacked yet again the following night, throwing men against the left of the French trenches and the left of the British trenches. Both sorties were repulsed after brisk but fierce fighting.

At 2 am on 15 January yet another sortie took place, amidst falling snow and with an icy wind blowing in from the north. Two parties of Russian troops converged on a sector held by the grenadiers of the French 74th Ligne. Fortunately, guards raised the alarm although they were not quick enough to stop the Russians from entering the trenches. Shots were exchanged as men fired blindly into the night at dark shadows, human forms lit up by the glare of muskets and rifles. Captain Bouton, of the 74th, was shot dead and several others hit. The regimental journal read:

> There were left alive in this little branch of communication, only three grenadiers and a corporal, namely Corporal Guillemin, who fought desperately in this narrow passage, and with his three men made head against the flood which was ready to overwhelm them.[3]

The second party of Russians attacked the trenches being guarded by the 1st company of the 74th, under Captain Castleman, who was bayoneted three times and killed. Lieutenant Rigaud drew his sword and ordered his men to charge and avenge Castleman's death. At this point they were joined by the 2nd company of the 74th,

> commanded by Sub-lieutenant Brachet. This officer, who was in advance of the section, came face to face with a Russian officer, both

> having their swords in their hands. They immediately attacked each other; and though Lieutenant Brachet received a thrust in his sword-arm, he soon recovered the advantage, and laid his adversary at his feet.[4]

As the opposing sides grappled with each other in the dark, confined spaces of the trenches, Commandant Rouméjoux came rushing forward with his own battalion to join in the fight. No sooner had he done so, however, than he was killed by a Russian bayonet thrust below the heart. But by now, the noise of the fighting had spread and French reinforcements came hurrying forward and after a further ten minutes or so of confused but bloody fighting the Russians withdrew, their retreat covered by their comrades in the Flagstaff Bastion. The French suffered nineteen killed, including two captains, and thirty-seven wounded. The Russians left behind five dead. At least one of the dead Russians was reported to have been carrying a hammer and a bag of headless nails, the intention being to spike as many French cannon as possible.

The Russian sortie of 15 January resulted in a curious exchange of letters between Canrobert and General Osten-Sacken, who commanded the garrison in Sevastopol. It came about as a result of a tactic which the French considered unlawful. Apparently, the Russians were divided into five platoons, of which four were armed whilst the fifth carried drag-hooks and boat-hooks. During the close-quarter fighting the Russians carrying the hooks and ropes would, apparently, 'harpoon' the knapsacks of the French troops in an attempt to drag them down. Others stretched long cords across the trenches in order to trip the French after which they would deal with them before they could get up. It was a tactic which the Russians frequently employed and which 'produced a feeling of painful surprise'. Considering the tactics to be underhand, Canrobert wrote to Osten-Sacken to complain about it. 'Permit me, Monsieur le Governeur,' he wrote,

> to direct your attention to a fact, of which you are doubtless not aware. It has been reported to me, that in the combats in the trenches, officers and soldiers have been dragged down by means of ropes and hooked poles. Our soldiers have no other arms than the musket, the bayonet, and the sword; and without wishing to affirm that the employment of these means is contrary to the rules of war, I may be allowed to say, in the words of an old French expression, 'that those are certainly not the arms of courtesy'. It is for you to judge of this.[5]

Needless to say Osten-Sacken defended the conduct of his men, replying to Canrobert:

> Our soldiers are recommended to make prisoners rather than to kill

> unnecessarily. As to the instruments which you mention, it is very possible that the labourers who usually accompany the sorties have employed their tools to defend themselves. Beyond this, the letters which I have forwarded to the Staff of the French army, from your own officers who are now prisoners with us, must sufficiently attest the manner in which they are treated in their captivity. It is for *you*, in turn, to judge of this.[6]

The exchange between Osten-Sacken and Canrobert gives us a curious insight into the minds of the Victorian soldier. In complaining about the use of hooks and ropes Canrobert was harking back to an age when wars were fought by gentlemen following agreed 'rules'. Naturally, there was an accepted convention between opposing sides and, by and large, armies kept to it. In the Crimea, however, the Russians evidently resorted to any means, fair or foul, to fight the invaders. When one considers the controversial treatment of Allied wounded on the battlefield – particularly the British at Inkerman – Osten-Sacken's claims that his men were 'recommended to take prisoners' is rather curious. Perhaps it demonstrates that, whilst the French remained firmly entrenched in the spirit of past glories, the Russians had embraced modern warfare and were using any means to defend their homeland.

The Allies were understandably wary of these sudden attacks, and not without reason. One Russian soldier wrote:

> Three English officers were dragged out of their dugouts with lassoes and throttled. Casualties on our side were two officers and eight other ranks killed, and thirty soldiers were wounded. The Tobolsky Regiment is so renowned for their bravery that Menshikov calls them the devils. The Allied prisoners claim there were three thousand men in the sortie and not five companies, so they were flogged by the Tobolsks. There are many English and Arab deserters. Recently a whole front line unit with an officer crossed over to us near the Chernaya river through starvation.[7]

Writing to his parents on 6 December 1854, Grand Prince Mikhail Nikolaevitch described a typical raid on the British lines.

> The other day some Black Sea Cossacks undertook a daring raid on the Allies. On the night of 24–25 [November] the skirmishers of the 8th Battalion, along with one commander, went across the Careenage Ravine to watch the enemy. They moved forward as far as the Sapoune Ridge and captured an English patrol of six men which was going from the lower redoubt to the upper one. The Cossacks immediately tied them up and took them with them. Meanwhile, the

> English raised the alarm and ran after them. The Cossacks then rushed back to the ravine, and came down to it just opposite the lower lighthouse, called for a boat from the ship and successfully returned to the city with their captives. The Prince awarded them with two crosses and some prize money. Tonight there was the first frost, of nearly 1.5 degrees, but the day was wonderful. It was very warm in the sun.[8]

One of the most famous exponents of these sorties was Seaman Koshka, who led several raids on the Allied trenches, taking prisoners and doing as much damage as he could to the besiegers' trenches. There were many other brave men like him. Koshka's exploits may have gained him great fame, but one of his escapades almost cost him his life, as Surgeon Pirogov, writing in February 1855, later recalled.

> Seaman Koshka is in the hospital in the dressing station. He became very famous and even the Grand Princes visited him. Koshka took part in all the sorties, and worked wonders under fire not only at night but during the daytime as well. The English had found two of our dead soldiers in their trenches and fastened them so as to make us believe they were sentries. During the day time Koshka crept along on his hands and knees to the trenches, found an English linen stretcher, and put one of the dead bodies on it. He cut holes in it, poked his hands through up to his shoulders, put the stretcher with a dead body on his back and then went crawling back. A shower of bullets was sent after him, and six bullets hit the corpse but he came safely back. Now he is in hospital. A bayonet wounded him in the stomach during one sortie but, fortunately, the bayonet came out under the skin and didn't touch the bowels. He is well now walking, and smoking cigarettes. Recently, he made one visitor pay him several kopeks for vodka. They say Timm [a Russian painter] came with the Grand Princes and painted a portrait of Koshka . . . The weather has changed again. After the early January frosts spring weather has come. Two days ago it froze slightly again but now there is a thaw and a southern wind is blowing. We had to open a balcony because the weather is like it is in Saint-Petersburg in April.[9]

Despite the series of almost nightly sorties the siege continued. Having failed in their attacks against the fortifications of the central part of Sevastopol, the Allies decided to direct their efforts against the Korabel'naia suburb. Originally, the chief French engineer, Bizot, had considered the Flagstaff Bastion to be the key to Sevastopol. With the bastion in Allied hands it would, he said, simply be a matter of time before the town fell. It was not a view shared by Burgoyne, however. As early as the very beginning of the siege he had identified the Malakhov Hill and the adjacent heights as the key to the Russian defences. With the Malakhov taken the Allies would be able to look straight along the eastern defences of Sevastopol and into the rear of the Redan. His case was argued at the meeting between himself, Airey and Bizot on 26 December, when the decision was taken for the French to take over the trenches on the British right. 'The Malakhov Hill was undoubtedly the only real target to attack; it was possible to command the whole of the Korabel'naia suburb from the position . . . Its capture would obviously result in the surrender of the Tower itself.'[10]

Unfortunately for the Allies, the defenders were one step ahead of them. Totleben and the Russians also appreciated the significance of the Malakhov and before the Allies could begin operations in front of it the Russians made their own move. On the morning of 22 February the French awoke from their slumbers to discover that the Russians had begun to dig in along the Careenage Heights as a precursor to the building of three redoubts there.[11] Major General Khrushchov recollected:

> At midday on 21 February on Malakhov Hill I was told by Prince Vasilchikov, the mayor, that I had to build the redoubts. Then I, Colonel Totleben and a commander of a scouts group, old Captain Danilenko, took a boat into Careenage harbour, turned round the cape and landed near the ravine of the 42nd naval depot. We climbed a hill and Totleben pointed to the place where the redoubts had to be erected . . . For the work they gave me three battalions of the Selenghinsky Regiment, and for a covering force four battalions of the Volynsky regiment.[12]

A line of white, chalky deposits sitting upon the ground provided good cover for the Russian workers who dug frantically whilst being screened by a line of skirmishers out in front. The French were taken aback somewhat by the Russian move and attempted to dislodge them from the positions on the night of 23–24 February. The attempts were unsuccessful, however, the Russians repulsing three attacks at bayonet point. General Khrushchov himself had a narrow escape during the fighting after being surrounded by some French Zouaves, whose officer had raised his sabre and was just about to strike the Russian general when Khrushchov's bugler, Semyon Pavlov, quickly grabbed a rifle from the hands of a dead Frenchman and thrust the bayonet into the French officer. The fortifications thus remained in the hands of the defenders. Two redoubts were built on the eastern side of the Careenage Ravine, the first, called the Selenghinsky, and the second, a new one built over the Georgievsky cellars, the Volynsky. Lieutenant Commander P A Shestakov, was given command of the first redoubt, and Lieutenant Commander M N Shvender the second.[13] For communication purposes Nakhimov ordered a bridge, made of barges, to be constructed across Careenage Ravine.

The construction of the two new forts, the so-called *ouvrages blancs* – the white works – was unpleasant enough to the Allies and was a rude shock. But the real surprise was yet to come. On the morning of 11 March the French were greeted by the sight of yet another work which had been built on a knoll on Victoria Ridge called the Mamelon, some five hundred yards in front of the Malakhov. This very distinguishable feature dominated the ground in front of the Malakhov and in the hands of the French would provide a superb position from which to bombard it. Conversely, if the Mamelon was held by the Russians it would provide a serious barrier to French progress. As the Malakhov was the key to Sevastopol, so the Mamelon was the key to the Malakhov. Totleben knew full well that the Allies would have to take possession of the Mamelon if they were to make a serious attempt on the Malakhov. The French knew it too, but when Bizot requested to be allowed to move against it Canrobert had refused, leaving the way open for the Russians to secure it. Once in his hands Totleben set his men to building a new work upon it called the Kamchatsky lunette which was completed on 21 March. This now effectively blocked the French approach to the Malakhov. Instead of directing their attention towards this latter work, which the Allies considered to be the key to Sevastopol, they now had another work to deal with.

All three fortifications had been built right beneath the noses of the Allies who could do little to retard their construction. The struggle for these fortifications would intensify during the next three months, for the Allies knew that without their possession they would never be able to capture the Malakhov Hill, and without the capture of the Malakhov they would never, of course, capture Sevastopol. Hence, the fighting for them became severe. Indeed, by the end of May 1855 the 'three boys', as the defenders called the Volynsky and Selenghinsky redoubts and the Kamchatsky lunette, had become the most dangerous places in Sevastopol, the French artillery shelling them throughout both day and night.

One of the main problems for the defenders of Sevastopol was a shortage of shells and gunpowder. They were also running short of men, largely due to the fact that, in their exuberance, they tended to expose themselves unnecessarily to the Allies' fire, and did not do enough to ensure their own protection. Indeed, on 14 March Nakhimov was forced to issue an order to the entire Sevastopol garrison reminding them of their responsibilities. 'The commanders,' he said,

> are reminded of their sacred obligation to take care that during the enemy's firing there should be no men out in the open without a job,

> and that the number of men serving the guns should be limited. I also ask the commanders to remind their soldiers that their lives belong to the Motherland and that they should try to realise the difference between real courage and simple bravado, which alone is of benefit and honour. Again, I take this opportunity to guard against the use of frequent and unnecessary firing. Inaccurate firing is a waste of powder and shells.[14]

The defenders in Sevastopol suffered a great blow on 19 March when Istomin was killed in the Kamchatsky lunette. He was killed instantly when he suffered a direct hit from a cannon ball which struck him in the head. Ironically, it was his birthday. The report on Istomin's death ran: 'Everybody considered Kornilov's bastion on Malakhov Hill to be unassailable because with Istomin present we were determined not to take one step back.' Nakhimov wrote to his relatives:

> The defence of Sevastopol has lost one of its main heroes, who inspired us with his noble energy and heroic determination. It was everybody's wish that we bury his body in the grave, which is sacred for the Black Sea sailors, in the crypt where the ashes of unforgettable Mikhail Petrovitch [Lazarev] lies along with the late Vladimir Alekseivitch [Kornilov]. I kept this place for myself but decided to give it to him.[15]

Nakhimov ordered a cross of cannon balls to be laid out on the spot where Istomin was killed.[16]

The construction of the *ouvrages blancs* on the Careenage Heights proved a real headache for the Allies who knew they would have to deal with them before they could even consider moving against the Malakhov. The Russians, on the other hand, suddenly realised just how exposed the garrison of the Kamchatsky lunette now was. A line of Allied guns was trained upon the lunette to pulverise it but it remained occupied by its garrison. Commenting on its forward position, General Semyakin wrote:

> In Sevastopol nothing has changed, only they do not know what to do with the Kamchatsky lunette. They built it out in front and now every day it sees a great loss as it is under fire from three sides. The enemy has built strong batteries from the previously insignificant trenches from the Sapoune ridge across towards the Careenage ravine. It was found to be difficult enough to take this height when there was not a single gun there, but now it is very heavily armed.[17]

The close proximity and concentration of Allied artillery ensured a high casualty rate amongst the defenders of the Kamchatsky lunette. On 5

April Nakhimov wrote to the father of an officer who had been killed there while keeping watch during the French attempts to approach it:

> Your own distinguished military career allows me to speak to you freely. Having agreed to your son's wish, you sent him to Sevastopol not for any awards or honours but by the sense of sacred duty which lies within each Russian and, in particular, each sailor. You blessed him for a deed for which he was inspired by his father's example, which he saw from his early childhood. You did your duty, he was honourably discharging his. He was given an important position, watching the troops placed in the lodgements in front of the Kamchatsky lunette. This was because it was difficult to find an officer in Sevastopol willing to do the task, but it was only as a result of his own wish. He was under fire every night but did not fail to remember the importance of his post. The effectiveness of his watch could be seen each morning, as from the minute he took up his post the enemy has not advanced a single yard. Enemy bullets could not touch him, but it was God's will that a stray shell was the cause of his death. He was killed at 1 am on the night of 22–23 March. Here in Sevastopol death goes unnoticed now, but your son was one of a very few who was worthy of the condolences of all the sailors and those who knew him. He was buried in the Ushakova ravine. While being taken to his grave I bore eyewitness to the genuine tears and grief of the men.[18]

Despite the artillery fire brought to bear upon the Kamchatsky lunette the defenders continued to hold on. No real attempts were made by the French to carry it and instead they concentrated on shelling it and on extending their trenches towards it. In fact, Bizot began pushing his trenches so close to the Kamchatsky lunette that Totleben decided a counter-measure must be made. Thus, it was decided to launch a sortie in order to throw the enemy back from their advanced positions. It was to result in one of the fiercest of all the midnight battles before Sevastopol.

The sortie took place at night on 22 March and involved some nine Russian battalions, nearly 5,500 men in all from the Kamchatsky, Dneprovsky, Volynsky and Ouglitz Regiments, under the command of Lieutenant General Khrulev, who had so recently come to grief at Eupatoria.[19] According to the French 'Journal of the Sieges', the sortie began at around 9 pm when a heavy fire of musketry was heard in front, after which dark Russian masses were seen moving forwards toward the French lines. There appeared to be three columns, one which headed directly for the French lines whilst the others were left and right, their intention being to turn the French flank, a move which involved attacking the right of the British sector. Waiting anxiously in the trenches for the

Russians were three battalions of Zouaves, under the command of Major Banon, who gave orders that his men were not to fire until the Russians were almost upon them. Whether or not the Russians thought they had reached the French trenches undetected is doubtful, but if they did they were given a rude shock when, just as they scrambled over the last few yards towards the French lines, the Zouaves rose and delivered a blazing volley into the night which dropped scores of Russians at close range. The fight was almost akin to the sort that would follow some seventy years later, as the Russians advanced across what might be called 'no-man's land' to attack the French trenches. The fighting was every bit as bloody too, the Russians, having been repulsed by the steady French volleys that illuminated the fighting, trying desperately to charge with fixed bayonets. Khrulev's men continued to pour forward and it was as much due to their sheer numbers, as well as their courage, that they finally hurled themselves into the French trenches where they engaged the Zouaves in some vicious hand-to-hand fighting.

The outnumbered Zouaves were only extricated from their position when Captain Montois brought forward his two elite companies which allowed the Zouaves to fall back and re-form. Major Banon then led his men forward again, only to be shot dead by a Russian bullet. It was desperate stuff. Colonel Janin, of the 1st Zouaves, was in the thick of it all, fighting away on the left of the French lines and cheering his men on despite being almost blinded by the blood that flowed into his eyes from a head wound, caused by a Russian ball, and by the numerous cuts to his face, caused by stones thrown by his assailants. General D'Autemarre was also in the trenches, leading by example, and fighting desperately to hold back the Russian tide. The fight for the French trenches lasted almost an hour until finally the Russians, having suffered heavy casualties, began to falter and dribble away into the night, and when the 4th Chasseurs came charging forward the outcome was decided in favour of the French.

While all this was going on in the French trenches in front of the Mamelon, the British trenches away to their left on the Vorontsov Ridge were being attacked. The difference was, however, that rather than send forward their troops en masse the Russians employed smaller numbers in four separate attacks. The British troops guarding the trenches that night numbered around 1,200 and consisted of detachments from each regiment of the Light Division, of whom 300, from the 7th, 23rd, 19th and 33rd Regiments, were placed in reserve. A further 300, again taken from all regiments in the division, were employed as a working party under the command of Lieutenant Colonel Tylden, of the Royal Engineers.[20] The remaining 600, from the 97th, 77th, 88th, 34th, 90th and the Rifle Brigade, came under the direct command of the senior field officer, Colonel Richard Kelly of the 34th Regiment. Kelly, who had celebrated his 40th birthday just two weeks before, had only arrived at Balaklava on 17

January but already was more than familiar with the habits and tactics of the Russians. Indeed, much of his time had been spent on duty in the trenches. When Kelly came on duty on the night of 22 March he was warned by both officers he was relieving, Colonel Farren, of the 47th, and Major Gordon, of the Engineers, that an attack might well be made upon the British trenches as the Russians were already attacking the French away to their right. Indeed, even as the officers talked the noise of battle could be heard loud and clear from across the middle ravine, which separated the Vorontsov Ridge from Victoria Ridge.

With so much activity away to the right of the British trenches the posting of sentries was carried out with more care than usual. In fact, Major Gordon accompanied Kelly as he went round posting his men. The usual procedure was to keep the sentries posted out in front until daylight, when they were drawn in. They would certainly need to be on their guard on this particular night, particularly with the Russians attacking the French. In fact, when Kelly returned to the British trenches he sensed that from the direction of the firing, the Russians had succeeded in getting into the French trenches. He now had a serious situation on his hands, for the Russians had only to turn to their right and they would be sweeping along the British trenches themselves. Kelly decided to counter this threat by forming up the detachment of the 77th, under Captain Rickman, facing east in skirmishing order towards the French lines, with their left resting on the British trenches. Supporting them was the detachment of the 88th. Meanwhile, Kelly's adjutant, Lieutenant Marsh, was sent off for reinforcements.

It wasn't long before the dark masses of Russians came sweeping down from the French trenches to attack Kelly and his men. There were some 800 Russians under the command of a naval officer, Captain Bonditschev, bearing down on Kelly's position, consisting of four companies of Greek Volunteers under Prince Morovli, the 6th Battalion of the Minsky Regiment, and a detachment of sailors. But just as they began to emerge from the darkness a huge cheer and a volley crashed out to the right front of the British trenches. As Kelly looked round he noticed Captain Hedley Vicars dashing forward at the head of his small detachment of no more than seventy or eighty men, of the 97th, with the regiment's bugler sounding the advance. Both Kelly and Gordon scrambled up and over the parapet to follow Vicars, although Gordon was almost immediately struck down by a musket ball that wounded him in the arm. Kelly meanwhile caught up with Vicars and was just turning to speak to him when Vicars was shot and killed. Vicars was an extremely popular officer who was renowned for his Christian preachings. His death, and the wounding of his subaltern, Hammond, left Kelly as the senior officer and rather than risk leading his small party into the midst of the much stronger Russians he brought them back to the British trenches. As it happened, Bonditschev pulled his men back also, leaving just the dead, dying and wounded out in the middle as both sides withdrew.[21]

The sortie had turned into a minor battle. One Russian eyewitness wrote, 'the Russian bayonet worked well. The success made the soldiers so angry that three times they ignored the signal to retreat until the admonitions of the celibate priest, Ioaniky, holding up a cross in his hands, persuaded them to retreat.' Ioaniky Savinov himself was quite a character. He was a celibate priest of the St George monastery in Balaklava, and was the priest of the 45th Naval Depot. He was badly wounded during the sortie and later died of the wounds he received. He was awarded the Order of St George of the 4th degree. He was the only clergyman to receive such a high award during the defence of Sevastopol. He was a serf of Count Sheremetiev and when the count heard about Ioaniky's deed and his death he gave his mother and his relatives their freedom.[22]

While Kelly had been driving off the Russian attack out in front, the detachment of the 77th had beaten off another attack, helped by the detachment of the 7th Fusiliers under Captain Browne. All appeared to be quiet for the time being but about an hour later another Russian column was spotted moving around to Kelly's left. Kelly quickly turned to Browne and asked him to bring his detachment of the 7th forward but a half-built trench obstructed their advance. Kelly then turned to Browne and told him he would go on alone to find the way and asked Browne to come forward as quick as he could. He never saw Browne again, for the 7th Fusilier was killed soon afterwards at the head of his men. Nevertheless, the 7th, along with a detachment of the 34th, under Lieutenant Jordan, charged and drove the Russians back once more. For the time being, therefore, the Russians were driven back and Kelly was able to return to the British trenches. As he climbed into the trench he saw before him a group of about seven or eight men, standing there in goatskin capotes. Naturally, Kelly thought they were his own men and ordered them to join Lieutenant Jordan's party. We may well imagine his shock and surprise when he discovered that they were, in fact, Russians.[23]

Kelly was armed with nothing more than a thick stick, which he always carried in the trenches, and his revolver which he quickly drew, hoping that if he shot the nearest man in the head the others would run away. Unfortunately, his revolver jammed and before he could try again he was set upon and beaten to the ground beneath a flurry of blows from the butt-ends of the muskets, and whilst he lay stunned at the foot of the trench he was bayoneted, receiving wounds in the shoulder and calf, and through his left hand. Fortunately, Kelly was saved by a Polish officer who jumped in to stop further punishment. He was then bundled away to the Russian lines as a prisoner of war.[24]

Meanwhile, the sortie continued. Away on the British left, yet another Russian column was advancing against the foremost trench on Green Hill.

Here, a detachment of the 20th Regiment was taken by surprise and driven back, leaving the trench in possession of the Russians. Working in the next trench was a group of 250 men under Captain Montagu of the Royal Engineers. These men were apparently so busy they failed to notice the advancing Russians who were on them before they knew anything about it. Fortunately, a young lieutenant of the 21st, Carlton, appeared on the scene with about fifty of his men, and together with a party of the 57th who had been gathered from nearby, he managed to halt the Russians, most of whom had remained behind in the front trench. A firefight then developed between the two sides, with Carlton's men gaining the upper hand. When the Russian fire began to slacken Carlton ordered his men to fix bayonets and charge, but when they reached the trench they found it deserted, and the Russians already on their way back to Sevastopol.

The future author and young lieutenant of artillery, Leo Tolstoy, took part in the sortie, which was the bloodiest of the war, something which did not become apparent until the following day when daylight revealed both the scale of the fighting and the tremendous casualties. The Russians admitted eight officers and 379 men killed and twenty-one officers and 982 men wounded. The French lost thirteen officers and 171 men killed, and twelve officers and 359 men wounded. A further four officers and eighty-three men were returned as missing, most being taken prisoner. The British got off relatively lightly, suffering just three officers and fourteen men killed and two officers and forty-four men wounded. Two officers – including Kelly – were taken prisoner.

It had been an astonishing and chaotic night, which is borne out by the heavy casualties. Indeed, it was necessary for a truce to be agreed the following day in order for the dead and wounded to be brought in. After the previous night's savagery it was a strange but not uncommon sight to see French, Russian and British officers walking and talking together, discussing the fight and the siege in general. 'The day was beautifully bright and warm,' wrote William Russell.

> White flags waved gently in the faint spring breeze above the embrasures of our batteries, and from the Round Tower and Mamelon. Not a soul had been visible in front of the lines an instant before the emblems of peace were run up to the flagstaffs, and a sullen gun from the Mamelon and a burst of smoke from Gordon's battery had but a short time previously heralded the armistice. The instant the flags were hoisted, friend and foe swarmed out of the embrasures. The Riflemen of the Allies and of the enemy rose from their lairs in the rifle pits, and sauntered towards each other to behold their grim handiwork. The whole of the space between the Russian lines and our own was filled with groups of unarmed soldiery. Passing down by the Middle Picket Ravine, which was then occupied

> by the French, and which ran down in front of the Light Division camp, I came upon the advanced French trench, within a hundred yards of the Mamelon. The sight was strange beyond description. French, English and Russian officers were walking about saluting each other courteously as they passed, and occasionally entered into conversation, and a constant interchange of little civilities, such as offering and receiving cigar-lights, was going on . . . While this civility was going on, we were walking over bloodstained ground, covered with evidences of recent fight, among the dead. Broken muskets, bayonets, cartouch-boxes, caps, fragments of clothing, straps and belts, pieces of shell, little pools of clotted blood, shot – round and grape – shattered gabions and sandbags, were visible on every side. Through the midst of the crowd stalked solemn processions of soldiers bearing their departed comrades to their long home. I counted seventy litters borne past me in fifteen minutes – each filled with a dead enemy.[25]

It had certainly been a determined attack by the Russians who had caused much havoc in the Allied lines, although not much lasting damage was done. Indeed, arguments raged as to just exactly what the Russians had achieved during the sortie. Kinglake certainly argued that, considering the numbers involved, the sortie had been a relatively useless exercise. However, the effect on morale of a successful sortie should not be underestimated. It may not have caused any great material damage to the Allied trenches but it gave the Russians a great lift. By carrying the fight to the Allies and by appearing to be the aggressor they could look forward to possible salvation and even victory. The other option was to do nothing and simply roll over and die, a course of action which was not only foolish but was a recipe for disaster. Totleben's aggressive defence became even more so when he began pushing out trenches in front of the Mamelon and the White Works, as the two new forts to the east of the Careenage Ravine were known. In typical sieges it was the besieger who advanced trenches whilst the besieged remained behind his walls and defences. By pushing forward his own trenches Totleben was, in effect, issuing a challenge to the Allies and was, in some ways, attempting to take away the initiative in what was for the Russians an almost impossible situation. And whilst the sorties gave the beleaguered Russian defenders a boost to morale these midnight battles did nothing for the Allies but increase their already high state of nervousness and tension.

NOTES

1 Baumgarten A 'Zametki k pis'mam knyazya A S Menshikova', *Russkaya Starina,* May 1875, 139–40.
2 Bazancourt, the Baron de (trans. by Robert Howe Gould). *The Crimean Expedition, to the Capture of Sebastopol. Chronicles of the War in the East* (London 1856), II, 173–4.
3 Ibid, II, 178.
4 Ibid, II, 179.
5 Ibid, II, 182.
6 Ibid, II, 183.
7 'Bumagi Shcheglovykh. Otryvok pis'ma D Shcheglova bez daty', *Archives of the Sevastopol Museum of Defence,* No. 5128, VI.
8 'Pis'ma velikogo knyazya Mihaila Nikolaevitcha avgusteyshim roditelyam'. *Central State Historical Archives,* Moscow, f. 728, op. 1, d. 1913a, l. 35–6.
9 'Sevastopol'skie pis'ma N I Pirogova. 1854–1855' (Sevastopol 2002), I, 346
10 Veigelt. *Osada Sevastopolya* (St Petersburg 1863), 115.
11 Where the Sevastopol district 'Abrikosovka' is situated today.
12 Khrushchov A P, *Istoriya oborony Sevastopolya* (St Petersburg 1889), 66.
13 *Russian State Military Historical Archives. – F.9196, description 22/285, unit 1.1855.*
14 Tarle E V, *Krymskaya voina* (Moscow 1941–1944), II, 343–4.
15 Nakhimov P S, *Documenty i materially* ( Moscow 1954), 478.
16 In 1904 a modest granite obelisk was erected on the Kamchatsky lunette by F N Erantsev. The inscription reads, 'Here on the 7th of March 1855 Rear Admiral V I Istomin was killed by a ball to the head.'
17 'Semyakin – Menshikovu, 25 March, 1855', *Central State Military Historical Archives, No.5757.*
18 'Pis'ma P S Nakhimova, 24 March, 1855, Sevastopol', *Archives of Sevastopol Museum of defence, No.5080.*
19 Bazancourt. *The Crimean Expedition* (II, 225) quoting Gochakov's report, gives the number of Russian battalions as being eleven, all naval.
20 Tait, W J, *An Officer's Letters to his Wife during the Crimean War* (London 1902), 445.
21 Ibid, 447–8.
22 Shavshin V G, *Bastiony Sevastopolya* (Simferopol 2000), 51.
23 They were not Russian troops but were actually Albanian Klephtis
24 Kelly survived his ordeal and was freed in time to take part in the latter stages of the war.
25 Russell, William. *The British Expedition to the Crimea* (London 1877), 246–7.

# CHAPTER EIGHTEEN
## 'A Stain of Revolting Disloyalty'

If there was one thing that really annoyed French marshals fighting Wellington in Spain and Portugal during the Peninsular War it was interference from Napoleon in Paris. The orders and despatches that managed to elude the clutches of the swarthy Spanish guerrillas usually took several days to reach Paris, by which time situations had often changed dramatically. When the emperor began trying to run the war from one of his several palaces things became almost impossible for his marshals who had a much better grip on reality. Hence, when Napoleon III began muttering about resurrecting French martial glory in the Crimea and started exercising his very limited military mind, memories were cast back forty years to the sort of situation that frequently hindered the French war effort in the Peninsula. Paris is a long way from Sevastopol and even given the technological developments in communications the thought of Napoleon extending his controlling hand over the theatre of war sent a shudder of dismay through his generals in the Crimea. Perhaps conscious of the problem of distance Napoleon then decided that he should come to the Crimea himself and place himself at the head of his army. Thus, on 26 February, the 'Imperial disturber of the peace of nations . . . imparted to the British Prime Minister the latest chimera of his teeming brain. Though he was not an expert in war, it took the form of a plan of campaign designed to subserve his personal glory.'[1]

Four weeks before his announcement Emperor Napoleon's confidant, General Adolphe Niel, arrived in the Crimea to 'plough the road' ahead of his master's arrival. Niel, a French engineer, had no concept of the situation in the Crimea but persuaded himself that he knew what had gone wrong to date and what was needed to bring about a successful conclusion to the campaign as far as the Allies were concerned. In fact, Niel was not so much a 'new broom' but was rather the emperor's 'spy in the camp'. Having discussed his plan to come to the Crimea with Niel, Napoleon despatched his lieutenant to the east to conduct what effectively amounted to a feasibility study. In their wisdom, Napoleon and Niel had decided that the Allies had committed a great mistake when they allowed themselves to be bottled up against the Black Sea with a substantial

Russian army hovering dangerously inland. They were also of the opinion that the Allies should have stormed Sevastopol in September, after the flank march, rather than allow themselves to be drawn into a long and costly siege. And by giving back to the Russians their line of communication with Batchki Serai and Simferopol the Allies had, in effect, hamstrung themselves. They came to the conclusion that it would be a sensible move for the Allies to cross the Chernaya river and retake possession of the Mackenzie Heights and the area farther north towards the Belbec river. This would effectively cut off the garrison of Sevastopol from the interior. From then on there would be no lifeline, no drip-feed of men and materials. Sevastopol would starve or surrender, with or without an assault. The siege, in any case, was to be considered a secondary operation, for the emperor was bent on engaging the Russians in the field in the traditional manner where glory and honour could be properly won, far away from the grubby business of siege warfare.

The brutal truth was, of course, that Niel was right. Sevastopol was always going to be a tough nut to crack so long as the line of communication with the interior remained open. And as long as the Russian Army remained out in the field on the Mackenzie Heights the siege operation was fraught with danger from the very start. But as for the Emperor Napoleon's grand design to win laurels for France in the field, this was certainly chancing it somewhat. After all, it required every available French and British soldier to man the siege lines and at the same time ensure the security of the overall operation. The solution was, of course, more men, and so on 3 February 1855 the French minister of war, Marshal Vaillant, ordered the concentration of thousands of French troops at Constantinople, ready to sail to the Crimea to implement the emperor's plan. In addition to the plan to move against the Russian field army Napoleon devised a second which involved bringing Omar Pasha and his Turks from Eupatoria to Alushta, situated on the south-east coast of the Crimea, where they would land before marching upon Simferopol. When fresh troops arrived from both Bulgaria and Egypt, Omar Pasha would indeed have been free to operate in what was effectively the Russian rear. It would have been a bold move to lift the tedium of the siege.

Bold French plans and ambitions were one thing. But when they directly affected the Allied war effort and compromised previously agreed arrangements made with the British it became a different matter altogether. According to the agreement made between the French and British on 1 January 1855 Canrobert's troops would take over the British siege lines on the Inkerman Heights, after which the French would make the Malakhov their objective, leaving the British to concentrate on the Redan. Niel's plan, to focus on completing the investment of Sevastopol by occupying the Severnaia – the northern side of Sevastopol – meant that the British would have to wait before the French took over the lines on the

Allied right. Niel had also instructed Canrobert to 'cool his ardour' and rather than undertake any aggressive moves that would – according to both Niel and the emperor – inevitably prove costly, they were to maintain the bombardment and approach by way of steady, deliberate and slow advances. 'If the assault of Sevastopol be impossible,' ran the new instructions,

> or likely to cost too many lives, without allowing us to take the entire town, you must hold yourself upon the defensive; and arrange in such a manner that it may be possible for you to take two divisions of infantry, the Imperial Guard, all the cavalry, and four field and four horse batteries; so that all those troops joined to a body of 40,000 men assembled at Maslak, near Constantinople, might, at the first signal, operate externally against the enemy.[2]

The difference between the old and the new plan was, in Kinglake's words, 'almost as wide as the difference between a sword and a scabbard'.[3] Furthermore, the adoption of Niel's plan by the obviously uneasy and uncomfortable Canrobert was enough to throw 'his whole spirit of warlike enterprise into lifeless abeyance, and render him morally powerless to execute the arrangements of the 1st of January with the daring, the firmness required for promptly seizing the Mamelon, and making it his path to the Malakhov'.[4]

But the real scandal was that Niel had orders not to convey the emperor's plans to the British. Everything was to be kept secret. Raglan was not to know. Hence, throughout February and March Raglan and the British began to wonder why the previous sense of urgency within the French camp had slipped into lethargy and inactivity. Instead of actively prosecuting the siege Canrobert was now being told to exercise restraint, and to cool his ardour, and to consider a move against the Russian field army as a priority and not the siege. 'It is,' wrote Kinglake harshly, 'under this aspect that concealment of the pith of Niel's mission from our Government and from Lord Raglan shows the stain of revolting disloyalty.'[5]

A series of meetings were held throughout March, attended by the Allied commanders-in-chief and senior members of staff. Plans were put forward and ideas discussed, but rarely was anything worthwhile agreed upon. Part of the problem was Raglan. The mild-mannered British commander was simply not hard enough on the French, and on Niel in particular, who blocked every suggestion relating to offensive measures, particularly those involving direct assaults upon Sevastopol. No, Niel was there specifically to see that nothing was achieved before the arrival of the emperor, who would sail from Constantinople at the head of his reinforcements to win the war for himself and for the Allies. The trouble was that Raglan, even if he had been a tougher personality, commanded such a weak army that his opinion carried very little weight. They didn't like it but the British were forced to accept the unpalatable truth that they were very much the junior partner in what was rapidly becoming a French operation.[6]

The pressure of keeping Niel's plans from Raglan certainly began to weigh heavily on Canrobert's mind, as did the prospect of having his emperor breathing down his neck. It was all too much for the French commander-in-chief. Writing to Lord Panmure on 24 March, Admiral Houston Stewart said:

> I declare to you that I never saw a man more decidedly *cast down* than Canrobert was yesterday. He happened to call on Lord Raglan whilst we were there. Only himself, Lord Raglan, Sir E. Lyons, and I were present. The dread of an attack seems to haunt him, and *defence* of our position to be allowed to supersede all operations of *offence* or advance. They say the Emperor is coming here; if he does (which I *very much* doubt) I do not believe Canrobert's tenure of the chief command would be worth many days' purchase.[7]

If Admiral Stewart had known of the secret plans of the French emperor he would certainly have reasoned why Canrobert was so downcast.

The interference from Napoleon and the presence of Niel led to a fractured relationship between the British and the French. Both armies began to aim derisory comments at each other and were the butt of jokes and jibes. Both gave as good as they got. The French were mocked for being little more than show, whilst the French looked down upon their dishevelled British allies as being hardly worth consideration. They were simply regarded as dead wood. Given the previous centuries of conflict between the two nations it is not surprising that old grievances should re-emerge despite their now being allies. Even Panmure, sitting secure in London, was moved to write to Raglan and advise guarding against French aspirations. 'I have sent you a long "secret and confidential" despatch,' he wrote, 'embodying my views and fears of the tendency of the counsels of our beloved allies. I have my suspicions of them, and I only hope you will not be induced to give way to them one inch more than you consider right.'[8] Panmure had every right to be suspicious. Admiral Stewart was certainly growing very wary of the French, and critical too. Despite noticing Canrobert's obvious slackness Stewart had yet to fathom the reason behind it, and could only conclude that 'matters [were] in a fix'. From his ship, HMS *Hannibal*, Stewart wrote on 26 March:

> They [the French] are, I fear, nearly at a standstill, and every day appears to add to the boldness of the Russians and to diminish the

> self-confidence of the French General, and (I doubt) the confidence of the French troops in their Generals, and especially so in Canrobert and Bosquet – the latter of whom stood high until the 24th ult., when he failed to retain possession of the Mamelon where the enemy have now a formidable work.[9]

The problem was exacerbated by the lack of influence Raglan could exercise over Canrobert. With so few troops at his disposal Raglan was powerless to do anything. Even a proposed expedition to Kerch, a vital Russian supply port in the Sea of Azov, was vetoed by the French commander, despite its having backing from both Sir Edmund Lyons and Admiral Bruat. It was massively frustrating. 'If the French General won't move,' wrote Stewart, 'we shall be looked upon as being asleep.'[10]

The Russians, meanwhile, lapped it all up and took advantage of the situation to improve the defences of Sevastopol and turn what was already an extremely strong fortress into an almost impregnable one. Menshikov was gone and the more diligent Osten-Saken had taken command of the garrison. Admiral Nakhimov, meanwhile, continued to inspire the defenders with his personal bravery, leading by example and always encouraging his men. Somewhat morbidly, he had already prepared his own grave, although this had been given up to Istomin when he was killed on 19 March. With thousands of men at their disposal the Russian defenders were able to take the initiative away from the somewhat divided besiegers. Indeed, there were almost as many workmen inside Sevastopol as there were British soldiers outside, so strong was the workforce and so weak the British. There was also a huge amount of raw material available to the defenders with which they shored up buildings, reinforced trenches and dugouts, made bombproof shelters and generally improved the all-round effectiveness of the defences. Totleben took the opportunity to capitalise on the Allies' inactivity by pushing forward a series of trenches of his own from the defences around Sevastopol. He had already wrested away the initiative from the Allies by his construction of the White Works on the Inkerman Heights and the Kamchatsky lunette on the Mamelon. Now, he began to push out towards the Allied trenches in an audacious move that created a sort of 'western front' battlefield, where Russian troops were continually raiding the Allied trenches. The almost nightly sorties kept morale at a high level whilst at the same time fraying the already taught nerves of the Allied troops in the trenches.

But despite the efforts of Nakhimov and Totleben, Gorchakov remained pessimistic about the chances of Sevastopol's survival. The constant Allied shelling gnawed away at his nerves whilst the prospect of relief by the main Russian field army in the Crimea appeared as remote as ever. It seemed to him only a matter of time before the Allies finally launched an all-out assault on the town and with the defences under continual bombardment the chances of successfully repulsing such an assault was slim. There was certainly no way either the garrison or the population of Sevastopol could escape to the south. Nor did there seem any chance of the Russian army breaking through to the town. The only possible escape route from Sevastopol lay across the harbour to the Severnaia to the north. The only problem was the several hundred yards of water between the north and south sides of the harbour. A pontoon bridge was needed and so Gorchakov, despite the obvious misgivings of Nakhimov, ordered General Bukhmeier to get to work and build a bridge capable of allowing the garrison and population bottled up on the south side of Sevastopol to escape. It needed to be a thousand yards long, and a thousand yards it was, although Nakhimov declared that he would never set foot on it.

Although the French displayed little inclination for offensive operations the much-pressed British at least maintained some semblance of activity, both in the field and off it. Sir John Burgoyne, that great, stalwart engineer, had finally gone home, removed from his position by an order of 16 February from Lord Panmure. His position was taken by General Sir Harry Jones. Burgoyne remained in the Crimea for a few weeks and helped Jones ease his way into his new position, but on 21 March, feeling uncomfortable and without any responsibility, he sailed for England. 'However disagreeable to quit the army here while in active operation,' he wrote on 12 March, 'I do not wish to linger on in the anomalous position in which I now find myself. Jones is being led rapidly into the full charge of every engineer operation, and any interference on my part may lead to a confusion in orders and opinions.'[11] On 21 March Burgoyne sailed home on board HMS *Banshee*, from where he wrote a very melancholy letter.

> Yesterday morning when I left the camp, it was cloudy, rainy and blowing a gale of wind. I got on board the *Royal Albert*, dined with Sir Edmund Lyons, and embarked on board this ship at 9 pm and put to sea; a beautiful clear starlight night, and the wind quite moderate; and this day is quite fine; we expect to reach the entrance to the Bosphorus during the night, and to anchor off Constantinople early in the morning. Everybody was civil at parting, Lord Raglan particularly so. Sir E. Lyons was full of attentions, as he always is; and, one of the last things, said, 'I will look after your son.' And thus I take my leave of this service, which has been a very interesting one; and I wish I could have seen it out![12]

Niel's grotesque mission to restrain Canrobert from overly offensive moves had placed the French commander-in-chief in an unenviable position. Privy to Niel's 'secret' orders Canrobert not only had to suffer the taunts from his British allies but also those from his own troops, none of whom really knew or understood what a difficult position he was in.

His natural offensive instincts told him to press on with the siege but dare he go against his emperor's wishes? He was torn between loyalty to both, which ultimately did neither any good. He could press on with the siege and with a second bombardment of Sevastopol, largely to keep Raglan happy and to satisfy his own sense of honour that something was actually being done by the French army, even if it meant defying the wishes of his master. On the other hand, his loyalty to Napoleon meant that he could not commit to an assault, even if the bombardment was successful and effective enough to warrant one. In the event he chose to go along with the agreed resumption of the bombardment of Sevastopol, largely to save face and keep his allies happy, not to mention the French people who had grown somewhat dismayed by the lack of progress by their army. Canrobert's decision to open a second bombardment was, of course, met with great relief by Raglan, although the British commander was much mistaken if he thought that an assault would follow.

By the end of the first week in April the Allied siege lines were bristling with 501 guns, primed and ready to deliver thousands of heavy metal shells on to Sevastopol and its defences. Of these guns, 132 were British and the rest French although the weight of the British guns being far heavier meant there was an effective ratio in terms of pound shot delivered of sixteen French guns to thirteen British.[13] Against this array of firepower the Russians could muster some 466 of their total number – 998 – which virtually put them on a par with the Allies. The drawback was, however, that the Allied guns could not really miss their targets. Any gun that was aimed against a particular point in Sevastopol's defences but which overshot and missed would obviously find a resting place somewhere inside the town. Hence the resulting high casualties. The Russian gunners, on the other hand, were aiming at a very narrow target in addition to which the besiegers had the relative protection of good entrenchments, unlike the Russians whose troops were crammed into the defences and the streets and buildings behind where even the wildest of inaccurate shots was capable of inflicting serious casualties.

Easter Sunday in 1855 fell on 8 April, a day when the defenders and the people of Sevastopol suffered little more than some sporadic firing from a few of the Allied batteries. In the meantime, the wives, sisters, mothers and daughters took themselves off to the bastions to kiss their menfolk and wish them well for Easter. In fact, 8 April was a fairly normal Sunday in Sevastopol, save for the odd shell and for the fact that much of the town was badly damaged. Otherwise, the usual church services were held, as were the normal Easter celebrations. It was a happy day, military bands played, soldiers donned new uniforms and paraded the streets, there was much dancing and, for the time being at least, the siege was forgotten. Monday 9 April was a different matter altogether.

It dawned grey and wet. There was thick fog and a heavy drizzle. It was

Inkerman weather. But as the light improved the unmistakable shapes of the Redan and the Malakhov started to become visible. The Allied gunners were wet through after a night of uncomfortable rain but they were cheered by the prospect of unleashing hundreds of shells upon the town and its unsuspecting inhabitants. At around 5.30 am the grey, gloomy dawn was lit by the flashes from the muzzles of over a hundred British guns that were followed in quick succession by even more French pieces, and before long the entire line of Allied trenches was a sheet of flame as the second bombardment got underway.

The Russians were evidently taken somewhat by surprise by the intensity of the bombardment and it took them over half an hour before they were able to react, their own guns replying in kind to the hundreds of Allied guns that barked out from the heights to the south of Sevastopol. The fiery flashes from the Allied guns were in stark contrast to the slate-grey sky overhead and towards the middle of the morning a heavy rain began to fall. There was no slacking in the Allied fire, however, and a steady stream of shells continued to rain down upon Sevastopol, pummelling the defences and inflicting heavy casualties upon the defenders at the walls and in the bastions. The new Russian works – the White Works – were smashed into piles of rubble, as was the Kamchatsky lunette on the Mamelon hill. The Flagstaff Bastion, meanwhile, was severely damaged and some of its guns silenced, whilst the Redan also took heavy punishment, barely resembling the sort of strong bastion it had been a few hours before. Sevastopol's defences were bruised and battered but they were not down completely. Indeed, frantic efforts were made during the night of 9 April and on the next morning, and when dawn broke on 10 April the Allies saw with some dismay that the Russians had repaired much of the damage caused the previous day. Any thoughts of an immediate assault were, for the time being at least, dispelled.

The Allied guns continued to blast away at Sevastopol throughout 10 April and even the magnificent efforts of the Russian defenders were not enough to keep pace with the rate of destruction being wreaked by the bombardment. Indeed, even Totleben was moved to comment that had Sevastopol been assaulted on 10 April he had little doubt that the assault would have proved successful. One of the reasons for the heavy casualties sustained by the Russians was that battalions of infantry and marines were forced to remain tightly packed and close behind the bastions because of the expected Allied assault. Totleben, of course, was not privy to the secret orders of the emperor's emissary, Niel, who was present at all Allied councils of war specifically to ensure that no assault should take place until the arrival of the French Army of Reserve from Constantinople. There he was 'the Spectre at the Feast', laying the hand of restraint upon the exasperated Canrobert whose natural instincts told him that now was the time to attack. Instead, the bombardment continued, as did the midnight battles in the trenches, with British and French casualties continuing to pile up, all because of Niel's evil influence. Worse still was the fact that as each day passed without an Allied assault the Russians were eventually able to recover and restore the defences to almost the same state as they had been in prior to 9 April. Indeed, the whole sad situation was best summed up by Kinglake who said the Allies' efforts were 'foredoomed to sheer barrenness by the spell of General Niel's mission'.[14]

In addition to the material damage done to Sevastopol the Allied bombardment inflicted severe casualties on the Russians. However, the Allies themselves did not get off lightly either, with the French in particular losing some senior officers including their chief engineer, General Bizot, who was mortally wounded on 11 April whilst visiting the British trenches with General Niel. We can only speculate on how things might have changed had it been Niel who was wounded. Bizot was shot by a ball which struck him in the cheek and 'fatally affected his brain'.[15] His death was mourned by all three armies. Commandants Masson and Saint Laurent followed Bizot to the grave, as did another well-liked French officer, Captain Mouhat, a holder of the Legion of Honour.

The Allied bombardment continued for the next eight days with the Flagstaff Bastion in particular coming in for continued heavy punishment. On 16 April more guns were brought forward and the Allies' rate of fire increased in preparation for the assault. Gunners worked furiously, sweating profusely even in the cold damp conditions in their efforts to reduce Sevastopol to a smouldering ruin. The Flagstaff Bastion was pulverised daily and by 18 April was considered even by the defenders to have become untenable. The nightly efforts by the defenders to repair the damage had become futile in the wake of such a heavy shelling, but in spite of the poor condition of the bastion Canrobert still refused to sanction an assault. On 19 April a ceasefire was declared in order to allow both sides to bury their dead. As was the case after the sortie on 22 March both French and Russian officers emerged from their respective positions to discuss the bombardment whilst standing out in the middle of what might be termed no-man's land. Once again, it was a strange spectacle to see men who, just a few hours before, had been trying to plough each other into the ground, now talking freely and politely with each other as gentlemen meeting in a park might do on a Sunday afternoon.

The truce marked the effective end of the general bombardment although there was no let up in the Allied shelling of Sevastopol and once again it was the Flagstaff Bastion that bore the brunt of the shelling. Totleben was particularly impressed by the power of the Allied mortars, which plummeted from the sky with extreme violence, hammering away at the bastion and reducing it virtually to a ruin. But if he was moved to comment on the power of the Allied mortars he was equally taken with the Allies' lack of resolve and was mystified – although obviously relieved – by the Allies' decision not to attack, particularly at a time when the Flagstaff Bastion lay virtually defenceless. 'The fall of the Flagstaff and the Central Bastion,' he wrote, 'would have necessarily rendered impossible all further defence of Sevastopol.'[16]

Raglan, meanwhile, was in a state of some despair, for he had still to fathom the reason for Canrobert's reluctance to assault Sevastopol. The bombardment could not last indefinitely. Surely it was time to consider an assault? At last, some semblance of sanity seemed to descend upon the French, for Canrobert, after a meeting with Raglan on 23 April, finally agreed to assault Sevastopol on 28 April. But despite this the surprised Raglan sensed a feeling of unease from Canrobert about his decision to assault Sevastopol. His suspicions were well founded, for just a day after the decision was made both Canrobert and Niel were writing to the Emperor Napoleon expressing their reservations about the plan, so much so, in fact, that on 25 April Canrobert did a complete turnaround and informed Raglan that the proposed assault would have to be postponed, citing the fact that because the French Army of Reserve was due to arrive from Constantinople in early May it made sense – apparently – to wait for their arrival. Raglan was in a state of some exasperation by now, and we may well understand his feelings. But there was little he could do so long as Britain remained the junior partner.

The second bombardment had been pregnant with the expectation of an assault but French prevarications had ensured this was not to be. Instead, there was nothing but a feeling of frustration, particularly amongst the British, although even the rank and file of the French Army, none of whom were privy to the designs of Niel and their emperor, were beginning to wonder why no assault was forthcoming. Indeed, the French now existed in a state of some mystification as to why their efforts had yet to result in an assault on Sevastopol. The Russians, meanwhile, continued to count their blessings and to repair and strengthen their pulverised works, whilst Totleben, that worker of wonders, saw to it that within days of the ending of the second bombardment the defences were back in as effective a condition as could be expected. Despite the abortive and unsatisfactory end to the bombardment it had once again proved to be a real trial for the defenders, for some 6,130 Russians were either killed or wounded, largely as a result of their having to remain in their dense ranks immediately to the rear of the defences least the Allies launch an assault. Allied casualties themselves were not exactly light, with the British sustaining 265 casualties and the French 1,585, the most serious of whom had been General Bizot, Canrobert's chief engineer.

By the end of April 1855 Anglo–French relations in the Crimea had become rather strained, largely as a result of Niel's restraining hand upon

Canrobert. Things were not improved by the prospect of having the Emperor Napoleon come out to the Crimea himself. In fact, the British were aghast at the idea. Even the French were not exactly over enthusiastic at the prospect. Nevertheless, Napoleon appeared determined to come out to the battlefield and lead his army to glory. A visit to London in April gave Napoleon the perfect opportunity to place before the British government his case for travelling to the Crimea himself, although at a council of war the assembled leaders did their best to dissuade him from this course of action. Napoleon arrived in England on 16 April, whilst back in the Crimea the second bombardment was a week old. His plan of action involved the formation of three Allied armies, with the first continuing the siege of Sevastopol, and the two others, the so-called '1st Army of Operation' to be employed in the field against the Russians, and the '2nd Army of Operation' which would come under Napoleon's direct command, to be used in a diversionary operation, landing on the south-east coast at Alushta before marching upon Simferopol. These armies were to have been strengthened by Omar Pasha's Turks and by the French troops assembling in Constantinople. It was these plans that had so caused the friction between the British and French, for, as we have seen, the emperor had sent Niel to the Crimea with the specific intention of seeing to it that Canrobert did nothing that would upset his plans. The emperor's plans initially met with a positive response from the various leaders in London, at least the creation of the new armies, but the plan to land at Alushta was considered to be 'wild and impracticable' by Lord Panmure who thought such a design would inevitably lead to the ruin of the French Army. Fortunately, none of these designs ever came to fruition and, indeed, no sooner had the emperor returned to Paris than he announced his intention to abandon his plans to travel to the Crimea.

The emperor's announcement that he would not be travelling to the Crimea after all did not put an end to his interference. Despite the vast distance between the Crimea and Paris Napoleon was soon able to reach out and touch his generals in the east by means of the 'new and dangerous magic'[17] conjured up by the laying of a cable between Varna and Eupatoria and also Varna and the Chersonese which became operational on the night of 3 May. This would allow the emperor to send a succession of orders at literally electrifying speed to Canrobert who, despite the vast geographical distance, was now within just a few hours of Paris. Ironically, the flurry of orders from Paris at all times of the day and night only served to hinder the Allied war effort and, indeed, would be one of the reasons behind the resignation of Canrobert, which was only a matter of days away.

The troublesome orders from Paris were only the prelude to a serious rift in the Allied camps. The real fallout occurred after the postponement by Canrobert of an Allied expedition to the Sea of Azov and the Kerch peninsula. The town of Kerch, some 150 or so miles from the Chersonese, lies at the far eastern end of the Crimean peninsula and commands the narrow straits between the Black Sea and the Sea of Azov. This in itself had little bearing on the operation around Sevastopol but it was certainly vital for another reason. Although Sevastopol was being blockaded it had not entirely been sealed off, or 'invested', and thus the Russians were able to drip feed men and supplies into the town. The problem facing the Russians was how to get the supplies to the Crimea in the first place, and so Kerch quickly became an important route into the Crimea for much of the Russian army's supplies and reinforcements, both from ships sailing from the Russian ports along the coast of the Sea of Azov and from the Caucasus to the east. Indeed, along with Perekop it soon became the main source of supplies keeping the vital artery flowing into the theatre of war and, in particular, the garrison of Sevastopol.

With the terrible winter now over and with the renewal of the Sevastopol bombardment the Allies looked to strengthen their hold on Sevastopol. It was, therefore, an obvious move to try to deny the Russians the vital stream of supplies that flowed into the Crimea through Kerch. Considering the importance of the place the Russian garrison was not particularly strong, despite the fact that they must have known that, sooner or later, the Allies would come knocking on their door. Commanding the 9,000-strong garrison was Baron Wrangel, whom we last met at Eupatoria. His garrison included 3,000 cavalry, two battalions of infantry and the majority of the remainder a sort of militia, including many Cossacks. It was not much of a match for the strong Allied force which had been designated to attack it.

The Allied force in question consisted of 12,000 troops under the command of Sir George Brown. The French contingent made up by far the greater part of the force, with the 1st Division of the 1st Corps under General D'Autemarre. The French, in fact, had only entered into the spirit of the expedition somewhat reluctantly. Canrobert, for example, was hesitant and not overly optimistic about its chances of success. But he went along with it. The British contingent consisted largely of the 42nd, 71st and 93rd, from the Highland Brigade, and a part of the 2nd Rifle Brigade. There was also a detachment of Turkish troops. Admiral Lyons and Admiral Bruat commanded the British and French squadrons respectively. The ships steamed off on 3 May, heading west towards Odessa in order to fool the Russians, but as soon as it grew dark the flotilla turned and sailed to the east and Kerch.

The expedition set off with high hopes of an Allied success. The problems and inertia of the past few weeks seemed to have been forgotten as the ships steamed off across the Black Sea towards the Sea of Azov, but hardly had the fleet boiled its way along the south-east coast of the Crimea than a telegram arrived from Paris – apparently it was the first to be received via the new underwater cable from Varna – ordering Canrobert to send every available ship to Constantinople in order to collect the waiting Army of Reserve and bring them to the Crimea. It was all part of the Emperor Napoleon's grand strategy for operating with three armies in the Crimea. Canrobert himself had expressed his doubts and fears as to the wisdom of the expedition in a meeting with Raglan which lasted well beyond midnight on 3 May. But when Raglan went to bed just after 1 am on 4 May he did so under the impression that he had soothed Canrobert's fears and that he would soon receive news of a successful attack upon Kerch. Unfortunately, he was not allowed to enjoy his blissful slumbers for long, for at about 2 am he was woken up by a French ADC who informed him that Canrobert was ordering the recall of the French ships. The order from Paris was, effectively, just what Canrobert needed to extricate himself from what he considered to be a dubious enterprise, but it may be easily imagined with what pain Canrobert reported the message to Raglan. He knew only too well of his master's deception and duplicity and, despite his own doubts as to the likelihood of success, Canrobert was finding it hard to keep it all from his friend and colleague, Raglan, who listened in despair not only to the emperor's order to send all available ships to Constantinople but also to his lofty designs for the future campaign. The ever diplomatic Raglan told Canrobert that a recall of the Allied ships bound for Kerch would reflect badly on the Allies but Canrobert's mind was set. Indeed, even as a weary Raglan struggled to take in the news Lieutenant Martin, one of Canrobert's orderlies, was boarding the *Dauphin* in order to sail after the fleet with orders for its recall.

The recall of the French fleet bound for Kerch caused a major rupture in Anglo–French relations in the Crimea. True, they must and would continue to work together, but interference from outside had pushed the British to the limit. The normally composed Raglan was beside himself with annoyance and irritation whilst Sir George Brown is said to have come very close to landing a blow upon the jaw of General D'Autemarre. It was all too much. Admiral Bruat was bound by orders and had little option but to turn round and sail back to Kamiesh, leaving Brown and Lyons to consider their options. Raglan, meanwhile, sent a message to them informing them that whilst he recognised that three-quarters of the Allied strength had been withdrawn there might yet be the opportunity for success, in which case Brown and Lyons were to proceed but only if they were absolutely certain they could achieve something positive. In the event both Brown and Lyons took the safe – and very wise – option of returning to Balaklava. The Russian forces at Kerch may well have been largely second rate but there was no sense in the British gambling the lives of 3,000 of their best troops in what would have been an extremely risky attack. Thus, the British ships sailed back to Balaklava. It all bore shades of the Grand Old Duke of York, leading his men out and leading them back again.

The repercussions began almost immediately with great disgust felt not only by the British but by the French who also felt a great twinge of embarrassment. Raglan himself reflected ruefully on Canrobert's decision to recall the ships. 'I did all I could to prevent it,' wrote Raglan to Lord Panmure, 'as I had previously done to persuade the General-in-Chief to undertake it. He never, however, liked the enterprise, and he availed himself of the inopportune arrival of the Emperor's telegraphic message to call Admiral Bruat and the French troops back.'[18] Panmure himself was livid, and highly critical of Canrobert, whom he considered weak, indecisive and not fit for command any longer.

> If he had refused his consent to the embarkation of the troops, he might have been forgiven, but to recall an expedition *after* it has sailed, and to expose your game to the enemy, shows him to be utterly incapable of high command, or of weighing the results of so false a move as he has made. Well may the Army and Fleet be disgusted. I only wonder Bruat obeyed so degrading an order. I never will believe that the Emperor's instructions were such as would leave General Canrobert no discretion.[19]

Admiral Houston Stewart followed the trend with his damning criticisms of the French and of Canrobert in particular. Writing to Lord Panmure, Stewart said that everything was going to plan and that 'there could not be one single reasonable doubt entertained of our complete success!' Captain Spratt, of the *Spitfire*, had surveyed the Russian defences at Kerch and had worked out the position and range of every one of the Russian guns and the depth of water. It was all going so well. 'Judge then of my amazement, on going on board *Royal Albert* by signal about 5 am, to find that Admiral Bruat had received by an express steamer, the letter from General Canrobert . . . No argument could prevail with him to go on.' Stewart then said that, had he been in Bruat's place, he would certainly have gone on. Indeed, he argued, as did Admiral Lyons, that having gone thus far it was madness to turn back. 'It was all in vain,' he wrote.

> I thought Lyons would have gone almost mad. Indeed, it was heart-breaking to us all, but to him in particular . . . Here we are again in perfect inaction, and mortified beyond expression in thus finding that, not only the French, but also the English Fleet is virtually under the control of a French General, whose dread of responsibility and indecision of conduct are the theme of complaint throughout the Allied Land and Sea Forces. Indeed, it is becoming very serious.

> Canrobert seems utterly unfit to be a Commander-in-Chief, and all confidence in his abilities has faded away in this quarter of the world . . . I blush to think of what is likely to be thought of our consistency or firmness of purpose by the Russians after this display![20]

Lieutenant Anthony Sterling, of the Highland Brigade, was just one of many British officers who was not only critical of the French but also of the British government, who he thought were doing nothing to help their army in the Crimea, and the high command itself. Writing from Balaklava on 7 May, and echoing the thoughts of many like him Sterling said:

> Well, to our astonishment, yesterday, back the whole concern came, recalled by telegraphic message from Paris and London. They [the expedition] were just preparing to land . . . What are our own people doing? Are there any more rational plans in progress for carrying on the war? Are any of the army appointments which turned out bad ones cancelled? Not one; confusion over all. We are in a mess; and I see no attempt at getting out of it. I am thoroughly disgusted with the state of things, and as Radical as you are, which is a strong phrase; but I see my country in danger of being sacrificed by incapables, and I have no power to do anything.[21]

It was not only the British who were angered by the countermanding of the expedition to Kerch. General Larchey, commanding the French Army of Reserve at Constantinople, was similarly enraged. 'All the world accuses the electric telegraph of having caused the failure of the Expedition to Kerch from which the best results were expected . . . Rightly or wrongly there is a general outburst of indignation at the counter-order of the Expedition to Kerch. Sailors and soldiers alike have been tearing themselves with rage.'[22] Napoleon himself, conscious of the accusing looks being aimed in his direction, simply sidestepped the issue claiming that the expedition to Kerch was 'incompatible with the offensive movement against the Russians'. By this he meant that he needed all available ships to bring his troops from Constantinople for *his* offensive. Napoleon's grand scheme to operate with three armies in the Crimea was discussed at conferences on 12 and 14 May, but in view of the strained relations between the Allies it was hardly likely to be adopted. Nevertheless, it was considered at length by Raglan, Canrobert and Omar Pasha. Raglan played his trump card by agreeing to Napoleon's plan but only if the Turks and French agreed to take over the British trenches in order to allow the British to take the field on a numerical par with their allies. Neither Omar Pasha nor Canrobert could agree to this and so Napoleon's plan was effectively ditched.

The refusal by Raglan to co-operate fully with Napoleon's plan was the last straw for Canrobert. The burden of command was becoming too heavy for him. Indeed, he had already offered the post of overall commander-in-chief to a naturally surprised Raglan, who declined, and it is even claimed that he had considered suicide, so bad had the situation become. The pressure was now too much for Canrobert – or 'Robert Can't' as he had become known to the British soldiers – and on 16 May he telegraphed the emperor informing him that the burden of command had become too heavy a responsibility for him and that he wished to step down and hand over command of the French army to General Pélissier. In his telegraph Canrobert actually stated ill-health as the main reason for his resignation.

> My enfeebled health no longer permitting me to retain the Commander-in-Chief, my duty to my Sovereign and my country compels me to ask you to transfer that command to General Pélissier, – an officer of great skill and experience. The army which I leave to him, is intact, warlike, ardent, and confident. I beg the Emperor to leave me the place of a combatant in its ranks, at the head of a simple Division.[23]

It was quite an astonishing situation. Here was the commander-in-chief asking to be replaced and put in command of a division, which says much for Canrobert's state of mind and the intense pressure he was under. But if ill-health was cited by Canrobert in public as the reason for his resignation he revealed what he considered the real reason to be in a private letter to the emperor three days later. In it, he left his master in no doubt that the lack of co-operation from Raglan in particular and was one of the real causes.

> The little relative effect produced by the numerous and excellent batteries of the Allies against Sevastopol since the reopening of the fire; the non-attack of our external lines by the enemy, – an attack which had appeared very probable and on which I had founded hopes of a success more decisive than that of Inkerman; the arduous difficulties which I have experienced in preparing the execution of the plan of campaign of your Majesty, now become almost impossible by the non-co-operation of the Chief of the English army; the very false position towards the English in which I have been placed, by the sudden recall of the Kerch expedition, to which I have since discovered they attached a great importance; the extraordinary moral and physical fatigues, to which for nine months I have not for an instant ceased to be subjected; – all these reasons, Sire, have produced in my mind the conviction that I ought no longer to direct in chief that

> immense army, the esteem, affection, and confidence of which I have been enabled to obtain.[24]

It was rather unfair of Canrobert to accuse Raglan of non-co-operation, especially considering the duplicity of the French, and in particular Niel. Had he come clean from the outset the problems might not, perhaps, have occurred. But at least Canrobert did admit to underestimating the importance of the Kerch expedition to the British, which resulted in the fatal breakdown in relations between himself and his allies. It was quite obvious to the French emperor that Canrobert was now in no fit state to command his army and thus, on the same day that he had written to Napoleon, Canrobert's resignation was accepted. Command of the army was given over to Pélissier, whilst Canrobert himself assumed command of Pélissier's former corps. It was a highly unusual situation but it at least had the merit of thrusting an aggressive, no-nonsense soldier into the spotlight at the head of the French army. On 19 May Canrobert duly summoned Pélissier and informed him that his resignation had been accepted and that command of the French army would pass to him, Pélissier, later that morning. The new commander then took himself off to see Raglan and expressed his desire to press on with the siege. Finally, at around midday, the French corps commanders, the Generals of Division, and the chief officers of the artillery and engineers, and General Staff, gathered in a hut to hear Canrobert say his farewells and announce the formal change of command. It was by all accounts quite an emotional meeting, during which Pélissier praised the efforts of the outgoing commander, but despite the emotion there were few left in any doubt that one of the main obstacles to progress against Sevastopol had now been removed. Now, perhaps, the Allies could finally move forward.

NOTES

1 Douglas, Sir George and Ramsay, Sir George Dalhousie (Eds), *The Panmure Papers; being a selection from the correspondence of Fox Maule, second Baron Panmure, afterwards eleventh Earl of Dalhousie, KT, GCB* (London 1908), I, 88–9.
2 Bazancourt, the Baron de (trans. by Robert Howe Gould). *The Crimean Expedition, to the Capture of Sebastopol. Chronicles of the War in the East* (London 1856), II, 264.
3 Kinglake, Alexander William. *The Invasion of the Crimea: Its Origin, and An Account of its Progress down to the Death of Lord Raglan* (London 1863), VII, 125.
4 Ibid, VII, 126.
5 Ibid, VII, 127.
6 Interestingly enough, the good people of Sevastopol still refer to the enemy as being the French, with barely any recognition – understandably – of the far less numerous British.
7 Admiral Stewart to Panmure, *The Panmure Papers*, I, 123.
8 Panmure to Raglan, *The Panmure Papers*, I, 125.

9 Admiral Stewart to Panmure, *The Panmure Papers*, I, 127–8.
10 Admiral Stewart to Panmure, *The Panmure Papers*, I, 128.
11 Wrottesley, The Hon. George (Ed). *Life and Correspondence of Field Marshal Sir John Burgoyne* (London 1873), II, 271–2.
12 Ibid, II, 280–1.
13 Kinglake, *Invasion of the Crimea*, VII, 132–3.
14 Ibid, VII, 137.
15 Bazancourt, *The Crimean Expedition*, II, 253.
16 Totleben quoted in Kinglake, *Invasion of the Crimea*, VII, 186.
17 Ibid, VII, 257.
18 Raglan to Lord Panmure, *The Panmure Papers*, I, 182.
19 Panmure to Raglan, *The Panmure Papers*, I, 183.
20 Admiral Stewart to Panmure, *The Panmure Papers*, I, 186–8.
21 Lieutenant Colonel Anthony Sterling. *The Highland Brigade in the Crimea* (Minneapolis 1995), 161.
22 Larchey, quoted in Kinglake, *Invasion of the Crimea*, VII, 271.
23 Bazancourt, *Expedition to the Crimea*, II, 306.
24 Ibid, II, 306–7.

# CHAPTER NINETEEN
# *Pélissier Takes Command*

General Jean Jacques Pélissier was one of the great characters of the Crimean War. A rough, tough, stocky, straight-talking soldier, Pélissier was devoid of any sort of diplomatic flair but was just the kind of aggressive commander to get the Allies' siege back on track. Born in 1794, Pélissier had entered St Cyr at the age of 20, since when he had seen a great deal of active service, particularly in Algeria. His men, who knew all about his fighting qualities, called him 'Tin Head'. He was not the sort of man to suffer fools gladly and, fortunately for Raglan and the British, the emperor's envoy, Niel, was one such fool. Pélissier had long since taken a dislike to Niel who he suspected was the root cause of Canrobert's sudden lapse into lethargy and caution. From now on Pélissier would call the shots. Niel would dance to his tune. If Niel so much as offered an opinion at future staff meetings Pélissier would turn on him, much to the embarrassment of any British officers who happened to be present. And as for the tedious and troublesome telegraphs from his interfering emperor, Pélissier would simply do his best to ignore them, citing a fault in the line as the excuse for his disobedience. In short, Pélissier was just the sort of man to carry the war to the Russians; a hard, no-nonsense soldier. He was a real son of Mars.

Despite the distractions and upheavals in the Allied camps throughout the first weeks of May, there had been no let up in operations before Sevastopol. The Russians continued to press at night with sorties whilst the shelling and counter-shelling continued in a desultory fashion. Meanwhile, the ever-energetic Totleben maintained his aggressive stance by pushing forward his trenches wherever possible, denying the Allies vital ground in front of Sevastopol and forcing them to redirect their attention upon new works and lines rather than the key points of attack, such as the Flagstaff Bastion, the Redan, the Mamelon and the Malakhov. The seizure of the Mamelon by the Russians and the construction of the Kamchatsky lunette had been particularly tiresome for the Allies, particularly the French, whose sector this was. This dominating mound would have provided a perfect field of fire for the Allied batteries which were to be directed against the Malakhov but being in possession of the

Russians it now became the object of Pélissier's desire, rather than the Malakhov itself. On the left of the Allied lines there were bouts of sporadic but heavy fighting, particularly on 22 and 23 May, when the French launched successive attacks against the Russian lines which Totleben had pushed out in front of No.5 (Central) Bastion towards the cemetery at the foot of the Zarogodnaia Ravine. It was important not to allow Totleben to retain the initiative but to drive him back, and thus Pélissier ordered two attacks to be made against the new Russian works.

The French attack was duly delivered at 9 o'clock on the evening of 22 May by two French columns; the first, under General Beuret, consisted of three companies of the 10th Foot Chasseurs, three battalions of the 2nd Foreign Legion, and a battalion of the 98th Ligne. The second column, under General La Motte Rouge, consisted of picked companies of the 1st Foreign Legion, supported by two battalions of the 28th Ligne, and having a reserve consisting of a battalion of the 18th Ligne and two companies of voltigeurs of the Imperial Guard. Beuret would attack to the left of the cemetery and La Motte Rouge, the right. The French infantry swept into the new Russian works, driving the Russians out at bayonet point. But no sooner had the Russians retired than they charged back again in massed ranks, getting stuck into the French with a vengeance. Two hours of hard fighting were needed before the French were able to secure the cemetery, despite the ground being swept by showers of grape shot from the Russian guns in the Central Bastion. The fight on the French right had been particularly severe.

> On all sides, according to their habit, is a terrible noise of drums, of piercing sounds of trumpets and bugle-calls, and of formidable yells, which spread from ravine to ravine and are re-echoed again and again. Our soldiers, now well accustomed to this noise, and to these savage yells, resolutely await the shock of the enemy's reserves. The Foreign Legion has established itself in front, and covers the line of our working engineers, who overturn the embankments and begin to turn the works, in order to transform them into shelter for us.
>
> The Russian masses arrive, imposing, compact, and impelled by their chiefs, and dash forward in their turn to retake the conquered ground. It is now no longer the dark and deep obscurity of the winter nights; there is still light in the heavens which plays fitfully upon the burnished steel of that forest of bayonets. A mêlée of fire begins to rage; then, a few minutes afterwards, another mêlée of men fighting against men. They fight with fury; our soldiers pierce those living walls which threaten to envelop them; but the breaches made by death in the front ranks are instantly closed up by the living. On all sides numerous battalions press forward, whose approach is protected by the undulations of the soil; our reserves are also ready;

> the battalions of the 18th, and the Voltigeurs of the Guard charge successively with an impetuosity which twenty times alters the aspect of that ever-varying combat. The remotest ambuscades are taken and retaken; the trenches are full of stiffened bodies and of inoffensive arms which dying men can no longer wield.[1]

The cemetery changed hands at least five times during the night following heavy Russian counter-attacks, but by dawn on 23 May it was finally in French hands. That night the French renewed their attacks on the trench running out towards the cemetery from the Central Bastion. Chiefly involved were the 46th, 14th, 80th and 98th Ligne, who managed to secure the trench before reversing the parapet so it that it turned from covering the defenders to providing cover for the besiegers. The capture of the work was achieved only after great sacrifice. Some 2,303 French soldiers were killed, wounded or taken prisoner. The Russians admitted to losses of 3,061. It is important to appreciate the nature and severity of these fights, and the heavy casualties sustained. They were not merely dashes out into the open by one side or the other. Nor were they akin to raids on each other's lines. They were full-blown actions where losses were comparable to those sustained during major battles.[2] In fact, when we compare the casualties on both sides during these two nights' fight with those sustained at Balaklava, for example, it certainly puts the latter action into perspective. Indeed, compared with these two fights in the Zarogodnaia Ravine the Battle of Balaklava looks like a very insignificant skirmish. When we consider that this type of war was waged by the Russians on an almost nightly basis we may well imagine the ferocity of the prolonged struggle for Sevastopol.

But before the Allies turned their attention to resuming active operations directly against Sevastopol's defences Pélissier decided to resurrect the expedition to Kerch, which had so shamefully been wrecked by the French earlier in the month. With the Emperor Napoleon now having abandoned the idea of coming to the Crimea himself and with his grandiose plans having been dumped, the main obstacles which prevented the postponement of the first expedition to Kerch were removed. Pélissier was naturally optimistic about the project which was in keeping with his aggressive instincts. Furthermore, other factors now came into consideration, such as the arrival during the middle of May of the first contingent of a 15,000-strong force of Sardinian troops under General Alphonse de la Marmora. This contingent, wrote the young Evelyn Wood, 'in its bright uniforms, perfect equipment, and generally well-organised system, formed a strange contrast to our men. The best feeling towards the British troops was evident in all ranks from their first arrival, and this increased as our acquaintance ripened.'[3] The addition of the Sardinian troops strengthened the Allies' right, particularly in the

Chernaya valley where the Russian field army continued to hover menacingly.

The new expedition to Kerch got underway on 22 May, the very day that the French and Russians were at each others' throats in the Zarogodnaia ravine. Once again the Allied force was commanded by Sir George Brown with the Highland Brigade, along with the addition of the 79th, providing the backbone of the British contingent which numbered 3,800. In addition there were 7,500 French under D'Autemarre, and 5,000 Turks under Reschid Pasha. There were also five batteries of artillery and fifty British hussars. Admirals Lyons and Bruat were again at the helm of the Allied fleet, no doubt hoping for a better outcome than that of the abortive expedition three weeks earlier.

By 24 May the Allied ships had reached their appointed rendezvous off Cape Takli, some twenty miles south of Kerch itself. The Russian garrison was as before, some 9,000 men of various qualities under Lieutenant General Baron Wrangel. The arrival of the Allied flotilla was reported to Wrangel shortly after dawn on 24 May at which he began making preparations to destroy his supplies and withdraw west towards Theodosia. He also despatched a messenger to Prince Gorchakov and to General Khomutov, commanding officer of the Russian troops in the eastern Crimea, informing them of the arrival of the Allied ships. Gorchakov's first thought was that this was part of an Allied invasion, intended to seal off the Crimea from the east, after which they would move north to Perekop and sever all communications between Russian and the Crimea. Units of Cossacks and Russian infantry were hastily despatched to the north to counter the threat which, as it happened, never materialised, not that it was ever part of the Allied plan anyway. In the meantime, Wrangel continued to prepare to abandon Kerch.

At about midday a British gunboat approached the Pavlovskaya battery, which lay on the southern side of the Bay of Kerch, and opened fire, to which the Russian battery answered with one of its 68-pounder naval guns. The exchange of fire lasted for fifteen minutes during which time other Allied ships approached Cape Kamysh-Burun, to the south-west of the battery. The Allied ships arrayed themselves parallel to the shore and opened up a heavy fire, whilst at the same time six battalions of infantry began to land, one of which was directed to the rear of the Pavlovskaya battery. In order not to be outflanked and cut off from his escape route the commander of the battery spiked his guns, blew up the powder magazines and fell back to the Theodosiyskaya road with his artillerymen and 218 men of the Karantinnaya Guards towards the main detachment of Lieutenant General Wrangel which had retired west after destroying large supplies of foodstocks and other provisions in the town.

At 1 pm the commanders of the coastal batteries, the Mac-Burunskaya, Gorodovaya and Karantinnaya batteries, likewise spiked their guns, blew up the powder magazines and also retreated to join the detachment of Lieutenant General Wrangel. An hour later two Allied gunboats glided into Kerch harbour just as the Russian ship *Argonaut* was leaving, with Rear-Admiral Wulf, the head of Black Sea coastline headquarters on board. The Allied gunboats fired at the ship but were driven off when the Enikalskaya battery opened fire on them. The *Argonaut* continued to leave the harbour, firing as it went, one of its shots damaging the engine of one of the Allied gunboats. Six more Allied ships then lined up to block the *Argonaut*'s exit but these were driven back by fire from the Enikale and Chushka batteries and from a second Russian ship, *Molodets*. The British gunboat *Snake*, under Lieutenant McGillop, also tried to stop the *Argonaut*, both ships employing intricate moves to try to gain the upper hand, but ultimately the *Snake* failed to halt the *Argonaut*, which sailed safely off into the Sea of Azov. McGillop was not done yet, however, for the *Snake* engaged three other Russian ships, the *Moguchy*, *Donets* and *Berdyansk*, which were anchored near the Admiralty building but were unable to put to sea. The crews were landed and the ships set fire to by the Russians themselves. Russian casualties were light, with the commander of the *Moguchy* and three seamen being reported wounded, whilst a Lieutenant Ushakov was listed as missing.

The fight between the Russian coastal batteries and the six Allied ships in the Kerch straits lasted until 9 pm when the commander of the Enikale battery, Lieutenant Tsehanovitch of the 17th artillery brigade, spiked his guns, blew up the powder magazines and fell back with his men to join the detachment of Lieutenant General Wrangel. The garrison of the Chushka coastal battery, meanwhile, had kept up a steady fire on the Allied ships throughout the day but when the columns of Allied infantry were seen, threatening their retreat, the garrison followed the example of the other batteries and retired after destroying their guns. In addition to the destruction of the coastal batteries some fifteen privately owned ships that were moored in the straits loaded with wheat, bread, oats and barley were also torched and sunk to prevent the supplies from falling into the Allies' hands. Those citizens who could do so chose to leave Kerch but many citizens had to stay, including many merchants who preferred to remain and guard their goods. It was a foolish policy. Finally, the mayor of Kerch, Lieutenant Colonel Antonovitch, and the town's head of police, destroyed all government and privately owned stocks of wheat, flour, hay and coal before leaving Kerch late on the evening of 24 May.[4]

By nightfall Kerch had been completely abandoned by the Russian army, not that there was much left to protect anyway, for the town was ablaze in many areas, leaving the Allies to approach against a fiery backdrop of flames and explosions. The majority of the population had also left, seeking shelter in neighbouring villages. The disembarkation of the Allied troops was completed before dawn on 25 May and by 6 am advanced units of Allied troops had begun to enter Kerch. The first task

Sir George Brown set his troops to was the destruction of an iron foundry used for the construction of guns, following which the systematic destruction of the vast quantities of grain began. Wrangel had already destroyed much of it himself, said to have been in the region of four million tons of corn and half a million tons of flour, all of which would have been mightily useful to the Allies, let alone the Russians themselves. But the destruction of Russian supplies was the name of the game and Brown's men duly carried out his orders. Unfortunately, some of the French troops set to work with far too much enthusiasm and before long had embarked upon a shameful orgy of looting and destruction, much against the will of Brown and other commanders who appear to have been powerless to prevent it. In his history of the Crimean War, Kinglake went to pains to point out that only 3,000 of the 15,000 Allied troops at Kerch were British and that the majority of the black deeds carried out at Kerch were perpetrated by the French and Turks. Well, that may be the case, but it is highly unlikely that the British element refrained from indulging in the time-honoured ritual of pillaging. The most infamous episode was the sacking of the Kerch Museum, during which hundreds of priceless artefacts were wantonly destroyed. Brown tried in vain to prevent this by posting hussars to guard the place but they appear to have been as bad as the rest of the Allied troops and simply joined in the plundering.

The pillaging and destruction continued unabated and with Kerch having been summarily turned inside out Sir George Brown turned his attention to Yenikale which lay six miles to the east. Sadly, the disorders continued during the march, the line of which was marked by plumes of smoke that rose from burning villages and hamlets. When Brown reached Yenikale on 26 May he was greeted by the Allied admirals who had already arrived there. The atmosphere in Yenikale was one of great self-congratulation. After the trials and tribulations of the traumatic winter and the abortive operations in spring, the Allies could finally congratulate themselves on a job well done. Not only had they captured or ensured the destruction of the Russian coastal batteries along the Kerch straits but they had destroyed a vast amount of valuable stores and supplies intended for the Russian Army. They had also effectively sealed the vital supply route into the Crimea via the Sea of Azov and Kerch.

For the next three weeks or so Captain Lyons, the son of Admiral Lyons, took his ships into the Sea of Azov and, having achieved total domination of the sea and the Russian fleet, enjoyed himself by raiding the coastal villages, burning them and destroying over two hundred Russian vessels of various kinds. With little or no opposition the Allies' landing parties of sailors and marines had a field day. The Allied incursions extended right up to Taganrog, a town at the very north-eastern end of the Sea of Azov, at the mouth of the Don river, where once again huge quantities of supplies were destroyed.

Just three weeks after the expedition had sailed for Kerch the Allies returned to the Chersonese, after leaving behind 7,000 troops, 5,000 of which were Turks, to maintain an Allied presence. The Allies rightly viewed the operation as a success, although one feels it was rather exaggerated in the wake of the previous few months' disappointments. The Russians themselves took a more pragmatic view of it all, considering it to have been more of an irritant than any major setback. The possession of the Kerch strait and the Sea of Azov did not bring the Allies any great benefit to themselves, but merely deprived the Russians of their vital artery through which flowed provisions to the Crimean Army through the Sea of Azov. Great attention had been paid to Kerch by Menshikov at the outset of the war largely because of its strategic importance. However, when the Russian High Command read the various reports drawn up by Russian engineers into what measures would be needed to get the town into a defensible state, the measures were considered too expensive. Thus, all that was done was the sinking of a few vessels, which proved woefully ineffective. In the event, over 200,000 roubles were spent on trying to improve the defences of the Kerch straits and soon after the war began they were declared impassable to Allied ships. Needless to say, when the Allied squadron passed through it, an investigation began into how this had happened. There was also a breakdown in communications between Menshikov and Gorchakov for the former had stated categorically that he would never allow Kerch to be occupied by the Allies and that reserves would be despatched there. Consequently, Gorchakov did nothing himself for the Kerch strait but relied upon Menshikov, who, in the event, did nothing either. Even more damning was the fact that, with Canrobert having already recalled the earlier expedition the Allies had shown their hand, whereupon it should have been obvious to the Russians that a second attempt would surely be made, as indeed it was. But despite this, no steps were taken to strengthen Kerch.[5]

The expedition to Kerch provided the Allies with a genuine cause for celebration after the trials of the late winter and early spring. Despite a certain amount of scorn poured on the success of the campaign by the Russians there was no denying that the closure of the supply route into the Crimea via Kerch was a great blow to them. Things were bad enough as they were and the severing of this vital artery only served to make matters worse for Gorchakov. The Allies themselves gained no great advantage themselves, other than the satisfaction of cutting the supply line. But more important was the boost to morale that the expedition to Kerch gave them. As we have seen, the irritating meddlings of the Emperor Napoleon and his envoy, Niel, had caused a great rift in the Allied camp between the French and British. But with the emperor's unwitting puppet, Canrobert, having tendered his resignation and with his replacement by the far more aggressive Pélissier, relations warmed again and thus the way was open for a fresh and far more vigorous approach to the war. Certainly, Raglan and the British could look forward to a renewed spirit of co-operation with the French. Kerch was the first example of this new spirit. Nevertheless, the success of the Kerch expedition cut no ice with the emperor who was still bent on seeing his grand designs carried out. His congratulatory telegram to Pélissier barely got above lukewarm, the emperor taking the opportunity to point out yet again that the real object of the game was to defeat the Russians in the field before concentrating on the siege of Sevastopol. Any other operations would have no effect, he said, other than to divide the Allied forces, which he considered potentially fatal. Fortunately, Pélissier's grasp on the real situation in the Crimea was far better than that of his meddling and distant emperor, for whom he had little time. No, Pélissier would do things his way and no amount of frantic bullying by Parisian telegrams could deter him.

The return of the expedition to Kerch put the Allies in good heart, and telegrams of congratulation came buzzing along the wire from London, including one from Queen Victoria herself who was delighted at the result. But even as the back-slapping continued an old enemy began to rear its head in the Allied camps, and in the camps of the Sardinian troops in particular. Ever since the Allies had arrived at Varna they had been ravaged by cholera, which continued to plague them well after they had landed in the Crimea itself. However, the disease had all but flown by the time of the Kerch expedition. But during the spring of 1855 it began to show signs of returning. It was the only real cloud on an otherwise clear horizon. The Sardinian commander, Marmora, had lost his own brother to the disease and his men were dropping like flies. Admiral Boxer, the man largely responsible for clearing the harbour of Balaklava, was dead too from the disease. On 12 June Raglan wrote to Lord Panmure, giving the latest state of affairs.

> I am extremely sorry to say that the cholera continues to make sad havoc in the Sardinian camp. There were ninety-nine fresh cases yesterday and between forty and fifty deaths. The troops, I am assured, are not dispirited, but this sad misfortune greatly affects General de la Marmora. His troops are encamped upon ground which looks all that can be desired. The accompanying paper shows the state of the cholera with us.

And then he ended ominously, 'You will observe with regret that it is still progressing . . .'[6] Fortunately, the dreaded and silent grey killer reached a peak during mid-July, although this was little comfort to the many Allied soldiers who were taken by the disease before then. It was fortunate that the improvements in the hospital system had begun to take effect and consequently the Allies were spared the massive problems that had so ravaged them the previous winter. It was just as well, for Raglan and Pélissier would need every man they could spare for the coming assault on Sevastopol which they planned for the first week in June. Indeed, even as the successful expedition from Kerch was returning to the Chersonese the Allies had already made their first moves which they hoped would lead to the fall of Sevastopol.

NOTES

1 Bazancourt, the Baron de (trans. by Robert Howe Gould). *The Crimean Expedition, to the Capture of Sebastopol. Chronicles of the War in the East* (London 1856), II, 325–6.
2 For example, the French casualty figure for the two nights of fighting for the cemetery and the Russian trench to the east of it was higher than all but eight of Wellington's great battles and sieges in the Peninsula between 1808 and 1814. The eight exceptions were Talavera, Albuera, Badajoz, Salamanca, Vittoria, Sorauren, Nivelle and Toulouse.
3 Wood, General Sir Evelyn. *The Crimea in 1854 and 1894* (London 1896), 265.
4 'Kopiya s otnosheniya generala knyazya Gorchakova voennomu ministru, 17 maya, 1855', *Central State Historical Archives, Moscow,* No.1357.
5 Miloshevitch N S 'Iz zapisok sevastopol'tsa', 1904, *Sevastopol* (Sevastopol 2002), I, 246–7.
6 Douglas, Sir George and Ramsay, Sir George Dalhousie (Eds). *The Panmure Papers; being a selection from the correspondence of Fox Maule, second Baron Panmure, afterwards eleventh Earl of Dalhousie, KT, GCB* (London 1908), Raglan to Panmure, I, 234–5.

# CHAPTER TWENTY
## *The Fall of the Forts*

The successful expedition to Kerch had put a spring back in the Allies' steps, whilst the appointment of Pélissier had boosted their flagging morale and given them greater determination to push forward and take Sevastopol. After weeks of French apathy things were finally looking good. But despite the change of command nobody within the Allied camps, British or French, was under any illusions as to the magnitude of the task that still faced them. The supply line into the Crimea via Kerch and the Sea of Azov might well have been severed but the investment of Sevastopol had still to be fully completed. Meanwhile, the Russians continued to feed in reserves of men and supplies to bolster the defences and feed the troops.

The beginning of June 1855 saw the Allies in a good position, with no fewer than 175,000 troops encamped to the south and south-east of Sevastopol, with some 588 guns trained on the town. The overwhelming bulk of these troops were French, of course, Pélissier's troops numbering just over 100,000. The British contingent had grown significantly since the dark winter days and now numbered 45,000, although the quality of many of these was nowhere near that of those who had landed in the Crimea the previous September. Indeed, many were considered to be mere boys, determined and keen to do their duty but lacking the hardened edge of battle that so marked out the veterans of the Alma and Inkerman. Sadly, most of these veterans had long since gone, taken either by sickness and disease or by the battles themselves. The Johnny Newcomers may well have been full of British pluck and spirit but these were of little use against Russian bayonets, guns and grape shot. The Turkish contingent numbered 10,000, mostly ill-used troops in whom Raglan had little faith and yet who might have made a great difference to affairs before Sevastopol had not the British commander marked them down as navvies, fit for little more than labouring work. The Sardinians, 15,000 strong, were liked by all, but suffered from the ravages of cholera. They would be given their chance, however, and would serve with distinction alongside their British, French and Turkish allies.

Facing this large host from behind their low walls and in their trenches and bastions, were seventy-eight battalions of Russian infantry, numbering around 45,000, as well as 9,000 naval gunners, who manned some 1,174 guns, 571 of which were heavy guns.[1] About half of these were concentrated in the Korabel'naia suburb, manning the line from the Careenage Ravine, down to the Malakhov and the Redan and on to the Flagstaff Bastion. With such a large number of troops in the suburb it was decided to send Nakhimov help and so Lieutenant General Khrulev, whom we last saw giving Menshikov ill-advice about attacking Eupatoria, was despatched to help organise the defence. The defenders were not only outnumbered by three to one but suffered from their cramped conditions. True, they had the benefit of good defences – when they were not being pulverised by Allied artillery – but the necessity of keeping them closely packed behind the defences inevitably ensured a frightening casualty rate. The Allied assault might come at any moment, so it was deemed necessary to keep them close behind what were marked down as the likely points of attack, such as the Redan, the Malakhov and the Flagstaff Bastion. The situation was eased somewhat by Totleben's aggressive defence, in which he pushed forward his own trenches from the walls of Sevastopol, turning the whole area outside the town into a scene that would not be unlike that to which the French and British would become accustomed some sixty years later on the Western Front. Totleben was, in fact, a real hero of the siege; uncompromising, clever, and seemingly aware of every move the Allies were considering. He was also acutely aware of the need to take the fight to the Allies, rather than just sit back and hope for relief, which was patently beyond Gorchakov. By grasping the initiative Totleben made life extremely difficult for the Allies who, in addition to the problem of attacking the walls of Sevastopol, now had the added problem of an extensive network of trenches, rifle pits and lunettes strung out in front of the walls.

In addition to the defenders of Sevastopol the Russians also had the services of the main Russian Field Army of some 21,000 men – largely from thirty-nine battalions of infantry – and a hundred guns, still hovering to the north of Sevastopol on the Mackenzie Heights. The threat from this force was very real and could not be ignored but, ultimately, it never materialised. The force remained a threat, but nothing more. Only in August would it flex its muscles and try something offensively. But for now it remained impassive, and in support, but little more. Although cholera reared its head in the camps of the Russian Field Army there was never any danger of it exploding into epidemic proportions, and the men generally had a relatively easy time of it. There was never any prospect of the Allies attacking them, nor did their own commanders show any inclination to engage the Allies themselves. So, they simply watched and waited whilst the siege wore on.

As the Malakhov was deemed to be the key to Sevastopol, so the key to the Malakhov was the Mamelon. Now, with Totleben having built the Kamchatsky lunette upon it and extended his web of trenches around it, Pélissier was faced with two obstacles. In addition to these there were the White Works, the two redoubts which Totleben had thrown up on the eastern side of the Careenage Ravine. These would also have to be taken before any serious attempt could be made upon the Malakhov. It was a difficult situation for the Allies, and for the French in particular, whose section this was. The simple geographical position of the Mamelon made it impossible for the French to bypass it. It couldn't be done, especially on such a narrow front. There was nothing for it but to attack directly.

The British, meanwhile, had their own problems. They knew full well that the Malakhov was the key to Sevastopol but their own objective, the Redan, was still capable of compromising any attack upon it. It is doubtful whether the capture of the Redan would have led to the fall of Sevastopol, but the capture of the Malakhov almost certainly would. Nevertheless, the Redan remained the prime objective for Raglan and his men, and if the Mamelon was the key to the Malakhov, then the Redan had its own small key, the Quarries, the name given to a work upon which the right of the Russian trenches was anchored, overlooking the Vorontsov Ravine. These trenches, 400 yards from the Redan at their narrowest point, effectively blocked the British approach from their lines between the Middle and Vorontsov Ravines, the area they called 'Gordon's Attack'. It was, in the words of Lieutenant Nathaniel Steevens, of the 88th,

> an 'ambuscade' which the enemy had constructed by strongly entrenching a quarry, which, as already stated, was situated on rising ground, about 110 feet above our nearest trench, and not more than 600 feet from it. The elevated position and close proximity of this ambuscade gave the Russians the advantage of a commanding fire, of which they persistently availed themselves with very harassing effect: many of our brave fellows here lost their lives, by incautiously exposing little more than their heads to the unerring aim of the ever-vigilant Russian marksmen.[2]

Once in their hands the British would be able to use the Quarries as their springboard for the attack against the Redan which would follow.

For once the Allied commanders were in complete agreement about their plan of attack. Pélissier and Raglan presided over a great council of war, attended by Generals Bosquet, Niel, Thiry, Lebouef, Beuret, Dalesme, Frossard, Martimprey and Trochu, on the French side and by Jones, Dacres, Airey and Adye on the British. Only Niel, somewhat predictably, and still clinging to his grand designs in the field, offered any real objections, but he was quickly savaged by Pélissier, much to the embarrassment of the British officers present. In fact, Pélissier felt so guilty about his treatment of the stunned Niel that he sent for him and apologised. Despite Niel's lame objections the council of war was a success. The objectives were clear to all; the White Works, the Mamelon and the Quarries. All that needed to be decided upon was the date of attack, which was set for 7 June.

Niel may well have been lashed by Pélissier's tongue but there was still the possibility that the emperor might yet intervene in the Allies' plans. And so it proved. On 5 June Napoleon sent a telegram to Pélissier reminding him once again that he should not commit his troops to a costly assault on Sevastopol, but should instead operate in conjunction with Raglan and Omar Pasha and take the field against the Russian Field Army. By now the tune was becoming a very tired one and Pélissier had no intention of listening to it any more. Any last, lingering hopes that the emperor might yet get his way vanished when Pélissier sent his own telegram to Paris, informing Napoleon of his decision to attack the defences in front of the Korabel'naia.

> I am to see Lord Raglan today (with whom, by the way, I am in perfect accord), in order to make the final dispositions for the assault which is to put in our power the White Redoubts, the Green Mamelon, and the Quarry in front of the Great Redan. According to my present reckoning, I shall commence this operation on the 7th, and I shall push it unrelentingly with the utmost vigour.[3]

The two messages must have crossed each other on their respective journeys along the wire, but there is little doubt which carried the most weight. The emperor's telegram cut little ice with Pélissier whose own telegram must have been a real slap in the face for Napoleon who was being told, in effect, that the commander-in-chief of his army in the Crimea was doing things his way, despite what the emperor thought himself.

Meanwhile, the Russian troops in the White Works and in the Kamchatsky lunette were in a desperate situation, largely due to the decision made on 3 June by General Zhabokritsky, who commanded in the Korabel'naia, when he reduced the garrisons of the redoubts and the lunette to a bare minimum. In the redoubts he left a battalion of 450 men and in the lunette some 350, hardly enough to man the works let alone defend them against a large French force. The garrisons would be further reduced by the sheer weight of Allied firepower that was about to open up on them. General Zhabokritsky's decision to reduce the garrisons would come in for bitter criticism from his own side later on, as would his own conduct.

6 June 1855 was a beautiful summer's day, with men on both sides no doubt lolling beneath a 'bright and cloudless sky'.[4] Inside the White

Works and the Kamchatsky lunette the Russians continued to labour at strengthening and repairing their works. Meanwhile, a few hundred yards from them the French quietly went about their business, bringing forward ammunition for their guns and making preparations both for the bombardment and the assault that would follow. The plan was quite simple. The Allied bombardment would last throughout the afternoon and evening of 6 June and continue throughout the next day. Hopefully, it would not only flatten the works themselves but would silence the guns inside. The Redan would also come under fire so as to ensure that the assault on the Quarries was not compromised. The bombardment was to be a short but violent one, after which it would be down to the time-honoured process of flinging men at walls and hoping for the best.

The afternoon continued, warm and tranquil, but at 2.30 pm the peacefulness was shattered when the Allies' guns opened up for the third major bombardment, this time against the works in front of the Korabel'naia.[5] The firing continued for the rest of the day, through the night and on into the next day, with shells screaming into the works and mortars dropping from the sky to pound and pulverise. The ditches were filled with debris and the ramparts smashed, leaving them resembling little more than mounds of earth, the guns silent and dismounted, and the defenders dazed and shattered. The fire of the British guns was particularly effective, by Totleben's own admission, the Royal Artillery firing with a 'dreadful exactness'. By 3 pm on 7 June, after some twenty-four hours of shelling, the Russian defenders and their guns had virtually been buried alive within their forts. The Allies' guns had reached a crescendo at about the same time and there appeared little to stand in the way of the waiting battalions of happy Allied infantry.

The Allied infantry had filed into their start positions from their camps to the south, marching slowly along the ravines whilst the crump of artillery continued to be heard in front of them. Confidence was high, and rightly so, for the bombardment had all but flattened the Russian works. Four French divisions were to be involved in the attack: the 3rd and 4th, under Generals Mayran and Dulac, and the 2nd and 5th, under Camon and Brunet, all of these divisions forming part of Bosquet's 2nd Corps. In fact, all arrangements for the assault were made by Bosquet himself. The British attack on the Quarries would be made by units of the 2nd and Light Divisions, commanded by Colonel Shirley of the 88th. Supporting the whole from the Careenage Ravine would be Omar Pasha's Turkish division.

Early on the evening of 7 June Russian observers noticed a great movement in the French trenches as their troops began to muster, whilst information gleaned from deserters indicated that an assault was about to begin. Several staff and regimental officers immediately rushed to General Zhabokritsky for orders but were somewhat taken aback when he declared himself unwell and departed for the other side of town, leaving no orders or instructions. Strangely, Russian historians do not consider him a traitor or a coward. It was simply that he was sadly lacking in military skills; he had no real talent and displayed nothing but indifference towards his task, 'the characteristics of a typical ambitious officer in the Russian Army of the period'.[6] With Zhabokritsky gone orders were quickly sent to Khrulev to take charge, but there was little he could do to stop the tide of red and blue once the assault got underway.

At 6.30 pm a succession of rockets arced their way into the blue sky above the Allied trenches at which the attacking Allied columns sprang forward to attack the Russian works.[7] Away on the Allies' right, General Lavarande's brigade left their trenches in the 2nd parallel and rushed forward across the three hundred yards of open ground to attack the Volynsky Redoubt, whilst away to their left General Failly's brigade dashed forward crossing twice the distance to attack the Selenghinsky Redoubt. Both brigades attacked under fire of grape and musketry, although this was not very effective, coming as it did from a combined garrison of barely 450 men. Nevertheless, the attacking French brigades still suffered from the Russians' fire, particularly Failly's brigade which came under enfilading fire from the Little Redan and from the Malakhov. The French brigades held their fire until they were almost upon the redoubts, all the time taking casualties from the desperate but accurate fire of the garrisons, but there was little the Russians could do against such an overwhelmingly numerically superior force and the French had little trouble in sweeping over the shattered ramparts and into the works. There was a brief struggle in the redoubts but the defenders were in a hopeless position and were quickly overrun, the commanding officer of the two redoubts, Chestakov, and his battalion commander, Bélaiev, both being killed amidst a flurry of bayonets.

Despite the relative ease of the French conquest the Russians were not about to let the new occupants settle for too long, for a battalion of the Muromsky Regiment came forward from the Korabel'naia to try to retake the redoubts, but once again French numbers told. The Russians were driven back and pursued by the French who, in their eagerness, continued another five hundred yards or so as far as the Zabalkansky battery which was sited at the very northern end of the Inkerman ridge, overlooking Careenage Bay. The five guns were quickly spiked and the battery destroyed before the French withdrew. Still the Russians refused to concede the redoubts without a fight and two more battalions of the Muromsky Regiment were sent out to cross the Careenage Ravine and climb the Inkerman Ridge before making a counter-attack on the White Works. Unfortunately, Bosquet had spotted this move and had already moved two battalions, under Lieutenant Colonel d'Orion, into the Careenage Ravine with the specific intention of cutting off the Russians and attacking them from the rear. No sooner had the two Russian battalions begun to ascend the Inkerman Ridge than d'Orion appeared in their rear, causing them to turn and fight their way out at bayonet point, but not before the French had secured over four hundred prisoners including twenty officers. This was the last attempt made by the Russians to wrench back the White Works from the French who remained masters of the redoubts. It had been a relatively easy fight. The attack on the Mamelon would not be so easy.

Whilst Failly and Lavarande were attacking the White Works three more French columns were attacking the Kamchatsky lunette on the Mamelon. On the right was Colonel Rose with a regiment of Algerian riflemen, in the centre came Colonel Brancion with the 50th Ligne, and on the left was Colonel de Polhes with the 3rd Zouaves. As with the White Works the Allied bombardment had pummelled the lunette into a series of earthen piles, vaguely resembling a small fort. The attacking troops had some five hundred yards of open ground to cover, but as the guns inside were thought to have been all but buried, little resistance was expected. Inside the lunette, its commanding officer, Timiryazev, made an entry in his diary.

> 7 June. 6 o'clock in the afternoon. It must be admitted that the situation of those of us who had to defend the lunette was very bad. There were 125 men with little but a prayer for God's help. But suddenly God sent Pavel Stepanovitch [Nakhimov] to the lunette. He never failed in such critical moments to visit those who needed his support desperately. I explained to the admiral the state of my lunette and the inevitability of an assault, but he ordered me to show him the damage caused to our artillery. As soon as we passed the fifteenth gun, the officer on duty, midshipman Kharlamov, reported that the assault was beginning, and I asked the admiral to take himself off and to send us reinforcements. But, instead, the admiral drew his hanger. I repeated my request and tried to persuade him that his presence here would be dangerous and that we would follow all his orders anyway.[8]

It is not clear whether Nakhimov remained behind to help defend the Kamchatsky lunette, but given the numbers of French troops now bearing down upon him it is unlikely that he remained so dangerously exposed for long, although eye-witness accounts do confirm that he was personally engaged in the fighting on 7 June. The three French columns poured forward from their 2nd parallel and covered the initial ground without much trouble as it was mainly dead ground, but when they broke out into the open they were immediately hit by a storm of grape and musketry, both from the lunette, from the Malakhov and even from the Redan. The guns in the Kamchatsky had not been silenced after all.

The Algerians, under Rose, managed to overcome a battery attached to the lunette and he quickly established a position there, firing upon the defenders of the Kamchatsky, while the 3rd Zouaves and Colonel Brancion, with the 50th, continued to drive forward through the storm of metal flying into their faces. Eventually, the French reached the ditch of the lunette whereupon they began scrambling up to the ramparts, again in the teeth of a withering fire from within. The 52 year-old Brancion himself was one of the first to climb on to the parapet, sword in one hand and the colours of the 50th in the other. It was a tremendous and inspiring sight for the other troops now scrambling and tumbling into the lunette behind him. Sadly, the inspirational Brancion was mortally wounded by a piece of grape shot that struck him down and left him lying inside at the foot of the interior of the lunette, grasping 'the golden eagle of the regiment' and leaving him 'enshrouded in his glory'.[9] Brancion's men could not be stopped, however, and more and more of them entered the lunette to drive the gallant defenders out, bayoneting them and shooting them down at close range. The Mamelon was in French hands, but not for long.

It was necessary to consolidate the hard-won and important position. Sadly, the enthusiasm of the victorious French got the better of them and, not content with one success, they pressed on towards the Malakhov itself. It was never intended that the French should actually attack the Malakhov. That would come later, once the Mamelon had been properly fortified and batteries established there. Nevertheless, history is littered with instances of soldiers taking advantage of good fortune to press home a successful attack and turn it into an even greater victory. But not here at the Malakhov. No, the Russian defenders were far too alert and resolute for that to happen. Instead the indiscipline of the French almost cost them the Mamelon.

The wild enthusiasm of the elated French drove them past the Mamelon and downhill towards the Malakhov. The ditch was a complete mess, with rubble and earth thrown up in huge piles as testament to the power of the Allied artillery barrage. But not for nothing had Nakhimov kept his battalions close to the bastions and now his policy paid off. True, it had cost him horrendous casualties as a result of Allied artillery fire ripping into the tightly packed ranks of Russians, but if they had been kept back in reserve away from the bastions there is little reason to doubt that the French troops who had already taken the Mamelon would have captured the Malakhov too. But it was not to be. Instead, Khrulev brought forward his battalions at the precise moment that the French were scrambling into the remains of the ditch. It was then a simple case of loading and firing as quickly as possible into the ranks of the exhausted French who were shot down in droves. A few volleys sufficed to send them reeling back in confusion, and when Khrulev led his own troops forward the retreat quickly turned into a rout. In fact, so panic-stricken were the French that the Russians drove on into the Mamelon which they quickly overran. All the hard-won efforts of men such as Brancion appeared to have been in vain had it not been for General Camon, who quickly brought forward his second brigade along with the 5th Division to support Wimpfen's brigade which was being slaughtered. General Brunet executed the orders with speed and precision and soon both his 1st Brigade and General Vergé's brigade were charging forward to meet the Russians. Now it was the turn of Khrulev's men to suffer. They had driven the French from the ditch of the Malakhov and had recaptured the Mamelon but had become exhausted in their efforts to do so. The two French brigades were fresh and had little trouble driving the Russians from the Mamelon once and for all, and after a few minutes' fighting the tricolour waved proudly over the hill once more. The Mamelon was retaken. It would not be lost again.

While the struggle for the Mamelon had been going on the British troops destined to attack the Quarries watched and waited anxiously for a positive result, for if the French attack failed it would severely compromise their own efforts, if indeed they took place. Thus, it was with no little sense of relief and excitement that they saw Brancion's tricolour fluttering above the Mamelon, which was the signal for the attack to begin. The attack itself would be carried out by 700 men of the Light Division and 600 of the 2nd Division, supported by the 62nd Regiment. Two separate bodies of 200 men from each division were to attack and carry the main Russian position, whilst the remaining troops were to attack the adjacent trenches.

With French cheers echoing across the Middle Ravine, the British sprang out of the 3rd parallel and hurried forward across the 400 or so yards of open ground towards the Russian trenches. The two storming parties, meanwhile, had a shorter distance to cover as they attacked from an advanced sap in front of the 3rd parallel. The British artillery had done a good job in shelling the Quarries and in suppressing the supporting fire from the Redan. It also raked the ground between the Quarries and the Redan in order to isolate the defenders in the former position from any help they might expect to receive from the latter. The effect of the fire on the tightly packed Russians was devastating.

> To describe the intense fury of the cannonade by which these operations were supported would be impossible; it was the admiration of every one. The sailors and gunners, rivalling each other in their exertions, worked the heavy guns and mortars with almost incredible rapidity. The effect of our fire upon the Redan was frightful to witness. The Russians, evidently expecting an attack upon that work, had brought all their men from their caves and hiding places, and massed them together in it. As one looked at the work from the

> Left Attack, the rays of the setting sun lighting up the mass of troops, the shells could be seen plunging and cutting gaps in the ranks, blowing the bodies of their victims into the air. Perhaps such an artillery fire was never before seen. For the hour that it lasted, it was the heaviest during the Siege.[10]

Unlike the French, who suffered heavy casualties in crossing the ground before their own objectives, the British stormers found it fairly easy going. It was clear that the supporting artillery fire had done its job. The two storming parties, one led by Major James Armstrong of the 49th, and the other by Colonel Robert Campbell of the 90th, were quickly into the Russian positions. The defenders were still dazed by the effects of the British bombardment but nevertheless put up a creditable fight which lasted the best part of thirty minutes. 'It was rough hard hitting, for about half an hour,' wrote Thomas Gowing of the 7th Royal Fusiliers. 'It was a little piece of work well done.'[11] After a sharp but relatively short fight the defenders were finally driven out, the Russians scurrying back towards the safety of the Redan pursued by small bodies of enthusiastic British troops. These quickly found cover and, taking up good firing positions, began an exchange of fire with the defenders inside the Redan.

The capture of the Quarries had been achieved fairly easily, and had gone off better than had been expected, but if the British thought the fight was over they were sadly mistaken, for the Russians made a series of counter-attacks upon the Quarries which lasted throughout the night. 'We routed the enemy,' continued Gowing,

> but we had hard work to hold our own, for they came on repeatedly with strong columns, and tried to retake them [the Quarries] from us. The fighting then became desperate, the bayonet was freely used on both sides, but although the enemy were three and four to one, they shrank back, and although their officers tried to lead them on, they could not be brought to a determined rush . . . We ran short of ammunition, and then we were in a nice mess; we used stones as we did at Inkerman, and as soon as they came close enough, we went at them with that ugly piece of cold steel.[12]

It was desperate stuff at times and the confusion in the darkness can easily be imagined. 'All was darkness,' wrote Hamley of the artillery, watching from the British trenches,

> except where the sparks of musketry were scattered as from a forge; then, with a flash and roar, a shell would climb the sky, passing the ridge of clouds lying on the horizon, mingling confusedly amid the stars, and then rotating downwards, when, as it disappeared behind

> the parapet aimed at, for a moment all was dark, till the explosion lit up the work, making it stand out in transient red relief from the surrounding blackness; or a shell from a gun would traverse the ground at a low angle, the burning fuse rising and falling in graceful curves as it bounded on, till its course ended in a burst of flame. Sometimes a bugle sounded shrilly in the still night; once or twice there was a cheer; and these sounds and the rattle of the small-arms showed the chief part of the combat.[13]

The counter-attacks continued throughout the night and when the sun rose on 8 June the Russians were still throwing men forward, desperately trying to recapture the works, but without success. The British held on, largely due to the pluck and courage of the private soldier, and to men like Major Armstrong who continued to direct his men despite being badly wounded, and to Colonel Campbell, twice wounded, whose bugler cleverly kept up a continuous call that gave the impression of greater strength, much to the dread and bemusement of the Russians who were ultimately beaten by Campbell's 'phantom soldiers'. Having repulsed the last of the Russian attacks British engineers set to work with spade and shovel to turn the place first into a defensible position and then to turn it round and make it a place of attack.

The Allied attacks on the White Works, the Mamelon and the Quarries had been a complete success, but it had come at a price. The French posted losses of some 5,500 and the British 700, of whom forty-seven were officers. The Russians themselves lost 5,000, 3,500 of whom were lost during the Allied bombardment. Again, these casualties, sustained during an important but relatively minor operation in terms of scale and duration, were on a par with major actions not only in the Crimea but in previous wars, thus emphasising the intensity of the fighting. The casualties for the British themselves could have been far worse, for the Russians had laid hundreds of 'fougasses' over the approaches to the Quarries. These were, in effect, a form of anti-personnel mine, which exploded when trodden on. By sheer good fortune the British stormers passed over them without setting too many of them off. Colonel Reynell Pack, of the Royal Fusiliers, described how well over a hundred were dug from the earth during a truce on 9 June. He also went on to describe this new form of weapon:

> The fougasse is a square or oblong case, made of metal or stout timber bound with iron hoops; in either case it is filled with gunpowder or gunpowder enclosed in bottles, grenades or shells, or a mixture of both, or all three. The case itself is buried from an inch to a foot below the soil. Gutta-percha or other pipes, filled with gunpowder, spring from each end; these rise above the surface, and are connected

> together by a few inches of glass tubing, containing at one end some phosphoric preparation, and at the other a few drops of acid, or perhaps altogether loaded with detonating powder. This glass tube, when broken either by the foot getting entangled in it, or by the direct pressure of the foot, ignites the charge, and an unexpected mine is fired.[14]

Unfortunately, Major Armstrong, who commanded one of the storming parties, had the misfortune of being one of the few to be wounded by a fougasse, not during the attack but when he was being carried off afterwards.

> He was wounded early, placed on a stretcher, and was being carried off by four men, a fifth and sixth following, when one of his bearers, treading on a fougasse, the Captain [sic] and the whole party were blown up. His hands, which were hanging outside the stretcher on each side, were sadly scorched, and the men were more or less severely injured, yet fortunately no life was lost; after a long detention in hospital all ultimately recovered.[15]

Compared with the French attack, with its resulting high casualty figure, the British attack can be considered rather more successful, although their objectives were nowhere near as daunting. There is, however, a negative aspect to this, one which perhaps reflects the great problem with Raglan as a field commander. For while the French were flinging whole brigades against their objectives Raglan, no doubt fearful of heavy casualties, chose to employ what amounted to two under-strength battalions which was something of a gamble, no matter how calculated. The danger here was, naturally, that the British force might not be strong enough to take their objective, and afterwards, supposing them to have been successful, might not be strong enough after their efforts to be able to fend off Russian counter-attacks. At the Quarries, for example, hardly any reinforcements were sent forward and the men in possession of the Russian works had to hold out until morning when the Russians finally gave up. One wonders whether it would not have been easier to send forward overwhelming numbers to ensure a successful attack. As it turned out on this occasion Raglan got away with it. He would not, however, be so lucky in future.

The Russian reaction to the loss of the White Works, the Mamelon and the Quarries was one of dismay, mainly because it could have been prevented. Indeed, the Russians did not consider the French to have taken their objectives so much as they themselves had given them up, this as a result of the failure of men such as Zhabokritsky, who shed his responsibilities on the eve of battle. One Russian officer, Uhtomsky wrote somewhat sarcastically:

> The wise order from the headquarters of the Crimean Army ensured the Allies' success in taking the Volynsky and Selenghinsky redoubts and the Kamchatsky lunette. While waiting for their assault the commander of the troops on the Korabel'naia side, General Khrulev, was recalled and General Zhabokritsky, a Pole, who did not support the war with the French, was appointed instead. On 3 June, and by order of this general, the garrisons of the three redoubts were drastically reduced, and as a result the redoubts were effectively sacrificed, leaving the entire left-hand sections of the defence in a helpless position. When Zhabokritsky excused himself from the battle, General Khrulev was appointed to command again, but the reserves came too late and the battle was lost. Admiral Nakhimov personally took part in the fighting and was nearly taken prisoner.[16]

The Russian historian, Tarle, was even more scathing. 'If Menshikov and Dannenberg saved the Allies at Inkerman, Gorchakov, Kotsebu [a staff officer] and Zhabokritsky guaranteed their success with the capture of the Kamchatsky lunette and the two redoubts.'[17]

The loss of the works was a serious blow to the Russians as it opened the way for a direct assault on both the Malakhov and the Redan. But it could all have been much worse. One Russian officer thought that Sevastopol could have fallen when the Kamchatsky lunette was lost, for it came as a great shock.

> At 5 pm we saw a mass of the enemy troops, threatening our left flank, but the fire was so strong that the smoke and dust darkened everything and there was no opportunity to watch their further movements. Soon after, we were informed by telegraph that the enemy had taken two redoubts, the Volynsky and Selenghinsky. A terrible fight began there and many troops were sent there from the city. The rifle fire continued till morning. At 6 pm news came that the Kamchatsky lunette was also taken. All these events affected everybody even worse than news of the rising number of dead and a sudden change was noticed in the voices of our men. Fortunately, there was an unbroken line behind the Kamchatsky lunette; had there not been, Sevastopol would have fallen.[18]

Reaction in England to the successful attack on the Quarries was one of joy. Coming as it did so soon after the success of the expedition to Kerch the queen, government and public really did begin to think that the tide had turned in the Allies' favour. 'These news are glorious indeed', wrote Queen Victoria to Panmure. 'Would Lord Panmure telegraph, either direct to him or through Lord Raglan, to compliment General Pélissier in her name on the brilliant success and gallantry of the French troops.'[19]

Raglan himself was happy at last. After the trials of the winter and all of the personal attacks upon him, it was a pleasure for him to write to Panmure informing him of the condition of the British troops. 'The troops are in the highest spirits. Their joy was excessive when the fire opened, and they are anxiously desirous of attacking Sevastopol.'[20]

The mood in France was quite different, at least in Paris. The Emperor Napoleon was much vexed at Pélissier's apparent refusal to listen to his counsels. For months now Napoleon had advised against a possible costly assault and had advocated destroying the Russian army in the field. It was simple enough, so why wasn't Pélissier listening to him? Not even the news of the successful French attack on the White Works and the Mamelon could sooth him. Instead there was nothing. Not a word. Telegrams had been buzzing down the wire from Paris for weeks now, sending unwanted orders and advice, most of which Pélissier had managed to ignore, but when a telegram of congratulation was expected there was nothing but cold silence. But with no communications from Paris Pélissier was at least left to bask in the glory of the capture of the forts amidst great optimism for a swift and successful conclusion to the campaign. He would have to make the most of it, however, for within eleven days the Allies' optimism would be ruthlessly crushed by the defenders of Sevastopol.

NOTES

1 Jocelyn, Colonel Julian. *The History of the Royal Artillery (Crimean Period)* (London 1911), 361.
2 Lieutenant Colonel Nathaniel Steevens. *The Crimean Campaign with the Connaught Rangers, 1854–55–56* (London 1878), 232.
3 Kinglake, Alexander William. *The Invasion of the Crimea: Its Origin, and An Account of its Progress down to the Death of Lord Raglan* (London 1863), VIII, 90.
4 Jocelyn, *Royal Artillery*, 364.
5 Bazancourt actually states that the guns opened up at daybreak on 6 June. However, we are more inclined to follow Jocelyn, *Royal Artillery*, 365.
6 Tarle E V, *Krymskaya voina* (Moscow 1959), II, 354.
7 Some confusion continues to reign over the timing of the attack. For example, MacMunn (*The Crimea in Perspective*, 191) claims the attack took place at 6.30 am on 8 June. One of the most recent historians of the war, Trevor Royle has the attack beginning at 6.30 am on the 7th (*Crimea*, 391). The majority of sources, including Kinglake, give the start time as being 6.30 pm on 7 June.
8 'Bumagi Timiryazevyh. Iz zhurnala, vedennogo Timiryazevym na Kamchatskom lyunete s 27 marta po 26 maya', *Archives of the Sevastopol Museum of defence*, No.5141, VII.
9 Bazancourt, the Baron de (trans. by Robert Howe Gould). *The Crimean Expedition, to the Capture of Sebastopol. Chronicles of the War in the East* (London 1856), II, 353.

10 W Edmund M Reilly. *An Account of the Artillery Operations conducted by the Royal Artillery and Royal Naval Brigade before Sebastopol in 1854 and 1855* (London 1859), 111
11 Gowing, Timothy, *A Soldier's Experience, or A Voice from the Ranks* (Nottingham 1903), 123.
12 Ibid, 123.
13 Hamley, E Bruce. *The Story of the Campaign of Sebastopol* (London 1855), 243–4.
14 Colonel Reynell Pack, *Sebastopol Trenches, and Five Months in Them* (London 1878), 154.
15 Ibid, 153.
16 Chernovye zametki Uhtomskogo', *Archives of the Sevastopol Museum of Defence*, No.5120, IV.
17 Tarle, *Krymskaya voina*, II, 361
18 *Sbornik rukopisey . . . o Sevastopol'skoy oborone* (St Petersburg 1872–1873), III, 380.
19 Queen Victoria to Panmure, Douglas, Sir George and Ramsay, Sir George Dalhousie (Eds). *The Panmure Papers; being a selection from the correspondence of Fox Maule, second Baron Panmure, afterwards eleventh Earl of Dalhousie, KT, GCB* (London 1908), II, 229.
20 Raglan to Panmure, ibid, II, 229.

# CHAPTER TWENTY-ONE
# *'Confusion and Mismanagement'*

Soon after the capture of the White Works, the Mamelon and the Quarries the Allies were ready to go again. This time their objectives would be the big two: the Malakhov and the Redan. Kerch had put the Allies in good spirits and the capture of the forts in front of the Korabel'naia only served to increase their optimism. Nobody was under any illusions as to the magnitude of the task facing them but there was an air of expectancy in the Allied camps, born of the successes on 7 June. Thus, hopes were high not only for the capture of Sevastopol but for an early end to the war itself.

And yet Pélissier was beset by problems. Ever since he had assumed command from Canrobert in May things had taken a turn for the better as far as the course of the war was concerned – at least for the Allies – whilst Anglo–French relations had improved immeasurably. However, since the capture of the forts on 7 June he had been beset with internal problems, none of which were helped by the ever present shadow of the emperor which continued to hang over him. The emperor still clung to his grand designs on the field and appears to have been unaware of the manner in which Pélissier was disregarding his orders and waging war the way he alone saw fit. In previous wars it was easy for a commanding officer to avoid interference from governments or heads of state for it usually took days, even weeks, for despatches to arrive, by which time they were usually outdated and useless. Thus, a commander-in-chief of an army was able to direct his campaign largely according to his own design. The introduction of the telegram changed all that. True, it still allowed a wily general to ignore unwanted orders and blame it on the new technology, but even Pélissier could not stretch things much farther. He had used up most of his plausible excuses and was now being backed firmly into a corner. Of course, he could always turn a blind eye to the emperor's telegrams by citing a problem with the line but it was a ruse he could use only sparingly. Sooner or later he was going to have to face up to his responsibilities to his emperor.

Pélissier's mood was not helped by the deafening silence from Paris, for despite the successes of 7 June there was still no word of congratulation from the emperor. Finally, on 14 June, a whole week afterwards, a telegram arrived 'congratulating' Pélissier on the capture of the forts. However, it was hardly congratulatory and was more akin to an admonishment. Indeed, it simply left Pélissier with a flea in his ear. Praise was very faint indeed, and evidently reluctant, and only offered after Napoleon had checked the casualty figure. Napoleon then went on to remind Pélissier once more that the game could only be won in the field. Pélissier was exasperated by this and not even the congratulations of the English queen could cheer him.

In fact, the emperor's telegram of 14 June was one irritating telegram too many for Pélissier who decided that, rather than play hide and seek with Napoleon's wishes, he would stand up and deal with the problem once and for all. If the emperor wanted him to carry out his orders for a campaign in the field against the Russian Field Army then he, Pélissier, would be forced into choosing between a dereliction of duty and dishonour to himself, by which he would go against the wishes of his Allies. If he were not allowed to command the army as he saw fit, then he would be left with little choice but to resign. It would be, he said sadly but sternly, 'impossible à exercer de concert avec nos loyaux allies, à l'extrémité, quelquefois paralysant, d'un fil électrique'.[1] Pélissier's unenviable position was summed up by Kinglake, who witnessed at first hand his anguish.

> In maintaining these struggles against his sovereign, Pélissier, after all, was resisting the then actual 'law' of his country; and, although this strong and proud man was accustomed to mask his sense of pain by outbursts of uncontrolled rage, he suffered, bitterly suffered, under words of rebuke and command, all importing that the terrible sacrifices of men he had made and was going to make would receive no sanction in France from the constituted Chief of the State. Writing to the War Minister, he declared himself to be 'afflicted' by the course that the Emperor was taking against him.[2]

To say Pélissier was in bad odour in Paris was putting it mildly but there was no reply from Paris, just silence. Pélissier was left in command but left also with a sour taste in his mouth. It was a bad time for the French commander-in-chief, for not only was he having difficulties with Paris but there were now divisions within his own camp, largely of his own making, divisions which his rough, undiplomatically caustic manner did little to heal. Niel, it will be recalled, had already been put firmly in his place, which came as no great surprise to the other French generals, but when Pélissier turned on Beuret, commanding the 2nd Corps artillery, and then Mayran, whom he considered to have lost control of his men during the assault on the Mamelon, the fallout really began. Both of these fine generals were reduced to tears by the lashings of Pélissier's tongue.

This was bad enough, but the fact that it was done in the presence of other officers simply wasn't on. Mayran, in particular, felt most aggrieved at his treatment, and rightly so.

On 10 June Raglan and Pélissier held a council of war to discuss the coming assault on Sevastopol. They had grasped the initiative and were keen to maintain the pace of attack. The new plan was simply to follow up the gains made on 7 June by making a direct assault on both the Malakhov and the Redan. It was also agreed that an attack should be made on the 'town' front, to the west of Sevastopol. By attacking both fronts at the same time the more numerical Allies hoped not only to break into Sevastopol via the Flagstaff Bastion but also to prevent the Russians from concentrating on the Korabel'naia front where the main Allied attacks would go in. The attack itself would be preceded by a short but intensive bombardment which it was hoped would silence the Russian guns and literally bury the defenders. Finally, the two men had to agree a date. In the event it was obvious. Indeed, there seemed only one possible date; 18 June. It was, after all, the fortieth anniversary of the Battle of Waterloo. Surely the omen was there for all to see? The old rivalry between the two great nations would be buried once and for all amidst this ultimate demonstration of Anglo–French co-operation. Cynics, however, might have seen it in another light. Perhaps it would be another example of friction between the two. It certainly evoked mixed feelings for Raglan. After all, it would also be the fortieth anniversary of the loss of his right arm, which the French had torn from him at Waterloo.

The signs – and indeed the omens – were good, but on 15 June, just a few days after the meeting, the first of three major, and some would say fatal, changes were made by Pélissier prior to the attack. The first involved the fiery Bosquet, who had rather unwisely kept in his pocket a plan of the Malakhov, which he had found on the body of a Russian officer following the attacks on 7 June. The two men had been rivals in Algeria and had little time for each other. Bosquet made no secret of the fact that he considered Pélissier's plans for the attack on the Malakhov to be flawed. He had also, again rather unwisely, been sending despatches back to Paris criticising his commander. We can well imagine Pélissier's mood when he found out about the 'hidden' plan that Bosquet kept from him. Therefore, it came as no great surprise when Pélissier removed him from command of his corps and gave him instead a unit which was to make a diversionary move in the Chernaya valley. The timing of this could not have been worse, for it came just three days before the Allied assault on Sevastopol. It was a clumsy and unfortunate move.

Bosquet's replacement was General Regnault St Jean d'Angely who commanded the Imperial Guard. D'Angely was certainly no slouch but to be pitched into the attack at the head of the troops who were to make the most important attack of the war so far was asking much of him. Unlike

Bosquet, who 'had for so many months studied the minutest details, and directed the attacks',[3] he had no detailed knowledge of the ground, nor did he really know his staff or the troops he was about to send into action. It was a grave error on Pélissier's part and it could all have been so easily avoided. We may well imagine the French reaction at this great change, and it had nothing but an unsettling effect on both officers and men alike. But despite this late and obviously damaging move, there still remained an air of great optimism in the Allied camps and it was amidst these high hopes that the fourth Allied bombardment opened up against Sevastopol.

The sun had barely got up on the bright, clear morning of 17 June when the guns crashed and roared into life and soon it was barely possible to see Sevastopol through the clouds of grey smoke that hung over the Allied trenches. Over 600 British and French siege guns opened fire added to which was the fire of several Allied ships which managed to get within range of the Russian defences. The important guns were the 114 French and 166 British guns that opened up on the Korabel'naia defences. The fire from these guns was absolutely crucial if the Allies were to take their objectives, the Malakhov and the Redan. The Russians replied from this sector with 207 guns. Once again, the Russian positions were buried beneath piles of earth and debris that were thrown up after every heavy exploding shell. It was a crushingly devastating bombardment. Conditions inside the Malakhov and the Redan were awful. An immense quantity of heavy metal shells were raining down upon them, heaving great swirls of debris high into the air, and crushing the life out of many a brave Russian waiting anxiously to defend the bastions. It was the same old problem. So many Russian troops were packed together, waiting in the rear of the bastions, that it was impossible for the Allied guns not to strike home. The ramparts were smashed and pulverised again, as they had been for days on end in the past, whilst Russian guns were dismounted or simply blown apart by the Allied deluge. With such a weight of metal being poured upon the Russian positions it seemed to the watching Allies that nothing could possibly be left alive, many of them no doubt harbouring secret thoughts that when the time came for the assault, it might prove to be a walkover. 'At length we were close with the enemy; the dreary vigils in the trenches, the wearisome life on the heights, were to be at an end, and, with the assured capture of the city, a new era would dawn for us and Europe.'[4] It was a forlorn hope.

A short time after the opening of the bombardment Pélissier visited Raglan to confirm the timings of the assault planned for the next day. The Allied guns would resume firing at daybreak on 18 June and continue for two hours in order to flatten any last lingering resistance in the bastions and to destroy any repairs the Russians would have made during the night. The attack would then follow at 6 am. Both men were very pleased at the progress of the firing and were satisfied with the arrangements for the assault. If all went according to plan they hoped to be masters of both the Malakhov and the Redan the next day. The new spirit of co-operation soon began to vanish, however, when Pélissier announced to a less than happy Raglan that he was ditching the plan to attack the town front and that he was concentrating instead on the Korabel'naia. An obviously nervous Pélissier was apparently worried that his men, if successful, would scatter once inside the town and run amok, and by doing so risked being driven back by a Russian counter-attack. It was the same understandable fear that had so concerned Wellington prior to the assaults on the great Spanish fortresses forty years before. More important, however, was the fact that the Russian defenders would no longer be so thinly spread along the defences but would be able to concentrate in and around the Malakhov and the Redan. It came as quite a shock to Raglan but there was little he could do. The British Army was by far the junior partner and he was left with no choice but to go along with the revised plan of attack. Even so, it made good sense to concentrate on just the Malakhov and the Redan. After all, Burgoyne, long since gone, had correctly identified the Malakhov as the key to Sevastopol. The Allies would need every available man if they were going to capture it, and it seemed pointless to thin this number by sending men on what would effectively be a diversionary attack on the town front. No matter how irritated Raglan was there were good military reasons for the Allies concentrating on the Korabel'naia front. But if Raglan was disappointed by the change of plan worse was to follow, for there was still one great, fatal change to come.

The Allied plan involved a French attack on the Malakhov and its adjoining defences, after which the British would tackle the Redan. Both of these were formidable positions and few were under any illusions that it would be anything but hot work. But with the bombardment continuing to pound away there was no reason to doubt that the attack would be anything other than a success. The French troops destined to attack the Malakhov and the Little Redan were from the 1st Division under D'Autemarre, the 3rd Division under Mayran, and Brunet's 5th Division, while the Guard Division under Mellinet would be held as a reserve. The plan was straightforward enough. Mayran's division would march north along the Careenage Ravine before turning to their left and, climbing out, would attack No.2 Bastion – the Little Redan – and the works on its left, including No.1 Bastion. Brunet's division, meanwhile, would advance from the French 2nd parallel, moving forward to attack the Russian defences to the west of the same bastion. Finally, D'Autemarre's division would march along the Middle Ravine and, emerging from the head of it, would ascend the ridge on their right and attack the Gervais Battery, which sat alongside the western or right flank of the Malakhov. In all, the French had amassed some 6,000 men in each column for the coming assault, in addition to which there was the Imperial Guard Division in reserve. This was fifteen times the size of the British attacking force.

The British troops destined to attack the Redan were drawn from the 2nd, Light and 4th Divisions, all of whom were placed under the orders of Sir George Brown. These were to be divided into three columns, although one, a covering force under General Barnard, would play no part in the assault. The two attacking columns, which would attack both the right and left flank of the Redan, were commanded by General Sir John Campbell and the fiery Colonel Lacy Yea respectively. Campbell's column consisted mainly of a storming column of 400 men of the 57th Regiment, supported by a reserve of 800 men of the 21st Fusiliers and 17th Regiment. In addition, there were a hundred riflemen covering the column, as well as scores of others who were detailed to carry ladders, fascines and woolpacks. Yea's column was likewise covered by a hundred riflemen and consisted of 400 men of the 34th Regiment, with a reserve of 800 men from Yea's own regiment, the 7th Royal Fusiliers, and the 23rd and 33rd Regiments. Again, they were accompanied by men carrying ladders and woolpacks. There would, therefore, be no more than 1,600 men attacking the Redan – in addition to which some 2,000 British troops under General Eyre who was to make a diversionary attack on the left of the main storming columns – which was far too few given the strength of the objective. Was this because of Raglan's fear of heavy casualties? The French, on the other hand, would be attacking with 6,000 men in each column, compared with 400 in each British column.

Waiting for the Allies behind the shattered walls of the Malakhov and the Redan were thirty-five battalions of infantry, commanded and inspired by Totleben and Nakhimov, and backed up by thousands of sailors and marines, all of whom were intent on killing as many British and French soldiers as was humanly possible. Their guns were all but silenced but if the Allies thought it was their own bombardment that had done this they were flattering themselves. No, the Russian gunners had long since decided not to play at counter-battery fire. They were saving their precious and short supplies of ammunition for a far grimmer and deadlier game. The guns were withdrawn from the bastions wherever possible and dragged to safety, waiting for the inevitable assault whereupon they would be towed out to be unleashed against the attacking Allies.

17 June continued warm and sunny, the Allied gunners sweating profusely as they continued to pound away at the Russian positions. All who witnessed the bombardment thought it so destructive that the coming assault could not possibly fail.[5] Over 12,000 rounds were sent crashing into the Malakhov and Redan on 17 June, almost the same number being fired the next day. It was all quite incredible. Even Raglan thought little could stop the Allies now, particularly as the Russian fire

had apparently been virtually silenced. The firing slackened towards evening and when night drew a veil over the scene most of the Allied siege guns reduced their rate of fire and left the business to the huge mortars which continued to drop shell after shell onto their targets. It was a real ordeal for the people of Sevastopol, as one eye-witness later recalled.

> Bombs, shells and missiles came screaming into the city; the fire was so continuous that it seemed that there were no intervals. The shells fell on the city like hail! It was impossible to imagine a more terrible picture of destruction. All hell had suddenly broken loose and terrified the inhabitants who, up until this very day, had stayed in the city despite the terrible conditions. In the middle of the night there came a terrible howling from the women and children who suddenly ran from their houses and rushed to the harbour. Death, in its fullest sense, was feasting at that very minute. One shell landed in a workshop where the cartridges were made, and where there were up to one thousand shells which immediately exploded.[6]

One Russian officer, Captain P I Lesli, later recalled just how terrifying the bombardment was for the people inside the town.

> I'll never forget that night. Our work was terrible; at least 2,000 men were crowded together in a small space trying to make room to repair the damage done during the day's bombardment, and not a minute passed without an explosion. Do you believe me, my friends, when I say that an assault is much easier to bear in comparison with a bombardment; it is better than having to stand around to see how people can be killed by just one shell. I'll never forget an incident when an embrasure in my battery was smashed; I arrived there and ordered the gunners, all nine of them, to repair it as quickly as possible and then get the gun firing again. They began to work, and I watched them for some time. I then went to another gun, but I had hardly gone a few steps when I heard a cry; I turned back and, well, can you believe it? All the gunners were killed by one shell. In a word, I saw such scenes on that day that it is no wonder we grow old at the age of thirty![7]

As far as the Allies were concerned, all was going to plan. The guns inside both the Malakhov and the Redan had apparently been silenced and only a few tame shots were lobbed out throughout the night. The ramparts had been smashed and the ditches badly damaged and partially filled in places by debris from the bombardment. Another council of war had been held and the timings confirmed. The attack would begin at daybreak, which was about 6 am. All had been settled and orders issued to the various storming parties, telling them where and when to muster prior to the assault. Raglan himself was in good cheer, for the results of the bombardment could clearly be seen, even before darkness fell. There was every reason to hope for a successful attack the next morning. But, right on cue, and just when Raglan was settling in for the evening, a messenger arrived from Pélissier with a despatch, which the British commander-in-chief read with great dismay. Pélissier had decided to change the hour of attack from 6 am to 3 am. Furthermore, it would take place without the required preliminary bombardment. Raglan had already been irritated by Pélissier's refusal to make a simultaneous attack on the town front, and whilst the sacking of Bosquet was an internal matter for the French, it had done nothing to help the Allied cause. This last change of plan was the last straw. There were barely seven hours before the attack was due to begin. To bring it forward by three hours left Raglan with no time whatsoever to alter his own plans or to remonstrate with Pélissier, not that it would have done any good. Once again, Raglan found himself very much the junior partner, dancing to the tune played by the French.

The change of plan would, in the opinion of Somerset Calthorpe, cause 'nothing but confusion and mismanagement'. But there was nothing Raglan could do at this late hour. It is difficult not to sympathise with him, and despite universal blame – at least from the British – being put upon Pélissier afterwards for changing the hour of attack, the French did have one valid point. Their own attacking columns were far more numerous than the British columns and as such it would take far longer to get them into position. Moreover, the generals commanding the attacking divisions were concerned that it would not be possible to conceal such large formations from the Russians when the day of days dawned next morning. And so it was that they asked Pélissier to bring forward the attack by three hours. Interestingly enough, French histories claim that this decision was reached at the council of war, held on the evening of 17 June at which Sir Harry Jones, Raglan's chief engineer, was present, and yet no objections appear to have been made then.[8] The resulting confusion can best be imagined. Some units were not in position on time whilst others were in the wrong place. Some officers were left with no orders at all.

The decision to bring the attack forward by three hours was bad enough, but coupled with the fact that it would take place without the preliminary bombardment it all added up to a recipe for disaster. Everybody in the Allied camps knew full well how adept the Russians were at repairing and shoring up their defences during the hours of darkness, and even making new works. Indeed, it was not unusual for the Allies to wake up the morning after an apparent successful bombardment to discover to their dismay that the work they had reduced to a mass of earth and rubble the night before now resembled an earthwork once again. Despite the heavy bombardment of 17 June Raglan knew full well that Totleben and his people would be working frantically throughout the night to clear the debris from the ditches and to repair the ramparts, and that if the Allies attacked the next morning without artillery support they were inviting disaster. But it was too late to change things now. Pélissier's mind was made up, his generals were content, and no amount of complaining from the British was going to change things. Raglan's men would simply have to do their best in what would undoubtedly be a desperate business.

The French divisions destined to attack the Malakhov began to file into their start positions throughout the night of 17 June and by 2 am most of them were crammed into the trenches and into the support areas behind. The far less numerous British were in position by 2 am also. The forward move had been carried out with as little noise as possible, and save for the shuffling of so many thousands of pairs of feet and the odd rattle of tins here and there, hardly any noise was heard. Or at least that is what the Allies thought. The Russians, however, had picked up the movement early on. Indeed, the noise of Mayran's division moving through the Careenage Ravine had been picked up by men of the Briansky Regiment in a forward listening post and reported to the commanding officer of the sector, Prince Urusov. Word was quickly passed along the line and Khrulev had his men brought quickly and silently forward into the Korabel'naia to await the Allied attack. The Allied troops mustering and massing in their trenches opposite the Malakhov and the Redan did so in the belief that their attack would not only be successful and decisive, but they thought it would catch the Russians by surprise. Sadly, and fatally for them, the Russians were completely prepared, and even as French and British officers checked their watches and saw to last-minute arrangements the defenders were priming their guns and cocking their muskets in readiness for the assault.

At around 2 am on the morning of 18 June 1855, Raglan mounted his horse and with his staff set off for his chosen vantage point which was to be one of the mortar batteries in the 3rd parallel. There is every possibility that he cast his mind back forty years to the great day when, serving alongside the Duke of Wellington, he had fought in the last great European battle of the Napoleonic age to help defeat the very army with which he was about to co-operate in what would prove to be his last battle. However, given the late changes to the Allied plan of attack which had effectively been forced upon him by the French it is highly likely that he had thoughts for one thing only; the coming assault. It was an ungodly hour to start out; it was cold and extremely dark, and the party could only proceed at a walking pace. Nevertheless, the 66 year-old commander duly made his way to his position from where he hoped to get a good view of an Allied success. Pélissier, also, was not in a particularly good mood for he had been late setting off for his own observation post which was the right Lancaster gun battery on Victoria Ridge. Like Raglan he found the going very difficult in the extreme darkness and it was soon obvious that he would not make it to his chosen position in time to give the signal for the attack to begin, which was to be the launching of a rocket from the French lines.

Pélissier's new and very fragile arrangements needed only one error or accident to derail the whole attack, and sure enough fate intervened to provide the very thing. General Mayran, who would lead the attack on the Little Redan, was already somewhat nervous about the coming assault and was still feeling the effects of his public dressing down from Pélissier a few days earlier. He waited anxiously in the trenches with his men, continually looking to the heavens for the signal rocket to appear. Then, at about 2.30 am, it duly did. The trail of a rocket was clearly seen arcing its way across the inky black sky. His staff, however, told him it was not the signal, but was simply the trail of a shell fired from a trench. Mayran was not convinced. 'It *is* the signal, and besides, when we attack an enemy, it is better to be before the time than after.'[9] He then gave orders for the attack to begin, sending word to General Failly, whose men were formed behind him, to prepare to advance also. Then, sword in hand, Mayran turned to his men and in hushed tones gave the order, 'Marchez!' The attack was underway.

Mayran should have listened to his staff, for the fiery trail he had seen in the sky was, unfortunately, not the signal for the attack to begin. It was, after all, just another shell fired blindly into the night. It was the fatal error that put the nail in the Allied coffin once and for all. The Russians, of course, cared little, for they were fully expecting the attack anyway. Bugles blared and drums beat frantically inside the bastions, calling the men to their positions and nailing any lingering hopes the Allies might have had that the defenders would be caught by surprise. A I Ershov was a Russian artillery officer positioned inside the Little Redan. Just after the 'signal' rocket was fired he jumped up on to the parapet. The sight that greeted him as he peered through the gloom took his breath away.

> Along the entire length of the enemy trenches in front of the Malakhov Hill a dense black avalanche of enemy assault troops was pouring forward. Officers with drawn sabres were running ahead of their men. It was an amazing sight! It was as if these violent hordes had sprung from the earth at that very moment.[10]

Pélissier, meanwhile, still hurrying to his vantage point, was beside himself with anger. What on earth was going on? It was only 2.30 am. The attack was not supposed to start until 3 am. They were starting without him.

Pélissier wasn't the only one to be taken aback by the early start. The newly appointed commander of Bosquet's previous command, General D'Angely, was so surprised to hear the sharp crackling of musketry in front of him, and believing it was a Russian attack, that he sent an aide to find out what was happening. He was mortified when he was informed that it was Mayran attacking the Little Redan, for he was powerless to do anything. He was 'extremely distressed', and was torn by indecision. Should he set off the signal rocket now and by doing so set in motion the other attacking French columns, or should he wait for Pélissier to arrive and leave Mayran to go on unsupported? It was, as they say, 'a tough call'. In the event, D'Angely chose to adhere strictly to his orders, and thus nothing was done to support Mayran. Eventually Pélissier himself arrived, 'in the shadowy light of the dawn', shaking with anger and demanding to know what was happening. He at once gave the order for the rocket to be launched, which was duly done. It was nearing 3 am.

With the signal rocket having spluttered and fizzed into the air the French attack officially got underway, but the damage was already done. By the time the divisions of D'Autemarre and Brunet were scrambling out of their trenches Mayran was already dead. As he dashed forward at the head of his men the 53 year-old general was struck in the elbow by a piece of grape shot, but bravely refused to hand over command to Failly. Soon afterwards he was killed by another grape shot which struck him in the chest. His men continued to attack, advancing over open ground, scores of them being mown down by grape shot and by intense musketry from the walls of the Little Redan which was defended by the Vladimirsky Regiment. Commanding the 1st Voltigeurs of the Imperial Guard was Colonel Boudville, whilst close by him were the 2nd Léger, led by the young Lieutenant Colonel Paulze d'Ivoy. Both men were struck down, the former by several wounds to the body and the latter by a musket ball in the face. The premature attack on the Little Redan was going disastrously wrong. It was impossible to get anywhere near the Russian defences and instead the attacking French infantry took up firing positions to try to maintain some sort of fire against the defenders, whilst trying also to find some way of getting forward. In order to get the attack going again Pélissier sent forward four battalions of the Imperial Guard, under Generals Mellinet and Uhrich, but even these could do nothing. They found the Careenage Ravine blocked by wounded and cowering French soldiers and could do nothing themselves but merely add to the growing casualty list. They also found themselves under fire from Russian ships moored in the harbour at the head of the Careenage Ravine. These were able to fire straight down the ravine and cause terrible casualties to the French.

Meanwhile, Brunet and D'Autemarre had begun their respective attacks. Attacking from the French 2nd parallel, Brunet's division had to cover almost 800 yards, passing the Mamelon, before moving into open ground to reach their objective, which was the sector between the west face of the Little Redan and the Malakhov. The result can be easily imagined. No sooner had they advanced into the open than they felt the full fury of the Russian guns which were loaded with grape and round shot. Brunet himself was killed almost immediately by a piece of grape shot which struck him in the chest, whilst Lieutenant Colonel de la Boussinière, commanding the artillery, had his head shattered by a round shot. The attack continued, however, with scores of Frenchmen being mowed down like corn before the scythe, leaving hundreds stretched out on the ground. The French attacked in two columns, the right-hand column veering too much to their right, heading straight for the Little Redan itself rather than the walls to the left of it. Despite their heavy losses and the amount of lead and iron being flung at them the French carried on but could get no closer than a hundred yards from the work, whereupon those that were not running back to the safety of their trenches took shelter in a fold in the ground to wait for support. The left-hand column of Brunet's division fared little better. These also came under heavy fire from the moment they began their advance and although some of the leading elements reached the ditch in front of the walls to the west of the Little Redan they could get no farther. Many threw themselves down and opened fire on the Russians from the shelter provided by the broken ground. The majority simply ran back to their trenches despite the best efforts of their officers.

Away to the left of Brunet's attack, D'Autemarre had gone forward to attack the west face of the Malakhov and the adjoining Gervais Battery situated to the left of it. Unlike Brunet, D'Autemarre had the benefit of being able to advance under cover along the Middle Ravine, and thus was spared the trial which had cut the other French columns to pieces. D'Autemarre's leading troops were the 5th Chasseurs, commanded by Commandant Garnier, and these advanced steadily along the ravine whilst the terrible noise from the other attacks above echoed along it. Garnier knew full well what awaited him and his men once they advanced into the open but knew also that they, more than any other, stood a better chance of succeeding owing to the cover the ravine had afforded them so far. 'There must be amongst us,' he said to his men, 'neither first nor last; but all together!'[11] Then, sword in hand, he led his men up the slope towards the Gervais Battery.

Garnier's action was to be one of the great epics of 18 June 1855 and was by far the most successful. No sooner had he broken cover than he immediately found himself charging into the midst of a shower of grape and musketry which laid low over a hundred of his men, but he pressed on and was soon jumping into the ditch before the battery, his men breathlessly following close behind. Then, with a great cheer, they were up and over the ramparts and were grappling with the Russian gunners inside and with the Poltavsky Regiment that manned the work. There followed a furious struggle between the French and Russians, with men of both sides slashing furiously at each other with bayonets, swords, axes and anything they could lay their hands on. Garnier himself was bayoneted in the arm and wounded by a musket ball, but he continued to fight on until they had taken the battery. It was a tremendous achievement. More French troops came forward to consolidate the position, including eighty sappers who began to turn the defences around to meet the expected Russian counter-attack from within. Garnier, meanwhile, re-formed his men and started to push carefully forward into the Korabel'naia suburb, taking possession of some half-wrecked houses despite fierce opposition by the Russians. 'They kill each other hand to hand, they seize each others' throats, and dash stones at each other.'[12] Not long afterwards, Garnier was joined by part of the 19th Ligne, under Colonel Manèque, which had also fought its way into the suburb. At last the French seemed to have a foothold in Sevastopol, but the Russians were not to allow them this luxury for long.

With Mayran's attack having been totally repulsed, Khrulev was able to leave just a small force of defenders there whilst sending the bulk of the other troops down to the Gervais Battery. Russian troops, including the Sevsky and the rallied Poltavsky, were brought back as well as others from the Redan which meant that Garnier and Manèque were being squeezed out from the flanks. And when Vasil'chikov brought forward four battalions of the Eletsky Regiment, Garnier's fate was sealed. The small French force slowly began to be driven back, despite heroic efforts to hold on. It was vital that support was sent forward but none came, largely due to the fact that three of the four messengers sent back to D'Autemarre by Garnier requesting support were killed. The fourth, Lieutenant Potier, managed to reach D'Autemarre, but only after his jaw had been smashed by a musket ball.

By now Garnier was suffering from his fifth wound, but he continued to fight on, although he and Manèque could do nothing to stop the Russians driving them steadily back. At length they were pushed back into the Gervais Battery and then, finally, over its parapets and down into the ditch outside. Here, the French came under tremendous pressure, the Russian defenders lining the parapets above and shooting down into the dwindling band of Frenchmen below. Seeing just how badly wounded Garnier was Manèque sent him back to the French lines. Garnier had barely left when Colonel Sorbiers appeared at the head of the 26th Ligne, and together they and the 19th made one last desperate attempt to take the Malakhov but it was all in vain. They reached the ditch but were flung back by a murderous fire of musketry and grape, fired into them at virtually point blank range. Manèque himself was hit twice, once by a ball which broke two of his fingers and once by a bullet in the thigh. Even the reinforcement supplied by the 39th Ligne could not help force the defences of the Malakhov and after a frantic attempt to get to the ramparts they finally gave way and fell back.

Raglan and his staff, and every other British soldier gathered either in the trenches or on the hills behind had watched the French attack anxiously. Initially, it was impossible to see anything. It was, after all, barely 2.30 am when the attack began. All they could see were the flashes of hundreds of muskets that flared and fired in the darkness, the explosions from scores of fougasses scattered over the approaches to the Malakhov, and the tongues of flames that lashed out from the muzzles of the Russian guns as they fired into the French columns. The noise of battle was clear enough; bugles blared, men cheered and shouted, there were the screams of the wounded and of those being killed and then there was the crackle of muskets and the crump of artillery. But as the attack wore on so the light began to improve, and soon the desperate struggles of the French could be seen through the dim grey light of dawn. It was a sight that shocked everyone. From the Little Redan in the distance to the Malakhov away to their right, the British troops could see the dark masses of French troops huddling together in the ditches or in dead ground and behind rocks. Hundreds more were limping and crawling back to the safety of their own lines. More still ran back. Even more lay dead and dying.

It was against this awesome backdrop that Raglan was faced with a mighty dilemma. The signal for the start of the British attack on the Redan was to be the occupation of the Gervais Battery by the French. Once secured, Raglan would launch his proud redcoats against the Redan, secure in the knowledge that at least they would not be taken in flank by Russian fire from this quarter. But with the French seemingly flung back at all points he now had to decide whether it was worth sending his men forward on what would surely be an impossible mission. What was he to do? If he launched the attack he knew he would be sending his men to almost certain disaster, but if he held them back he would face the backlash from his French allies and would be forever accused of turning his back upon them. Even Raglan himself was coming under fire from Russian grape shot. Indeed, Sir Harry Jones was wounded in the neck while talking to him, and others close by were also wounded. The whole Allied plan was tumbling into tragic farce, and from a military standpoint there was only one sensible decision to make; to stop the attack. Only someone bound by an overwhelming sense of decency and great loyalty to their allies would send their men on such a foolhardy errand. Unfortunately for the waiting British columns Raglan was just such a man. The attack would go ahead.

The British soldiers waiting nervously in the Quarries and in the adjoining lines were not the men of the Alma. Nor were they the men of

Inkerman. These heroes had long since gone, taken by sickness and by cholera or the wicked winter weather. The once proud regiments that had fought in the previous September, October and November had been so reduced in number as a result of the great battles and by the winter, that they were barely recognisable as those who had so bravely stormed the Great Redoubt on 20 September or had defended The Barrier on 5 November. There were of course still plenty of good, solid veterans about but by and large the regiments were now full of 'Johnny Newcomers' and young boys, many of whom had barely learned to shave, let alone stick a bayonet into the body of a burly Russian if need be. But at least they could count on the experience of the men who would lead them, Lacy Yea and Sir John Campbell, both of whom were 'enjoying' what would prove to be the final moments of their lives.

It was with great anguish, and more from a sense of loyalty to his allies than any great belief in probable success, that at 3.15 am[13] on 18 June, the fortieth anniversary of Waterloo, Raglan ordered the signal rockets to be fired for the commencement of the British attack on the Redan.[14] The whole business lapsed into confusion almost immediately. On the left of the British attack Sir John Campbell's column had just over 450 yards to cover before they reached their target, the west face of the Redan. In the event, the men had barely tumbled from their trenches before they began to drop, struck down by Russian artillery. It was all a mad scramble; the men were encumbered with ladders, woolsacks, fascines and other bundles of necessary equipment to be used in getting across the ditch and into the Russian works. The men were also wearing their knapsacks. In Wellington's day, whenever the men were required to undertake an assault on a fortress, they were allowed to leave their packs behind and go in with just the minimum of required equipment, but not here. And if the ladder parties and those carrying other equipment had trouble getting out of the trenches, the actual storming parties themselves had equally difficult problems, for hundreds of British soldiers, not required for the assault, had crept out of their camps and had filled the trenches to watch, leaving regiments like the 57th to pick their way round in the open before beginning their attack. It all added up to unfortunate and unnecessary delays.

Whilst the ladders parties, the men carrying woolsacks, and the covering parties of riflemen struggled out in front, the main storming column finally emerged behind them. The 57th, under their commanding officer, Colonel Shadforth, advanced into the open making for the Redan and immediately came under fire from Russian artillery. One by one the riflemen, scurrying from position to position in front of the main column, began to drop as grapeshot swept the ground, seeking out targets. Leading the main column itself was 47 year-old Sir John Campbell who went into the attack, 'glowing with that warlike ardour that comes with the blood of the Scots'.[15] Unfortunately, Campbell had covered only a few of the 450-odd yards that would lead him to his objective before he was killed. The column was then placed in the very capable hands of Colonel Shadforth, but barely had he given his first word of command than he too was stretched out on the turf, killed by a Russian gun. The engineer officer chosen to guide the column, Lieutenant Murray, was also killed. Everything was going horribly wrong. Some Russian accounts claim that the British troops threw away their ladders the moment they got out of the trenches, and that so many British officers were killed whilst out in front, trying to inspire their men by example, that the young men following them were wracked with indecision and quickly lost heart.

With both Campbell and Shadforth dead, command of the column now passed to Lord West, who was with the reserve back in the trenches. He was too far back at the moment to influence the outcome of the attack but two other officers, Major Inglis, of the 57th, and Colonel Warre, were at least trying to do something, but with little effect. The 57th and what was left of the protective screen of riflemen had seen the apparently impassable abattis, a barrier formed of sharpened branches of trees that lay eighty yards in front of the Redan, and decided to avoid this by skirting along the top of the Vorontsov Ravine to pass by its right flank, after which they would be able to attack the western face of the Redan. At this point they were joined by scores of other British troops from various other regiments – 'lawless intruders' as Kinglake called them – who had come forward without orders to join the attack. Warre and Inglis duly led this ever-dwindling band past the abattis, all the time under a vicious fire from the Briansky Regiment inside the Redan and, in particular, from the guns of the Artakov battery, which lay in the re-entrant angle of the west face of the Redan. Despite the storm of shot being poured on them the British stormers got to within thirty yards of the Redan's ditch before they were brought to a halt, whereupon Warre had them lie down and take cover as best they could using the folds in the ground and the debris that lay scattered about. From here they were at least able to hit back and fire upon the embrasures but there was little chance of any further progress. In the meantime, Inglis was sent back to request reinforcements.

Whilst Warre and his men clung desperately to their hard-won position Lord West busied himself trying to pull together reinforcements to go forward in support, but it was all in vain. Although many men did go forward including what remained of the ladder party under the future General Sir Gerald Graham, then just plain Lieutenant Graham of the Royal Engineers, it proved impossible to get others to leave the safety of their trenches. 'In vain the officers stood up amid the iron shower and waved their swords; in vain the engineers returned to bring up the supports; the men could not be induced to quit the parapets in a body. Small parties of half a dozen, or half a score, ran out only to add to the slaughter.'[16] The men knew full well what awaited them on the other side and Lord West simply could not induce them into 'climbing over from Life to Death'.[17] Even urgent pleas to Sir George Brown for reinforcements fell on deaf ears. Instead of sending reinforcements Brown simply told West to re-form his column and assault again, something which was out of the question. Thus, Warre was left stranded, under fire, being showered with grape, musketry and hand grenades, and unable to get forward. Faced with such a hopeless position he reluctantly ordered his men to return as best they could to the trenches, all the time under fire. Nothing whatsoever had been achieved, save for the slaughtering of almost half of Campbell's column.

Whilst Campbell's men were being cut to pieces on the left, the right British column, under the fiery Lacy Yea, of the Royal Fusiliers, was faring little better. There were few braver men in the British Army than Lacy Yea. There were few more unpopular men either. His rough, tough attitude was admired by many but loathed by even more, but in such a situation like this he was just the sort of fighter that was needed. Like Campbell's column, Yea's was preceded by a screen of riflemen and 180 soldiers and sailors whose duty it was to carry forward the ladders and woolsacks which would be used to get over the abattis and in and out of the ditch beyond. The 34th Regiment provided the four hundred men of the storming column, backed up by eight hundred men of the 7th and 23rd Fusiliers and the 33rd Regiment. Guiding the column was Lieutenant A'Court Fisher, of the Royal Engineers.

Like Campbell's column away to their left, Yea's men came under heavy fire as soon as they left the relative safety of their trenches. Grape shot whistled through the air, round shot came bouncing in to smash and maim, and when they got within range the defenders opened up with a blaze of musketry. It was fearful stuff. Even Raglan, who had seen more than a few heavy bombardments during his career, was moved to write: 'I never had a conception before of such a shower of grape as they poured upon us from the Russian works.'[18] Nevertheless, Yea pressed on, sword in hand at the head of his column, until the leading elements emerged from the storm to find their way blocked by the abattis, eighty yards in front of the ditch. The future Field Marshal Sir Evelyn Wood, then just a young midshipman, was one of those brought up by the abattis.

> The obstacle was in itself about four feet thick and from four to five feet high, the stoutest portions of the wood being from six to eight inches in diameter. There were one or two places where we could have pushed through one man at a time, but even then, after crossing the open space intervening between the abattis and the ditch there was a still more serious obstacle. The ditch, 11 feet deep and some 15 feet broad, was in itself a difficulty to overcome; but 26 feet above its

> bottom, there was the huge earthen rampart, on which the Russians were standing ready for us.[19]

Riflemen searched desperately for a way through, as did the men of the 34th when they arrived at the barrier. A'Court Fisher noted with dismay that the Allied bombardment had done nothing at all to damage the abattis. There were, however, one or two places where men could get through, or crawl under the abattis, but Russian riflemen quickly marked these down as their killing ground, and concentrated their fire upon them.[20] The young engineer officer was soon joined by Yea, who was stalking the abattis, trying to see whether there was a way through. A'Court Fisher told him who he was and asked whether he should advance. Yea did not even have the time to answer, for he was suddenly flung backwards, struck in the head and stomach by grape shot and killed instantly. Thus, both of the attacking British columns had lost their commanding officer. Timothy Gowing, of the 7th Fusiliers, was in the thick of the action.

> At another signal we went off at a rapid pace, with our Colonel in front, sword in one hand and revolver in the other; they let us get well out into the open so that we had no cover, and then, reader, such a fire met us that the whole column seemed to melt away. Still on we went, staggering beneath the terrible hail. Our Colonel fell dead, our Adjutant the same, and almost every officer we had with us fell dead or wounded, but still we pressed on until we were stopped by the chevaux-de-frise, and in front of that our fellows lay in piles. We were there met with a perfect hell of fire, at about fifty yards from us, of grape, shot, shell, canister, and musketry, and could not return a shot. Our men could not advance and would not retire, but were trying to pull down the barrier of chevaux-de-frise. We might just as well have tried to pull down the moon.[21]

It was complete chaos at the abattis, with scores of British troops trying to find a way past it. Another engineer officer, Jesse, came up to A'Court Fisher and asked what was to be done. No sooner had the words left his lips than he too was shot in the head and fell dead. It was a nightmare. To his immense credit, A'Court Fisher remained at the abattis and tried to gather together as many troops as he could to make another assault but there were so few survivors it was a pointless exercise. Like Warre away to his left, A'Court Fisher withdrew the survivors to a position which afforded some protection from the deadly Russian fire and there await reinforcements. It speaks volumes for the unsatisfactory arrangements that a junior engineer officer was now in command of regular British infantry at the most important place on the battlefield. There was simply no other officer there to assume command. A'Court Fisher's small band was dwindling by the minute. They were just eighty yards from the ditch of the Redan but it was impossible to advance, and with no reinforcements coming from the British lines A'Court Fisher was left with no other option but to order his men to retreat, which was done under a heavy fire from the jubilant Russians. In fact, many survivors were already running, panic-stricken to their own lines having thrown away their arms and equipment to assist them in their flight. In the chaos, more than a few British officers and men found themselves cut off from their own lines, as one Russian soldier later recalled.

> One English officer was leading his men forward, running towards our battery, and trying to keep their lines in check in order to try their luck against the parapet of our fortification. But his efforts were in vain. Everybody ran away and he was left behind them! 'Boys,' the commander of the Okhotsky regiment, Colonel Malevsky cried, standing on the banquet of the Brylkin battery. 'Look! That officer has become detached.' 'Yes, he has, sir!' several happy voices answered. A soldier of the 7th Chasseur Company, Gladikov, rushed to the embrasure, and quickly reached the Englishman, struck him in the neck with the butt of his rifle, disarmed him and dragged him back to the bastion. The English soldiers nearby began to fire on them. A small ditch was not far from them and so Gladikov dragged the Englishman over to it, pushed him down and jumped down himself, but at that very moment he was wounded in his leg with two bullets while the English officer was wounded in his head. Gladikov told the Englishman that he needed to be dressed, took a scarf from his neck and dressed the Englishman's head. But he had nothing to dress his own wounds with and in any case he had no time to do it. Unable to climb up the ditch, which was exposed to English fire, Gladikov held the Englishman with one hand and began to demolish the lodgement with the other one in order to get inside, but as soon as they got over the semi-demolished parapet, a ball from an enemy field gun, which was probably aimed at them, hit the lodgement and covered them both with a heap of stones whilst Gladikov was badly cut up and bruised in his shoulder and arm. Our guns replied to the enemy with several balls. Meanwhile, Gladikov brought the half dead, worn out Englishman directly to the regiment commander.[22]

The British officer was badly wounded but survived his capture. The only bright spot on an otherwise very black morning was the success achieved by General Eyre who, advancing along the Picket House Ravine with a brigade of around 2,000 men, consisting of the 18th, 38th and 44th Regiments, with the 9th and 28th in reserve, managed to drive off units of the Iakoutsky and Tomsky Regiments who were holding the rifle pits and a small cemetery at the head of the ravine. Despite coming under heavy fire from the Peresyp and Barrack Batteries Eyre's men continued to press on, their ranks thinning from enemy fire, capturing some houses right beneath the Barrack Battery. The houses were quickly reduced to rubble as a result of the heavy fire opened upon them by the Russians, but Eyre remarkably continued to hold on until about 5 pm when he withdrew his men, handing over the captured ground to the engineers. It was the only successful action on an otherwise fearful day, but it had come at a tremendous price. Of the 2,000 or so men led into the Picket House Ravine no fewer than 562 were either killed or wounded, thirty-one of whom were officers including Eyre himself who was badly wounded in the head, but lived to tell the tale.

By about 6 am it was all over. For the Allies it had been a bloody shambles; for the Russians a complete triumph. The Russians admitted some 1,500 casualties on 18 June, including Totleben who received a leg wound that put him out of the remainder of the campaign. A further 4,000 were lost the previous day during the bombardment, which bears testament once more to the price they were prepared to pay for keeping their men so concentrated in readiness in rear of the threatened bastions. The French lost some 3,500 killed and wounded, including Generals Mayran and Brunet, both of whom were killed. The British paid for their folly at the Redan with 1,505 killed, wounded and missing, including Campbell, Yea and Shadforth, all of whom were killed.

Far from cementing Anglo–French relations and burying the ghost of Waterloo once and for all, the failure of the attack on 18 June only served to heighten tensions and widen the divisions. Notwithstanding the fact that their own attacks had failed elsewhere, the French felt that they might have succeeded in exploiting their partial success in the Gervais Battery had the British carried off their attack on the Redan with a bit more aggression. There were veiled criticisms in the French camp and blatantly open ones. 'The men [the British] were unwilling to leave the trenches, and their officers had to drive them out . . . by deeds of the most extreme severity.'[23] Another French officer complained bitterly: 'The English came to grief on the Redan; their army is now like a cannon-ball chained to our feet; we should arrange to leave them out of the reckoning so far as the trenches are concerned.'[24] Even the Russians were aware of the arguments between the Allies.

> The English are being blamed by the French for not carrying into action fascines when they assaulted. Frankly, on a field littered with dead English bodies, their arms and ammunition, I didn't see any fascines, but what benefit could they have been when nobody even reached the ditch of the 3rd bastion [the Redan], and the bravest fell no farther than the abattis in front of the salient angle?[25]

Naturally, everyone in the Allied camps was extremely distressed and disappointed at the failures of 18 June, and although it was not the time to point the finger of blame it did not stop all parties from doing so. Even the broken-hearted Raglan could not refrain from playing the blame game.

> The determination of General Pélissier not to attack the Russian right, that is, the town of Sevastopol, whereby the enemy were enabled to concentrate a larger force in the faubourg of Korabel'naia was very unfortunate. The change of the hour of attack was also a great mistake. General Pélissier said here, on Sunday morning, that it was desirable that the Artillery should have a couple of hours after daylight the following morning to destroy any repairs the Russians might have made in the night . . . The greatest mistake is the partial attack of Sevastopol. If the attack had been general, the enemy's troops must have been scattered, and there could have been no great massacre there, and if confusion on their part had ensued, total defeat would have been the consequence; whereas, had we succeeded yesterday [18 June], the town itself would have remained to have been assaulted.[26]

He also admitted to launching his attack partially to appease his Allies.

> I always guarded myself from being tied down to attack at the same moment as the French, and I felt that I ought to have some hope of their success before I committed our troops; but when I saw how stoutly they were opposed, I considered it was my duty to assist them by attacking myself . . . Of this I am quite certain, that, if the troops had remained in our trenches, the French would have attributed their non-success to our refusal to participate in the occasion.[27]

It is a sad reflection on the whole situation, therefore, that Raglan only committed his troops to the attack to avoid upsetting the French. As one historian noted dryly:

> [Raglan] still retained one powerful trump card; he had all along (knowing the Redan to be untenable without the Malakhov) reserved to himself the timing of the British assault. If all went well with the French, what reason was there to suppose the British would not succeed? If the French failed, a British attack would be quixotic and useless. Unhappily, it was a card Raglan was too much of a gentleman to play.[28]

The French themselves were not entirely blameless. In fact, the errors had all been theirs from the word go. Pélissier's behaviour towards his own officers, his decision to sack Bosquet and the poor timing of it, his abandonment of the plan to attack the town front of Sevastopol, his policy of attacking without a prior bombardment and, finally, the very late change of start time, all added up to a recipe for total disaster. And then, of course, there was Mayran and his unfortunate error in mistaking the stray shell for the signal rocket. The late decision by Pélissier left the British with no time to alter their own arrangements for the assault. Major Patullo, of the 30th, summed up the problems this created when he said that,

> many of the details were made out and superintended by staff men who (you will hardly believe it) had never been in the trenches before and I hardly need tell you that it needs considerable experience of the trenches to move men in and about them; the dullest subaltern who daily does duty there would have made a better commander than the shrewdest staff man without experience of the ground.[29]

But the question should be asked whether, once the decision to attack had been made, Raglan committed enough troops into battle. The answer was almost certainly no. Thus, both attacking British columns were left to fend for themselves once their assaults had broken down. It also had a knock-on effect, in that they were unable to support the French who had actually made it inside the Gervais Battery. True, this may well have increased their casualties but it might also have enabled them to get over the abattis and into the Redan. We will never know.

While the finger of blame was being pointed in the British and French camps the Russians were enjoying their great victory. After the loss of the Mamelon and the crushing Allied bombardments the total repulse of the Allied assaults came as a huge boost to their morale. It was needed too, for when the Allied guns opened up yet again after the failed assault many of the soldiers, unable to stand the bombardment any longer, ran to the roadstead and fought over the small boats that would take them to Severnaia, the north side of Sevastopol. Indeed, despite the victory there were still those who believed that when the Allies attacked again they would certainly succeed. In the end, it was largely through the efforts and exhortations of the priests that fresh hope was instilled in the hearts of the waverers.

The people and garrison in Sevastopol had long since felt abandoned by the main Russian Field Army which had done little to come to their aid. They had now come to believe that their only real salvation lay in their ability to withstand the Allied assaults. 18 June had proved they could do it and gave them every confidence that they would be able to do so again when called upon. Needless to say, the news of the Russian victory was received in St Petersburg with immense joy. It was such a change to read news of a Russian success after so many depressing reports had come from the Crimea. The czar responded by heaping rewards upon the leading figures involved in the defence. Vasilchikov, Totleben, Khrulev, Urusov, Semyakin, Osten-Saken and, of course, Nakhimov, were all handsomely rewarded, although Nakhimov, who received an increase in pay, typically responded by saying he would rather have received more powder than be given a pay rise. Most welcome of all, of course, was the victory itself. The Russians had defeated the Allies once and now had no reason to doubt they could do it again, and although powder was short, confidence was high, even if the resumption of the Allied bombardment on 18 June only served to remind them of the great problems they continued to face.

Nobody was more distressed at the failure of the attack on 18 June than Lord Raglan. The British commander-in-chief always had the interests of his men at heart and was devastated to see so many of them cut down before the Russian defences at the Redan. It affected him tremendously. From a strategic viewpoint the failure of the Allied attack, and in particular the British effort, was a real setback to him. It was also a personal blow, for having spent virtually all of his army life serving in the shadow of the great Duke of Wellington he felt almost obliged to deliver the kind of glorious victories his old chief had done on countless occasions. But it was not to be, and the fact that the disaster came on the fortieth anniversary of Waterloo only served to compound his misery. Nevertheless, the Allied guns were back in action before the morning of 18 June was out and the bombardment got underway once more. No matter how distressing the Allied defeat the siege had to go on.

The failure of the attack on 18 June was just the latest in a series of crippling setbacks that would have made many a younger man buckle, let alone a man of 66 years. Raglan had seen his army ravaged by cholera, had seen them storm the heights of the Alma and defy Dannenberg at Inkerman. He had witnessed the destruction of the Light Cavalry Brigade and had watched, virtually helpless, whilst his army suffered the traumas of a wicked winter. He had come under personal attack from those in England, including the queen herself, and had endured savage criticism from the English press. He had also battled and fought against the secret designs of the French, particularly Canrobert, and the well-meaning but ultimately frustrating and exasperating Pélissier. The slaughter of his men before the Redan was the final straw. Those close to him noticed a great change in his appearance; it was the look of a man who had not long to live. On 24 June his close friend and confidant, the adjutant general, Sir James Estcourt, died after contracting cholera three days earlier. Raglan too was now ill, too ill in fact to attend the funeral of his great friend on 25 June. By the afternoon of 28 June Raglan was at death's door, and his staff began to gather at his headquarters. General Airey, the author of the fatal order that had sent the 'valiant lunatics' to destruction at Balaklava, heard his last words. 'Sir, you are very ill,' said Airey, quietly stating the obvious. 'Whom would you like to see?' he asked, to which Raglan whispered feebly, 'Frank'. This was Lady Raglan's nephew, Lord Burghesh. He then lapsed into unconsciousness. Burghesh duly arrived, but although Raglan briefly regained consciousness he never spoke to his nephew. 'We went in,' wrote George Paget in his journal, 'and remained with him till all was over, his death taking place about 7 pm, calm and peaceful.'[30]

The following morning the commanders of the Allied armies and the admirals of the fleets came to pay their respects. Canrobert came of course, but the most affecting scene involved Pélissier, the man who had done so much to get the Allied campaign back on track but who had so upset arrangements for the attack on 18 June. Pélissier stood at the foot of Raglan's bed for over an hour, crying like a child. Meanwhile, the news of Raglan's death spread throughout the Allied camps and struck home like a thunderbolt. It was a great blow for Raglan was more of a father figure than a warrior. Timothy Gowing of the Royal Fusiliers likened it to the passing of a close relative than the commander of the army. But that was the problem. Virtually all of the tributes that were made at the time, and have been ever since, only serve to emphasis Raglan's reputation as being a true English gentleman, a man of great honour, dedicated to the service of his country, and the man who, more than any other, preserved the often fragile alliance with the French. But few, if any, could actually bring themselves to add Raglan's name to the list of great generals Britain has produced over the years.

On the warm and sunny afternoon of 3 July the staffs of the Allied armies gathered at Raglan's headquarters and waited in respectful silence as his coffin was brought out, draped in a Union Jack, and placed on top of a 9-pounder gun carriage. Then, as the carriage trundled off towards the port of Kazatch the bands struck up the *Dead March*, whilst drums slowly beat out a muffled roll. The route was lined by men from all British regiments. The French turned out too. Even the Russians stopped firing for the day, as if by way of paying their own respects to their adversary. The body was then taken aboard Raglan's yacht, *Caradoc*, and whilst the Allied guns barked out their final tribute the yacht steamed slowly out of the harbour and before long was slipping silently over the horizon. Raglan was gone.

NOTES

1 'It will be impossible to exercise in concert with our loyal allies, at the sometimes paralysing extremity of an electric wire.'
2 Kinglake, Alexander William. *The Invasion of the Crimea: Its Origin, and An Account of its Progress down to the Death of Lord Raglan* (London 1863), VIII, 133.

3 Bazancourt, the Baron de (trans. by Robert Howe Gould). *The Crimean Expedition, to the Capture of Sebastopol. Chronicles of the War in the East* (London 1856), II, 274.
4 Hamley, E Bruce. *The Story of the Campaign of Sebastopol* (London 1855), 258.
5 History was certainly repeated on 1 July 1916, when similar optimistic thoughts were expressed before a similarly tragic British assault.
6 Dukhonin N 'Pod Sevastopolem v 1853–1856 godah', *Russkaya starina*, October 1855, 90.
7 'Pis'ma kapitan-leytenenta P.I. Lesli', *Sbornik rukopisey . . . o Sevastopol'skoy oborone* (St Petersburg 1872), II, 376–80.
8 See for example Bazancourt, *The Crimean Expedition*, II, 382.
9 Ibid, II, 385.
10 Ershov A I, *Sevastopol'skie vospominaniya* (St Petersburg 1858), 207–9.
11 Bazancourt, *The Crimean Expedition*, II, 395.
12 Ibid, II, 396.
13 W Edmund M Reilly. *An Account of the Artillery Operations conducted by the Royal Artillery and Royal Naval Brigade before Sebastopol in 1854 and 1855* (London 1859), 121.
14 Sources differ as to whether it was Raglan or Sir George Brown, ostensibly commanding the assault, who gave the order for the rockets to be fired. Certainly Reilly, who actually fired the rockets, said he was given the order to fire by Brown. The responsibility, however, was clearly Raglan's.
15 Kinglake, *Invasion of the Crimea*, VIII, 171.
16 Hamley, *Campaign of Sebastopol*, 260.
17 Kinglake, *Invasion of the Crimea*, VIII, 178.
18 Raglan to Panmure, Douglas, Sir George and Ramsay, Sir George Dalhousie (Eds), *The Panmure Papers; being a selection from the correspondence of Fox Maule, second Baron Panmure, afterwards eleventh Earl of Dalhousie, KT, GCB* (London 1908), I, 246.
19 Wood, General Sir Evelyn. *The Crimea in 1854 and 1894* (London 1896), 321.
20 This sad episode will certainly strike a chord with students of the First World War, particularly the Battle of the Somme when, on 1 July 1916, British infantry were mown down whilst searching for gaps in the undestroyed German wire, much in the same way that British infantrymen were killed whilst searching for gaps in the abattis in front of the Redan.
21 Gowing, Timothy. *A Soldier's Experience, or A Voice from the Ranks* (Nottingham 1903), 125–6.
22 *Sbornik izvestiy, otnosyashchihsya do nastoyashchey voyny, book 32* (St Petersburg 1855), 469. Dated: Sevastopol, June 6, 1855.
23 Colonel Desaint, quoted in Vulliamy, C E *Crimea: The Campaign of 1854–56* (London 1939), 287.
24 Moré de Pontgibaud, ibid, 287.
25 *Sbornik izvestiy, otnosyashchihsya do nastoyashchey voyny, book 32* (St Petersburg 1855), 485.
26 Raglan to Panmure, *Panmure Papers*, I, 245.
27 Raglan to Panmure, *Panmure Papers*, I, 246.
28 Pemberton, Baring. *Battles of the Crimean War* (London 1962), 196.
29 Ibid, 197.
30 Paget, Lord George. *The Light Cavalry Brigade in the Crimea* (London 1881), 104.

# CHAPTER TWENTY-TWO

# *'Castles in the Air'*

The death of Lord Raglan brought about yet another change of command in one of the armies fighting in the Crimea. Already the French had lost Saint-Arnaud to cholera, whilst Canrobert had been simply replaced of his own accord, his role being taken by Pélissier. The Russians had lost two of their heroes, Kornilov and Istomin, to Allied shell fire, and had seen Menshikov replaced as commander-in-chief by Gorchakov. Raglan was not to be the last major casualty of the war, however.

When the British army landed in the Crimea in September 1854 it did so with Sir George Cathcart holding the so-called 'dormant commission', under which he was to assume command in the event of anything untoward happening to Raglan. Although Sir George Brown was nominally the second-in-command of the British army the gifted Cathcart was the government's preferred choice, but as Cathcart had been killed at Inkerman it was all academic anyway. Instead, the very ordinary, polite and somewhat retiring 63 year-old Sir James Simpson assumed command. Like Raglan, he had last seen major action during the Peninsular War and Waterloo campaign. In fact, he was badly wounded at Quatre Bras, two days before Waterloo. Since then he had served in India under Sir Charles Napier, but that was about it. He had, it will be remembered, been sent out to the Crimea by the government in the wake of the winter troubles to weed out the rotten eggs from Raglan's staff but was obviously too polite to do so and instead simply confirmed that all was well with the army personnel. Simpson was an unfortunate choice as commander-in-chief – upon visiting the Crimea the Duke of Newcastle called him a raving lunatic – as he himself was reluctant to assume the position. In the event, he was to remain in command for just four months before he tendered his resignation.

The French continued to press on with the siege of Sevastopol, waging war underground as well as on the surface. Mine shafts were dug deep into the earth, moves that were met by the Russians with their own tunnels, and thus a strange, dark war was waged out of sight of the armies above. The French, in fact, were troubled by internal disputes in the summer of 1855 as Napoleon continued to lean on Pélissier, whom he held responsible for the heavy casualties sustained on 18 June. It was even suggested that Niel, who continued to make trouble for Pélissier, take over command, although this foolish idea was wisely averted when Marshal Vaillant intervened. Despite Canrobert's removal from command he continued to enjoy great popularity with his men and wield influence with Paris, so much so that Pélissier had begun to tire of his troublesome presence. It resulted in Canrobert being recalled to Paris in July, his place being taken by another veteran of the wars in Algeria, General Patrice de McMahon. Even the stout Omar Pasha had his troubles, for whilst he and his army were playing their part in the siege of Sevastopol the Turkish city of Kars in Armenia was putting up a brave resistance to a large Russian army under General Muraviev. It was only natural, therefore, that he requested something be done to help his countrymen but with his requests falling upon deaf ears he took drastic action and, on 14 July, left for Constantinople.

Just over two weeks after Raglan's death it was the turn of the Russians to suffer a mighty blow. Admiral Pavel Stepanovich Nakhimov had been one of the most dominant and inspirational figures in Sevastopol since the very opening of the siege. He was, of course, a household name in Russia, largely because of his famous victory at Sinope in November 1853. The sight of him walking or riding round the bastions, inspecting the defences and encouraging the defenders was always a reassuring one. It is said that the first thing most of the defenders wanted to know after the attack of 18 June was how Nakhimov was.

> Even those who had been badly or even mortally wounded did not forget their beloved leader. One of the wounded soldiers of Count Dibitch-Zabalkansky's regiment lay on the ground near the Malakhov. 'Sir! Sir!' he cried to an officer who was riding to the city. The officer didn't stop. 'Wait, sir!' The wounded soldier was crying out in pain and was obviously dying. 'I am not asking for your help, but I must ask you something very important!' The officer came back to the wounded soldier, as did a sailor. 'Tell me, sir, was Admiral Nakhimov killed?' the soldier asked. 'No, he wasn't'. 'God be praised! Now I can die easy'. These were the last words of the dying man.[1]

But despite the fact that his men loved and respected him, Nakhimov was still tough enough to drive them on. After all, the last thing he needed was his men going soft and he was constantly inspiring them, both by his personal example and by stern lectures. If a sailor on duty in the bastions, whether he was sick or simply tired and exhausted, ever asked for permission to be relieved for a short period, Nakhimov would refuse, and after receiving the request on one such occasion turned on the enquirer adding:

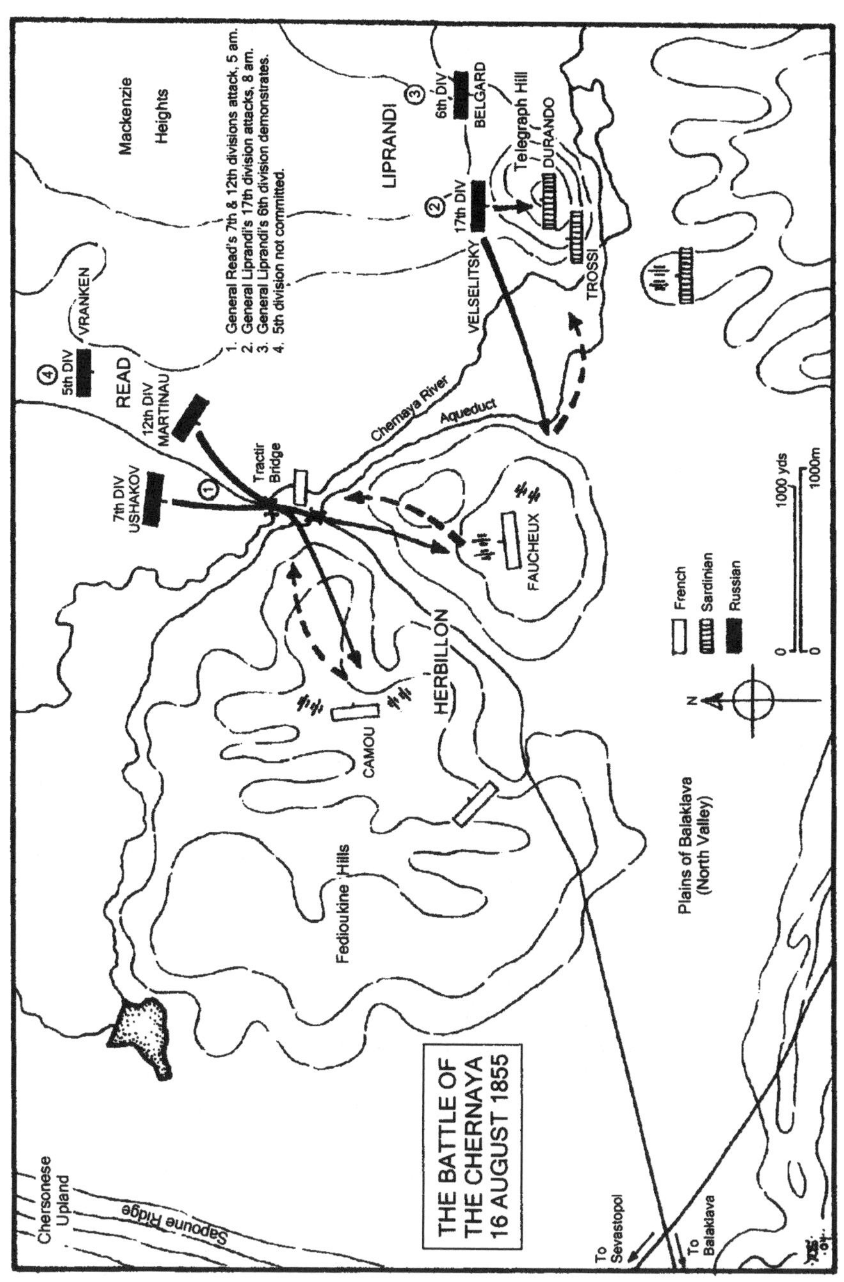
THE BATTLE OF
THE CHERNAYA
16 AUGUST 1855
1. General Read's 7th & 12th divisions attack, 5 am.
2. General Liprandi's 17th division attacks, 8 am.
3. General Liprandi's 6th division demonstrates.
4. 5th division not committed.
Mackenzie
Heights
LIPRANDI
6th DIV
BELGARD
Telegraph Hill
DURANDO
17th DIV
VELSELITSKY
TROSSI
VRANKEN
5th DIV
READ
12th DIV
MARTINAU
7th DIV
USHAKOV
Tractir
Bridge
Chernaya River
Aqueduct
FAUCHEUX
HERBILLON
CAMOU
Fedioukine Hills
French
Sardinian
Russian
1000 yds
1000m
N
Plains of Balaklava
(North Valley)
Chersonese
Upland
Sapoune Ridge
To
Sevastopol
To
Balaklava

> What! Do you want to leave your post? You must die here, you are a sentry, and you will not be changed! All of us will die here; remember that you are a Black Sea sailor and you must defend your native city! We'll leave nothing for the enemy except our dead bodies and ruins; we must not retreat! I've already chosen a grave for myself; my grave is already made! I'll lie near my commander Mikhail Petrovitch Lazarev. Kornilov and Istomin are already there. They did their duty and we have to do it as well![2]

Nakhimov knew his business well, and with Totleben was one of the main reasons why the British and French had been unable to make much headway in their attempts to take Sevastopol. Like Kornilov and Istomin before him he was not averse to putting himself in the line of fire for his country. Indeed, both of these great admirals had already paid the ultimate price and had sacrificed themselves for their cause. They were certainly not to be found skulking in the rear in some bombproof shelter during times of crisis. No, both Kornilov and Istomin were men who led by example, and when the Allied shells came raining down on the town they were to be found in the front line, being splattered with mud and blood and covered with the grim grime of battle. Their luck would only run so far, however, and it had come as no surprise to their men – albeit it was still a great shock – that both men had been killed in action.

Like his two great friends Nakhimov was no stranger to danger but he continued to tour the defences and expose himself to Allied fire, much to the consternation of his staff who warned him on numerous occasions not to keep putting himself in harm's way. Some even believed that he wanted death. Indeed, Prince V I Vasilchikov said:

> There is no doubt that Pavel Stepanovitch did not want to survive the fall of Sevastopol. He alone remained alive of his brave fellow-fighters [Kornilov and Istomin]; he was looking for death. During his last days he began to display himself on the parapets of the bastions, accompanied by his staff and wearing his glittering epaulettes. This attracted the attention of the French and English skirmishers.[3]

It was inevitable that death would finally catch up with him, and so it proved. On 10 July Nakhimov rode out with his two aides-de-camp to inspect the Redan and Flagstaff bastions. As he rode through the streets of Sevastopol he issued a series of mundane orders after which he proceeded to the Redan where he had to see to the appointment of a new commander, Lieutenant Vikorst, the previous incumbent having lost a leg to an Allied shell. Afterwards, Nakhimov and his other aide-de-camp, Lieutenant Koltovskoy, visited Nikonov's battery, after which they returned to Admiral Panfilov's dug-out in the Redan where they drank some lemonade before setting off, this time with Panfilov, and 'under the most terrible fire', to the 4th section of the defences. Nakhimov, who was apparently in a more cheerful mood than usual, then returned once more to the Redan.

In the past Nakhimov had repeatedly warned his staff about the need for self-preservation, and to beware when moving around the bastions, particularly with Allied riflemen so close by. When he arrived at the Redan Nakhimov sat down on a bench near Admiral Panfilov's dug-out. A group of officers were soon standing round him, talking to him, when suddenly a sentry shouted 'bomba!', at which everybody rushed to the dug-outs except Nakhimov who remained seated on the bench The shell exploded close by but Nakhimov was unhurt, and after calling for his horse he mounted and rode off to the Malakhov, the very bastion where Kornilov had been killed on 17 October. When he arrived there Nakhimov jumped off his horse to the cheers of the seamen and soldiers inside the bastion, who were happy to see their favourite commander. The men gathered round Nakhimov and he spoke to them, after which he gave an order to the battery commander. Finally, he began to take the first few steps of the fatal walk towards the parapet at the top of bastion in order to inspect a fire-step. Aware that he was in great danger if he dallied too long on the fire-step, officers rushed to him and did their best to stop him. The commander of the 4th section assured him that everything was fine and that he had nothing to worry about and should leave the bastion immediately, but, undeterred, Nakhimov said nothing and continued towards the parapet.

Captain Kern tried to think up an excuse to prevent Nakhimov from putting himself in danger. The best he could do was to tell the admiral that a religious service was being held in the bastion. The next day was, after all, the holiday of St Peter and St Paul (Nakhimov's name day). Kern suggested they should attend, but Nakhimov, aware of the ruse, snapped back: 'I'm not stopping you from going.' When they reached the fire-step Nakhimov took a telescope from a sentry's hands and stepped up, his head and shoulders clearly visible to the Allies outside. His tall, round-shouldered figure, resplendent in his admiral's uniform with its gold epaulettes, was easily seen by the British and French riflemen and provided them with a very close and very tempting target. Kern and the aide-de-camp made one last attempt to persuade Nakhimov to keep low or to go around the sandbags and watch the Allies from there. But Nakhimov remained silent and stood absolutely motionless, watching the French through the telescope. Inevitably, a bullet came whizzing at him, thudding into the sandbag, and just missing his left elbow. Nakhimov simply said: 'They are shooting rather accurately today.' The words had barely left his lips when he suddenly tumbled backwards without uttering a sound. A bullet from a rifle had struck him in the face, smashed into his skull and exited through the back of his head.[4]

Although his men had feared such a disaster they were still stunned by the sight of their beloved Nakhimov weltering in his own blood at the foot of the rampart. They rushed to him and found him still alive, despite the severity of his wound, although he was unconscious. He was gently picked up and carried back to his quarters. From time to time he opened his eyes but he neither spoke nor moved. Meanwhile, crowds gathered anxiously at the house, waiting for news. The best doctors in the town gathered and tended to Nakhimov but there was little hope of a recovery. He lingered for two days until the fatal day, 13 July. One eye-witness at Nakhimov's bedside later wrote:

> I went into the room where the Admiral lay and found there the same doctors that had been there the previous night, along with a Prussian doctor who had come to see whether his medicine had had any effect. Usov and Baron Krudener were there; the Admiral was breathing and from time to time opened his eyes, but at about 11 am his breathing suddenly became more intensive; there was silence in the room. Doctors went to his bed. 'Death is coming here,' said Sokolov, loudly and distinctly. The last minutes of Pavel Stepanovitch were running out! The Admiral stretched out for the first time and his breathing became infrequent and irregular. After several more sighs he stretched himself again and sighed slowly. The dying Admiral made a convulsive movement and he sighed three more times. Nobody noticed his last sigh. After several moments, everybody looked at their watches and then Sokolov said in a loud voice: 'He has passed away.' It was seven minutes past eleven; the hero of Navarino, Sinope and Sevastopol had finished his glorious walk of life.[5]

News of Nakhimov's death quickly spread throughout the stunned town. Even though they knew it would be only a matter time before he exposed himself to danger once too often it was still a great shock to the defenders. Nakhimov's quarters were soon engulfed by sailors and soldiers – at least those who got permission to leave their posts – eager to pay their respects. They changed shifts with each other in order to get away, returned to their bastions, then went back to the coffin as soon they could do so. It was a tremendous outpouring of grief. The seamen crowded around the coffin both by day and night, kissing the dead admiral's hands. And it is pleasing to record that, as the Russians ceased firing during Raglan's funeral procession to Kazatch, so the Allies stopped pounding away at Sevastopol, long enough for Nakhimov to be laid at the side of his two great comrades, Kornilov and Istomin, on St Vladimir hill. One of the nurses of the Sisters of Mercy described his funeral:

> In the second room there lay his coffin, decorated with golden brocade and many cushions with orders on them. At his head three admiral's flags were grouped together. He was covered with the flag, shot through and torn, which was flying from his ship on the day of the Battle of Sinope. Tears were running down the bronzed cheeks of the sailors. I have yet to meet a single sailor who would not say he would gladly die for him. I will never forget the deeply sad impression of his funeral; the sea with the numerous threatening enemy ships; the hills with *our* bastions where Nakhimov went endlessly, cheering and encouraging the defenders more with his example than with words. And the hills with *their* batteries, from which they were mercilessly smashing Sevastopol and from which they could fire on the funeral procession. But they were silent and respectful and there was not a single shot fired during the funeral.[6]

Totleben, still suffering from the severe wound sustained on 18 June, heard about Nakhimov's mortal wound on 11 July. He wrote to his wife:

> Yesterday evening Nakhimov was badly wounded in his head whilst on the Malakhov Hill. This sad event has affected me terribly. I loved Nakhimov like a father. This man did us all a great service. He was loved and respected by everybody. Thanks to his influence over the fleet we achieved much that seemed to be impossible. He was a genuine patriot; he loved Russia and was ready to sacrifice everything for its honour, just like the noble patriots of Ancient Rome and Greece. At the same time he had a tender heart, he looked to the care of all of the wounded men; he visited everybody and helped everybody.[7]

The death of the great and inspirational Nakhimov came as a huge blow to the defenders of Sevastopol. It was true that life had gone on after the deaths of the two heroes, Kornilov and Istomin, who had similarly inspired the garrison but Nakhimov had been there from the beginning. He was the last of the great trio of fighting admirals. With him now gone and Totleben wounded, the burden now fell largely on the shoulders of the garrison commander, Osten-Saken.

The Allies had been firmly ensconced to the south of Sevastopol since the beginning of October the previous year, since when they had achieved no real gains. Instead, they had seen their armies ravaged by cholera and other sickness, had experienced great hardships throughout the winter, and had seen the relationship – at least between the British and French – tested to the very limits. They had also seen their great assault of 18 June go terribly wrong. The Russians, on the other hand, had experienced different problems. Their forces inside Sevastopol had suffered tremendous losses due to the Allied bombardment, whilst their attempts to break the Allies' stranglehold had come to a bloody end at Inkerman. Sickness was rife in the Russian Field Army, which itself had done little to help the garrison of Sevastopol. But at least they could point to a very successful repulse of the Allies on 18 June which was every bit as much a triumph for them as it was a disaster for the Allies.

The defence of Sevastopol on 18 June had caused mixed feelings in Sevastopol, because on the one hand the garrison had great faith in their ability to repeat the exercise when called upon to do so, but on the other they were being slowly demoralised by the continuous Allied bombardments, which were making life in Sevastopol very difficult. 'You know what Sevastopol has borne during the last hard three weeks,' wrote one disgruntled inhabitant,

> but you, perhaps, cannot imagine its real state. We seem to be approaching a critical period when all physical and moral strength may yield to terrible fatigue for the want of hope for help. When it will end, only God knows, but it is possible that the day is very near. The number of sailors still standing on their feet is dwindling every day. Many rumours tell us that in Saint Petersburg the difficulties and dangers of our present situation are not accurately recognised. Is it not possible to give us sufficient reinforcements which would allow the Crimean army to make some sort of attempt to advance? All these questions worry everybody and are the constant topic of all discussions. It seems that everybody forgot about the dangers, even ourselves, the citizens of the Severnaia side. There is no place now that is not touched by either a rocket or a ball.[8]

Furthermore, it seemed to them that Gorchakov's field army was doing nothing to help them. They were effectively on their own. Thus, the situation had reached stalemate, with the Russians in particular becoming increasingly tired of the war and looking for a way out.

Internal differences were now beginning to cloud judgements within the Russian camp, which was becoming increasingly divided into those who wanted to take the offensive and those who wanted to sit tight and simply continue to counter whatever attack the Allies hurled at them. The problem was that both camps had little faith in a positive result for Russia. The czar, Alexander II, was looking for a way out of the war. He was sick and tired of it, and of the manner in which his army was being allowed to waste away both on the Belbec and inside Sevastopol. The siege was becoming an almighty drain not only on Russian manpower but also on the economy, Russia finding it impossible to keep pace with Britain and France who could commit huge chunks of their budgets to the war effort. Alexander was growing desperate and by now was pleading with

Gorchakov to do something, anything, to move the war forward. But although he hoped to end the war by a peaceful solution he still wanted to fight a decisive battle to bring about a peace conference. He had been mightily pleased by the success of 18 June but wanted to draw the Allies out into the field and defeat them in a battle which would not only bring fresh glories to Russia but would also force the Allies to sue for peace. In some ways his designs were not that dissimilar to the Emperor Napoleon's who also wished his army would take the field in a more conventional manner. However, the commander-in-chief of the Russian Field Army, Prince Gorchakov, had little faith in such a policy and was most unwilling to take the field. After all, there was nowhere his army could attack the Allies except for the position which they held on the banks of the Chernaya river. But with the French having been for many months in occupation of the Fedioukine Heights, which overlooked the river, they would be attacking troops who were well dug in. Then there was Osten-Saken, commander of the garrison in Sevastopol. Osten-Saken was no military genius but he was a good soldier. However, the death of Nakhimov had really shaken him. He thought it madness for anyone to be contemplating an offensive. On the other hand, he was equally depressed about his chances of holding Sevastopol and went so far as to advocate a withdrawal to the Severnaia, on the north side of Sevastopol harbour. Thus, the Russians were faced with three choices; to take the field and win a decisive victory, to maintain a continued defence of Sevastopol as they had done for the past ten months, or to abandon the southern side of Sevastopol and cross to the Severnaia.

It was a tough call and one which Gorchakov was unwilling to make. Even Czar Alexander would not commit himself definitely to an offensive in the field. Instead, he restricted himself to vague suggestions and intimations that Gorchakov should take the field. In the end Alexander, faced with such divisions and with a reluctant commander-in-chief, suggested that if Gorchakov would not make the decision then a council of war should be held to do it for him. On 3 August Alexander had written to Gorchakov, urging him to do something and suggesting he convene the council of war.

> The daily losses to the Sevastopol garrison, which are proving difficult to replace, have convinced me of *the necessity to undertake something decisive to put an end to this terrible slaughter* [the czar had underlined the words shown in italics]. Given the importance of the situation and in order to ease your responsibility I suggest you to take council with your experienced staff-officers.[9]

It was just what Gorchakov needed as it took the decision out of his hands. It was also what the czar wanted, and in order to see that his wish for a decisive battle was carried by the council of war he sent his envoy, General Adjutant Baron Pavel Alexandrovich Vrevsky, to lean on Gorchakov and see to it that the offensive took place. He also informed Gorchakov that he had embodied and despatched to the Crimea the *opolchenie,* a sort of Russian home guard, which could be called out in times of great crisis. These were not quality troops but they would at least bolster Russian numbers and give the wavering Russian commander more confidence.

The council of war was duly held on 9 August, with the issue being the next course of action. The three options – to continue the defence, to take the field and fight a decisive action, or abandon the southern side of Sevastopol and retreat to the Severnaia – were discussed openly but no decision was made. Instead, all those in attendance were asked to commit their thoughts to paper and present their reports the following day. When the council reconvened and the reports had been submitted it was clear that the delegates were split into two camps, those in favour of an offensive and those against. The project to abandon the southern side of Sevastopol appears not to have been a viable option, although Osten-Saken argued for it. Even those who were in favour of an attack on the Allies, including Liprandi and Khrulev, were aware of the dangers attached to a move against the Allies. Realistically, there was only one place where they could attack, and that was across the boggy Chernaya river against troops strongly entrenched and with powerful artillery. But when the votes were cast Gorchakov, who himself was in favour of an action having been influenced by the czar and Vrevsky, won the day and thus it was decided – almost certainly against his better judgement – that an attack should take place to draw the Allies into the field and, hopefully, give them such a beating they would sue for peace. It was hugely ironic that the decision to fight the great hoped-for battle was made not by Napoleon or the French, but by the Russians themselves.

Having agreed, or rather having been coerced, into undertaking to attack the Allies, Gorchakov fixed the date of the attack for 16 August. But there was still one twist. Gorchakov was evidently still unsure about the wisdom of attacking the Allies in such a strong position, and so, just two days prior to the attack, he visited Totleben who was still recovering from his wound in his house on the Belbec river. With Gorchakov were Vrevsky and P E Kotsebu, the general adjutant of the Crimean Army. Totleben may well have been the master of defence and siegecraft, but he was certainly no slouch when it came to offensive operations either. Upon being informed of the decision to attack Totleben could not help but express his dismay, considering it not only foolish but arguing that, even if the attack were successful, which he doubted, it would make little difference to the Allies. True, it might well cramp their sphere of operations somewhat, but it would do little to compromise their lines of communication which ran via the ports of Balaklava, Kamiesh and Kazatch. At best Balaklava and the British supply port would certainly come under pressure but the Allied troops on the Chersonese would hardly be affected by a Russian victory at the Chernaya. Nevertheless, Vrevsky was determined to see the attack go ahead, and when Gorchakov began to waver once more Vrevsky turned on Totleben and angrily accused him of trying to derail a project that had already been sanctioned by the council of war that had been held on 9 August. It was a disgraceful way to speak to someone who had been at the very heart of the defence of Sevastopol, unlike Vrevsky himself, who had only recently arrived in the Crimea. Despite his grave misgivings Totleben's warning went unheeded and when Vrevsky left he did so in the knowledge that he had got his way once more. Gorchakov, however, was left feeling as insecure and confused as ever and was apparently bent on postponing the attack. The commander of the Sevastopol garrison, Osten-Saken, also thought the decision to attack to be the wrong one. Reflecting on the fatal council of war some twenty years later, he condemned the decision. 'The decision to attack the Fedioukine Heights was an unhappy one; the heights would be impossible to hold for any length of time even if successful.'[10] But once back at his headquarters the ever-forceful Vrevsky merely confirmed the date of the attack and thus Gorchakov was left with no option but to begin planning its execution. It was a thoroughly unsatisfactory way of preparing for what might prove to be the key battle of the war.

Gorchakov planned to attack the Allies on the Chernaya with 50,000 infantry, 10,000 cavalry and 168 guns. General N A Read, who was in overall charge of the operation, was to command the right of the Russian attack, his force consisting of twenty-four battalions of infantry from Ushakov's 7 Division and Martinau's 12 Division. These were supported by a battalion of riflemen, eight squadrons of lancers and six *sotnia* of Cossacks. He also had two brigades of artillery and four Don Cossack guns. The left attack was to be commanded by General Liprandi, whose force also consisted of twenty-four battalions of infantry, from Bel'gard's 6 Division and Veselitsky's 17 Division. These were in turn supported by a battalion of riflemen and six *sotnia* of Cossacks. Two brigades of artillery completed his force. Vranken's 5 Division, of sixteen battalions of infantry and forty-eight guns, was to remain in reserve on the road leading from the Mackenzie Heights. In addition to these 50,000 infantry a further reserve infantry division, the 4th under Shepelev, was positioned even farther back but played no part in the battle.[11]

The Chernaya battlefield actually formed part of the old Balaklava battlefield of October 1854. Indeed, it was upon the very heights now being held by the French that the Russian guns that had fired into the left flank of Cardigan's Light Brigade had been positioned. That was now a distant memory, however. Indeed, it seemed as if years had passed since the 'valiant lunatics' had made their famous charge. The Fedioukine

Heights ran in a south-east to north-west direction and spanned a distance of about 3,000 yards. They were now held in strength by three French divisions, Camou's, Faucheux's and Herbillon's, around 25,000 men in total, commanded by General Herbillon himself, supported by forty-eight guns, with entrenchments at the foot of the heights which were themselves protected by the Chernaya river and, closer to the heights, by an aqueduct. The last 900 yards of the southern end of the heights were separated from the main sector by the road that ran from Balaklava to the Mackenzie Heights, crossing the aqueduct by means of an old wooden bridge and the river itself by the Tractir bridge. Farther to the south-east lay a gap about 900 yards wide before another height rose on the south side of the river, the Gasfort Height. This was held by the 6,000-strong Sardinian 2nd Division, under General Trossi, who was in turn supported on his right by the Sardinian 1st Division, also 6,000 in number, under General Durando. A further 3,000 infantry, under General Jaillet, were positioned to Durando's right. The Sardinians were also bolstered by some thirty-six guns and four squadrons of cavalry, in addition to which there were 10,000 Turkish troops from Osman Pasha's division, and twenty-four squadrons of British cavalry under Scarlett. A Sardinian detachment had been placed on Telegraph Hill, an isolated position on the north bank of the Chernaya, just to the west of Chorgun.

The Allied position on the Chernaya was, therefore, a very strong one, both in terms of geography and in the numbers of troops holding it. It didn't help the Russians either that their plans were well known to the Allies. Various Russian officers had been seen examining the position for days beforehand, whilst deserters also brought in information, and it was no secret that an offensive was coming. There were lapses too in Russian security which also favoured the Allies. Indeed, on 15 August, the day before Gorchakov's planned attack, Lord Clarendon in London received a telegram from the British ambassador in Berlin, Lord Augustus Loftus, which read: 'I am informed confidentially that a telegraph has been received this day from St Petersburg stating that orders have been sent to Prince Gorchakov to take the offensive against the Allies at all costs.'[12] This news was immediately relayed to Simpson in the Crimea. Finally, a patrol of D'Allonville's Chasseurs d'Afrique picked up the Russian movements late on the evening of 15 August and reported back to Herbillon. Thus, there was little chance of the Russians repeating the surprise which had been sprung on 5 November at Inkerman. It was against this background of Allied preparedness, pressure from St Petersburg, of doubts and internal wranglings in Sevastopol, not to mention his own self-doubt, that Gorchakov brought forward his troops on 15 August ready for the attack the next day.

Given the way in which Gorchakov had been virtually forced into undertaking the offensive it is no surprise that his plan of attack was as vague as it was confusing for those who had to execute it. It was bound to lead to confusion and so it proved. The 'plan' involved an advance by Read with 7 and 12 Divisions, attacking with his artillery the French bridgehead, which had been established around the Tractir bridge, and the French positions on the Fedioukine Heights, and preparing the way for an attack across the Chernaya river itself. However, he was on no account to cross the river until he received further orders from Gorchakov. Liprandi, meanwhile, was to advance in two columns, his left column, Bel'gard's 6 Division, was to advance to Chorgun and shell Telegraph Hill and the Gasfort Heights, whilst his right column, formed of Velselitsky's 17 Division, was to drive the enemy outposts from Telegraph Hill but, like Read and Bel'gard, was not to advance any farther until he received definite orders to do so from Gorchakov. It was, therefore, a movement order rather than a plan of attack. More important was the fact that nobody on the Russian side, Gorchakov included, actually knew what they were to do once they had advanced to the river. It all smacked of a 'hit and hope' plan.[13] Few, if any, of the Russian commanders had any faith in the plan of attack.

> All the experienced Russian generals were absolutely certain that the next day would be a disaster. 'General Read has had a premonition that he will not survive tomorrow,' said his orderly. When Colonel Skyuderi, the commander of the Odessky regiment, heard it he said, 'Read has had the same premonition as we have. Mind you, many of us, including myself and Bel'gard will be annihilated tomorrow.[14]

The Russian attack was scheduled to begin at 4 am on 16 August but ran into problems almost as soon as it started. It was a misty morning, and silent too, and when a very nervous Gorchakov arrived on the ground with his staff he was irritated to find that neither Read nor Liprandi had opened their bombardment on the Allied positions. He immediately sent off an aide, Lieutenant Krasovsky, to tell them both that it was high time they began their attack. Unfortunately, before Krasovsky reached either of them they duly ordered their guns to open fire. Gorchakov must have breathed a sigh of relief as the guns barked into action, but his problems were about to begin. The fire from Read's guns was falling short of its target and was landing instead at the foot of the Fedioukine Heights. As there was little point in continuing with the bombardment, Read ordered his guns to cease firing. He was peering through the mist, looking at the results of the bombardment, when Krasovsky arrived bearing Gorchakov's order to start the attack. Gorchakov's verbal order was not for the attack proper to begin, but only the initial advance. The problem was, that Read saw it differently. When Krasovsky told him it was 'time to start', Read replied by asking him, 'time to start what?' The question completely threw Krasovsky who had no idea. The artillery bombardment had already begun. Therefore, Read thought this must be the order to advance across the river. Sadly, it wasn't.

Prince S Obolensky was one of Gorchakov's aides-de-camp. He had also commanded the Don Cossack battery of artillery at Balaklava. He took part in the Battle of Chernaya and described it in a letter to his father-in-law, Count S Sumarokov. Of the fatal misinterpretation of Gorchakov's order he wrote:

> At dawn the C-I-C was in the valley with the troops. General Read accordingly ordered the artillery, which was moved forward, to open fire on the Fedioukine Height. Despite the order not to advance until told to do so, the C-I-C sent his aide-de-camp to tell General Read to begin the action. When the aide-de-camp gave the order to General Read the artillery was already in action. General Read thought that this was the order to advance and attack the Fedioukine Heights with his infantry. He asked the aide-de-camp if he understood the order of the C-I-C correctly. The aide-de-camp answered that he didn't know but he repeated word for word the order from the C-I-C 'to begin the action'. General Read then asked the chief of staff, General Veimarn, how he interpreted it. The latter said that, as he understood it, they ought to cross the river.[15]

Interestingly enough, another account claimed that Veimarn, 3 Corps' chief of staff, pleaded with Read to wait and asked for clarification. Veimarn apparently left Read to join Gageman, the corps artillery commander, and when he returned was surprised to find Read deploying for the attack.[16] Read apparently told Veimarn that as far as he was concerned it was the order to advance across the river. Krasovsky meanwhile returned to Gorchakov to query the order but was dismissed by the commander-in-chief who said simply: 'General Read knows exactly what he has to do.'[17] The trouble was, that what Gorchakov thought Read was about to do differed enormously from what Read himself thought he had to do.

After apparently clearing up the confusion surrounding his order to Read, Gorchakov took himself off to congratulate Liprandi, whose troops had driven the Sardinians from Telegraph Hill with relative ease, thus clearing the north bank of the Chernaya river of almost all the Allied troops, save those at the bridgehead at the Tractir Bridge. Vranken's 5 Division was then ordered to come forward to take possession of the hill which would give them a superb tactical advantage, for as they looked across the river they were staring directly at the gap between the French right and the Sardinian left. Gorchakov could use the hill as a pivot for assaulting the Allied position. But even as Gorchakov savoured this brief moment of success things were beginning to go horribly wrong farther to the north where Read's men were starting to across the river. The sounds of heavy fighting suddenly began to echo along the valley, heralding the start of Read's advance, but Gorchakov had barely time to wonder what all the noise was when one of Read's aides-de-camp came galloping up to inform the somewhat surprised commander-in-chief that Read was already across the Chernaya and was requesting reinforcements. Gorchakov's shock can easily be imagined, but he quickly recovered himself and decided to change his mind. Instead of attacking the Allied right he would move against their left. He therefore despatched a messenger to Vranken ordering him to forget Telegraph Hill and instead march to reinforce Read who was obviously struggling to maintain his position on the south bank of the river. It was the start of an unfortunate day for Vranken and his division.

Read had brought forward both Martinau's and Ushakov's divisions, both of which struggled to get across the river owing to a lack of bridging equipment. The far more powerful French guns on either side of the bridge, commanded by Captains Vautré and Sailly, cut swaths through the oncoming Russian columns as they struggled out of the water with the help of planks, ladders and 'flying bridges' and crossed the marshy ground beyond. Martinau's 12 Division – the Odessky, Ukrainsky and Azovsky – found the going extremely tough. They drove out the French defenders in the bridgehead at the Tractir bridge but found progress extremely hard going as they advanced on either side of the road to Balaklava which passed through the Fedioukine Heights. Nevertheless, the Russians pushed on against Failly's division, struggling with them on the hillside whilst Herbillon hurried reinforcements to the scene. The 73rd Ligne came up on Failly's left whilst General Cler brought forward two battalions of the 62nd and a further battalion of the 73rd up on to the hill on the right of the road. Two weak battalions of the 3rd Zouaves and some companies of chasseurs came forward also as the fighting intensified. The French recovered and unleashed a withering fire into the Russian ranks, stretching hundreds of them on the wet, boggy ground, including the commanding officer of the Odessky, Skyuderi, the man who had taken one of the redoubts from the British at Balaklava. The Azovsky, who had taken the first redoubt at Balaklava, had also suffered terrible losses and were now falling back. The French themselves lost heavily, losing some four hundred men including Commanders Darbois and Alpy, both of whom were mortally wounded. But French pressure told and Martinau's men slowly began to give way and fall back, re-crossing the aqueduct and the Chernaya river under fire from Failly's men.

Thomas Buzzard was a British surgeon serving with the Turkish army in the Crimea. He had ridden out from his camp on the morning of 16

August having heard the sound of artillery fire and arrived to see Read's columns attacking the Fedioukine Heights.

> The rise of the curtain which had been formed by the morning mist enabled us to see that from the Fedioukine Heights immediately facing us at a distance of about a mile, and from all about the valley of the Chernaya river and the undulating ground to the right of it, rolling clouds and globular masses of white smoke from very many cannon were constantly mounting and dispersing. To the west of the road from Mackenzie's farm, we could trace the fire of the many guns in the large Russian battery to which the French had given the name 'Gringalet,' and again, still more to the left but nearer, continually recurring clouds of smoke showed where the French were busy with their artillery on the summit of the larger Fedioukine height. To the right, about Mount Gasfort and the hillocks near Chorgun, the guns and musketry of the Sardinians added their share to the white clouds which were constantly ascending and marking the scene of what was evidently a fierce engagement.[18]

Away to Martinau's right, Ushakov's 7 Division had been having an equally tough time against General Camou's division. All three of his battalions, the Mogilevsky, Vitebsky and Polotsky, had struggled across both the river and the aqueduct only to come under intense rifle and artillery fire from Wimpfen's and Sencier's brigades on the left flank of the French position. Grape shot flew through their ranks, round shot ploughed into them, and when the 50th Ligne and 3rd Zouaves launched a counter-attack with charged bayonets Ushakov's men were brought to a halt. The 82nd Ligne then came up on Ushakov's flank and, caught between the two fires, the Russians broke and ran, splashing their way through the Chernaya river and running back as far as the foot of the Mackenzie Heights. It was a total rout. Martinau's battalions were also driven back having achieved nothing whatsoever, and by 7.30 am there were no Russian soldiers on the west bank of the river, save for the dead, dying, wounded and those taken prisoner. Thomas Buzzard again describes the Russian attacks.

> Presently we could see from the lower and nearer part of the Fedioukine height a line of columns of infantry, recognisable as Russians, breasting the steep ascent to the left in its way to attack the French position on the crest of the hill. The line was advancing in admirable order, and was presently followed at a few yards' distance by another line parallel to it and in similar formation. So much could easily be seen, whilst with a field-glass we were near enough to discern the officers a few yards in front of their men cheering them on.

> Even with the naked eye we could see here and there, as each line continued its steady course upwards, numerous little dark masses (at the distance suggesting lumps of broken earth) suddenly appear on the ground behind it. With the field-glass these little masses became resolved into more or less shapeless heaps of dead or wounded men.
>
> Not more than a few minutes had elapsed, and the first line had only covered about a third of the distance required to bring it in contact with the French artillery on the summit of the height, when, overwhelmed by the murderous fire which it encountered, and yielding to the pressure of the French charging downwards, it turned and swept backwards and downwards in disorder, with what was evidently great loss.
>
> Then it was met by the second line which was advancing to its support, and these two together again faced the ascent. It appeared at first to us that this second attack, reinforced by the weight of the supporting columns, might prove successful, but after a few minutes, and when little more than half the required distance had been surmounted, the sweeping fire of the guns and impetuous rush of French infantry, pressing upon them down the hill, overpowered the ascending troops, and after a gallant resistance these turned and fled back in disorder towards the river.
>
> But even after this repulse the Russians were apparently undismayed. A few minutes passed and a third line came into sight advancing for a renewed attack, whilst such was its persistence that it succeeded in mounting to the crest of the hill in a furious rush. There, however, it encountered the French, who again charged and drove it down the slope in great disorder.[19]

There was no joy either for Gorchakov on the Russian left. Vranken's 5 Division, it will be remembered, had been ordered to the Russian left to occupy Telegraph Hill but had then been redirected to the Russian right once Read's attack had got underway. Vranken had yet to reach the front line and already Martinau and Ushakov had been bloodily repulsed. Read was in no mood to throw away yet another division and instead chose to attack with a single regiment only, the four battalions of the Kostromsky, with a single battalion of the Galitsky out in front to screen their advance. Considering two whole divisions had already been repulsed with heavy loss, it is a mystery why Read thought he could now succeed with just a single regiment supported by a single battalion. But it got worse. Even as the Kostromosky formed up in order to advance Read changed his mind yet again and decided to send in the single battalion of the Galitsky alone. It was the beginning of a tragic episode.

The Galitsky crossed the Chernaya under French artillery and rifle fire, and by the time they emerged on the west bank their numbers had been whittled away dreadfully. A few more yards sufficed to convince the Galitsky of the futility of their advance and they fell back, leaving behind scores of dead and wounded. The Kostromsky watched all of this with a mixture of sadness and horror, for the Galitsky had barely returned to their own lines when the Kostromsky were ordered to resume their march and attack themselves. The regiment went forward under fire, unflinching and determined to succeed, and in the absence of Vranken, who had been wounded, were led by Veimarn, the 3 Corps chief of staff. The result of their attack was as predictable as it was tragic, for over half the regiment became casualties in executing an attack which lasted just a few minutes and achieved nothing at all. Veimarn himself was among the dead. Worst still was the fact that Read, undeterred by the bloody failures of these attacks and seemingly bent on self destruction, ordered the poor survivors of the Galitsky to attack once more. The fragile battalion showed no outward signs of disobedience but formed up with the intention of crossing the river and attacking once more. Virtually all of the battalion's officers were down, and the men were led by Major Chertov, who had already had his horse shot beneath him, and who limped forward on foot, picking his way over the shattered remnants of the earlier attacks. Needless to say the attack, or rather advance, came grinding to a halt in the teeth of a heavy and sustained fire. What remained of the Galitsky then turned and fell back slowly, having given their all for Mother Russia.

The retreat of the Galitsky might have been far more costly had it not been for the swirling mist that prevented the French from firing their guns accurately. The mist also led Gorchakov to attack yet again. The Russian commander-in-chief was actually directing operations now, since Read had been killed by a French shell. One of his first moves was to bring forward all four regiments of 5 Division, being the Kostromsky, Arkhangelogorodsky, Volgogodsky and the remaining three battalions of the Galitsky, and have them attack the Tractir bridge before crossing the river once more, this time under cover of the mist, to attack the Fedioukine Heights. Once again the initial moves proved successful, with French defenders being forced from the bridge, after which the Russians began to clear the river. However, just when Gorchakov started thinking his battalions were making good progress the mist cleared, revealing to the French a mass of Russian infantry at which the French batteries were redirected. The ensuing fire was most destructive. Casualties in 5 Division were horrendous. The divisional commander, both brigade commanders, the four regimental commanders, and nine battalion commanders, were all killed, as was Read himself, struck down by a French shell. It was 8 am, and the Russians had made no progress whatsoever.

With Read dead, Gorchakov assumed personal command of his army. So far the day had gone horribly wrong for the Russians, but given his lack of military skill the fact that the commander-in-chief was now in control of affairs was hardly likely to change things. Undeterred by the total repulse of his troops, Gorchakov decided to continue with the attacks on the French-held Fedioukine Heights. Velselitsky's 17 Division, reinforced by the Odessky Regiment, was moved across from Telegraph Hill to attack the eastern end of the Fedioukine. The Russians drove forward and a fierce fight ensued between them, the French and the Sardinians of Marmora who were soon heavily engaged. General Trotti's 2nd Division was brought forward to bolster the defences, his men lining the banks of the aqueduct to fire on the stalling Russians. General Montevecchio was killed during the fighting but his brigade continued to fight on, reinforced by French troops from General Faucheux's division. The Odessky regiment suddenly surged forward out of the mêlée and began to drive between the French and Sardinians, but General Cler was on hand with two battalions to halt the advance and send them tumbling backwards. The attack ended in a bloody repulse, with eight Russian battalion commanders being wounded. It was hopeless.

Fortunately for Gorchakov, fate lent a hand in the shape of a French artillery round which killed Vrevsky, the man who had pushed him into attacking in the first place. With Vrevsky dead there was nobody left for Gorchakov to answer to, and even with his own limited grasp of military tactics he could see that any further attempts to force the Allied position would only end in even heavier casualties. There was only one thing to do; order a withdrawal. Thus, at around 10 am, six hours after the battle had started, the Russians were in retreat, returning to their positions on the Mackenzie Heights covered by their cavalry and artillery which, despite being outgunned, had performed well under difficult conditions. 'Our artillery was handled well,' wrote Obolensky,

> but fired from very disadvantageous positions; nearly all the batteries had to fire uphill because they were located in the valley of the Chernaya River. The descent from the Mackenzie mountain was so difficult that by the time the reserve artillery was coming down the action was already over (it lasted nearly three hours). That's why it was impossible to reinforce the artillery. The retreat was carried out in good order and the enemy did not follow us. The cavalry covered our retreat but was not engaged. We occupied our former position without having caused any damage to the enemy. But we suffered great losses.[20]

Russian casualties on 16 August were tremendous. 2,273 were returned killed, including Read, Veimarn and Vrevsky with 4,000 wounded. A further 1,742 were recorded as missing, most of whom were taken prisoner. It was a bloody day and a great setback for Gorchakov and the Russians, who had experienced their worst day since the Battle of

Inkerman ten months earlier. The French lost a total of 1,800 killed and wounded, whilst the Sardinians returned light casualties of 250 with just fourteen killed. Such were the heavy losses sustained by the Russians that it took a truce of two full days to collect and bury the dead. 2,129 Russian soldiers were buried by the French and a further 1,200 by the Russians themselves.[21] The dead and wounded lay thick on the ground after the battle and when Thomas Buzzard passed over the battlefield afterwards he found the scenes, 'scarcely possible to exaggerate'. It was indeed a horrifying sight.

> On the banks of the aqueduct, on the bridge which crossed it, and also, but less frequently, in the water below, were heaps of Russian dead and wounded. The Tractir bridge, too, which is larger than that over the aqueduct, was literally blocked with and for a time rendered impassable by a pile of corpses, numbers of dead and wounded also being strewn about the banks of the river, the water of which I could see in places running red with blood. Amongst the dead and dying were quantities of weapons – muskets, swords, and bayonets – besides helmets or caps, crosses, icons and other religious emblems, and, perhaps not less pathetic, loaves of black bread scattered upon the ground or half exposed in the haversacks in which they had been carried by the weary soldiers during a very long night's march. Here and there some bottles were also to be seen.
>
> In many classical paintings of battlefields which I have seen the dead soldier has been usually depicted lying upon his back, with face upturned. I noted that in this tragic scene the dead in, I think, the majority of instances, lay on their faces, literally, to use the Homeric phrase, 'biting the dust.' These men had been shot whilst advancing up hill, and their bodies ceasing to be under the control of life would naturally fall in the direction in which they had been moving when struck.[22]

The smoke had barely drifted from the Chernaya valley before the recriminations began. Gorchakov knew full well he would be criticised by the czar, even though he had carried out his master's wishes and had attacked. After all, was not the battle fought to end the war, and thus avoid further losses? Fortunately for Gorchakov he had a scapegoat. As Lucan, Cardigan and Raglan had Nolan to blame after Balaklava, so Gorchakov had Read to act as culprit, and there is never anything better than a dead scapegoat. After all, they cannot answer back and speak for themselves. Nevertheless, Gorchakov's criticisms of Read were valid – just. He had attacked across the Chernaya river without first having received orders to do so, as had Liprandi, and by doing so had derailed the Russian plan from the word go. Conversely, faulty staff work on

Gorchakov's part had played a great part in the confusion that led to the attack in the first place. His aide-de-camp, Krasovsky, was not experienced enough to appreciate the significance of the order and should have been in a position to answer Read correctly when pressed by him for clarification. Instead, he simply allowed Read to interpret the order as he saw fit. Unfortunately it was the wrong interpretation. In the event, Alexander refused to condemn Gorchakov and simply said that Russia had to be prepared to suffer such heavy losses if it were to place itself in a position to end the war on favourable terms. However, the old commander-in-chief of the army, Marshal I F Paskevich, was not so forgiving. The old man was at death's door but mustered enough strength to dictate a letter to Gorchakov, accusing him of failing to stand up to the czar and for not sticking to his own beliefs as regards Russian strategy. Like Totleben and other doubters, Paskevich thought Gorchakov's plan to be flawed and doomed from the start. It was, he said, 'castles in the air', adding that the plan, unconvincing and doubtful from the start, had resulted in almost 10,000 Russian casualties, which they could ill afford. And when Gorchakov characteristically sought to shift the blame by claiming he was simply following the czar's directions, Paskevich retorted by saying that Gorchakov should have therefore resigned, which would have saved himself from having the stain of 10,000 lives forever on his conscience. He also attacked Gorchakov for his cowardice in trying to blame the dead Read and Veimarn.

The Battle of Chernaya brought about a change in Alexander's perception of the war. The defeat, however painful and costly, had shown that the Russian soldier was still prepared to sacrifice himself for the czar and for Russia, as Obolensky observed in his letter to his father-in-law. 'It is very sad to write about the battle but it is comforting to know that they [the French] could not break the spirit of our troops, whilst in Sevastopol they remain determined to fight on and repulse all the enemy attacks.'[23] Alexander was disappointed but not dismayed at the outcome of the battle. Indeed, it gave him greater strength to continue the struggle. If he ever considered abandoning Sevastopol in favour of a campaign in the field those thoughts were well and truly banished. Sevastopol must not fall, and even if it did Russia would continue the war until it forced the Allies to come to the peace table. In the meantime, Pélissier could at least rest easy that the battle which the Emperor Napoleon had craved had finally been fought, not that the Allies had done anything to bring it on. With the pressure now off Pélissier could turn his attention once more to the siege of Sevastopol.

NOTES

1 *Admiral P S Nakhimov* (St Petersburg 1872), 26. Edition of the Sevastopol Department of the Polytechnic Exhibition.
2 Bogdanovitch M *Vostochnaya Voyna* (St Petersburg 1876), III, 413.
3 *Admiral P S Nakhimov*, 26.
4 Tarle E V, *Krymskaya voina* (Moscow 1959), II, 411–13.
5 *Kronshtadsky vestnik*, 1868, No.17.
6 'Izvlechenie iz pis'ma Krestovozdvizhenskoy obshchiny sestry G.B.', *Morskoy sbornik*, 1855, No.9, 72–4.
7 Shil'der N *Graf Eduard Ivanovitch Totleben, ego zhizn' I deyatel'nost'* (St Petersburg 1885–1886), I, 78.
8 'Izvlechenie iz pis'ma iz Sevastopolya, 26 aprelya, 1855', *Central State Historical Archives, Moscow*, sh. 130.
9 'Alexander II to Gorchakov. Petergof, 20 July 1855', *Russkaya starina*, July 1883, 211–12.
10 Osten-Saken D, 'Voenny sovet pri oborone Sevastopolya', *Russkaya starina*, October 1874, 331.
11 These figures are taken from Major-General V Sterneggs, *Schlachten-Atlas, des XIX Jahrhunderts, Der Orientkrieg 1853–56 in Europa und Asien* (Leipzig, n.d.) Nr.6, 3.
12 Lord Loftus to Lord Clarendon, Douglas, Sir George and Ramsay, Sir George Dalhousie (Eds). *The Panmure Papers; being a selection from the correspondence of Fox Maule, second Baron Panmure, afterwards eleventh Earl of Dalhousie, KT, GCB* (London 1908), I, 350.
13 Gorchakov's plan brings to mind a similarly disastrous plan, conceived by Lt. Gen. John Whitelocke when attacking Buenos Aires in July 1807. His columns were sent into the city with orders to advance as far as the Rio de la Plata and then wait for orders. Needless to say, no orders arrived and the whole attack ended in disaster.
14 'Iz vospominaniy A N Suponeva', Russkiy Arhiv, 1895, No.10, 262.
15 Tarle, *Krymskaya voina*, II, 442–5.
16 Albert Seaton. *The Crimean War: A Russian Chronicle* (London 1977), 202–3.
17 Ibid, 203.
18 Thomas Buzzard, MD. *With the Turkish Army in the Crimea and Asia Minor; A Personal Narrative* (London 1915), 138–9.
19 Ibid, 140–1.
20 Tarle, *Krymskaya voina*, II, 445.
21 Pélissier to Vaillant, in Bazancourt, the Baron de (trans. by Robert Howe Gould). *The Crimean Expedition, to the Capture of Sebastopol. Chronicles of the War in the East* (London 1856), II, 435.
22 Buzzard, *With the Turkish Army*, 144–5.
23 Tarle, *Krymskaya voina*, II, 445.

# CHAPTER TWENTY-THREE
## *Final Preparations*

The new commander-in-chief of the British army in the Crimea, James Simpson, might well have felt a degree of sympathy for Gorchakov if he had known how much pressure was being put on him to do something positive and carry the war to the Allies. The resulting battle on the Chernaya river on 16 August had been the result of Czar Alexander's pressure and what had it achieved? It had achieved nothing, save the loss of almost 10,000 Russian troops, not to mention a couple of thousand French and Sardinians. By the late summer of 1855 Simpson was being subjected to the same kind of pressure as his opposite number in Sevastopol. With the prospect of a second winter in the Crimea looming, the Allies, and in particular the British, wanted positive action, and they wanted it sooner rather than later. Panmure and his government, not to mention the queen, expected the new commander to push on with the siege and bring the operation to a successful conclusion, but instead the siege continued at pedestrian pace. The plain truth of the matter was that Simpson was simply not the man for the job.

Ever since the death of Raglan Simpson had expressed doubts about the wisdom of appointing him as commander. Indeed, even before he had officially assumed command of the army, he was writing to Panmure, expressing his concerns that he might not be up to the job.

> I have put myself in Orders to command until instructions from England shall come; but my health is sure to give way, as I have constant threatenings of gout in spite of all the care I take, and it may come some day too hard for me to bear! I cannot conceal this from my own conviction, and therefore hope soon to be relieved from work that is too much for me.[1]

These admissions immediately set alarm bells ringing in London and rather than leave the army 'in trembling hands', Panmure was soon discussing a probable successor to Simpson. How desperate the government was, and how short of gifted officers the British Army was can be judged by the list of candidates Panmure drew up. It was headed by the 76 year-old Lord Seaton, the man who had done so much to defeat the Imperial Guard at Waterloo forty years before. Lord Hardinge, another Peninsular War veteran, was also considered, as was the younger Duke of Cambridge, whose only military experience had come at the Alma and Inkerman. Even Sir Harry Smith was mentioned. To think that all the Army had to offer was a list of legends who had cut their teeth fighting in another age was quite remarkable. In the event, Panmure earmarked Major General Sir William Codrington as Simpson's successor, should the day ever come, which seemed increasingly likely.

Simpson's position was not made any easier by the pressure being brought on the British government itself. The Tulloch-McNeil commission set up after the winter debacle had presented its findings, whilst the report submitted by the Roebuck Committee was due for debate also. Thus, things were slightly prickly in England to begin with. In the meantime Simpson plodded on, barely able to stay awake during some of the briefings, as Admiral Houston Stewart pointed out in one of his gossipy letters to Panmure.

> With respect to the *Military Authorities*, I ventured to tell you what General Simpson said himself of his own unfitness for the Command-in-Chief, and certainly the three or four times we have since met have in no degree tended to make me think he had estimated his own physical powers *too lowly*. On the contrary. He has already grown to look half-a-score years older, and to carry a more anxious, *chirpit* [feeble] countenance. Indeed, it is evident to the most careless observer who sees and talks to him for five minutes that he is *completely* over-weighted and much oppressed. I have attended two conferences with him, and in neither of them has he addressed one single word or remark. In short, it appears to me, and I may add to Sir E[dmund] L[yons], that it is quite impossible the good General and worthy old soldier has enough in him to maintain either the interest, or the honour and credit, of the English Army under the present most trying circumstances, and I ardently hope that you may have taken him at his word, and believing his own representation of inability, have appointed some younger, more accomplished, and energetic officer.[2]

This was followed on 28 July by Panmure writing to Simpson in which he effectively told him to get a grip of himself. Panmure understood the problems Simpson faced in the Crimea but said, 'you must *lead*. You must not be oppressed by care nor daunted by difficulty . . . So, shake off the black dog, and make yourself respected by the Allies and obeyed by your own people.'[3] It was all quite astonishing for a minister of war to be lecturing the commander-in-chief as a father would his son. The thought of anybody in England, including the prime minister, writing to the Duke of Wellington, for example, in the same way does not bear thinking about. It just would not have happened. But such was Simpson's lack of confidence and ability that he was constantly in need of chivvying up. Finally, on 31 July, Simpson received a despatch from Panmure which also contained a 'dormant commission' for Codrington, appointing him to command should anything happen to Simpson. 'In the event of your illness or absence,' wrote Panmure, 'you will present the commission to Codrington and have him put in orders.' He then added cheerily, 'In case of a bullet having your billet marked on it doing its work, you had better enclose the commission in a packet to be immediately delivered to Codrington.'[4]

It was against this backdrop that Simpson was expected to press ahead with the siege of Sevastopol. There was no real progress at all. True, Pélissier and the French continued to push forward their works, new mines were dug, and batteries established, but in the centre of the siege lines, which were manned by the British, little headway was made due to a combination of a lack of drive and the hard, rocky soil that made digging extremely difficult. It made life dangerous too, for the men digging the trenches had little or no cover, save for the somewhat weak barriers provided by the many gabions and fascines. The French, on the other hand, were able to dig deep and pile up the spoil to make far more effective cover for themselves. The Russian attack at the Chernaya river on 16 August at least had the effect of galvanising the Allies into stepping up their operations, and on 17 August, the day after the battle, the Allied guns swung into action once more to open the fifth bombardment of Sevastopol. Their targets were primarily the Redan and Malakhov, first to smash the works into oblivion and, second, to suppress the heavy fire from the Malakhov which the Russian guns had been pouring on the French saps being pushed forward towards it from the Mamelon. Some 456 French and 182 British guns duly opened up on their targets, the Redan and Malakhov, with 586 Russian guns replying.[5] The Russian forts were quickly buried beneath a storm of iron, the earth ramparts crumbling under the sheer weight of iron being hammered into them. O Konstantinov later described the ordeal in the Russian trenches during the first days of the August bombardment.

> The volleys from the enemy batteries and their rifle fire were taking their toll of our men. The curtains, made of rope, were smashed and the bullets struck the gunners through the embrasures. We were losing from 600 to 1,500 men each day but we continued to repair the damages at night, all the time under fire from case-shot fire from the nearest attacking batteries. Our work was wasted, for the stones and dry earth would not mix properly and each blow of a shell destroyed everything that had been repaired; all this effort had cost us terrible

> sacrifices. The mounds of earth afforded little shelter to the defenders; they were killed in thousands but continued with courage to stand fast under the deadly fire, waiting for the moment when the enemy would rush to the attack. Then they would stop their attack and drive them back them with their bayonets, out of the ruins of their trenches.[6]

Despite the punishment the Russians were taking from the bombardment they were still able to reply to the Allies' fire. Not content to simply sit back and wait for the assault, Osten-Saken and his men did their very best to carry the fight to the Allies, both by means of their own artillery and by the sorties which continued to plague the besiegers. They also enjoyed the odd piece of good fortune. On the night of 28 August a Russian shell, fired blindly into the night, came bouncing very conveniently – for the Russians at least – into a powder magazine on the Mamelon. Around 15,000lbs of powder were stored in the magazine which immediately exploded, sending a vast fountain of fire into the black night sky, much as a volcano would when erupting. The roar was tremendous, and the Mamelon was ripped apart by the explosion, the ground rocking violently all around it. Over a hundred Frenchmen were killed or wounded by the explosion and by the tons of debris that were flung high into the air, some of which landed within the walls of Sevastopol itself.

It was not only those in the front line who suffered from the Russians' fire. Lieutenant Frederick Vieth, of the 63rd Regiment, had not long arrived in the Crimea and found his sleep disturbed one night by a Russian cannon ball, despite his billet being some three miles from Sevastopol.

> Although three miles away, the Russians reminded us occasionally of their presence in anything but an agreeable manner. On the first night I slept in a tent in our camp, a huge round shot from one of their batteries fired at a great elevation struck the tent of the captain of my company which was adjacent to mine – luckily at the time not occupied – smashing a new saddle, fresh from England, that stood on a rest within, demolishing sundry articles of furniture, and splitting and knocking the tent over.[7]

The main bombardment lasted for four days, although the firing was continued right into the first week of September, albeit at a much reduced rate. Henry Clifford was just one of many who believed the final act would not be long in coming. In a letter to his father on 20 August, Clifford wrote:

> The shelling from the English Batteries on the Redan and Malakhov by day and night has been quite wonderful. At night, I have often

> counted as many as ten shells in the air at once going into the Redan, and for the first time a constant fire of Musketry from dusk in the evening until daybreak in the morning has been kept up from our advance trench in the Redan, so that the enemy has not been able to send out working parties to repair the damage during the day. Both the Redan and Malakhov are much knocked about outside but the fire from them, though diminished is not subdued. The Tower of the Malakhov is no longer to be seen above the parapet.[8]

The damage caused by the Allied bombardment was immense, and the feeling that a successful attack was now possible spread throughout the increasingly optimistic Allied camps. But what was more worrying for them was the sight of several rafts, moored in the harbour of Sevastopol opposite Fort Nicholas. It was quite obvious that these were for the purpose of throwing a pontoon bridge across the harbour, connecting the Severnaia with the south side of the town. Its purpose, however, was misinterpreted by the Allies, who naturally feared the worse for it would allow Gorchakov to transfer troops from the north to the south of the town at his will. 'The Russians have begun a bridge across the harbour,' wrote Clifford, 'made by large rafts. It will be finished in a day or two, and it is no doubt built for the purpose of moving large bodies of troops from the North side to attack the trenches on this, and I have no doubt we shall have a row ere long in consequence.'[9] Hamley was another officer who feared the worst.

> Thrown from the shore of the north side of the harbour opposite Fort Nicholas, the rudiments of a bridge appeared, made of rafts, moored side by side. After the battle of the 16th, the work proceeded with increased diligence, and about the 26th or 27th it stretched completely across to the point of rock on which Fort Nicholas is built, and was speedily put into operation, great trains of vehicles moving incessantly across, conveying articles, apparently of furniture, to the north shore. We had looked attentively for the completion of this bridge; rumour said that, as soon as large bodies of troops should be enabled to move across with ease and celerity, a simultaneous attack would be made from the town, and by the army on the heights, the latter aiming at Balaklava, while the force sallying out from the town would distract out attention, and, if successful, effect a junction with their comrades across the plateau.[10]

Simpson merely confined himself to a couple of lines in a despatch to Panmure, in which he, like so many others, saw the bridge as a threat, although he was at least moved to admit that it was a fine piece of work. 'The enemy has very nearly completed the bridge across the harbour – a splendid work – portending mischief.'[11] An attack on the Allies, which men such as Clifford and Hamley and even Simpson feared was never really an option, however, for in spite of their fears Gorchakov had more than just offensive moves in mind when he ordered the bridge to be constructed, if indeed he had any at all. Gorchakov, in fact, was still wracked with indecision. On the one hand, he still believed Sevastopol to be indefensible and was convinced that the only real option was to evacuate the south side of the town and take up a position to the north. On the other hand he had his duty to the czar who, ever since the Chernaya battle, had become bent on fighting on and preserving the town. Gorchakov was certainly willing to continue the fight for as long as the czar wished him to, but he was forced to write to Alexander to point out that whilst he was prepared to fight on he would only do so until such time as Russian casualties and Allied gains made the situation in Sevastopol impossible. In fact, Russian losses were running at around 2,000 a day, a situation which could not go on indefinitely. In spite of the dreadful conditions inside Sevastopol hundreds of men made their way there to help with the defence. N S Miloshevitch was one of them.

> In July 1855 I was appointed to the staff of Sevastopol garrison at my own request. I was frequently asked the question; what made me, a married man, offer myself to Sevastopol where I would most likely be killed, leaving my family without any means? I had already gone through the years of enthusiasm and passion during my previous nine years service in the army and was fully cured of the dream of getting a baton. I answered by saying I had no intentions. I was simply a son of my time, that great time when the spirit of great patriotism and honour prevailed in Russian society. In this respect I was no different from anyone else. Each of my friends was ready to do the same. In the reign of Emperor Nikolay Pavlovitch the feeling of military valour was regarded very highly in the Russian army. The unequal struggle with the Allied coalition raised that feeling even higher and it was that which sent our soldiers to Sevastopol despite the prospects. If the private advantages and privileges enjoyed by the Russian officers had prevailed in Sevastopol, the siege would have become impossible for us.[12]

The ordeal of the defenders was well known in St Petersburg, where everyone feared the worse but could do little about it. Anna Fyodorovna Tyutcheva was a maid of honour at the czar's Court. On 31 August she wrote in her diary:

> After the failure of our army on the Chernaya river our situation is becoming more and more desperate from one day to the next. The

> bombardment is becoming increasingly stronger; we are losing a lot of men. Sevastopol has turned into hell; it is showered with a rain of fireballs by day and night. Rumours are spreading that it has been decided to evacuate the Yuzhnaya side of the city. We spent the evening in a gloomy and sad mood and hardly spoke. Each of us had only one thought, and nobody has either the wish or courage to speak. I tried not to look at the Emperor and Empress in order not to see the deep anxiety on their faces.[13]

On 3 September, with the fifth Allied bombardment winding down, the Allied commanders held a conference at which plans for what they hoped would be the decisive attack on Sevastopol were discussed. Not that there was much discussion, of course, for Pélissier knew exactly what needed to be done and had drawn up plans accordingly, plans that were laid out rather more for British approval than for discussion. Given the overwhelming numerical superiority of the French over the British this was hardly surprising, however. Also present with the commanders-in-chief were Generals Bosquet, Thiry, Martimprey and Frossard. The chief British engineer, Sir Harry Jones, was in attendance also. And then there was General Niel. Pélissier had made little secret of his dislike for the emperor's 'spy in the camp', but all that appeared to have passed. Indeed, after outlining his plans to the assembled officers Pélissier handed everything over to Niel for a final briefing.

> We are 25 metres from the place [the Malakhov]; but, to reach this point, we have made immense sacrifices; moreover, the Commander-in-Chief of the Artillery will tell you, that we are almost out of ammunition. At present, the Malakhov is the only issue of the siege; its capture will give us the faubourg, and the faubourg will give us the town. The assault presents itself in the most favourable aspect that I have dared to hope.[14]

The admission by Niel that ammunition was running low must have shocked everyone although it probably made no difference to them when each was invited to step forward and give his opinion. Pélissier could, if he wished, wait for the arrival of 400 mortars, but this would only add to the delay. All wanted the attack to take place as soon as possible. It was a unanimous decision. With the discussions at an end Pélissier got to his feet and announced sternly: 'The attack shall be made.'

The great attack was fixed for 8 September, and was to be preceded by a bombardment of three days, beginning on 5 September, and to ensure that the Russians were given no opportunity to prepare for the assault, Niel insisted that the date for the attack remain a secret, and that the hour of the assault not be fixed until the last possible moment. It was a sensible move. Aware that certain indiscretions had apprised the Russians of the date and time of the attack on 18 June Niel was very anxious that such a sensitive piece of information should not leak into Russian hands this time.

By the evening of 4 September the Allies had amassed 806 guns in their batteries in front of Sevastopol. Of these 627 were French and the remaining 179 British; 129 guns faced the Flagstaff Bastion, 134 the Central Bastion, eighty-three were ranged against the Quarantine Bastion, and a further 267 guns were directed at the Malakhov, the key to Sevastopol. The remaining fourteen guns were to be found in two other French redoubts but would not be firing upon the town. The British guns were distributed with seventy-one in the batteries of the right attack, and 108 in the batteries on the left.[15] Despite the lack of ammunition in the French camps it was an awesome array of firepower. The Malakhov and the Redan would bear the brunt of the fire, but unlike the attack in June the Allies' fire would consume every inch of Sevastopol's defences. Pélissier realised now that it had been a mistake to attack on one front only, an error which enabled the Russians to move troops from other parts of the town across to the Korabel'naia to help defend the two great forts in that sector. This time he intended attacking the Flagstaff, hence the French guns were turned upon the town front also. In addition, the coming bombardment would not only range over all parts of the defences but would also 'affect a certain irregularity' in order to conceal the hour of attack. Then, shortly before the actual assault, the guns would lift their fire from the forts themselves and concentrate on the rear areas where the Russian reserves would inevitably be waiting.

The coming assault would be the supreme test for Gorchakov, and in particular Osten-Saken and the defenders of Sevastopol. Gone were the inspirational figures like Kornilov, Istomin and Nakhimov, all three of whom lay together on St Vladimir's Hill. The military genius of Totleben was gone too, but at least he was still alive, recuperating at his house on the Belbec from the wound he had sustained back in June. The defence of Sevastopol rested squarely with the dwindling force of soldiers, sailors and marines who had kept the Allies at bay for the best part of a year. Osten-Saken was there directing the defence, ably supported by men such as Khrulev and Semyakin, who could be relied upon in times of crisis. The defenders themselves had seen their numbers slowly whittled away, despite the steady trickle of reinforcements that had been fed in throughout the siege. On the eve of the great assault Osten-Saken could count on the services of ninety-six battalions of infantry, three *opolchenie* – a sort of 'home guard' – and one battalion of riflemen, in addition to which there were 2,200 sappers, 2,000 artillerymen and 4,000 naval gunners, a combined total of almost 50,000 men.[16]

Wednesday 5 September dawned fine and clear. As one historian put it:

> There was every prospect, as far as nature was concerned, of a tranquil and refreshing day. No ripple silvered the lucid unmurmuring sea, no breath of air shook the blue, thin lines of smoke which lightly ascended from the town, the front or the camps. Nor, for a time, was there any unusual noise of war; only the occasional crack of a sniper's rifle, scattering the wheeling seagulls or startling the herons in the Chernaya sedge. But there was a busy movement in the French batteries; mantlets were drawn away from the narrow embrasures, uncovering the guns; men were brisk on the slippery platforms, hauling on ropes, piling shot or filling shells, ready to handle sponge or rammer, preparing for action.[17]

At 5 am the peace and tranquillity of the autumn morning was shattered as over six hundred heavy Allied guns roared into action. It was deafening, and quite unlike anything the Allies had unleashed against Sevastopol before. The French batteries firing at the town front were directed by General Leboeuf, whose guns,

> opened fire with a unity and violence not to be described. All our lines, the enemy's works, and the town itself, are soon wrapped in a thick cloud of smoke; the cannon of our allies respond energetically to our own, and the Malakhov attack begins its fire. The roar of the artillery often becomes suddenly silent, and then recommences with additional fury. It was . . . now a succession of salvoes, now a continuous rolling fire of artillery. During the night our cannon continue to fire, to prevent the enemy from repairing the injuries inflicted upon his works, or replacing his disabled guns.[18]

By mid-morning Sevastopol, its defences and its defenders were wrapped in smoke and reeling beneath the power of the bombardment, the intensity of which surpassed anything they had previously experienced. The walls of the Redan and Malakhov crumbled away at every blast, ditches filled with earth and guns were dismounted or simply blown apart. It was hell. Even Gorchakov was stunned, and in letter to the czar wrote:

> Beginning with the 5th of September the assailants augmented, in an incredible manner, their cannonade and bombardment; breaking down and destroying our works, along our whole line of defence, sometimes by sudden salvoes from all their batteries, sometimes by a continuous rolling fire of artillery. This infernal fire, directed against our embrasures and merlons, clearly showed the enemy's intention to dismount our guns and destroy our works, and then to assault the town. It was no longer possible to repair our fortifications; – and we

> restricted ourselves, consequently, to embanking the powder-magazines and stockades. The falling parapets filled up the ditches; the merlons crumbled to pieces; it was, every moment, necessary to repair the embrasures; the gunners perished in great numbers, and it became exceedingly difficult to replace them. At this period, the loss was enormous. From the 5th to the 8th of September, four field officers, forty-seven subalterns, and 3,917 men were killed or disabled.[19]

With so many battalions of defenders packed necessarily into the bastions and in rear of them, it is no surprise that casualties were so heavy. Pyotr Alabin recalled an incident during the bombardment that was, perhaps, typical of many that occurred on 5 September.

> Yesterday [5 Sept] a great accident happened in the 3rd bastion. As soon as the bombardment began, the commander of a company of the Kamchatsky regiment, Lieutenant Maevsky, received an order to take his company up to the Nikonov Battery, and to position it under the parapet in order for his people to have a rest. He did so and afterwards sat with the battalion commander, Major Milevsky, in a shed to play cards. The bombardment was becoming heavier when all of a sudden a corporal rushed into and cried: 'Sir! The company is destroyed!' 'Who are you talking to? Major Milevsky exclaimed.' 'To Lieutenant Maevsky, Sir.' 'Who is this man? Milevsky asked Maevsky.' 'The Sergeant Major,' was the reply. 'He can't be a sergeant major because he is a fool! Is it impossible! What are you gabbling about?' 'Sir, they've been killed.' Then everybody rushed from under the shed, ran to the place where the company had been sheltering and saw a terrible picture. The parapet was turned upside-down by the explosion of several shells which fell simultaneously, and the men that were sleeping under the parapet now covered the ground, along with gabions and sandbags. Everybody rushed to dig them out and found sixteen dead bodies and barely twenty only just alive, who were sent to hospital.[20]

After the disastrous attack of 18 June Pélissier and Simpson were taking nothing for granted and wanted to ensure that when their troops attacked the Redan and Malakhov again they would find the going much easier. It was vital, therefore, that not only were the guns inside the bastions silenced but that the defenders were unable to repair them during the night. After all, the last thing the attacking troops wanted to find when they arrived at the ditch in front of the Russian works was a deep excavation, into which they would have to jump, before then scrambling, usually by means of ladders, out the other side in order to get at the ramparts of the forts. What they really wanted to find was a ditch filled with the debris thrown up by the bombardment. They wanted to find the embrasures smashed and the guns destroyed, and they wanted to find nothing but dead gun crews inside. The abattis that had thwarted the British when they attacked the Redan on 18 June was a particular target for the guns. This had proved as effective in halting the red-coated British infantry as barbed wire would their khaki-clad descendants sixty years later. Hence, the bombardment was more intense than anything that had gone before. Everything, forts, guns, ditches, walls and the defenders inside them, had to be flattened. It was as simple as that.

After just two hours' firing the guns in the Malakhov fell silent, although, ominously, those in the Redan continued to reply. Watching from Cathcart's Hill was William Russell, and the view from here provided him with wonderful material for his readers. 'The iron storm,' he wrote,

> tore over the Russian lines, tossing up, as if in sport, jets of earth and dust, rending asunder gabions, and 'squelching' the parapets, or dashing in amongst the houses and ruins in their rear. The terrible files of this flying army extending about four miles in front, rushed across the plain, carrying death and terror in their train, swept with heavy and irresistible wings the Russian flanks, and searched their centre to the core. A volley so startling, simultaneous, and tremendously powerful, was probably never before discharged since cannon were introduced.[21]

By now Gorchakov knew the Allies were planning to attack. He had no idea when it would come but the intensity of the bombardment left nobody in any doubt that the attack would be launched very soon. Indeed, despite Niel's insistence that the date and hour of the attack remain secret, the French themselves did little to conceal their movements. Despite attempts to conceal or camouflage their trenches, French troops were observed gathering and moving forward on the Inkerman Heights on the very day the bombardment began.

Although the Malakhov and the Redan were the main targets of the bombardment other bastions came in for terrible punishment. No.2 Bastion, the Little Redan, was situated just to the north of the Malakhov and on 5 September came under heavy fire from the French guns. One French shell blew up the bastion powder-magazine, which badly damaged the left flank of the fort and knocked out several guns. There was not a single safe place in the bastion, and because of the Allies' fire it was impossible to carry the wounded to the dressing station situated in No.1 Bastion during the hours of daylight. Instead, they could only move by night. It is said that, when anybody in Sevastopol mentioned the words, 'hell, crush or slaughter', the people knew they were talking about the Little Redan. Gorchakov himself visited the bastion during a rare lull in the bombardment and asked the soldiers of the 8th Division who were defending it, 'Are there many of you here, at the bastion?' The reply came back, 'Yes, but only for three days perhaps, Your Highness.' Command of the Little Redan changed hands fairly regularly during the bombardment. After Ershov had been wounded, command passed in turn to Lieutenant Commanders P Nikitin and M Esaulov, and Lieutenants Ladyzhinsky, Veizenberg and Fedorovitch. During twelve hours of bombardment on 5 September every third man out of the 600 defenders was killed or badly wounded. In fact, so badly damaged was the bastion that preparations were made to blow it up, should the enemy get anywhere near to capturing it. Therefore, mines were laid beneath battery No.127, the Gennerih battery, the wires being laid by men from the 3rd Field Engineer Battalion under the direction of Lieutenant M Frolov.

By the end of the first day of the sixth bombardment, the Russian defenders inside the bastions and in the streets behind them had been well and truly deafened by the roar of the shelling. They were covered in dust and debris, and many were smothered and splattered with the blood and brains of those of their comrades who had been smashed by Allied shells. There was hardly a yard of frontage that had not been hit by a shell of some sort and it came as a great relief to them when darkness brought about a slight lull in the firing. The heavy Allied guns stopped firing, but if the Russians thought they could emerge from their shelters and begin repairing their works in safety they were mistaken, for when the siege guns stopped the mortars took over, launching their huge shells into the air to come crashing down out of the night sky on to the Russian works. Pyotr Alabin described the Redan at the end of the first day.

> During the bombardments the English fired on the 3rd Bastion with incredible power. By the end of the evening the bastion had become a heap of earth, on which it was difficult to make out the traces of fortifications. But during the night the guns, covered up with earth, were dug out, the ditch was emptied; the walls, soaked with the blood of the workers, were raised again.[22]

When darkness descended on the evening of 5 September the Allies could congratulate themselves on an astonishingly powerful bombardment. The Malakhov and the Redan were now barely recognisable as the sort of works that had denied them on 18 June. The Allies' fire had even reached out to the Russian ships moored in the harbour.

> Suddenly, an immense glare of light reddens the whole heaven. In the direction of the harbour is seen the blaze of an enormous fire, the

> circle of which increases every instant, while sparks and flakes of burning matter fill the air in all directions. It is a Russian vessel, which is burning in the harbour.[23] The fire lasts for several hours.[24]

The Allied bombardment continued throughout the following two days, by which time the defences were in a terrible state. As early as Thursday 6 September, the second day of the sixth bombardment, the defences of No.4 sector, which included the Malakhov, were reported to be so badly damaged that the commanding officer, Karpov, told Gorchakov that unless reinforcements were sent straight away the sector would fall by the end of the week. There was no let up during the next two days as the Allied bombardment reached a crescendo of noise. The ramparts of both the Redan and the Malakhov were in a severe state of disrepair, two thirds of the Russian guns in this sector were knocked out, whilst hundreds continued to be slaughtered by the Allied guns. Critically, the Allied artillery fire on 6 September had been so intense, even into the night, that the garrison had been unable to carry out any repairs. It was, as one historian put it, 'the first time that this had happened during the 349 nights of the siege'.[25]

At the conference held on 3 September Niel, it will be remembered, had requested that the date for the attack, 8 September, should remain a secret known only to Pélissier and a handful of generals. But now, on the eve of the great attack, it was time for the date to be made known to the divisional and brigade commanders who would lead their men the next day. The secret meeting duly took place on the afternoon of 7 September, with Bosquet in attendance along with senior staff officers, the generals of division and of brigade, together with the heads of the artillery and engineers. Bosquet, in fact, had been restored to favour by Pélissier and would oversee the attack on 8 September. Pélissier explained to them the plan of attack, and requested that each of the officers who would lead a unit should go and study the ground over which they were to attack. It was a sensible suggestion. Then, as those who had still to be told the date and time held their breath, Pélissier announced gravely that it would take place at noon the following day. 'I have long known you all for brave soldiers,' he said to them, 'and I have entire and unlimited confidence in you. Tomorrow the Malakhov and Sevastopol will be ours'.[26]

The main objective for the French was the Malakhov, the Little Redan, and the adjacent Russian defences. Their plan of attack involved dividing their front into three zones, from where the three attacking columns would advance. On the right would be Dulac's division, supported by the Chasseurs of the Guard and a brigade of D'Aurelle's division. Their objective was No.2 Bastion, the Little Redan. The middle column would consist of La Motte Rouge's division which was to attack the curtain wall which connected the Little Redan with the Malakhov. The left column would consist of McMahon's division, supported by the Zouaves of the Guard, and Wimpfen's brigade of the 2nd Division of the 2nd Corps. McMahon's objective was the Malakhov itself. The Imperial Guard was to be held in reserve, and in order to allow them to arrive at the works in an effective compact mass, engineers had cut a way through the trenches. The cuttings, some forty yards wide, were hidden from view by gabions and earth. Each of the attacking columns was to be guided by a detachment of sixty sappers led by a major and three other officers. The sappers, as well as half a battalion from each of the regiments in the columns, were to carry tools such as axes and crow-bars as well as ladders to help get across the ditches. Finally, each column was joined by fifty artillerymen led by a captain and a lieutenant. Their job was to go forward with the attacking columns and spike the Russian guns or, if possible, to turn them on their former owners. In addition to the main French attacks on the Little Redan and the Malakhov diversionary attacks were to be made by them against the town front to the west, along the line of the Quarantine, Central and Flagstaff bastions. This was a major departure from the plan of attack of 18 June.

The objective for the British was the Redan. It had denied them in June; they were determined it would not happen a second time. The troops selected to attack the work were drawn from the Light and 2nd Divisions. First to go forward from the Light Division would be a covering party of a hundred men from the 2nd Rifle Brigade, commanded by Captain Fyers. These were to be followed by the first storming party, 160 men of the 97th under Major Welsford. This party would be carrying ladders and would be the first to try to storm the Redan. 'They must be good men,' ran the Divisional Orders, 'and true to their difficult duty.' The next storming party would consist of a further two hundred men, also from the 97th, under Colonel Handcock, along with three hundred men of the 90th, under Colonel Grove. The supports consisted of 750 men of the 19th and 88th Regiments. These would be followed by a working party of one hundred men from the 90th under Captain Perrin. The 2nd Division's stormers consisted of a covering party of a hundred men from the 3rd (Buffs) under Captain Lewes, followed by a further 160 men from the same regiment who were to form the scaling party carrying the ladders. The men destined to storm the Redan numbered 260 men, also from the Buffs, 300 of the 41st, and 200 from the 62nd. The working party would consist of a hundred men of the 41st. The remainder of the Light and 2nd Divisions would be held in reserve. Although they would not be part of the storming divisions the 1st and Highland Divisions were to be formed in the 3rd parallel adjoining the attack on the French right.

The problem with the British arrangements for the assault can best be reflected in the numbers used by them, compared with the French. Pélissier was attacking the Korabel'naia front with around 25,000 men, reinforced by a further 5,000 Sardinians. The town front, meanwhile, was to be attacked by around 20,000 men. Simpson, on the other hand, was committing no more than 1,500 to the actual assault on the Redan, with reserves of no more than 3,000. It was not enough. Raglan had come unstuck on 18 June when he committed far too few troops to the attack. Surely the lessons had been learned? It would seem not. And so, whilst the French were able to throw thousands into forcing home the attack and supporting it afterwards, the British had barely enough men to get inside the Redan, let alone reinforce and hold it. But that was not the only problem. Including the covering party, the storming parties and the supports, no fewer than five different units would attack the Redan. It was, therefore, doomed to be a very fragmented attack. Then there were the problems caused by the engineers who, unlike their French counterparts, had made no attempt to cut a wide channel through the trenches in order to allow the attacking troops to get forward quickly. Instead, they would make their way into the front line trenches at a snail's pace. And even when they did arrive in the jumping off trench they were extremely crowded, for the front line trench from which the 1,500 stormers would attack was barely nine hundred yards long. The final folly was the two hundred yards of open ground the British troops would have to cover before reaching the Redan. The French, on the other hand, had pushed their trenches to within thirty yards or so of the Malakhov. Thus, when they emerged from their trenches on 8 September they literally stepped straight into the Malakhov.

The planning problems were compounded, sadly, by the quality of the men – or rather boys – chosen to make the attack. It was all very well choosing the Light and 2nd Divisions, after all, they had been operating in front of the Redan for the last few months and had a good knowledge of the ground. But the fact that these same two divisions had been most active in front of the Redan also meant they had suffered more than their fare share of casualties. These had been made good by raw recruits, many of whom were regarded as mere boys, and whose only real training thus far had been in the trenches themselves where they had learned little other than to keep low and hide from Russian bullets. Gone were the men of Inkerman and the Alma. This was a very different army. 'The courage of our men,' wrote Henry Tyrell, 'has too often redeemed a series of neglects and errors in those who commanded them. Unhappily, this firmness and valour of the soldier failed the nation in the great event we are about to describe.'[27] The same writer went on to cite the 97th as a prime example of the sort of troops which now made up a large part of the British Army.

> In a recent petty sortie of the Russians, some raw recruits of the 97th, when their officers bravely led them to repulse the enemy, hesitated

> then turned, leaving only eight or ten men with the officers, one of whom paid for their desertion with his life, while two others were dangerously wounded. The matter was inquired into; a well-deserved rebuke was administered to the offenders; and the men of the 97th regiment, as punishment for the recent misconduct for some of them in the trenches, were told off to *lead* the assault. We shall speedily see the result of this surprising and most painful error.[28]

It is not clear whether the 97th were indeed chosen to lead the assault as a kind of punishment, but if true, it was a remarkably short-sighted and ridiculous decision. It was a fatal one too. Indeed, when the officers destined to lead the attack read the orders there were those who simply shook their heads and said ominously, 'This looks like another 18th of June.'[29]

Unlike the attack on 18 June the great assault on 8 September was planned to go in at noon, at a time when the Russians would hopefully be eating their midday meal. This actually worked in the Allies' favour, for not only did it give their artillery a whole morning to hit the defences of Sevastopol with everything they had, and by doing so make things easier for the attacking troops, but it should give the Russians little clue as to the timing of the assault. Once dawn – the usual hour of assault – had come and gone the Russians would naturally assume the attack would not be launched that day – hopefully. Although the Allied bombardment slackened during the night of 7 September and the next morning, the pressure was maintained by a continuous stream of heavy mortar shells which were dropped on to the Russian defences. Behind the lines everything was a scene of great activity as final preparations were made for the assault. Ladders were gathered in and tools collected, ready to be used once the Allies were inside the works. Watches were checked, weapons oiled and extra ammunition issued. The stormers no doubt wrote their wills, just in case the worst happened, they wished each other good luck and shook hands, and in general did all those things that men about to go into battle had done for centuries, until finally the first few streaks of daylight began to appear over the horizon away to the east. 'The night was one of feverish impatience. Day at length dawns. A northerly wind sweeps along the ravines, and mingles its sharp whistle with the thunder of our cannon.'[30]

Throughout the morning of 8 September the Allied gunners worked their guns once more, smashing and ploughing into the earth any repairs the Russians had managed to carry out during the night. The last few hours of firing gave the waiting Allied troops immense confidence. Not only was it continuing to kill and main the defenders but it wrecked the defences and tore away the repairs. It also cleared away the large sections of the abattis which had so confounded the British on 18 June. In the Allied camps all was set. Everything was ready. They were ready in Sevastopol too.

> The English have worked hard to destroy the third bastion, [wrote Alabin] and today they had to take it at any price in order to make amends for the last disappointment. They *had to* take this terrible stronghold at any price, and do it alone, for they did not want to share their triumph with anybody. They *had to* cover those mighty walls of the so-called *'Great Redan'* with fresh English blood, and wash away with their triumph the bloodstained soil which had yet to dry up, much to the shame of England, since 18 June. At last there came the moment for the fatal combat.[31]

NOTES

1 Simpson to Panmure, Douglas, Sir George and Ramsay, Sir George Dalhousie (Eds). *The Panmure Papers; being a selection from the correspondence of Fox Maule, second Baron Panmure, afterwards eleventh Earl of Dalhousie, KT, GCB* (London 1908), I, 257.
2 Stewart to Panmure, *Panmure Papers*, I, 297–8.
3 Panmure to Simpson, *Panmure Papers*, I, 317.
4 Panmure to Simpson, *Panmure Papers*, I, 321.
5 Colonel Julian Jocelyn. *The History of the Royal Artillery (Crimean Period)* (London 1911), 411–12.
6 Konstantinov O 'Shturm Malakhova kurgana', *Russkaya starina*, November 1875, 573–4.
7 Vieth, Frederick Harris D *Recollections of the Crimean Campaign and the Expedition to Kinburn in 1855* (Montreal 1918), 30.
8 Clifford, Henry. *His Letters and Sketches from the Crimea* (London 1955), 247.
9 Ibid, 247.
10 Hamley, E Bruce. *The Story of the Campaign of Sebastopol* (London 1855), 291.
11 Simpson to Panmure, *Panmure Papers*, I, 361.
12 Miloshevitch N S, 'Iz zapisok sevastopol'tsa' (Sevastopol 2002), I, 246–7.
13 Tyutcheva A F, *Pri dvore dvukh imperatorov. Vospominaniya. Dnevnik* (Moscow 1928), II, 43.
14 Bazancourt, the Baron de (trans. by Robert Howe Gould). *The Crimean Expedition, to the Capture of Sebastopol. Chronicles of the War in the East* (London 1856), II, 443.
15 Bazancourt, *The Crimean Expedition*, II, 447.
16 Seaton, Albert. *The Crimean War: a Russian Chronicle* (London 1977), 210.
17 Vulliamy, C E. *Crimea: The Campaign of 1854–56* (London 1939), 311.
18 Bazancourt, *The Crimean Expedition*, II, 448–9.
19 Ibid, II, 450–1.
20 Alabin P V. *Pohodnye zapiski v voinu 1853–1856 godov* (Moscow 1892), 523
21 Bentley, Nicolas (Ed). *Russell's Despatches from the Crimea 1854–1856* (London 1966), 249.
22 Alabin, *Pohodnye zapiski v voinu*, 536.
23 The ship set ablaze in the harbour was in fact the *Marian*.
24 Bazancourt, *The Crimean Expedition*, II, 449.

25 Seaton, *The Crimean War*, 210.
26 Bazancourt, *The Crimean Expedition*, II, 453.
27 Tyrell, Henry. *History of the War with Russia* (London n.d.), II, 251.
28 Ibid, II, 252. This incident was almost certainly the fight that cost the celebrated officer, Hedley Vicars, his life.
29 Ibid, II, 252.
30 Bazancourt, *The Crimean Expedition*, II, 454.
31 Alabin, *Pohodnye zapiski v voinu*, 336–43.

## CHAPTER TWENTY-FOUR
# 'The Mortal Blow'

It was 8 September 1855. The great battles of 1854 were now only memories. Since then there had been the terrible winter with all its attendant troubles. A rift between the British and French had opened and closed, though not totally. Then there was the failed assault on 18 June. By now both sides were staggering and reeling like boxers, unable to land the knock-out punch. With both sides growing weary of the struggle it looked very much as though everything would rest upon the outcome of the assault about to take place.

The morning of the 8th was no different to those which had preceded it. The majority of the Allied gunners had hardly stirred from their breakfasts and so the early morning's shelling of the Russian positions was carried on at a much reduced rate. But while the shells flew into the Russian lines French and British troops were beginning to muster for the great attack. Away to the east, on the French right, over 20,000 troops were to take part in the attack, which made it virtually impossible for the movements to go undetected. Despite great efforts to conceal their movements the French were simply unable to do so. In fact, shortly after dawn Russian listening posts picked up the sound of large formations moving about, and although nothing was seen the defenders were rushed into the bastions where they massed, waiting for the attack. But nothing came. Instead, there was simply an intensification of the bombardment as the Allies laid down their final bombardment prior to the attack. The consequences for the defenders were, of course, disastrous. Once again, their massed ranks were easy targets for the Allied gunners whose shells ploughed into them, killing and maiming hundreds. But still no attack came. Then, at 8 am, three mines were exploded in front of the Malakhov in order to dispose of any mines that might lie in wait for the attackers and to bring down any tunnels that might hinder the attack. While great pillars of earth were sent rising into the air the Russians in the bastions gripped their muskets and rifles tighter, expecting clouds of skirmishers to begin stealing their way through the dust and debris towards them. And yet still the Allies did not come. And so as more and more defenders began to fall to the increasingly heavy Allied bombardment, the order was given to the reserves to pull out and await further developments.

Even as the three mines were being set off Bosquet's Order of the Day was being read to the troops who were about to attack the Malakhov.

> Soldiers of the 2nd Corps and of the Reserve! On the 7th of June, you had the honour to strike the first blows aimed directly at the heart of the Russian army. On the 16th of August, you inflicted, on the Chernaya, the most shameful humiliation upon their relieving troops. Today, it is the final stroke – the mortal blow, – that you are about to strike, with that strong hand, so well known to the enemy, – by robbing him of his line of defence at the Malakhov, – while your comrades of the English army and of the 1st Corps will commence an assault upon the Great Redan and the Central Bastion. It is a general assault, – army against army. It is an immense and memorable victory with which you are about to crown the young eagles of France. Forward then, soldiers! The Malakhov and Sevastopol are ours! *Vive l'Empereur*![1]

The troops then began to file off into the trenches and their various jumping off positions, their movements partly masked by the dust thrown up by a strong wind. 'The elements themselves seemed to come to our aid, and to say to us, that Heaven supported our cause.'[2] Then, whilst the Allied gunners turned up the heat of the bombardment, the attacking French troops began to settle down in their trenches, hoping that, when the time came, the attack would pass off without any trouble. Bosquet took himself off to his chosen vantage point, which was in the 6th parallel, the most advanced of the French trenches. He arrived there at 10 am. Pélissier and his staff, meanwhile, rode over to the Mamelon, along with Niel, Thiry, Martimprey and several other staff officers. Last minute orders were issued, watches checked, and anxious glances exchanged. All was set. There was nothing to do now but wait until noon.

Inside the Malakhov things were stirring. Despite the dust thrown up by the wind the defenders had seen suspicious movements within the French lines. Away to the east on the old Inkerman battlefield, Russian lookouts had seen large formations of French troops moving forward, information that was immediately relayed back to Sevastopol. However, the signal was given little credence initially, and was apparently returned for clarification. After all, the Allies had always attacked before dawn hadn't they? It was now approaching noon and the chances of the Allies attacking in broad daylight were slim. And so it was that many of the defenders were pulled back or simply went about cooking their midday meal. It was, after all, going to be just another day. Pyotr Alabin was in the Redan throughout the morning, and recalled the tense atmosphere in Sevastopol. His account confirms the confusion over the report from the Russian lookouts over at Inkerman.

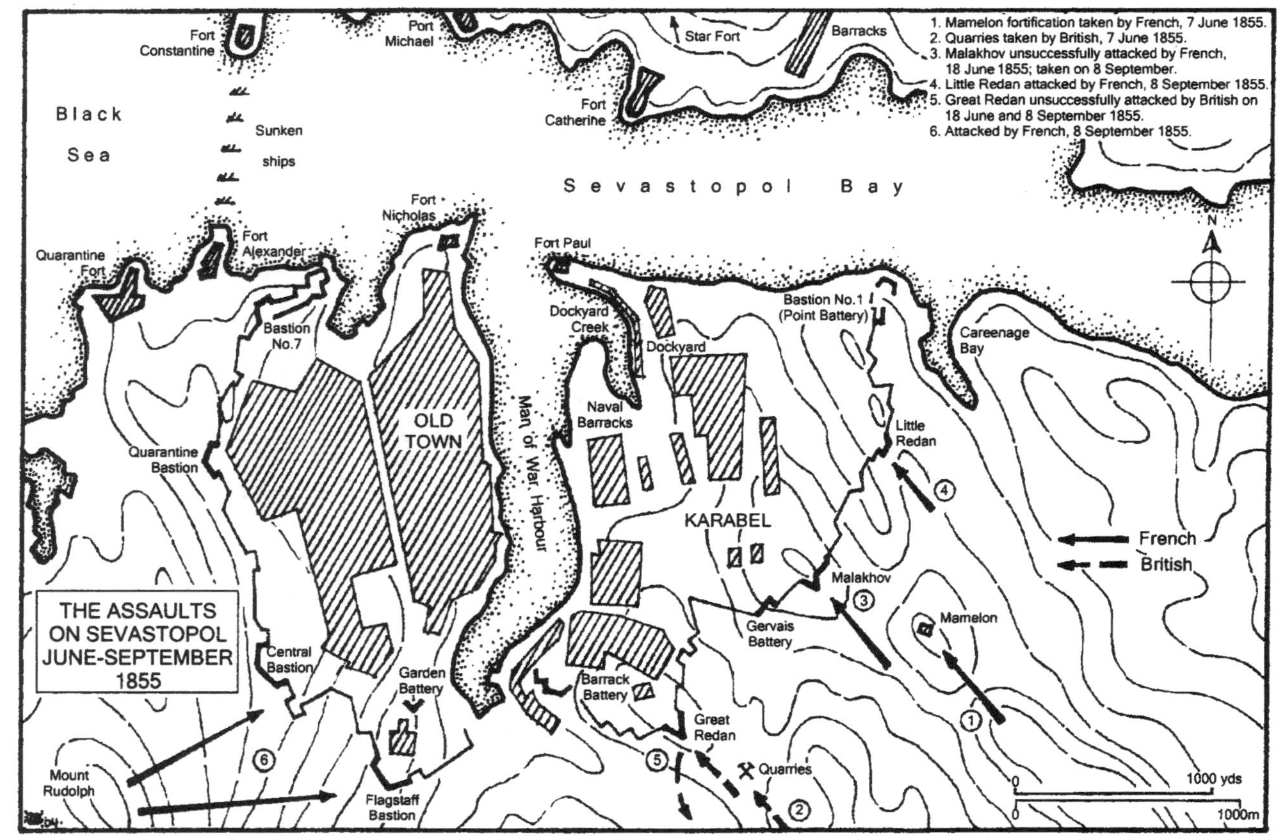
THE ASSAULTS ON SEVASTOPOL JUNE-SEPTEMBER 1855
1. Mamelon fortification taken by French, 7 June 1855.
2. Quarries taken by British, 7 June 1855.
3. Malakhov unsuccessfully attacked by French, 18 June 1855; taken on 8 September.
4. Little Redan attacked by French, 8 September 1855.
5. Great Redan unsuccessfully attacked by British on 18 June and 8 September 1855.
6. Attacked by French, 8 September 1855.
French
British
N
1000 yds
1000m
Black Sea
Sevastopol Bay
Fort Constantine
Sunken ships
Port Michael
Fort Catherine
Star Fort
Barracks
Quarantine Fort
Fort Alexander
Quarantine Bastion
Bastion No.7
Fort Nicholas
OLD TOWN
Central Bastion
Garden Battery
Flagstaff Bastion
Mount Rudolph
Man of War Harbour
Fort Paul
Dockyard Creek
Naval Barracks
Dockyard
KARABEL
Barrack Battery
Great Redan
Quarries
Gervais Battery
Malakhov
Bastion No.1 (Point Battery)
Little Redan
Careenage Bay
Mamelon

> On the morning of 8 September the 15th Reserve Infantry Division and the Modlinsky, Prazhsky and Zamostsky regiments (each of them consisting of two battalions) stood in the centre of the Malakhov Hill. The Lyublinsky Regiment, which also had two battalions, was working on completing the mines beneath the bastion, none of which were armed yet. In case of an assault the Lyublinsky Regiment was to leave a reliable sentry at the entrance to the mine gallery and then join the reserve of the Malakhov's garrison. The right flank of the fourth section, under command of Captain Kern, consisted of the famous Gervais battery, which was guarded by the chasseurs of His Imperial Majesty Grand Prince Mikhail Nikolaevitch's Regiment under command of the colonel of the Kamchatsky Regiment, Kitaev. The Muromsky Regiment, under the command of Major General Bussau, guarded the left flank of section up to the barrier (on the curtain). At dawn, the lookouts in the watchtowers on the Inkerman heights noticed an unusual movement of the enemy and so Prince Gorchakov informed the garrison's commander about it. Although a strong dusty wind hid what was going on in the enemy's trenches, we observed, at about 10 o'clock in the morning, that the French were carrying short logs and boards to their trenches and assumed that they were carrying the materials in order to lay their mine gallery under the hill. The tireless Lieutenant Wulfert was the Malakhov's most faithful guard from the very first shots right up until today. He and the fort were inseparable and he had experienced eleven bloody months there. He galloped to General Khrulev with a dispatch informing him of the French movements. The general, having listened to his report, barely had time to bring forward the regiments of the reserve, the 9th Division. He heard the alarm but rushed to the 2nd bastion because he didn't see the blue flag on the Malakhov Hill, which was a pre-arranged signal of a French assault. The French were increasing their fire and at 11.15 changed its direction and began to fire upon the area behind our batteries where our reserves were waiting.[3]

The withdrawal of the reserves from the Malakhov did not take them out of harm's way, for, as Alabin relates, at about 11 am the Allied bombardment began searching the rear areas where the reserves had mustered. The Malakhov was now occupied by its gun crews and a company of riflemen, and despite the sightings and reports of French movements it seemed as though the day would pass like any other. Out of sight of the French guns Major General Bussau was busy awarding crosses of the Order of St George to various soldiers, men talked and smoked their pipes, whilst most simply sat down to begin their midday meal. With the Allied bombardment having virtually ceased it was, in fact, quite a pleasant sunny Saturday afternoon. Not even the sudden crashing of a salvo of French shells could stir the Russians into anything other than curious onlookers. But when loud French shouts were heard out in front of the redoubt, all suddenly changed into a scene of wild commotion. It was twelve noon; the attack had begun.

The French trenches in places were barely thirty yards or so in front of the Malakhov and when the French charged forward they virtually jumped straight into the wrecked ditch of the work itself. 'The generals spring forward, waving their plumed hats; – living signals, they leap upon the parapets, the first to show themselves, entirely unprotected above the breastworks, – and shout, "Soldiers! Forward! *Vive l'Empereur!*" That cry, a thousand times repeated, thrills upon every lip. It is the signal of assault.'[4] In an instant, the ramparts of the Malakhov were crowded with a seething mass of Frenchmen who surged forward from their trenches to snatch the bastion from the for once unwary Russians. Alabin again:

> The distance from the last trench to the bastion ditch was only 25 metres (nearly 36 paces) – only a few leaps for a Zouave! The French covered the distance in a moment, not having experienced any canister shot because all the guns were loaded with balls and shells. There was no time to reload them with case shot. Those who had time fired but because they were aimed at the French batteries they sent their shells way above the heads of the attackers. Moreover, the French hadn't experienced any rifle fire because there was nobody on the banquet except for the skirmishers, who were firing at the trenches. There was no way that a large group of men could stand on the hill with their cocked muskets and wait for the assault. The drum on the hill hardly had time to sound the alarm before the French had taken the curtain and the rampart on the front of bastion and had overthrown the units of the Prazhsky Regiment. At that very moment the triumphant enemy, supported by the crowds of their comrades and the shouts of the huge reserve columns, using the ladders to cross the ditch, overran everyone who dared to oppose them. They dislodged our soldiers from each beam, which cut the interior of fortification, and occupied the whole upper part of the hill up to its gorge. That gorge, fortunately, was closed with a wide and deep ditch, which crossed it, and a parapet. The French were stopped by our fire and did not pursue us further.[5]

The men of McMahon's division covered the ground between the front French trench and the Malakhov easily and quickly and were up and over the ramparts without any problem. The real fighting began once they were inside, for they immediately came face to face with the Russian reserves who came dashing frantically forward to stem the French tide. The

Modlinsky Regiment hit the French running and violent hand-to-hand fighting ensued. The French were inside and they were not about to let go, nor were the Russians prepared to give it up without a fight. Although his regiment, the Muromsky, was away to the left of the bastion defending the curtain wall, Major General Bussau was still inside the Malakhov when McMahon's men came over the ramparts. He had still been preparing to present medals to some of the defenders and was caught unarmed. Instead, he picked up some rocks and began throwing them at his assailants until he was shot down. The commanding officer of the Malakhov, Karpov, was wounded also and taken prisoner, whilst the Prazhsky Regiment lost its commanding officer, Colonel Friend, killed during the fighting. It was all total chaos.

McMahon's Algerians had entered the Malakhov without too much trouble, catching the defenders completely off guard. But once inside they found themselves set upon by hundreds of Russian troops who flung themselves at their enemies, fighting desperately to keep them out. Even the lowest ranker knew that if the Malakhov fell their beloved town would be unable to hold on much longer. The fighting was bitter and savage, and when the two sides closed it became impossible to load their weapons and instead both sides set about each other with whatever weapons they could lay hands on. Lumps of wood, rocks, axes, crow bars, artillery ramrods and sponges, and, of course, the butt end of many a musket, was used during the fighting. Needless to say the dreaded 'white weapon', the bayonet, was using unsparingly and ferociously. But no matter how hard and how desperately the Russians fought they could not drive the French out, and by 12.30 the Malakhov was taken. Even so, small groups of Russians continued to defy the odds and fight on. In one notable incident, a Russian general[6] was cut off along with a small group of his men by a unit of Zouaves. Upon being summoned to lay down his arms the Russian officer simply swore at his enemies and thrashed at them with his sword. The Zouaves tried to rush them but only ended up being skewered by Russian bayonets. Eventually, they were left with little choice but to shoot them down.

Elsewhere, a small group was holding out in the tower of the Malakhov. Inside were Lieutenants Yuny, Danilchenko and Bogdazevitch,[7] with two naval officers and thirty men of the Modlinsky Regiment, who had been placed there to guard the pile of ammunition that had been left inside the tower. These men cleared away the rifle embrasures in the tower and barricaded the doors and opened up a withering and well-aimed fire on anyone who dared to come within view. The French suffered many casualties here and only succeeded in forcing the defenders to surrender by threatening to burn them out with bundles of blazing fascines. The French rush to the curtain had been so quick that the men of the Lyublinsky Regiment had no time to get out of the mine shaft they had been constructing. The sentry at the entrance to the gallery was quickly overthrown and those inside the gallery were forced to surrender.

With the Malakhov now in their possession, the French attempted to move to their left and attack the Gervais Battery but came face to face with the Kazansky Regiment, who were driven back losing their commanding officer, Kitaev, in the fight. The French were prevented from advancing any further, however, by the arrival of the Kostromsky and Galitsky Regiments that came dashing up from inside the town. With them was A A Vyazmitinov, who found himself trying to stem the French tide pouring from the Gervais Battery.

> We rushed forward and forced the leading French detachments back. Many were killed by their bayonets. We had no idea of the object of our attacks and didn't ask ourselves whether we would be successful. We simply rushed forward, drunk with the ardour of battle, and forgot that we were trying to take the very place which we had lost half an hour before. But there seemed no possibility of us holding out ... A narrow area between beam and parapet was covered with blood. A mixture of blood and dust covered the ground like a brown-red coloured paste ... I had taken part in many battles, but never before had I heard such a hail of bullets as I heard during the last assault of Sevastopol. Usually, as densely as the bullets fly, one can hear the difference between their whine. But here only one long hissing sound was heard. It seemed to be like a stream, flowing with bullets. We couldn't aim at the French because of the thick smoke. We were firing into the smoke, trying only to direct our bullets parallel to the ground.[8]

While the attack on the Malakhov was going on, Le Motte Rouge's division had attacked the curtain between the Malakhov and No.2 Bastion, the Little Redan. Once again the Russians were caught tucking into their midday meals, but as the French had a greater distance to cover to reach the curtain the defenders were warned by the opening of the attack away to their right, at the Malakhov, and were able to load their guns and open fire. The ground was swept by canister that knocked over scores of French troops but before long they too were up and over the wall and setting about the Russian defenders. Colonel Chabron, at the head of the 11th Léger, drove his men over the wall and on to the second line of Russian defences before being flung back, although the curtain wall remained in French hands in spite of the gallant efforts of the Olonetsky, who saw their commanding officer, Alekseev, captured, and the Muromsky, whose commander, Nichik, was wounded.[9] 'The French rushed the curtain and barrier at the same time as they attacked the Malakhov,' wrote Alabin.

> The resistance of the Muromsky Regiment that defended them was in vain, for there were ten French soldiers for every one of ours. They took the curtain, the barrier, and the 12-gun battery and pursued ours up to the second line of fortifications. But there they were met by the heavy artillery fire of the Henrikh Battery and by the Sevsky Regiment, which threw them back at bayonet point and pursued them to the barrier. The Sevsky Regiment, however, couldn't hold out there because they came under fire from enemy in the trenches in front and from those firing into the flank from the Malakhov Hill. Our regiment retreated to the second line and opened up a heavy fire from there against the French, who retook the 12-gun battery and barrier. Suddenly, to our great delight, a shell, fired probably from the Henrikh Battery, flew into powder magazine of the 12-gun battery and the battery blew up, along with many uninvited guests and covered a huge area with a cloud of smoke, sand and dust. The French who were left alive near this point, rushed to their friends in horror because they now thought that all the area taken by them was mined. There was turmoil at the Malakhov Hill as well – the French on the Malakhov Hill thought that we were blowing up the mines and they would share the fortune of those who had been inside the 12-gun battery. That turmoil nearly turned into a stampede and our regiment decided to use that moment of panic and fear and to advance. The French saw us coming, however, and regaining their senses met us from behind the parapet with a deadly fire. They realised the explosions had stopped and inspired by the example of their commanders returned again to the barrier. A great number of soldiers were killed by that explosion and General La Motte Rouge was wounded.[10]

With the curtain wall to the [Russian] left of the Malakhov, along with the Malakhov itself, now in French hands, things were looking very bleak for the Russians. At the other end of the curtain wall the Little Redan, part of No.5 sector under Captain Mikriukov, was attacked by Dulac's division, which was led by Generals Saint Pol and Bisson. The Little Redan was defended by two battalions of the Olonetsky, with one battalion each from the Aleksopolsky, Poltavsky and Kremenchugsky Regiments held back in reserve. It was a strong garrison but, like the defenders at the Malakhov, they had been allowed to drift off for their midday meal. Thus, when the French came storming forward at noon the garrison inside the bastion was way below strength. Major General Sabashinsky was acting bastion commander and he was apparently having an argument with a messenger sent to him by Khrulev when the French suddenly burst out of their trenches barely fifty yards away. Dulac's division was quickly inside the Little Redan but, unlike the attack on the Malakhov, things did not go quite as smoothly for the French. The Russians, in fact, now began to stabilise the situation, for the reserve battalions were beginning to arrive, rushing up from the rear areas, charging straight into the French who were brought shuddering to a halt. There was a fierce crossing of bayonets before slowly but steadily the Russians began to gain the upper hand. Then, aided by twenty guns on the flanks of the work and in a nearby cemetery, the French began to fall back, leaving behind them scores of dead and wounded. One of those killed during the attack was the 59 year-old Colonel Dupuis, who had fought the Russians once before – during Napoleon's ill-fated 1812 campaign. The majority of the French retreated to the safety of their own trenches, just fifty yards or so away, although some remained lying in the ditch at the foot of the work, including the chief of the divisional staff, Lieutenant Colonel Magnan, who was mortally wounded.

Despite being driven out Saint Pol and Bisson re-formed their battalions and attacked the Little Redan once more. Again they forced themselves over the ramparts and into the bastion but they could not hold it. Saint Pol himself was killed and Bisson wounded, whilst scored of others were shot down or bayoneted by the Russians. The Chasseurs of the Guard attacked, rallying the broken battalions around them, but they fared little better. General de Marolles then led forward his brigade, consisting of two battalions of the Grenadiers of the Guard who swarmed up and over the ramparts, forcing the defenders to withdraw to the safety of their second line. But, like all those before him, Marolles was unable to maintain his position in the teeth of such a murderous fire of grape and canister, and the hail of musket and rifle balls being poured out from the Russian second line. The Russians then counter-attacked, flinging themselves at the French using swords, bayonets, fists, boots, and anything that came to hand. Marolles himself was killed and his body found the following day, mutilated by several severe wounds. General de Pontèves was killed here also.

Thus, the Little Redan remained in Russian hands, and now Sabashinsky began trying to clear the French from the curtain wall which connected it with the Malakhov. His attempts met with some success but the French remained in possession of most of it. But despite their efforts to hold the Little Redan and to drive the French from the curtain wall the Russians knew full well that unless they retook the Malakhov all their efforts would come to nothing. It was the key to Sevastopol and Khrulev knew that unless he did something, and did it quickly, the town would become untenable.

When the first alarm had sounded General Khrulev and his staff mounted their horses and rushed to the weakest point, which they considered to be the 2nd bastion, the Little Redan. But before he arrived he learned to his dismay that the Malakhov had fallen and so rode there instead, gathering around him the 9th Division that was in reserve. It was to be the crucial action of the day. When he reached the Malakhov Khrulev took command of the Ladozhsky Regiment and led it forward in an attempt to break in using a kind of drawbridge which had been thrown over the ditch in the gorge. He got no farther than the ditch, however, where he was met by a storm of rifle bullets from behind the parapet closing the gorge. The bridge remained but its passageway was blocked and his men had no way of getting back inside the Malakhov. The Ladozhsky soldiers were on the point of rushing the bridge but the French concentrated all their rifle fire on it. General Khrulev was wounded at once and the Ladozhsky repulsed. One of his aides-de-camp, Captain Voeykov, then rushed forward at the head of one of their battalions but was killed with a bullet in his chest. It was possible to enter the bastion only through two entrances; the first one led towards the Little Redan by way of a wooden bridge across the ditch, and the second towards the Gervais battery. The entrances were immediately blocked with gabions, fascines, inverted guns and sandbags. The only way to assault the bastion was from the gorge itself or to go right round the Malakhov and attack it from the front at the same point which was attacked by French, as Alabin later recalled.

> In the first case we had to cross the ditch that closed the gorge. That ditch was rather deep, was 2 *sazhens* wide and had near vertical walls, which had been made in the stony soil of the hill with great effort. Then we were to take a rampart, which was in perfect condition and virtually inaccessible. We hadn't got any gabions or fascines, or even scaling-ladders. It was much more difficult to assault the hill from this side than from that by which it was taken by the French. It was no great effort to get over the ditch, which crumbled greatly in some places as a result of the bombardment.
>
> In the second case we had not only to deal with an experienced enemy that was in the bastion but also with the approaching crowds of French that would strike our rear and flank at the very moment of our assault. Finally, to take the hill we needed one commander who, in a decisive moment, could command the troops, who could work out the plan of action, and who was popular with the troops. He also needed strength and skill to execute that plan himself. But, unfortunately, there was no one commander at this point for a long time. As I have already said, General Khrulev was wounded in his left hand at the beginning of our attack and, suffering greatly, went to the dressing station. He ordered his assistant, Major General Lysenko, to take command. The Ladozhsky soldiers took cover behind a parapet formed of the dead bodies of their comrades, they hid in the ruins of houses around the hill, and behind the stones and heaps of earth, and began to exchange fire with the French in the Malakhov.

> At this point the last reserve regiments came, the 48th squad of the Kursky irregulars. Everybody was eager to fight, and burning with the desire to dislodge the enemy with their bayonets but nobody could reach the enemy. The fire from the parapet stopped everybody. General Lysenko was badly wounded in his leg with a bone shattered and a contusion in his stomach, which resulted in his death. The troops in front of the hill again lost their commander. Meanwhile, we could see the whole enemy armies approaching the hill. The field artillery came and opened fire. Each moment that passed the enemy strengthened their possession of the hill.[11]

Whilst Khrulev was battling in vain to save the Malakhov, Gorchakov was watching anxiously from the Severnaia. Although it was possible to observe events from the northern side of Sevastopol it was impossible for him to know the true state of affairs at the bastions. Nevertheless, he had the sense to send the Azovsky, Ukrainsky and Odessky Regiments across the pontoon bridge to the Korabel'naia to bolster the defences. By the time they arrived Khrulev had been wounded and command passed over to General Martinau although, like Khrulev before him, he could make no impression on the French who were strengthening their hold on the Malakhov. Like Khrulev, he was also to fall to a French rifle bullet, as Alabin recalled:

> The rifle fire was terrible in the gorge of the Malakhov Hill and Gervais battery, one part of which was in our hands and the other in the enemy's. There was a desperate fight here with soldiers throwing grenades, and fragments of stone at each other. The rifle bullets from the Malakhov were flying around the Korabel'naia side and found many victims, especially in the second line where the masses were crowded. They exchanged fire with the French, but to little effect, having no opportunity to attack them with cold steel. The 12th Division came bravely forward and advanced to the Hill. They stopped soon afterwards, however, because they plainly saw how it was impossible to take the Hill from that side, and this only increased the crowd of soldiers in the second line. The heroic commander of that division, Lieutenant General Martinau, who succeeded General Lysenko in command of the left wing troops, was at that moment badly wounded by the rifle bullet. His arm was smashed near the shoulder. With incredible courage he endured the wound and went back, supporting his broken arm by his good one. He then sent word to the garrison commander telling him to appoint a new commander to troops on the left side.
>
> He was *the third* general to fall in front of the Hill that day. Two generals had already perished here! But this time we were equal with

> the enemy: I was told by the French staff officers that the French had sent eighteen generals to attack the Malakhov Hill. Five of them were killed, eleven were wounded. Only General McMahon, who attacked the Hill, was left unharmed and later took command of the detachment which attacked our left half when General Bosquet was wounded.
>
> The C-in-C, was constantly receiving dispatches containing bad news from the 4th section, and went there himself to see the state of affairs. He reached the second line and watched things for a long time and saw for himself the great difficulty there would be in recapturing the Hill. He saw there was no possibility of its success, and knew that rivers of blood would be spilt in vain because the abandoning of the Yuzhnaya side of Sevastopol was already decided upon anyway. Having made sure that the French capture of the Hill would not prevent our retreat – and having made sure that the 3rd bastion, a so-called key to our retreat, was in our hands – he ordered us not to recommence the attack on the Hill but to withdraw troops from the second line in order to avoid losses.[12]

The struggle for the Little Redan and the Malakhov, and the curtain wall connecting them, reached crisis point for the Russians at around 5 pm, by which time the key to Sevastopol, the Malakhov, was firmly in French hands. By now, Gorchakov himself was on the scene. With so many of his commanders having been killed or wounded he was forced to come across and see the situation for himself. It was not good. The curtain wall to the left of the Malakhov was also in French hands but Sabashinsky and his men continued to hold off the French at the Little Redan. On the 'town front' away to the west, the Russians had enjoyed good fortune. Although the attacks here were little more than diversionary ones they had still come on in good strength. General de Salles, commanding the French 1st Corps, had attacked along the whole length of the front, with the main attacks being directed against the Central Bastion and the Flagstaff Bastion. The French attacks were preceded by the detonation of two large mines beneath the Central Bastion at which the French brigades dashed forward to the attack. The rushes were met with a hail of grape, canister and musketry which scythed down hundreds of French troops, including De Salles himself, who was shot through the head. By 3 pm it was clear that the attack on the 'town front' had failed and all French troops were ordered back to their trenches. Leboeuf's batteries then took over, shelling the Central and Flagstaff bastions in preparation for a second attack, this time by D'Autemarre's division and by General Cialdini's Sardinians. But when Pélissier saw that the Malakhov was firmly in French hands the attack was suspended. It was a wise decision. After all, the renewed attack on the 'town front' would only result in the unnecessary loss of hundreds more lives, for with the Malakhov in his grasp Pélissier knew the town was as good as taken. The price of victory was high, however, for no fewer than 145 French officers and 1,489 men had been killed, with a further 254 officers and 4,259 men wounded. Ten officers and an astonishing 1,400 were listed as missing, many of whom were killed.

The capture of the Malakhov by the French effectively signalled the end for Sevastopol. Once inside, the French would be able to fire into the rear areas, into the Redan, and into the harbour and town of Sevastopol itself. Everyone, both Russians and Allies alike, knew the Malakhov was the key to everything, and with the key now safely in the hands of the French they were ready to unlock the defences and bring an end to the siege. But first there was one last tragedy to be played out, for even though the Malakhov was taken it was still considered necessary for the British to do their bit and attack the Redan. British honour demanded it.

Eager to avenge the disaster of 18 June, the British were ready and waiting to go. The Redan, that great and powerful earthwork that had cost them so dearly during the previous assault, lay uphill on the far side of almost 250 yards of open ground. The signal for their attack to begin was to be the hoisting of the French tricolour inside the Malakhov, which would be done as soon as it was taken. A flight of rockets would be shot up also. The troops selected for the task assembled in the trenches early on 8 September. It is almost certain that a good number of them were terrified of the ordeal that lay before them. Many of them had barely learned to shave, let alone kill. They were little more than boys, and whilst many probably looked upon life in the British Army as a great game few could have had any idea of the sort of nightmare they were about to be plunged into. This was no game. Not any more. It would be sheer slaughter.

NOTES

1 Bazancourt, the Baron de (trans. by Robert Howe Gould). *The Crimean Expedition, to the Capture of Sebastopol. Chronicles of the War in the East* (London 1856), II, 455–6.
2 Ibid, II, 456.
3 Alabin P V, *Pohodnye zapiski v voinu 1853–1856 godov* (Moscow 1892), 546–7.
4 Bazancourt, *Crimean Expedition*, II, 459–60.
5 Alabin, *Pohodnye zapiski v voinu*. 547–8.
6 Major General Yuferov possibly
7 These three lieutenants were awarded with the order of St Great Martyr Georgy of the 1st degree
8 Vyazmitinov A A, 'Sevastopol ot 21 marta po 28 avgusta 1855 goda', *Russkaya starina*, April 1882, 54–6.
9 Seaton, Albert. *The Crimean War: a Russian Chronicle* (London 1977), 213.
10 Alabin, *Pohodnye zapiski v voinu* 554–5.
11 Ibid, 545–57.
12 Ibid, 545–57.

# CHAPTER TWENTY-FIVE
# 'Shame, Rage and Fear'

For the British army in the Crimea, 8 September 1855 was to prove one of the defining moments of their war. The battles of Inkerman and the Alma were glorious days and had demonstrated the British soldier at his very best. But the battles and their consequent huge losses had severely weakened the army, since when the winter troubles and the siege of Sevastopol had brought upon it a tremendous strain. Despite the victories at the Alma and Inkerman they had not resulted in overall victory in the war against Russia, whilst the siege itself had failed to break the resolve of the gallant defenders, to which the failed attack on 18 June provided ample testament. It all seemed to come down to the attack on 8 September. It was, as one British historian put it, 'the Day of Days'.[1]

The British troops destined to attack the Redan watched anxiously from their front-line trenches, looking for the signal for their attack to begin. At noon they watched as, right on time, McMahon's troops sprang from their trenches and swarmed over the Malakhov. Although they were unable to see what was happening in the bastion there was every sign that the French had succeeded in establishing themselves inside it as thousands of French troops, Algerians and Zouaves, made their colourful way forward, cheering, and shouting, and wishing long life to their emperor. Waiting and watching from inside the Redan was Pyotr Alabin, and in his diary, written the day after, he recalled the moment the attack began.

> Suddenly at midday, the piquets shouted: 'They're coming! They're coming! They're attacking the Malakhov!' The dreaded news of the beginning of the assault on the Malakhov Hill immediately spread throughout the bastion. Although the blue flag, which meant 'assault', wasn't raised over the tower in the Malakhov, the alarm was sounded in the third bastion and everybody began to watch the first moments of the assault. Our hearts beat faster than ever. We could clearly see that crowds of men were running forward from the trenches on the Kamchatsky lunette, and from other trenches. We saw them rushing to the Hill, and saw the Zouaves climbing up it, standing on the backs of their comrades and helping each other up.

> We saw a three-coloured banner rise over the Malakhov Hill and were now ready to share our bloody feast with our guests.[2]

Anxious glances were no doubt exchanged in the British lines whilst senior officers craned their necks looking for the signal. Then, suddenly, a tricolour could be seen through the smoke, fluttering back and forth on the ramparts of the Malakhov. It was followed soon afterwards by a cluster of rockets that were sent into the bright late autumn sky. It was ten minutes past twelve. It was time to go.

At the word of command the men of the 2nd and Light Divisions scrambled out of their trenches and began making their way out into the open, heading for the Redan which lay about 250 yards in front of them. The advance was uphill and there was virtually no cover. The covering party of the 2nd Rifle Brigade, under Captain Fyers, took the lead, spreading out in front of Major Welsford and the 160 men of the 97th Regiment who made up the first storming party. Some of the men carried ladders, and what a cumbersome burden they proved to be. Men cursed and sweated as they stumbled forward, weighed down by what were, in fact, vital pieces of equipment, for without them there would be little hope of scaling any serious obstacles they might find in their way. Following behind Welsford came the second storming party, a further two hundred men of the 97th, under Colonel Handcock, along with three hundred men of the 90th, under Colonel Grove. Following gamely behind were the supports, the 750 men of the 19th and 88th Regiments, whilst Captain Perrin and his one hundred-strong working party from the 90th brought up the rear. The 2nd Division's stormers sprang forward at the same time, attacking to the right of the Light Division. They were led by Colonel Charles Windham, who had tossed a coin with Colonel Unett for the honour of leading them. The covering party of the 3rd (Buffs), under Captain Lewes, led the way followed by a further 160 of their comrades, many of whom carried ladders. Behind them came 260 men from the Buffs, 300 of the 41st, and 200 from the 62nd. Warren's brigade, the 30th and 55th, formed the reserve.

It was a spectacular sight to those who had gathered to watch from Cathcart's Hill. Amongst them was the wife of Colonel Handcock, of the 97th, who watched the tiny red specks charge forward, many of them tumbling and falling as the Russians opened fire. Little did she know that one of the fallen was her own husband. Unlike the French, whose trenches extended to within barely thirty yards of the Malakhov, the British stormers had to cover almost 250 yards, which gave the Russians ample time to prepare. The defenders were also warned, of course, by the attack on the Malakhov. Thus, there was no chance of achieving the sort of surprise that the French had. In fact, the Russian defenders in the Redan had been on the alert throughout the morning following reports of unusual movements in the British trenches.

The British attack got off to a bad start. The 1,400 or so men selected for the actual storming – a woefully inadequate number – were crammed together in a fairly short stretch of trench, and it is said that the men from at least two regiments, possibly the 97th and 19th, went forward prematurely, having mistaken a 'cautionary word' for the order to attack. Others claimed that once the French tricolour was seen above the Malakhov the British troops simply could not be restrained any longer, and poured out of their trenches in a disorderly rabble, even overtaking the men carrying the ladders. Indeed, many of these men were knocked down in the scrimmage and the ladders simply thrown aside. Whatever happened, it certainly upset the arrangements and sent everyone forward in a disorderly manner. Once in the open the stormers came under heavy fire from the Russians. Grape shot swept the ground in front of the Redan whilst the defenders lined the ramparts, unleashing a withering fire into the advancing British. As on the occasion of the failed attack on 18 June the British troops went into action still wearing their packs on their backs, whereas all they really needed was a rifle, bayonet and plenty of ammunition. This was not the time to be carrying spare shirts and mess kits. They struggled up the slope towards the Redan, officers in front, yelling and pointing to the front, whilst men dropped on all sides, ripped apart by grape shot or simply shot dead by musketry. Leading one of the ladder parties was major George Ranken, of the Royal Engineers, who left one of the most vivid descriptions of the assault on 8 September.

> Our men were no longer restrained; before there was time to get the ladders to the front, and before the sappers could advance to cut away the abattis, they rushed in a struggling line over the parapets, and dashed on towards the salient. I hurried up my sappers as fast as I could, shouting to them till I was nearly hoarse, and ran forward with them and the ladder party, with a drawn sword in my hand (my scabbard and belt I left behind). In the hurry and confusion many ladders were left behind. There was, however, little excuse for this, as the men had had their places distinctly assigned to them, and should not have left the trench without their ladders. It was of course impossible to perceive that anything of the kind had occurred, and still more impossible to rectify it had it been known. The only word was – 'Forward' the only course to pursue – to advance as rapidly as possible. Nearly 200 yards of rough broken ground and an abattis had to be crossed under the enemy's fire. The men advanced with the greatest spirit. I could see bodies dead and wounded lying along and strewing the ground on each side of me, as I pressed forward, shouting continually to the men to advance, and not to pause for an instant. When I came to the abattis, I found five men nearly exhausted

> carrying a ladder and trying to get it over the opposing branches; the remaining three men composing the party of eight had probably been killed or wounded in the advance. I leant them my aid and urged them on.[3]

The Redan itself was shrouded in thick grey smoke which bellowed from the muzzles and barrels of the Russian guns. Inside the defenders worked the guns and loaded their rifles and muskets, determined to repeat the successful defence of 18 June. This time, however, they did not have the benefit of the abattis which had so thwarted the British on that occasion, for the artillery bombardment of August and September had swept it aside and hardly any of it remained in place. Despite the tremendous fire being poured into them the British could not be stopped and soon they reached the ditch, breathless, sweating and eager to break in and avenge the previous failed assault. Pyotr Alabin again:

> The welcome which the English received was terrible! A lava flow of lead and cast iron was poured on them. Our enemies fell like autumn leaves in a storm and they rushed back away from the batteries where the Minsky, Volynsky and Kamchatsky regiments met them with a deadly fire of artillery and a shower of bullets. The English on the left flank fled; they didn't even reach the ditch, so dreadful was the fire of the Iakoutsky regiment. But the English who survived in the centre of their attack, inspired by their brave officers, entered the damaged salient angle of the bastion and drove back the Vladimirsky regiment and the 47th [the Kursk *opolchenie*] that defended this position! A small part from the Sousdalsky regiment came running up to them but the triumphant English crushed them also. They went from success to success; they took the dugouts, artillery, the whole angle up to the gorge, which was, fortunately, blocked with a small ditch and parapet.[4]

The British reached the ditch at the salient angle of the Redan and found it wide and deep, despite the intense bombardment of the last few days. However, George Ranken thought it nowhere near as difficult as had been expected.

> The edge of the ditch was soon reached, and I was relieved to find the ditch not nearly so formidable as it had been represented, and as I had good reason, from the solidity and extent of the Russian defences, to suppose it was likely to prove. I was prepared for a broad ditch, flanked by caponieres, and for military pits, chevaux-de-frise, palisades, and all kinds of obstacles. The dreaded ditch of the Redan, however, proved nothing but a simple trench, perhaps fourteen or

> fifteen feet deep at the counterscarp, and twenty or more at the escarp. I kept my ladders rather to the right of the salient angle, having been warned that the flanking fire would probably be severe up the proper left face. Half-a-dozen or so were lowered and reversed in a minute, and the men poured up them with eager haste. I set to work with every sapper I could get hold of, or to whom amid the din I could make myself audible, to tear down the rubble stone work with which the salient of the escarp was revetted, and form a practicable ramp for ascent without ladders.[5]

The ditch was fifteen feet deep, in fact, but much debris lay here and there and it did not prove to be too difficult to get down into. Ladders were thrown down and pushed against the other side, whereupon the men, led by their officers, began to scale the other side and enter the Redan itself. Others simply scrambled up, pulling their comrades up and helping them through the embrasures. Charles Windham reached the ditch and crossed it without much trouble, although there were only three other men with him, one of whom, Mahoney, was shot through the head as soon as he climbed through the embrasure in front of him. Windham, meanwhile, turned and called to the rest of his company to hurry up and move on. He waited until about fifteen men had got across before he entered the Redan itself, 'entering at the second or third embrasure to the right, the first being on fire'. Windham then dropped into the Redan itself. The problem was that no one followed him. 'To the best of my belief,' he wrote later, 'I was followed by no one.'[6] One man from the 88th did in fact follow him, along with two men from the Rifle Brigade, but that was about all. Elsewhere, however, other British troops were getting inside the Redan despite the intensity of the Russian fire. They managed to scramble over the ramparts and through the embrasures and were soon tumbling into the main work itself. It was quite an achievement, even though there were very few of them. Meanwhile, George Ranken and his men began to get to grips with the task of tearing down the ramparts and opening up the embrasures.

> The long continuance of dry weather which preceded the assault must be regarded as a very favourable circumstance. The gabions staked to the ground with wooden spikes (with which the counterscarp was revetted) were torn down, and used in forming with rocks, stones, and debris, a small parapet across the ditch of the proper left face, and a similar counter-caponiere thrown up also on the other side. I had to work, however, with my own hands.[7]

The Russians had retrenched at the rear of the Redan, so that if the British got into the bastion they would have to face a second defensive line, formed of a long entrenchment, lined with Russian guns and infantry. It was common practice. Indeed, during the Peninsular War, the last time British soldiers had been called upon to fling themselves at fire and stone, the French had a bad habit of doing the same, retrenching, so that Wellington's men had a second barrier to pass, should they be fortunate enough to negotiate the first. The Russians inside the Redan drew back to their entrenchment leaving their guns behind them and the bastion open and inviting to the crowds of British troops hurrying towards it. Now, more than ever, was the time to get forward the reserves and get men into the bastion to consolidate the position. Several British officers were now inside the Redan, and the number was growing by the minute. But very few of their men followed them, barely a hundred at most. Instead, they moved along the ramparts a short way or, as in the case of the vast majority, they lay down behind the ramparts and contented themselves with exchanging fire with the Russians to the rear of the place. Despite the haranguings of their officers they simply would not go on.

> Our men, having got into the little chambers were by necessity cut up into small parties; and as the Russians held in force the proper right and the four flanking guns, the only thing to do was to get our men out of that position and take the second line – an easily transversed ditch – by a dash, which would have induced all followers to come into the battery instead of into the salient . . . I tried three times. Many of the men could not see me, others were busy firing; only two came out with me when I went forward, and took a shot, by my order, at a Russian officer . . . But in spite of the most approved theatrical attitudes, and *strong* language, I could never succeed in getting attended to.[8]

To the Russians, fearful they had lost the place, it came as a blessed relief. The British had got into the Redan but in no great numbers, and those that were inside remained concentrated within the salient angle, with none moving beyond the third or fourth gun on either side of the angle. No matter how hard their officers tried the men would not advance any farther, whilst those outside would not enter. More and more British soldiers had succeeded in reaching the Redan but remained outside. They simply could not be induced to enter, as Henry Clifford recalled. 'The scaling ladders, for many men got there, were placed against the parapet, and many officers and men of these regiments got into the Redan. Supports were sent up, which also suffered much crossing the open to the Redan, but these instead of rushing on when they got to the parapet, lay on it outside. The Russian reinforcements came up, and drove the storming party out.'[9] Those British troops who did venture into the Redan at least tried to do something positive, and set about spiking the guns and on destroying as much of the work as possible, as the watching Pyotr Alabin later recalled:

> The English were sitting on the guns and spiking them; they were looting the dugouts; they were drinking rum from the camp flasks; they were lighting up their cigars with our fuses, cutting the gun-carriages, setting fire to the gabions and fascines in the embrasures, breaking everything they could but still carried on a severe exchange of fire with our soldiers. All of a sudden, the thundering of drums was heard. A great 'hurrah' was heard and the first carabineer company of the Kamchatsky chasseur regiment, brought from the batteries by its commander, Lieutenant Colonel Artemyev, came running forward with levelled bayonets through the destroyed part of the parapet. The bayonet charge was terrible. It was supported with the same terrible determination by the grenadier company of the Iakoutsky Regiment with part of the Sousdalsky regiment and the remains of the Vladimirsky Regiment. After fierce fighting they threw the English out of the bastion. Our soldiers were throwing stones, shouting swearwords and firing their muskets.[10]

Captain John Hume, of the 55th, had had a very lucky escape when his company went forward to attack the Redan. No sooner had he left his trench than he was struck in the breast by a grape shot that glanced off his prayer book, cut through his sword belt and gave his light company whistle an almighty dent. It could have been far worse, however. Hume pressed on and arrived at the Redan to find the ramparts crowded with soldiers from various regiments.

> I found it quite impossible to get my men through the crowd on the salient in any kind of formation, so the only thing to be done was to get through as best we could; but it was fatal to our chance of doing much to be stopped in our advance, and whatever formation we had was destroyed; it was too late, under the heavy fire we were exposed to, to try another part of the work.[11]

It was the same story everywhere; the more determined British units simply could not get through the masses crowding together on the outside of the ramparts. Hume eventually managed to get some ladders and scale another part of the Redan. There appeared to be no Russians in front but Hume noticed many on his flanks. 'Ah, sir, let us charge them!' said Private Whelan, who was with him. 'If these men will go with us we will; three of us are not enough to do any good.'[12] Sadly, none of the men from the other regiments would follow him, and so they remained with the others, crowding together on the ramparts. It was chaotic. Hume was then struck on the back of the head by a Russian grenade and flung backwards into the ditch. A man of the 41st, who had been shot through the head, then fell down on top of him. At length Hume managed to extricate himself, all the while suffering from the blow to the head, and he lay down at the back of the ditch with many other men of the 55th who were firing up at any Russians they could see.

Hume's story is typical of the attack on the Redan. Instead of attacking in battalion strength the 55th had been ordered to send forward just the light company and No.6 company. The 55th's commanding officer, Major Cure, waited in the trenches for the remaining companies to arrive from the rear but found they had already gone over piecemeal, taken out by their own officers. He managed to gather about a hundred men together and set off himself for the Redan where he found the newly promoted Lieutenant Colonel Cuddy trying to organise a group of men from different regiments. Cure then went back to try to find the rest of the 55th but most of them were already scattered around the Redan. Cure then returned to the Redan, crossing the 250 yards of open ground for a second time, all the while under fire. This time he was not so lucky, for he was badly wounded by a musket ball which broke his arm. He returned to the British lines leaving Cuddy to assume command. The unfortunate Cuddy was not to enjoy his newly won rank, however, for he was shot dead in the ditch soon afterwards, his body tumbling down to rest amongst the scores of other corpses which were piling up there. The 55th were leaderless once again, but they were not the only ones. Numerous British officers had been shot down and killed, leaving their men bereft of leadership, and with no supports coming forward from the trenches they began to waver.

> It was difficult to get any one to do anything; the men, as they struggled up to the assault in support of the advance, seemed stunned and paralysed – there was little of that dash and enthusiasm which might have been looked for from British soldiers in an assault; in fact, it required all the efforts and examples of the officers to get the men on, and these were rendered almost ineffective from the manner in which the various regiments soon got confused and jumbled together. The men, after firing from behind the traverses, near the salient, for half-an-hour at the enemy – also firing behind his parados and traverses, – began to waver. I rushed up the salient with the view of cheering them on, and the officers exerted themselves to sustain them; the men gave a cheer and went at it afresh. The supports or reserves, ordered to follow, straggled up in inefficient disorder, but were unable to press into the work, as the men in advance, occupying the salient, refused to go on, notwithstanding the devoted efforts of the officers to induce them to do so. Whether it was that they dreaded some secret trap, or some mine which would destroy the whole of them at once – whether it was that the long and tedious siege works had lowered their '*morale*' – or whether it was owing to the dreadful manner in which their Division (the Light, *most* injudiciously selected

> to lead) had been cut up in the previous actions – it is a melancholy truth that the majority of the assaulting column did not display the spirit and dash of thorough good soldiers, when assaulting the enemy. They refused, however, to retreat, and seemed to look round for aid; I trembled when I saw no one coming, and looked continually, anxiously, round for the reserves I considered, as a matter of course, would be advanced immediately it was perceived that the leading columns had failed to carry the position and were commencing to waver.[13]

The growing number of Russian troops gathering behind their breastwork had little difficulty in shooting down the British officers who were trying vainly to get their men to advance. It was only a matter of time before the Russians counter-attacked and, sure enough, they duly obliged, driving the British back over the parapets and into the ditch beyond. It would have helped enormously if the French, instead of spiking the Russian guns inside the Malakhov, had turned them on the retrenchment at the rear of the Redan but nobody appears to have considered this. It was now vital that the reserves were brought up and, some did indeed get forward, but they suffered considerably from Russian fire, particularly from the batteries on either flank. Sergeant Timothy Gowing, of the 7th Royal Fusiliers, was one of those who braved the defenders' fire to reach the Redan.

> We, the supports, moved forward to back up our comrades, but anyone with half an eye could see that we had not the same cool, resolute men, as at Alma and Inkerman; though some of the older hands were determined to make the best of a bad job; and I am happy to record that the old Inkerman men took it very coolly; some of them lit their pipes, I did the same. A brave young officer of ours, a Mr Colt, told me he would give all he was worth to be able to take it as comfortably as some of our people did – it was his first time under fire – he was as pale as death and shaking from head to foot, yet he bravely faced the foe. The poor boy (for he was not much more) requested me not to leave him; and he fell dead by my side, just outside the Redan.[14] Our people were now at it in front; we advanced as quickly as we could until we came to the foremost trench, when we leaped the parapet, then made a rush at the blood-stained walls of the Redan – we had a clear run of over 200 yards, under a murderous fire of grape, canister, and musketry. How any one ever lived to pass that 200 yards seemed a miracle, for our poor fellows fell one on top of the other; but nothing but death could stop us. The musket ball whistled by us more like hail than anything else I can describe, and the grape shot cut our poor fellows to pieces; for we had a front and two cross

> fires to meet. It seemed to me that we were rushing into the very jaws of death, but I for one reached the Redan without a scratch. While standing on the brink of the ditch, I considered for a moment how best to get into it, for it appeared to be about twenty feet deep, with no end of our poor fellows at the bottom, dead and dying, with their bayonets sticking up; but the mystery solved itself, our men came rushing on with a cheer for Old England, and in we went, neck or nothing, scrambled up the other side the best way we could, and into the redoubt we went with a shout truly English. The fighting inside the works was desperate – butt and bayonet, feet and fist; the enemy's guns were at once spiked; some of the older hands did their best to get together sufficient men for one charge at the enemy, for we had often proved that they were no lovers of cold steel, but our poor fellows melted away almost as fast as they scaled those bloody parapets, from a cross-fire the enemy brought to bear upon us from the rear of that work. The moss of that field grew red with British blood.[15]

The problem remained; the British officers could not get their men to advance beyond the parapets and through the embrasures in order to attack the Russians deeper inside the Redan itself. They simply wouldn't do it. It is almost certain that most of the officer casualties occurred whilst they were standing up trying to get their men forward. Some of the reserves refused to go forward, whilst the others only served to add to the chaos. Of the senior officers who led the initial attack Colonel Unett was wounded and carried to the rear, Major Welsford had his head blown off when trying to get through an embrasure, whilst Handcock was mortally wounded, shot in the head. He later died in the arms of his young wife. The 31 year-old Captain Maximilien Hammond, of the Rifle Brigade, had only landed at Balaklava some two days before the assault, having returned from sick leave in England. Hammond was a God-fearing soldier, a true Christian, well liked by all who knew him. Despite his lack of experience in the Crimea he was at the head of his men when the attack on the Redan took place, and was last seen helping a colour-sergeant through an embrasure. A fellow officer of the Rifle Brigade saw him on the ramparts of the bastion, thrashing away with his sword before he finally fell amidst a flurry of Russian bayonets. His body was recovered later, punctured by several wounds.[16] But these were just four of innumerable British officers and men who fell attacking the Redan. There were hundreds more. It was developing into a regular bloodbath. Worse still, as far as the British were concerned, not only were the casualties mounting alarmingly, but the Russians were clearly getting the upper hand once more. Indeed, the defenders were more than pleased with the way they had dealt with their assailants.

> It seemed to us that our counter-attack had been successful. The English attack was repulsed; our triumph was complete! But General Pavlov was not so sure. He sent two companies of the Selenghinsky regiment from the reserve to the salient angle. Before they had time to get there the English attacked the bastion again and once again took it despite the desperate resistance of our garrison. The English took the parapet and were firing upon the whole bastion. They even charged forward and tried to attack us with their bayonets but the Selenghinsky regiment came up at that point, supported by the Kamchatsky, Iakoutsky and Vladimirsky. At the same time as this second attack on the salient angle the English struck at Yanovsky's battery. The Sousdalsky regiment was there. The British bravely passed through the cross-fire and, leaving heaps of dead bodies behind, climbed the battery with their scaling-ladders but were met by the defenders. The Sousdalsky couldn't withstand the great numerical superiority of the English but the Iakoutsky came forward just in time, struck the enemy's flank and threw them back from the battery taking two officers and twenty seven other ranks prisoner. They then sent the retreating English on their way amidst a very heavy fire. The English finally escaped and retreated to their trenches. Their casualties were enormous. Near the bastion there was not a square *sazhen* [Russian measure of length = 2 m 13 cm] of ground where there was not a dead or wounded soldier.[17]

Sergeant Gowing's great concerns about the lack of experience among the British soldiers who had come out to the Crimea since the winter were well-founded. Now, more than ever before, were needed the men of the Alma and of Inkerman, but these were long gone. The blend of youth and experience was distinctly one-sided, with the ranks being swelled by fresh-faced young men who were barely willing, and certainly not able to do the job. They had covered the ground between their trenches and the Redan in good time but it had struck the fear of God into them. Once at the Redan they were gripped by indecision and fear, and instead of pressing on they stood around in groups, looking confused and lacking leadership. They were too petrified to go forward into the Redan but were disciplined enough – at this point anyway – to remain behind the ramparts, firing over them at the ever-growing number of Russian troops inside.

It is said that a rumour was going round that the Redan had been heavily mined, which may well have contributed to the reluctance of the British rank and file to follow their officers and get forward. This particular theory is not without substance, for the use of mining and counter-mining had been one of the features of the siege of Sevastopol so far. Had the Russians simply retreated to the rear of the Redan in order to draw the British into a trap? Few were willing to find out. There was massive confusion and disorder. The British soldier, in the heat of battle, has habitually followed the orders from whatever officer happened to give them, but at the Redan it seems as though they would listen only to their own officers. The men of one regiment, for example, would not obey the orders from an officer of another. Thus, the misery was compounded. No order, no discipline, and nobody willing to venture deeper into the Redan. And all the time more and more of them were shot down by the Russians.

> We must again remember that our 'men' in this case were mostly boys who had been walking in the streets of London or down the quiet country lanes of England only a few weeks previously; and we may ask, perhaps, whether, in the circumstances, they were not behaving as rationally as those who were responsible for their awful situation.[18]

Meanwhile, Windham was desperately trying to get his men forward but had been fighting a losing battle and, along with the three men who had followed him into the Redan, had been forced back to the ramparts. 'We fell back,' he wrote, 'and on my getting upon the parapet, the men were nearly taking a panic. I accordingly ran to the top of it (amongst their muskets) and assured them there was no cause for fear, and implored them not to fall back; they gave me a cheer and all seemed right.' At that point Windham sent one of his officers, Roger Swire, back to the British trenches to ask Codrington for the reserves to be sent forward, for it was clear to him that unless they were received soon he and the other British troops at the Redan would be driven out. But just as Windham thought things had settled down his men wavered once more.

> Then another panic came on and I thought they would all be off. I shouted to them to stand firm and a bugler of the 62nd sounded the advance, the men cheered and all was again quiet. I now, after hitting a man with my fist for firing through the burning embrasure, tried to get the men away from the salient where they were crowded, along the proper left face of the work; but beyond a dozen it was no go.[19]

A succession of officers was sent dashing back to Codrington requesting support. Some were killed, but others made it. But still Codrington dithered. Some reinforcements managed to get forward but they went over piecemeal and only served to compound the confusion at the Redan. Finally, and in great despair, Windham decided he would have to go himself and, turning to a young officer, Crealock, said, 'I have sent five times for support . . . Now bear witness that I am not in a funk but I will now go back myself and try what I can do.'[20]

Windham was, of course, acting with the best of intentions, but it was a mistake. His pleas for reserves fell on deaf ears. Indeed, Codrington simply said, 'come down Windham, you'll only get killed there. My good fellow, they won't go and I have no number to send.' It was a frighteningly frank admission by Codrington who was taking what appears to have been a very detached and relaxed view of it all. British soldiers were being slaughtered at the Redan and all he could do was play the part of the typically nonchalant British officer in a time of crisis. Unfortunately, Codrington appears not to have realised just how big a crisis it was. In the meantime, Windham appealed to General Markham, commander of the 2nd Division, who suggested he take the Royal Scots. Windham then returned to Codrington and, climbing the parapet, asked him to give the order to go forward again. Incredibly, Codrington pulled him back, saying, 'Come down, Windham, and don't be in such a hurry. Let's see what the French are about.'[21] Codrington's attitude should come as little surprise given the eccentric manner in which other senior British commanders conducted themselves on 8 September. Sir Harry Jones, for example, was suffering from a severe attack of rheumatism and, unable to move either hand or foot, was carried on a litter wearing a red nightcap. Sir Richard Airey watched the assault wearing a large white handkerchief tied over his cap and ears to shield himself from the biting wind. Simpson, meanwhile, suffering from some illness, just sat in a trench, 'with his nose and eyes just facing the cold and dust, and his cloak drawn over his head to protect him against both'.[22] Sadly, by the time Windham was ready to lead the Royals forward it was too late for the British were pouring back like so many frightened rabbits.

It had suddenly dawned on the Russians that, despite the crowds of British soldiers on the ramparts, in the embrasures, and in the ditch, they were not going to advance and push deeper into the Redan. The Russians had little trouble shooting down the few officers inside and were now more than comfortable holding their retrenchment at the rear of the Redan. Furthermore, their reinforcements were now arriving, not only from inside Sevastopol but also from the Malakhov, from where those who were not involved in the attempts to recapture the bastion now came. The Russians could sense the fear in the British troops and realised that a counter-attack was all that was needed to send their wavering enemies back to their own lines. Guns were primed, loaded with grape shot, muskets and rifles loaded and bayonets fixed. Then, at the word of command, a tremendous fire crashed out from the rear of the Redan sweeping away scores of British soldiers. Those that survived the deadly blast had barely regained their senses when, suddenly, from the depths of the smoke that slowly rolled away in front of them, there came hundreds of grey-clad Russian soldiers, their bayonets charged, and their officers, sword in hand, cheering them on. For the British, reeling backwards on the ramparts, it was the last straw.

> What brought matters completely to a crisis I have never exactly ascertained: I heard directly after I regained our trenches that three officers of the 41st, after vainly striving to induce the men to advance, rushed forward together, and were all three shot down like one man by the cross fire of the Russians behind their parados. This was the turning point, according to this account, of the men's indecision – they wavered and fled. I was near the counterscarp when I saw the whole living mass on the salient begin reeling and swaying to and fro; in a moment I found myself knocked down and lying on my face, with a number of men scrambling over me – their bayonets running through my clothes. I expected to have been stunned and bayoneted, and to have been left insensible in the ditch, or shot by the enemy before I could drag myself out of it. However, at last I saw an opening, and holding on by my hands and knees, managed to force my way to it through the moving mass, and regain my legs. I ran then as fast as I could towards our advance trenches, the grape whistling past me like hail, and the Russians standing on top of their parapets, and firing volleys into the crowds of fugitives.[23]

The sight of the fierce-looking Russian infantry, letting out their now infamous long drawn-out howl, was too much for the shell-shocked young boys who had expended their last ounce of courage. Despite the efforts of the remaining officers and the more experienced NCOs they refused to stand, and, turning their backs on the advancing Russians, they looked to safety, to the ditch below, and to their own lines that lay 250 yards in the distance. At first there was a dash from those at the back, then, as those at the front tried to get through and off the ramparts there was panic, pushing and, finally, a mad disorderly stampede. Scores of British troops tumbled into the ditch, others simply fell as the ramparts and the gabions on them gave way under the pressure of hundreds of heaving bodies. The side of the ditch itself gave way and in an instant both the earth and the troops all came down together, crashing down onto those still in the ditch, many of whom stood with their bayonets upturned. Many of the British were impaled on their comrades' bayonets, others were crushed and scores knocked unconscious. It was pure mayhem. It is not difficult to picture the writhing red mass, struggling and boiling to get out of the ditch, men desperately fighting with each other, the living trampling on the dead and dying, the shouts and cries of the wounded, the swearing, the screaming and the sheer hell of it all. And then, just when things couldn't get any worse, the Russians arrived on the ramparts, heavily armed and looking straight down into the ditch at the heaving mass of helpless British infantry.

The slaughter in the ditch can easily be imagined, the Russians unleashing a destructive fire into the panic-stricken British soldiers who were struggling to get out. Hand grenades were tossed down, exploding and killing dozens, the ladders were kicked away from the ramparts and gabions rolled down. Pieces of wood, stones, lumps of debris, anything that came to hand, in fact, was hurled down into the mass, whilst anyone lingering on the ramparts was quickly dealt with by a bayonet or the butt of a musket, or they were simply shot down. The British continued to struggle and fight their way out of the ditch, until finally, one by one, they began scrambling out, first just a few, then a steady stream, rolling and stumbling forward in their desperation to escape the carnage. Then began the desperate dash for salvation, the men flinging away their knapsacks and even their rifles in order to facilitate their flight; it was every man for himself. To the watching crowds on Cathcart's Hill it all seemed so unreal as hundreds of small red dots came running back to their own lines. Those in the trenches themselves could hardly believe what they were seeing, and braced themselves for the impact of so many terrorised soldiers who literally threw themselves into the trenches until they lay 'four deep upon each other'. It had been a complete disaster, and utter shambles, but not to the Russians. For them, it was a sweet victory. Amongst the cheering, defiant Russian defenders was Pyotr Alabin, who was overcome by it all.

> The bravest English remained in the bastion ditch and kept up a galling fire that prevented our men from showing themselves above the parapet. However, we had to drive away these brave fellows as they would become very useful for the English if they began the assault again. We couldn't waste any time. Ensign Dubrovin took forty-eight riflemen of the Vladimirsky regiment, went down the ditch and rushed on the English. Nobody escaped: those who were not killed were taken prisoner, and the ditch of the third bastion was completely cleared of the enemy. The English finally retreated to their trenches. It was hard to believe that they would dare to attack the bastion again.
>
> The day was fading. There were no attacks from the English side any more. You can hardly imagine that great joy, that delight, which everybody on the third bastion, from General Pavlov to the last soldier, was filled with! For a moment, we forgot that the greater part of Sevastopol was cut off from us, and that the Malakhov Hill could, in two or three hours, be belching a flow of cast iron on us! Nobody paid any serious attention to the new bombardment. All the officers and soldiers were in ecstasies of delight. Everybody thought that the retaking of the Malakhov was possible, that at night regiment after regiment, brigade after brigade, would go to it, fill the gorge with their men, pass along the bloody bridge to the fortification and wrest it from the enemy's hands.[24]

Another of the defenders, Miloshevitch, was similarly overjoyed, and justifiably proud of the way in which he and his comrades had defended the Redan. He was also critical of the British failure to consolidate their initial success.

> The English attack under command of Colonel Windham on the 3rd bastion began soon after the French attack on the Korabel'naia side. The 3rd bastion was not a good place to be, for throughout the whole of August the enemy were shelling it mercilessly. But to its great honour, no other bastion defended itself so successfully. It defeated the enemy whereas others failed. Not even the tremendous enemy fire succeeded in silencing its guns. Right until the very end the bastion was ready to reply to the enemy guns, round for round. The English, supported by large reserves, rushed forward in extended order to the salient angle of the bastion and to the left face of it, entered into the embrasures and forced the Vladimirsky regiment back. But then, instead of taking advantage of their success and taking further measures to consolidate, they began to cut the gun's mounts and tear off the boards from the platforms. They were doing this when the Selenginsky and Kamchatsky regiments suddenly arrived and threw them out at bayonet point. They attacked twice more but with no success; some English remained in the ditch but the riflemen of the Vladimirsky regiment turned them out. The defeat of the English was absolute. It is remarkable that they attacked only with fixed bayonets.[25]

The British attack on the Redan had ended in total defeat, a misery compounded by the French success at the Malakhov, for although its capture left Sevastopol at the mercy of the Allies the French would have the laugh of their British allies, not that they dwelt long on the failure of the British at the Redan, nor did they have any reason to. Doubtless there was a degree of smug self-satisfaction amongst the French army but they could content themselves with a job well done, and in any case they had long since regarded the British army with disdain, as the junior partner and a partner they could do just as well without. Reaction in the British trenches was one of depression and anger, but also of relief for the survivors, as Ranken wrote:

> In our trenches all was shame, rage, and fear – the men were crowded together and disorganised. It was hopeless to attempt to renew the attack with the same troops. My sappers all went to the Quarries, but I remained for more than half-an-hour in the most advanced trench with the shattered remains of the assaulting column. An officer of the 97th came up to me and shook me by the hand, saying that he was

> glad to see me safe and sound, and that of his regiment he was the only officer left, Major Welsford and Colonel Handcock (whose wife, poor thing! was then in the Crimea) having both been killed, and several others wounded.
>
> Finding there was to be no attempt to renew the attack, and mentally returning thanks to God for my wonderful preservation from imminent peril, I returned to join my party at the Quarries. On my way I passed General Sir William Codrington, who was charged with the direction of the attack, sitting in one of the trenches with his aides-de-camp about him. I repeated to him a few words I had heard fall from the lips of an officer of the 33rd, to the effect, that if it were possible to collect the men of the various regiments together, under their own officers, he would be willing to renew the assault. Sir William said the fire of the grape was too heavy to admit of the attack being repeated that day. I was received with very kind and hearty congratulations by one friend or brother officer after another, whom I encountered in my progress through the trenches – Anderson especially, who was attached to the same company as myself, said he had been particularly anxious, and when he found I did not return with the sappers, thought it was all over with me.[26]

British casualties were horrendous, considering the numbers involved in the attack. A total of twenty-nine officers and 361 men were killed and 129 officers and 1,914 men wounded. One officer and 176 men were listed as missing, although it is likely that the majority of these were killed. The Russians, meanwhile, lost fifty-nine officers and 2,625 men killed, 279 officers and 6,964 men wounded and twenty-four officers and 1,739 men listed as missing, all these casualties coming at all points attacked on 8 September. French losses were listed in the previous chapter. It all added up to an extremely bloody day, with casualties certainly on a par with full-pitched battles. William Russell was moved to comment that, although the assault on the Redan had lasted about an hour and a half, the British lost more men in that time than they had at Inkerman, where the fighting lasted over seven hours.[27] The scenes in the British trenches afterwards shocked those who witnessed them, and defied all but the most descriptive of pens. 'The engineers' hut, near the Quarries,' wrote Ranken,

> presented a most lamentable spectacle when I reached it. Every stretcher had been put into requisition for carrying off the wounded. Some of the men employed as bearers, it was said, had not returned – remaining away to avoid the danger (for death and wounds were rife through every part of the lines on this day, and men were actually killed in the stretchers on which they were being borne wounded to the rear).

> Several poor fellows, more or less grievously wounded, were lying helpless and in agony in the trench. Inside the hut was a poor gunner with his leg badly shattered by the splinter of a shell. In front, in the centre of the roadway, lay a rifleman dying, covered with blood about the head and face, and foaming at the mouth – a most ghastly spectacle. Near me was a poor fellow shot in the small of the back, in great pain: I managed to raise him up, with some empty sandbags, to make his position easier – this was all I could do. Three or four more victims lay groaning round or faint and silent around; while the inexorable roar of cannon and shot continued, and death remained busy at his work.[28]

The British, meanwhile, looked to a post mortem. The history of the British Army is littered with acts of incredible bravery, and of tremendous feats in the face of great adversity. Indeed, the phrase 'against all odds' crops up time and time again. Britain had – and still has – a tradition of great deeds on the battlefield. It was what the public expected, that their armies would do their best. But at the Redan the question was asked: had British troops really given it their all? Had they really done their best? The brutal truth was that they probably hadn't. It was true that men like Windham had done everything that had been asked of him and got inside the Redan but hundreds more had failed at the vital moment. As Codrington himself had said, 'they wouldn't go'.

The failure of the British attack at the Redan certainly could not be put down to a single cause. There were a whole cluster of errors that, when put together, resulted in the disaster of 8 September. The 250 yards distance the British had to cover in order to reach the Redan was certainly a factor but it was not the major reason, even though it did give the Russians more time to inflict heavier casualties on the stormers. The inadequate number of stormers certainly was a major factor. Barely 1,400 British troops made up the initial attacking force which compared badly with over 25,000 French who attacked their objectives. Then there was the inexperience of the troops themselves. These were not the men of the Alma or Inkerman; a great many were very young men, boys almost, who lacked the experience needed in times of crisis. Many company officers were also fresh and relatively new; their grip on a deteriorating situation was somewhat slack, and they appear to have been unable to grip their men as they should even if the latter had been gallant enough. They were certainly not of the calibre of soldier needed in the confusion that reigned on the ramparts of the Redan. It was a point touched upon by Henry Clifford, who wrote to his father the day afterwards:

> I can only account for the sad conduct of the men thus. First, they are almost all young soldiers, and many of the Officers being very young

> have but little influence over them. Taken from perfect peace and quiet in England to the Trenches before Sevastopol, they have been taught to look for shelter and not expose themselves to fire. Day after day, friends and comrades have fallen in cold blood in those very trenches, by shot or shell from that Redan, by their side.
>
> Some of them went at the Redan on the 18th and were driven back with great loss. Was it prudent to send these two Divisions, that had never been a moment out of the trenches, to take the Redan? Second, was it right to send any men two hundred yards in the open against a place like the Redan, with guns vomiting forth grape, and when hundreds of their comrades fell long before they ever got to the Ditch? The French, with older and more tried troops, would not assault the Malakhov again till they had silenced the fire of the guns and brought their trenches within twenty yards of the Ditch from which the sharpshooters could keep down the fire from the parapet.[29]

But although most eye-witnesses tended to put the finger of blame upon the inexperience of the private soldier the principal failure was not the men themselves, even though the youth and inexperience of many of the first attacking echelon would not have helped. No, the failure seems to have been a combination of poor planning, bad leadership and a lack of command and control, all of which were indeed compounded by the poor quality of the men themselves.

To be fair to them, the men were badly let down by a lack of support, for the job of a first wave of attackers is to storm their objective and then wait for reinforcements to come up and pass through and continue the attack. In effect, the initial wave was to 'pass on the baton' to the second wave and leave them to it. After all, the first wave of attacking troops would have been tired after their efforts anyway, and would certainly not be in any great shape to advance beyond their initial objective, the Redan. Moreover, the British soldier has traditionally excelled when put on the defensive. Thus, when faced with the Russian entrenchment at the Redan it suited his mode of fighting to settle down behind the ramparts and wait for the Russian counter-attack, rather than drive on deeper into the work. It was something which William Russell touched upon.

> Lamentable as it no doubt is, and incredible almost to those who know how well the British soldier generally behaves in presence of the enemy, the men, when they reached the parapet, were seized by some strange infatuation, and began firing, instead of following their officers, who were now falling fast. Most men stand fire much better than the bayonet – they will keep up a fusillade a few paces off much sooner than they will close with an enemy. It is difficult enough sometimes to get cavalry to charge, if they can find any decent excuse

> to lay by their swords and take to pistol and carbine, with which they are content to pop away for ever; and when cover of any kind is near, a trench-bred infantryman finds the charms of the cartridge quite irresistible.[30]

As for Charles Windham, well, he was in a very difficult position. Having been driven to despair by the apparent lack of reinforcements he had taken off to do it for himself, a move which largely contributed to the flight of the remaining British troops from the Redan. Whilst it is easy to sympathise with Windham his move ought to be questioned, for it appears to have left the men still at the Redan with no real officer in overall command. If Windham knew there was no hope of success unless support was got forward he should have called it a day and brought his men off in good order, after all there was little point in remaining in the Redan if the only prospect was either death or capture by the Russians. Furthermore, a high proportion – possibly even the majority – of the British casualties sustained at the Redan occurred in the ditch and in the flight afterwards. Had Windham got his men off in good order it is likely that, whilst the attack would still have failed, the losses would nevertheless have been smaller. The inexperienced British troops have been criticised for not obeying orders from anyone other than their own officers – certainly Windham could not get them to follow him. But herein lay another problem. These troops, without officers, confused and lacking direction, are suddenly asked to follow into the Redan an officer who is standing on top of the ramparts, waving his sword round, shouting and swearing like a madman, and using 'approved theatricals' – all this is from Windham's own report. Think about it; scores, if not hundreds of men have already been shot dead or wounded by the Russians. Do you follow this 'madman' and risk adding to the growing number of dead or do you ignore him and wait for direction from your own officers? Well, for the young men clinging on by their eyelids on the ramparts of the Redan there was only one answer. Thus, Windham was ignored and, ultimately, forced to give up and return himself to the British trenches in search of reinforcements.

As for the planning, it is a prime military tenet that any attack has to consist of more than one echelon of assault troops, and that enough troops are to be made available for the task in hand. The 1,400 British attackers were far too few, particularly compared with the French. When the leading attackers got to the Redan and lay down they had done their bit really. Running under fire across 250 yards with their kit and rifle was exhausting enough and they were shattered at the other end. When they reached the Redan their job was to hold the ground taken and suppress the defenders with their fire while the second echelon moved up, moved through and exploited their success. This was the classic 'grand' tactics for the attack – applying more than one echelon of attackers and enough troops for the job. Unfortunately, the British attack on the Redan met with neither of these requirements. The stormtrooper style of tactics ignores this whole echelon concept, with the attackers pushing as far as they can against any weak spot while ignoring the strong, and trickling through into an enemy rear area without waiting for the second echelon. This, however, calls for high morale, mental flexibility and careful training of junior leaders, the NCOs, in particular, and was a concept not really brought into effect until circa 1916. It was certainly not uppermost in the minds of the military strategists in 1855.

On the face of it, the British troops seem to have got it about right, and Windham and Russell may have got it wrong. Indeed, when Russell uses expressions like 'lamentable' he shows his ignorance of tactics. What he wanted was solid lines of red-coated infantry advancing to victory at a steady measured pace with colours flying, etc. Well, faced with defences like the Redan, a rush of infantry to get over the ground and into good fire positions is the order of the day, and it seems the first echelon did just that. The next phase was down to the second attacking echelon – the supports – and they were not coming forward. Those that did venture forward simply advanced in dribs and drabs, which was no good at all. The occasion demanded a concerted effort by all supports together but it was not to be, and men like Ranken were left to wait for the supports which failed to come.

> It was in vain, however, to look; our Generals had left their reserves about an hour's march in the rear, so that even if our soldiers had charged forwards, as they should have done, they would probably have found themselves compromised, surrounded by the enemy, and immolated, before any assistance could have been brought to them.[31]

This brings us to leadership. The question should be asked, why was the Highland Brigade, the 3rd Division or even the Brigade of Guards not ordered to move forward? Did they not know the first echelon had 'succeeded' in their limited role? If so, why were they not told? Codrington must have known – through Windham's messages, at least those that got through – that the second echelon was needed as soon as possible. And it really was not for Windham to go back and try to sort things out, for things would go to pieces at the Redan as soon as the commanding general 'left' the field and he must have known it, hence his comment to Crealock that he was 'not in a funk'. Whilst Windham deserves a degree of sympathy, given his predicament, it was probably a mistake for him to go back; his men saw this and drew their own conclusions. After all, how did they know he was not simply running away?

Poor planning also had an effect on command and control. Divisional

Orders for the attack on the Redan allowed for little beyond the actual storming of the position, i.e. the order of advance for the British troops. There was no subtlety in the 'plan'. Thus, the officers and NCOs of the attacking echelon had no idea of their tasks beyond the actual storming of the Redan. Did they believe they had 'done their bit' and were now to wait for the second echelon? If so, they – the junior officers and the NCOs in particular – might well have been disinclined to follow officers who, although quite senior like Windham, they might not have known well if at all, and perhaps have thrown into confusion the 'plan' for the second echelon to move through and exploit.

Considering the hellish state of affairs in the Redan Codrington probably made the right decision not to reinforce defeat. It was probably the only correct thing he did all day, but even this decision was forced upon him by the state of affairs in the trenches, for it was only the terrible chaotic congestion there after the failed assault that prevented the other divisions from being brought forward in time, otherwise the slaughter might well have been greater. With a bit more forethought and planning, combined with greater determination, he might have succeeded if he had sent forward a specific second echelon rather than allow the supports to go forward piecemeal. In the event the planning, from Simpson's choice of attackers through to Codrington's handling of the assault, appears to have been woeful, with nothing more imaginative than simply throwing men forward in the time honoured fashion, and hoping for the best. Sadly for the British stormers, it simply wasn't enough.

In the meantime the recriminations went on. Henry Clifford was distraught at what he had seen on 8 September.

> And what almost breaks my heart, and nearly drove me mad, I see our soldiers, our English soldiers that I was so proud of, run away. I shall not be able to read over what I write, and so you in England reading it quietly, you will hardly think that every word is what I feel and that no language I can make use of can convey to you an idea of what I have seen and felt since yesterday.[32]

Others felt equally ashamed of what they had seen. 'I am sorry to say the men behaved in a most cowardly and rascally manner,' wrote another spectator, 'left their officers to be killed and failed entirely . . . We were entirely repulsed . . . and disgracefully repulsed . . . The men held back or ran, the officers were all obliged to go to the front and were shot like dogs, not being able to get the men to advance.'[33] It was typical of the many comments on the disaster. Indeed, by far the most depressing aspect of the attack was the apparent refusal of the men to go deeper into the Redan. According to Windham himself it was, 'the greatest disgrace which has ever fallen on the British soldier. I could have forgiven them if they had been beaten out, but they would not go in.[34] Anthony Sterling thought much the same, but was far more scathing of the British high command. The attack was,

> the greatest, and perhaps the only, disgrace of this sort which has ever befallen the British arms. Are we not to ask how, and why? Is the English army and nation to endure the discredit which has fallen upon them, solely from the appointment to supreme command of an incompetent person in himself, and the more incompetent because he has not moral energy enough to break through the trammels of a clique which hung about headquarters?[35]

He then went on to say,

> it was, indeed, truly hopeless ever to make an attack with such troops; a set of raw recruits – undisciplined, unacquainted with one another and with their officers, and of different regiments mixed together. But the British Government chose the Commander-in-Chief, and he chose his own General, and his chosen General's own division, to make this attack, and to risk and lose the honour of England.[36]

Remarkably, the incompetent Simpson claimed in his official despatch that the attacking troops had been 'supported to the utmost', adding that his men displayed 'the greatest bravery'. Given that Simpson sat in a trench throughout the attack, with his cloak drawn about his head, we may safely say that he was simply going through the motions when he wrote his report, not that it was every likely to reflect much truth anyway. Pélissier, too, claimed in his despatch that the British had fought well, and that it was an unequal contest. He also said that after two hours' fighting, 'the English decided upon evacuating the Redan', and claimed that 'they did this with so firm a front that the enemy did not dare to follow them'. Both despatches were quite astonishing. It was one thing to tone down a defeat in order to spare the feelings of a hopeful and expectant British public, but these reports were works of pure fiction.

All in all it had been a bad business – a 'disaster and disgrace', according to the historian of the British Army – made all the more painful for the British by the success of the French at the Malakhov. But if the British thought they would have an opportunity to restore their bruised and battered pride they were to be sadly mistaken. There would be no second chance at Sevastopol, no more opportunity for glory, for the fight for Sevastopol was about to come to a sudden and unexpected end.

NOTES

1 MacMunn, Sir George. *The Crimea in Perspective* (London 1935), 206.
2 Alabin P V. *Pohodnye zapiski v voinu 1853–1856 godov* (Moscow 1892), 536–7.
3 Ranken, W. Bayne (Ed). *Six Months at Sebastopol; Being selections from the Correspondence of the late Major George Ranken, Royal Engineers* (London 1857), 49–50.
4 Alabin, *Pohodnye zapiski v voinu*. 537–8.
5 Ranken, *Six Months at Sebastopol*, 50–1.
6 Mansfield, H O. *Charles Ashe Windham; A Norfolk Soldier* (Lavenham 1973), 231.
7 Ranken, *Six Months at Sebastopol*, 52.
8 Mansfield, *Windham*, 151.
9 Clifford, Henry. *His Letters and Sketches from the Crimea* (London 1955), 256.
10 Alabin, *Pohodnye zapiski v voinu*, 538.
11 Hume, John R. *Reminiscences of the Crimean Campaign with the 55th Regiment* (London 1894), 164.
12 Ibid, 165.
13 Ranken, *Six Months at Sebastopol*, 51–3.
14 Colt's gravestone can still be seen inside the British Memorial on Cathcart Hill, just outside Sevastopol.
15 Gowing, Timothy. *A Soldier's Experience, or A Voice from the Ranks* (Nottingham 1903), 161–2.
16 Hammond, Capt. M M. *Memoir of Captain M M Hammond, Rifle Brigade* (London 1858), 344.
17 Alabin, *Pohodnye zapiski v voinu* 336–43.
18 Vulliamy, C E. *Crimea: The Campaign of 1854–56* (London 1939), 323.
19 Mansfield, *Windham*, 232.
20 Ibid, 232.
21 Ibid, 233.
22 Tyrell, Henry. *History of the War with Russia* (London n.d.), II, 253.
23 Ranken, *Six Months at Sebastopol*, 53–4.
24 Alabin, *Pohodnye zapiski v voinu* 336–43.
25 Miloshevitch N S, 'Iz zapisok sevastopol'tsa', (Sevastopol 2002), I, 281.
26 Ranken, *Six Months at Sebastopol*, 54–5.
27 Russell, William Howard. *The British Expedition to the Crimea* (London 1877), 355.
28 Ranken, *Six Months at Sebastopol*, 55–6.
29 Clifford, *Letters and Sketches*, 259.
30 Russell, *British Expedition*, 347.
31 Ranken, *Six Months at Sebastopol*, 53.
32 Clifford, *Letters and Sketches*, 259.
33 Lieutenant Fletcher, RN, quoted in Pemberton, Baring. *Battles of the Crimean War* (London 1962), 225.
34 Vulliamy, *Crimea*, 319.
35 Sterling, Lieut.Col. Anthony. *The Highland Brigade in the Crimea* (Minneapolis 1995), 209.
36 Ibid, 212.

## CHAPTER TWENTY-SIX
# 'Flame, Smoke and Ashes'

Although the Russians had given the British a dreadful beating at the Redan the loss of the Malakhov to the French effectively meant that Sevastopol was no longer tenable. They had fought bravely and defended their town to the hilt for the best part of a year but the loss of the Malakhov was, as Pélissier had hoped, 'the mortal blow'. Gorchakov knew as much by the early evening of 8 September. Indeed, he had crossed the bridge linking the Severnaia with Sevastopol in order to take a look at the situation at the Malakhov himself. Needless to say, he got nowhere near it, the bastion having long since been secured by the French. Gorchakov knew full well the consequences the loss of the Malakhov would have for the defenders of Sevastopol and no sooner had he arrived back on the Severnaia than he issued the fatal order for the evacuation of the town. It was 6 pm.

As distressing as it was for the Russians they knew full well, as did the Allies, that the capture of the Malakhov by the Allies left the defenders with few options. In fact, it left them with only one; to evacuate the town as ordered by Gorchakov. Allied minds were no doubt cast back to the early days of the siege and to Burgoyne's belief that once the bastion was in Allied hands Sevastopol would follow soon afterwards. His prediction was about to come true. With the Malakhov in their hands the Allies would now have a simple task of turning round the guns and bringing forward their own, after which the remaining defences would be at their mercy, for the bastion completely dominated the town and its defences along its southern and eastern sides. Gorchakov may not have been the greatest of military geniuses – not that there were many in this tragic war anyway – but he was not that stupid that he did not recognise a lost cause when he saw one, and a prolonged defence of Sevastopol with the Malakhov in French hands was certainly a lost cause. Thus, the order was given for the defenders to make their way as best they could down to the Roadstead in order to begin the evacuation of the town by way of the pontoon bridge across to the Severnaia.

Like the other defenders of the Redan Pyotr Alabin had fought hard to defeat the British, only to have his efforts undermined by the fall of the

Malakhov. Things had gone well at the Redan but during the evening rumours began to circulate that Gorchakov had given the order for the evacuation of Sevastopol. It was a bitter pill to swallow for Alabin and his comrades.

> Vague rumours about an order to abandon the southern side began to circulate in the garrison. That sad news was soon confirmed by official command, but we were ordered to wait for the order to do so. How gloomy our souls became; how sore were the hearts of the defenders of Sevastopol! Nobody complained to the Prince at all! Everybody knew his high spirits: everybody believed in him, everybody knew that he loved our Sacred Russia even more than us, and that he would do nothing that was not in accord with its honour. Everybody saw the necessity of leaving the southern part of the town. Everybody clearly knew there was no other way out for us from the semi-circle in which we were put by the power of circumstances; our only way out was across the harbour. There, on the Severnaia side a glimmer of hope was still glowing for us . . . Nevertheless, everybody took the news of the retreat with great sadness.
>
> How could we give up the sacred graves of our brothers to the enemy? How could we give them fortifications, which were built by our heroic friends from dust soaked with their blood, the guns, and the piles of shells? You see, they will take all these with them as salvage to lay before the world as evidence of their triumph over Russia, which was never defeated. And what of the houses, and the large buildings? The enemy will make their homes in them; they will laugh at us and will say, 'Russia prepared our winter houses for us!' But no, it will never be so! We cannot give trophies to the enemy; we will repeat the Moscow fire; we'll blow up everything that is of worth! Flame, smoke and ashes – that is what our enemy find in Sevastopol![1]

The evacuation was carefully managed, each stage signalled by rockets sent up from the old town. It was a dark, windy night, which reflected the gloomy aspect of those crossing the bridge. Slowly but steadily, and without any disorder, the defenders began crossing the bridge to the Severnaia. There was no panic, no hurrying, simply a sad resignation that all of their great efforts had been in vain. They had been unable to hold on to Sevastopol. N C Miloshevitch had been sent to Sevastopol at his own request in July 1855 and arrived on the day of the Chernaya battle. On the evening of 8 September he received orders to abandon his post and cross the roadstead to the Severnaia.

> At about 8 pm I left the 5th bastion with my field guns, and was ordered to take my camp case across to the Severnaia side, and with

nothing else to do I took a stroll along the Sevastopol streets. There I met the teams which had been ordered to burn the buildings and for some time I directed their work. Then I went to the Nikolayevskaya battery; it was absolutely empty. Only the hospital remained full of people. They had already begun to set fire to the furniture and other inflammable materials in the casemates. It was with great reluctance that I threw onto the fire some wonderful carved furniture, brought from Marseilles, which came from the room of the former commander of the garrison artillery in Sevastopol – the soldiers didn't dare break it. Then I went back to the temporary bridge and began to watch. The blazing fires lit the gloomy faces of the defenders of Sevastopol on the bridge. Silhouetted against the fiery background was the dark monument to Kazarsky; and from the darkness on the enemy's side flames flew up from time to time and disappeared in the harbour. Here the seamen with bundles of belongings started to move across one after the other. I moved up to the bridge barrier: I wanted to know how the heroes felt as they were leaving their native city, but there was an unusual silence in their ranks; the silence was broken only now and then by somebody crossing themselves or whispering the words of a prayer . . . After a while, the bridge slowly became deserted and there was silence where before there had been the noise of crowds of soldiers . . . Anguish, an unbearable anguish, oppressed my soul . . . The impressions of the day still lingered vividly in my mind, the last events in particular . . . and I begrudged leaving Sevastopol; we had grown accustomed to its bastions and to the bombardments. Our struggle, so full of glory and hardship, overwhelmed my soul to such extent that all further events seemed to have no meaning. Even though I was leaving Sevastopol safe and sound it did not have any meaning to me owing to the uncertain future . . .

Having crossed to the Severnaia, I absentmindedly strolled two versts past the Mikhailovsky fort, and tried to discover the whereabouts of my battery but nobody could answer me. Where was I to go? There were no lights before me, the darkness was impenetrable and the anguish was growing more and more . . . I returned to the city, and visited the Nikolaevskaya battery, from where they were taking the last of the wounded . . . I again took shelter near the bridge and remained there till the very dawn when a sapper officer told me that dismantling of the bridge had begun. I was the last to cross the bridge. I found the bivouac of my battery. The officers greeted me with surprise and I was the first who brought them the terrible news that the evacuation of Sevastopol was over.

The enemy didn't disturb us in our retreat at all, although every now and then a bomb or a rocket fell in the harbour or on the

> Korabel'naia. Before dawn the rear guard passed and then they took the bridge away. At midday on 9 September the Pavlovskaya battery exploded; the Nikolaevskaya battery remained intact because the order to charge the mine shafts below it came too late and there was no time to do it. On 10 and 11 September the steamer-frigates *Vladimir, Bessarabia* and *Chersonese* were sunk. Their commanders asked for permission to go to the sea to try to force their way through to Nikolaev or to perish in battle with the enemy's vessels which sealed off the harbour entrance on 9 September.
>
> I can imagine the astonishment of the advanced units of enemy troops when, on the morning of 9 September, they found both the fortifications and ruins of Sevastopol to be empty! For the first few days only gangs of French marauders were to be found in the town, and some of our seamen joined them, mourning for their native ashes. The fire continued and from time there were explosions caused by powder magazines. These explosions caused the enemy some alarm for they feared the town might be mined, which is why the city remained unoccupied for several days. By the evening of the 9th our wounded, handed over to us by the French, were brought from the Malakhov Hill and the last seamen left Sevastopol.[2]

While the garrison trudged wearily down to the pontoon bridge demolition teams set about destroying as much of the works and defences as possible. Thirty-five powder magazines were blown up along with several batteries, whilst several ships were sunk in the Roadstead. Houses were torched and gutted and other key buildings destroyed. It was all reminiscent of the burning of Moscow forty-two years before. Indeed, the explosions certainly made the French think twice about entering Sevastopol until they were absolutely certain they would not be walking straight into a heavily mined town. The comparison between Moscow in 1812 and Sevastopol in 1855 was not lost on the defenders as they retired from the place. 'The conflagrations were the consequences of the invasions of both Napoleons,' wrote one of them.

> Moscow burnt down and now long-suffering Sevastopol is also blazing. The glowing of the fires is being reflected in the still harbour water, and it is seems as if water, earth and sky have all become set ablaze. Frequent explosions of powder magazines on the bastions and in the batteries shake the stony Sevastopol ground. The deafening crackle of powder explosions announced to the whole world that the struggle is not finished and will be renewed again.[3]

Another defender, A A Vyazmitinov, likened the burning of Sevastopol to that of Rome and Pompeii. 'It seemed to me as if Old Rome Pompeii was dying again before me,' he wrote. In fact, he later visited Pompeii and thought it much less destroyed than Sevastopol![4]

Meanwhile, the evacuation continued, with whole regiments shuffling slowly across the bridge whilst barges and steamers helped speed the flow from south to north by ferrying troops across to the Severnaia. It was a delicate operation and one that caused no small degree of apprehension amongst the Russians, for although the French and British were wary of entering Sevastopol in case of mines the Russians did not know this and feared the Allies might move down upon them at any moment. But they need not have worried. The only threat to their retreat came via the odd shell tossed into the town or at the bridge, the shells throwing up huge columns of water on either side of it. Leo Tolstoy was just one of thousands of Russians saddened at having to leave Sevastopol at the mercy of the Allies. 'All along the line of the Sevastopol bastions,' he wrote,

> which for so many months had been seething with extraordinary vigorous life, which for so many months had seen heroes come and go, one after another, removed by death, and which for so many months had inspired the fear, hatred, and finally, the admiration of the enemy – the Sevastopol bastions were now deserted. All was dead, deserted, ghastly – but not quiet: everything was still undergoing destruction. The ground, ploughed up by fresh explosions, was strewn with shattered gun mountings, pinning down human corpses – Russian and enemy – heavy iron cannon now silenced for ever, hurled into pits with frightful force and half-buried by earth; shells, cannon balls, more corpses, pits, shattered logs, blindages, and again corpses in grey and blue greatcoats. And all this was often disturbed again and lit up by the lurid glare of explosions that continued to rend the air.
>
> The enemy saw that something inexplicable was taking place in grim Sevastopol. The explosions and the deathly silence on the bastions made them shudder; but they dared not believe, remembering the cool and stern resistance they had met with that day, that their dauntless foe had vanished, and they waited with suspense and trepidation for the end of this gloomy night.
>
> The Sevastopol army, heaving and tossing like the sea on a dark and stormy night, contracting and stretching and shivering with alarm down the whole length of its body, swaying to and fro on the shore of the bay, the bridge and the Severnaia Side, moved slowly in a solid mass away from the place where it had left so many of its courageous brothers, away from the place that was all drenched with its blood, away from the place which, for eleven months, it had held against a foe twice its strength and now was ordered to abandon without a fight.

> The first reaction of every soldier to this order was one of bewilderment and pain. The second was one of fear of pursuit. The moment the men left the places where they had been accustomed to fight, they felt defenceless and they huddled frightened in the dark at the foot of the bridge, which swayed in the powerful wind. Clicking their bayonets as they jostled each other, the infantry pushed on, regiments, vehicles and militia; mounted officers carrying dispatches pushed their way through the seething crowds; inhabitants and orderlies carrying baggage wept and pleaded to be allowed to pass; the artillery with clattering wheels, pushed its way to the shore, hurrying to get away. Notwithstanding their various preoccupations, the instinct of self-preservation and the desire to get away from this grim scene of death as soon as possible were uppermost in everybody's mind. This was felt equally by the mortally wounded soldier lying among five hundred others on the stone floor of the Pavlovsky Quay and entreating Heaven to send him release, by the militiaman who with all his might was pressing into this solid mass of humanity to make way for a General on horseback, by the General who was firmly controlling the crossing and restraining the haste of the soldiers, by the sailor who had been caught up by a moving battalion and was having the breath crushed out of him by the swaying crowd, by the wounded officer borne on a stretcher by four soldiers who were forced to stop and lower the stretcher to the ground at the Nikolayevsky Battery, by the artilleryman who had served at his gun for sixteen years and was now, by an order from above which he could not understand, with the aid of his comrades, pushing his gun over the steep cliff into the bay, and by the sailors who, after scuttling their ships, were now vigorously rowing away from them in their longboats. On stepping off at the other end of the bridge nearly every soldier took off his cap and crossed himself. But at the back of this feeling of relief there was another, oppressive, aching and more profound feeling, akin to penitence, shame and anger. Nearly every soldier, on looking back at abandoned Sevastopol from Severnaia Side, heaved an inexpressibly bitter sigh and shook his fist at the enemy.[5]

Tolstoy was not alone in feeling sad at leaving Sevastopol, the town which had been defended so gallantly for the best part of a year. A N Suponev was another;

> It is difficult to describe what the defenders of Sevastopol felt in their hearts in those moments . . . Emotions and feelings ran high and many tears were shed. The old seamen were sobbing like children . . . Shells and bombs were falling into water every now and then on both

> sides of the temporary bridge ... The weather was calm; the stars were shining in the sky but they dimmed against the background of the brightly burning buildings and fortifications and the no less bright trail of balls, which were forever crossing the sky in different directions.[6]

The day after the evacuation of Sevastopol Gorchakov wrote to Alexander, informing him of the evacuation and trying to put as brave a face on affairs as possible.

> From the morning of 5 September the enemy's shells rained down upon us like hail and our losses exceeded 2,500 people every day. Yesterday, after a severe bombardment, huge enemy forces advanced to the assault from all sides and were repulsed everywhere except at the Malakhov Hill. The area here was very disadvantageous and we were unable to dislodge the enemy and, moreover, the commanders, Generals Khrulev and Lysenko, were both wounded. There was nothing left but to use that impression, our courage produced on the enemy, and to vacate the western side, on which we were losing more than 2,500 men every day even without a battle. The fire of the enemy was so great that we stood to lose half the army within ten days.[7]

The loss of Sevastopol was a blow to Alexander, although it can hardly have been totally unexpected. Nevertheless, he put a brave face on it and tried to encourage Gorchakov by evoking the spirit of 1812, just as Nicholas had done throughout the war. 'Don't give up,' was his message to Gorchakov, 'remember the year of 1812 and trust in God. Sevastopol is not Moscow and the Crimea is not the whole of Russia. Two years after the Moscow fire our triumphant troops were in Paris. We are the same Russians.'[8] It was true that the Russians of 1855 were much the same as those who had defeated Napoleon in 1812 but on that occasion they were part of a coalition against France. They were not fighting alone. On this occasion, however, it was Russia which was alone, with France as the senior partner in a coalition fighting against them. Alexander was, therefore, now in a somewhat bad position both politically and militarily, and despite his declared intention to fight on the war was as good as lost. The destruction of Sevastopol was always a main war aim of the Allies and with the town in their hands – and Gorchakov in no apparent position to reverse the situation – they could look to the dismantling of the dockyards and the fortifications. Gorchakov himself was one of the last to leave the burning town for the Severnaia. He had given orders for the bridge to be broken up, after which he was rowed across in a small boat, no doubt reflecting on the defence with a mixture of pride and bitterness, although he was realistic enough to know a lost cause when he saw one, and the loss of the Malakhov to the French certainly meant that any prolonged defence of Sevastopol was futile.

As Gorchakov's small boat glided gently across the Roadstead and the last of the Russian outposts were withdrawn, the Allies watched in awe as Sevastopol, their great prize and the object of the game for the last year, erupted amidst a series of deafening explosions. The night sky was lit up by huge red flames that burst from key points in and around the town as magazines and ammunition dumps exploded. Watching from the hills around Sevastopol the Allies gazed on, and for a while the British troops forgot all about their bitter failure at the Redan. 'I was standing on the top of the parapet, wrote Frederick Vieth,

> looking towards the Redan, which the dawn was just revealing in outline, when a terrific explosion behind it took place, followed by others close by. In the midst of flame and smoke ascending skywards, one could see vast numbers of shells, which exploded in the air, stones, earth, logs of wood, and no doubt many bodies of our own and the enemy's dead and dying went up with this mighty upheaval. It was a terrible sight.[9]

The mood in the French camp, meanwhile, was far more upbeat. Pélissier was delighted with the outcome of the attack on the Malakhov and even the repulses along the town front and the heavy losses generally could not dampen his enthusiasm. 'The bulwark of the Russian power in the Black Sea no longer exists,' he declared to his men in an Order of the Day on 9 September. 'On that day [8 September] you gained for your eagles new and imperishable glory.'[10] But even Pélissier knew there would be no further glory for his men. Indeed, in the same Order he declared that his men would soon be returning to their wives and families. In his eyes the game was as good as over, and there did not appear to be any reason to doubt his optimism. The dismantling of Sevastopol had indeed been the great aim of the Allies in the Crimea, and now that moment was at hand.

But first, the Allies had to ensure that Sevastopol was a safe place to enter. The past months of siege warfare in front of the town had given them great cause to be wary of mines and it was hardly likely that the Russians were about to let them simply enter their town without leaving them some sort of welcoming present. Or would they? The capture of the Malakhov had been unexpected and sudden, and there had barely been time to make arrangements for the evacuation, let alone set about a sophisticated setting of mines in order to blow up the first Allied troops as they entered the town. Instead, the priority had been to set the place ablaze and blow up the magazines. If they could not leave the place as a death trap the Russians could at least leave it a smouldering wreck. The first Allied patrols entered Sevastopol early on the morning of 9

September to find the town deserted by everyone except the wounded. Sentries were then posted to prevent plunderers and sightseers from entering the place, not that there was much left to see, and although some officers with passports were allowed to enter the ruins it was not until 12 September that the Allies officially took possession of Sevastopol. The sights were both sickening and saddening, particularly for the British who found scores of their comrades dead in piles at the Redan.

> The bodies of those slain in the assault were collected in the ditch of the Redan. Riflemen and soldiers of the line lay together in all postures, some shattered, some with their wounds not visible; here a bearded sergeant, there a boy-recruit lying on a tangle of blood-stained bodies, fragments of limbs, and protruding stumps; amid which appeared here and there, in frightened contrast to such ghastly pillows, a face calm as in calmest sleep. The dead Russians were placed together at one end, and when all were collected, the earth of the slope was shovelled over, and the rampart they had fought for formed above assailant and defender a common funeral mound.
>
> The interior of the Redan was a wide level space, filled with debris of all kinds – fragments of gabions, broken guns and carriages, beams hurled from exploded magazines, and chasms made by bursting shells . . . At two or three places a heap of slain Russian gunners were collected behind their batteries, whose bodies wore terrible marks of shot and shell; numbers were headless, some cut absolutely in two, with the upper or lower half wanting; some torn open, some with great holes in their skulls; and detached from the group might be sometimes seen a human thigh or shoulder.[11]

There were equally appalling sights along the eastern side of Sevastopol, where the French had attacked. Naturally, the sights were worse at the Malakhov, as William Russell later recalled.

> Inside the sight was too terrible to dwell upon. The French were carrying away their own and the Russian wounded, and four distinct piles of dead were formed to clear the way. The ground was marked by pools of blood, and the smell was noisome; swarms of flies settled on dead and dying; broken muskets, torn clothes, caps, shakos, swords, bayonets, bags of bread, canteens, and haversacks were lying in indescribable confusion all over the place, mingled with heaps of shot, of grape, bits of shell, cartridges, case and canister, loose powder, official papers and cooking tins.[12]

Some of the worst sights were reserved for the hospitals in which were found hundreds of wounded, dead and dying soldiers, mainly Russian, although there were many British and French also. Despite the efforts of men like Pirogov, his colleagues, the Sisters of Mercy and other nurses, the intensity of the Allied bombardment had been so great that the Russian medical services had been simply overrun. When the order was given to abandon Sevastopol as many of the walking wounded as possible were withdrawn but hundreds more remained behind with little more than a few carers and letters from the Russians asking the Allies to look after the wounded as best they could. But with the town ablaze and the Allies reluctant to enter until things calmed down, vital days were lost, during which many died. William Russell visited one of the main hospitals situated inside the dockyard, and found it in a horrendous condition, a real 'chamber of horrors'.

> Entering one of these doors, I beheld such a sight as few men, thank God, have ever witnessed. In a long, low room, supported by square pillars arched at the top, and dimly lighted through shattered and unglazed window-frames, lay the wounded Russians, who had been abandoned to our mercies by their General. The wounded, did I say? No, but the dead – the rotten and festering corpses of the soldiers, who were left to die in their extreme agony, untended, uncared for, packed as close as they could be stowed, some on the floor, others on wretched trestles and bedsteads, or pallets of straw, sopped and saturated with blood, which oozed and trickled through upon the floor, mingling with the droppings of corruption. With the roar of exploding fortresses in their ears – with shells and shot pouring through the roof and sides of the rooms in which they lay – with the crackling and hissing of fire around them, these poor fellows, who had served their loving friend and master the Czar but too well, were consigned to their terrible fate. Many might have been saved by ordinary care. Many lay, yet alive, with maggots crawling about in their wounds. Many, nearly mad by the scene around them, or seeking escape from it in their extremest agony, had rolled away under the beds, and glared out on the heart-stricken spectator – oh! With such looks! Many, with legs and arms broken and twisted, the jagged splinters sticking through the raw flesh, implored aid, water, food, or pity, or, deprived of speech by the approach of death, or by dreadful injuries in the head or trunk, pointed to the lethal spot. Many seemed bent alone on making their peace with Heaven. The attitudes of some were so hideously fantastic as to appal and root one to the ground by a sort of dreadful fascination. Could that human being, or that burnt black mass of flesh have ever held a human soul? It was fearful to think what the answer must be. The bodies of numbers of men were swollen and bloated to an incredible degree; and the features, distended to a gigantic size, with eyes protruding

> from the sockets, and the blackened tongue lolling out of the mouth, compressed tightly by the teeth, which had set upon it in the death-rattle, made one shudder and reel round.[13]

By the middle of September the Allies were in full possession of Sevastopol, at least the southern side of the town. The Russians, meanwhile, occupied the Severnaia from where they continued to send over the odd shell every now and then, although this proved more irritating than damaging. Consideration then had to be given to the next course of action; should the Allies turn their attention to Gorchakov's forces to the north or should they sit tight and wait for directions from London and Paris? In reality the Crimean War was as good as over on 9 September when Sevastopol was taken, for as far as the Allies were concerned the great object of the game had now been achieved. There were those, of course, who wished to see the war extended deeper into Russia but few wished – or had the inclination – to see it escalate into a wider conflict. Also, opinions were greatly divided as to how the war should continue. Thus, with the Allies at odds with each other as to their next course of action, and with Austria in particular pressing for an acceptance of its peace proposals, things were now set for the closing stages of the Crimean War.

NOTES

1 Alabin P V. *Pohodnye zapiski v voinu 1853–1856 godov* (Moscow 1892), 544.
2 Miloshevitch M S, 'Iz zapisok sevastopol'tsa' (Sevastopol 2002), I, 286–8.
3 'Vospominaniya D V. Ilyinskogo', *Russkiy arhiv*, 1893, No.4, 334.
4 Vyazmitinov A A 'Sevastopol ot 21 marta po 28 avgusta 1855 goda', *Russkaya starina*, April 1882, 61–2.
5 Tolstoy, Leo. *Tales of Sevastopol* (Moscow 1950), 152–4.
6 'Iz vospominaniy A N Suponeva', Russkiy Arhiv, 1895, No.10, 267–8.
7 'Gortchakov to Alexander II. Severnaya side of Sevastopol. 9 September 1855', *Russkaya starina*, July 1883, 216.
8 'Alexander II to Gorchakov. Moscow. September 3 1855', *Russkaya starina*, July 1883, 220.
9 Vieth, Frederick Harris D, *Recollections of the Crimean Campaign and the Expedition to Kinburn in 1855* (Montreal 1918), 39.
10 Bazancourt, the Baron de (trans. by Robert Howe Gould). *The Crimean Expedition, to the Capture of Sebastopol. Chronicles of the War in the East* (London 1856), II, 499–501.
11 Hamley, E Bruce. *The Story of the Campaign of Sebastopol* (London 1855), 316–17.
12 Russell, William Howard. *The British Expedition to the Crimea* (London 1877), 364.
13 Ibid, 366–7.

# CHAPTER TWENTY-SEVEN
## *Five Points to Peace*

Although neither the Russians nor the Allies knew it at the time, the fall of Sevastopol to the Allies effectively marked the end of the Crimean War. Of course, this view is taken with the benefit of hindsight, and although efforts and plans would be made to continue the war it is tempting to suggest that, even in September 1855, those responsible for prosecuting the war suspected, for a variety of reasons, that this was the case.

Even as the conflagration took hold in Sevastopol news was buzzing down the telegraph wires to Paris and London, informing the respective governments of the fall of the town. Naturally, the news was welcome but it was greeted very differently in the two capitals. In Paris there was tremendous joy and celebration. The capture of the Malakhov seemed a fitting reward for the great effort put into the war by France and her army, many viewing the capture of Sevastopol as the beginning of the end – if not the end itself – of the war. It was not, however, a view shared by Napoleon. Although he was delighted that Sevastopol had finally been taken he looked to far greater things, to defeating the Russian army in the field and to rekindling the spirit of the great era of the Napoleonic Wars. Sevastopol was, in his opinion, only the beginning of greater things to come. In the meantime, he sent profuse congratulations to Pélissier and made him a Marshal of France.

In London, meanwhile, celebrations were far more muted. Initially, there had been wild rejoicing, particularly in London, when the news of the fall of Sevastopol was received on 10 September. Theatre performances came to an abrupt end, public houses emptied on to the streets and large crowds gathered to cheer and rejoice at the news. But when the real truth of the events of 8 September began to filter through the mood quickly changed. True, the capture of Sevastopol had long since been the main Allied objective in the Crimea, but the British repulse at the Redan had tempered any thoughts of celebration and, indeed, a sense of shame and dismay descended upon England. The French had taken the Malakhov but Queen Victoria's soldiers had failed to deliver their part of the bargain. Britain's pride was severely dented and not a moment was to be lost in trying to rectify the situation by pushing on with the war and driving the Russians out of the Crimea altogether. The people's anxiety was increased by the great fear that the war might yet end without the British army having the opportunity of righting a terrible reverse. Surely, her people asked, the war was not to end now, not before Victoria's soldiers could show what they were really made of. Even the queen herself was dismayed at the prospect. The Turks, meanwhile, were delighted, and looked to a prolonged campaign in the Crimea which would free their forces to act elsewhere in Asia. The Russians remained similarly optimistic and believed that the loss of Sevastopol was nothing more than a setback. Russia had triumphed in 1812 despite losing Moscow and, claimed Czar Alexander, was in no worse a position now. The fight would go on.

Both Britain and France, meanwhile, looked to finishing off the job. Sevastopol – or at least the southern side of the town – might well have been taken but the Russians continued to dwell on the Severnaia, from where they continued to toss shell after irritating shell across the Roadstead and into the old town, increasing its ruined state and causing the Allies the odd casualty here and there. Something had to be done to extend the campaign across the Roadstead and from there north, driving the Russians out completely. The problem was how to take the war deeper into the Crimea and prevent the sort of stalemate that had proved so costly throughout the winter of 1854–5 from setting in once more during the coming months. Indeed, the prospect of spending a second winter on the dreaded Chersonese plateau was enough to send scores of British officers applying for leave home to England. They had endured one winter: they were damned if they were to do it again.

It soon became apparent in the afterglow of the capture of Sevastopol that the road ahead for both Britain and France lay in different directions. Despite Napoleon's desire for further glory and to pursue an aggressive campaign deeper into the Crimea, he realised that the capture of Sevastopol had cost thousands of French lives. Did he really want to risk his throne by throwing away the lives of thousands more on a campaign just to satisfy his own vanity? Furthermore, as the capture and destruction of Sevastopol as a Russian naval base had always been one of the main war aims of the Allies, would this satisfy French honour and public alike? With the prospect of a negotiated peace in the offing maybe it was time for France to call it a day whilst they were ahead. Thus, Pélissier consolidated his position and began preparing from the destruction of the dockyards in Sevastopol, leaving his British allies to decide upon their own next course of action.

As far as the British government was concerned there was only one course of action left – Russia must be humbled, and it must be humbled soon. The disaster at the Redan had caused deep dismay, shock and shame in England, and the prospect of simply settling the war with a grubby, albeit successful, siege, was one which the government simply could not conceive of. Instead, they wanted to see battalions of redcoats swinging out over the Crimean plains in pursuit of the Russian army, driving on to Simferopol and to the north beyond. Sadly, Simpson was not the man to see this through. It was obvious that the reluctant British commander was way out of his depth and was not the sort of man to carry out the government's wishes. Instead, Simpson was more concerned with arrangements for the coming winter and with the reconstruction of Sevastopol. Given the terrible state of affairs during the previous winter his caution and concerns were well founded, but if the British – and indeed the Allies – were to benefit from the capture of Sevastopol they had to get out and get on in pursuit of the Russians who could not be allowed to remain on the other side of the Roadstead. They had to be driven out and given a good thrashing. Unfortunately, Simpson quickly lapsed into a state of inactivity, one which puzzled and alarmed an exasperated government. On 17 September Panmure wrote to Simpson:

> We cannot tell here why you are resting on your oars. You neither fire nor lay plans for attack, nor tell us what you are doing with what you have got. The public will be on you to keep you alive, and while all the daily press are praising the Army, they are loudly crying out to 'run into the fox.'
>
> I tell you this at more length on paper than I can by telegraph, for I dare say, before it reaches you, it will be stale and some deed will be done. I don't want to urge you to rashness, but mind, if you conceive a great scheme which can be executed by your own troops and those of Marmora with the aid of any Turks, I don't want you to play second fiddle to Pélissier. Only tell him plainly your plans, and don't make yourself a General of Division to him, Maréchal though he be.
>
> We speculate here that you should try to turn the McKenzie Heights by Baidar, and to cut off his [the Russians'] communications with his rear, but so much must depend on your own information that all we can really say is, 'Don't waste yourself in idleness.' I do not say that your best policy may not be to delay and to press on the enemy's rear when he retires; but you must be ready to do so, and always have some strong position behind you, to fall back upon should he turn to rend you.[1]

The British government's concerns can be easily understood, but so too can Simpson's frustration at having to endure interference from London by ministers who had little real grasp of the situation in the Crimea. The trouble was that the government had every reason to be concerned at Simpson's apparent lethargy, in the same way that Raglan had been alarmed by Canrobert's inactivity the previous spring, and as much as

Simpson hated been told what to do by men thousands of miles away he probably knew, deep down, that he ought to be doing something to keep up the pressure on the Russians, although he would act only when he and he alone was ready. He wrote:

> It is very easy for people in England to say, 'Follow up your success', but Marshal Pélissier and I are responsible, and we are convinced that we are acting the wise part in pausing until we can see the plans of our enemies. It would be rash in us to attack the Russian position, as strong as any that can be imagined, fortified at every pass, and defended by an army stronger than our own! A little time will show, and as the telegraph will announce our movements before this reaches you, I will say no more.[2]

But there were to be no more moves, not at least against the Russians on the Severnaia. And so the criticisms began to mount at home, which an increasingly agitated Simpson found more difficult to deal with. Even though confined to his sickbed through gout Panmure managed to attack Simpson and his 'dry manner of narrating' compared with Pélissier's 'voluminous and . . . ably composed despatches'. Indeed, there was more skirmishing between Simpson and Panmure than there was between the Russians and the Allies until finally, unable to accept further criticism, Simpson resigned. On 1 October 1855 Panmure acknowledged Simpson's resignation and, with an air of satisfaction, suggested that poor health should be put forward to account for it unless Simpson himself wanted to state other reasons. Almost immediately there began the quest to find his successor, which was no easy task given the list of candidates, all of whom had factors which weighed for and against them. Various names went into the hat, Campbell, Codrington – who carried the 'dorment commission' anyway – Bentinck, Rokeby and Brown among them. Despite his poor showing during the attack on the Redan on 8 September, Codrington was named as Simpson's successor with effect from 10 November. It was a decision which did not go down too well with some of the candidates, particularly Sir Colin Campbell who eventually went home to England rather than serve under an officer junior to himself. Panmure touched upon the point in his last letter to Simpson as commander-in-chief, written on the first anniversary of Inkerman.

> I see you have let Sir Colin Campbell come home on private affairs. I presume either that some words have passed between you, and a rupture occurred, or that the old Highlander has smelt a rat and determined to be off before any change take place. Be that as it may, his absence will make the change easier, and I have every hope it will do well.[3]

In the meantime the Allies finally decided to attack the Russians, although the attack was to be launched not against Gorchakov's forces to the north of Sevastopol but against the town of Kinburn, east of Odessa, which commanded the estuary of the Bug and Dnieper rivers. Kinburn boasted three not particularly strong forts that had been built by the Turks in the previous century, and a garrison of 1,400 men under Major General Kokhanovitch, although it was not Kinburn itself that attracted the attention of the Allies. Situated some eighty miles up the Bug river lay the town of Nicholaev, an important Russian naval base and a major centre for Russian shipbuilding and recruiting. If Kinburn were to fall to the Allies they would have command of the estuary which would effectively deny the Russian fleet access from Nicholaev to the Black Sea.

Although some 10,000 infantry embarked for the expedition – 6,000 French troops and 4,000 British – the expedition was largely a naval operation, and was one which had been of French conception. 'It will be something for the Navy to do', wrote Panmure, 'and they have been in sad want of it for some time back'.[4] The expedition was to be commanded by General Bazaine, with Admiral Bruat commanding the French squadron and admirals Lyons and Stewart the British. It was a powerful naval force, which included six battleships mounting a total of 583 guns, in addition to which there were numerous steam frigates, sloops, and gunboats. There were also a number of mortar vessels, floating batteries and rocket boats. It was all quite spectacular.

The expedition sailed on 7 October and arrived off Odessa the following day. The inhabitants were naturally alarmed at the sight of the powerful Allied fleet and at the prospect of a serious bombardment and a good deal of chaos ensued. They need not have worried, however, for it was all part of the ruse designed to draw Russian troops away from Kinburn, and despite remaining at anchor for the following five days there was no bombardment. On the morning of 14 October the fleet was off Kinburn, poised to begin its bombardment of the forts. First of all, the forts had to be sealed off and on 15 October the Allied infantry were landed to the south and rear of the main work, Fort Kinburn. Frederick Vieth was with the 63rd, which he claimed was the first regiment to set foot on Russian soil.

> An exciting race was run between the boats filled with men of the different regiments, each striving to touch land first. Those containing my Regiment and the 17th led the van, and every nerve was strained as the sand beach got nearer and nearer.
>
> I was the subaltern that day carrying the Queen's Colour, Lacy, my chum, having the Regimental one. Scarcely had the boat touched, when grasping the staff, I jumped into the water and wading on shore drove the end of the staff into the sane, letting the colour float on the

> breeze. It has been said that a boat of the 17th Regiment landed first, but the fact remains that the Queen's Colour of the 63rd Regiment was the first British flag on the soil of Russia proper.[5]

With the Allied infantry ashore there was no chance of the garrison being reinforced from outside. The wind got up on the same day as the landings, which prevented the Allied ships from opening fire, but on 17 October, on the anniversary of the opening of the first bombardment of Sevastopol, the ships opened fire. Before long, Fort Kinburn found itself being pounded not only by the Allied ships but also by the floating batteries of mortars and rockets. After about an hour's firing the fort was ablaze and soon afterwards the Russians' reply, which had so far been relatively ineffective anyway, ceased altogether. After another thirty minutes of pouring shot and shell at the fort the Allied ships ceased fire and two small boats were launched, one each from the British and French fleets, carrying an officer and interpreter, demanding that the garrison surrender.

A short parley followed after which Kokhanovitch disappeared inside the fort to discuss the surrender with his officers. There was evidently some difference of opinion as to whether the garrison should fight on, with at least one officer, a Pole, declaring he would rather fight on and blow up the magazine if necessary rather than surrender to the Allies. Eventually, the disputants were led away and Kokhanovitch agreed to surrender the fort. The surrender of the garrison was, by all accounts, a dramatic affair. The Russian flag was run down the flagpole and a white flag, followed by a tricolour and a Union Jack, run up instead. Then, Kokhanovitch himself marched out, with a pistol in one hand and a sword in the other. As he approached the waiting Allied officers he discharged both his pistols into the ground at his feet before handing them and his sword over to his captors. The two other forts surrendered soon afterwards. Of the 1,400 garrison some forty-five were killed and 130 wounded. Allied losses were trifling.

A reconnaissance to the north revealed no Russian troops, save for isolated bands of roaming cossacks. The forts were then garrisoned by French troops whilst the British sailed back to Sevastopol. The Russian prisoners, meanwhile, were sent to Constantinople. The expedition to Kinburn was a great success, for it deprived the Russians of the use of the Bug and Dnieper estuary and with it access to the Black Sea from Nicholaev. The operation had gone off without a hitch and had demonstrated that the British and French could work together successfully. Certainly, there was none of the trauma that accompanied the first abortive expedition to Kerch. For some strange reason however, it was barely noted in any of Panmure's despatches. One almost feels that, despite his hopes for a renewal of hostilities against the Russians, he sensed that the serious fighting in the Crimea was at an end, that the

Allies' appetite for prolonged war was well and truly on the wane, and that expeditions such as Kinburn, no matter how effective, were little more than footnotes to the greater story of the war in the Crimea. The same applied to one of the final actions of the war which took place on 20 October when a French cavalry force under General D'Allonville attacked a larger Russian force at Eupatoria, inflicting heavy casualties on them.

The onset of winter in the Crimea certainly saw a marked change in attitudes to the war within the Allied camps. No matter how much Napoleon wished to see his armies on the offensive against the Russians it was impracticable. Gorchakov's position on the Mackenzie Heights was an extremely strong one, with every approach to it blocked and with the position resembling a fortress. The French had suffered heavy casualties in taking Sevastopol and the public's interest in the war was steadily on the decline. As far as they were concerned France's thirst for glory had been sated. The destruction of Sevastopol as a Russian naval base had been achieved, and with little likelihood of further operations interest in the war began to slip from the front pages of the Parisian newspapers. In fact, as early as mid-September Napoleon was having discussions with Austria about the best way of bringing about an end to the war, but when he asked Palmerston's government whether they would be prepared to work with him in order to do the same he was met with a flat refusal. It was the last straw as far as an exasperated Napoleon was concerned. He saw no sense in prolonging a war that was evidently going nowhere, and as the British position was clearly at odds with his own he simply gave up and lost interest in the war.

What Napoleon failed to judge correctly was the temper of the British public. It is true that many felt much as Napoleon did and were frankly tired of the war. Sevastopol had been taken and Russia chastised, and perhaps it was now time to talk peace. But these were strictly in the minority. Most Britons looked upon the capture of Sevastopol as merely the springboard for further operations in the Crimea and, indeed, in Russia. Most people felt that British honour demanded more effort and that the disaster at the Redan on 8 September should be avenged.

Four weeks after the capture of Kinburn Napoleon again tried to steer Britain towards pulling out of the war, which only served to drive the two Allied countries farther apart. Palmerston was livid, particularly when he discovered that Napoleon had been working closely with Count Buol, the Austrian foreign minister, on an ultimatum to be delivered to St Petersburg which carried the threat of Austrian intervention if it was not accepted unconditionally by Czar Alexander. There he was, fully expecting a resumption of operations in the spring, only to hear that Napoleon was suggesting that the Allies give up. In the event, Palmerston agreed to the submission of Austria's ultimatum to Russia – but only after Britain had made significant changes to it – but the manner in which it had been engineered rankled with him and only served to illustrate the fact that the two sides had two completely different outlooks. The problem was cleverly solved by the British ambassador in Paris, Lord Cowley, who suggested that a council of war be held in Paris to discuss the future course of the war. It was a suggestion that diffused the tension between the two allies and allowed them to sit down together to discuss the best way of continuing the war. Sadly, it was a decision which condemned the French, many of whom expected to return home early, to an extended period of anguish on the Chersonese plateau.

The winter of 1855–6 saw a reversal of fortunes for the two Allied armies in the Crimea. Twelve months earlier the British army had been ravaged by sickness, the commissariat system had broken down and the army left in an appalling state. It also brought down Aberdeen's ministry. The French, on the other hand, had not only come through in good style but had been forced to shoulder the burden of the siege, taking over half of the British siege lines. The winter of 1855–6, however, was a completely different situation because the British troops enjoyed ample supplies of food, clothing and other essentials, as well as generally good health. The second winter had proved to be nothing like the traumatic winter the previous year and by the time early spring arrived in 1856 the British army was raring to go once more, its soldiers fit and healthy and eager for the fight. The young men who had failed so miserably at the Redan were now well drilled and disciplined and were in good condition. 'Old sweats', invalided home in 1854 and 1855, began to return and a good, beefy backbone was added to the raw material that had now been moulded into a fighting army to be proud of.

The French army, on the other hand, was no longer the tower of strength it had been the previous year. Pélissier's men had been stricken by cholera and dysentery, suffering every bit of the ill fortune that had so dogged their allies the previous winter. Indeed, it is estimated that as many as 40,000 French troops died of disease during the winter, far more than had ever been lost in action. Now it was their turn to endure the miseries of a breakdown in the army system and despite the best efforts of the British to help them they had enormous difficulties in maintaining themselves at Sevastopol. And so, while the British looked to renew the campaign after the winter sojourn, there was no longer anybody fit enough to fight alongside them.

Whilst the French suffered on the Chersonese, both military and political leaders of Britain and France gathered for the council of war. The meeting began on 10 January 1856, shortly after the Austrian ultimatum had been delivered to St Petersburg. At the meeting fanciful plans were suggested and discussed, usually with Napoleon leading the way with his longed-for offensive, including a plan for a pincer-movement from east and west against Simferopol. The British, meanwhile, looked to the Baltic, to Kronstadt and a possible strike against St Petersburg itself. Indeed, hundreds more gunboats were built with the specific intention of striking out in the Baltic. Whether anyone seriously believed these plans would actually be put in motion is debatable. However, even as they laboured long and loud over their war plans for 1856 Czar Alexander and his ministers and advisors were meeting in St Petersburg where momentous decisions were about to be made.

By the end of 1855, Russia – or at least Czar Alexander – realised it would be extremely difficult to continue the war without completely draining Russian resources, both financial and military. The war had simply become too expensive to continue. But he had yet to abandon all hope and was still inclined to draw on the Russian experience of 1812. If he could not achieve a satisfactory military solution to the war he could at least negotiate one from a position of strength which he believed he held. He was also swayed by his advisors who, like the czar himself, clung to past glories and to the spirit of 1812. Fresh regiments could be raised and plans were drawn up, and when news of the Russian capture of the fortress of Kars reached St Petersburg at the end of November 1855 the mood in the Russian camp became as buoyant as it had ever been. Sadly, it was, as Paskevich had described Gorchakov's action at the Chernaya, 'castles in the air'. It was just wild and misplaced optimism. Indeed, three days after Christmas Day, and even as Alexander and his ministers and advisers were stoking up the fires of war once again, the Austrian ambassador, Count Valentin Esterházy, arrived to douse the embers by delivering the Austrian ultimatum.

On New Year's Day 1856, Czar Alexander called a meeting of his ministers and advisers in order to discuss the implications of the Austrian ultimatum. It contained the original four points which had been discussed and rejected by the Russians in Vienna in the spring of 1855. The first point demanded that Russia give up her protectorate of Wallachia, Moldavia and Serbia, whilst the second would remove all obstructions from the Danube and that there should be freedom of navigation upon it. The third point demanded that the Black Sea become a neutral zone and be opened up to the commerce of all nations. Under the terms of the fourth point Russia was to give up all claims to its protectorate over the Orthodox population of the Turkish Empire. Given the situation in which Russia found itself Alexander realised he had little option but to accept the four points. It would be a bitter pill to swallow but he had little alternative. The problem was that a fifth point had been added, apparently at Britain's insistence, which allowed the Allies the right to raise other issues at any future peace conference, and despite Esterházy's assurances that no territory would be lost by Russia it was a point which Alexander could not accept. After all, any points that might be raised at a future peace conference might not be possible for Russia to reject. This fifth and final point, Alexander decided, was not acceptable. The problem was that if all five points were not accepted by Russian by 18 January Austria would enter the war on the side of the Allies. It was a real hammer blow but it was one which Alexander hoped he could avoid. However, when Prince A M Gorchakov, Alexander's new foreign minister and cousin to M D Gorchakov, the commander of the Russian Field Army in the Crimea, delivered Alexander's partial acceptance of the ultimatum to the Austrians in Vienna on 11 January he was told bluntly once again that either all five points were accepted by Russia or Austria would be declaring war. Gorchakov was also reminded in no uncertain terms that Russia had five more days before the Austrian declaration would be made. This was bad enough, but the consequence of Austrian intervention would mean that Prussia, too, would no longer be able to sit on the fence. They also would be forced to take up arms against Russia. The odds were now stacking up fast and furiously against an embattled Alexander.

On 15 January Alexander once again called together his ministers and advisers at the Winter Palace in St Petersburg, amongst whom were Prince Vorontsov, Counts Orlov, Kiselyov, and Bludov, the minister of war Prince Dolgorukov, Grand Duke Konstantin, Count Nesselrode and Pyotr Meyendorf, who was invited as he was a former Russian ambassador in Vienna and an expert on Austrian affairs. Although no minutes of the meeting were taken Meyendorf left a detailed description of what happened during that historic meeting in the Winter Palace. The atmosphere at the meeting, which began at 8 pm, was tense and a sense of great sadness hung over everyone present, each and every one of whom had a sense of deep national pride, none more so than Alexander, but they were realistic enough to accept that Russia had been fought to a standstill and that there was little way out. The sacrifices at Sevastopol had been as great as they had been in vain, for despite the efforts of men such as Kornilov, Istomin, Nakhimov and Totleben, the Allies were even now crawling all over the southern side of Sevastopol. Furthermore, the Russian armies had yet to achieve a single victory against the Allies, and even the capture of Kars was regarded as scant reward for all of their mighty efforts. The consequences of a prolonged war were dangerously obvious: not only did Russia stand little chance against the nations now arraying themselves with one another but defeat would have great and disastrous repercussions in Russian-controlled countries like Finland and Poland.

The issue to be debated was, of course, Austria's ultimatum, which was explained fully by the czar to the assembly of advisors and ministers, after which he gave over the floor for discussion. Nesselrode was decidedly in favour of accepting the Austrian suggestions. There was little hope of a Russian victory, he said, and to prolong the war would only bring more nations in against Russia. And if Austria joined the coalition the new conditions which they would impose would almost certainly be worse than those on the table at present. Nesselrode also reminded his colleagues that not even the Allies themselves were fully in favour of the Austrian ultimatum as they felt it did not go far enough. Accept now, he argued, while there was still a chance of negotiating a favourable peace settlement.

Prince Vorontsov then took the floor. The old governor of the Caucasus found the ultimatum very painful for Russia but like Nesselrode he also realised that there would be little chance of securing a more favourable peace as long as the war continued. A continuation of the war would demand new sacrifices and greater expense and, perhaps, the loss of Poland and Finland, not to mention almost certain financial ruin. It was better to accept peace now, he argued, than to be forced to accept it later on.

The third speaker was the wily Count Orlov who was an advocate of accepting the proposals. He knew that the Bludovs, both father – the minister of war – and daughter, were trying to influence the czar and czarina, keeping them informed of the mood in fashionable patriotic circles and convincing them not to agree to peace. Orlov attacked the 'ill-intentioned and ignorant people' who produced objections to peace. In Orlov's opinion these objections were not worthy of any attention. The majority of the population, tired of the sacrifices that the war demanded, would accept the news of peace with joy. The government did not need to take notice of idle talk and of the cries of the public (*des criailleries du public* – the whole meeting was held in the French language). Orlov also drew the meeting's attention to the fact that not half a century had passed since Poland and Finland had become part of the Russian Empire, and that they had yet to become tightly bound to it, so it was not clear how they would be influenced by the further expansion of the Allies. 'In comparison with such dangers the sacrifices, we are now demanded to make, are insignificant and minimal and we must agree with them.'[6]

After Orlov had finished the floor was taken by Count Kiselyov, although there is no record of what he said in Meyendorf's letter. Meyendorf himself spoke at the meeting, and as he frequently mentions the words spoken by Kiselyov we may assume that the latter had spoken in favour of accepting the Austrian proposals. Kiselyov's argument was, apparently, based upon the fragile state of the Russian economy, a theme picked up by Meyendorf who pointed out that war inevitably leads to bankruptcy. Not only was the financial deficit huge, but in many regions there was a lack of hands for agriculture. If Russia persisted with the war, he said, it would find itself in a weak condition, much as Austria had been in after the Napoleonic Wars and Sweden after the wars of Charles XII. Meyendorf also contended that the peace conditions, suggested to Russia, would do little to prevent the development of its economic resources, and would not in the least cause any damage to Russia in the near future. He was certain that in a few years' time Russia would be as strong as it was before the war but this would not be possible under the present conditions. It was a view that was supported by Alexander.[7]

The meeting went on into the early hours of 16 January and despite much gloomy discussion everyone present realised there was little choice but to accept the Austrian ultimatum in full. News of Russia's acceptance of all five points was relayed to Vienna and afterwards to Paris and London. On 1 February 1856 a protocol was signed at Vienna by representatives of all the warring factions, save for Sardinia, which called for an armistice and that all parties should meet within the following three weeks before drawing up the official peace treaty. All that remained of the preliminaries was the venue for the peace conference. Even that proved contentious, but eventually all parties settled for Paris, with the negotiations set to begin on 25 February.

When news of Russia's acceptance of the Austrian ultimatum began to filter out on to the streets of St Petersburg the capital was plunged into two very different moods: relief and despair. The great majority of ordinary Russian people, and many of those at the Court of Czar Alexander, wished to continue the war. However, the people that really wielded the power, including the czar himself, opted for peace. But not all at the Court of the Winter Palace agreed with him. A maid of honour, Anna Fyodorovna Tyutcheva, who was very influential in the czar's Court, was one of many who advocated continuing the war. She committed her thoughts to her diary, which was published seventy-three years later. On 18 January 1856 she wrote:

> I am in absolute despair. Today everybody was repeating loudly that very soon a peace would be signed and that the Emperor had agreed to accept an offer from Austria. Only yesterday they said that Esterházy had left St Petersburg as a result of our refusal to accept the Austrian proposals but today they are speaking about a peace. Now I understand the Emperor's irritation during these days; perhaps he was conscience-stricken by the fact that he had yielded and had put his signature to the document to the shame of Russia.

The following day Tyutcheva wrote, 'Only yesterday it was rumoured that we had agreed to the peace on humiliating Austrian conditions . . . I can't repeat everything I heard during the day. Men were crying of shame.' Tyutcheva could not contain herself and the following day she went to the czarina, Maria Alexandrovna, Alexander II's wife.

> She [the czarina] told me that although the peace would prove costly Russia could not continue the war any longer. I appealed to her and pointed out to her that everybody considered the finance minister

> and war minister to be incompetent and that it was necessary to try other people before compromising Russian honour.

Her entry for 23 January read:

> I determined not to keep silent . . . I told her that everybody was in despair and thought that the Emperor was probably given a drug to make him sign the conditions so shameful for Russia after he had rejected them outright four times and after it was elucidated by all the European newspapers. I told her about an incident that happened yesterday in the Russian theatre during a performance of 'Dmitry Donskoy'. At the very moment when an actor pronounced the words, 'Ah, it is better to die in battle than to accept a dishonest peace!' all the spectators burst into a storm of applause and cries, so that the actors had to stop their acting for a while, and booed off an actor who played the one who advised making peace. Here was a real public demonstration![8]

But the following conversation between Tyutcheva and the czarina showed that in the struggle between the two factions the peace party prevailed over patriotic feelings:

> Why do those people, who stood for this peace, instead of feeling shame and humiliation, pretend to become triumphant as if they had gained a victory over the country? Why do they throw mockery and insult into the faces of those who mourn the shame of their country? Why does Prince Dolgoruky in your salon tell Countess Razumovskaya with a happy look, 'I congratulate you, Countess, in spring you'll be in Paris'? Why does Count Nesselrode, at a dinner, tell an Italian singer Lablash, 'Let's congratulate each other. This year we'll come to you to eat macaroni.'[9]

These pleadings and arguments, coming as they did from a most faithful and loving woman, upset the czarina. In a frighteningly frank admission she told Tyutcheva bluntly:

> The tragedy is that we cannot tell our country that this war was begun in error owing to a tactless and unlawful event, the occupation of Principalities, that it was conducted badly, that the country was not ready for it, that there were neither guns nor shells, that all the branches of administrations are badly organised, that our finances are exhausted, that our policies had been flawed for some time and that all these led us to the present situation. We can't say anything, we can only keep silent.[10]

But even those who considered peace to be shameful understood that to continue the war would be pointless. The alternative was clear to everyone.

> The shameful peace will not take place, and the war will begin again, this sluggish, agonising, absurd war. God is leading Russia through severe trials of self-consciousness, in order to understand the source of the troubles and disasters it is suffering from. The warriors were happy at the thought of peace but when they discovered that it was bought at the cost of such shameful concessions they said they would be ashamed to return home, and that in Russia they would be ridiculed. But everything is in the order of things: it is necessary to dishonour the governmental Russia, to unmask it completely; it would be unfair and illogical if it happened differently.[11]

The Paris peace conference duly opened on the appointed day, 25 February, with representatives from all of the major belligerents present. There were twelve in all, including the British foreign minister, Lord Clarendon sitting alongside Lord Cowley, the British ambassador in Paris. France was represented by Count Alexandre Walewski, its foreign minister, and the Comte de Bourqueney. Count Camillo di Cavour was there on behalf of Sardinia, as was the Marquis de Villa Marina. Turkey was represented by the Grand Vizier, Ali Pasha, and Mohammed Djemil Bey, Turkey's ambassador in Paris. The Austrian foreign minister, Count Buol, was present, along with the Austrian ambassador in Paris, Count Hubner. These latter two gentlemen were the only representatives from a non-combatant nation, although two Prussian representatives, Prime Minister Manteuffel, and the Prussian ambassador to Paris, Hatzfeldt, were admitted to the negotiations at a later stage. The chief Russian negotiator at the peace conference was Count Alexei Orlov who, supported by Count Brunnov, proved a skilful negotiator. Indeed, given the situation Russia was in he did remarkably well in what was effectively a damage limitation exercise. This was due in no great part to the splits within the Allied camp. Indeed, the old jealousies and agenda that had been rife before the war surfaced once again as the French, British and Austrians pulled first one way and then the other, playing right into the hands of Orlov who quickly seized upon the divisions and took great advantage of the situation. Given the diversity of interests at stake for the Allies and Russia's fears of a massive loss of territory it is remarkable that an agreement was signed at all. Nevertheless, after five weeks of verbal skirmishing, all parties had managed to thrash out the final document which was formally signed on 30 March 1856. Russia finally had peace but it was greeted with mixed feelings, as D A Milyutin later recalled:

> Though the news on signing of peace treaty was reported in St Petersburg in its usual way – by cannon shots from the Petropavlovskaya fortress and with a Te Deum – it could not be considered a joyful event. Although it put an end to the sufferings of war the peace was bought at a high price. Russian national feeling was outraged. The young czar had to pay for the misfortunes of the war that he did not start.[12]

Under the terms of the treaty Russia was forced to hand back the fortress of Kars to Turkey whilst Sevastopol and other Russian towns occupied by the Allies were in turn given back to Russia. The neutralisation of the Black Sea was confirmed, with its waters being opened up to the commercial vessels of the world, in addition to which both Turkey and Russia were forbidden to maintain any sort of military arsenal or dockyard along its shores. Some Russian territory in Bessarabia at the mouth of the Danube was ceded to Moldavia, whilst the Danube itself was opened up and all nations given freedom of navigation along it, the river coming under international supervision. One of the initial causes of the Crimean War, foreign interference in the ailing Ottoman Empire was resolved with hardly any effort at all, with the Sultan himself issuing a decree which guaranteed all the privileges and rights of all Christian and non-Moslem subjects. Ironically, there was not a single reference within the treaty's thirty-four clauses to the great question that had sparked off the whole conflict in the first place: the question of possession of the keys to the Holy Places.

Considering its predicament Russia didn't do too badly, and Orlov came out of the proceedings not only with a great deal of dignity but also with great praise and respect. Indeed, after emerging from the negotiations the Comte de Bourqueney was moved to remark 'When one reads the Treaty of 30th of March there is nothing to show who is the victor and who the vanquished.'[13] Both Britain and France, and latterly Austria, had feared Russian expansion and the quest to curb it had been one of the main Allied war aims. The terms of the treaty, however, barely achieved this. As one historian put it 'The loss of the Crimean War hardly retired Russia's frontiers – it merely held them temporarily in check.'[14] Indeed, barely three years after the signing of the Treaty of Paris Russia was on the move again, making extensive land conquests between the Black Sea and the Caspian Sea, and when the Franco–Prussian War broke out in 1870 Russia took the opportunity of repudiating the treaty altogether, citing the infringement of certain Russian rights that no longer bound Russia to the treaty. The Treaty of Paris had lasted just fourteen years.

NOTES

1 Panmure to Simpson, Douglas, Sir George and Ramsay, Sir George Dalhousie (Eds). *The Panmure Papers; being a selection from the correspondence of Fox Maule, second Baron Panmure, afterwards eleventh Earl of Dalhousie, KT, GCB,* (London 1908), I, 389–90.
2 Simpson to Panmure, *The Panmure Papers*, I, 395.
3 Panmure to Simpson, *The Panmure Papers*, I, 477.
4 Panmure to Simpson, *The Panmure Papers*, I, 452.
5 Vieth, Frederick Harris D. *Recollections of the Crimean Campaign and the Expedition to Kinburn in 1855* (Montreal 1918), 58.
6 Tarle E V *Krymskaya voina* (Moscow 1959), II, 505–6.
7 Central State Historical Archives. *Iz pisem P.K. Meyendorfa*, le 3/15 janvier 1856.
8 Tyutcheva A F *Pri dvore dvukh imperatorov* (Moscow 1929), II, 98–105.
9 Ibid, II, 98–105.
10 Ibid, 98–105.
11 Letter of I S Aksakov to his parents, dated January 25 1856, Arhiv instituta istorii russkoy literatury, arhiv Aksakovyh. No.27, sh. 84. Pis'mo I S Aksakova roditelyam.
12 Lenin State Library, manuscript department, Manuscripts of D A Milyutin, No.33, p.376
13 Vulliamy, C E. *Crimea: The Campaign of 1854–56* (London 1939), 349.
14 Seaton, Albert. *The Crimean War: a Russian Chronicle* (London 1977), 225.

## CHAPTER TWENTY-EIGHT

# *First of the New or Last of the Old?*

With the fall of Sevastopol to the Allies all thoughts turned to the longed-for and expected offensive deeper into the Crimea and, possibly, into Russia itself. But during the days and weeks that followed, the great optimism that the capture of Sevastopol had brought began to evaporate, and by the spring of 1856 all thoughts of further fighting had long since been replaced by a feeling of frustration and by a sense of massive anti-climax, particularly amongst the British troops. The winter of 1855–6 had not proved the trial it was expected to have been, but the improvement in the weather brought no improved prospects of renewed fighting. Thus, the British army was denied the opportunity to avenge the great disaster at the Redan on 8 September the previous year. It was simply not to be. Instead, thoughts turned to peace, to the end of the war, and to a return home. And so it was that, on the morning of Wednesday 2 April 1856, the Allies awoke to the news that the peace treaty had been signed in Paris and that the war was officially over. It was, as Frederick Vieth wrote, 'the happiest event of the whole war'.

> The news arrived in the morning, and soon after midday salutes from all our own, and the French and Sardinian batteries awoke the echoes in the shattered town below, and resounded along the Chernaya valley. The Fleet of the Allies at Kamiesh and Kazatch bay, decked in holiday attire with many coloured flags, thundered out their welcome of the joyful event. Even the merchant vessels in Balaklava harbour sent up aloft what stock of bunting they possessed to do honour to the occasion. A genuine gladness spread everywhere, with one marked exception, not a gun was discharged by our late enemies by way of salute, not an extra flag did they display, and though one would have thought that they, most of all, would have had reason for rejoicing – for had not the proposals for peace emanated from their own government – yet along the whole line of their defences they preserved a sullen silence.[1]

With peace having been concluded between Russia and the Allies all prospect of further fighting ended. Nevertheless, it would be three months before the last of the Allied troops finally left the Crimea, during which time the business of soldiering continued. Although piquet and patrol work was no longer necessary there was still much work for the men, particularly for those from each division whose job it was to go round collecting the expended Russian shot which lay scattered about the ravines in their thousands. This shot was eventually gathered and piled up, after which the Land Transport Corps conveyed them by train and horse down to Balaklava from where they were taken back to England. Other duties included endless rounds of drilling and inspections, roads were built or improved, whilst the men also took the opportunity to improve their own living conditions as best they could. Horse racing was a popular pastime – it had been during the war anyway – particularly amongst the officers, whilst plays kept both officers and men entertained during the monotonous spring days.

The cessation of hostilities also meant that the Allies were able to indulge in a spot of sightseeing without fear of interference from the Russians. It is true that passes were deemed necessary for most areas – the interior of Sevastopol was still deemed to be off limits to most – but officers in uniform were allowed to cross to the Severnaia unhindered and without passes. Popular excursions included Yalta and Batchki-Serai, whilst some even ventured as far as Simferopol. The old battlefield of the Alma, by now a distant memory, was a popular haunt also. Fraternisation was commonplace. Frederick Vieth later recalled an outing with a brother officer who crossed over the Tractir Bridge before riding down to the Severnaia to inspect Sevastopol's northern defences.

> In the rear of some of these [the fortifications] several regiments were quartered, not under canvas but in rude huts, many living in what were simply holes dug in the face of the hill. Most of the men we met did not strike us as having very prepossessing countenances. Many were fine looking chaps and well built, but to me they seemed to have a downcast look as if their lot was not a happy one by any means. Lots of them wanted us to buy from them small articles as relics, or begged tobacco. One small fellow with a merry face – a singular contrast to the others – amused us very much. Even the group of his morose looking comrades about him caught the infection and actually laughed. Having enlisted our attention, he proceeded to indicate in clever pantomime the relative value of the marksmanship of a Russian, a French, a Turk and a British soldier. Throwing his arms and legs into the attitude taken in firing a rifle, he exclaimed 'Russ' – then 'bang' or some word for it. We were to understand this to mean a Russian had discharged his piece. Shielding his eyes with his hand, he looked as if to see the effect of his shot, finally shaking his head and gesticulating to show us the Russian had missed his object. These

> manoeuvres he repeated as a Turk, and Frenchman firing, prefixing 'Turcos' and 'Français' in each case. But when he described in pantomime an Englishman shooting at a Russian, he fell on his back and closed his eyes to represent the fatal effect of the English bullet. It was a very grotesque performance, his mimicry and expression being capital, and we could not help laughing heartily at his sly way of trying to get a tip out of us. He succeeded.[2]

It was not uncommon, during the period after the peace had been signed, for Allied and Russian officers to be seen riding together. Even General Lüders, the new Russian commander-in-chief, was able to ride into the French lines, being greeted by a guard of honour by his former adversaries. It was all rather civilised after the previous year of bloody fighting. The tedium continued until 12 July when the last of the Allied troops left the Crimea, and when the ships puffed away from its rugged shores there were few looking back who had landed at Eupatoria in September 1854. Indeed, the Alma, Balaklava and Inkerman were fast-fading memories, blurred by the miseries of a terrible winter and by the horrors of a prolonged and bloody siege.

The defence of Sevastopol and the Crimean War generally had cost Russia dear in human terms. In the 328 days of the siege between 4 October 1854 and 27 August 1855, Totleben himself estimated Russian losses at Sevastopol alone to be 31,708, almost half of which were killed. The casualty rate was, therefore, almost one hundred per day.[3] However, research suggests total Russian losses to be far higher. L G Beskrovny calculated that in addition to the 1,123,583 men Russia put into the field in 1853, a further 870,000 men were conscripted, making a grand total of 2,001,583. Given that the total strength of the Russian army at the end of 1855 – after the cessation of hostilities – was 1,527,748, a total of 473,835 lost their lives either through sickness or in battle.[4] It is a shocking figure. The pressure that was put on Russian surgeons was tremendous. Over 500,000 Russian soldiers were admitted to hospitals in Sevastopol during the war, 152,733 of whom were cured. 44,711 died, 272,484 were transferred to other hospitals. The remainder were either transferred to other units or were still in care when the figures were computed.[5]

The Allies, whilst not suffering anywhere near the number of casualties of the Russians, lost large numbers also. Some 95,000 French troops died in the Crimea, 20,000 of whom were killed in action. The remainder died of sickness, over 40,000 dying during the winter of 1855–6 alone. British battle casualties were put at 4,000, whilst a further 18,000 died of sickness, making a total of around 22,000. Turkish losses were even greater, at around 45,000, although another estimate puts this figure at 30,000, which is still much larger than the British figure, and includes casualties sustained during the campaign on the Danube. Sardinian losses were very light, with only twenty-eight casualties at the Chernaya and a further 2,000 deaths caused by sickness. The total death toll for the Crimean War was in the region of 640,000, a figure which topped even the more protracted American Civil War.[6]

The political consequences of the war have been examined in the previous chapter. But what about the military? The majority of historians look at the Crimean War from the post-war years, considering it to be the first of the modern wars. However, in many ways the Crimean War was the last of the old wars. It is true that the war saw the development and first real use of such weapons as the Minié rifle, and of powerful steam and screw-driven ships. Artillery was more powerful and more effective than ever before. The Russian army's use of 'anti-personnel mines' in front of the Sevastopol bastions was a new development – it was certainly the first time the British had encountered such interesting devices. The use of the telegraph brought the Allied governments right into their respective headquarters at the front, whilst photography brought the war home in all its stark reality. The care and nursing of sick and wounded soldiers saw great improvements also. But these latter three aspects were more social developments than military.

There is little doubt that great improvements were made in the military technology but when the Allies attacked the Russians on the Alma river on 20 September 1854 the British and French infantry went forward in much the same way as the great Emperor Napoleon's troops had done at Waterloo forty-one years earlier, and the Duke of Marlborough's redcoats had done at Blenheim 150 years before. And when the two sides got stuck into each other with their bayonets at Inkerman they were fighting in the same way that generations had fought before them. Indeed, both Wellington and Marlborough would almost certainly have felt at home at Inkerman and the Alma. Balaklava also bore echoes of the past, with the charge of the British Heavy Brigade proving a glorious re-run of the same brigade's great charge at Waterloo.

In fact, it was to Waterloo and the Peninsula that the British looked throughout the war. Raglan, a veteran of both campaigns, based much of his strategy and tactics in the Crimea upon the events that took place in Spain, Portugal, France and Belgium between 1808 and 1815. As we have seen in an earlier chapter, the British army was led by veterans who – save for a precious few – had only ever fought under Wellington. Thus it was only natural that they looked to former glories when they embarked upon the great expedition to the Crimea. The French were no different, and constantly looked to reviving old glories of the Napoleonic Wars. Indeed, it was the reason that almost drove Napoleon III to go to the Crimea himself. It is ironic that the Allies sought to use the Crimean War to cement Anglo–French relations by attacking on the fortieth anniversary of the one battle that brought to an end the previous Great War in Europe;

Waterloo. The Allied politicians may well have been looking to the future but the military were firmly entrenched in the past. The Russians were exactly the same. The French had come to grief in 1812 when they unwisely chose to attack Russia, a defeat that eventually led to the downfall of Napoleon. Now, forty-two years on, both Nicholas and Alexander, not to mention the Russian generals, all chose to draw upon the memories of 1812 for inspiration. All sides looked back to an age which, ironically, the Crimean War would end.

For the British Army, the Crimean War came as a timely wake-up call. Rotten after years of neglect and decay, reforms were introduced too late to save it from disaster during the terrible winter of 1854–5. But, as the old saying goes, 'the British Army always trains for the last war', and so if the Crimean War exposed the massive shortcomings in the British Army's system it certainly sobered it up in time for a similarly savage conflict that awaited it the following year in India. The tragedy was that, having recovered superbly from the disastrous first year of the war, it was denied the opportunity to avenge the shame of 8 September at the Redan by the armistice and subsequent peace treaty signed in Paris. On the wider front the Crimean War had barely dented Russian aspirations in the east, which was one of the main war aims for the British government. It was all massively frustrating for both the army and the country in general. Thus, Britain turned away from Europe and looked farther a field and to her empire, which would keep her armies busy for the next half century.

The Crimean War had ended in triumph for Napoleon III and France, although the war was tinged with the frustration of not being allowed to go on and achieve an ever greater triumph. When Britain failed to support Napoleon's vision for an expansion of the war deeper into the Crimea he quickly lost interest and the French had to make do with being the victors of the assault on the Malakhov on 8 September. Their large army had been the senior partner in the alliance throughout and had demonstrated its professionalism in the trenches and in the field. It was not easy for Napoleon, forging an alliance with France's most ancient enemy, but although the relationship became frayed at times it remained intact long enough for the Allies to see out the campaign relatively successfully. The trouble was that the war gave Napoleon an over-inflated opinion of himself and when he took on the might of Bismarck's Germany fourteen years later it resulted in his humiliation, defeat and fall from power.

The two great powers that sat on the fence throughout the war – Prussia and Austria – enjoyed mixed fortunes as a result of the Crimean War. The former profited from it, largely as a result of Austria's own position in Europe which was certainly weakened by the war. Having failed to be attracted by offers from both Russia and the Allies to join them in the Crimean War, Austria subsequently saw her influence reduced both by her refusal to enter the war and by the rise of nationalism in Italy. And, like France, she succumbed to defeat when she took on Bismarck's Germany in 1866. With Austria weak and with the other major European powers static after the end of the war Prussia took advantage and began the drive which would eventually lead to German unification.

Finally, we must look at Russia and the effect of the Crimean War in Russian history. It can be divided into two periods; pre- and post-Crimean War. The first period can be defined as an era that saw the progressive rise of the political and military strength of Russia, particularly in the wake of Russia's defeat of Napoleon's legions in 1812. It also saw Russia assume the mantel of a sort of 'gendarme of Europe', with Czar Nicholas I adopting the role of 'chief of police', one of his main roles being to protect 'the sacred' order in Europe.

The second period, which followed the end of the Crimean War, can be characterised by the demolition of the czarist self-consciousness of the Russian people. Before the war, as P A Valuev stated, Russia was 'a plain field where the will of the government met no opposition and did as it saw fit'.[7] After the war a gradual reform of the autocratic regime was started, beginning with the abolition of serfdom. It was no accident that the Crimean War fell almost exactly halfway between the Great French Revolution (1789) and the Great October social revolution (1917).

A great deal of responsibility for the war lies with Czar Nicholas 1. So assured was he of Russian might that he allowed this to obscure his judgement, as a result of which he often acted in contradiction to his empire's best interests, following the principles of agreements between other monarchs even though they were not suited to Russia's own situation. For example, his decision to give military aid to Austria in 1849 prolonged the existence of its most treacherous enemy for decades, and gave rise to a general mistrust and even hatred of Russia, which was viewed as a barrier to progress amongst European liberal bourgeois and revolutionary circles. By the middle of the nineteenth century Nicholas was sure he had weakened the major European states – save for Britain – and saw the opportunity of solving Russia's ancient responsibility of protecting the Orthodox subjects of Turkey from their oppressive rulers. A voluntary settlement with Britain over the future of the ailing Ottoman Empire appeared to be the easiest solution. Sadly, he was mistaken.

In many ways, the Crimean War was Nicholas's own war; Russia's defeat meant defeat for himself. He was certain of his own infallibility and steered Russia on to treacherous and potentially mortally dangerous rocks. The Russian ruling class, which considered itself to be a part of European aristocracy, was shown the door from what they considered to be their European home and were given to understand unequivocally that they were now strangers in that home. The Crimean War drew a clear line of division between Russian and European civilizations, and ensured

European spiritual, cultural, historical and political estrangement from Russia.

Today, those divisions are fast vanishing, as east draws closer to the west. The collapse of the old Soviet Union led to a thaw in east–west relations and with it came far greater freedom of movement, not only for Russian citizens but also for westerners wishing to visit the old Soviet bloc countries. The militarily sensitive and secretive towns of Sevastopol and Balaklava, which had been closed to outsiders – both Russians and foreigners – for decades, were opened up and now encourage visitors. The Crimea is, in fact, no longer part of Russia but belongs to the Ukraine.

The old battlefields themselves are easily visited today. The Alma has not changed much at all. True, the river is now little more than a wide stream in places, but otherwise the visitor will easily pick out the undulating folds in the ground that mark the site of the Great Redoubt. Today, an obelisk stands erect inside it, commemorating the battle, whilst a short distance away stands a memorial to the brave fighters of the Vladimirsky Regiment. An old British memorial to the 23rd Royal Welsh Fusiliers stands not far away. Inkerman remains much as it was, covered with scrub and small trees. A radar station now stands atop Fore Ridge whilst the remains of the Sandbag Battery can only be found with difficulty amongst the trees. Visitors will marvel at the stamina of the Russian troops who attacked up the St Clements Ravine and at the bravery of the British troops who steadfastly held on at The Barrier on that memorable, misty November morning. Balaklava is, and always will be, probably the most famous battlefield in British military history. Twenty minutes of madness will never diminish the bravery of the men of the Light Brigade, whose valley of death is now divided into two by a couple of somewhat ugly tower blocks. The scene of the climax of the famous charge is much as it was, however, and the visitor will easily imagine the Russian guns being overrun by Cardigan's cavalry. The South Valley, the scene of the charge by the Heavy Brigade, is easily visited and defined, and one is left wondering how on earth Scarlett and his men ever managed to cut their way through the Russian mass, charging uphill from a standing start. And where once a forest of ships' masts choked Balaklava harbour, luxury yachts are moored side by side with small fishing boats that still ply their trade in the Black Sea. How different it all is from the filthy, unhealthy cesspit that Fanny Duberley described in her diary back in 1854. Finally, there is the proud city of Sevastopol, still scarred after its devastation at the hands of Hitler's legions during World War Two. The outlying ravines are easily recognisable, particularly the Vorontsov Road, featured in the famous Fenton photograph. The redoubts and bastions have long since gone but their positions are still marked by walls which assume the shape of their former selves. A memorial stands inside the forbidding Redan, outside which scores of British soldiers still lie buried.

The Malakhov, too, remains, dominating the Sevastopol skyline, whilst the Flagstaff Bastion hosts the famous Panorama and the great painting by Rubo depicting the defence of Sevastopol on 18 June 1855. And no visit to Sevastopol is complete without including the St Vladimir Cathedral in which lie interned the three great defenders of Sevastopol, Kornilov, Istomin and Nakhimov.

The Crimean War remains an enigma, famous on the one hand, and yet so mysterious on the other. In Britain, for example, there are few people who have not heard of the Charge of the Light Brigade and Florence Nightingale. Indeed, for all of its futility, the charge at Balaklava is arguably the most famous event in British military history. Scores of public houses, the length and breadth of the country, are named after battles such as the Alma, but few will be able to recall the other great events and personalities of the war. The situation is no different in the Crimea, where the 'heroic defence of Sevastopol' is viewed as a separate event from the wider war. The people of Sevastopol cannot fail to be aware of the defence of their city, surrounded as they are by reminders of the epic event, but like their British cousins few can recall the other battles or even the reason why the war was fought. France, meanwhile, has her own reminders that can be found in numerous Parisian bridges and streets that bear the names of Crimean battles and generals, but again, the events of the war itself remain relatively obscure.

There are those who argue that the Crimean War should never have been fought, that it was a useless effusion of blood, and that it was a squabble between two sets of monks that escalated into war. Others cite the mounting tensions between the various empires, and Russia's growing ambitions in the east, and claim the war was inevitable. Whatever the viewpoint, the Crimean War remains one of the great conflicts of modern times, a war which, coming as it did almost half way between the Napoleonic Wars and the First World War, marked the passing of a bygone military age and the beginning of another as Europe lurched forward into a far more dangerous era. Indeed, the consequences of the war helped the spiral of events that would eventually lead to Armageddon in 1914. Thus, the Crimean War, the clash of empires that raged between 1853 and 1856, was at the same time the last of the old wars and the first of the new.

NOTES

1 Vieth, Frederick Harris D. *Recollections of the Crimean Campaign and the Expedition to Kinburn in 1855* (Montreal 1918), 88.
2 Ibid, 89–90.
3 Russell, William Howard. *General Todleben's History of the Defence of Sevastopol 1854–5, A Review* (London 1865), 311–21.

4 Baumgart, Winfried. *The Crimean War 1853–1856* (London 1999), 216.
5 Hubbeneth, Dr K Y. *Service Sanitair des Hopitaux Russes Pendant La Guerre de Crimée* (St Petersburg 1870), App. 2.
6 These figures come from various sources and were compiled in Baumgart, *The Crimean War*, 215–16.
7 Valuev, P, 'Thought of the Russian', *Rodina*, 1995, No. 3–4, 144.

# *Bibliography*

## Manuscript Sources


'Bumagi Shcheglovykh. Otryvok pis'ma D Shcheglova bez daty', *Archives of the Sevastopol Museum of Defence.*

'Bumagi Timiryazevyh. Iz zhurnala, vedennogo Timiryazevym na Kamchatskom lyunete s 27 marta po 26 maya', *Archives of the Sevastopol Museum of Defence.*

'Chernovye zametki Uhtomskogo', *Archives of the Sevastopol Museum of Defence.*

'Izvlechenie iz pis'ma iz Sevastopolya, 26 aprelya, 1855', *Central State Historical Archives, Moscow.*

'Kopiya s otnosheniya generala knyazya Gorchakova voennomu ministru, 17 maya, 1855,' *Central State Historical Archives, Moscow.*

'Na Severnoy storone u 4 batarei, Nikolay Nikolaevitch Alexandru Nikolaevitchu, 26 oktyabrya 1854', *Central State Historical Archives, Moscow.*


## Printed Books


A British Officer. *The Powers of Europe and Fall of Sebastopol* (Boston, 1856).

Adkin, Mark. *The Charge; The Real Reason why the Light Brigade was lost* (London, 1996).

Adye, Lt. Col. John. *A Review of the Crimean War* (Wakefield, 1973).

Alabin P V. *Chetyre voiny. Pohodnye zapiski v 1849, 1853, 1854–1856 i 1877–78 godah* (Moscow, 1892).

Anglesey, The Marquess of (Ed). *'Little Hodge.' Being extracts from the diaries and letters of Colonel Edward Cooper Hodge written during the Crimean War 1854–1856* (London, 1971).

Astley, Sir John Dugdale. *Fifty Years of My Life* (London 1894).

Auger, Charles. *Guerre d'Orient; Siège de Sébastopol; Historique du Service de l'Artillerie* (Paris, 1859).

Barthorp, Michael. *Heroes of the Crimea; The Battles of Balaklava and Inkerman* (London, 1991).

Baumgart, Winfried. *The Crimean War 1853–1856* (London, 1999).

Bazancourt, the Baron de (trans. by Robert Howe Gould). *The Crimean*

*Expedition, to the Capture of Sebastopol. Chronicles of the War in the East* (London, 1856).

Bell, Sir George. *Soldier's Glory; being Rough Notes of an Old Soldier* (London, 1856).

Bentley, Nicolas, (Ed). *Russell's Despatches from the Crimea 1854–1856* (London, 1966).

Bogdanovitch M. *Vostochnaya Voyna* (St Petersburg, 1876).

Bonham-Carter, Victor (Ed). *Surgeon in the Crimea, The Experience of George Lawson, recorded in letters to his family, 1854–1855* (London, 1968).

Brunon, Jean. *Balaclava; La Charge de la Brigade Légère* (Marseille, 1955).

Buzzard, Thomas, MD. *With the Turkish Army in the Crimea & Asia Minor* (London, 1915).

Calthorpe, S J G. *Letters from Headquarters* (London, 1857).

Calthorpe, Lt Col. Somerset J Gough, and Cadogan, Gen the Hon. Sir George. *Cadogan's Crimea* (London, 1980).

Chambers, W R. *Pictorial History of the Russian War, 1854–56* (London, 1858).

Chesney, Kellow. *Crimean War Reader* (London, 1975).

Clifford, Henry. *His Letters and Sketches from the Crimea* (London, 1955).

Cowley, Henry Richard Charles Wellesley, First Earl of. *The Paris Embassy during the Second Empire* (London, 1928).

Curtiss, John Shelton. *Russia's Crimean War* (Durham, NC, 1979).

David, Saul. *The Homicidal Earl; The Life of Lord Cardigan* (London, 1997).

Douglas, Sir George and Ramsay, Sir George Dalhousie (Eds). *The Panmure Papers; being a selection from the correspondence of Fox Maule, second Baron Panmure, afterwards eleventh Earl of Dalhousie, KT, GCB* (London, 1908).

Doerig, J A (Ed.). *Marx vs. Russia* (New York, 1962).

Dubrovin, N F. *Materialy dlya istorii Krymskoy voinyi oborony Sevastopolya,* (St Petersburg, 1871–1874).

Dubrovin, N F. *Istoriya Krymskoy voiny i oborony Sevastopolya,* (St Petersburg, 1900).

Elphinstone, Captain H C. *Journal of the Operations Conducted by the Corps of Royal Engineers* (London, 1859).

Ershov, A I. *Sevastopol'skie vospominaniya* (St Petersburg, 1858).

Fletcher, Ian. *Gentlemen's Sons: The Foot Guards in the Peninsula and at Waterloo, 1808–1815* (Speldhurst, 1992).

Fletcher, Ian. *Galloping at Everything: The British Cavalry in the Peninsular War and at Waterloo, 1808–1815* (Staplehurst, 2000).

Fortescue, The Hon. J W. *A History of the British Army* (London, 1899).

Goldfrank, David M. *The Origins of the Crimean War* (London, 1994).

Golikova, L. 'Syostry miloserdiya Krestovozdvizhenskoy obshchiny', *Sevastopol Encyclopedic Directory* (Sevastopol, 2000).

Gooch, Brison D. *The New Bonapartist Generals in the Crimean War; Distrust and Decision-making in the Anglo-French Alliance* (The Hague, 1959).
Gouttman, Alain. *La Guerre de Crimée 1853–1856* (Paris, 1995).
Gowing, Timothy. *A Soldier's Experience, or A Voice from the Ranks* (Nottingham, 1903).
Hamilton, Lt. Gen Sir F W. *The Origin and History of the First or Grenadier Guards* (London, 1874).
Hamley, E Bruce. *The Story of the Campaign of Sebastopol* (London, 1855).
Hamley, General Sir Edward. *The War in the Crimea* (London, 1892).
Hammond, Capt M M. *Memoir of Captain M M Hammond, Rifle Brigade* (London, 1858).
Harris, Stephen M. *British Military Intelligence in the Crimean War, 1854–1856* (London, 1999).
Hibbert, Christopher. *The Destruction of Lord Raglan* (London, 1964).
Higginson, Sir George. *Seventy-One Years of a Guardsman's Life* (London, 1916).
Hodasevich, Captain R. *A Voice from Within the Walls of Sevastopol; A Narrative of the Campaign in the Crimea and of the Events of the Siege* (London, 1856).
Hubbeneth, Dr K Y. *Service Sanitair des Hopitaux Russes Pendant La Guerre de Crimée* (St Petersburg 1870).
Hume, John R. *Reminiscences of the Crimean Campaign with the 55th Regiment* (London, 1894).
Ishchenko, N A. *Krymskaya voina 1853–1856 godov: ocherki istorii i kul'tury* (Simferopol, 2003).
Jocelyn, Colonel Julian. *The History of the Royal Artillery (Crimean Period)* (London, 1911).
Judd, Dennis. *The Crimean War* (London, 1975).
Khrushchov, A P. *Istoriya oborony Sevastopolya* (St Petersburg, 1889).
Kinglake, Alexander William. *The Invasion of the Crimea: Its Origin, and An Account of its Progress down to the Death of Lord Raglan* (London, 1863).
Klembowsky, Colonel W. *Vues des Champs de Bataille de la Campagne de Crimée* (St Petersburg, 1904).
Loy Smith, George. *A Victorian RSM: From India to the Crimea* (Tunbridge Wells, 1987).
Lukashevitch, Klavdia. *Oborona Sevastopolya i ego slavnye zashchitniki: iz istorii Krymskoy voyny 1853–1856* (Moscow, 1995).
Lummis, William M and Wynn, Kenneth G. *Honour the Light Brigade* (London, 1973).
MacMunn, Sir George. *The Crimea in Perspective* (London, 1935).
Mansfield, H O. *Charles Ashe Windham; A Norfolk Soldier* (Lavenham, 1973).

Maurice, Sir Frederick. *The History of the Scots Guards* (London, 1934).
Mawson, Michael Hargreave (Ed.). *Eyewitness in the Crimea; The Crimean War Letters of Lieutenant Colonel George Frederick Dallas* (London, 2001).
Mercer, Patrick. *Give Them a Volley and Charge! The Battle of Inkerman* (Staplehurst, 1998).
Mercer, Patrick. *Inkerman 1854* (London, 1998).
Miloshevitch N S. 'Iz zapisok sevastopol'tsa, 1904,' *Sevastopol* (Sevastopol, 2002).
Moyse-Bartlett, H. *Nolan of Balaclava; Louis Edward Nolan and his Influence on the British Cavalry* (London, 1971).
Nakhimov, P S. *Documenty i materialy* (Moscow, 1954).
Niel, General Adolphe. *Siège de Sebastopol; Journal des Operations de Génie, Publié avec l'Authorisation du ministre de la Guerre* (Paris, 1858).
Nolan. *History of the War Against Russia* (London, n.d.)
Oman, Carola. *Sir John Moore* (London, 1953).
Pack, Colonel Reynell. *Sebastopol Trenches, and Five Months in Them* (London, 1878).
Paget, Lord George. *The Light Cavalry Brigade in the Crimea* (London, 1881).
Palmer, Alan. *Banner of Battle* (London, 1987).
Pemberton, Baring. *Battles of the Crimean War* (London, 1962).
'Pis'ma K R Semyakina', *Sbornik rukopisey o Sevastopol'skoy oborone* (St Petersburg, 1876).
'Pis'ma kapitan-leytenenta P I Lesli', *Sbornik rukopisey o Sevastopol'skoy oborone* (St Petersburg, 1872).
Ranken, W Bayne (Ed). *Six Months at Sebastopol; Being selections from the Correspondence of the late Major George Ranken, Royal Engineers* (London, 1857).
Reilly, W Edmund M. *An Account of the Artillery Operations conducted by the Royal Artillery and Royal Naval Brigade before Sebastopol in 1854 and 1855* (London, 1859).
Robson, Brian. *Swords of the British Army* (London, 1996).
Rous, William John. *Letters from the Crimea. 1854–1855.* Typescript copy kindly loaned by the late Sir William Rous.
Royle, Trevor. *Crimea; The Great Crimean War 1845–1856* (London, 1999).
Russell, William Howard. *General Todleben's History of the Defence of Sevastopol 1854–5, A Review* (London 1865).
Russell, William Howard. *The British Expedition to the Crimea* (London, 1877).
*Sbornik izvestiy, otnosyashchihsya do nastoyashchey voyny, book 32* (St Petersburg, 1855),
*Sbornik rukopisey o Sevastopol'skoy oborone* ( St Petersburg, 1872–1873).
Seaton, Albert, *The Crimean War: a Russian Chronicle* (London, 1977).
Shavshin, V G. *Bastiony Sevastopolya* (Simferopol, 2000).

Shavshin, V G. *Nad 'Dolinoy Smerti' (Balaklavskoe srazhenie)* (Simferopol, 2002).
Shepherd, John. *The Crimean Doctors; A History of the Medical Services in the Crimean War* (Liverpool, 1991).
Shil'der, N. *Graf Eduard Ivanovitch Totleben, ego zhizn' I deyatel'nost'* (St Petersburg, 1885–1886).
Small, Hugh. *Florence Nightingale; Avenging Angel* (London, 1998).
Steevens, Lieutenant Colonel Nathaniel. *The Crimean Campaign with the Connaught Rangers, 1854–55–56* (London, 1878).
Stephenson, Frederick Charles Arthur. *At Home and on the Battlefield; Letters from the Crimea, China and Egypt, 1854–1888* (London, 1915).
Sterling, Lt Col. Anthony, *The Highland Brigade in the Crimea* (Minneapolis, 1995).
Sterneggs, Maj Gen V. *Schlachten-Atlas, des XIX Jahrhunderts, Der Orientkrieg 1853–56 in Europa und Asien* (Leipzig, n.d.).
Sweetman, John. *Raglan: From the Peninsula to the Crimea* (London, 1993).
Tait, W J. *An Officer's Letters to his Wife during the Crimean War* (London, 1902).
Tarle, E V. *Krymskaya voina* (Moscow, 1941–1944.).
Thomas, Donald. *Charge! Hurrah! Hurrah! A Life of Lord Cardigan of Balaclava* (London, 1974).
Tidsall, E E P. *Mrs Duberley's Campaigns; An Englishwoman's Experiences in the Crimean War and Indian Mutiny* (London, 1963).
Tolstoy, Leo. *Tales of Sevastopol* (Moscow, 1950).
Tolycheva, T. *Rasskazy starushki ob osade Sevastopolya* (Moscow, 1881).
Totleben, E I. *Défence de Sebastopol* (St Petersburg, 1864).
Totleben, E I. *Opisanie oborony goroda Sevastopolya* (St Petersburg, 1863–1872).
Trevor-Barnston, Michael (Ed). *Letters from the Crimea and India* (Chester, 1998).
Tyrell, Henry. *History of the War with Russia* (London, n.d.).
Tyutcheva A F. *Pri dvore dvukh imperatorov. Vospominaniya. Dnevnik* (Moscow, 1928).
Veigelt. *Osada Sevastopolya* (St Petersburg, 1863).
Vieth, Frederick Harris D. *Recollections of the Crimean Campaign and the Expedition to Kinburn in 1855* (Montreal, 1918).
Vulliamy, C E. *Crimea: The Campaign of 1854–56* (London, 1939).
Ward, S G P (Ed). 'The Hawley Letters: The Letters of Captain R B Hawley, 89th from the Crimea, December 1854 to August 1856,' in *The Journal of the Society for Army Historical Research*, Special Publication No.10 (London, 1970).
Warner, Philip. *The Crimean War; A Reappraisal* (Newton Abbot, 1972).
Warner, Philip (Ed), *The Fields of War; A young cavalryman's Crimea campaign* (London, 1977).

Wilkinson-Latham, Robert. *Crimean Uniforms; British Artillery* (London, 1973).
Wilkinson-Latham, Robert. *Uniforms & Weapons of the Crimean War* (London, 1977).
Wood, General Sir Evelyn. *The Crimea in 1854 and 1894* (London, 1896).
Woodham-Smith, Cecil. *The Reason Why* (London, 1953).
Wrottesley, The Hon. George (Ed), *Life and Correspondence of Field Marshal Sir John Burgoyne* (London, 1873).
Zayonchkovsky, A M. *Oborona Sevastopolya. Podvigi zashchitnikov* (St Petersburg, 1904).

### Articles, journals and newspapers

'Alexander II to Gorchakov. Petergof, 20 July 1855', *Russkaya starina*, July 1883.
'Alexander II to Gortchakov. Moscow, 3 September, 1855', *Russkaya starina*, July 1883.
Arbuzov E. 'Vospominaniya o kampanii na Krymskom poluostrove v 1854 i 1855 godah.' *Voenniy sbornik*, April 1874.
Baumgarten A. 'Zametki k pis'mam knyazya A S Menshikova', *Russkaya Starina*, May 1875.
*Collection of manuscripts, introduced to His Imperial Highness Crown Prince (Cesarevitch) about the defence of Sebastopol by its defenders.* (St Petersburg, 1872.)
Dukhonin, N. 'Pod Sevastopolem v 1853–1856 godah', *Russkaya starina*, October 1855.
'Intendantstvo: iznanka kampanii', *Rodina*, 1995.
'Izvlechenie iz pis'ma Krestovozdvizhenskoy obshchiny sestry G B', *Morskoy sbornik*, 1855.
'Iz vospominaniy A.N. Suponeva', *Russkiy Arhiv*, 1895.
Konstantinov, O. 'Shturm Malakhova kurgana', *Russkaya starina*, November 1875.
Koribut-Kubitovitch 'Vospominaniya o Balaklavskom dele 13 oktyabrya 1854 goda', *Voenniy sbornik*, 1859.
Kurpikov, Major. 'Epizod iz Inkermanskogo dela', *Collection of the manuscripts about the Sevastopol defence*, St Petersburg, 1872.
Osten-Saken, D. 'Voenny sovet pri oborone Sevastopolya', *Russkaya starina*, October 1874.
*The Cottager's Monthly Visitor.*
*The Times*
'Vospominaniya, D V. Ilyinskogo', *Russkiy arhiv*, 1893.
Vyazmitinov, A A. 'Sevastopol ot 21 marta po 28 avgusta 1855 goda', *Russkaya starina*, April 1882.
'Zapiski doktora A Genritsi.' *Russkaya starina*, November 1877.

# Index